DATE DUE

NIGHT TALES REMEMBERED

NIGHT TALES REMEMBERED

Fables from
the Shammas

Michael Jay Katz

Jason Aronson Inc.
Northvale, New Jersey
London

The Night Tales Trilogy

Night Tales Remembered: Fables from the Shammas is Volume II of *The Night Tales Trilogy* by Michael Jay Katz. Volume I, entitled *Night Tales of the Shammas,* contains Alef, Bet, and Gimel in the story cycle. Volume III, *Night Tales from Long Ago,* concludes with Zayin, Het, and Tet.

Copyright © 1990 by Michael Jay Katz

10 9 8 7 6 5 4 3 2 1

Library of Congress Cataloging-in-Publication Data

Katz, Michael Jay, 1950–
   Night tales remembered : fables from the Shammas / Michael Jay Katz.
     p.   cm.
   Vol. II of the Night tales trilogy.
   ISBN 0–87668–816–4
   1. Legends, Jewish.   2. Jews–Germany (West)–Rhineland––Miscellanea.   I. Title.
BM530.K38   1990
296.1'9–dc20
                                                   90–167
                                                    CIP

Manufactured in the United States of America.
Jason Aronson Inc. offers books and cassettes. For information and catalog write to Jason Aronson Inc., 230 Livingston Street, Northvale, New Jersey 07647.

CONTENTS

DALET 1

Stories of

Rabbi Abraham Achselrad
Rabbi Hayyim

HEY 205

Stories of

Rabbi Abraham Achselrad
Rabbi Joel
Rabbi Eliazer of Worms
Rabbi Hayyim

VAV 379

Stories of

Rabbi Abraham Achselrad
Rabbi Eliazer of Worms
Rabbi Asher

ood evening, Rabbi. Of course–please sit here by the stove; the late night fire helps me to become sleepy also. You and I are not blessed like old Reb Elbaum. Once again I saw him nod off during the last prayers this evening. He has learned to sway piously even while asleep; he must have inherited some magic from the mystic Abraham Achselrad. I suppose that you and I could use a dose of Achselrad ourselves tonight. My grandmother said that he could put men into a sleep trance by waving a gold coin before their eyes.

Yes, this was the same Rabbi Abraham ben Alexander who headed the Jewish community of medieval Cologne in the last half of the twelfth century. Rabbi Abraham was a student of Eliazer ben Judah, the mystic rabbi of Worms, and Abraham ben Alexander was somewhat of a mystic himself. But even in those far distant days, the ordained rabbi–the *semikhah*–concentrated on pious scholarship. He was the head of a medieval Jewish university, and first and foremost, he interpreted the holy literatures.

In addition, medieval rabbis were also the official judges for the Jewish community. By that time, the legacy of historical rabbinic decisions was vast. These decisions were built on the Holy Scriptures and on the Talmud, and the same style of reasoning was used for legal matters as for purely spiritual analyses. Thus, rabbis were full-time thinkers and writers. The work of a rabbi required a careful and reasoned preservation of years and years of accumulated learning – in a great many ways, the medieval rabbi was a curator of the Jewish "museum of knowledge."

Old Abraham Achselrad was the "curator" in Cologne. During the late Middle Ages, it was Cologne and the other German communities along the River Rhine that quietly held the orthodox faith. It was the Northern European Jews who maintained the old traditions that came from the Holy Lands, and these traditions are the roots of today's religion. You see, Rabbi, in the German Rhinelands, the Jewish schools were quite isolated. They had little interaction with the neighboring Gentile communities. To the south, especially in Spain, the Jews freely adopted the ideas of their Moorish surroundings. In contrast, in the north the Jewish schools had little to copy – for instance, there were no Christian universities in Germany until the middle of the fourteenth century.

Cologne, Worms, Mainz, and the other Rhineland Jewish communities were insulated and conservative. It is true that, with their ears the German Jews heard foreign ideas. But in their hearts they listened mainly to their own thoughts. And to what did this lead? Outside the synagogues were many dark days; but inside the synagogues old magical threads began to glow, and mysticism became interwoven in the fabric of that old philosophy known as Judaism.

Yes, Rabbi, the Middle Ages brought many dark days. Nonetheless, mystical magic often brightened the mornings in the Jewish communities, and there were always pockets of happiness and laughter. (You know the Jewish expression, Rabbi: "Laugh in the morning, and you will grow fat and happy in the evening.") My grandmother once told me a medieval tale about laughing. It was the story of Elijah and of Salomo ben Aleydis ha-Kohen, a gardener who lived and laughed in medieval Cologne at the time of Abraham Achselrad; let me tell it to you:

Once upon a time, said my grandmother to me, there was a pious and happy young man named Salomo ben Aleydis ha-Kohen. Salomo was a gardener; he grew vegetables and he sold them in the market.

Salomo often laughed out loud. When no one was about, he some-times skipped down the road. At the same time, Salomo was self-conscious; frequently he did not dare to act as happy as he felt.

Now, over the past few years, Salomo had noticed that when Rabbi Abraham gave the seder on the first night of Passover, the Rabbi was so full of ecstatic joy that he smiled and he shivered. One year, when Salomo saw how happy the Rabbi was, Salomo waited until the seder was over and then he jumped up from the table. He laughed out loud. He clapped his hands with great joy, and he shouted, "Hallelu-jah!"

Salomo jumped. And the people around him jumped too. But the people jumped because they were startled and even frightened. "You are a strange man," they said to Salomo ben Aleydis, shaking their heads.

"What? Is this really so strange?" wondered Salomo. "Then perhaps there is something terribly wrong with me." Salomo worried and worried. He looked at other people – they seemed much calmer than he. At times, Salomo danced for no reason at all. Often he could not resist smiling. "Yes, I am definitely a strange man," thought poor Salomo. So eventually Salomo went to the synagogue to consult the local sages. Salomo came to the old Cologne synagogue in the spring-time, with a giddy tickle to his step and with the hint of future gardens deep in the corners of his pockets.

Salomo stepped in the front door. He went through the ante-room, and he walked into the main prayer hall, which was filled with wooden benches. He smiled as he passed the twelve stained glass windows with their colored lions and snakes. Happily, he looked up at the Holy Ark made of stone. Then he walked to the door of the back study room. There, the Rabbi was bent over a book. Was he studying? No, old Rabbi Abraham was dozing, for he had stayed awake all night writing in his mystical tome of Kabbalistic lore, the *Keter Shem Tov.*

Various scholars were sitting on the wooden benches along the wall. The old men greeted Salomo. Salomo gave them a little bow and he sat on an empty bench. Politely, the scholars listened to Salomo's worries about his excessive happiness. Then they offered their advice – to begin, white-haired Baruch ben Jacob said, "Salomo, my good friend, think carefully now: Exactly why are you so joyful?"

Before Salomo could answer, a younger scholar, Elisah ben Samuel, said, "Yes–and why do you dance at the slightest provocation?"

"And why do you always clap your hands?" asked Joshua ben Eliezer.

The other scholars were nodding, and Lewe ben Anselm said, "Simply put, Salomo–Why is it that you are so happy?"

"Well . . ." began Salomo, but Menahem ben Joel interrupted and said, "My young friend, you are like Psalm 29":

> Lebanon skips like a calf unpent
> Mount Hermon jumps like an oxen child
> Assyria romps like a frisky infant
> While Palestine floats full free and wild.

"Exactly," said Moyses ben Nathan. "Is something tickling you into an ecstasy?"

And Old Shimshon ha-Zaken coughed and he said, "Tell us, Salomo: What makes you so giddy?"

Salomo ben Aleydis ha-Kohen tapped his chin, and he thought a moment. He looked around the room. Then he stood up and he said, "Why, gentlemen, it is simply because of Rabbi Abraham. You see, it is like babies."

"*Babies*?" asked Baruch.

"Yes," smiled Salomo, "I cannot help smiling when I see a little baby laugh. And in the same way, I cannot help laughing and jumping when I see Rabbi Abraham happy and smiling."

The seven sages of Cologne looked at one another. The Rabbi was sleeping calmly at his desk. The old men looked at the Rabbi, they looked at Salomo, and they shook their heads. They stroked their beards. They muttered among themselves. Just then there was a noise outside and suddenly Rabbi Abraham awoke. Salomo looked at old Achselrad; then he asked, "And what is your opinion, good Rabbi?"

Abraham Achselrad looked a bit confused. "What is my opinion?" he asked.

"Yes, Rabbi," said Salomo. "What do you think? Why am I irrepressibly happy?"

Rabbi Abraham sat up in his chair. He pushed a book back on his desk. "What do I think?" he repeated. Old Achselrad stroked his beard, and he looked at the wall. He nodded as if listening to a far-off voice. "Salomo," said the Rabbi, "you are a gardener, are you not?"

"Yes, Rabbi, I am."

"Ah, of course you are. Well, you know the old Hebrew proverb: 'As is the garden, so is the gardener,' " said Rabbi Abraham.

Salomo ben Aleydis looked puzzled, and the Rabbi continued. "I think, Salomo, that one should always put his trust in the good Lord God (blessed be He). Trust in the Lord, and you will always be happy."

"Amen," agreed the sages.

Then Salomo said, "Of course, Rabbi – but I have discovered that I am joyously happy because I see that *you* are joyously happy."

The Rabbi smiled, and he tapped his fingers on his desk. "Well, yes, Salomo, I am often happy too. For instance, I am very happy at Passover. And, young man, I will tell you why: I have seen the Prophet Elijah. I have seen him sit and eat with us at the seder, and he has filled me with a most warm and happy feeling."

Salomo ben Aleydis opened wide his eyes. "You saw Elijah?" he asked.

The Rabbi nodded and smiled.

Salomo became sad. "Now I feel terrible," he said. "At the last seder, I was sitting right by you, Rabbi. Clearly I was not worthy enough to see the great Prophet. To me, his chair looked empty."

"It may have *looked* empty," said the Rabbi, "but it was not empty at all. Yes – in fact, if I recall properly, the Prophet was sitting nearer to you than to me, Salomo."

"That is worse," said Salomo sadly, and he sat down heavily on a bench.

Then white-haired Baruch ben Jacob said, "Salomo, I do not know why you are suddenly so sad. The Prophet Elijah does not come to be seen. He is not a balm for the eyes. No, my young friend, Elijah comes to counsel and to protect common folk. He whispers in your ear. He is an invisible household guardian – he is a gentle and helpful spirit."

Elisah ben Samuel continued: "You see, Salomo, Elijah is always roaming about the earth on missions of mercy. But he is a *feeling* – he is not a vision."

Joshua ben Eliezer nodded and he said, "Exactly, Reb Elisah – the Prophet Micah reminded us that Elijah would be sent as a forerunner of the Messiah. That means that he will be visible only when the Messiah is just about to arrive."

And Lewe ben Anselm added, "However, Elijah is also an Angel of the Covenant. He comes to all ritual ceremonies, such as circumcisions. Unfortunately, he is still invisible – and we still await the coming of the Messiah, amen."

"Amen," said Menahem ben Joel. "Therefore, Salomo, the prophet Elijah is still invisible when he joins us at the Passover seder."

Moyses ben Nathan nodded. "But remember, Salomo," he said, "the wondrous invisible Elijah comes to *all* the Jewish festivals in the home."

"Yes," said old Shimshon ha-Zaken, "Elijah symbolizes the happiness of the Jew at home."

The Rabbi nodded and stroked his beard. "True, good friends – and," he said, " 'symbolizes' is an apt word, Reb Shimshon. Salomo, I think that you misunderstand how you should see. It is with your *heart* that you 'see' joy and warmth and happiness. So do not be discouraged if you do not 'see' Elijah with your *eyes*."

"Exactly what do you mean, Rabbi?" asked young Salomo.

"I mean exactly this, Salomo: you are young," said Rabbi Abraham. "You are young – but you are a fine young gardener. Gardening can be a joyous profession. I would not worry about mystical visions yet."

Rabbi Abraham ben Alexander again looked off into the distance. "Salomo, you are a good and pious man," said the Rabbi. "Rest assured, my friend: you will have a happy place in the Great Hereafter. Someday you will be old – older than me – and *then* you will see wondrous visions galore. But that shall not come to pass until the far, far distant future. Now enjoy being a young gardener; do not be in a hurry to become an aged mystic. Mysticism is a two-edged sword – visions can be terrifying as well as holy. Be calm, Salomo, and be patient. Garden, be happy, and trust in the good Lord God (blessed be He), amen."

"Amen," repeated the many scholars sitting on the benches and nodding their heads.

Salomo ben Aleydis ha-Kohen looked at the bearded men sitting along the wall. "Perhaps," he said, "it is Elijah who has been tickling me all along."

The Rabbi smiled at Salomo. "Perhaps he has," said old Achselrad.

Salomo looked at the scholars. He looked at the Rabbi. He felt a warm and happy glow – and he felt a little irrepressible tickle. Salomo smiled, and he thanked the many sages of Cologne for their advice. Then he left the Rabbi's study room and walked into the main prayer hall, which was filled with wooden benches. Salomo looked at the Holy Ark made of stone. Sunlight filtered through the twelve stained glass windows with their colored lions and snakes, and Salomo felt the warm sun on his back.

Salomo ben Aleydis ha-Kohen walked out the front door and began to walk home. It was springtime. He wandered about the cool bright streets thinking of the various counsels that he had heard, remembering the words of the Rabbi and the sages in the Cologne yeshiva, in the little Jewish university of medieval Cologne. Finally, Salomo reached his house. He went out into his yard and he gardened, fine and quiet and proud. Happily he dug and he weeded and he pottered about, among the beans and carrots, the chicory and endive, the lettuce, the mallows, the orach, and the sorrel. And Salomo smiled, as he remembered the saying from the Book of Proverbs:

> Work out-of-doors before you rest
> Garden neatly with your wondrous plants,
> Found at first a plentiful harvest –
> And only *then* begin your household dance.

O h, good evening again, Rabbi. Yes, I know—it is always hard to sleep on the night of a bright half moon. Just put your feet up on the side bench here and I will open the stove door. Let me push the coals back. There is nothing like that white glow; it washes away the cares of a hard day.

I heard your final benediction tonight, Rabbi; clearly, you are overworked. Oh yes, even a shammas like me can tell. I kept one eye on you when I was cleaning the dishes, and I saw that you were watching the door, hoping that Reb Elbaum would leave early. But then Reb Anton stayed to talk about that scriptural passage, Psalm 6:

> Do not condemn me to sickness and worry;
> Please be merciful, I am aching—
> Do not punish me in Your anger and fury—
> Heal me now for my very bones are shaking.
>
> My soul shivers in dread and dismay—
> O Lord, please remember me;
> Deliver me through Your love, I pray,
> And set my feverish body free.

I am weak and ill and dazed,
Save me from the precipice –
For who can sing Your glorious praise
Beyond the pale, in Death's black abyss?

This is painful verse and your analysis was a draining exercise; so of course you are still worn out. What is that? A story from me? Rabbi, all I know are the children's tales, the grandmother fables. You need something new and fresh to keep your mind keen. Otherwise you will become a dreamy old man like me and you will find yourself constantly musing and dozing and nodding off in front of the stove.

What do you mean you are already an old man, Rabbi? Do you really think that sixty years is old? You are still a child. When you reach eighty, *then* you will be old. You doubt that you will live to see eighty years? If so, Rabbi, then you will never grow old. . . . All right, all right, I know no special stories but listening to you and Reb Anton put me in mind of shivering, and shivering reminded me of a tale that my grandmother told me about the strange shivering of Hiyyah ben Jacob:

Once upon a time, began my grandmother, in medieval Germany along the wide River Rhine, there lived a pious and somewhat mystical scholar named Abraham ben Alexander, Achselrad of Cologne. Rabbi Abraham had a yeshiva, and one of its poor but faithful members was a man named Hiyyah ben Jacob ha-Levi. Hiyyah once shivered, and that was the beginning of his troubles.

What is the problem with shivering? Well, Rabbi, I used to think that shivering was simply caused by the cold. But that is not the reason at all. You shiver when the spirits of the dead are about. Apparently, Hiyyah knew this, for when poor Hiyyah began to shiver uncontrollably one warm spring day, he became very, very worried indeed.

Hiyyah ben Jacob shivered and he shook and he trembled, and he ran to the old Cologne yeshiva. He stepped in the front door, he went through the anteroom, and he walked into the main prayer hall, which was filled with wooden benches. Hiyyah passed the twelve stained glass windows with their colored lions and snakes. He looked up at the Holy Ark made of stone, and he walked to the door of the back study room. There, Rabbi Abraham was bent over a book, lost in his reading.

"Rabbi," said Hiyyah quietly.

"Yes?"

"Rabbi, I have had an upsetting experience," said Hiyyah.

The Rabbi looked at Hiyyah and carefully closed his book. "Please, sit down and tell me about it," said Rabbi Abraham.

Hiyyah was pale. He sat on an edge of one of the worn benches along the wall and he told his story. Earlier that morning, said Hiyyah, in the bright warm light of the springtime sun, he had been walking by a field. Suddenly he began to shiver uncontrollably. Hiyyah stopped in fear. He looked around.

After a moment, Hiyyah ben Jacob saw a misty-looking man sitting under a tree. Could it be Isaac ben David? No, that was not possible. Isaac ben David had been dead for many years. Hiyyah feared the worst and he wanted to run away, but the man called out to him.

"Do not be afraid of me," said the spirit. "Although I am dead, I will not hurt you. As you know, I am Isaac ben David."

Hiyyah remained frozen. Did he dare speak to the dead?

"Hiyyah," called the spirit, "do you not remember me?"

"Yes, I remember you," said Hiyyah, hesitantly. "But, Isaac, you have been dead for a long time. Whatever are you doing here?"

And Isaac said, "I will tell you once and I will tell you twice, and I will tell you the truth; for the spirit of a dead man cannot lie. When I was alive, this field was mine, and I had taken it away from its owner by force. Now I have no peace. All night long I must walk the edges of the field—night after night after night." The spirit sighed. There was silence. A chill wind blew, and Hiyyah shivered and he shook. There were no clouds in the sky, but a dimness grayed the horizon.

"I was a moneylender," continued Isaac. "I gave money both for small projects and for large. One day, a man came to me for money to buy seed for the next season. When he returned in a few months, he could not pay me back. I threatened him; finally I called him into court. I was awarded his field, and I took it as payment. It was this very field."

The field itself seemed to waver, and Hiyyah rubbed his eyes.

"Legally," said Isaac, "this field was mine: the man could not pay back the money that I had lent him. I even extended the due date for many months. The reason that he could not repay me, however, was that his son had become ill. Unfortunately, there also had been a very bad harvest. The poor man had absolutely no cash, and he had sold almost all his valuables in order to pay for some healing charms—which, I am sorry to report, did not work. Still, I insisted on my money. The man could not pay, so I had the local officers confiscate his field." Again the spirit sighed, and again there was silence. The chill wind blew, and Hiyyah shivered.

After a little while Isaac went on: "Therefore, Hiyyah, I am condemned. Forever I must walk around this field—nightly, I face my cruelty to a neighbor who had done me no real harm. But, Hiyyah, you can save me from this eternal fate. Go to my wife, Leah. Tell her what I have done. Beg her to return the field to its rightful owner."

Hiyyah did not reply. He was afraid. He shivered and he shook, and he ran back to the old yeshiva building in Cologne to tell his story to Rabbi Abraham.

The Rabbi stared at Hiyyah, he stroked his beard, and then he said, "Good Hiyyah, you must do as this spirit has asked."

Hiyyah felt weak. He could not stop shivering, but he did as he was instructed. Hiyyah ben Jacob went to the house of the dead man. He knocked on the door. Isaac's wife opened it and she said, "Well, Hiyyah, it has been a long time since I have seen you. Why are you here? And why are you shaking? Why are you so pale?"

Hiyyah's throat was dry. In a faint voice he briefly explained what he had seen.

The woman looked at Hiyyah strangely. "Hiyyah, I am certain that you are a fine man, but you have been seeing things," she said. "My husband is long gone and buried, and much as I wish differently, he will never return. Please do not pretend such things to me."

"But, Leah, I am telling you the truth," said Hiyyah.

"Then it is a cruel truth," she answered, and she went back into her house.

Hiyyah waited for a moment on the steps; then reluctantly he returned to the field.

The spirit of the dead man was sitting under the tree. The air was silent and cool, and although no clouds covered the sky, the horizon was gray. Hiyyah looked at Isaac. "Your wife will not believe me," Hiyyah reported.

"Listen, Hiyyah," said the spirit, "I have no one else to turn to. Leah must help me out. I cannot leave this field, but to show her that this is the truth, have her come here tomorrow morning. She will find me sitting by this tree." And the ghost said no more, but with a grievous groan it vanished in a cloud of mist and left Hiyyah all alone.

Now Hiyyah's very bones were shivering. Again he returned to the house of the dead man. Hiyyah knocked at the door. No one answered. Hiyyah knocked once more. Finally Leah opened the door. She stood there uncertainly. Her hand shook a bit on the latch. Her eyes were red.

Hiyyah took a deep breath. "Leah," he began, "I really apologize for continuing to bother you."

Leah stood trembling and she said nothing. A dog barked somewhere, far away. Hiyyah shifted his weight: he too was shaking. "Listen, my good woman," he said, "your husband Isaac says that he was a moneylender. Is that correct?"

"Yes," said the woman in a thin voice.

"Leah," said Hiyyah, "your husband has returned from the dead in order to atone for his bad deeds as a moneylender. He has begged us to help him. We can soften the eternal penance to which he has been condemned. He claims that tomorrow morning you will find him sitting under the oak tree by the edge of the field that you own. Go to him and listen to his story—then please do as he asks."

Poor Leah was very upset by this whole idea. Hiyyah wondered, "Will she go to the field, or will she just try to ignore this reawakening of her old sad feelings?"

The next morning Hiyyah went to the field. Soon, Isaac's wife appeared there too. The two people stared at the oak tree. At first only a mist was visible—then the mist coalesced into the figure of a man sitting under the tree. It was Leah's dead husband, Isaac. Her eyes opened wide. She could not say a word; instead, she ran away.

Fearfully, Leah ran to the Cologne cemetery, the *Am Toten Juden*. Usually the medieval Jewish cemeteries were comforting places. They were the last refuge from those day-to-day storms that thundered down upon the battered Jewish communities. Although the cemetery was a burial ground, it also was a fine park. Jews would spend hours sitting peacefully in this "Garden of Life"—a sacred sheltered spot for the living, as well as for the dead. But on that particular day, the Garden of Life brought Leah no peace at all. Leah ran in the front gate and hurried blindly past the other visitors. She went directly to her husband's grave. The dirt was disturbed. Leah reached down into the soil. She knocked on the coffin–but it returned only a hollow empty ring. Then Leah knew that the grave was empty of the spirit of her dead husband Isaac.

Leah shivered and she shook, and she trembled uncontrollably. Slowly, she walked back to the field where her husband sat. Leah was silent and fearful. She stared at the specter. A cool wind blew from afar and Leah shivered again. Still there was silence–a blank and dismal quiet lay throughout the field. And the spirit of Isaac ben David wavered silently under the oak tree at the edge of the field on that strange spring day, long, long ago.

Eventually, Leah spoke. "Why are you here?" she asked in a voice that could barely be heard.

"Leah, my fine and faithful wife, the spirits of the dead can mix into the lives of the living," said her husband. "And the future is an open book to us, the inhabitants of the Great Hereafter–like the demons and the angels, we departed humans can hear the decisions of the Golden Court on High."

After a moment, Isaac continued: "We spirits flit and float through the universe. Sometimes we can even intercede in order to right wrongs and to prevent misdeeds. My good wife, I committed a sin when alive. I would like to rectify it now. Please, I beg of you, return this field, which I wrongly took from its former owner. Then, my dearest one, I shall finally rest in peace."

Leah listened silently. She nodded her head and agreed to do as her husband asked; then she returned home. There she sat on the bed, feeling weak for many hours. After a long time, Leah felt a bit stronger. Then she stood and she walked into the town to try to return the field. However, Leah soon learned that the original owner was now dead.

This was too much for the poor woman. She could not face her dead husband again, and she said nothing to anyone. Days came and days went, and Leah did nothing more. However, Hiyyah passed the field every day. Every day he saw that Isaac ben David remained sitting under a tree. And every day Hiyyah shivered and he shook. Finally, he asked Leah what had happened, but the woman refused to speak to him. So once again, Hiyyah returned to the Rabbi.

Rabbi Abraham listened silently to the whole story. He closed his eyes. He nodded his head. Then he opened his eyes and he stroked his beard. "Hiyyah," said Rabbi Achselrad, "I do not like the sound of this."

"What shall we do?" asked Hiyyah ben Jacob.

"First," said the Rabbi, "Isaac's wife must give the field to the children of the original owner."

Hiyyah returned to Leah. She appeared gray and worn. Hiyyah looked at the poor sad woman who answered the door, and gently he reported the Rabbi's words to her. At first Leah hesitated. But Rabbi Abraham was a holy and respected man and therefore Leah built up her courage, found the heirs of her dead husband's client, and formally signed over the field to the children.

Now Hiyyah no longer saw the spirit of Isaac ben David— however, he still shivered as he passed the field. Meanwhile, poor Leah began to have problems. She had cruel dreams and cold sweats in the dead hours of the night. Lights flickered in the corners of her house. Objects moved at night of their own accord. Then a neighbor's child became ill for no reason.

Leah was worried. Then she became frightened. Finally, she went to the mystic Achselrad. Rabbi Abraham listened to the latest developments. He closed his eyes, he opened his eyes, and he stroked his beard. Old Abraham Achselrad said, "It is time for you to return to the cemetery and to fix these matters once and for all."

"Rabbi, I am tired of this sad business," said Leah. "Also—I am afraid."

"There is no other way, my good woman," said the Rabbi. "Evil spirits have intervened. Now we must exorcise them."

The woman shivered and she sighed, but finally she asked, "All right, what must I do?"

The Rabbi said, "Now listen carefully. Tomorrow in the morning, go to your husband's grave. Take off your shoes. Sit down on the top of the mound of dirt, and say the following":

> By the will of the good Lord God (blessed be He), and by my own will, I do not intend to go along with you yet or with any other deceased or with any spirit whatsoever. Do not come after me. Do not torment me. My desire is to . . . .

"Just a moment, Rabbi," said Leah. "Can you write this down for me?"

"Certainly, Leah," said Rabbi Abraham. So in a neat and tiny script, the Rabbi wrote:

> By the will of the good Lord God (blessed be He), and by my own will, I do not intend to go along with you yet or with any other deceased or with any spirit whatsoever. Do not come after me. Do not torment me. My desire is to live in this world at peace for now.
>
> So, with the consent of the celestial and the earthly tribunals, I solemnly command you in the Name of the good Lord God and by all the holy names of the angelic Host—Aniel, Gabriel, Hasdiel, Kabshiel, Metatron, Michael, Rahab, Raphael, Ridyah, Sandalfon, Shamriel, and Uriel—that you must stop troubling me.
>
> Your body, O my beloved husband, must lie calmly in its grave until Resurrection. Your soul must rest in that place where it properly belongs. I command this upon you with a sacred oath, now and forever, amen.

Rabbi Abraham gave the charm to Leah, who read it quietly to herself. Then the Rabbi said, "After you recite this incantation, pat the grave seven times. Put your shoes on again, and, without looking back, return home. When you get home and before you enter your house, wash your hands and your eyes and your face three times, as if you had just come back from a funeral."

"I must sit on the grave, recite the incantation, pat the grave seven times, and then wash three times at home?" asked Leah.

"Exactly," said the Rabbi. "Then, my good woman, light a candle in your bedroom each night for seven nights."

The woman repeated the entire procedure to the Rabbi. Rabbi Abraham stroked his beard. He listened and he nodded, and he wished Leah well; then he went back to his reading. The woman stood for a moment in the doorway of the old yeshiva. "Why must I have dealings with the spirits?" she thought sadly. Leah shivered. She shook her head, and she left the synagogue.

The next morning, Leah returned to the *Am Toten Juden*. She shivered in the gray light, but she followed the Rabbi's instructions; then she went home. That night Leah felt a cool breeze pass through her bedroom. She began to tremble and she opened her eyes—but she saw nothing. Later that very night she began to feel better, and she slept well. The next morning dawned bright and sunny. Leah felt that a weight had lifted from her soul. The weeks passed gently and smoothly, and she never heard from her dead husband again. Hiyyah, however, could not walk by the field without shivering, even in the warm and hopeful springtime suns of many years thereafter.

ood evening, Rabbi. I see there is no sleep for the weary – yes, that is what my grandmother said, and she said it almost nightly. If you are cold, my old friend, then sit down here on the bench and I will stoke up the oven. This stoker? It is one of the iron shoe-scrapers from the front hall; you probably do not recognize it because it is covered with soot. Of course, there are still two scrapers in the anteroom for dirty shoes. But I myself am of the old school, Rabbi: I think that all pious men should pray barefoot in the synagogue. Did you know that Moses of Leon – Moses ben Shem-Tov – prophesied that the Messiah will appear barefoot? Well, we can always hope.

As my grandmother said to me, "We must always hope, my little one. Some say that hope is a delusion – but it does not matter, for hope is happiness." Grandmother said this often, and of course how could you question a great saying like that? She also told me stories about hope. In particular, I remember grandmother's tale about Moses ben Shem-Tov and the great book of hope, the *Zohar*.

Hope comes in the springtime, and, said my grandmother, it was one medieval springtime that young Moses ben Shem-Tov came to Cologne. Moses ben Shem-Tov was a Jewish scholar from Spain. He was born in Leon in the middle of the thirteenth century, and he died at Arevalo. Reb Moses claimed to have translated the most influential of all Kabbalistic works, the *Zohar* (the "Radiance"). This a book filled with hope–the hope that wondrous mystical magic is alive in the world, amen.

Yes, when Moses of Leon came to northern Germany, it was a warm spring evening with cool breezes as only the River Rhine can give. Do you know the springtime fable that Moses ben Shem-Tov wrote in another of his books, *Tasks and Joys*? It goes like this:

Old Winter blew a bitter wind and criticized the Spring:

"When you appear," said Winter, "no one can stay calm. No one remains firm or stable or in one place. People run off to the meadows or the woods or the streams. They pick crocuses, jonquils, lilies, and violets. They twine long knotroot grasses around their fingers. They put green bellwind leaves into their pockets."

Winter rumbled and grumbled. Spring looked off toward the clouds, smiling.

"Are you listening?" asked Winter, shaking his snowy head. "In the springtime, people leave the solid land and take to their boats. They roll across the waves; they tack in the puffs and catspaw breezes. They actually laugh aloud as the sails snap taut in the wind. And then what of the rains? Why, no one seems troubled by a sudden drenching springtime rain."

"Ah," said Spring, "that sounds fine to me."

"Fine?" roared Winter. "That weak-willed, daydreaming, soft treatment sounds fine? Frankly, it sounds terrible. What is the purpose of living, if you just wander about from here to there with no goal, with no resolution, with no determination. *You* encourage men to look to the ephemeral wispy clouds. But *I*, on the other hand, force men to look down at the firm and steady rock-hard earth":

> January brings the wretched days
> With gales fit to skin an ox
> The cruel frosts drip an icy glaze
> And bleak winds rake the frozen rocks;
>
> High in the oaks' tall tangled crowns
> Blustering winds assassin-like
> Rip branches off and crash them down
> And fill the glens with wooden spikes.

The vasty woodlands groan and call,
In cold waves the open fields drown;
The animals both large and small
Run for cover with their tails down.

In thick coats men shiver and hurt
Walking bent and grim in snows,
Stumbling along the hardened dirt
Following their long thin winter shadows.

The Spring shrugged. "Well, old Greybeard, at least you can see yourself honestly in the cold hard light of a bitter winter's day," said Spring. "But, my friend, I would offer you a different picture in return":

Garden early, after snows withdrawn —
Awaken in the light blue dawn
And turn the soil beyond the lawn.

Now the flowers are still just dreams
The vegetables but golden gleams
The shoots and stalks like green moonbeams —

But root among the brown wood chips
And hints of autumns cool and crisp
Will lightly brush your fingertips;

Plant the tiny pale white seeds
And the tang of harvest reeds
Jumps up to touch your nose indeed;

Then as you dig you realize
That summer winds and fireflies
Are just beyond my springtime skies.

"Bah – that is weak and spineless!" growled Winter. "You peddle dreams and mysticism. You tease men with elusive hopes."

"Perhaps," said Spring, "but in springtime people are happy."

"Happiness is not everything," said Winter.

"Oh – I think that it is," said the Spring.

Is it, Rabbi? I am not certain myself. In any case, my grand-mother would often say that happiness comes from hope – and hope came to Cologne during many springtimes, even in those dark medi-eval days. For example, once upon a time, said my grandmother to me, in the town of Cologne on the wide River Rhine, lived a pious rabbi named Hayyim ben Yehiel. Rabbi Hayyim was the Chief Rabbi of medieval Cologne many, many years ago. Late in his life, he headed the delegation that negotiated with Emperor Rudolph for the release of the hostage Rabbi Meir of Rothenburg. But one day, before those complex international events, Rabbi Hayyim was reading late in his study in the synagogue building. It was a mild springtime evening, and a strange thin traveler arrived in the back room of the Cologne yeshiva where Rabbi Hayyim was hard at work.

As you know, Rabbi, all manner of barefoot and pious pilgrims came through Germany each week from the Holy Land in those old medieval times. Strange men would appear in the Cologne yeshiva at any time of the day or night, for wandering pilgrims were constantly returning from the southern, Mediterranean regions. These travelers came wide-eyed and worn, and they came filled with wondrous tales and with deep religious hope.

The wanderer who appeared to Rabbi Hayyim one springtime evening was a young man, white-robed, thin, and fair-haired. He removed his shoes in the anteroom. And why did he take off his shoes? It was honest humility before the Divine presence. (As you know, when Moses heard the holy call from the burning bush he was told by the Almighty Lord God: "Come no nearer. Take off your sandals: the place where you are standing is My sacred ground.")

So with pious humility the young stranger padded in on stock-inged feet. He entered the main prayer hall, which was filled with wooden benches. He passed the twelve stained glass windows with their colored lions and snakes, he looked up at the Holy Ark made of stone, and he walked to the door of the back study room. There, Rabbi Hayyim ben Yehiel was bent over a book, lost in his reading.

"Rabbi," said the stranger quietly.

"Yes?" said the Rabbi.

"Rabbi, my name is Moses ben Shem-Tov. May I come in?" asked the pilgrim.

"Certainly, young man, please come in and sit down," said Rabbi Hayyim. "I do not recognize you. Are you from the Rhine regions here?"

Moses ben Shem-Tov sat down on one of the worn benches. He put his knapsack on the floor by his feet.

"Originally, Rabbi, I am from Leon in Spain. I have come north through France, and now I am traveling home again, down the Rhine valley."

Rabbi Hayyim nodded. Neither man said anything. Moses closed his eyes, resting–after a few moments, he said, "Rabbi, I have been traveling, collecting information. You see, I am compiling a book–well, actually I am translating a work of Rabbi Simeon ben Johai. Do you know of him?"

"I certainly do," said Rabbi Hayyim. "Simeon ben Johai was a famous Tanna."

"Exactly," said young Moses. "He was a rabbi during those wonderful years in Palestine, almost a millennium ago."

Rabbi Hayyim nodded again, and he said, "I have heard that he lived alone for twelve or thirteen years, when he was hiding from the Roman government after the unsuccessful Bar Kochba rebellion."

The Rabbi looked off toward those golden southern lands. "The old stories say," he continued, "that Rabbi Simeon lived in a cave, a warm dry cave in the suntanned hills of the Holy Land, and that he spent his days in quiet gardening and meditation. I remember hearing that he took particular pride in his sweet-roots and that he would haul barrels of water on his shoulder each morning from a nearby stream in order to water his many fine green sweet-root plants."

"Yes," said Moses of Leon, "and during those years of isolation, Simeon was instructed by angels. They revealed to him the profound Divine meanings hidden within the seemingly clear words of the Torah. They taught him the Kabbalah.

"Ah, the great and glorious Kabbalah," continued young Moses reverently. "The Kabbalah is the 'reception': it is the occult truths received from the angels."

But Rabbi Hayyim shook his head and said, "Actually, Moses, 'Kabbalah' means 'doctrines received by tradition.' Most rabbis would say that the Kabbalah is simply all our religious doctrines outside of the Torah itself – especially the oral traditions received through scholarly teachings."

"So I have heard," said young Moses ben Shem-Tov. "But, Rabbi Hayyim, 'Kabbalah' really means something else. The Kabbalah is our special *mystical* oral tradition. It is the tradition received from angels, and it is steeped in personal secret magical knowledge."

Young Moses lowered his voice a bit. "Rabbi," he continued, "the Kabbalah is not earthly knowledge: the Kabbalah unravels the nature of the great Lord God (blessed be He), it recounts the many Divine emanations (that is, the ten *sefirot*), it delves into the creation of angels and of man, and it explains the hidden details of the revealed Law."

Rabbi Hayyim sat back in his chair. He stroked his beard, and he listened without saying anything.

Moses of Leon looked at the Cologne Rabbi, he looked down at his hands, and then he said quietly, "Have you ever heard of the *Zohar*, Rabbi?"

The Rabbi said nothing for many minutes. He stared intently at the young man sitting across from him, a young man who had wandered into the old Cologne yeshiva with no introduction, a young man who had come through all the cosmopolitan centers of medieval Europe. The *Zohar* was a name that glowed and shimmered. It was a mystical name. Frequently it was whispered in the evenings, and then men would nod knowingly. But the actual book itself was strangely elusive. Who had ever seen it with his own eyes? "Yes," said Rabbi Hayyim ben Yehiel of Cologne, after a time, "I have heard of the *Zohar.*"

Moses ben Shem-Tov nodded. He looked down at his feet. The night was deepening. Moses moved his shoulders and he stretched. He blinked his eyes. Finally he continued: "As you know, Rabbi," he said, "the *Zohar* is a commentary on the Torah. It complements the other Kabbalistic books, especially the *Sefer Yetzirah* and the *Bahir.*"

Rabbi Hayyim looked at the young traveler. "Have you ever seen the *Zohar*?" asked the Rabbi.

Moses of Leon looked around him at the little back study room. He looked at the worn benches, he looked at the piles of prayer books, and he looked at the Rabbi's desk, which was cluttered with manuscripts. After a moment, he said softly, "Good Rabbi, I have at home in Guadalahara a copy of the *Zohar* itself."

Rabbi Hayyim closed his eyes and then he opened his eyes; he stroked his beard, but he said nothing aloud.

Young Moses was continuing: "You see, Rabbi, I spent many years with the famous mystic, Isaac the Blind ben Abraham of Posquieres. Perhaps you have heard of old Isaac?"

"Yes," said Rabbi Hayyim, "actually, I met him on more than one occasion." Hayyim ben Yehiel smiled. "His outer world was dark, but clearly his inner world was light and bright and holy."

Again, Rabbi Hayyim looked off, far away. Was he seeing sunny Posquieres? "I remember Blind Isaac well," said the Rabbi. "He liked to sit in the afternoon sun. He would recount how souls passed from body to body after death. He said that although he could not see material objects, he had traded his vision for the ability to discern whether men possessed new and fresh souls.

"Of course new fresh souls come directly from the world of the Heavenly spirits. In contrast, old souls are in the midst of migrating and wandering from body to body. And why would they be wandering? It is in order to recover their original purity. The holy souls seem to get a bit dirty in the bodies of us weak and wilsome mortals. . . . Ah, young man, I have certainly heard much speculation about the migration of souls; recently, two of the followers of old Blind Isaac – Reb Azriel and Reb Ezra, the mystic Kabbalists of Gerona – have been in the Jewish communities here in Germany explaining these ideas in some detail."

Rabbi Hayyim nodded to himself. "But I did not mean to change the subject," he said. "Tell me – you have obtained a copy of the mystical *Zohar*? I had not heard that there was a copy anywhere in Europe."

"Well, Rabbi, undoubtedly it is a rare treasure," said young Moses ben Shem-Tov. "I, too, knew nothing of this manuscript for many, many years. Then one evening after I had helped the holy man of

Posquieres to write down some of his revelations, I was rooting among the old manuscripts in his storeroom and I found this collection of writings."

"It was the *Zohar*?" asked Hayyim ben Yehiel.

"Yes," said young Moses.

The Rabbi raised his eyebrows again. "Then tell me about it," he said.

Moses ben Shem-Tov settled into his seat. "Well, Rabbi, where can I begin? The *Zohar* is a personal account. In the *Zohar*, the great Mishnaic teacher, Rabbi Simeon ben Johai, reports about his discussions with departed spirits and with celestial angels.

"There is no doubt that this is a controversial work. However, its radiance will win over even the skeptic. The author, Rabbi Simeon himself, says: 'When the *Zohar* becomes widely known, then people will read it in all manner of lights. But no matter how one views the work, it will nourish all minds to the end of their days.'

"Now," continued young Moses of Leon, "I have had a difficult time deciphering the entire work, and I must confess that I am not entirely certain of my translation. The manuscript is in Chaldee, a rather obscure language. But even in my poor rendition, the truth of the words shines through with Heaven's radiant light, amen."

Moses ben Shem-Tov smiled, and he closed his eyes. "Yes, good Rabbi, the *Zohar* assures us that there is great magic and mystery abroad in the world. All is not what it seems on the surface. Nonetheless, there is hope for us – through study, we can see into the depths of this holy realm. Even the most esoteric doctrines of the Kabbalah come directly from the Holy Scriptures. True, these wonders do not jump out at the uninitiated. That is both the mystery and the hope – there are always more hidden joys for the hard-working thoughtful man. The most profound and enrapturing meanings lie hidden beneath the surfaces of the letters and the words of the Holy Scriptures – and the truly pious student can find these treasures forever.

"This is how Rabbi Simeon puts it: 'What if the Law were simply ordinary expressions and narratives and stories? What if the Truths were the direct, plain, and unadorned words of Esau, Hagar, Lavan, the ass of Balaam, or Balaam himself? In this case, we could not call it the "Law of Truth" or the "Perfect Law" or the "True Witness of the good Lord God Almighty" or just "*The* Law."

" 'But this is not the case. We have been given a holy, inexhaustible *Law of Truth*. It is a Law for all times. It is a Law for all of our world, our vast, thick, eternal, and incondensably complex world. God's *Law* is not a simple law – it is a Law that is as incondensably complex as the situations to which it applies. The Law is written in the Torah. And each word of the Torah represents a sublime inexhaustible source. Each narrative points not only to the single instance in question but also to an infinite number of cases.

" 'All of the written symbols of the Lord's Holy Torah have an unplumbable depth. The words are rich and thick and multi-layered. We can study and study and study and never exhaust *The* Law – just as Jews can live and live and live and never exhaust the myriad opportunities to apply the Truths of the unknowable Lord God. In other words, we must search and study and question and pray. And we must not stop as long as breath is in our bodies and as long as Jews live upon this earth, amen. . . .' "

What is that, Rabbi? The *Zohar* is a forgery? Yes, I too have heard that said. Apparently, Moses of Leon was a romantic. He was careless with his money. He gave things away with little regard to his future or to the future of his family. He also wandered about – first he lived in Guadalahara, then in Viverro, next in Valladolid, and finally in Avila. And everywhere, he wrote; for instance, he composed the book of mystical religious poems, parables, and stories called *Tasks and Joys*. These and other books were reprinted, but they were not known widely – and young Moses remained quite poor. Suddenly, however, after he published his translation of the *Zohar*, Moses ben Shem-Tov found himself with a regular and comfortable source of income.

Had Moses of Leon actually written the *Zohar* himself? Had he himself compiled the myriad secret, arcane, and oral doctrines of the Kabbalah? Did Moses ben Shem-Tov take the liberty of putting these ideas into the mouth of an older authority, taking care to make the coloring and style appropriately archaic? This, Rabbi, is the suspicion that I have heard bandied about.

In later years, after old Hayyim ben Yehiel had retired and when the young Rabbi Asher (sometimes known as "Rosh") had assumed the rabbinate of Cologne, two influential Spanish Jews, David Rafan and Joseph of Avila, reported that the *Zohar* was a forgery. Reb David and Reb Joseph claimed that neither the wife nor the daughter of Moses of Leon had ever seen an original Chaldee version of the manuscript. These men thought that the *Zohar* was composed entirely by Moses ben Shem-Tov.

Was it a creation of Moses ben Shem-Tov, or was it a revelation to Rabbi Simeon? Whichever was the case, the *Zohar* soon became a new text. The *Zohar* was an irreversible step in the evolution of Judaism. Previously, the Kabbalistic doctrines had been elusive; they had been protean and aethereal. Now they became stable and permanent. With the *Zohar*, a mystical current flowed into the traditional legal dust-dry talmudic studies. Now holy study could involve magic and ecstasy. Now Jewish theology could include intimate personal prayer and all the ineffable emotions that go along with it.

Hayyim ben Yehiel was not a mystic and he was not a Kabbalist. After young Moses ben Shem-Tov told his tale to Rabbi Hayyim, the old Cologne Rabbi only nodded and tapped a finger on his desk and he stroked his curly beard. Moses of Leon ate a late meal with the shammas and stayed the night. Young Moses spent the night on the floor next to the stove, and in the morning he left after prayers. The morning was bright and cool and clean, and quietly and peacefully Moses ben Shem-Tov walked from the synagogue. And although young Moses left the city, the happy hopeful barefoot spring had slipped gently into Cologne, once again and forever.

ood evening, Rabbi. You are having difficulty sleeping again? Put your feet up on the side bench and I will open the stove door. Let me push these coals back; the white glow will wash away all the cares of your hard day.

I heard your final prayers tonight and there is no use denying it— you are overworked. Even an old shammas like me can tell. I kept one eye on you when I was cleaning the dishes; I saw that you were watching the door, hoping that Reb Elbaum would leave early. But then Reb Anton stayed late to argue with Reb Etan about the talmudic passage (the one from the *Abodah Zarah* chapter in the fourth tractate of the *Mishnah*):

Humility is the greatest of all virtues. As it is said in the Book of Isaiah:

> The spirit of the Lord whispered a word
> When He appointed me to speak—
> And, O humble men, I have heard:
> "God will uplift the meek."

Note that it is not said that the saints or the heroes will be uplifted: It is the modest, the humble, and the meek who will be redeemed and who will rejoice. It is the modest who can inherit the earth.

And, Rabbi, that talmudic passage reminded me of old Jehuda ben Saul. (Rabbi Jehuda? He was two rabbis before you.) I remember how one day Rabbi Jehuda was lecturing to his yeshiva students. "Respect the modesty of the *hakham!*" he declared suddenly. The boys looked puzzled.

"*Hakham!* I say," said Rabbi Jehuda.

He nodded his head. "*Hakhamim,*" said the Rabbi, "they are the rabbinical interpreters of the Law!" He pounded on his *almemar*–his reading desk–and he looked sternly at the young men on the benches. The Rabbi stared at the boys, the boys looked at the floor, and there was silence; so the Rabbi said, "Let me say to you, young men– quoting from the beautiful Song of Songs–"

> Attend, O Jerusalem's children;
> Israelites come out–come away
> And welcome wise King Solomon
> Who wears the headband gay
> With which his mother crowned him
> On his wondrous wedding day.

Again, the Rabbi stared down at his charges. "Need I say more?" asked Rabbi Jehuda.

The yeshiva students hesitated. After a moment, young Moshe ben Samuel said, "Good Rabbi, certainly it is a beautiful verse. But what does it have to do with *hakhamim?*"

Rabbi Jehuda stepped back. He raised his eyebrows. "What does it have to do with *hakhamim?*" he asked. "Have I heard you correctly, Moshe? Why, this verse is the very modesty of the *hakham* incarnate!"

The Rabbi struck his fist on his desk. "Young men, fledgling scholars, the great rabbinical interpreters of the law have a golden crown, they have a headband of gay jewels. It is the *Torah* that crowns the *hakham* on the day of his teaching and on the day of his indoctrination into the Law of the Lord, amen."

The students settled in for a lecture. "Listen, my untutored boys," continued the Rabbi, "let us investigate this verse from the Song of Songs.

"Now, first the great singer says: 'Come out–come away and welcome wise King Solomon.' In other words, we Jews should go out and welcome the *hakham.* But this immediately raises questions: Where should we go? Should we go outside of our homes? Should we go into the marketplace? Should we leave the yeshiva?"

Rabbi Jehuda surveyed his charges. No one spoke. After a moment, the old man continued: "No, of course you should not go *outside*–at least not outside any building. Instead, you must go outside yourself. It is your own personal home–your self-important domain–it is your own self interest that you must leave. In other words, do not be too proud. Be modest. Humbly come outside of yourself."

The Rabbi closed his eyes. "Blessed be the Almighty Lord God, for you young Jews are all potential *hakhamim,*" he intoned, as he bowed his head.

"Ah, boys," sighed the Rabbi, opening his eyes again, "sometimes I think that I am not worthy of addressing a sermon to you, even when you listen. Perhaps you should be thought of as fish."

There was a long silence. Finally, young Moshe ben Samuel asked, "How are we like fish, Rabbi?"

" 'How?' you ask. How are you like fish? I will tell you how and I will tell you why. In the Book of Genesis you were compared to fish in the blessing with which Jacob, your forefather's forefather, had blessed you through his children. I remind you":

Then Jacob blessed his son Joseph. Next, he said of the two boys, Ephraim and Manasseh:

God is my eternal shepherd
  Always gently guiding me
He delivered me from harm
  And saved me from adversity.

May the great Lord God Almighty–
  With Whom my fathers talked
And in Whose smiling sunshine light
  Abraham and Isaac walked–

May He gently bless these boys
   May my own name be their name
(And my fathers' names theirs too)
   And may He give them lasting fame;

May they become a mighty people
   Under fragrant cedar trees
And let them multiply like the fish
   Which fill His plentiful seas.

"Yes, my good young men," continued the Rabbi, "you too are like these fish. And why is that? It is because the fish do not drink their own water. Instead, fish wait for rain to drop from the sky—and so do you. You see, my boys, while swimming in the water, fish do not drink. But as soon as the storm clouds gather, they raise their heads out of the water; then they drink the rain."

The students looked puzzled. Rabbi Jehuda looked at his fingers, then he looked at the ceiling. "Do you wonder about this, young men?" he asked. "Then I will explain. You see, fish find rainwater more tasty than their own water. And although *you* have the potential for generating many fine words yourselves—in fact, you continuously swim in an ocean of words—you too desire new words, words that seem to fall magically from the sky. You, my wide-eyed young scholars, are fish, and you hope for the tasty mystical rainwater of the *hakhamim*."

The Rabbi sighed. "However," he said quietly, almost to himself, "our words are no more magical than are yours."

Wearily, the Rabbi put his head down on his desk. The boys looked at one another. They began to stand and to gather their books. Suddenly Rabbi Jehuda looked up and said, "And now to return to the Song of Songs. Well, young men, how do we know that 'Jerusalem's children' actually refers to the rabbinical interpreters of the Law, the *hakhamim*?"

The students sat down again, but they did not know what to say. "I will tell you how we know this," answered the Rabbi. "We begin with the holy Psalm 87":

> Among towns, there is none
> God loves like Jerusalem
> Under the golden sun
> Within the gates of Zion.
>
> Jerusalem is built
> Upon the holy hill,
> God chose her for Israel
> As His peaceful domicile.

Rabbi Jehuda nodded and smiled. "Of course, it is all clear now," he said.

The boys looked at one another. Finally young Moshe said, "It is not entirely clear to me, Rabbi."

"Oh, it is not? Does the verse not say that the good Lord God (blessed be He) loves the gates of Zion?" asked the Rabbi sternly.

"Yes," said Moshe.

"Obviously, Moshe, this means that He loves those who are distinguished in studies of the gates of Judaic religious law," said the Rabbi. "It means that the Almighty One loves the *hakham*."

"And then," continued old Jehuda, "consider the words 'Welcome wise King Solomon' in the Song of Songs. This indicates that Solomon was a *hakham*. In fact, this is why he is called 'wise King Solomon'—for it says in the Book of Proverbs":

> Through Wisdom
>   Kings rule strongly;
> With Wisdom
>   Just laws are made.

"In other words, kings reign by the support of the Lord God's mighty Torah. Furthermore, all Israel are sons of kings, hence they are all potential *hakhamim* as well. Even you boys may conceivably become learned rabbinical interpreters of the Law," said the Rabbi, "– someday."

Old Rabbi Jehuda shook his head; he seemed worn out from this analysis. His voice faded. His eyelids drooped. He put his head in his hands and he closed his eyes. The yeshiva students waited politely for a few minutes. A thick silence lay on the walls, on the floor, and on the benches. Finally, the boys began to stand and to shuffle out. Two boys started to whisper. Suddenly the Rabbi awoke. He looked down at the boys. He stared at them and he said, "And consider the Song of Songs further, young men. How do we know that the line 'the headband gay, with which his mother crowned him' actually refers to the Torah?"

Again, the students sat down on the old benches. Rabbi Jehuda was saying, "Is it not said in the Holy Scriptures: 'Call Wisdom your mother'? And also it is written in the Book of Proverbs":

> Attend, my son, in the Holy place
>   To the teachings of the Lord,
> These sacred words are a headband of grace
>   And a golden necklace as reward.

The Rabbi nodded to himself. "Now," he said, "the hidden meanings of the Song of Songs are certainly beginning to shine forth." He nodded again and he spoke a bit louder: "And in this light, the line 'on his wondrous wedding day' obviously means the day of his teaching. Why is this? On a wedding day, the mother and the family rejoice. It is exactly the same with the members of a yeshiva – you should rejoice when a *hakham* visits you. Yes, my young and unformed charges, you should be happy that I am still alive to take the time to talk to you – old as I am, and young as you are."

The Rabbi seemed to be staring somewhere far away. "But, my boys, is it worth all the effort that I must make?" Rabbi Jehuda looked off sadly. "Often I think of the lament from the Book of Proverbs":

> This is the Scholar's Doubt:
>   I am weary O Lord;
> I am tired and worn out.
>
> I am an aged creature –
>   I scarcely am a man,
> I've learned nothing from my teacher.
>
> No wisdom do I retain,
>   I have no true insight,
> All facts seem quite profane.

I am weak, I am undone:
We mortals can't understand
The world of the Holy One.

"How true that is," sighed Rabbi Jehuda ben Saul. Then old Rabbi Jehuda put his head down on his desk, and he seemed to fall asleep.

Ah, the great Jehuda ben Saul is a warning to us all, Rabbi: scriptural analysis is filled with difficulties. A biblical passage is a complex thing; a scriptural verse is not what it appears at first. Even the *hakhamim* must work and work at it – and in the end they can never be certain that they have a full understanding. Therefore, a scholar must always remain modest. As the old Hebrew proverb reminds us: "Whisper your virtues in a low voice and proclaim your faults aloud."

Yes, scriptural analysis is more complex than it might appear to the novice. No one knew this better than old Rabbi Abraham ben Alexander, the mystic Achselrad of Cologne. He was always looking deep into matters, peering below the surfaces in his strange mystical way. Rabbi Abraham saw the handiwork of the Divine One at every turn. He saw the incontestably incomprehensible interventions of the good Lord God (blessed be He) in everything – even in the linens of the synagogue.

No, I am not making this up, Rabbi – my grandmother told me every detail. You see, one evening Rabbi Abraham was studying the fine craftsmanship of the tablecloths in the yeshiva. He looked closely at the tablecloths, and he began to see the faint outline of a face. It was the face of Jhida ben Moshe ben Joseph ha-Kohen, a dealer in fine woven cloths. And why did he see a young man's face in a piece of linen? It is a strange tale that my grandmother told to me long ago; now I will gladly tell it to you:

Once upon a time, said my grandmother, when Abraham ben Alexander was the Chief Rabbi, there lived in the Jewish Quarter of Cologne a pious man named Moshe ben Joseph ha-Kohen. Moshe was a dealer in fine woven cloths. By now Reb Moshe had grown quite old, and he had no children. Daily he prayed and prayed: Would the most beneficent Lord God grant him a son, even in his old age? If so, then the old man promised that the boy would study the Torah above all else.

When she heard these prayers, Moshe's wife raised her eyebrows. Then she patted her husband's hand, and she said, "Well, my dear, I suppose that all things are possible, if only we have faith."

I am happy to report, Rabbi, that it is true: all things *are* possible, and wonders *do* occur. The good Lord God (blessed be He) heard Moshe's prayer, and He gave the old man a son. Moshe named the child Jhida. When Jhida ben Moshe grew up, he was trained in the Torah – his father scrimped and saved and he spent all his money on teachers for his son. However, even with all his teachers' efforts, Jhida remained a rather modest student.

Then one day old Moshe ben Joseph died. After a sad week of mourning, the mother said to her son, "You have had the opportunity to study for many years. Now it is time to support the family. Follow my advice: Take the money that your father left and continue in the cloth trade so that we can live comfortably."

Jhida listened, but he also decided to consult with the sages of the Jewish community. He went to the old yeshiva in Cologne and stepped through the front door. He went through the anteroom, and he walked into the main prayer hall, which was filled with wooden benches. Jhida passed the twelve stained glass windows with their colored lions and snakes, he looked up at the Holy stone Ark, and he walked to the door of the back study room. There, the Rabbi was bent over a book and a group of scholars was sitting talking quietly.

"Good morning, gentlemen," said Jhida. He sat on one of the benches. "Now that my father (blessed be his memory and name for ever and ever, and may I be an atonement for his decease, amen) has died, my mother advises that I go into business. I know that studying the Torah is important – in fact, my father always dreamt that I would be a great *hakham*. However, my mother says that I must now support the family."

The old men talked among themselves. Then white-bearded Baruch ben Jacob said, "Jhida, as the Talmud tells us":

> The Holy Scriptures declares that honoring one's parents is equal to honoring the Omnipresent One (blessed be He). For it is said in the Book

of Exodus: "Honor your father and your mother; in this way, you will live long in the land that the Lord your God is giving to you."

The sages nodded and they murmured "amen." Then a younger scholar, Elisah ben Samuel, said, "Likewise, in the Book of Leviticus, it says":

You shall revere and honor, each of you, his mother and his father. And you shall keep My Sabbaths – I am the Lord.

"Exactly, good Elisah," said Joshua ben Eliezer. "Now, Jhida, two different actions are commanded here: namely, *revere* and *honor*. And the Talmud tells us clearly what these mean: By 'revere' is meant that you should not criticize or contradict their well-intentioned statements."

Lewe ben Anselm nodded and said, "And then, Jhida, what does the Talmud mean by 'honor'? 'Honor' means that you should provide your parents with sustenance. Give them food, drink, clothing, and shelter. Support them, and help them out of any difficulties."

"Therefore," continued another sage, Menahem ben Joel, "by all means follow your mother's wishes. Go into business and support her."

The other men nodded. And Moyses ben Nathan said, "Moreover, young man, we all wish you well. So we offer you the two scriptural passages for a prosperous business. The first is":

If the good Lord, the God of my father, the God of Abraham, and the Fear of Isaac, had not been with me, then you would have sent me away empty-handed and with no success. But God saw my labor and my hardships; thus, He has sustained me and He shall make me prosper in my work.

"Amen," said Baruch.

Old Shimshon ha-Zaken coughed and cleared his throat and he said, "Yes, amen. And the second passage is":

Joseph gave his steward this order: "Fill the men's packs with as much food as they can carry, and put each man's silver at the top of his pack."

"So, Jhida, we old men offer these thoughts now, with our best wishes and with the blessings of the good Lord God, amen."

"Amen," responded the other scholars, smiling and nodding and stroking their beards.

Jhida thanked the scholars, and he returned home. And so Jhida ben Moshe ha-Kohen followed his mother's advice–he went into business. Like his father, Jhida became a dealer in fine woven cloths. But Jhida decided to specialize–he concentrated his trade on samite, a heavy silk fabric with a warp of six threads interwoven with gold. In those days, Cologne was famous for its fancy woven silks, which were used for ecclesiastical garments and for fancy cushions and stoles and maniples and orphreys, and young Jhida went into business buying and selling finely woven narrow bands of samite silk.

As you might suspect, this was a very limited type of business, and it took a tremendous effort to make it work. Jhida ben Moshe tried, but he did not enjoy his life. Other businessmen cheated him. Tradesmen and weavers made false claims. Often Church buyers did not pay him. Soon, Jhida found that he himself had to bend the truth; he invented accounts, and he gave inaccurate and incomplete statements. To obtain the cloths he needed, Jhida had to pay bribes, and even then Jhida rarely received cloth of the quality that had been promised–frequently he was given only remnant pieces.

One day Jhida went to Bonn on a buying trip, and he returned empty-handed. That evening he walked into the front door of his house with his shoulders slumped. His mother asked, "And where are all the cloths that you should have bought?"

"Mother," he said, "I cannot take this life any more. The world of business is a nightmare. I am surrounded by lies. Everyone promises, but no one lives up to his claims. Every single businessman cheats in some way. I have tried my best, but I simply cannot remain a cloth merchant. Instead, let me study the Torah, which is the best trade of all, amen."

His mother sighed. "Listen, Jhida, you are the only child I have," she said. "If you wish to study the Torah, then so be it–I will not stand in your way."

Jhida sat at the kitchen table. He looked at his hands. "You know, Mother," he said, "actually I am a talented man. Father (may his memory be a blessing for me and for all my children forever, amen) gave me the opportunity to study, and now I know quite a bit of Halakhah. I am certain that I can become a well-known and respected scholar."

Jhida's mother said, "A scholar is fine – but 'well-known and respected' is not really important."

"It is important to me," said the young man. Jhida ate his dinner, and he went to bed. The next morning he packed a knapsack, and then Jhida ben Moshe ha-Kohen went off into the world in order to study the Torah. It was springtime and the world felt new and fresh and clean.

Jhida thought that he would begin by walking and thinking. Perhaps he could make a pilgrimage to some well-known centers of study, places such as the mystic yeshivas of Worms or of Regensburg. Jhida walked and walked. After a while, he came out into the open country and he saw an old man ploughing. The man was walking slowly and awkwardly: a book was lying open on the plough in front of him.

Jhida went up to the man and said, "Hello, good sir, may the Lord be with you – blessed be the Most Holy One."

The old man returned the greeting: "May the good Lord God bless you also."

Then Jhida asked, "For whom are you ploughing? Who lets you work and study at the same time?"

"Well," said the old man, "I plough and I sow and I weed and I hoe for myself. I give the corn to the poor, and I give the wheat and the oats to scholars. Nonetheless, there is always enough food left over for me."

"Ah, *I* belong to that class of people," said the young man.

"You are poor?"

"No – I am a scholar. In fact, I would have to say that I am a young *hakham*," said Jhida.

"Well, well – that is fine," said the old man, leaning against his plough. "I love to meet scholars. Tell me something that you know; then I can learn from you."

Jhida thought for a moment. He looked around at the rich field in which they were standing. "I know that Moses told us how the good Lord God (blessed be He) gave us water, land, stones, and food as our due," he said.

The old man was quiet. Then he said, "Do you mean that wealth and fertile land and good food are owed to us?"

"Certainly," said Jhida, "that is what the Holy Scriptures says."

Again the old man was quiet. After a moment he said, "Perhaps you are referring to the verses in the Book of Deuteronomy where Moses, in his great farewell address, tells the children of Israel":

> For the Lord your God is bringing you to a rich land, to a land of streams, of springs, and of underground waters gushing out in hill and in valley. It will be a land of wheat and barley, of vines, fig trees, and pomegranates, a land of olives, cream, and honey. It will be a land where you will never live in poverty nor will you want for anything. It will be a land whose common stones are iron ore and gold and from whose hills you will dig copper. You will have plenty to eat, and then you will bless the Lord your God for the rich warm land that He has given you.

"Yes, exactly," said Jhida.

Then the old man said, "You are still young; perhaps you can return later, when you know more."

Jhida opened his eyes wide and he said angrily, "What do you know, old man!"

But the old man said only, "I must return to my studies now." And he resumed the slow ploughing of his fields.

Jhida stalked off and continued on his way. Suddenly it began to rain and rain. Jhida was drenched. A fog arose. It seemed as if the surrounding fields had disappeared. Jhida wandered about, but he could see neither man nor road.

Jhida walked and he walked. Eventually he found himself, dripping wet, by the side of a small hut. He went to the door. There was no one to be seen. After listening quietly, Jhida knocked and an old woman answered.

"Excuse me," said Jhida. "May I come inside to get out of the weather?"

"Certainly," said the woman. "My goodness, you are wet and cold. I have a little cold porridge here. Are you hungry?"

"Yes, I am," said Jhida.

The woman ladled some of the cold cereal into a bowl. Jhida was very hungry, but just as he was about to eat, the old woman put up her hand and she said a blessing:

Blessed be You, O Lord our God, King of the world—You Who feeds the whole world in Your goodness, with grace, kindness, and mercy. As the psalmist sings:

> God gives food to all His creatures,
>   And His love endures forever;
> God gives shelter to His children,
>   And His love endures forever;
> So give thanks to the God of Heaven—
>   For His love endures forever.

And with Your great love and goodness, we have not lacked food, and we will not lack food for ever. For the sake of Your great and ineffable Name, take care of all and do good to all and provide food for all Your humble creatures. As the psalmist sings:

> The eyes of all lift in hope to You
> And You give them food when it is due,
> With open arms and a bountiful hand
> You give full meals to the hungry man.

Blessed be You, O Lord our God, Who feeds us all.

Then there was silence. Jhida began to eat—but then he looked at the old woman. Suddenly he felt very uneasy and much less hungry.

"Where is your bowl? Are you not hungry yourself?" Jhida asked.

"Yes, I suppose that I am," answered the old woman.

"Then why are you not eating?"

"There is only enough food for one person. You are young. You will live longer than me; you deserve the food."

Jhida was hungry, but as he looked at the old woman he found that he could not eat. So he got up and thanked the woman, and he left.

The rain was lighter now, and Jhida ben Moshe continued walking. He felt cold and miserable. Soon he came to another small wooden house. Again, he went to the door. He knocked, and this time an old man answered.

"Excuse me, sir," said Jhida. "May I come in to get out of this rain?"

"My goodness—you are wet! Please come in," said the man. Jhida stepped into the small room.

"I have some lentils on the stove," said the man. "Are you hungry?"

"Yes I am," said Jhida.

The old man ladled some of the beans into a bowl. Jhida was extremely hungry, but just as the young man was about to eat, the old man put up his hand and said a blessing:

Blessed be You, O Lord our God, King of the world—You Who feeds the whole world in Your goodness, with grace, kindness, and mercy. As the psalmist sings:

> God gives food to all His creatures,
>   And His love endures forever;
> God gives shelter to His children,
>   And His love endures forever;
> So give thanks to the God of Heaven—
>   For His love endures forever.

And with Your great love and goodness, we have not lacked food, and we will not lack food for ever. For the sake of Your great and ineffable Name, take care of all and do good to all and provide food for all Your humble creatures. As the psalmist sings:

> The eyes of all lift in hope to You
> And You give them food when it is due,
> With open arms and a bountiful hand
> You give full meals to the hungry man.

Blessed be You, O Lord our God, Who feeds us all.

The old man had been reading a prayer book. Now he returned to his reading—and there was silence. Jhida began to eat, but then he looked at the old man. Suddenly Jhida felt very uneasy.

"Are you not hungry yourself?" Jhida asked.

"Yes, I suppose that I am," answered the old man.

"Then why are you not eating?"

"I am old now, and food is not as important as study."

Jhida ben Moshe ha-Kohen looked down at his bowl. He could not eat. Instead, he got up and thanked the man, and then he left the house.

The weather was cloudy, but the rain had stopped. Jhida looked at the sky. He looked at the fields and the trees. He noticed the small green leaves on the tangleberry bushes. Then Jhida turned back down the road.

Jhida returned to Cologne. Instead of going directly home, he went to the yeshiva first. Jhida ben Moshe stepped through the front door of the old synagogue building. He removed his wet shoes in the anteroom. He walked into the main prayer hall, which was filled with wooden benches. Jhida passed the twelve stained glass windows with their colored lions and snakes, he looked up at the Holy Ark made of stone, and he walked to the door of the back study room. There, the Rabbi was bent over a book and seven old sages sat on the worn benches along the edge of the room.

White-haired Baruch ben Jacob looked up and said, "Jhida, why are you here?"

Jhida answered, "Reb Baruch, I am not at ease with myself. Let me sit here a moment and talk to you." Jhida sat on one of the worn benches. "I thought that I was a scholar," he said. "But now I am not convinced that I really am. I thought that I could live comfortably with just my studies—but somehow it does not seem to be the right life for me after all."

The sages were quiet for a moment. Then the youngest sage, Elisah ben Samuel, said, "Jhida, the true scholar need not be a brilliant *hakham*, and the true scholar need not be an ascetic. Many fine men in many comfortable occupations are true scholars under the eyes of the good Lord God (blessed be He)."

And Joshua ben Eliezer added, "That is well said, Reb Elisah."

"Amen," said Lewe ben Anselm.

Then Menahem ben Joel nodded and he said, "Jhida, recall the scriptural Proverb–"

> The first step to wisdom's reward
> Is reverence for the holy Lord,
> Knowledge of God's true word
> Is mightier than the iron sword.
>
> Through His endless love sincere
> Your days will be rich and deep
> And many happy comforting years
> Will be yours before you sleep.

And Moyses ben Nathan said, "Yes–and you can live this long, happy, and holy life in any clothes, Jhida; it does not matter if you wear an immaculate Sabbath robe or a torn and dirty workman's tunic."

Finally, old Shimshon ha-Zaken nodded and said, "Exactly, Reb Moyses–just hold firmly to the holy teachings, Jhida; that is all that is truly important. Recall the scriptural Proverb":

> Listen My students
> Take My teachings as guide
> Know My commandments
> Study Law at My side–
> And the years of your life
> Shall be far multiplied
> As the lights in the Heavens
> Thick with stars far and wide.

Jhida nodded and he turned to Rabbi Abraham. "And what do *you* think, good Rabbi?" asked the young man.

Old Abraham Achselrad woke with a start. "What?" he asked. Then he said, "What do I think? Well–one should always trust in the Lord."

Rabbi Abraham squinted and he blinked his eyes. He stared at a linen tablecloth lying on the edge of his desk. Was Jhida's face lightly outlined in the stitching? The Rabbi looked closely, and he smiled. He tapped his desk with one finger, he stroked his beard, and he said, "Yes, Jhida, trust in the good Lord God. And then remember: temperance, balance, modesty, and humility. You really do not need much else in this life. In the Book of Proverbs, it is said":

> These things I hope that God concedes—
> Keep lying and immodesty afar,
> Also give me just my basic needs:
> Shelter, food, and the evening star.

Jhida nodded once and then he nodded twice, and he thanked the Rabbi and the other sages. Then Jhida left the small study room of the yeshiva. He went back out into the anteroom. He put on his wet shoes, and he walked the streets of Cologne. Jhida ben Moses walked for more than an hour, up one street and down the next, and eventually he found that he had reached his home.

Jhida walked into the house. His mother was preparing dinner. Jhida sat down and ate a good meal. He felt better, he read the Torah, he said his prayers, and he went to sleep. And Jhida dreamt the happy dreams of a man at peace.

The next morning, Jhida set out for the marketplace; there, he bought many varieties of special woven cloths. Jhida took his time. He chose carefully, and he smiled when he felt the careful workmanship. He bought fine pieces of baldachin, ciclatoun, damask, kincob, samite, sendal, and velvet. The prices he paid were too high, but that did not worry him; and later in the week, when he sold the cloth, he made only a very small profit. In the evenings, when he returned home, he helped his mother to prepare dinner and then he read the Torah quietly to himself. Each day, Jhida ben Moshe ha-Kohen went to sleep content. Humbly, he asked for only small things from life—and he received them. And then Jhida was happy for the rest of his days, amen.

What is that, Rabbi? I was just resting my eyes—please, join me here by the stove. (I think you will be too warm on that bench; try the one nearer to the wall.) An old man like me can doze forever by a warm stove; I suppose that is because of the green stones at the bottom of the stove feet.

What do I mean? Why, Rabbi, certainly you know the power of *Yahalom*, the green emerald stone. *Yahalom* is the princely stone, the stone of Zebulun. And in fact all green jewels are stones of Zebulun: they are all princely. Green stones help your businesses, they preserve tranquility and peace, they soothe people and bring good will—and they encourage sleep.

My grandmother kept a special green stone by her bed. She had found the stone in the river when she was young, and she claimed that it helped her through many a sleepless night. Did that stone really have magical powers? Frankly, I do not know, but my grandmother said that the restful sleep given by the green stone accounted for her amazingly good health even when she was older than I am (and I am eighty, you know). Of course, grandmother always reminded me that the main cause of sleeplessness is demons—they make noises at night.

Demons live in the backs of pantries and under heavy furniture and in wells and in cellars, and they hiss and they rustle and they keep you awake at night. Fortunately, however, green stones repel demons.

Most of the time the cellar-demons are the worst. On the other hand, sometimes even cellar-demons can surprise you by doing good deeds. For instance, my grandmother told me that once upon a time, in the congregation of Rabbi Abraham ben Alexander, Achselrad of Cologne, there was a devout man named Machir ben Aleydis ha-Kohen, and Machir was helped by the demons living in his cellar.

Machir was a goldsmith. He was a quiet man, and he lived alone; in fact, Machir had absolutely no relatives living in Cologne or any-where nearby. One day Machir became very ill and he thought that he was about to die. He was too weak to stand. He was sweaty and hot. His head would spin if he made the slightest movement. After a while, Machir could no longer eat, and day by day he became weaker and weaker and weaker.

Machir ben Aleydis could barely move. The house demons from his pantry and from under the furniture and from the well and from the cellar all began to feel sorry for him. The spirits from the cellar had a conference, and they decided to help. These cellar-demons brought food and water to Machir every day. One day passed, and a second came and went. Machir's fever subsided. His skin became drier. His eyes became clearer. Yes, Machir got stronger, and eventually he recovered.

After two more weeks, Machir was completely well again. The goldsmith was so grateful that he decided to will his house to the demons living in his cellar–now they would have a place to live for ever and ever. Therefore, carefully and legally, Machir wrote a brief will:

To the officials whom it may concern:

I am Machir ben Aleydis ha-Kohen. In the blessed Name of the Al-mighty Lord God, Whose memorial will be exalted and praised for ever and ever, I declare that I have no known living relatives. Therefore, I will and bequeath my house on Unter Goldschmied Street in the city of

Cologne to the kind demons who live in the cellar, from this day and after my death, amen.

Signed,
Machir,
the son of Aleydis ha-Kohen

Many years later Machir died quietly. The women from the Burial Society came and prepared the body, a small funeral was held, the house was closed, and the cellar remained locked and heavily barred.

After a while, a pious Jew moved to Cologne from Bonn. The newcomer was a box-maker. His name was Reuben ben Samuel and he had a wife and two sons, Aaron and Lemhule. The family was welcomed by the Jewish community. It was pointed out that Machir's house was empty. Machir had had no relatives, and no one had seen a will; therefore, the parnas of the congregation had taken charge of finding a new occupant for the house. Reuben arranged to buy the house, and the parnas ruled that the money would go toward community charity.

Of course, one must be cautious when moving into a new house, and in his meeting with the community elders in the back room of the old Cologne yeshiva, Reuben ben Samuel heard much wise advice. White-haired Baruch ben Jacob said, "Let me remind you, young man, if you build, then use wood. Any change bothers the local demons, but a stone house has an air of stability and permanence—therefore it is certain to irritate the demons. (Although even a house of wood can bring on problems.)"

A younger scholar, Elisah ben Samuel, nodded, adding, "If the new house is on the site of an old one, then be careful to put the windows and the doors in their exact former positions. Again, this is a courtesy to the local demons: their habits have become fixed, and they are bound to be upset by changes."

Next, Joshua ben Eliezer said, "Those are important rules, gentlemen. However, I always say that it is better to build as an investment. Because of pre-existing demons, it is wise not to move into a new house at all—you are certain to irritate the spirits somehow. So, sell a new house if you possibly can."

And Lewe ben Anselm said, "Exactly, Reb Joshua. And as a general principle, Reuben, always let new developments settle a bit.

The local spirits need time to get accommodated to new things. Always leave a new house uninhabited for a time."

Reuben ben Samuel raised his eyebrows, but he listened politely and attentively. Then he said, "Good rabbis, thank you for this advice. However, I am not building a new house. I am just moving into an old house; it is already well established and quite settled."

Menahem ben Joel stroked his beard and said, "In any case, you should be careful, Reuben: every house has hidden demons. Remember, when you first arrive, bring bread, salt, and sugar for protection and for good luck."

"In addition," added Moyses ben Nathan, "before entering the door for the first time, you must recite the three 'new house' verses from the Holy Scriptures."

Reuben looked puzzled. "What are the three 'new house' verses?" he asked.

The sages looked to old Shimshon ha-Zaken. Shimshon coughed and he cleared his throat and said, "Well, Reuben, these verses are:

"*One*: 'So Jacob lived in Canaan, the country in which his father had settled.'

"*Two*: 'Thus Israel settled in Egypt, in Goshen. There, they acquired land, and they were fruitful and increased greatly.'

"*Three*: 'On the first day of the first month, you shall set up the Tabernacle, the Tent of the Presence.' "

Reuben repeated the verses, and he nodded his head. Then he thanked the Cologne sages and he left the back room. Reuben passed the Holy stone Ark. He walked by the twelve stained glass windows with their colored lions and snakes. He went through the main prayer hall, which was filled with wooden benches. Finally, he walked through the anteroom, and he stepped out into the alley leading to Judengasse Street in the old Jewish Quarter of medieval Cologne.

A few days later, Reuben ben Samuel and his family moved into Machir's house. They brought bread and salt and sugar on the first day for luck, and they recited the "new house" verses as they stepped across the threshold. For a time everything went well. The house was large and Reuben's family had few possessions, and for a few weeks the new owners did not investigate the attic above or the cellar below.

However, children are curious, and Aaron, the older son, was an especially bold young boy. One day he forced open the cellar door. In the dark, Aaron tripped and he fell down the seven broken steps and he was killed. It was a black day in the family, but after the funeral and a week of mourning, Reuben and his wife and their other son Lemhule slowly began to recover. And slowly but as surely as the sunrise, life went on.

Seven days came and seven days went. The family slept poorly. Hisses and rustlings wafted up from the cellar at night. Strange happenings began to occur during the day. In the kitchen, when food was cooked at the hearth, gray ashes appeared in the pots. Candlesticks fell and broke, and vases tumbled and smashed on the floor. Doors would stick unexpectedly or they blew open when there was no wind.

Another week came and another week went. After five weeks, after six weeks, after seven cycles of seven days, the problems continued—they seemed even to grow worse. So one morning, Reuben and his wife and his son Lemhule went to consult the elders of the community. The seven sages of Cologne were sitting along the benches in the back room of the yeshiva, where the Rabbi was dozing. After listening to the entire story, the old men shook their heads, they stroked their beards, and they murmured among themselves. "This is a serious matter," said old Shimshon ha-Zaken.

"What do *you* think, Rabbi?" asked Reuben ben Samuel.

Rabbi Abraham awoke with a start. "What do I think?" he asked. He looked around at the sages and at Reuben and his family. "Ah, good Reuben, I think that we must all trust in the glorious Lord our God (blessed be He)." And the sages nodded and they stroked their beards and they murmured "amen."

Reuben thought about that sentiment for a moment. Then he said, "But Rabbi, what can I do about my house?"

"Your house?" asked the Rabbi. "Clearly, in order to advise about your house, Reuben, I must go and see it for myself."

Then Rabbi Abraham put on his hat and his coat, and he walked out into a sunny morning in the Jewish Quarter of Cologne, on the wide dark River Rhine. It was the springtime. Light winds played through the streets. Was there the sound of ships from warm ports, far, far away? The Rabbi stood a moment. He bent his head and he listened. On some gentle-winded days, the Rabbi thought that he could hear the sounds of the Mediterranean or even of the suntanned Holy

Lands beyond. Old Achselrad thought that he heard faint voices and he often listened to the winds:

> He would monitor the gentle breeze
> Through ancient atmospheric seas
> And map the clouds adagio
> From far below.
>
> Now, this springtime wisp of wind right here
> Peeking in the window mirror
> To whisper, then to disappear—
> Do you hear?
>
> Once it came from David's golden tongue
> Another spring; the world was young
> When first he breathed the holy word
> That we've just heard.

Yes, Rabbi, old Achselrad listened, and he thought that he heard ancient holy words. Angels carry those words in the light breezes, and Kabbalists say that holy gentle winds continue blowing forever, mixed and intermixed into our everyday weathers and flowing eternally and everywhere throughout our vast, thick, and incondensably complex world, amen.

In any case, Abraham ben Alexander stepped out the front door of the synagogue, and he listened to the winds; he looked down the road, and then he began to walk toward Reuben's house. The Rabbi walked down Judengasse Street. He turned west onto Engegasse Street, and he went around the corner of Unter Goldschmied Street to the house that once had belonged to Machir ben Aleydis of Cologne and that now belonged to Reuben ben Samuel, formerly of Bonn.

The old house was stone; it was gray and moss-covered. The doors were heavy and barred. Along the side was a courtyard with a vegetable garden, a shed, and a well. Inside, two dark rooms took up the whole first floor: a kitchen in the back and a sitting room in the front. There was a narrow winding staircase leading to the bedrooms upstairs, and the cellar door was in the back. Now the cellar door remained latched and the damp dark underground room was filled with a crush of demons.

Rabbi Abraham walked toward the back door. He listened to the winds and a chill breeze seemed to come from the cellar, carrying the voices of two demons speaking to one another—may the good Lord God protect us from such evils.

As the Rabbi stood listening and wondering, he heard one demon cough and hiss and ask the other demon: "Ah, you malevolent spirit, where is that irritating Jewish family that has invaded our house?"

"It is strange that you should ask me that question now," said the second demon. "But you are a strange and wicked creature, so I will answer. The entire family went to the Cologne synagogue. They hope to enlist the aid of that meddlesome Rabbi Abraham. Apparently, Reuben ben Samuel is still intent on remaining in this house—in *our* house—and undoubtedly he will continue to bother us endlessly."

"I cannot understand him," said the first demon in a rustling dry voice. "Have we not already killed one of his children? Must we kill the other son or the wife or even Reuben himself?"

"Ah, you hairy dybbuk, I fear it may yet come to that," answered the second demon, hissing and coughing and spitting and laughing.

When Rabbi Abraham heard this, he had no doubts about what he should do, for it is said in the Talmud:

> We are told in the Book of Deuteronomy: "Then all who dwell on earth shall see that you have the Name of the Lord, and they shall go in fear of you." And in this passage, the word "all" includes demons, dybbuks, devils, and other evil spirits.

So, with this in mind, Achselrad invoked the Name of the Lord in order to protect Reuben ben Samuel. The holy man sat down, right there on the ground, and he wrote out a holy charm. First, he took a small piece of white parchment from his pocket. On one side, he wrote the *Shema* followed by seven mystical words. Then he turned the paper over and he wrote:

> Mighty is Yahweh-Elohim of Israel. By all the virtues of the Lord's holy Name, *Shaddai*, may Reuben ben Samuel and every member of his

family remain safe and sound. May they be protected from all manner
of malign spirits. May their home be a haven from evil, and may they
live in the shelter of the good Lord God (blessed be He) forever. Then
may all their children and grandchildren grow up in health and study the
Torah and marry and raise families and find a quiet, happy old age.
Amen, eternally hallelujah – thus shall be Your will, *selah* and amen.

The Rabbi rolled the parchment into a tight scroll; he tied the paper
with seven white threads, and in each thread he put seven neat knots.
Next, he strung the small packet on a slender white rope, and he tied
the parchment amulet onto the cellar door of the house, pronouncing
seven mystical Names of the Lord God Almighty.

    After a moment, a wind arose. It came from inside the house,
from the bowels of the dank dark basement, and it blew the demons
out into the street, scattering them in a rush – hither, thither, and yon.
A gabbling crush of hairy demons and evil spirits flew about wildly,
shrieking and hissing and coughing and crying. And even the holy
Rabbi stood back a moment, pushed aside by the pressure of the vast
throng of cold cruel angry spirits.

    They flew about like a storm tide, these demons – and to the
uninitiated eye, it seemed as if a wild wind had blown up suddenly,
tearing through the branches of the trees and blowing the dust of the
yards and the streets. One of the cellar-demons coughed and spat and
hissed and shrieked, and it came over to Rabbi Abraham and said, "You
merciless old man – you have banished us from our house! Rightfully,
that house was ours. We inherited it legally. Now we demand justice.
We demand a hearing in the *Bet Din*."

    As you know, Rabbi, even demons have a right to be heard in the
Bet Din, the religious court. So Rabbi Abraham nodded, and he said,
"Very well – we will hear your case this afternoon." And he turned and
walked back to the yeshiva.

    This was a Thursday, court day in the the Juden Viertels, the
Jewish Quarter of Cologne. Rabbi Abraham ben Alexander and the
two other judges sat upon a bench by the Holy stone Ark in the main
prayer hall. After the other cases had been heard and decided, the Rabbi
stood at the *almemar* – the synagogue's main reading desk. Then he said,
"At this time, we shall hear the case of the spirits that have been

residing in the house of Reuben ben Samuel, now of Cologne and formerly of Bonn."

The synagogue seemed to darken; a misty cloud flowed in from the anteroom and hovered in a far corner. A cold damp feeling crawled along the floor and the walls, and even at a distance, all the people felt fearful.

For a moment there was silence. Finally a rustling dry voice hissed and coughed, and it said, "Listen, you cruel and inconsiderate people. We spirits have lived in the house on Unter Goldschmied Street before any of you were born. We lived in the cellar and in the corners and in the attic; we lived in the chimneys and in the walls. This has always been our home. Usually it was quiet—and that is exactly what we want. We cannot sleep during the day if there are noisy children running about. We cannot stand the smell of Jewish cooking. And all this constant Jewish praying is like an insect buzzing and buzzing and buzzing in our ears."

But Reuben ben Samuel said, "This is *our* house now. We bought it—and it is a human house, not a demon house. You will just have to go somewhere else; you have no right to live there."

"No right?" asked the demon. "No right?" it repeated, hissing and laughing. The demon shrieked and it coughed and it whipped out the written will of old Machir ben Aleydis, and to the assembled people who could not see the demons it seemed as if a wind had suddenly blown a parchment paper into the room and onto the floor. The shammas picked up the paper. He handed it to the Rabbi, who read it carefully.

The demon continued: "I will tell you about our rights! We soft-hearted spirits saved the life of the last owner, a Mr. Machir Aleydis. To repay us, he willed us his house. This was our due. And now we claim the house legally. You will see, Rabbi, that the last will and testament of Machir is in perfect order. Therefore, rabbis and judges, we demand that you remove this bothersome person and his noisy family from our house. In fact, we also expect compensation for all the grief that we poor spirits have suffered."

The Rabbi was a very holy man; unlike the others, he could see the demons. He stared at them intently for a moment. Then he looked at Reuben and he asked, "And what have you to say, Reuben?"

Reuben stood up. He felt a bit shaky, but he built up his courage and he said, "Good rabbis, I knew nothing of this document. I came to Cologne with my family, and in accord with all the appropriate and legal requirements, I bought Machir's house from this very congregation. Our house is a Jewish house, and it is in the Jewish district. We are good Jews. We have followed all the local Jewish rules. Therefore, in the first place, I think that we are legally entitled to own and to live in the house."

The demons hissed and coughed, and a cold damp chill wind whirled and twirled in the dark corner of the old synagogue of Cologne. Reuben swayed but he remained standing. "In the second place," he said, "demons should live away from people. We have enough troubles as it is, without having to fend off evil spirits too."

Reuben looked at the dark and empty space in the synagogue occupied by the demons. Nervously he rubbed his hands along the purple fringes of his small prayer shawl, his *tallis katan.* "Moreover," said Reuben, "the claimants are demons. Even if they do possess a legal will, I think that human law cannot be applied here. I think that these spirits can never inherit human property."

The demons hissed and they coughed and they spat and they shrieked, and the humans in the synagogue felt quite afraid indeed.

The judges sat silent, listening quietly to both sides of the argument. When no more was to be said, the three holy men stood and they withdrew to the small back room of the yeshiva.

One of the judges said, "What do you gentlemen think?"

The three old men were silent a moment. Then Rabbi Abraham said, "Traditionally, when one enters a new house, he should say (from the Book of Genesis): 'So Jacob lived in Canaan, the country in which his father had settled.' And later in the Book of Genesis, it is written: 'Thus Israel settled in Egypt, in Goshen. There, they acquired land and they were fruitful and increased greatly.' "

The other judges stroked their beards and nodded. "Clearly," continued Rabbi Abraham, "these verses refer to Israelites – that is, to men and not to demons. Therefore, in matters of occupancy, the good Lord God (blessed be He) favors men over demons."

The other judges nodded again. "In addition," said Rabbi Abraham, "the Law of the good Lord God requires demons, devils, dybbuks, and all other malign spirits to avoid the habitations of men and to disperse themselves and to live only in solitary places."

Again, the two assistant judges nodded and one of them said, "True, Rabbi."

"The house in question is a Jewish house in the midst of a Jewish district in a populous town. Therefore," concluded the Chief Rabbi of Cologne, "I suggest that demons can hold no legal title to the house of the goldsmith, Machir ben Aleydis ha-Kohen."

And both of the other judges said, "Amen."

The three old sages returned to the main prayer hall. Rabbi Abraham ben Alexander looked at the demons and he looked at Reuben. "Men are inherently good," began Achselrad. "Also, the Talmud reminds us: 'God is only goodness–evil never comes from Heaven.' In contrast, demons and evil spirits are inherently bad. Thus, demons are not protected within the sphere of the good Lord God's favored children."

There was silence. One of the demons spoke up: "Listen, Rabbi, regardless of your moralizing and name-calling, we have a valid will here."

The Rabbi looked at the demon for a moment. Then the holy man said, "In regard to this specific claim, Rabbi Jochanan ben Baroka wrote in the talmudic tractate *Baba Batra* that if inheritance statements refer to one who is not entitled to inherit, then the statement is invalid–no matter how properly it is written.

"In the Book of Leviticus, the Almighty Lord God spoke to Moses and He commanded":

> Do not resort to ghosts, spirits, or demons. Do not make yourselves unclean by seeking them out or by associating with them in any way: they are not among My sphere of holy children–and I am the Lord.

"We judges have concluded that demons cannot inherit human property. Therefore, the will is invalid."

The demons angrily hissed and they coughed and they flew about in a dark misty wind. The evil spirits refused to stay still and they refused to depart. Rabbi Abraham removed a small square amulet from his robe. He waved the amulet over his head. In a stern voice, he pronounced seven holy words. And then he chanted:

Was a graveyard where you've grown,
Rising in Dumah's sacred ground?
It matters not—I send you home;
Return there, evil ones: sink down!

Is rotting soil what you choose?
Then return to crumbling fetid clay,
Go back to mud and dirt and ooze:
Sink there for ever and a day.

Kings have vanished in graveyard clay
And so shall you—mud is your home.
Or are you from the black sea spray?
Were you born in wave and foam?

Then fly off to the Antipodes
And drown beneath cold vortices
Churned to froth by the frigid breeze
Of vast and heartless open seas.

Go back to Sheol's cruel abyss
With thick muds for your nighttime bed;
Fall over the dank, black precipice
Where cold winds will shriek around your head.

Let us never hear your laugh afar,
Your wicked, dusty, hissing cry,
As long as sun and moon and star
Light up God's wide celestial sky.

At this, the demons shrieked in terror and they were swept together, rising up like one black wave. The cold cloud of evil spirits rushed from the holy wooden building, and they fled to the darkest forest in the outlying countryside, never to haunt Cologne again.

All the assembled people felt the fearsome creatures pass before them like a grim bleak wind. Tiredly, Rabbi Abraham ben Alexander sat down, and for a few minutes no one spoke. "Are we safe now?" asked Reuben weakly.

"Yes," said the Rabbi.

Uncertainly, Reuben looked at his wife and his son. The Rabbi watched the family. He tapped his finger on the bench. Then he went into the back room and he returned with a small shiny green stone. He gave this stone to Reuben, repeating the priestly benediction:

> May the Lord bless you and watch over you
> May the Lord make His face to shine upon you
> May the Lord be gracious and good to you
> May the Lord look kindly on you
> And may He give you peace, amen.

Rabbi Abraham instructed Reuben to have his wife sew the small green stone into the hem of his *tallis katan*. The good woman did that, right then and there. Then Reuben ben Samuel and his wife and his son Lemhule left the synagogue. The family went home – they moved back into the house that had once belonged to Machir the goldsmith. The green stone remained sewn into the *tallis katan*. And the parchment amulet remained tied to the cellar door handle of Reuben's home, where gently it blew in the wind for years and years and years. And Reuben's family lived in the house uneventfully ever after.

abbi, I am glad to see you here alone. I want to apologize for my outburst during the service this evening. It was just that I heard Reb Anton say that he was jealous of Reb Elbaum's good fortune. Imagine—Reb Anton let himself be envious, and in the synagogue no less!

No, Rabbi, I do not think that casual comments are an acceptable excuse. In the olden days, in the strict and pious days of our fathers, Reb Anton would have been ordered to leave and never to return. Remember, at that time the last prayer each day was:

May this be acceptable before You, O Lord my God and God of my fathers and my forefathers: let no hatred toward us enter the heart of any man nor hatred of any other man enter our own hearts; and may no envy of us enter the heart of any man nor envy of any other man enter our hearts. May Your Torah be our occupation all the days of our lives, and may all our words be well received by You, amen.

As my grandmother always told me: "Envy is simply not allowed, my little boy." Then she would repeat the scriptural Proverb:

> Envy only those who truly believe –
>   Those who revere the Lord –
> Then you too shall eventually receive
>   A long and fine reward:
> The golden thread of your life's great weave
>   Will remain an uncut cord.

She would also quote from the Talmud:

> Plagues occur from seven ill causes: envy, bloodshed, pride, robbery, slander, unchastity, and vain swearing.

and:

> Envy, excess indulgence, and hatred of his fellow creatures put a man outside of the Almighty Lord's good world.

So, Rabbi, you can see why I find envy such a serious fault. . . .
    What is that, Rabbi? Well, I will tell you: envy is the quiet insistent whispering of the evil Samael himself. Grandmother once told me a very sad story of envy; apparently, it was originally related to Abraham Achselrad by Rabbi Petahiah. Yes, exactly – that was Petahiah ben Jacob. Petahiah was the brother of Rabbi Isaac ben Jacob ha-Lavan (Isaac "the Wise") of Prague, who wrote a profound commentary on several talmudical treatises. Petahiah was a wanderer; in fact, he toured the entire world. Petahiah traveled through Poland, Russia, the land of the Khazars, Armenia, Media, Persia, Babylonia, and Palestine, and then he wrote about his adventures in a book called *Sivuv ha-Olam* ("Around the World").
    Rabbi Petahiah's travels were at the end of the twelfth century, in the days of old Achselrad and well before Asher ben Yehiel was the Chief Rabbi of Cologne. Why do I introduce Rabbi Asher? It is simply this: When he was the leading scholar in Cologne, Asher spent most of his time writing and reading. Rabbi Asher studied the Torah and the Talmud in the little back room of the yeshiva – this was the room where the Cologne rabbis had passed endless hours working and thinking and arguing with themselves. Above the back study room was a loft for storage. One spring morning, on a day that he felt should

be devoted to organizing and to piling papers, to dusting off books and to setting things in their neat and orderly places, a day with little time for difficult thought – on that gentle dreamy day, Asher ben Yehiel was rooting around among the manuscripts in the loft. After a while, Rabbi Asher found an old letter from Rabbi Petahiah of Regensburg to Rabbi Abraham ben Alexander, Achselrad of Cologne.

"My dear Rabbi Abraham – [began the letter]

"I have just met a fine young man, a Jew from Worms. He has agreed to carry this letter to my good friend, Rabbi Jacob ben Elijah of Worms, who I am certain will then arrange to transport it to you. I write to wish you and your family well, to convey my fondest greetings to all the Jews of your blessed community in Cologne, and to praise the good Lord God (blessed be He) and His Almighty Name for ever and ever, amen.

"I will not trouble you with the details of my many wagon rides and my subsequent sea voyages. Suffice it to say that they brought me here safely to the Oriental regions, regions that are so near to the great Holy Land where someday the Messiah shall return and deliver us and resurrect all souls and rebuild the Temple on Zion, amen. I write now in order to record for you some details of the lands and the peoples that I have seen in these old and foreign realms. The bright and glorious hand of the good Lord God is visible everywhere, if only we look – praise the Lord Yahweh-Elohim.

"As I mentioned, my old friend, I have had many, many adventures in arriving here. I hope – with the good Lord willing – to relate these events to you in person. For now, let me just say that after touring the Holy Lands of Palestine, I turned north. In fact, I took ship again, and recently I have ventured onto the island of Cyprus.

"Cyprus is the largest island in this part of the world. It is directly north of the Holy Lands, and ever since the crusading princes invaded Jerusalem, the island of Cyprus has been under the control of various European kings. I landed at the southeastern port of Larnaca. Much of the island is occupied by two mountain ranges. Between the mountains lies a broad plain, extending across the island from the bay of Famagusta to the bay of Morpheu; this plain, the Mesaoria, is watered by streams from the mountains on either side. Today, corn fills the open fields throughout the Mesaoria – however, the natives claim that at one time the whole area was clothed in thick forests, dense with tall trees. I find this hard to imagine as I look at the almost endless low horizons that stretch afar until they are finally edged by the distant mountains (which, by the way, are named Adelphi, Olympus, Papoutsa, and Troodos).

"There are some unhealthy swamps scattered about inland, but the coasts are quite fresh. Most of the islanders are farmers, growing barley, raisins, and wheat. The soil is very fertile; carob, mulberry, and olive trees are everywhere. Vineyards are also common, and the natives carry wine in tarred skins which give it (to my mind) a poor taste. I have seen only a small amount of livestock, but there is a breed of Cyprian mule that is exported and is well known in the mainland countries. Besides agriculture, the island has many mines: copper mines, salt mines, silver mines, and marble quarries.

"Early on, I spent some days in the main city, Nicosia, in the north central part of the island. Nicosia is the capital of Cyprus. The town is old and walled, and it is filled with many churches. Tanning and silk and cotton-weaving seem to be the main industries. Most of the people of Nicosia are Mohammedans and Christians, but I did find a small community of Jews, and one of them told me a sad story that took place here, sometime during the last century. I suppose you could say that it is a story of children, good Abraham. The scriptural proverb reminds us –"

> A girl or a boy
>   Delights his father and mother,
> And parents can enjoy
>   Their children forever.

"And fortunately 'forever' can roll out beyond the grave, as my sad story attests:

"The tale begins with a young Jewish wife named Hannah. Hannah was the daughter of Lavan ibn Elizaphan. After her parents died, Hannah married Ephod, a wealthy shipowner in Nicosia. Hannah wanted many, many children, but the couple had only one child, a sickly boy named Itzchak. Itzchak seemed a dull child to Hannah, and he could never learn much in school. Nonetheless, Ephod loved young Itzchak dearly, and the two smiled together when they walked hand-in-hand through the streets and the fields, amen.

"Hannah got older, and no more children arrived – and year by year Hannah became very jealous of her sister-in-law Miriam. Miriam was the wife of Ephod's brother Ammihud, who lived in the neighboring town of Kythraea. Miriam had twelve fine children. Yes, Abraham – Miriam had twelve lovely children, and all of them were noble and handsome and bright and all the boys were scholars. Hannah could not bear to think about it. Why was Miriam blessed, and why was Hannah cursed? Hannah thought of Miriam at night, and Hannah could not sleep. After a while, Hannah could think of nothing else but the unfairness of her life.

"How could she rid herself of these feelings? When Hannah looked at her husband, she thought of his brother Ammihud; then the thought of Ammihud reminded her of the twelve bright and brilliant children of Miriam. These children seemed like mocking stars that shone down on Hannah each night. Hannah could not bear to see her nieces and nephews. She could not stand to hear their names. Hannah tossed and turned in her bed every single night. Then one bleak night, Hannah decided that she must do something – she must do something extreme – in order to put these overwhelming feelings to rest. Hannah decided to kill Miriam's eldest son, Hannah's nephew Yehudi.

"The two families visited each other frequently, and during these visits, Hannah became a woman possessed. She seemed distant and strange. She did not always speak when she was spoken to. The husbands looked at each other, and they shook their heads. One day, the family of Ammihud was visiting Nicosia. As usual, Itzchak was playing with his cousin Yehudi late into the evening. The boys decided to trade beds that night, and Miriam's son Yehudi slept on the mat that was the bed of Itzchak, while Hannah's son Itzchak slept under the covers in the corner that was normally reserved for the visiting cousins.

"The day had been hot. Hannah was feeling weak and dizzy. She could not sleep; for hours she tossed and she turned. And now it was the dark dead depths of the night. Hannah pushed off her covers. Quietly she stood up. Bright stars were shining in the sky, cold and blinding. Was there a dim light somewhere in the house, or were her eyes remembering the firelight from another room and from an earlier hour? Hannah rubbed her eyes. A shimmering curtain of light glowed at the edge of her vision.

"Hannah was barefoot. She walked quietly down the hallway. The house was thick with old silence, but a dog whined outside somewhere far, far away. Hannah peered into the darkness. There stood a shadow, a black figure. The figure turned—it turned, and Hannah saw that it was Dumah, the Angel of Death, and it stood covered from head to foot with unwinking eyes. Dumah held a drawn and bloody sword, and his breathing was like the sound of dry leaves, rustling and rustling in the blank autumn wind.

"Dumah, the Angel of Death, turned slowly. He turned slowly and silently and smoothly and darkly. Was he speaking? Hannah thought that she heard the words of the Most Holy One from the Book of Genesis":

> What have you done, Cain? Listen! Your brother's blood that has been shed is crying out to Me from the ground. Now you are accursed forever: you are banished from the ground that has opened its mouth wide to receive your brother's blood—his blood that you have shed.

"Were those words actually spoken, or was Hannah just remembering having heard them at some distant time and in some far-off place? By now the stars had gone out in the sky, and Dumah, the Angel of Death, stood and waited, with his unwinking eyes and his drawn and bloody sword. Hannah was not afraid: she knew that the black angel should be there. Hannah looked down at her hand. She had a knife. She moved the knife and she killed the sleeping boy in the corner of the room. Then without looking back, she hurried out of the room and went to bed.

"In the morning, great cries of anguish arose. Children and maids came running, and Hannah discovered that she had killed her own son Itzchak. She opened wide her eyes. The sky was glaring and it was gray. Hannah could not move—and then she made a strange crying sound. It was the noise of a bird, the cry of a nightingale or a warbler. A local poem recounts":

Hannah of Nicosia
  Sadly cried with fright
Like a despairing warbler screaming
  In the weak and cold starlight
Through the long bleak empty
  Late hours of the night
On a thick-leaved ancient tree
  Beyond and out of sight.

She cried and trilled and wailed
  In a twittering bird-like run
Chirping high and low and wild –
  First loud then softly sung –
Mourning for her Itzchak mild
  Now lost in oblivion,
He was mad Hannah's only child
  And Ephod's beloved son.

"Yes, mad Hannah could not speak; she could only cry in a bird-like voice.

"The entire household was in shock – and the child's body lay for nine days unburied. The men were completely numb. The other children were taken in by neighbors. The servants were afraid to come to the house. A strange and unspeakable horror had occurred – but no one knew why it had happened. A stupor descended, like a thick and muffling cloud, on both grief-stricken families.

"The first day passed and then somehow the second ended too. Then nine days came, and nine days went. And finally, the fierce Lord God looked down from Heaven. The great and awesome Lord God Almighty stared down at the bleak household in Nicosia, and He waved His mighty arms. And on the night of the ninth day, the body of young Itzchak was changed into stone. On the tenth day, Hannah herself died and suddenly she crumbled into dust.

"What was happening? The family could not comprehend. Neighbors stayed far away. Poor Ephod was like a man struck and stunned by heavy blows. He sat in shock. He could not speak. He could not eat.

"Again, the Almighty Lord God looked down from His eternal Throne of Glory in Heaven. The Most Holy One is strong and fierce, but He is merciful and just. The Lord stared down at the devastated household in Nicosia. 'The memory cannot be erased,' He thought. 'It will glow forever like the cold full moon in the deep hours of the most lonely of nights.' Therefore, the great Lord God waved His mighty arms, and Ephod was turned into a stone also. Finally, the Most Omnipotent One sent down two angels from Heaven: the angels Raphael and Uriel came and carried the two stone bodies, Itzchak and his father Ephod, up to a quiet spot high on Mount Troodos. It is said that water now falls continuously from the two rock figures – but I myself have not seen that sight, good Abraham, and so I can only report to you what has been told to me, amen.

"In any case, the father and son are forever side by side, and they must be smiling together once again as they walk hand-in-hand in the streets and the fields of the Great Hereafter. Of that, my friend, I am quite certain.

"Well, let me end my letter, dear Abraham. I close my eyes and I can see you reading this in your holy study in Cologne. I think of you often, old friend – do you think of me too? Do you remember how once *we* walked smiling hand-in-hand on the banks of the wide River Rhine, happy as the grass was green in the light of our blue-skied childhoods? I remember, and I know that someday we shall walk together again.

"Your childhood friend,
Petahiah, the son of Jacob"

ello, Rabbi, I will be with you in a moment – I cannot leave until every tablecloth is folded, otherwise the day has not ended properly.... There, now I am finished at last, and I can sit next to you by the stove. Tomorrow night begins the holy Sabbath again, gently raining down joy upon our peaceful resting faces – praise the great Lord God, amen.

Ah, the holy gentle Sabbath; it is a day forever being filled with customs. It is strange, Rabbi – the Sabbath symbolizes the wondrous endless rest of eternity, floating among the clouds, free from mundane cares and chores. But here in this mortal world we busily clutter the Sabbath with ritual and with tradition. Why, in the Middle Ages, the mystic Rabbi Achselrad introduced hosts of special customs to the Sabbath days of medieval Cologne. He also inserted new Kabbalistic poetry into the synagogue service on certain Sabbaths in the spring, when he had his congregants read the poetry of Kalir from his *Shiv'ata*.

Of course, these are all beautiful poems. For instance, do you know Kalir's little poem about the Sabbath Angel? It goes:

White and cool with footsteps light
She slips into our weekend prayers,
The Sabbath Angel pure and bright
Bringing rest from wordly cares.

On Friday night the Angel wise—
The Sabbath with her cool gray eyes—
Rains sleep and peace in calming guise
To ease our long hard sacrifice;

She whispers warming lullabies
Of gentle dreams and quiet sleep,
She lightly seals our weary eyes
She soothes our limbs from aches sown deep

She lays her hand in ours.

What a fine holy restful Sabbath picture. Are you falling asleep, Rabbi? No? I am not sleepy either. But I am relaxed, because I enjoy these hymns, the ones that come down to us from those old pockets of Jewry in medieval Germany. In those days, the poetical hymns—the *piyutim*—of the Hebrew poet Eleazer Kalir were just appearing in German synagogues. Kalir was the first major poet to contribute original verse for the service. . . . What is that? Kalir came from the ninth century? Well, to tell you the truth, I am not certain, Rabbi. I think that the exact age in which Kalir lived is unknown. It was sometime during the Geonic era—but did he live at the beginning of the Dark Ages, or was he from the end? No one knows for sure.

Kalir was actually Eleazar ben Rabbi Kalir, and this name "Kalir" is a strange one. At one time, the scholars of Palestine and their pupils would eat small cakes inscribed with biblical verses, in order to make their studies more successful. The cakes were called *kollyrim*. Eleazar was a scholar—was the name "Kalir" derived from his *kollyrim*? Or perhaps "Kalir" is a variant of Cagliari, the capital of the island of Sardinia, where Eleazar ben Rabbi Kalir was born.

In any case, it is certain that there *was* a poet named "Kalir," also referred to as Kaliri. He was a student of the Hebrew poet Jannai. Kaliri wrote over one hundred and fifty religious poems—he wrote poems for all the Festivals, penitential prayers for the Holy Days, and sad songs of lamentation. Kaliri's poems are filled with grammatical puzzles, with rare words, and with obscure phrases – in fact, some of them are almost indecipherable riddles. But in spite of their complexities, Kaliri's poems all have a lovely sound, and they were soon included in the liturgies of the Italian, French, and German Jews. In the German synagogues, Kaliri was considered a poetic sage, and the German Jews crowded his poetries into their various Festival prayers. A few of his poems are quite mystical. Some deal with angels – and it may have been the very Sabbath poem that I just recited to you that set the old scholars to talking about angels one day in medieval Cologne.

It was a springtime day, a fine warm afternoon once upon a time in Cologne on the River Rhine. It was the day before the Sabbath, and the men were sitting and talking idly in the rabbi's little study room. Yes, Rabbi, it was the gentle restful springtime. The windows were open, a light cool breeze blew in, and it felt to the old men like holy spirits and Sabbath angels were washing through the worn wooden yeshiva. One of the scholars, old Shimshon ha-Zaken said, "How glorious are the holy angels!"

The other sages nodded, and Lewe ben Anselm said, "Amen, Shimshon – the holy, holy angels, blessed be they."

Again the men nodded, and they murmured "amen."

Then old Reb Joshua said, "God's Heavenly Host is a myriad of holy angels. Gloriously they populate the Holy Scriptures. Each angel is a messenger of the good Lord God – each comes to earth on a specific errand, and then he disappears. The blessed angels do not wander about the world frivolously."

"Amen," said Reb Lewe quickly.

"Amen," repeated Joshua, who continued: "The angels are all created to the greater glory of the wondrous Lord God. As it is said in the Book of Isaiah":

I saw the Lord seated on His Great Throne of Glory, high and exalted, and the skirt of His robe filled the temple. About Him were attendant seraphim, and each of these angels had six wings. One pair of wings covered his face, one pair covered his feet, and one pair was spread in flight. And these angels were calling ceaselessly to one another:

Holy, holy, holy is the Lord of Hosts:
The whole earth is full of His glory.

The men in the little back room sat quietly for a moment, each thinking his own holy angelic thoughts. Then white-bearded Baruch ben Jacob said, "Angels live in Heaven, so they have access to the founts of mystic lore. It is through angels that our mystics learn their secret wisdom – the mystic turns to angels for his holy inspiration. And it is the angels who grant the requests of these pious holy men."

A younger scholar, Elisah ben Samuel, said, "Amen, Reb Baruch. Undoubtedly, this is how our own holy Achselrad keeps in touch with the Divine Mysteries. Rabbi Abraham told me that he first learned the details of angels from his teacher, Eliazer ben Judah of Worms. Rabbi Eliazer actually possessed a copy of the book *Raziel* – as you know, all our information about angels was told to Adam by the angel Raziel, and, subsequently, holy scribes wrote the facts into a book."

Joshua ben Eliezer nodded. "Ah, my friends," he said, "there is no doubt that it is through the angels that the most Holy One maintains a close contact with His mortal world."

"That," said Elisah, "is exactly my point: Angels are God's messengers."

"But, good Elisah," continued Joshua, "communication can go both ways. Angels can carry messages to Heaven also."

"Did I ever suggest otherwise?" asked Elisah.

"Well, Elisah, we should say this out loud: we should make this point explicitly," said Reb Joshua. "Angels are the way to reach the ear of the Heavenly court. Mystic rabbis call on angels directly – and to do this, these holy men use the secret values hidden inside the letters of the Holy Scriptures."

Lewe ben Anselm stroked his beard and said, "Joshua, you are taking this too far. Perhaps angels can carry our hopes back to Heaven – on their return journeys – but clearly that is not their primary mission. No less an authority than Rabbi Eliazer himself has written: 'The angels are the messengers of God. He impresses His will upon them. He sends them forth to do His bidding.'"

"Yes, Reb Lewe," said Menahem ben Joel. "This is my understanding also: angels can do nothing of their own free will. They act only upon the command of the good Lord God (blessed be He)."

But Joshua shook his head. "No, Menahem – I am afraid that is an outdated view. Angels have a considerable degree of autonomy. The omnipotent Lord cannot be bothered with all manner of petty decisions. The Almighty One depends entirely on the angels: they relieve him of minor daily problems."

And Moyses ben Nathan said, "I agree, Reb Joshua. In fact, we find the old Sages saying":

> There are many acts that angels can perform of their own accord, without a special, Divine order from above. It is for this reason that men can write amulets in order to enlist the angels in earthly matters.

The scholars began to mutter among themselves. Old Shimshon ha-Zaken coughed. He rubbed his cheek, he stroked his beard, and then he said, "This may be true, gentlemen, but we must maintain our perspective. Angels are primarily *malakhim*. They are messengers of the Lord. They are holy emissaries.

"Most angels have quite specific functions. There is a division of labor among the great Host: each angel has a certain field of activity, and the Divine orders are assigned to particular angelic specialists. In all cases, my scholarly friends, the first priority of an angel is to be a messenger in his own particular realm. Is this not true, Rabbi?"

The scholars looked to the Rabbi – but the Rabbi was asleep. Old Rabbi Abraham had been writing all night in his book on mystic Kabbalistic lore, the manuscript entitled *Keter Shem Tov*. (As you know, Rabbi, this work has never been printed; to this day it remains hidden in the loft above the rabbi's little study room in the yeshiva of Cologne.) The Rabbi was breathing heavily and his eyes were closed, so after a while Elisah asked loudly, "And what do *you* think, good Rabbi?"

Achselrad awoke with a start. "What do I think?" he asked. The Rabbi looked around him. He winked and he blinked, and he said, "I think that we must always trust in the good Lord God (blessed be He), amen."

The Rabbi looked at the men sitting on the worn benches. The old scholars murmured "amen," but they seemed a little puzzled. Elisah ben Samuel said, "And as to *angels*, Rabbi?"

"Of course, Reb Elisah," said the Rabbi, "I was just coming to that. The Talmud tells us":

> There are myriads of angels. And why is that? It is because an angel is created with every utterance that issues from the mouth of the most

Holy One (blessed be He). We learn from Psalm 33 in the Holy
Scriptures:

> By the word of the Lord
> Were the Heavens made –
> All the Heavenly Horde
> Formed from words that He said.

"Thus, the angels are *malakhim*; that is, messengers. They are
physical embodiments of holy commands."

The Rabbi smiled, and he looked somewhere far away. "On the
other hand, once let loose, the angels seem to take on lives of their own,
gentlemen. Yes, they take on complex lives of their own," said Rabbi
Abraham ben Alexander. And a light angelic breeze blew gently
through the back room of the old medieval yeshiva.

The Rabbi continued: "These angels – initially commands of the
wondrous and mystical Holy One (blessed be He for ever and ever) –
the Lord's angels act out dramas and passions as amazing as any of
which one might conceivably dream."

The old sages raised their eyebrows and looked at one another,
but Rabbi Achselrad did not seem to notice. "Now, one time, my
scholarly friends, I had a very strange experience," said the Rabbi. "It
was a very strange experience indeed. I was working on a manuscript,
and it was late at night. I was hardly paying attention to anything
around me. Suddenly I noticed that the candlelight was flickering. I
looked up, and there in the doorway stood Shifra, the widow of Vyvus
ben Moshe.

" 'Rabbi,' she said to me, 'I need to talk with you.'

"I set down my pen, I invited her in, and I listened to her story.

"Shifra was a beautiful young woman. Sadly, her husband Vyvus
had died of a fourth fever during a hard cruel winter. Shifra continued
to earn a living as a seamstress; also, she had a small vegetable garden
behind her house. As a girl, Shifra had heard magical stories – and now
she dreamt magical dreams as she sewed and as she gardened. Shifra
dreamt of flying and of immortality. She imagined herself floating far
and wee, among the glorious fluffy clouds for ever and ever, praise the
Lord, amen.

"One day, a handsome man came to her door and asked her to

sew him a coat. He returned in two weeks, he marveled at the fine stitchery, and he paid her ten gold coins. Imagine, my wise friends – ten gold coins for a coat! Shifra was overwhelmed. She tried to thank him, but the man hardly spoke to her. A few months later, though, he returned and he asked her to make him an identical coat. Shifra spent day and night working. When he came back for the new coat, the stranger was obviously delighted with it, and he gave her twenty gold coins. At this rate, Shifra did not need to take on other sewing tasks. She worked very slowly, she gardened more often, and she day-dreamed for long, long hours.

"It was a few weeks after Passover when the stranger returned again. What did he want this time? Of course, he wanted another coat. 'How could he need so many coats?' wondered Shifra. She shrugged her shoulders and she smiled at the man. The man nodded silently, and then he left. Again Shifra set to work. Shifra was a skilled seamstress, and she made a neatly stitched beautiful black coat. When the man came back in two weeks, he took the garment and examined it carefully from top to bottom. He looked at the sleeves and the pockets and the edges and the lining. He looked at the coat – and then he looked at Shifra. Shifra felt embarrassed. She looked down at her hands.

"Neither person spoke. After a few minutes, the stranger said, 'This is a very fine coat, young woman.' Shifra said nothing. Suddenly the man confessed that he had fallen in love with her. Shifra did not know what to say. Then the stranger said a most amazing thing: 'Young woman, I am an angel.' "

The seven sages of Cologne, sitting on the worn benches, began to murmur among themselves. Eyebrows were raised, and beards were stroked.

The Rabbi looked at the old sages. "Yes, gentlemen," he continued, "it was an angel – the angel Yofiel. The angel Yofiel had fallen in love with Shifra, the widow of Vyvus ben Moshe of Cologne. Shifra could not look up at him, and after a few minutes, Yofiel abruptly left. The little tailoring room was suddenly very empty. 'Has this been a daydream?' wondered Shifra. Was Yofiel just a vision, like the clouds that she seemed to see so clearly whenever she sewed?

"One week passed and then two – seven days came, and seven days went. Suddenly it was seven weeks later, and Shifra was convinced that she had merely dreamt a fine dream one day many weeks ago. The weather was nice and Shifra had the door open. She could just see two towering white clouds above the rooftops far away. A gentle angelic breeze blew in, and then Yofiel appeared again at her door. Shifra felt a shiver in her back. Yofiel stepped in, and all was warm and quiet. After a moment, the angel said to the young woman: 'Shifra, this is my last visit; I cannot return again. But I can give you one wish. Is there something that you desire more than anything else in the world?'

"Shifra opened wide her eyes. She looked at this handsome stranger. He was wearing a coat that she had sewed for him. She remembered the coat–the sleeves, the pockets, the lining, the edges. She remembered the many hours of sewing and of thinking of clouds. The thick white cottony clouds were free from our dusty earth. They floated forever happy and restful. 'Yofiel,' she said, 'holy angel–if that is truly what you are–then I should like to live forever.'

"Yofiel only nodded, and then he turned and left.

"Shifra did not know what to make of this incident. She wondered and she worried. Was it evil or was it holy? Was she a bad person? Or was she blessed? After many long days and after many long nights, she finally came to see me. When she told me this story, I too was not certain what to make of the tale. Had the poor woman imagined everything?"

The Rabbi stopped his story for a moment, and he stroked his beard. Then he went on: "As you know, my respected colleagues, the Kabbalah teaches us that all souls are immortal. They were created once upon a time long, long ago by the Great and Omnipotent Holy One. Each soul has an earthly career. It passes into a human body. It is tried and examined and tempted and tested. Can it remain pure, in spite of all the temporary taints and mars? If so, it will ascend, fully repurified after death, to the domain of the spirits, and there it will merge into the blessed aethereal world of the *sefirot*.

"On the other hand, if the soul is not sufficiently strong, if it absorbs the vulgar, crude, and ugly vapors of our mortal world, if it develops serious imperfections, then another fate awaits. The tainted soul is recycled. After death it is repurified, and it returns in a new body–until, after repeated tests and repurifications, finally it can soar aloft forever. As it is written in the Holy Scriptures":

On that golden jubilant day
A trumpet blast will sound aloud,
Abyssinia and Egypt will hear it play;
The horn will waken from their shrouds
Dead souls who'll fly up far away
To Zion under God's white clouds.

"Amen," said Reb Baruch.

"Yes, amen," repeated the Rabbi. "In any case, my friends, the soul is immortal. But Shifra asked for something more. Shifra wanted her personal existence to go on forever. She was young and she was beautiful. She thought of clouds and of springtimes and of floating free eternally, just as she was then. She recalled a poem of the hymnist Kaliri":

There are riches high in Heaven
And bright white clouds as a reward
For all eternal children
Who trust the celestial Lord.

In the sky their city sits
With streets like starry bands
Where windswept cotton cloudlets
Flow gently through the lands;

They are dressed in glorious gowns
Whiter than the gentle snow,
They all have rainbow crowns
Ashine with sunlight and moonglow.

And God looks on them gently
And they praise the Lord on high
Floating lightly in His blue sea —
His cloud-like children in the sky.

"And Shifra thought, 'Now I can live like that forever, here on earth.'

"Shifra sat on those very benches where you sit now, gentlemen.

And silently I looked at the young woman. Truly, friends, I did not know what to say. I only shook my head, and I returned to my manuscript, for there was nothing for me to do. Matters were in hands more powerful and more holy than mine."

Rabbi Abraham shook his head, and he mumbled something to himself; then he returned to reading his book. The sages around the small back room looked at one another. Eyebrows went up. Beards were stroked. After a while, the young scholar Elisah ben Samuel said, "Excuse me, Rabbi – what happened next?"

The Rabbi looked up. "What happened next?" he repeated. "Nothing happened next: Shifra still lives happily on Engegasse Street." Then the Rabbi looked down at his book and soon he was lost in his reading.

Well, Rabbi, I know that you, too, are wondering. My grandmother said that she had heard more of this story. After Shifra told her tale to the mystic Achselrad, she felt better. She left the yeshiva, and she returned home. Shifra did not do anything new or special. She sewed, and she gardened. For a time, she was quite happy. She was hopeful. She watched the thin shining clouds in the winter. She followed the fluffy clouds of spring and the thick and cottony clouds of summer. In the fall, gray clouds raced across the sky. Shifra smiled. She watched the sky, she sewed, and she gardened. She made fancy dresses and elegant coats. She puttered among the mustard greens and the endive, the sorrel, and the peppergrass. She edged tablecloths with lace. She tied up the vines in her garden and she weeded and she hoed – and the years went by, and Shifra lived and lived and lived.

Shifra lived and lived and lived. But, too late, she realized that she had not asked to continue to be young. Shifra had asked only to live – and live she did. Over the years, Shifra began gradually to shrivel. Her skin became as thin and spotted as fine parchment. Her hair was like lightly spun white wool. Her voice became weak and shaky. What was to come next? It was simply more of the same: Shifra continued to grow thinner and tinier and more wrinkled. After decades, she was as thin as a broom straw, and she was as wrinkled as an old, old raisin. Shifra was reduced to a whispery shivery rustling dried stem of grass, and when people would come across her, they could no longer understand her raspy thin and shriveled voice. And, Rabbi, Shifra may be alive to this very day, but she would be so thin and so tiny that, if you saw her, then I am certain you would mistake her for the faint, faint shadow of an old dried straw from a medieval German broom.

ood evening, Rabbi. Of course—please sit here by the stove, the night fire helps me to become sleepy also. You and I are not blessed like old Reb Elbaum; once again, he nodded off during the last prayers this evening. He has learned to sway piously even while asleep. Undoubtedly he acquired some magic from the mystic Achselrad. Yes, Rabbi, we too could use a dose of Achselrad tonight—my grandmother said that he could put men into a sleep trance by waving a gold coin before their eyes.

As you remember, Achselrad was a pupil of Eliazer ben Judah, the mystic of Worms. Strange and mystic visions visited old Rabbi Abraham in the synagogue of Cologne. I doubt whether he would be tolerated nowadays, but my grandmother said that Rabbi Abraham was also a scholar, and he always claimed that his visions came from devout and pious study. Many an astonishing event took place in his yeshiva—or so grandmother (blessed be her memory) was told. Of course, there were also some very ordinary events. As my grandmother often said, "Life is ordinary, when it is not extraordinary."

Much of his workaday life was ordinary, but Rabbi Abraham spent his free time immersed in the extraordinary. You see, old Achselrad worked night and day writing an extraordinary set of Kabbalistic tomes of mystic knowledge. And one morning in the early light, while working on one of these extraordinary books (the *Keter Shem Tov* – a work that was never published and that now exists only as a secret manuscript hidden in the loft of the old Cologne yeshiva), Rabbi Abraham heard a noise and looked up. There, in the light of the doorway, he saw the dejected figure of a wealthy member of his congregation – it was Martel ben Aaron ha-Kohen.

Reb Martel was a pious man, and he had three fine and pious sons. However, Martel was now very upset with them. Each son wanted to marry a woman with a bad trait: one woman was greedy, one was lazy and always ordered others about, and one complained continuously about other people. The young men were hopelessly in love. They would not listen to Martel's counsel. Poor Martel could not keep from thinking of the sad fates awaiting his sons, and finally he came to the yeshiva to talk with the sages.

Martel ben Aaron stepped into the back study room. There, the Rabbi was bent over a book, and a group of scholars was seated on the worn benches along the wall.

"My good friends," began Martel sadly, "I am in a terrible quandary."

"Yes, Reb Martel," said old Shimshon ha-Zaken, "we can see that you do not look happy."

"I am more than unhappy," said Martel sitting down heavily. "I am devastated. My sons, my good and favorite young boys – the future of my lineage – these children all want to marry women with evil traits."

Martel shook his head and he clasped and unclasped his hands.

"It cannot be as bad as you say," said white-bearded Baruch ben Jacob.

"That is true," responded Martel. "It is not as bad as I say – it is worse. These young women are the complete opposites of good wives. You know how in the Book of Proverbs the Sages tell us":

> Who can appraise a capable wife?
>   Her worth is beyond all else in life –
> Like a ship that is laden with merchandise
>   She brings from afar good food and spice;

> And for the needy she always opens her door:
> A good wife is generous to all the poor.

"Well, gentlemen, these young women break all the rules that follow. For instance, the Proverb goes on to say":

> The husband trusts his wife
> And her children feel secure;
> She leads a model life –
> Her truthful words endure.

"Yet, I am sad to say, one of my sons' choices is a thief."

"No?!" said a younger man, Elisah ben Samuel.

"Yes," said Martel sadly, "I am afraid that it is true. And you know how the Proverb continues":

> She is ever on her feet
> As household shepherdess
> She never stops to eat
> The bread of laziness.

"Well, another of my sons' choices is completely lazy."

"How awful," said Joshua ben Eliezer, shaking his head.

"Exactly," said Martel. "And then the Proverb also points out":

> When a good wife speaks aloud
> There is wisdom to be heard,
> Honest truths are the proud
> Foundations of her word.

"I must report, friends, that the third woman is a liar and a slanderer."

The many sages shook their heads. "This is sad, Reb Martel. In fact, it is quite sad," said Lewe ben Anselm. "But it is not irreparable."

Martel looked up at old Lewe. "There is hope?" he asked.

"Certainly," said white-haired Baruch ben Jacob, "greed can be cured. Remember the Hebrew proverb":

> Never happy is the king
>> Who wants to own each little thing
>> That he takes to fancying.

> Forever happy is he alone
>> Who does not want or e'er bemoan
>> The things he cannot hope to own.

Martel looked a bit puzzled, and Elisah ben Samuel, a younger scholar, quickly said, "Yes, Martel, what Reb Baruch means is this: give these young women their ideal existences, and they will reform. Remember: 'When the mouse is full and satisfied, then cheese and flour seem tasteless to him.' "

And Joshua ben Eliezer said, "Exactly. Put their coins directly on the table. It will work to cure all the faults of these women. 'Deeds speak louder than words – a barking dog does not bite.' "

Martel looked from one man to the next. "What are you gentlemen suggesting?"

"Listen, my friend," said Reb Lewe. " 'A job is fine, but it interferes with your free time.' "

"And in the same vein," continued Menahem ben Joel, "there is the wise adage: 'A heavy purse makes a light heart.' "

Moyses ben Nathan nodded twice. "Amen, good Menahem," he said. "Moreover, do not forget, Martel: 'What need of honey, when sugar is sweet?' "

The scholars all stroked their beards and murmured among themselves. Finally, Old Shimshon ha-Zaken coughed and he cleared his throat and said, "Yes, friends – and then there is another very apt saying: 'If he is no good to the next fellow, then he is no good to himself.' (Or, perhaps it goes: 'If he is no good to himself, then he is no good to the next fellow.' At the moment, I forget which it is.)"

Now Martel felt quite puzzled indeed. He looked from one scholar to the next and then he looked at Rabbi Abraham.

The Rabbi was listening to the advice. The old sages continued to stroke their beards and to murmur among themselves. After a few minutes, Rabbi Abraham asked, "Tell me, Reb Martel: Will your sons marry regardless of what you say?"

Martel looked sad. "Undoubtedly they will," he answered.

"Well," said Rabbi Abraham, "you know the old proverb: 'If you cannot get up, then get down. And if you cannot get across, then go around.'"

Martel creased his forehead. "These many proverbs are making me a bit dizzy, Rabbi," said Martel ben Aaron. "Exactly what do you suggest that I do?"

Rabbi Abraham sat back in his chair. "Let me ask you another question, Reb Martel," he said. "Do these women have other vices?"

"I must think a moment, Rabbi," replied Martel ben Aaron. He tapped his chin, and then he said, "No–I think that each woman has only one especially bad trait."

"I see. And you are wealthy–are you not?"

"Well, let me just say that I can provide for all my wants and also contribute a significant amount to charity," answered Martel.

The Rabbi nodded. He drummed his fingers on his desk, he pursed his lips, he thought a moment, and then he said, "Then let these women marry your sons, with your blessings."

"What?! How can I ignore the facts, Rabbi? I must be honest with my children. I do not think that it will be good for them to marry these difficult women–in fact, I am certain that it would be a sad, sad mistake."

"My advice, good sir," said Rabbi Abraham, "is to let the marriages proceed. You cannot fight your children. Remember–they are now grown men. They must be allowed to live their own lives and even to make their own mistakes."

Martel looked down at his feet dejectedly.

"Do not be so sad, Martel," said the Rabbi. "You are not powerless here. I did not say to take *no* action: I only advise that you not fight a battle you are certain to lose."

"But what can I do, Rabbi?"

"Well, my friend, here is one possible course of action," said Rabbi Abraham. "After the marriage, give the keys to all your money to the first woman. Soon she will satisfy her greed and she will have no reason to steal. Remember the old proverb: 'You always have a good appetite at someone else's feast.'"

The old scholars nodded approvingly and murmured "amen."

"Moreover, Martel," continued the Rabbi, "sharing your wealth with your children is really a very holy way of life. It is advocated by the Talmud, which advises us":

A man should spend less than his means on food and drink for himself. He should spend up to his means on his clothes. But he should spend above his means on honoring his wife and his children. These people are dependent upon him, while he himself is dependent on the good Lord God – the God Who only need have spoken once and the entire World came into being.

Martel frowned. "Are you certain that this will work?" he asked.

"No," said the Rabbi.

"No?" asked Martel.

"No," said the Rabbi. "Who can tell the future in a thing like this?"

Martel felt defeated. "Then why do you give this advice?" he asked.

Rabbi Abraham smiled. "The world is complex, Martel – it is incondensably complex. The good Lord God (blessed be He) has woven our world with a thick detail and with such variation that none of us will ever understand it fully. Nonetheless, we are obliged to do our best: we can never give in and we can never sit by idly. We must try, even when the end of this effort is unknown."

"Amen," said Baruch ben Jacob.

"Amen, Baruch," said the mystic Achselrad. "Yes, we must do our best, Martel. And in these efforts, we use the principles that have been worked out during the past ages – in fact, that is the point of all these proverbs and time-tested sayings.

"For instance, in relation to the money for the first of your potential daughters-in-law, the Talmud says: 'Where there is no meal, there is no Torah.' This means that when we feel hungry, when we do not have sufficient sustenance, we cannot learn that which is essential to the fulfillment of the Divine will. Specifically, this woman must taste her fill of money before she can fully taste holy knowledge."

"I see," replied Martel ben Aaron slowly. "But what about the second woman? I recall that the Talmud has warned us":

Among those whose life is not a good life
Is the man who is ruled by a domineering wife.

"Listen, good Martel," said the Rabbi, "give many servants to the second woman. Arrange it so that there are no chores that she *must* do. She will have plenty of free time; then we will invite her to be in charge of the community charity. This is a position of honor. It will not appear as an assignment; instead, it will seem to be a reward. Eventually, benevolence will improve her spiritually – as the Talmud says: 'Whoever practices charity and justice fills the whole world with loving kindness.' "

"Amen," said Baruch ben Jacob.

"Yes, amen," said the mystic Achselrad. "And, Martel, when we set this woman up as the head of the Benevolent Society, we will give her many helpers. Apparently, she likes to order people around. She must have a managerial temperament. Let us take advantage of it. We will channel it into constructive activities. I would not be surprised if she becomes a very hard worker – remember the proverb: 'Hire a servant, and then you will do it yourself.' "

Martel ben Aaron was tapping his chin. "I see," he said. He thought about this advice, and then he asked, "What about the third woman, Rabbi?"

"As to the third woman, undoubtedly she lies out of insecurity. Not only should you give her wealth, but also you should treat her honorably. Make her welcome in your home and also in your business. Talk kindly to her, and treat her with importance. The Book of Proverbs reminds us that":

Kind words are like golden honey:
On the tongue they taste sweetly
And they nourish the whole body.

"Amen," said Baruch ben Jacob.

"Yes, amen, good Baruch," said the mystic Achselrad. "Martel, be certain that you and your son consult this woman on business matters. The Talmud tells us: 'If your wife is tall, then stand on a chair and talk to her. If your wife is short, then bend down and whisper in her ear.' This means that a man should not think himself too superior to consult his wife about his affairs. Trust this woman, Martel. Involve her in serious discussions, and soon she will not lie or slander at all.

"And then, my friend, set a holy and honorable example by continuing to follow this principle. Consultation is the basis of trust, and trust is the basis of truth. Remember the old proverb: 'As you look at a man, so will he appear. And as you talk to a man, so will he talk.' "

Martel ben Aaron thought for a bit. Then he said to the Rabbi, "Rabbi, your advice sounds good."

The many scholars sitting on the benches nodded and murmured "amen," and there was much stroking of beards all around.

The Rabbi smiled, and he bent down over his papers again.

However, Martel did not stand up to leave. He rubbed his hands on his legs, and then he said rather quietly, "Rabbi, your advice certainly sounds good. I appreciate it, and I do not mean to question it."

Rabbi Abraham looked up. Martel was uncomfortable, but he continued: "I am now getting on in years, and I must say, Rabbi, I recall other times when I have heard fine-sounding advice about such complex matters. But those elegant words sometimes led to ends that were not quite as fine as I had hoped."

The scholars began to frown, and Martel hesitated. There was silence in the back study room. Still, Martel continued: "I mean no disrespect, good Rabbi. But I have noticed that sometimes the theorizing done in advance was simply wrong. What if, by some small chance, your ideas do not work out?"

Martel looked to the Rabbi, but there was silence. The Rabbi had a faraway look in his eyes. Perhaps the Rabbi had not heard Martel. Or if he had heard, then it did not seem that he was about to answer. Finally, old Shimshon ha-Zaken coughed and he cleared his throat and he said, "My friend, there is an important saying from the Talmud":

Among those who will never behold the cruel face of Gehinnom in the afterlife is he who has a bad wife. Through his exceptional suffering, such a man has expurgated fully his sins in this world.

"Therefore, take heart, Martel—if your sons marry these women, then they will end up all right, no matter what courses their lives take."

At this point in the story, my grandmother looked up at me, Rabbi. She looked up from her embroidery—the handwork with which she busied her old fingers each day when she sat at the edge of her mother's grave. Grandmother stopped her sewing, she smiled, and then she said, "I do not know if the old mystic Abraham ever answered Martel's question. But, my golden little one, Martel need not have worried. All marriages are preordained: they are made in Heaven. The Talmud tells us that forty days before the formation of a child, a *Bat Kol* (a holy Daughter of the Voice) announces, 'This tiny person – this little spirit of a child – is destined to marry a particular person named such-and-such.'"

Grandmother looked down at her embroidery again. "And," she continued, "thus shall it always be – regardless of what the parents think or do or say or fear. With the blessings of the good Lord God ringing gently in their ears, the preordained young couple will marry. Then the glowing white pure radiance of Heaven and all the everlasting joys beyond will bless forever that wondrous marriage. And the couple will be eternally happy, like the magnificent white clouds of the summer sky, for ever and ever, amen." . . . Yes, Rabbi, I remember that this is what my grandmother said to me, when sitting beside her mother's grave in the old Jewish Garden of Life Everlasting.

h, good evening again, Rabbi. I know that it is always hard to sleep on the night of the new moon. Put your feet on the side bench here and I will open the stove door. Let me push the coals back: the white glow will wash away all the cares of your hard day.

I heard your final benediction tonight, Rabbi – clearly you are overworked. Oh yes, even a shammas like me can tell. I kept one eye on you as I cleaned the dishes, and I saw that you were watching the door, hoping that Reb Elbaum would leave early. But then Reb Anton stayed to review the scriptural passage, the ending of the Book of Job:

> After Job had prayed for his friends, the Lord made him prosperous again and gave him twice as much as he had had before. All his brothers and his sisters and everyone who had known him before came and ate with him in his house. They comforted and consoled him over all the trouble that the Lord had brought upon him, and each one gave him a piece of silver, a gold ring, and fresh-baked loaf of bread.

> Then the Lord blessed the latter part of Job's life more than the first part. He had fourteen thousand sheep, six thousand camels, a thousand yoke of oxen, and a thousand donkeys. And also he had seven sons and three

daughters. The first daughter he named Jemimah, the second Keziah, and the third Keren-Happuch. Nowhere in all the land were there found women as beautiful as Job's daughters, and their father granted them an inheritance along with their brothers.

After this, Job lived a hundred and forty years: he saw his children and their children to the fourth generation. And when he died, he was old and full of years and happy.

Yes, Rabbi, the Book of Job takes one on an exhausting emotional journey: of course it would wear you out. . . . What is that? A story from me? Rabbi, all that I know are the children's tales, the grandmother fables. You need something new and fresh to keep your mind keen. Otherwise you will become a dreamy old man like me, and you will find yourself constantly musing and dozing and nodding off in front of the stove.

What do you mean you are already an old man, Rabbi? Do you really think that sixty years is old? You are still a child. When you reach eighty, *then* you will be old. You doubt that you will live to see eighty years? If so, Rabbi, then you will never grow old. . . . All right, all right, I know no special stories but listening to you and Reb Anton speak of Job's advanced age reminded me of the postponed death of Gottheil the baker of Cologne. It is a tale that was told to me by my grandmother—now where shall I begin?

Once upon a time, said my grandmother to me, in old Cologne in the days of Rabbi Abraham ben Alexander, there lived a very wealthy baker, a widower named Gottheil ben Jesse ha-Levi. Gottheil's father Jesse had been a fine and well-loved *hazan*, but Gottheil did not have his father's gift for music. Instead, Gottheil became a successful baker, and after some time, he also inherited much money from his wife's family. Gottheil had no children, and now he was a widower without kith or kin.

Gottheil was an unusually kind man, and he always gave out free bread. "Yes, friends," Gottheil said to his colleagues in the yeshiva, "as the Holy Scriptures reminds us, bread is not only a staple of life, it is also a warm and golden gift to the Lord. The Book of Leviticus says":

Take fine flour and bake twelve loaves of bread. Then set the loaves in two rows, six in each row, on a table of pure gold before the Lord. This bread is to be set out before the Lord regularly, Sabbath after Sabbath, on behalf of the Israelites as a lasting covenant. It belongs to Aaron and his sons, who are to eat it in a holy place because it is a most holy part of their regular share of the offerings made to the Lord.

Being independently wealthy, Gottheil gave his bread free to anyone who came into his bakery, and every day he felt happy when he gave out the fresh-baked warm bread. This had been his practice for many years. His helpers shook their heads in amazement, but by the great Lord's blessing, his business still managed to make money. (You see, Rabbi, Gottheil also sold all manner of other baked goods besides bread.) I suppose that it is just as the Book of Proverbs tells us –

> The kindly man is blessed
>   For sharing his daily bread
> With the poor and the distressed.

One day an old recluse, a local Jew named Moses ben Baruch, came to see the good baker. Moses often had visions and he was said to be somewhat of a seer. "Reb Gottheil," said Moses ben Baruch in a low and serious voice, "I have been granted a vision, a holy omen about you." Gottheil stopped his work and he raised his eyebrows. Moses then proceeded to tell the baker that the previous night, in the dark dead hours, he had been passing the alleyway leading to the synagogue. He had glanced toward the old building. Was there a dim light in the main prayer hall or were his eyes tricking him? Slowly, Moses walked toward the building. He tried the front door. It was unlocked. Had the shammas forgotten to lock the synagogue?

Moses stepped inside the building. He removed his shoes and he walked into the main prayer hall. The building was thick with old silence, but a dog whined outside somewhere far away. Moses peered into the dark hall. There, past the worn wooden benches, beyond the twelve stained glass windows with their colored lions and snakes, stood a dark figure at the Holy stone Ark. The figure turned – it turned, and Moses saw that it was Dumah, the Angel of Death. The black angel stood at the Ark, covered from head to foot with unwinking eyes. He held a drawn and bloody sword. His breathing was like the sound of dry leaves, rustling and rustling in the chill of a blank autumn wind.

Dumah, the Angel of Death, turned slowly. He turned slowly and silently and smoothly and darkly. Was he speaking? Moses ben Baruch thought that he heard the holy words from the Book of Lamentations:

> This I always think of
>   And thus I have hope after all:
> "Because of God's great love
> We recover from every fall.
>
> "God's all-sheltering peace
>   Will never be withdrawn –
> In fact it is increased
>   With every radiant dawn."
>
> And I remind myself meanwhile:
>   "The good Lord cares for me."
> So, like a contented child
>   I await Him patiently;
>
> Our God is compassionate
>   Protecting faithful men –
> And quiet and calm I now await
>   His salvation once again.

Yes, there stood the Angel of Death and in the oldest and dustiest voice of all, he said, "Finally, the time has come for the baker, Gottheil the son of Jesse."

Moses ben Baruch shivered. Dumah, the Angel of Death, continued: "You must tell Gottheil ben Jesse that his deeds of charity have been fine and that they have been blessed by the Most Holy One. As a reward, the great God Almighty will remove Gottheil from this world of sin, suffering, and sorrow, to live in the glorious Paradise of the Great Hereafter before the end of the year."

Moses felt weak and afraid. Dumah said no more, and the dark shape became a shadow; then slowly it dimmed and it faded away completely. After many minutes, Moses ben Baruch backed out of the room and he hurried home. Then the old recluse climbed into his bed, but he did not sleep at all that night.

The next day, Moses ben Baruch went to Gottheil ben Jesse – and now Gottheil was listening carefully to the entire story. Moses braced himself for the reaction, but Gottheil smiled and said, "Ah, blessed be the good Lord God, amen." Then the baker instructed his assistants that from that time forward, they would charge nothing at all for any of their baked goods. Instead, they were to spend all of Gottheil's money, until he ran out of funds. Next, Gottheil sat down and made out a will – "All my remaining money," he wrote, "should be used to buy bread for needy people." Moses ben Baruch watched, he shook his head, and he left the baker, who was now very busy setting in motion his final preparations.

Gottheil was a man at peace. He was happier than ever when he went into the bakery every day. Each morning, he himself would bake a little dab of dough in the oven first thing, as a holy offering. This was in accord with the scriptural commandment from the Book of Leviticus:

> When someone brings a grain offering to the Lord, his offering is to be of fine flour. He is to pour oil on it, to put incense on it, and to take it to Aaron's sons the priests. Then the priests shall take a handful of this mixture and burn it as a memorial portion on the altar – it will be an offering made by fire, an aroma pleasing to the good Lord God.

After burning this tiny bit of dough, Gottheil would take another small portion of dough and he would reserve it as a starter for the next batch. Finally he would set to work, and he would bake his daily loaves. There were others who could help him with the baking, but Gottheil liked nothing better than to make bread. After he took the loaves from the oven, he would say a prayer over the newly baked bread, and he would taste one slice (for the sake of the good Lord God) after it cooled. Ah, Rabbi, I can almost taste that chewy crust myself!

Soon, the end of the year began to approach. Gottheil felt healthier than ever. Each morning he awoke under the sunshine smile of the good Lord God, and he looked forward to the bright cool autumn days. The old year ended. *Rosh Hashanah* came and went. Then the Day of Atonement was upon them. Gottheil ben Jesse ha-Levi was whole and sound, and he continued his baking chores day after day. Another week passed and then several more. After seven cycles of seven weeks, Gottheil ben Jesse ha-Levi, the wealthy baker, was still alive and well, and he was as happy and as prosperous as ever. . . .

What? Of course there is more, Rabbi: I only closed my eyes for a moment–can an old man not take a little rest? Now you have interrupted my thoughts. Let me see, where was I? Yes, yes–as my grandmother said, "Death does not come until finally it comes." Did you ever hear her say that, Rabbi? You never knew her? That is too bad; you missed a fine woman. Ah, well–anyway, Rabbi, I first heard about the delayed death of Gottheil the baker from my grandmother, may her soul visit happily with the souls of her parents forever, amen. . . . What is that? Just be patient, Rabbi.

Once upon a time, said my grandmother to me, in the earliest days of the Jewish communities in Germany, there lived in Cologne on the River Rhine, an old reclusive scholar named Moses ben Baruch. (Please do not interrupt me, Rabbi.) This solitary man had predicted the death of the baker, Gottheil ben Jesse ha-Levi–in fact, Reb Moses had even reserved a grave for the baker in the Jewish cemetery, the Cologne *Am Toten Juden.*

Month after month passed, and Gottheil the baker remained alive and well. Moses ben Baruch was mystified. He even became worried and annoyed. Had he really seen Dumah? Could Dumah have told him an untruth? Where could a pious person put his faith, if not in the word of an angel?

The prayers of Reb Moses grew longer and longer. Sometimes he went without food for one or two days. Often he would stand from morning until night. And, eventually, another holy vision came to him. In the vision, Moses ben Baruch found himself sitting on a worn bench in the small back study room of the Cologne yeshiva. Rabbi Abraham was hard at work on his mystical treatise, the *Keter Shem Tov.* Suddenly the candle flickered and a dark shape wavered in the doorway; it was Dumah, the Angel of Death.

Moses ben Baruch said to the black spectral figure, "Good angel, how is it that Gottheil the baker is still alive?"

And Dumah, the Angel of Death, turned to Reb Moses and said, "Moses – Moses ben Baruch – you are a devout man."

This appeared to be a question, and Moses replied, "I try to be, O Angel."

"Yes," replied Dumah, the Angel of Death, "you do try. And of such devout men as you there are scores who try, who fast, who pray, and who spend sleepless nights longing for Heaven and for the rewards of the Great Hereafter. Unfortunately, these men often look down upon others who take a more practical and less ascetic course of action."

With his fathomless black eyes, Dumah stared at Moses ben Baruch and said, "Some men, Moses, remain immersed in the affairs of their fellows, helping and attending and working and doing charity. The world needs a great variety of men, Reb Moses. The awesome Lord God (blessed be He) loves all who revere Him – He loves the pious ascetic, and also He loves the active worker among men."

In the dream, Rabbi Achselrad watched and he listened in silence.

"Gottheil the baker is an active man," said Dumah, the black Angel of the Lord. "He goes out into the world. He bakes, and he works. He lives day by day, as if each day were his last. He uses each day for the benefit of others. Before these recent events, he had been a fine and upstanding man – now he is acting like a saint. True, your fame as a seer has suffered by the continued longevity of Gottheil, but especially in these evil times the Almighty Lord God cannot spare Gottheil from his fine service here on earth."

There was a moment of silence. "As I have said, it is true that your fame as a seer has diminished," repeated Dumah. "This is not a matter with which the Omnipotent One has concerned Himself. However, Moses, I might say a few words to you on my own: it is not too late to save yourself from a sad and early death." Then Dumah, the Angel of Death, faded slowly from sight, and soon he disappeared completely.

The room remained dark and silent. Moses ben Baruch looked at Rabbi Abraham. The Rabbi looked at the empty doorway, and then he looked at the old recluse. "What did Dumah mean, Rabbi?" asked Moses.

Rabbi Abraham stroked his beard. "Let me remind you, Reb Moses: *Tzedakah Tatzil Mimavet*," said Achselrad. "From the Book of Proverbs, we learn":

> Wealth is a light commodity
>   On Judgment Day,
> But goodness, alms, and charity
>   Shall heavily weigh.

> Generosity and virtue,
>   Kind words with each breath–
> These will protect you
>   From a sad and early death.

Then Rabbi Abraham nodded to himself, and he went back to working on his manuscript.

Moses ben Baruch awoke from his vision and he looked around. He too nodded his head; he knew what he must do. He walked down the street and he went to the shop of Gottheil the baker, and he asked to be taken on as an assistant. Gottheil ben Jesse raised his eyebrows; then he patted old Moses ben Baruch on the shoulder and he welcomed him into the shop. And Moses worked from that day until the end of his long life as a baker's helper. Moses ben Baruch worked for Gottheil ben Jesse serving the good Lord God (blessed be He) through the fresh-baked warm bread of life.

And, Rabbi, my grandmother said that both men lived for many, many years more. Then one Sabbath morning, Gottheil died and Moses inherited the shop. Yes, Gottheil died gently and contentedly, and he was reunited with his parents in the Great Hereafter. Gottheil prayed and studied in the land of Eternity. All his brothers and sisters and everyone who had known him before were there, and they ate with him in his house. And of course he saw his wife and his nieces and his nephews and their children to the fourth generation. And then, too, old Gottheil was young again, and he heard the beautiful voice of his father Jesse the *hazan* singing him soft songs at night as he baked bread. And Gottheil sat at his father's feet, smiling and waiting happily for a taste of the fresh-baked warm bread of Heaven. So, hallelujah, Rabbi – and I wish you forever a warm fresh-baked heavenly amen.

ood evening, Rabbi. I see there is no sleep for the weary—yes, that is what my grandmother often said. If you are cold then sit down here on the bench, and I will stoke up the oven. This stoker? It is one of the iron shoe-scrapers from the front hall. Of course there are still two scrapers in the anteroom for dirty shoes. But I myself am of the old school: I think that all pious men should pray barefoot. Did you know that Rabbi Samuel ben Meir said the Messiah will appear barefoot? The famed Samuel ben Meir himself once wrote that very news from the city of Troyes in France.

Have you ever been to Troyes, Rabbi? It is a trading city southeast of Paris. Troyes is a pretty town. Branches of the River Seine cross through its neatly gardened interior. In the olden days, Troyes had famed fairs, and its canals ensured that goods flowed in and out easily through all seasons and in all weathers.

Troyes has always been filled with Jews. In the Middle Ages, Jews were international merchants: they were bankers and they were middlemen, importing gems, glassware, jewelry, linens, and spices. Jewish merchants were also postmen and marriage brokers. And of course Jewish travelers hoped to breathe the atmosphere of the great rabbinical luminaries; therefore, visiting Jews sought out the local yeshivas – and in Troyes, they would rush to sit at the feet of Rashi or his descendants.

All foreign Jews felt a great reverence for the rabbis of Troyes, and the custom of attending barefoot at even the casual rabbinical discussions was strictly followed. Today, this ritual piety remains in only a few ceremonies. The *Kohanim* remove their shoes when they bless the congregation in the synagogue. Mourners remove their shoes during the seven sad days of mourning. And on the Day of Atonement and on the ninth day of *Av*, all pious Jews pray without their shoes. But shoelessness was once the standard: it was a universal symbol of devotion and of pious humility.

In any case, Rabbi Samuel ben Meir – who is also known as "Rashbam" – was one of the most venerated scholars of medieval Troyes. Rabbi Samuel had no doubt that when the Messiah would walk finally into our lives, he would come barefoot. Rashbam wrote this in a letter that answered a request of the mystic Rabbi Abraham ben Alexander, Achselrad of Cologne.

Ah, what a writer was old Abraham Achselrad! Grandmother said that the good Lord God had taken possession of the right hand of Rabbi Abraham: he could not stop writing. Achselrad wrote reams of letters to other scholars (such as Rashbam). In addition, he wrote a number of lengthy Kabbalistic tomes. The most famous of these works was the *Keter Shem Tov*. Unfortunately, this book remains unpublished; to this day it exists only as a crumbling manuscript somewhere in the loft above the back study room of the central yeshiva in Cologne.

At an earlier time, the two rabbis – Rashbam and Achselrad – had met in Cologne. My grandmother said that it was on a mild springtime morning. The sun was yellow and gentle, the sky was blue and cool, and an old traveler walked into the back room of the Cologne yeshiva, where Abraham Achselrad was working. As you know, Rabbi, in those far-off days, all manner of pious pilgrims came through Germany each week. They came from the East, from the Mediterranean shores, and from the Holy Lands, and it was not unusual for strange men to appear at odd hours of the day or night in the Cologne yeshiva.

It was morning, and Rabbi Abraham was writing intently when he thought he heard a noise. The Rabbi looked up. There in the doorway stood a man whom he did not recognize.

"Yes?" said the Rabbi.

"Are you Rabbi Abraham?" asked the old stranger.

"I am," answered Achselrad.

"My name is Samuel ben Meir. May I come in?"

Rabbi Abraham raised his eyebrows. Samuel ben Meir was a name well known to him. Rabbi Samuel was a famous commentator on the Holy Scriptures and on the Talmud; in fact, he was the foremost French scholar of critical scriptural analysis early in the twelfth century – also, Rabbi Samuel was a grandson of the great Rashi himself.

"This is an honor," said Rabbi Abraham, standing and offering his seat to Rabbi Samuel. Samuel ben Meir smiled, but he sat on one of the worn benches. Rabbi Abraham ben Alexander sat on a side bench also, rather than at his desk.

The two men talked and argued about many matters. Eventually they began to discuss points of scriptural interpretation.

"You know, my friend," said Rabbi Samuel, "I do not completely accept all the interpretations put forth by my esteemed grandfather Rabbi Shelomo."

"So I have heard," said Achselrad, sitting back and stroking his beard. "Many of the issues seem too recondite for me to follow. But, Rabbi Samuel, I have also heard that you take a strange position on a very basic subject – the matter of 'days': What is this about the day starting in the morning? You cannot truly believe this."

"On the face of things, I know that this sounds radical," said Rabbi Samuel. "But listen, my friend: it seems to me unavoidable that day begins at dawn. Day does not begin at the previous sunset –"

"But, Rabbi Samuel," interrupted Rabbi Abraham, "this is as fundamental a precept as –"

"Just a moment, good Rabbi," said Rabbi Samuel. "The *nighttime* beginning of daytime is not merely a paradox of words – it is also a distortion of the Holy Scriptures. A nighttime beginning for the day is merely a tradition – and it is a mistaken tradition, I might add. It is only a Jewish custom that has been passed to us from the deepest antiquity.

"The first verses in the Book of Genesis say":

And the holy Lord God (blessed be He) saw that the light was good, and He separated the light from the darkness. He called the light "day," and the darkness "night." So evening came and morning came, the first day.

"You see, Rabbi Abraham, it says: 'He called the light "day." ' Therefore, day begins with light."

"Ah, my good Rabbi Samuel," said Rabbi Abraham, "the verses also say: 'So evening came and morning came, the first day.' Therefore, the day must begin with the evening first."

Rabbi Samuel shook his head. "Rabbi Abraham, you are falling prey to the same old argument. Step back a moment and think. Look within yourself. Is it natural for the day to begin at night? Do you not feel, somewhere deep within your holy soul, that the night is an ending and that the morning is a beginning? Trust your soul, my friend – for your soul is as close to divinity as you and I can get in this dusty mortal world of ours."

And what could old Achselrad answer to that? . . .

What is that? Rashbam and the Messiah? Yes, yes, Rabbi – I am about to continue. I was just thinking quietly here, in the glow of the stove. Now, where was I? Oh yes, my grandmother told me that old Rabbi Abraham had written once to Rashbam. This was a few years after the two men met in Cologne. Achselrad had written to ask the famous philosopher about odd numbers, and this is Rashbam's reply:

"To my dear friend and holy colleague,
Abraham, the son of Alexander –

"I thank you for your letter, which I received last month. It is good to hear of the thoughtful scholarship that flourishes under your direction in the Jewish communities of the rich valley of the River Rhine. I know that the good Lord God (blessed be He) has shined down His warm smile and His loving-kindness and His benevolent radiance upon you and all your colleagues and upon the eager young children in your yeshivas, amen.

"You ask about odd numbers. This is a difficult subject, for we must carefully separate vague mysticism and untested folk beliefs from the more holy natural truths about numerology. I have, as you know, been taught by my grandfather Rabbi Shelomo ben Isaac (may his name be forever blessed) to seek explanations of difficult matters in the Holy Scriptures and in the Talmud. For his understandings, Rabbi Shelomo looked to the words and to their precise grammar, and I have tried always to follow his lead. (In fact, I have done this meticulously in the commentary on the Book of Job, which he began and which I have just completed.)

"In all cases, I try to stay with simple clear explanations. My philosophy is: Do not read more into a work than is allowed by the actual words and by their actual organization. As you know, this has led me to some controversial interpretations. Sometimes I have taken a stance that varied from the traditional readings of the Holy Scriptures, as put forth in the Talmud. But this is not contrary to the spirit of Judaism. The Talmud is, of course, a work of men—and men differ in their visions of the world, praise the Lord.

"Yes, my friend, we each see the world through our own eyes. At the same time, we must be open to learning things from our hearts too. We are blessed with holy souls; often we must look *within* ourselves for understandings. This requires a balancing act: we search the Holy Scriptures, and simultaneously we search our holy souls. The good Lord God did not have the space to inscribe all Truths in the Holy Scriptures—some He wrote within our immortal souls.

"The Truths written in our souls are what we might call the 'natural rules.' And how do we actually recognize these natural rules? First, thoughtful men put potential Truths into words. Then the words are tried and tested by tradition. Finally, the best of these natural rules are retained; they are recorded in the peripheral literature and even in folk beliefs and common sayings. And *this* is the realm, good Abraham—the realm of our natural and human 'literature'—where the number rules have been recorded. Much of the number lore comes to us from the peripheral books of our great Jewish culture. The mystical virtues and powers of numbers, for instance, are thoroughly discussed in the *Sefer Yetzirah* and also in the Kabbalah—these texts reiterate many, many natural rules that have been with us for years immemorial.

"Having moved from the Holy Scriptures to the holy soul, we can now ask: What are the natural rules for numbers? Let me begin with a passage from the sacred literature. In the Talmud, it says: 'Incantations that have not been repeated the prescribed number of times must then be said 41 times in order to be effective.' Now, good Abraham, is there something special about 41? Is 41 better than 3 or 7 or 72 or 221? I think not. Rather, the Talmud is emphasizing repetition: it is the continual *repetition* that gives an incantation its special power.

"Thus, one essential rule is: *many* is more powerful than *one*. This is a natural rule. It agrees with our natural inclinations – it feels right. I saw this so clearly in my young children, Rabbi Abraham. Children are innocent. Their souls are much more exposed than those of adults, who are scarred and hardened and whose souls are cloaked and bandaged and wrapped and sometimes hardly visible at all. As you remember, children love repetition and rhyme and chant, and nothing catches their ears more than singsong repetitions and reiterations.

"Clearly, repetition itself is powerful. In addition, however, particular numbers of repetitions color this power in individual ways. Traditionally, we learn that good luck comes from odd numbers. In contrast, the Talmud warns that even numbers are not merely unlucky, they are actually dangerous. Even numbers attract the attention of demons, dybbuks, and devils. Undoubtedly, you have heard the folk rules: A man should not eat or drink in a group where there is an even number of people. Or, one should not do things two at a time – never take fire twice from the hearth when there is a sick person in the house, and never marry two couples on one day in the same community.

"Thus, as a general rule, avoid even numbers. Odd numbers, on the other hand, have helpful uses. Three is clearly the most mystical odd number. Most actions and incantations should be performed three hours before sunrise or three days before the new moon or three days in succession. Furthermore, as you may know, my grandfather Rabbi Shelomo disclosed to me in a dream the correct pronunciation of the ineffable, incommunicable Name of the wondrous Lord God (blessed be He): this Name is built of threes – it consists of three times three times eight clusters of three holy Hebrew letters.

"Yes, threes are undoubtedly mystical. And as for sevens? They, too, have many fine uses. For instance, you will recall the talmudic prescription for the cure of certain fevers":

Take seven prickles from seven palm trees, seven chips from seven beams, seven nails from seven bridges, seven ashes from seven ovens, seven scoops of earth from beside seven doors, seven pieces of pitch from seven ships, seven handfuls of cumin, and seven hairs from the beard of an old dog. Mix these ingredients, put them in a packet, and tie it to the neck-hole of your shirt, using a white twisted cord containing seven tight knots.

"Moreover, God has set seven planets in the sky. And, as you know, the Hebrew verb 'to swear an oath' means literally 'to come under the influence of seven things'—thus, Genesis tells us that the oath between Abraham and Abimelech at Beersheba was sealed with seven female lambs. (Of course, I need hardly mention that the original Creation required seven days and that each of our Great Festivals also lasts seven days.)

"Apparently, my friend, threes and sevens are the most powerful odd numbers. Threes and sevens are 'naturally' holy numbers: somehow, they are close to the soul. I myself cannot find much Divine numerology directly written in the Holy Scriptures. But I must admit that in the quiet of the evening, I nonetheless often fall to musing over these mystical and powerful numbers. The magic of numbers warms me in a deep and unexplainably spiritual way—and that is how I would offer their use. Warm yourself, good Abraham, at the hearth of special numbers.

"And now, old friend, as I close this letter, let me make a secret confession: my favorite warming number is 'seven.' If I am to put any faith in mystical numbers and if I am to play a game, guessing when holy events are to occur, and if I would use the warm glow of 'seven,' then let me quietly, and just for fun, tell you this—I would not be surprised if on that glorious day when the Messiah shall walk barefoot and holy into our lives and when he will once again reawaken the sleeping mother Jerusalem and redeem all our souls, then it will be on the seventh day of the seventh month of a year of sevens. Hallelujah, good Abraham—hallelujah and amen seven times over.

"Your humble friend and colleague,
Samuel, the son of Meir"

ood evening, Rabbi. Are you having difficulty sleeping again? Put your feet up on the side bench here and I will open the stove door. Let me push the coals back; there is nothing like that white glow to wash away the cares of a hard day.

I heard your final prayers tonight. Clearly you are overworked — even an old shammas like me can tell. I kept one eye on you when I was cleaning the dishes; I saw that you were watching the door, hoping that Reb Elbaum would leave early. But then Reb Anton stayed late to argue about the "scholar's doubt" section from the Book of Proverbs:

> This is the Scholar's Doubt:
> I am weary O Lord
> I am tired and worn out.
>
> I am an aged creature
> I scarcely am a man
> I've learned nothing from my teacher.
>
> No wisdom do I retain
> I have no true insight
> All facts seem quite profane.

I am weak, I am undone—
　We mortals can't understand
The world of the Holy One.

Has any mortal ascended
　To Heaven and then returned?
Do you know him or where he's ended?

Has a man ever held a windstorm
　In the hollow of his palm
Or carved out a mountain's form?

Has anyone dared to crowd
　The seas inside his pocket—
Or jumped from cloud to cloud?

Has someone planted wildwood
　Filled with living things?
Is there such a mortal? Could

You tell me now his name
　Or do you know his son
Or the country from which he came?

Is there such a man?
　Then tell me now his name—
If, in fact, you can.

Did you hear Reb Anton talking with Reb Lavan? Reb Lavan
was saying that the "doubting scholar" in this verse was simply
overwhelmed by the wealth of knowledge in the Book of Proverbs—
and that reminded me of a story told by my grandmother. It was a
story about a wealth of proverbs. Grandmother was relating an incident that occurred long ago, in the small back study room of Achselrad
of Cologne. Achselrad (that is, Rabbi Abraham ben Alexander) was my
grandmother's favorite rabbi; he was a mystical scholar from those dim
medieval days in Germany along the wide dark River Rhine. Did you
know that Rabbi Abraham began his Kabbalistic treatise—a book called

the *Keter Shem Tov*—with the "scholar's doubt" verses from the Book of Proverbs?

Anyway—where was I? Oh yes, in medieval Germany along the wide dark River Rhine, there was once a famed yeshiva headed by Abraham ben Alexander, the mystic Achselrad of Cologne. (Just be patient, Rabbi—I am not really repeating myself, I only wanted to be certain that you knew to which mystic I was referring.) In any case, Rabbi Abraham's yeshiva was always filled with sages and scholars, and each of these wise old men believed in living by the holy proverbs.

In those days and in that community, there lived two brothers who were twins. One was named Solomon and one was named Simon, and both were sons of Isaac ha-Levi. Solomon and Simon were devoted to each other totally—and now that we are speaking of proverbs, there is a fine scriptural saying about such brothers:

> A friend loves you at some times,
>   But a brother's love is bountiful—
> A brother is like the sunshine
>   Which helps you heal your deepest trouble.

Now let me tell you a story about the brothers Solomon and Simon of Cologne:

Once upon a time, said my grandmother to me, when Abraham ben Alexander was the Chief Rabbi of Cologne, there lived in that town twin brothers, Solomon and Simon ben Isaac ha-Levi. These brothers loved and trusted each other, and they remained together even after they had grown up. One brother, Solomon, married and had many children, but he was poorer than his brother. The second brother, Simon, never married, and he became quite wealthy. However, each brother was happy and neither envied the other.

Solomon and Simon were merchants. Both traded in grain—and this was the full extent of Solomon's business. On the other hand, Simon had prospered, and now he traded in grain and horses and other goods, including glassware, gold, pearls, roses, and silver.

One day, the two brothers were walking together down Judengasse Street, when an old scholar named Gabriel ben Hayyim stopped them and said, "Boys, I have had my eye on you."

"You have?" asked Solomon.

"Yes, I have," said Reb Gabriel. "Now, do you know that it is your duty to share with each other?"

"Of course it is," said Simon.

"Yes, it certainly is," said the old scholar, frowning at them.

"Well, sir, we *do* share," said the brothers.

"Ah, but not properly," admonished old Gabriel. "Remember the scriptural Proverb":

> A wise servant can take precedence
> Over a disgraceful son
> Even inheriting from the parents
> As a brother would have done.

The brothers raised their eyebrows and they looked a bit puzzled. Old Gabriel ben Hayyim squinted at them, and he said, "And in the Book of Leviticus, the great Lord God (blessed be He) says":

> When your brother is reduced to poverty and sells himself to you, then you shall accept his help, but you shall not allow him to work for you as a slave.

The brothers looked at each other. Then Reb Gabriel said, "I think that you two are on a Course of Destruction. You had best consult with Rabbi Abraham and his colleagues at once."

The brothers did not know what to say. They had thought that they were behaving honestly, uprightly, and lovingly. Perhaps, however, they were sinning inadvertently. Solomon and Simon became worried. They continued on their way, but early the next morning they went to see Rabbi Abraham.

Solomon and Simon stepped in the front door of the synagogue building. They went through the anteroom, and they walked into the main prayer hall, which was filled with wooden benches. The brothers passed the twelve stained glass windows with their colored lions and snakes. They looked up at the Holy Ark made of stone, and they walked to the door of the back study room. There, in the light of the early morning, they found the Rabbi sleeping at his desk, for he had worked all night on his mystical treatise the *Keter Shem Tov*. The yeshiva scholars were sitting on the worn benches, talking quietly among themselves.

Solomon and Simon stood uncertainly in the doorway.

"Yes, gentlemen?" said old Baruch ben Jacob.

Solomon looked at Simon, and Simon looked at Solomon.

"I am Simon, the son of Isaac ha-Levi. This is my brother, Solomon," began Simon.

Simon looked at Solomon. "We were advised to come and ask for your counsel," said Solomon. "Apparently, we have not shared properly between ourselves."

The sages stared intently at the two young men. Some of the old men nodded, some tapped their feet, and some raised their eyebrows. The scholars whispered among themselves; then white-haired Baruch ben Jacob cleared his throat.

"You have not shared properly?" he asked. "Well, the Holy Scriptures certainly encourages brothers to live together amiably and helpfully. As it is said in the Book of Proverbs":

> Six things the good Lord hates –
>   Yes, seven does He despise:
> Haughty spirits and proud eyes
>   Vile tongues that criticize
> Hands that cause an innocent's demise
>   Hearts that wicked crimes devise
> Feet that hurry for an evil prize
>   False witnesses telling slanderous lies
> And those who incite fights unwise
>   Between brothers, where they should ne'er arise.

A younger scholar, Elisah ben Samuel, nodded. "Yes, good friends," he said, "there is much wisdom in the practical words of the Holy Scriptures. For example, I remind you of the famous scriptural Proverb":

> An offended brother is more unyielding
>   Than a strongly fortified city,
> And disputes among brothers arguing
>   Are the fiercest in their intensity.

"In other words, the strength of emotions generated between brothers exceeds the strongest wood and iron that build the great cities."

Then Joshua ben Eliezer tapped a finger on one of the benches and he said, "Amen, good Elisah. Moreover, as the old Hebrew proverb says: 'If one of you had not lifted up the stone, then the other would not have found the jewel.' That is, the success that each of you enjoys in business is due in part to the other."

The many scholars nodded, they stroked their beards, and they murmured "amen."

After a moment, Lewe ben Anselm said, "And I would also recall the Proverb":

> In the midst of many others
>   A man can still find ruin alone,
> But two loyal brothers
>   Will guard and protect their own.

"This means, of course, that there is none closer or more trustworthy or more protective than a true brother."

And Menahem ben Joel said, "Yes, gentlemen, the Proverbs tell us much about such relationships. For instance, there is also the scriptural Proverb":

> If even a man's own brothers
>   Find him hard to stand,
> Then certainly he will be shunned
>   By others near at hand.

Menahem's colleague, Moyses ben Nathan, stroked his beard and he said, "Proverbs are all well and good, my wise friends, but I myself turn to the Psalms for the deepest insights. And it is written in Psalm 133":

> How blessed and how sanctified
> For brothers to be close allied
> And to worship quietly side by side.

Finally, old Shimshon ha-Zaken nodded and coughed, and he said, "Reb Moyses, as you know, the Book of Proverbs follows the Book of Psalms. Thus, a Proverb should always follow a Psalm. And so, I remind you of the related scriptural Proverb":

A friend is a companion everywhere
Throughout the gentle weather –
But brothers have been born to share
Even difficult days together.

The various scholars nodded and murmured and stroked their beards – and old Rabbi Abraham continued to doze.

This was certainly a wealth of proverbs, although they left Solomon and Simon at somewhat of a loss as to how to proceed. The sages did not seem to have more to offer. The Rabbi remained asleep. Solomon and Simon raised their eyebrows and they looked at each other. Then the two men nodded to the sages and they returned home. And as they worked and ate and slept, over the next few days, the brothers Solomon and Simon thought about what they had heard.

Solomon and Simon shared a grain warehouse in the Alter Markt district, just to the east of the Juden Viertels – the Jewish Quarter of Cologne. A week after they had consulted the sages, the brothers found themselves working together in their warehouse late one night. Earlier they had divided the day's shipment of grain and had put it in sacks. Then they had loaded the sacks onto the distribution wagons. Now it was late, and Solomon and Simon were left with the money and the goods that they had received in payment. The two brothers were hot and covered with grain and they were quite tired. They dismissed their helpers, and they decided to sleep together in the warehouse in order to protect their valuables.

In the middle of the night, Solomon awoke, and he thought to himself, "My brother Simon is single. But I, by the blessing of the Highest One, have a good wife and four fine and lovely children. I know joys that my brother will never experience. It is not right that I should receive a share equal to his from our work together."

Solomon nodded to himself, and he thought that perhaps a holy word was in order here. Therefore, he repeated the first passage in Genesis that is traditionally recited for a prosperous business:

If the good Lord, the God of my father, the God of Abraham, and the Fear of Isaac, had not been with me, then you would have sent me away empty-handed and with no success. But the Lord saw my labor and my hardships; thus, He has sustained me and He shall make me prosper in my work.

Solomon felt a holy spirit invade his soul. He stood up. He took fully half of his share of the receipts, and he put it in his brother's pile. Then he smiled and went to bed happily.

The night wore on. A while later the other brother, Simon, awoke. It was the late dark hours. Simon took to musing, and eventually he thought to himself, "My brother Solomon is a married man; he also has children to look after. On the other hand, I am single, and I have no responsibilities other than myself. It is not right that I should receive a share equal to his."

Simon nodded to himself, and he felt that he should say a blessing or some other pious verse. All that he could remember at the moment was the second passage in Genesis that is traditionally recited for a prosperous business, so he repeated that verse:

Joseph gave his steward this order: "Fill the men's packs with as much food as they can carry, and put each man's silver at the top of his pack."

Simon felt a holy spirit creep into his soul. He stood up. He took a third of his share of valuables and he put it in his brother's pile. Then he smiled, and he went to bed happily. Now the piles were once again equal.

The next morning, the two men arose. They looked at one another, and they patted each other on the shoulder. Then each man packed up his valuables: each took home an equal share of the previous day's receipts. Yes, Solomon ben Isaac ha-Levi and Simon ben Isaac ha-Levi were good men, and they were brothers—and more importantly, they remained fast friends to the end of their days.

At this point in the story, my grandmother looked up at me, Rabbi: she looked up from her embroidery—the handwork with which she busied her old fingers each day when she sat at the edge of her mother's grave. Grandmother looked up at me, she smiled, and then she said, "Ah, my golden boy, Solomon and Simon were fine and faithful brothers. And brothers, my little one, are a wondrous security. They protect us against the strange forces that hide in the shadows of this complex tangled world of ours. These dark forces are ever present. They are the strange forces that make even the scholars doubt, when they wake alone in the late, late hours of a deep black night."

ood evening, Rabbi. I was just resting my eyes – please feel free to join me here by the stove. (I think you will be too warm on that bench: try the one nearer to the wall.) An old man like me can doze forever by a warm stove; I suppose that is because I often forget to trim my fingernails.

What is that, Rabbi? Well, fingernails induce sleep: fingernail trimmings can be used in sleeping potions, you know. You did not know this? Oh yes – my grandmother told this to me many times. Discarded parts of bodies are powerful ingredients in profane magic. Although Jews have always stayed away from such heathen practices, the medieval Jews certainly knew about them; during the Middle Ages, in the neighboring Gentile communities, parts of corpses were used in the black magic of thieves and other malefactors. Jews, on the other hand, relied on parchment amulets and charms. . . .

What? No, no – do not get up on my account, Rabbi: I was just resting my eyes a moment. I was resting and musing. . . . Well, to tell you the truth, Rabbi, I was remembering an event – an encounter – from Cologne, a small happening from those dim old days of Rabbi Abraham ben Alexander, the mystic Achselrad of Cologne. This incident had to do with amulets and charms. You see, Rabbi, in those days, Jews always carried charms in order to protect themselves against malicious spirits.

This particular encounter took place once upon a time, long, long ago, in medieval Cologne. There, on the western outskirts of the city, lived a young man named Nachum ben Anschel ha-Kohen. Nachum was a dairy farmer who owned only three cows, and he made a meager living selling butter, cheese, cream, and milk. One morning, Nachum was taking a trip to visit his sick brother in Bonn. As he walked along the River Rhine, the air got darker and darker and the sky sank lower and lower. Soon it began to rain very heavily. Nachum was cold and wet and muddy. He felt miserable, and he stopped under a tree.

Rain and mud and cloudy times are made for imps and demons. Dybbuks and fallen angels fly about. Dark spirits and wraiths haunt the countryside. Nachum was drenched and he shivered uncontrollably. As Nachum leaned back against the tree, he suddenly stepped on a stick. The stick cracked, and there was a hiss and a laugh and a grim demon appeared. It said, "Evil man – you have broken my walking stick. You will suffer for this wicked deed."

Nachum was very frightened, but he remembered that a demon could not touch anything that is tied in a sack. Quickly, he pulled his cloak around himself, and managed to tie himself within, just like a sack. (Now do not ask me how Nachum did this, Rabbi, for I confess that I am mystified myself.)

The demon jumped up and down: it was frustrated and angry. It called and it taunted, but Nachum sat there, wrapped in his cloak like a large tied-up sack. The demon hissed and it spat. The man peeked out from between the folds, watching the demon carefully. Eventually, the demon began to fiddle with its pointy clawed toes, and it looked away. Then quick as a wink, Nachum reached out and he caught the demon – for he knew that if the demon remained securely held then it could not control him. A demon has no power over anything sealed, tied, or bound in any fashion, and a demon loses its power when it itself is sealed or tied or bound.

Again, the demon hissed and it spat, and it said, "Let me loose this instant! I am just about to change you into a pile of mud!"

Nachum ben Anschel said nothing; he only held on tightly. The demon wriggled and it squirmed, it waved its legs and it howled.

Then the demon coughed and it shrieked and it said, "If you do not let go of me, I will turn you into a toad with one eye!"

Of course, Nachum was frightened, but he was wearing his protective amulet. This was a small sheet of fresh lead, strung on a new white thread around his neck. On the metal was etched:

> Deny a witch or a sorceress life;
> Life to a witch must be denied;
> Deny the life of a sorceress;
> A witch is to be denied her life;
> Life is denied to a sorceress.

I charge you, the angels Mchashpiel, Ktasiel, and Sandriel, in the name of what I am and what I shall be, and in the ineffable Name of the Lord God Yahweh, the Lord of Hosts Who presides over all angels, that He and they shall nullify any sorcery committed against Nachum, the son of Anschel ha-Kohen, from now until Eternity—amen and *selah*.

Nachum felt weak, but he took heart in the charm and he held on to the demon with all his might. Now the demon began to change its shape. It turned into a lion, a serpent, a leopard, and a boar. Then it became a tree, a flame, and even water. However, somehow Nachum managed to hold fast through all these changes.

At last the demon returned to its usual hairy evil form. It hissed and it spat and it called out, "I give in, you cruel man—if you release me, then I will reward you."

Ah, but Rabbi, could you believe a demon? Nachum knew that the demon would keep its promise only if it swore an oath on the holy Name of Yahweh. "Swear by Yahweh that what you say is true," demanded the man.

"I swear," said the demon.

"That is not good enough," insisted Nachum ben Anschel. "You must swear by the Name of the great Lord God Yahweh (blessed be He)."

"All right!" shouted the demon angrily. "I swear on the Name of Yahweh that I will reward you if you release me."

But Nachum hesitated. He hesitated—and well he should have. "With what will you reward me?" he asked.

The demon hissed and it spat. "I will reward you with disease," said the demon bitterly.

"Then I shall never release you," said the man.

"You will tire eventually," said the demon.

"Perhaps," said Nachum ben Anschel.

The two sat there in a stalemate for many hours. Nachum ben Anschel was worried that his hands would become numb and that they would no longer do as he wished. Finally the demon said, "All right, all right–I give in. I will reward you with money."

"How much money will you give me?" asked Nachum.

"Five gold coins," said the demon.

"That is not enough," said the man.

"You are greedy," said the demon.

"Perhaps," said Nachum ben Anschel.

The two sat and sat and sat. One hour passed, and then a second came and went. It was late morning. Or was it the early afternoon? Nachum was hungry, and his head began to spin. All at once, the demon said, "You are an evil man, but I will reward you with fifty gold coins."

"And you will do me no harm?"

"Very well–I will not harm you," said the demon.

"Let me hear you declare this as an oath," said Nachum.

"All right, all right–have you no mercy on a poor spirit? I swear by Yahweh that I will give you fifty gold coins and I will do you no harm if you release me," hissed the demon.

"I accept," said the man. He let go of the demon, who spat and hissed and coughed and disappeared in a puff of foul gray smoke.

Nachum was tired and shaken. He returned home and lay down, and immediately he fell asleep. Nachum slept a dreamless sleep for many, many hours.

The next day dawned brightly, and Nachum felt better. He looked out his window. A wispy cloud, a bit of celestial cotton, floated far and high. A bird squeaked and cheeped behind a yellow-green leaf. Nachum dressed and washed, he said his prayers, and he had (praise the good Lord God) an entirely uneventful day. And then, the next week also passed calmly and easily.

Not long afterward, one of Nachum's cows became weak. Soon it was unable to stand, and Nachum took it to the *shochet* to be slaughtered. The *shochet* recited the appropriate ritual prayers, including the phrase from the Book of Leviticus: "They shall no longer sacrifice their slaughtered beasts to demons." Then the animal was swiftly killed. In its stomach, the *shochet* found a wallet with fifty bright gold coins. Nachum gave one coin to the *shochet* and he gave twenty-five gold coins to charity. Then Nachum said a brief prayer, he smiled, and he kept the remainder of the money for himself. Nachum ben Anschel ha-Kohen remained a good and pious man. He always wore his lead amulet—and, although the world is crowded with throngs of cruel hairy demons, Nachum never saw an evil spirit again.

abbi, I am glad to see you here tonight: you bring holy thoughts to my mind. You see, when I am alone I find it hard to remember all the holy things that I should know. And this is in spite of the comforting words of the good Lord God (blessed be He) in the Book of Deuteronomy:

> The commandments that I set for you this day are not too difficult for you – and they are not too remote. My Truths are not in Heaven, so that you must say: "Who will go up to Heaven for us to fetch them and to tell them to us in order that we can keep them?" They are not beyond the sea, so that you must say: "Who will cross the sea for us to fetch them and to tell them to us?" These things are very near to you – in fact, they are upon your lips and in your heart, ever ready to be kept.

I know this verse quite well. Nonetheless, Rabbi, when you are here, then I feel much better: now the holy truths really *do* feel near to me.

Ah, rabbis are a great strength and comfort to us all. They guide us. They uphold us. And, notwithstanding the optimism of the Almighty One, I think that we need them nearby. My grandmother always spoke warmly and respectfully of these holy men. Of course, her favorite rabbi was the old mystic Abraham ben Alexander, Achselrad of Cologne. Every day, Rabbi Abraham was called upon to bring the commandments of the good Lord God near to the members of his Jewish community. Because of old Abraham Achselrad, holy things did not remain remote in Heaven or distant across the sea; the sacred Truths became interwoven with the daily lives of the Jews of Cologne. Why, even in practical matters of commerce or in common daily disputes, when the Rabbi intervened, the decisions and the interactions were elevated to more sacred levels. For example, I remember one elevating story that my grandmother told – in this tale, Rabbi Abraham used his holy insight to resolve a monetary argument among three brothers in old medieval Cologne:

Once upon a time, said my grandmother to me, there lived in Cologne a very pious and wealthy man named Joseph ben Kalonymus. Reb Joseph had three sons – Simon, Gabirol, and Elia – and all of them were clever and all were talmudic scholars. Of course, just as with you and me, Rabbi, Joseph ben Kalonymus eventually grew old and weak. Yes, Joseph grew old, and before his death he called together a number of the sages from the Jewish community of Cologne.

It was a fine morning, late in the spring month of *Iyar*, when Baruch ben Jacob, Menahem ben Joel, and old Shimshon ha-Zaken came to the house of Joseph ben Kalonymus. These three scholars were longtime friends of Reb Joseph. In their presence, Joseph told his sons, "My dear children, Simon, Gabirol, and Elia, after my death I will leave you my wealth. It should be enough to last each of you all your life, if the good Lord God (blessed be He) does not send you any serious troubles and if the great wheel of fortune does not revolve unpredictably."

Old Joseph coughed, and he rested. Then he said, "Of course, we can never be protected completely against the future. The omnipotent Lord whirls our little earth in His holy palm. The great wheel of fortune revolves inexorably. Hopefully, none of you will suffer. However, I think that I can afford extra protection for only one child against some unforeseen disaster. But for whom shall this be? I love you all. Therefore, I will leave you an additional locked chest for an emergency. Inside, there is enough money for one of you. Who will need it? Only the good Lord God knows for certain."

There was silence. After a moment, Joseph ben Kalonymus continued: "I want each of you to pledge that you will not open this oak box except in the case of extreme need. In order to protect the chest from temptation, I set up these conditions: you will take turns keeping the chest, and when one of you has the task of holding the chest, then a different son will be responsible for the key."

At this point, Joseph opened the chest and he showed the men that it contained seven hundred gold coins. Then he closed and locked the fine oak box. The old sages murmured "amen," and the sons promised to adhere to this regimen of caretaking for the money – thus, in the presence of the community elders, the sons Simon, Gabirol, and Elia solemnly agreed to carry out their father's last wishes.

Old Joseph was a pious man. He had been kind and generous and very charitable throughout his lifetime, and one Sabbath morning he died quietly and peacefully. After a sad week of mourning, the three brothers divided the inheritance money. And to begin, Simon kept the sealed chest and Gabirol kept the key. Then the sons set themselves up in various businesses, and they were each comfortably wealthy.

After some time, the youngest son, Elia ben Joseph, who was a great spendthrift and (I am sorry to say) a gambler, lost all his money. Now he was poor. Elia's wife and his family were unhappy; their clothes became old and ragged and sometimes they did not have enough food. Elia could think of no way to earn a comfortable living. Therefore, he asked his brothers to open the oak money-chest and to give him the contents. The other brothers hesitated. It did not seem to be a dire emergency. The oldest brother, Simon, said, "Listen, Elia, rather than take this irrevocable step, I will lend you seven hundred gold coins. In fact, we will not call it a loan – you are my brother, so you may pay me back or not as you please."

Elia smiled and he took the seven hundred gold coins. When his wife discovered the loan, she said, "Please, Elia, invest this money in some steady business." Elia promised, but soon he fell into his old habits. In less than a year the money was gone completely. When he had spent the money, Elia again found himself poor. Still, he was unwilling to work seriously, so he turned to his two brothers for a second time.

Elia walked into Gabirol's house one evening. Simon was sitting at the table, talking business with his brother. Elia said to the two men,

"My good brothers, Simon and Gabirol, let us finally open the chest that Father left us. Through the unfathomable wishes of the Almighty Lord God (blessed be He), I am afraid that my fortunes have turned sour. Now it is time to rescue me. Father could not be resting peacefully in the Great Hereafter if he knew that one of his favorite sons was suffering."

The two older brothers looked at each other sadly, and they shook their heads. Gabirol, the second brother, said, "Listen, Elia, I cannot accept the idea of opening the chest. You are not a responsible person, but I will give you some money rather than break Father's will because of your bad habits. Here are seven hundred gold coins. It would be nice if you could pay me back; otherwise, consider it a gift."

Again Elia was happy. But Elia's wife said, "How many chances will you get, you spendthrift? Listen to me. If necessary, give the money to one of your brothers to invest for you. But whatever you do, do not spend it yourself."

"Yes, yes, good wife," said Elia. However, that week he heard from a friend that it would be possible to buy a large quantity of ornate spice boxes at a very low price. Elia spent five hundred gold coins, but the boxes turned out to be of poor quality – and in any case, at that time there was little demand in Cologne for expensive spice boxes.

Soon Elia had gone through the remaining money as well. Now he found himself stuck. He was certain that his brothers would not give him any more money. Therefore, Elia waited until it was his turn to keep the key, and secretly he had a copy made – when the key passed to him, he took it to Bonn on a business trip and had a locksmith craft an exact duplicate. Later he gave the original key to his brother Simon in exchange for the chest. Elia now had both the chest of money and a key.

One night, after his wife and children had fallen asleep, Elia took the counterfeit key and he opened the oak box. Inside were the seven hundred gold coins. Elia removed the money, and he substituted an equal weight of stones. Then he carefully closed and locked the chest, and he buried the extra key in the back yard.

Again, Elia had a great quantity of money. Gabirol looked at Simon, and Simon looked at Gabirol. Apparently Elia had reformed. His brothers were surprised, but they were happy. Somehow, Elia was prospering, and a great weight had been removed from the brothers' minds. However, Elia was still Elia, and within a year he used up all the money that he had taken from his father's locked oak box.

Elia tried to borrow money from friends and he tried to borrow money from relatives, but he could raise very little cash. He began to sleep fitfully and to eat poorly. He became alternately short-tempered and sad, and eventually he went back to his brothers. He said to them, "I thought that I would not have to bring up this subject again. As you know, I have not complained for quite a while, and I have managed to live comfortably without bothering you. Is it the will of the good Lord God, or have I been born under an unlucky planet? Whatever the cause, the wheel of fortune has revolved and once again I have been left in the mud. In fact, I am now penniless – through no doing of my own. You are my brothers. Give me some money so that your own family's family will not starve."

The brothers looked at one another. Finally Simon said, "Elia, we *have* helped you – both Gabirol and I have been overly generous. However, you must grow up now and become responsible for your own actions."

Then Gabirol added, "Simon is right, Elia. You are an able-bodied man. Find work, and stop being so wasteful. That is the best course."

Simon continued: "Listen, Elia – we will not always be around to rescue you. It is time that you took responsibility for your own life. You must finally grow up and become more reliable."

And the two men refused to give any more money to Elia.

Elia stared at his brothers. A hot wave passed over him. "So," he thought, "now they are turning against me. It is easy for them: they have plenty of money. They have been lucky in the world. In their hearts, these two have always looked down on me, but now their true selfishness is finally revealed." Elia hit the table with his hand. "All right," he said out loud, "if that is the way you are going to act, then I declare that it is time finally to open the oak chest and give me the emergency money!"

The two older brothers looked at each other. "You are pushing this to a crisis," said Simon. "Let us wait awhile and see if your fortunes take a turn for the better."

"Yes," said Gabirol, "do not rush into this. Once the chest is opened, the money will be exhausted forever. Be patient, Elia."

But Elia was angry. He said to them, "You are hard-hearted men.

It is written in Father's will that in the case of absolute necessity – if one of us falls on extremely hard times – then we must open the chest and use the money. Unfortunately, that time has come."

When the other brothers saw that it was inevitable, they finally agreed. The next day, the three brothers went to the elders of the community; they carried the locked chest with them into the synagogue. Simon, Gabirol, and Elia stepped through the front door of the old yeshiva building. They went through the anteroom, and they walked into the main prayer hall, which was filled with wooden benches. The brothers passed the twelve stained glass windows with their colored lions and snakes. They looked up at the Holy Ark made of stone, and they walked to the door of the back study room. There, a group of scholars and sages was sitting and talking on the worn benches along the wall.

"Good day, gentlemen," said Simon. The old men nodded and murmured greetings.

Gabirol looked around him. "Unfortunately," he said, "we find ourselves obliged to open this money-chest. Perhaps you remember the will of our father, to which some of you were witnesses. The chest contains a special fund for emergencies. Elia, our youngest brother, now insists on opening the box; he has become destitute, and Simon and I have stretched ourselves to the limits helping him out financially."

The elders nodded. During the last year, Gabirol had been in charge of the key and Simon had been in charge of the box. In the presence of the venerable old men of Cologne, Gabirol gave the key to white-haired Baruch ben Jacob. Reb Baruch opened the box, which was still in the hands of Simon. Baruch lifted the lid – and everyone saw that the chest was filled entirely with stones.

Elia ben Joseph immediately pushed Simon aside. Angrily he said to the old scholars, "Look at this! My older brothers have cheated me. I see now why they had refused to open the chest before. And now it is also clear why they have given me their own money. Simon and Gabirol have stolen my inheritance! That is why they are rich and I am poor. These two had charge of the box and the key during the last year; my brothers must have taken out the money and put stones in its place. I insist that they immediately pay me full restitution. I demand my seven hundred gold coins!"

The other brothers were astonished. They had seen their father lock the box originally, many years ago. Now they were unsure as to who was the culprit, and they looked at each other suspiciously. The community elders stroked their beards. They muttered and they murmured among themselves. Some mischief was afoot, but who was guilty? Had one brother deceived the other two? Were two brothers in collusion against the third? Or were all three brothers trying to take advantage of the community? The elders could not decide. Therefore, the sages waited for the Rabbi to hear the story.

Not long afterward, Rabbi Abraham walked into the small back study room. The air felt uncomfortable. The Rabbi looked around him intently, and then he sat down at his desk. Elia spoke first; then each of the other brothers presented his case. Rabbi Abraham stroked his beard and listened carefully without speaking. Then he said, "My friends, you must remain here awhile, for I cannot shake the decision out of my sleeve."

Old Abraham Achselrad walked back into the main prayer hall, which was crowded with wooden benches. He looked at the Holy stone Ark. He saw the sunlight sifting through the twelve stained glass windows with their colored lions and snakes. Then he sat and prayed quietly. After a moment, he recalled a verse from the Holy Scriptures, in the Book of the Prophet Malachi:

> "I am the Lord unchanging, and you, too, have not ceased to be sons of Jacob. From the days of your forefathers, you have been wayward and have not kept My Laws. But if you will return to Me, then I will return to you." Thus says the Lord of Hosts, blessed be He.

Then Rabbi Achselrad closed his eyes and he opened his eyes. Slowly he stood, and he returned to the brothers in the back study room. "Let me begin by telling you a brief story and then asking your opinions," he said.

The brothers looked at one another. The old sages remained silent. And Rabbi Abraham ben Alexander began his tale:

"Once there were two friends as close as brothers. One of these men had a daughter; the other man had a son. The fathers agreed that their children should marry one day, and they wrote this charge into their wills.

"Inevitably, the wheel of fortune turned in unpredictable ways. It came to pass that the son grew up to be penniless, while the girl grew to be very, very rich. Not only did the boy's family lose all their money, but every business that the young man tried failed miserably – in fact, he seemed almost cursed.

"When it came time for the marriage, the fathers had long since died. The young man said to the young woman, 'Although our fathers have decreed that we should marry each other, I am afraid that I cannot marry you. I have no money. Furthermore, I have terrible luck in business and I will only be a drain on your resources. This cannot be the true intent of our fathers.'

"The girl was heartbroken, and she said, 'Do not worry. I have enough money for the two of us. I would rather marry you and not break our fathers' wills.'

"The young man listened, but he said, 'May the good Lord God bless you and give you good fortune. Find another husband. Now you can choose anyone that you want. Pick a scholar, pick a rich man – make your life as wonderful as it can be – but stay away from me, I am bad luck.'

"The young woman did not know what to do, and although she received many fine offers of marriage from other men, she turned them all down. Many years later, she died unmarried and childless.

"Moreover, one day during her long lonely life, a robber came and took all her money. But just as he was about to leave, she told him her sad story. Then, through the intervention of the good Lord God (blessed be He), the robber suddenly had a change of heart and he could not take the money; instead, he left with no valuables whatsoever.

"Then the woman said a silent prayer. Ever after, she had a great fear of robbers, so she hid all her money. In the end, the woman died wealthy, but the money was hidden. No one got any of the money, and to this day no one knows exactly what happened to all of her wealth – amen."

The Rabbi closed his eyes. There was silence in the small back study room.

"That is a strange story," said Gabirol.

"What is the question that you wanted to ask us about it?" said Simon.

Rabbi Achselrad opened his eyes. "Well," he said, "in the story, none of the people ended up happy. I would like to know each of your opinions – which person made the biggest mistake?"

The Rabbi looked first at Simon ben Joseph. Simon frowned a moment, and then he said, "Clearly, the young man made the biggest mistake. Although he was penniless, he was basically good-hearted. He would have made a fine husband, so he should have married the woman."

Next, the Rabbi looked at Gabirol. Gabirol said, "Clearly, Rabbi, the young woman made the biggest mistake. Although she wanted to respect both the young man's wishes and her father's wishes, she should have made the best of her life. If she could not force the young man to marry her, then she should have married another man and had a family. In this way, at least she would have carried on her father's lineage – besides, she could always have remained friends with her childhood sweetheart."

Finally, the Rabbi looked to Elia ben Joseph. Elia looked at his brothers and he looked at the seven old sages sitting on the benches along the wall. Then he said, "I think that the robber made the biggest mistake. The woman hoarded her money. She had no one to spend it on, and in the end there was no one to inherit it. The robber was too soft-hearted; he should have taken the money. No one else was going to use the wealth. At least *he* could have used it and the money would not have been wasted."

Elia saw that one of the scholars, old Shimshon ha-Zaken, had raised his eyebrows, so Elia quickly added, "Of course if I were the robber then I would have given some of the money to charity too."

Then the Rabbi nodded his head, and he said, "Ah, my boys, it is written in the Holy Scriptures – in the introduction to the Book of Proverbs – 'If a wise man listens, then he will learn much.' "

At this point, the Rabbi was not looking at the young men and he was not looking at the scholars. I am not certain exactly where old Abraham ben Alexander was looking; but again he nodded his head, and then he said, "Therefore, blessed be the Lord Who lets all tongues tell the truth."

"Amen," said old Baruch ben Jacob.

Rabbi Abraham Alexander looked at the three brothers, one by one. "I see," he said to Elia, "that you, the youngest son, have somehow managed to take your father's money from the chest. Hold on a moment, young man. I know that it is you who is guilty – do not protest. Further lies will not help. So here is my ruling. . . ."

The Rabbi looked up at the ceiling, and he began to intone, almost in a chant, "We begin with the Book of Exodus, where the omnipotent Lord God commands us: 'Do not spread a baseless rumor. Avoid all lies.' "

"Amen," said old Baruch.

"Amen, Reb Baruch," repeated the Rabbi. Then he continued: "Honesty is an elemental and holy virtue. Remember that the Talmud tells us: 'Jerusalem was destroyed because honest men ceased to reside therein.'

"And the Talmud goes on to say":

> There are seven kinds of thieves, and chief of all is he who deceives his brothers. The most Holy One (blessed be He) hates a person who says one thing with his mouth but who knows another thing in his heart.

The Rabbi looked sternly at Elia. "Now, young man, exactly what shall we do with you?" he asked. There was silence. The Rabbi tapped his finger on his desk. "The Book of Leviticus says":

> When one of you is reduced to poverty and sells part of his patrimony, then his next-of-kin who has the duty of redemption shall come and redeem what his kinsman has sold. . . . When your brother is reduced to poverty and sells himself to you, then you shall accept his help, but you shall not allow him to work for you as a slave.

Rabbi Abraham was silent. Then he said, "Elia, I interpret these scriptural verses to mean that you must work for each of your brothers for one year, as a paid workman. This is my ruling and my decree."

The old scholars nodded their heads, and they murmured "amen."

The three brothers looked at one another, and they turned to go. But the Rabbi stopped them. "Just a moment, young men, I have more to say."

The three brothers turned back. "Simon and Gabirol have been more than fair," said the mystic Achselrad. The scholars stroked their beards and they nodded their heads.

"However," continued the Rabbi, "the Almighty Lord demands yet *more* from the two of you. The Book of Proverbs tells us":

> Do not rejoice at a victim
>> Or when your enemy's prayers are ignored;
> Be modest and humble and help him —
> We are all children of the Lord.

"Simon and Gabirol, if you do not forgive Elia, then you will continue the bad feelings and the enmity," said the Rabbi. "You two brothers must make a supreme holy effort: remove this evil from your family. Harmony and love come from strength and hard work. Remember, family is more important than money. In the end, it is the blessings and the love of the good Lord God that are the true riches — and we are all members of God's blessed family."

Then the Rabbi nodded to himself, and he turned back to his manuscript and became lost in thought.

And, Rabbi, I remember distinctly that, after telling me this tale, my grandmother said, "This has been a story about proverbs, my golden little boy. Proverbs are tiny gems that we can carry about in our pockets — so let me give you one more scriptural Proverb, a little gemstone for your small pocket":

> It is the blessings of the Lord
>> That bring to us our best reward,
> Our soul's most treasured grace.
>
> God stores his blessed things close by —
>> They are in your heart in rich supply
> And in your child's embrace.

ello, Rabbi, I will be with you in a moment—I cannot leave until every tablecloth is folded, otherwise the day has not ended properly.... There, now I am finished at last and I can sit next to you by the stove. Tomorrow night begins the Sabbath again, praise the great Lord God, amen.

To me, the Sabbath always means mystical poetry. My grandmother said that it was the mystic Rabbi Abraham Achselrad who first introduced Kabbalistic poetry during the synagogue service for certain Sabbaths in the springtime. On the Sabbath *Zakhor*, before *Purim*, and on the Sabbath *Parah*, just thereafter, Rabbi Abraham had his congregants read the poetry of Eleazar Kalir from his *Shiv'ata*. Achselrad also loved the poetry of Meir ben Isaac of Worms and the poetry of Rabbi Bahya ben Joseph ibn Pakuda of Saragossa. Do you know any of Bahya's hymns? One that I remember is Bahya's prayer for the Sabbath:

> I saw a homestead new bedight
> On one holy Friday night
> Where passed a peaceful angel wight,
> A silvery restful Sabbath sprite.

A celestial shaft of pure cool white –
The Sabbath angel's clear moonlight –
Slipped through the window on that night
Down from Heaven's starry height;

It set the children all alight
With their faces wide-eyed, bright
And blessed within Your holy sight
O radiant Lord, our God of Might.

Yes, each week the children slight
Are robed again in purest white
And loved anew and loved aright
By the gentle Sabbath sprite.

I wonder if old Rabbi Abraham ever read that poem. I am certain that he would have liked it. Although he was very pious, he was also a mystic – and to be honest, he was a romantic. In his younger years, Abraham tried many wild and romantic things, and he traveled far and wide. Once, he visited King Ferdinand II of Castile. Ferdinand II was King of Leon. His reign of thirty years was unremarkable – although there was constant petty fighting until he beheaded some unruly local nobles. King Ferdinand was a simple man with no political talents. When he died at age sixty-one, Ferdinand II was thought of as a good knight and a stalwart soldier. But I cannot help wondering: Did he die happy? As my grandmother once told me: "The truly happy man, the man with God's warm blessing, is he who ends a full life contented with himself."

What is that, Rabbi? Old Abraham ben Alexander? As I said, my grandmother reported that he had spent one Sabbath in the royal court at Leon, in northern Spain. There, surrounded by the courtiers, he dissolved an attendant pageboy: he made the young man disappear by dispersing him in thin air after dinner. No, Rabbi, I am not inventing this – my grandmother said that this is exactly what she had heard.

And this same strange Rabbi Abraham was a prolific writer too. Unfortunately, his most famous Kabbalistic tome, the *Keter Shem Tov*, a book of mystical lore, has never been published; now it lies in the Cologne yeshiva as forgotten crumbling papers above the rabbi's study room. Old Abraham Achselrad was always writing in this manu-script—although I do not know whether the mystic Achselrad was continually writing new things or whether he merely polished and rewrote the old. In any case, my grandmother said that it was in the dark early hours of the morning, while he was working on the *Keter Shem Tov*, that Rabbi Abraham looked up, and in the yellow light of the candle on his desk, he saw a holy sight.

At that time, Abraham ben Alexander was seventy years old. In his later years he had written many books, he had thought deeply for many long hours, and he had seen many strange and wondrous sights. But his favorite memories were still of early days; they were spring-time days when he and Petahiah had been young yeshiva students. Long ago, the two boys had played in the fields outside the city walls. They had lain on dusty banks of the wide River Rhine in warm weathers, with rains falling gently all around. Old Abraham Achselrad suddenly thought back, and he remembered those fine times. Abraham smiled. He felt a cool wind. He saw a springtime light. Was it like this long ago, on a warm afternoon when the rains fell like mist on his face? The candle flickered lightly, and Rabbi Abraham ben Alexander thought that there, in the doorway of the old yeshiva of Cologne on the River Rhine, stood a stooped and ancient man with a dusty beard.

"Hello?" said the Rabbi.

The figure remained silent in the doorway. Rabbi Abraham blinked and winked and he rubbed his eyes. The specter wavered dimly. Was it the candlelight? Were Achselrad's old eyes playing tricks?

Achselrad was an old man. He sat with an old man's slouch, and he waited with an old man's patience, watching with old man's eyes. Eventually the specter in the doorway smiled and spoke, and it talked in a quiet ancient voice.

"Greetings, good Rabbi. My name is Bahya ben Joseph ibn Pakuda. I am a rabbi from the south, far away from the cold winters of the River Rhine," said the spirit.

Rabbi Abraham knew the name well, for Bahya ben Joseph ibn Pakuda had written some of the fine poetry that Achselrad himself read on the springtime Sabbaths. Rabbi Bahya had been a spiritual philos-opher, living a century earlier in Saragossa, Spain. Bahya had written a treatise in Arabic called *Guide to the Duties of the Heart*. The book was translated into Hebrew and into French, and its intense pure spirituality gave the emotional passions of mysticism a beautiful Judaic foundation.

"Rabbi Bahya," said old Achselrad, "why are you here?"

The specter wavered a bit, ebbing and flowing in the doorway; then it smiled again. "Good Abraham, I am a pilgrim. I am a wayfarer, an all-night walker. You might say that I am a dream-stalker, wandering through this hard world of cliffs and canyons and rocky cracks, a world thick with demons and dybbuks and devils."

A little breeze seemed to skitter through the corner of the old study room. "I am walking, barefoot," said Rabbi Bahya, "toward the Holy Land. It is a bright and warm region toward which we all go eventually. But I am patient; I am in no hurry. Now I am passing by Cologne, and I have come to give you fond greetings and to stay a moment in order to share our warm and holy thoughts, amen."

"You are on your way to the golden sands and the suntanned hills of the Holy Land," said old Achselrad.

"Yes," said Bahya.

Abraham ben Alexander sat quiet, thinking softly. Did the rain fall lightly on your face in the Holy Land just as it did here beside the River Rhine? Rabbi Abraham closed his eyes, and he smiled. Time moved ever so calmly. After a few minutes, Rabbi Abraham opened his eyes. He shook his head gently, and he asked, "Tell me, friend: Have you been wandering long?"

The specter shimmered in the doorway. "I do not remember, good Rabbi," it said. "For I am totally consumed and enveloped in thinking of the good Lord God and all of His commandments. There is nothing of more importance than to focus on the holy purposes directed by the great Lord God. Continuously, I am wrapped in a cloud of awe and of thanks to the Lord. As Psalm 145 says":

> Every day I bless my King
> Both night and day I laud His Name,
> I praise my God again each morning:
> His greatness is beyond acclaim.
>
> God forgives, His love endures—
> He is good-hearted and aware;
> He watches over all His creatures,
> All earth receives His tender care.

My tongue shall evermore proclaim:
"The Lord is far beyond compare!"
All men will bless His holy Name
Both here and everywhere.

Rabbi Abraham nodded. He was silent, thinking quietly. His mind mused idly. There seemed to be no hurry in the rabbi's room at the edge of the wide River Rhine. Abraham's head nodded; his breathing became slow and regular. Had old Achselrad fallen asleep? After a while he seemed to wake again, and he said, "Holy Rabbi, praising the Lord is fine and good. Yes – to revel in the joys of the great Lord God is certainly wondrous."

The spirit smiled, and it nodded. Old Achselrad continued: "But I also wonder, my friend: Is this sufficient?"

And Bahya, the specter, answered from the doorway: "Is it sufficient? I would not exactly ask the question that way. Instead let me say, good Abraham, it is the essential first step. Prayer – devout, fervent, and all-consuming prayer – is the soul's longing for the amazing grace of the good Lord God (blessed be He). Before all else, we must humble our soul to Him. We must let our inmost heart extol the Creator with praise and with gratitude to His name. Cast your burdens on the Lord, I say, and take your spiritual sustenance in return."

Rabbi Abraham sat with his hands resting on his desk. Papers and books were piled everywhere. The Rabbi looked at the specter. He looked at the worn benches. He looked at the prayer books in the corner. Rabbi Abraham looked about the room, and he said to the spirit of Bahya: "Tell me, my good Rabbi: What about study and learning and scriptural analysis?"

Again, the spirit nodded. "Certainly those are fine pursuits, Abraham. But they must be secondary pursuits. Biblical exegesis, grammar, speculative philosophy – all the activities with which the scholars busy themselves – these are subordinate exercises."

The specter wavered in the doorway. "To be honest," it continued, "I think that even the study of the Talmud seems a rather weak pastime. In Judaism, it is more important to add deep spirituality to our lives. The duties of the heart – the dictates of our innermost conscience – are infinitely more important than the ritual duties prescribed by any legal code.

"True Judaism is purely religious, Abraham. The codes and injunctions and the ceremonial laws and rituals, these are just fancy clothes. They cover the real faith. The ceremonies are like the temporary grasses and the seasonal fields which cover the eternal rolling hills of God's great earth immemorial, amen."

The seasonal fields? The rolling hills? Abraham Achselrad smiled, and he remembered a time long ago. It was a springtime when he and young Petahiah had basked in the sand and the sun; it was a springtime when they had caught gray grasshoppers outside the cemetery by the wide and ancient River Rhine.

But Rabbi Bahya ben Joseph ibn Pakuda was talking to Achselrad again: "Abraham, are you listening? I was saying this: For all these many centuries, great rabbis have unraveled and explained the Law — and I revere their thoughtful words. But in the end the intellectual discussions always must be woven into a Jew's inner life. The practical analytical operations are only tools. Rational explanations are useful, but they should be considered as a perpetual river, running clean and pure and deep through our inmost being. Scholarship, my friend, waters the holy soul. But it cannot substitute for true spirituality."

A clean pure deep river? Why, so it is, mused old Abraham Alexander, and he looked beyond the specter in the doorway. Rabbi Abraham looked back through many years. Again he saw the warm springtime afternoons when he and young Petahiah lay on the bank of the clean pure deep River Rhine and rain fell gently on their faces, for ever and a day. And in the little back study room in the yeshiva of Cologne, even the walls seemed to fade into far away and long ago.

After a time Bahya began to speak, but he was very quiet. Abraham ben Alexander was not certain that he heard all the words of the holy spirit from the south. "Surrender," said Bahya. "Give in to a pure and selfless life. That is the meaning of the laws of the Nazirite, which are written in the sixth Chapter of the Book of Numbers. Nazirites must not cut their hair. They must not drink wine. They must keep far from the dead. Such rules are sacred reminders that we must turn away from external pleasures and pains. You see, my friend, most men need the help of asceticism and seclusion in order to lead a deeply contemplative life."

The specter paused. It wavered in the doorway. "Of course, it is impossible that *all* men should live as complete ascetics. If this were the

case, then civilization would stop. Utter desolation would follow – and
certainly this was never intended by the good Lord God. The world
needs its diversity; thus, God created a vast and wondrous variety of
men. Do you remember this verse?"

> People are distinct, complex and rich
> And multiform like snowflakes which
> Are each unique – through people rife
> Diversity is brought to life.

"Yes, Abraham, the Almighty One has populated our world with
endless heterogeneity, with incondensable complexity. But at one end
of the spectrum of mankind there must always be certain exemplary
selfless pious Jews. We continually need a few ascetics, Rabbi. These
men demonstrate how the natural distracting earthly passions can, in
fact, be ignored."

Bahya continued: "I say 'Jews,' good Rabbi. But really I mean all
God-fearing men. In my day, scores of years ago, there was a fine
young Mohammedan scholar named Ghazali. Ah, I remember him
well.

"Ghazali was Muhammad ibn Muhammad Abu Hamid
al-Ghazali, an Arabian philosopher and theologian. He was brilliant.
At the age of thirty-three, he was appointed professor in the Persian
college in Baghdad. Then, suddenly he began to worry – actually, he
began to wonder. Ghazali wondered about the oceans and about trees
and babies and clouds. He thought deeply about why music could bring
on ecstasy. He was baffled by the strange shapes of rocks. He marveled
at the unidentifiable sounds of the summer nights and the eternal
silences of the dark hours of the winter. Ghazali was constantly
mystified, and he found that his soul yearned for God.

"One day, four years after his meteoric rise to a professorship, he
suddenly quit. He gave up his academic chair, he left home and family,
and he became an ascetic. Ghazali was a pious mystic in search of God.
He ate sparingly. He dressed in a simple robe, and he walked barefoot.
He prayed three times a day. Over the years, he took pilgrimages to
Alexandria, Damascus, Hebron, Jerusalem, Mecca, and Medina. He

studied, he meditated, he wrote, and he prayed. Yes, good Abraham,
the holy Ghazali became an ascetic and an example to his people and,
I would say, to all men – even to Jews."

Rabbi Abraham listened quietly, but now Bahya was silent. So
old Achselrad asked, "And what happened to the Mohammedan
Ghazali?"

"As time passed, he traveled less and less," said the spirit of
Bahya, "but he lived quiet and happy. Occasionally, he would go by
sea to the various Mediterranean ports. He even spoke to small collec-
tions of people about the nature of a completely holy contemplative
life. From one trip he never returned. Did he die at sea? That is the
rumor – and I am certain that it is correct: Ghazali had a gentle sea-
borne death, a death soft like tears."

Soft like tears? Rabbi Abraham remembered the verses from an
old poem. Was it one that Bahya had written, a century ago?

And then, fair friend, a sea-borne death
Awaits for you like mist –
Quiet, gentle, soft like tears
Drifting in now to assist
When you are tired with seventy years;

Then all your children's children's race
Will be forever blessed with grace
And gentle winds will them embrace,
While soft rains you will forever taste
Upon your peaceful sleeping face.

Now Rabbi Abraham, too, was seventy gentle years of age; he
smiled, and he closed his eyes.

But Bahya was continuing to speak. "Yes, Rabbi," said the
specter, "all men and all faiths need such examples. For instance, we
Jews have the 'Mourners of Zion.'"

Rabbi Abraham opened his eyes. He looked puzzled. "The
'Mourners of Zion'?" he asked.

"I am referring to a group of Karaites who lived ascetically a century before my time," said the spirit of Bahya. "As you know, the Karaites – the Children of the Text – adhere strictly to the Holy Scriptures. They ignore all the oral and talmudic legacies; the Karaite liturgy is composed entirely of scriptural verse, with no other prayers or hymns.

"Now, good Abraham, in the central community of the Jews in tenth-century Jerusalem, sixty Karaites left their homes, their property, and their families to live in holy simplicity together. They refused to eat meat or to drink wine. They went barefoot, and they dressed in plain tunics. They spent all day fasting and praying. These ascetics called themselves the 'Mourners of Zion,' and each man followed his signature with the descriptor 'The Mourner.'

"It was these very 'Mourners' who set the Karaites on the severe ascetic course that we sometimes see today. The Mourners followed the Levitical laws to the letter. In addition, they avoided any contact with Gentiles: they would buy no food from Gentiles, and they would not eat anything that had been touched by a non-Jew. Some of the Mourners became so extreme that they looked on their more worldly brother Jews as blasphemous sinners who were also to be avoided assiduously."

The specter wavered and seemed to sigh. "Ah, my good Rabbi, even the best-intentioned behavior can become distorted. Our world is so thickly tangled with strange byways and with unusual geographies that we pilgrims can only trudge on with hopeful hearts. We do our best. We listen with our inmost soul, we trust in the good Lord God, and then we walk ever onward, all day and all night."

The mystic Rabbi of Cologne nodded. His eyes were closed, and he heard the gentle ancient voice of old Rabbi Bahya chanting a poem; it was the famous poem that introduces Bahya's book *The Humble Mendicant*:

> I am just a simple stranger
> Wandering wide-eyed, poor and true
> A humble walker who fears no danger
> A quiet barefoot traveling Jew.

I am a pilgrim on ancient tracks
Through this world of winding paths,
Of canyons, cliffs, and rocky cracks
Tangled thick with demon wraiths.

I walk by night – past field and tree –
Toward that golden holy place
The ancient sunny Promised Country
With no sickness or disgrace.

And I am going to see my mother
Then I will rest, no more to roam,
I'll bring my baby and her brother –
We are all going back to home.

I'll walk south and then I'll cross
The holy River Jordan's foam –
And in those lands with sun-baked gloss
I'll finally know my Eternal Home.

Therefore God of pedestrians
Grant warm winds at your command
Let my children hold my hands
And walk with me to the Promised Land;

Give us blue skies with white clouds
Let my children laugh aloud
Make them hop, as we walk free
And have them smile and look up at me.

The ancient voice faded away. Old Rabbi Abraham opened his
eyes. The specter was gone. But it did not matter: my grandmother
said that Abraham ben Alexander knew this poem by heart. In fact, he
wrote it into his *Keter Shem Tov*, and often he recited it quietly on
springtime Sabbaths when there were no other special hymns.
Abraham Achselrad would repeat this little poem to himself, as the
back study room lightened in the old yeshiva – yes, he would recite it in

the medieval Cologne dawn. Then once again it would be the morning of a gentle bright holy Sabbath with her restful warming arms, arms that embraced even the cold Rhinelands of Europe from afar in the golden south, where lie the holiest of the Holy Lands.

ood evening, Rabbi. Of course—please sit here by the stove: the night fire helps me to become sleepy also. You and I are not blessed like old Reb Elbaum. Once again, I saw him nodding off during the last prayers this evening. He has learned to sway piously even while asleep; undoubtedly he acquired some magic from the mystic Achselrad. I suppose that you and I could also use a dose of Achselrad ourselves tonight. My grandmother said that he could put men into a sleep trance by waving a gold coin before their eyes: as you know, Rabbi Abraham ben Alexander, also called Achselrad of Cologne, was a pupil of Eliazer the mystic of Worms.

Old Abraham Achselrad was always conjuring visions in the synagogue. I doubt whether he would be tolerated nowadays, but my grandmother said that Rabbi Abraham was also a scholar—and he himself claimed that his visions came from devout and pious study. Many an astonishing event took place during his rabbinate—or so my grandmother (blessed be her memory) was told. One day, his vision from Ecclesiastes saved poor Lavan ben Anselm ha-Kohen. . . . Yes, I will gladly tell you about Lavan—although he had nothing to do with Spain.

Did you not ask about Spain? Then I suppose that I was drifting off–for a moment, I was thinking of the time when Rabbi Abraham visited the Spanish King Ferdinand II in his court in Leon; during his stay there, Achselrad made a young pageboy disappear during dinner. Oh? You knew this already? Then perhaps you have heard about Achselrad's vision about birds, from the Book of Ecclesiastes. You have not heard about this? Then I will tell you exactly what I learned from my grandmother:

As you know, Rabbi Achselrad is the author of that mystical treatise called the *Keter Shem Tov*. It is a wondrous magical Kabbalistic book. Unfortunately, it was never published; now it exists only as a secret manuscript hidden in the loft of the old Cologne yeshiva. Grandmother said that it was early one summery morning in the month of *Tammuz,* while he was writing this very book, that Rabbi Abraham looked up, and in the light of the candle he saw Lavan ben Anselm ha-Kohen standing in the doorway, pale and shaken. "Rabbi," said Lavan weakly, "I need your help. I am about to be arrested for murder."

Now, Rabbi, let me tell you what actually had happened:

In medieval Cologne, the Jewish Quarter was just north of the Christian parish called St. Laurence, and just beyond St. Laurence was St. Albans parish. Lavan ben Anselm was a rather dreamy Jew who lived in the St. Albans parish. Over the years he had wandered throughout Europe; he had heard the famed tale-tellers and song-singers in Jewish communities from France to Russia and from Germany to Spain. Deep in his heart, Lavan felt the warm and gentle tug of holy verse, and in the evenings he composed poetry for himself.

The previous evening had been very hot. Lavan could not sleep, and he had walked late into the night. Now it was almost morning. Lavan was not paying attention to his surroundings–instead, he was thinking of how to capture in a single line of verse the endless yellow and white jonquil gardens that edged the suntanned hills of Paradise in the Great Hereafter. As he passed by a corner, somewhere near the southern edge of the St. Albans district, Lavan heard a strangled cry. He looked up. There he saw an old man being attacked by a robber. The old man had been coming home from work. He had a full wallet. The robber took the old man's wallet and also his belt and hat and shoes.

After he had robbed him of everything, the robber said, "Now I am going to take your life also."

"No! Please do not hurt me!" cried the old man.

The robber said coldly, "Listen, old fool, if I let you live then you will report me; you will identify me and I will lose my *own* life. I have no choice: I must kill you."

The old man said, "Let me live. I promise that I will not report you. I will just close my eyes. I will not follow you. You can go off safely and disappear – and if I ever do see you again, I will just look the other way!"

But the robber said, "I cannot believe you; of course you will promise anything now."

"Please, trust me!" said the old man, crying. "Besides, if you kill me, then undoubtedly somebody will see you. Why – why, think of the birds! They will have seen your crime, and they will tell. In the end, you will lose your life too."

"Ah, now you are making fun of me," said the robber angrily, and swiftly he killed the old man. Suddenly the robber spotted Lavan, whom he recognized. However, instead of running, the robber laughed and he called out, "Murderer! Lavan is a murderer!"

What should Lavan do? He heard the city guard running toward them. The robber stood shouting and pointing at Lavan. Lavan ben Anselm began to tremble and to shake, and then he ran and ran and ran. Back went Lavan toward the Jewish Quarter, and he did not stop until he came to the synagogue and the reassuring figure of old Rabbi Abraham ben Alexander.

Rabbi Abraham listened to Lavan's story. Then the mystical old man closed his eyes. After a moment, Achselrad opened his eyes again. "Lavan," said the Rabbi, "there is a well-known Hebrew proverb: 'Do not speak of secret matters in a field that is full of little hills.' "

"What does that mean, Rabbi?" asked Lavan.

"It means that you should be careful of what you say when someone may overhear you," answered Rabbi Abraham.

"Is that relevant to my problem, Rabbi?" asked Lavan.

"We will see what we will see, Lavan," said the Rabbi.

Rabbi Abraham stood, and he put on his hat and his coat. Without glancing backward, he left the small study room of the yeshiva and he walked through the main prayer hall, which was filled with wooden benches. The Rabbi passed the twelve stained glass windows with their colored lions and snakes, he went by the Holy stone Ark, he stepped out of the main door, and he strode off to the ecclesiastical courthouse, with Lavan ben Anselm hurrying behind.

And what was happening with the robber during all this time? He was determined to play his role as the innocent witness. However, before going to the court to file a formal report of the murder, the robber stopped at a city inn for a meal. The robber felt confident and at ease. He ordered meat and turnips, with ale to drink. The innkeeper nodded and brought a plate of chicken. When he saw the chicken, the robber thought of birds, and he began to laugh. The innkeeper was standing nearby. "And what is so funny about my food?" he asked.

"Oh, it is nothing," said the robber. "I was just thinking that these birds will never tell their tale again."

The innkeeper was puzzled. There was no full moon. Was this a madman? "The chickens will never tell a story?" asked the innkeeper.

The robber drank some ale, and he chuckled. "Listen, friend," he said to the innkeeper. "A certain person, who I shall not name, happened to kill an old man. This person had taken the man's wallet and some of his clothes. Unfortunately, the old man could identify the robber so the robber had no choice but to silence him permanently. But before the robber could take care of this last detail, the old man wildly claimed that birds would tell the tale of the killing. Imagine that! Of course, this unnamed person was too clever for the old man." Then the robber laughed again.

The innkeeper was silent, but he noticed that the robber carried an extra belt and an especially fancy wallet full of money. After he finished eating, the robber paid from the full wallet, and calmly he walked off to court to swear that the Jew, Lavan ben Anselm, was actually the killer.

The robber came to the court before the Rabbi arrived. In angry words, he explained how he had witnessed a terrible crime and how he had immediately called the city guards. The guards confirmed that a known Jew, Lavan ben Anselm, had been seen running from the scene of the murder.

After a while, Rabbi Abraham appeared, with Lavan following worriedly behind him. The two men came into the court where the Archbishop himself was presiding—this was Archbishop Adolph of

Cologne, a noble and honorable prelate. Archbishop Adolph knew Rabbi Abraham. "Rabbi," said the Archbishop sadly, "one of your Jews has killed an old man. We have an accuser who witnessed the entire crime. I see that you have brought the murderer, and I appreciate this – but I am afraid, Rabbi, that Mr. Lavan Anselm must be imprisoned and hanged."

"I see," said Rabbi Abraham. Abraham Achselrad looked at the witness, he looked at Lavan, and he looked at the Archbishop. Rabbi Abraham closed his eyes a moment, and then he asked, "Have you a Bible here, good Archbishop?"

"Of course," replied the Archbishop, and he instructed one of the court officers to pass a leather volume to Rabbi Achselrad.

"Now, let us read from the Book of Ecclesiastes," said the Rabbi.

"I respect your religious views, Rabbi," said Archbishop Adolph, "but is this really necessary now?"

Rabbi Achselrad was holding the Bible. Suddenly his eyes opened wide. Then they closed tightly. He became weak and he sat down on a nearby chair. His body trembled. After a moment, the Rabbi gently set down the Bible.

The Archbishop began to stand. "Are you all right, Rabbi?" he asked.

Rabbi Abraham opened his eyes. He looked toward the ceiling. "I have just had a vision, Your Honor. I have seen the bird-filled Heavens; doves and egrets fluttered nearby, eagles and ospreys soared far and high, and all were smooth wisps of wings amidst the celestial sky. I have seen the good Lord God (blessed be He), Master of all creatures in the field, in the sea, and in the air. And now I have seen also that Ecclesiastes of the Holy Scriptures is quite important," said Abraham Achselrad. "If you will be so good as to hand me that Holy Book again, then I will read a bit of the appropriate verses":

> Do not speak ill of others or lie
> For birds can carry your voice with ease,
> Eventually winged heralds will certainly cry
> Your words atop the towering trees –
> The birds which fly through the Heavenly sky
> Will tell your secret to the traveling breeze.

And the true robber felt a shiver in his back.

But Archbishop Adolph was watching the Rabbi intently. "It is beautiful verse," said the Archbishop. When Rabbi Abraham remained silent, the Archbishop added, "And certainly that is a noble and holy sentiment, Rabbi."

"You are a noted cleric, Archbishop Adolph. What would you say that this verse means?" asked the Rabbi.

"Clearly it means that you should watch your tongue."

"I agree, Your Honor – and I would say that it means even more," said the Rabbi.

"You would?" asked the Archbishop. "Then pray tell, Rabbi Achselrad: What more do you read into this verse?"

"First, I would say, Archbishop, that one should speak carefully and thoughtfully – as the old proverb relates: 'Do not speak of secret matters in a field that is full of little hills.' In addition, we are warned that the creatures of nature, and especially the birds of the good Lord God, carry tales and that they will reveal the truth in the end."

"Exactly what are you saying, Mr. Alexander?" asked the Archbishop.

"I am saying this, Archbishop: I have had a vision. I have seen that birds will solve this crime and will free the innocent man."

One of the court officers laughed, and he said, "You have read all this Jewish mysticism in one verse of the Bible?"

"Yes, I have," said the Rabbi. "And, Archbishop, I shall prove it to you."

"What do you propose?" asked Archbishop Adolph.

"It appears to me that birds will reveal the true killer. An old man lay dying, and I am certain that, in the end, he called upon the birds to avenge his death," said Rabbi Abraham. "I am as certain of this as I am of the eternally repeating dawn: birds shall unveil the murderer."

Archbishop Adolph creased his forehead and he looked at the Rabbi. "How will the birds do this?" asked the Archbishop.

"I have had a vision," repeated the Rabbi. "If you will order the guards to close the court doors and to ask for silence, then I think that I can share my vision with you."

The Archbishop conferred with his councilors. After a brief argument, the Archbishop of Cologne agreed to try Rabbi Abraham's idea. The guards stood before the doors, and the robber became very worried indeed.

Meanwhile, the Rabbi sat down, and he wrote seven mystical names on a small piece of white parchment. He tied the paper with seven white threads, and in each thread he put seven neat knots. The Archbishop watched intently. Then the Rabbi strung the small packet on a slender white rope. Gently, Rabbi Abraham placed the parchment necklace around the shoulders of the Archbishop. Rabbi Abraham pronounced certain mystical Names of the Lord God Almighty, and he said to the Archbishop, "Good sir, just close your eyes and take a deep breath. Then concentrate on birds. Try to picture birds."

The Archbishop closed his eyes, and he took a deep breath. He tried to picture many birds flying in the sky. At first he saw doves. Then he saw egrets. Suddenly the Archbishop saw the murderer. The evil man was calmly sitting in an inn in the St. Albans parish. The Archbishop looked up. He seemed to be able to see through the walls and the ceilings, and he saw that doves and egrets had collected on the roof of the inn. Then the Archbishop looked at the evil robber, and he saw that the man was eating a plate of chicken. The robber laughed and he confessed his crime to the innkeeper, who was standing at his side.

Archbishop Adolph opened his eyes, and he shook his head. He was silent for a moment. As he looked around the courtroom, it seemed to him that the man sitting as a witness was in fact the murderer whom he had seen in his vision. Could this be true? Or was it all some deceptive Jewish magic? The Archbishop frowned. He tapped his desk. Finally he said to the guards, "There is an inn in the St. Albans parish, not far from the scene of the crime. Bring the innkeeper to me."

Two guards hurried off. The true murderer began to shake uncontrollably. The courtroom remained silent. In less than half an hour, the soldiers brought the innkeeper back to the court. "Do you know anything about a crime committed near your inn earlier this morning?" asked the Archbishop.

The innkeeper saw the robber. The robber was staring directly at him, and the innkeeper thought to himself, "This man is already a murderer. He will kill me too if I dare to speak against him." So the innkeeper hung his head and he said nothing.

It was clear what was happening, and Archbishop Adolph said to the innkeeper, "You are safe here in the court. However, if you lie, then you will face a sterner Judge than me on that final Day of Judgment in the Great Hereafter."

The innkeeper could not bring himself to look at the robber. But finally he said, "I can only say that I heard a strange story from this man, as he ate at my table this morning. He said that there had been a murder and that a wallet and some clothes were stolen and that the victim had claimed that birds would tell about the killer."

"Do you know who the killer was?" asked the Archbishop.

"Well," said the innkeeper slowly, "this man here told me the story. He seemed to know all the details. He was quite pleased with himself, and he had a fancy wallet full of money – also he had an extra belt."

"Why did you not come forth with this information before?" asked Archbishop Adolph.

"Frankly, good sir, I hope that you will have mercy on me. I am an honest businessman. But I was afraid. You see, if the man was brazen enough to kill someone on the open street – why, he might then kill me just as easily instead of paying for his meal. Or later he might come after me at night. I was afraid for my own safety."

The murderer jumped up and he shouted, "You are right! I should have killed you while I could!" He rushed at the innkeeper, but he was seized by the guards and arrested immediately.

The Archbishop said to him, "Stand up before me – for now it is clear who you are and what you have done."

The murderer stood weakly. He did not know what to do or what to say. Rabbi Abraham shook his head sadly, and he said, "The Almighty Lord cannot forgive these sins. As it is said in the Book of Proverbs":

> Never rob a defenseless man –
> Aid him selflessly,
> And never scorn a hungry man
> Nor plague his family.

> God is our Protector
> He shields the humble and the weak,
> He will punish the wicked braggart
> Then He will redeem all the meek.

The Archbishop said, "Amen, good Rabbi." Then he turned to the court.

"This man has killed another," said the Archbishop.

There was silence. "Moreover, he has attempted to implicate Mr. Lavan Anselm, who is an innocent man," continued Archbishop Adolph.

"Therefore," declared the Catholic cleric, "we find this man guilty of murder and of deceit."

After a moment of silence, the Archbishop said quietly, "I pronounce a sentence of hanging."

Then the sky seemed to darken – and, said my grandmother, the sound could be heard of many birds flying off, far away beyond the distant clouds.

Ah, good evening again, Rabbi. Yes, I know – it is always hard to sleep when there is a bright half moon. Just put your feet up on the side bench and I will open the stove door. Let me push the coals back: there is nothing like that white glow. It washes away the cares of a hard day.

I heard your final benediction tonight, Rabbi. There is no use denying it – you are overworked. Oh yes, even a shammas like me can tell. I kept one eye on you as I cleaned the dishes, and I saw that you were watching the door, hoping that Reb Elbaum would leave early. But then Reb Anton stayed to discuss the scriptural passage from the Book of Isaiah:

> This is the basic meaning
>   of the Atonement Fast
> That I require of you:
>   Save food for the outcast,
> Take the homeless poor
>   into your house, and feed
> And clothe the ragged man –
>   Attend first to others' needs.

If you do this then you too
  will shine like the dawning sun
And you will grow strong and wise
  from the charity that you have done,
Then your righteousness will march
  before you like a shield
And the glory of the Lord
  shall protect you far afield.

Ah, selfless charity – it is a continuous duty. You are a charitable man, Rabbi: you give freely of your time and your energy – and I see that you are still worn out from all the charity that you have done this evening. . . . What is that? A story from me? All that I know are the children's tales, the grandmother fables. You need something new and fresh to keep your mind keen, otherwise you will become a dreamy old man like me and you will find yourself constantly musing and dozing and nodding off in front of the stove.

What do you mean you are already an old man, Rabbi? Do you really think that sixty years is old? Why, you are still a child: Adam lived to be nine hundred and thirty years, you know. Perhaps you will feel old when you reach eighty or ninety. You doubt that you will live to see eighty years? If so, Rabbi, then you will never grow old. . . . All right, all right, I know no special stories but listening to you and Reb Anton discuss charity put me in mind of Reb Suskind, the false miser of Mulheim. . . .

What? Of course there is more, Rabbi: I only closed my eyes for a moment – can an old man not take a little rest? Now you have interrupted my thoughts. Let me see, where was I? Yes, yes – as my grandmother (may her soul visit happily with her parents forever) told me:

Once upon a time along the wide and dark River Rhine, there lived a pious scholar named Rabbi Abraham ben Alexander, Achselrad of Cologne. (Now do not interrupt, Rabbi.) As I was saying, Rabbi Achselrad was the spiritual head of all the communities up and down the northern Rhineland – communities such as Gladbach, Kalk, and Mulheim. In the village of Mulheim, just north of Cologne on the other side of the River Rhine, there lived a rich Jew. His name was Suskind ben Johel ha-Levi. Although he was quite wealthy, old Suskind seemed to be the worst of misers: he never contributed any charity and he never gave money to the poor.

For instance, once a man came to Suskind and asked for money. The poor man also hoped for some food or some old clothes. The beggar could not walk straight. His eyes were blurry. He was weak. He wore a ragged coat and torn pants, and he had no shoes. The rich man looked at the dirty wanderer, and he asked, "Oh – so you want my charity? Do you think that I spend all my time earning money for you? Get a job. Take some responsibility for yourself. And tell me: Where is your real home?"

The stranger stood for a moment, and he wrinkled his forehead. "My *real* home?" he asked.

"Yes, yes – where do you come from?" asked Suskind.

"I live here – well, actually, I spend most of my time in the streets of Cologne," answered the beggar.

"Then go back to Cologne. Everyone in Mulheim knows that I do not give charity," said the rich man.

"But I am absolutely destitute," pleaded the beggar. The poor man seemed to shake, although the weather was not very cold.

"That is not my fault," said Reb Suskind. "Go try the shoemaker." And the rich man went into his home and closed the door. The beggar stood a moment. He looked down at the tiny blue wildflowers growing beside Suskind's door. Then he slowly turned, and he walked away in search of the shoemaker.

The shoemaker in question lived in a poor part of town; he was a Jewish cobbler, and his name was Kaleb ben Ephraim. Kaleb surprised everyone because he was a great benefactor. With open hands, he gave alms and clothes and food to everyone who turned to him. When this particular beggar located Kaleb's home, Kaleb welcomed the worn-out man, and gave him bread and soup. Then Kaleb reached into his box of leather scraps and he took out two gold coins, which he also gave to the wanderer.

The poor man had tears in his eyes as he left Kaleb. Kaleb looked after the wretched old creature, but did not ask why this drifting man was ever born or why the great wheel of fortune had slowly revolved to crush him. He did not wonder why the beggar had been left to creep through endless streets. Such questions were for other people–for rabbis, perhaps. Rabbis ask and ask and ask these questions. But long ago Kaleb had decided he could not understand the differences in people's fates. Maybe the wise rabbis knew more than he. Kaleb only sighed and he shook his head and turned back to his work.

Kaleb worked long hours, yet poor people in Mulheim relied on him and he never failed them. Yes, Kaleb the shoemaker helped a great many needy people, amen. Years passed and one day the rich man, Suskind ben Johel, died. Suskind had no immediate family, but there were some distant relatives. Out of an obligation to the dead, a few of these relatives gathered with the local Mulheim neighbors and went through the appropriate ceremonial rituals–for a week, family and visitors sat on the floor, they spoke quietly, they wore slippers, and they did not wash.

On the first day, the women of the Burial Society came. Reb Suskind's body was laid out on the floor with a candle at its head. Although no one's heart was really in it, the women of the Burial Society did their duties: they sat all night and sewed a white shroud with tiny gentle stitches–stitches so small that no hurt could come to the spirit of the dead man. Although the men could say no kind words about him, nonetheless they said no unkind words either. Silently they glued the coffin together, using no nails, which might snag the spirit of the dead man. Kaleb came and wept quietly. But other than the charitable shoemaker, it seemed that no one else really had good feelings toward the dead man.

The burial itself was in the *Am Toten Juden* of Cologne because there was no Jewish cemetery in Mulheim. Rabbi Abraham presided. Suskind had never attended the Cologne synagogue, and Achselrad had not known the man. However, the Jews of Cologne who did know Suskind ben Johel ha-Levi had decided that they should bury the old miser in a far corner of the cemetery, near the fence. And the Jews of Cologne still felt so angry at the old man that few of them followed the funeral procession to the cemetery. Afterward, a small group of mourners returned to the home to sit for the old man. When they entered the house, the shoemaker and the distant relatives and a few neighbors followed tradition and took a bite of an egg dipped in ashes.

Then the mourners sat in silence. The people of Mulheim had bitter feelings: they could speak no evil aloud about Suskind, and so they said nothing at all. Only Kaleb had tears in his eyes.

The next morning the sun shone brightly, and within a week soothing rains came. One week passed, and then came two. Soon, seven weeks had come and gone, and during that time a number of poor men and beggars came to the shoemaker in order to ask for alms. Kaleb was sympathetic, but he said to them, "I am afraid that I cannot help. I have nothing to give you."

"How is this possible?" said one old beggar. "You have always been so generous before."

"Yes, what has happened, Reb Kaleb?" asked another poor man.

Sadly Kaleb shook his head, but he said no more. When the people of Mulheim realized that Kaleb had suddenly stopped being generous, they tried to imagine all possible explanations. What had happened? What was the problem? Even under repeated questioning, the shoemaker would not give a straight answer. Eventually word reached Rabbi Achselrad. "This sounds strange," thought the Rabbi. "I wonder if Kaleb has found himself in some difficulty with which I could help?"

Therefore, old Abraham ben Alexander sent word to the shoemaker asking that he come and see him. It was a hot afternoon in the summer month of *Tammuz* when Kaleb ben Ephraim reported to the synagogue. He stepped in the front door, he went through the ante-room, and he walked into the main prayer hall, which was filled with wooden benches. Kaleb passed the twelve stained glass windows with their colored lions and snakes. He looked up at the Holy stone Ark, and he walked to the door of the back study room. There, the Rabbi was bent over a book, and a number of scholars sat along the benches, talking among themselves.

The old scholars greeted Kaleb politely. Kaleb sat down. He felt a little weak in the presence of the sages of Cologne. The sages sat quietly for a few minutes. Finally, white-haired Baruch ben Jacob asked the first question: "Kaleb, you are a fine and pious man. All of us respect you, and we appreciate your contributions to the Jewish community of Mulheim. But we cannot help wondering why you have stopped helping the local poor people?"

Kaleb looked at his feet: "Good Rabbis, this is rather difficult to explain."

Kaleb volunteered no other information. Therefore, a younger scholar, Elisah ben Samuel, said, "Now, now, Reb Kaleb, do not be shy. Obviously, you have given much charity: you have given well beyond your means. We are not criticizing you. We are only wondering at this abrupt change. Have you run into some troubles? Do you now need *our* help?"

The windows in the old synagogue building were open. A breeze blew lightly into the back room and it tickled a paper on the Rabbi's desk. The Rabbi was listening quietly, stroking his beard. Joshua ben Eliezer leaned back on his bench. He looked at Kaleb, and he said, "It is the complete stopping of all charity that puzzles us, good Kaleb. Remember, my friend, the amount of charity is not important. It is only the act of giving that is important. Recall Psalm 41":

> Happy is he who tends the helpless –
> The Lord will spare him from all sickness:
> God gives him health and protects from harm,
> Guarding him with His sheltering arm
> Holding at bay his enemies
> And keeping him safe from cruel disease.

Lewe ben Anselm nodded, and he said, "Exactly, Reb Joshua – moreover, Kaleb, I would point out that you must take a long-term view of these things: the benefits of charity are really only seen in retrospect. Charity makes one's life worthwhile when it is *remembered* – when remembered by the giver, when remembered by his friends and relatives, and when remembered by the good Lord God (blessed be He)."

"Amen," said Baruch. Then Menahem ben Joel added, "Yes, amen – as it is said in the scriptural Proverb":

> Wealth is a light commodity
>   On Judgment Day,
> But goodness, alms, and charity
>   Shall heavily weigh.

Generosity and virtue,
  Kind words with each breath –
These will protect you
  From a sad and early death.

Again the scholars nodded. Next, Moyses ben Nathan said, "Because of these things – things that we know so deeply and that we believe so strongly – we are worried.

"Now, Kaleb, I hasten to say we are not worried that you are too poor to give as much as you did before – previously, you exceeded all possible expectations. No, good Kaleb, we are worried only that you have forgotten this: when all else goes, when money and clothes and fancy belongings are stripped away, at that point it is only the fine and warm memories of your good deeds that are left. These are the most precious of heritages. Do not give them up."

The scholars all nodded and murmured "amen," and there was much stroking of beards. Finally, old Shimshon ha-Zaken coughed, and he said, "Exactly, Moyses. As the scriptural Proverb says":

Do not worship wealth and ease;
  Be sensible and give up greed.
Before you turn, up comes a breeze –
  Gold disappears, wealth will recede,
Money grows swift wings and flees
  Like an eagle, a fleet bird of speed.

Meanwhile, the Rabbi sat quietly, listening to all this counsel. Kaleb hung his head, and he looked at his feet. After a few moments he said, "Good rabbis, you all knew Suskind ben Johel, who passed away a few months ago – did you not?"

The old scholars nodded. "Well," continued the shoemaker, "I am sorry to say that he was known as a miser. I say 'known' because in truth he was not a miser. Certainly he was gruff, but he was not really a bad man. I must admit that Suskind was not very sociable: frankly, he was rather unfriendly. I think that he had had an unhappy childhood. In any case, when he came here from Arnheim, many, many years ago, he would talk with me sometimes. I became an acquaintance of his. In fact, I was probably his only acquaintance."

Kaleb paused, and then said, "Yes, I can only say 'acquaintance.' Unfortunately, old Suskind had no real friends – he was abrupt and harsh even with me."

The seven sages of Cologne sat quietly, stroking their beards.

Kaleb continued: "When Reb Suskind moved to Mulheim, he brought with him much money, but he did not really need it. He had no immediate family. In business, he was a middleman so that it was not necessary for him to own a large stock of merchandise. His personal wants were minimal. What was he to do with his money?"

"Why did he not simply give it to charity?" asked old Reb Baruch.

Kaleb creased his forehead, and he nodded his head. "Ah, gentlemen, now we come to the problem. Reb Suskind was a man of iron ideas. Somehow he had learned that in King Solomon's Great Temple there was a Chamber of Secret Charity. In those days, devout and pious Jews put their contributions into this room secretly. Then the poor – especially if they had originally been members of well-to-do families – could take the money without embarrassment, and therefore they were supported in secrecy. Knowing this, old Suskind always insisted: 'Charity must be secret.' "

The sages of Cologne stroked their beards. Reb Elisah said, "That is like the little talmudic story":

> A rabbi once saw a man give a gold coin to a beggar publicly. The rabbi reprimanded the donor: "It is better that you had given him nothing than that you gave him money in public. Now you have embarrassed him by making his poverty known to one and all indiscriminately."

"Exactly," said Kaleb, "and as I was the only person whom Reb Suskind knew in the town of Mulheim, he asked me to distribute his money to charity. In this way, his donations could remain anonymous."

"*You* gave away Reb Suskind's money?!" exclaimed Reb Joshua, and all the scholars' eyes opened wide.

"Yes," said Kaleb, "but there was one condition: I must not disclose where the money came from. Suskind was adamant. I promised him that I would not reveal his secret – and so it was. And as he began to trust my confidentiality, he gave me more and more money."

"Now, Reb Kaleb, exactly how did this secret giving work?" asked Reb Lewe.

"Friends, it was quite simple: old Suskind gave me money on the day following each Sabbath. It was he, not me, who was the real benefactor of Mulheim. After Suskind's death, I have not had a penny to give because I never took any of the money myself, and I am really a very poor man," answered Kaleb ben Ephraim the shoemaker.

Kaleb looked down at his feet. "I have struggled with this secret since the day that old Reb Suskind died. I hope that when now he hears that I have told you, he will forgive me."

The sages stroked their beards, but they said nothing.

Rabbi Abraham looked at Kaleb, and he smiled. "Do not worry, good Kaleb," said the Rabbi. "I am certain that the Almighty Lord God (blessed be He), Who is the true and final Arbiter, forgives and loves you as much as He ever did."

The old mystic Rabbi had a faraway look in his eye; he stared off into space, he nodded his head, and he said, "Suskind did his best. It is quite true that the Talmud points out that secret charity is selfless charity. Also, there is no doubt that the Almighty One admires humility. Reb Suskind lived up to his Jewish ideals, and I think that we have all misjudged the man."

The scholars in Cologne nodded, and quietly they murmured "amen." Rabbi Abraham stepped from behind his desk. He patted Kaleb on the back. Then he set his hands on the shoemaker's head and he pronounced a blessing:

> May the Lord bless you and watch over you
> May the Lord make His face to shine upon you
> May the Lord be gracious and good to you
> May the Lord look kindly on you
> And may He give you peace, amen.

Then the shoemaker returned home to Mulheim, relieved and happier.

Kaleb had come to Cologne on a Thursday. On the next Sabbath, Rabbi Abraham made an announcement in the synagogue. He proclaimed that Reb Suskind had been a true, honorable, and righteous Jew, he praised the old man's memory, and a bench near the Holy stone Ark was dedicated to the name and the memory of Suskind ben

Johel ha-Levi. When the full story was told, the Burial Society planted two green bushes on each side of Suskind's grave. Ever after that, the place near the fence where Suskind was buried became the preferred area for burial: all pious members of the community requested to be buried near Reb Suskind. My grandmother said that small blue wild-flowers always grew on the grave of Suskind ben Johel ha-Levi. And, Rabbi, the writing on the tombstone may be worn after all these centuries, but to this day the grave can still be recognized by its tiny blue flowers—flowers that are the color of God's celestial Heaven, amen.

ood evening, Rabbi. I see there is no sleep for the weary. If you are cold then sit down here on the bench and I will stoke up the oven. This stoker? It is one of the iron shoe-scrapers from the front hall – you probably do not recognize it because it is covered with soot. Of course, there are still two scrapers in the anteroom for dirty shoes. But I myself am of the old school: I think that all pious men should remove their shoes when they enter the synagogue. Did you know that someday the Messiah will walk barefoot into the city of Jerusalem? It will be through the third gate to Heaven, because the Talmud tells us that there are three entrances to the *Gan Eden*: the first is in the wilderness, the second is in the sea, and the third is in Jerusalem, amen.

My grandmother said that each of these gates has a *mezuzah* – the most holy of the Jewish amulets – on its gatepost. Now, now, Rabbi – do not look at me like that, I mean nothing irreligious. Even the serious Rabbi Tam was a great promoter of amulets. And of course the mystic Abraham Achselrad wrote in detail about such sacred charms in his great work, the *Keter Shem Tov*. I suspect that Rabbi Abraham learned many of his sacred and mysterious details about amulets when he was visited by the French Rabbi, Jacob ben Meir Tam. You do not know about that visit? Then let me tell you exactly what my grandmother told me:

Once upon a time, said my grandmother to me, in the town of Cologne on the wide River Rhine, there lived a pious and mystic rabbi named Abraham ben Alexander. This was in the Middle Ages, and as you know, Rabbi, all manner of pilgrims came through Germany each week in those olden days. Strange men might appear in the Cologne yeshiva at any time of the day or night; for in medieval Europe, wandering pilgrims were constantly returning from their foreign travels. These wayfarers came wide-eyed and worn, and they came filled with tales of ever new potential Messiahs. Of course, all Jews remained hopeful: the Messiah was never far from their thoughts. Thus, there was always a bit of wonder about the appearance of even the most pale and ill-clad of these peregrinating specters.

It was late on a hot summer night in the month of *Tammuz*. The winds were asleep and the air was heavy. An old man, dressed in white, walked quietly into the Cologne yeshiva. He removed his shoes and he walked barefoot into the prayer hall, where he stood silently praying. It was in the dead of the night. Rabbi Abraham had been reading in the small back study room. After a while, the Rabbi thought that he saw a glow in the main hall. Rabbi Abraham stood up from his desk and walked out of the little study room. There, in front of the Holy stone Ark, stood the old stranger, thin and pale and dressed in white.

Abraham Achselrad stared intently. After a moment, he asked quietly, "May I help you, my good sir?"

"I am Jacob ben Meir Tam. I come from Rameru in France, Rabbi," answered the stranger. "May I spend the night?"

Rabbi Abraham opened wide his eyes. Jacob Tam was one of the most famous of the talmudic commentators – moreover, Rabbi Tam was a grandson of the great Rashi. Yes, Jacob Tam was a *Tosafist*, but although he was from northern Europe, he was not a conservative talmudist. Rabbi Tam had a romantic streak: he could not resist the magical pull of secular studies. The medieval Spanish Jews talked of rocks and stars and fish and profane poetry, and Rabbi Tam listened intently to all the southern visitors passing through Rameru. Of course, even in the north, Jews were living more closely with their Gentile neighbors in those days. And it was Jacob Tam who formalized the Jewish rules for those interrelationships – many of these practical ordinances were set out in his books the *Takkanot* and the *Sefer ha-Yashur*.

In addition, Rabbi Jacob Tam was a grammarian and a poet. He studied the Spanish techniques of Hebrew poetry, and he wrote poetic prayers and mystical poems. He wrote back and forth to Abraham ben Ezra, the Spanish philosopher. They exchanged poems and criticized each other's verses. Rabbi Tam followed his studies wherever they led. His immersion in poetry led him to study the Hebrew language – and soon he became a recognized expert in Hebrew grammar and in the roots of Hebrew words. His poetry also led him to philosophy, and then philosophy led him into sacred mysticism. After a time, Jacob Tam found himself studying amulets and charms. Eventually he gave amulets an academic credence: he took charms from underground folk practices into the open intellectual sunlight. Maimonides and his followers had swept rationalism into Judaism, but Rabbi Tam helped to keep the parallel stream of mysticism alive.

When people asked him how he could mix mysticism and rationalism, Jacob Tam would say: "I recognize neither mysticism nor rationalism – I recognize only Knowledge and Wisdom. As we are told in the Book of Proverbs":

> I am Wisdom – it is humility I teach –
> I build knowledge and also prudence;
> For presumption, pride, and glib speech
> Are emptiness and pure pretense.
>
> I have force and power and weight
> Understanding, sense, and wit;
> Through me rulers command their state
> And kings make laws both just and fit.
>
> I reward him with a thoughtful view –
> He who searches for my truths;
> I set forth a path of virtue
> Lined with insight for all youths.

What is that, Rabbi? Abraham ben Alexander of Cologne? Yes, yes, just be patient – I am coming to him. As you recall, Jacob ben Meir

Tam, the grandson of Rashi, walked into the old Cologne yeshiva late one summer night and asked for a place to stay.

"Please, make yourself comfortable in the small study room," said Rabbi Abraham. Then he led his guest through the back doorway and into the rabbi's study. Rabbi Abraham cleared the wooden pallet, which was covered with books and manuscripts, and he helped Jacob Tam to settle on a blanket. Rabbi Tam thanked old Achselrad. Then he began to recite the *Shema*. As Achselrad left the yeshiva, he could hear Rabbi Tam ending his evening devotions with the "night verse" from Psalm 3:

> Therefore I can lie down then
> Sleeping without dread or fright
> And I will awake tomorrow again
> Calm and warm and sound and tight –
> For the good Lord holds me safely when
> I brave the terrors of the darkling night.

The next morning dawned blue and bright. When Abraham ben Alexander arrived at the synagogue, Rabbi Tam had finished his morning prayers. The two men sat together, and they talked quietly in the back room.

"The *kameya*, that is, the Hebrew amulets," Rabbi Tam was saying, "are not magical: they are holy. Sadly, Rabbi, the world is filled with difficulties, diseases, and dangers. When these problems come from unholy forces, such as evil spirits, then you have no choice: you must take holy countermeasures – and some of the best sacred defenses are the *kameya*."

Rabbi Abraham nodded. Jacob Tam continued: "Of course, this has long been an accepted view. For instance, the Talmud tells us that one can use whatever holy objects or incantations are needed for healing – even those that some people regard as superstitious. Why, a healing amulet may even be carried on the Sabbath.

"However, the amulet must be holy. It must have the Divine Name and also the *Shema*. And what else is permitted on the charm? Certainly the names of the seven major angels may be included; these are Gabriel, Metatron, Michael, Nuriel, Raphael, Tzadqiel, and Uriel. Then, as you know, particular symbols increase the force of a written amulet. Two important symbols are the *Magen David* and the 'Hand of Might'—a diagram of the right hand. (You can ensure that these symbols are holy by writing the name *Shaddai* along their edges.)"

Jacob ben Meir Tam was reciting, almost as if giving a sermon. Rabbi Abraham sat quietly and listened. "Yes, good Abraham," said Rabbi Tam, "from my careful researches, I am convinced that Judaism can accept the use of sacred amulets as protections, especially in order to heal the body and to prevent disease."

Rabbi Tam looked at Rabbi Abraham. "But I suppose that you already knew this," said Jacob Tam.

Rabbi Abraham thought for a moment. He stroked his beard, and then he said, "Well, Rabbi, it is true that I have had dealings with amulets, charms, and incantations. However, there is always much to learn. Perhaps you would show me how *you* go about making an amulet."

"Gladly," said Jacob Tam. He stood and closed the door to the back room, so that the two men would not be disturbed.

"We begin with the optimal times," said Rabbi Tam. "Writing is most effective at certain times, on certain days, and under the conjunction of particular stars."

Jacob Tam sat down at the Rabbi's desk. He tapped the worn tabletop with his finger. "My studies indicate," he said, "that not all times are good for the writing of amulets. Of course no writing whatsoever is permitted on the Sabbath; in addition, however, only certain days of the month are acceptable and safe for inscribing an effective amulet. Let me make you a list." And he wrote:

time of day	day of the month
all day	1, 4, 12, 20, 22, 25, 28
mornings only	5, 7, 8, 11, 14, 16, 21, 24, 27, 30
evenings only	17

Rabbi Abraham studied the paper. He nodded, and he looked back at his companion.

"The most useful amulets seem to be the traditional ones, the ones that can be worn as necklaces," continued Rabbi Tam. "The holy words are written on parchment. But the parchment must be protected. Roll the paper into a tight scroll, or put it in a small hard case—

this will keep the charms safe from foul weathers and from prying eyes. Now, Rabbi Abraham, have you a clean parchment from a kosherly slaughtered animal?"

Rabbi Achselrad took a square of calf parchment from his drawer, and he handed it to his colleague.

"First, there is the benediction," said Rabbi Tam. Old Achselrad listened closely, for this was new to him. Jacob Tam closed his eyes, he put a clean handerchief on his head, and he recited:

Praised be You, O Lord our God, King of the world, Who has sanctified Your great and revered Name. You have revealed this Name to the pious ones, so that they may invoke Your power and Your might by means of Your Name and Your word and the words of Your mouth, both oral words and written words. Praised be You, Lord, King, Holy One – blessed be You. May Your Name be extolled for ever and ever, amen.

"Amen," said Rabbi Abraham.

Next, Rabbi Tam wrote the *Shema* followed by seven mystical words on one side of the white parchment. Then he drew a triangle, and inside this figure he wrote: *In the Name of the merciful and compassionate God.* Underneath, he wrote these words from Psalm 91:

No disaster however slight
Shall befall you late at night
For God has charged His angels bright
To guard your paths through dark and light.

Angelic hands will guide each trip,
You shall walk safely without a slip,
Stepping fearlessly on scorpions –
And deadly snakes will seem your friends.

Rabbi Tam blew gently on the writing, waiting for the ink to dry. Then he turned the parchment over. "On the other side," he said, "we write our specific charm. For example, here is a fine holy prescription --" And Jacob ben Meir Tam, the rabbi from France, wrote:

Mighty is Yahweh of Israel. By the virtues of these holy signs and seals and in the Name of the good Lord God (blessed be He), may the bearer of this charm be saved from ill winds. May he and his family be protected. May his children grow happily, free from all diseases and from evil occurrences and from extraordinary death. May his children be brought up on the Torah. May they reach the marriage canopy in health. And may they do good works eternally.

O blessed Lord our God, may You let these children to grow into a long life. And then may they all age calmly, with a quiet mind, living a gentle life, now and forever. Amen, eternally hallelujah – thus shall be Your will, *selah* and amen.

Silently, the two holy men read over this devout request. Then Rabbi Tam rolled the parchment into a tight scroll; he tied it with seven white threads and in each thread he put seven neat knots. Finally, he strung the small packet on a slender white rope, and gently he laid it on the rabbi's desk, there in the back room of the old yeshiva in Cologne, once upon a time long, long ago.

Yes, Rabbi, medieval Jews loved amulets. In those days all people – Jews and Gentiles alike – were fascinated by arcane scripts and signs and symbols. And come to think of it, amulets are still woven into the lives of us Jews today. What do I mean? Why, I am referring to *mezuzahs*, of course. A *mezuzah* is a piece of parchment inscribed with holy scripts and signs and symbols, and it is protected by a small hard case, just as is any other amulet.

My grandmother told me that in the Middle Ages *mezuzahs* kept the myriad evil spirits at bay. The famous medieval Rabbi Meir of Rothenburg said, "If Jews knew how useful the *mezuzah* is, then they would not lightly disregard it. For instance, no demon can have power over a house upon which a *mezuzah* is properly affixed. In our house alone, I believe that we have at least twenty-four *mezuzahs*."

My grandmother also pointed to the authority of the Talmud, which warns: "A premature death visits the homes of those who fail to observe meticulously all the laws relating to the *mezuzah*." Likewise, Kabbalists claim that the word *mezuzah* was originally built from the two words *zaz* and *mavet*, meaning "death depart." Therefore, my grandmother said that when you move, your first act should be to fasten a *mezuzah* to your doorpost – otherwise you may bring an early death upon your children. On the other hand, attending to your *mezuzah* is like having two thousand eight hundred servants, and it ensures that all your children shall be forever blessed. As it is written:

> Then all your children's children's race
> Will be forever blessed with grace
> And gentle winds will them embrace,
> While soft rains you will forever taste
> Upon your peaceful, sleeping face.

Yes, good fortune comes from our most sacred holy amulet, our *mezuzah*. "Remember, my little child," said my grandmother to me, "the purpose of a *mezuzah* is to provide a Jew with a continuous reminder: even in the privacy of your own home, you live under the all-seeing protective eye of the good Lord God (blessed be He). The Lord loves you, and He will ensure that – no matter where you are – His warm and gentle grace will rain softly forever on your peaceful, sleeping face. So, amen, my golden little boy, amen and sleep well."

ood evening, Rabbi. You are having difficulty sleeping again? Put your feet up on the side bench here, and I will open the stove door. Let me push these coals back: the white glow will wash away all the worries of your hard day.

I heard your final prayers tonight, and there is no use denying it, Rabbi—you are overworked; even an old shammas like me can tell. I kept one eye on you when I was cleaning the dishes. I saw that you were watching the door, hoping that Reb Elbaum would leave early. But then Reb Anton stayed late to argue about the passage in the Book of Ecclesiastes:

> As He deals with mankind
> God tests them continually,
> Thus He can clearly find
> Their true spirituality.

Yes, Rabbi, we each know the trials and the tests posed by the Almighty Lord God (blessed be He). The Lord tests—and sometimes things work out well, but sometimes they do not. I remember a story that my grandmother told me about the Lord's trials and tests; it was the story of Mordecai ben Simon ha-Levi and his son Jethro:

Once upon a time, said my grandmother to me, there lived in Cologne on the wide River Rhine, a man named Mordecai ben Simon. Mordecai was a good man and a learned man. He studied day and night. He prayed fervently, and undoubtedly he found favor in the eyes of the Omnipotent Lord God. Mordecai had an only son, who was a very fine lad, and the boy was named Jethro.

One hot summer night in the month of *Av*, Dumah, the Angel of Death, came to Cologne. It was in the dark dead hours of the night. Mordecai lived across the alleyway from the yeshiva. For some reason, Mordecai could not sleep. He looked out his window at the synagogue building. Was there a dim light in the main prayer hall, or were his eyes playing tricks on him? Mordecai pulled on his clothes. He walked across the street to the synagogue building. The front door was unlocked. This was strange—had Chayim, the shammas, forgotten to lock the door last night? Was there a robbery in progress? Mordecai was a brave man. He opened the door and he stepped into the anteroom. There was silence throughout the building.

As always, Mordecai removed his shoes. Then he walked into the main prayer hall. The building was thick with old silence, but a dog whined outside somewhere far, far away. Mordecai peered into the dark hall. There, past the worn wooden benches, beyond the twelve stained glass windows with their colored lions and snakes, stood a dark figure at the Holy stone Ark. The figure turned—it turned, and Mordecai saw that it was Dumah, the Angel of Death. Dumah stood covered from head to foot with unwinking eyes. He held a drawn and bloody sword, and his breathing was like the sound of dry leaves, rustling and rustling in the blank autumn wind.

Dumah, the Angel of Death, turned slowly. He turned slowly and silently, smoothly and darkly. Was he speaking? Mordecai thought that he heard the holy words of Psalm 103:

> As children are by their father known
> Likewise God understands His fold—
> The good Lord knows our inmost bones
> For He formed us from the dust of old.

> God made man like the wildflowers,
> We blossom in a springtime roar
> But after windy autumn showers
> The fields have no flowers anymore.

The Angel of Death stood there with his unwinking eyes and with his drawn and bloody sword, and in the oldest and dustiest voice of all, he said, "The end has come for your son Jethro. I have been sent by the Almighty Lord God to tell you that the time for your son's death has been decreed—and now it has arrived."

Mordecai ben Simon ha-Levi hung his head. After many minutes, he replied, "What God desires, no man can prevent, amen."

Dumah, the Angel of Death, said nothing.

Mordecai continued: "But I pray you, O Dumah—have one final mercy on me. Let me first marry my son. Then you can do what you have been commanded. With all my heart I would like to lead my only son under the wedding canopy. Please, let me see him married."

"I am not certain that I can honor this request," said Dumah, the Angel of Death. "The Great Almighty One has issued a Decree of Death."

"Ah, good angel, I do not ask that you contest the will of the Lord. Just give me a little more time before you fulfill the incontrovertible Decree. Remember that the Talmud tells us":

> Any man who has no wife lives without joy, without blessing, and without goodness.

"So, for the sake of the short remaining time in my son's life, I beg you to allow him to be married," said Mordecai.

Dumah, the Angel of Death, was silent for a moment, and then he replied, "Very well—your wish is granted: I will wait until the marriage ceremony. However, the wedding must take place within one month's time."

Dumah disappeared in the shadows, and Mordecai went sadly home. Yes, Mordecai went home, but he did not sleep for the rest of the night. Early the next morning he met with the parents of a fine young woman, and he announced the betrothal of his son, fixing the wedding to take place in four weeks. The neighbors and the friends and the relatives were puzzled. Why was a marriage arranged so soon? Mordecai merely said that it was the will of the good Lord God (blessed be He). Mordecai ben Simon ha-Levi was a very devout and pious man; therefore the people around him took him at his word.

The next day, Mordecai sent his son Jethro to invite people to the wedding. On his way, Jethro met Rabbi Abraham ben Alexander. The Rabbi said, "Hello, Jethro. Where are you going this morning?"

Jethro ben Mordecai answered, "I am on my way to invite people to my wedding."

The Rabbi closed his eyes. He felt weak. He began to sway. Then he took a deep breath, and he sat down on a rock. "Rabbi," said Jethro, "are you all right?"

Rabbi Abraham opened his eyes. He stared at Jethro, and then he said, "Frankly, young man, I must speak with you. Please sit down here a moment. I have had a vision. I think that the black Angel of Death will appear at your wedding ceremony. At that time, the Almighty Lord God wishes to take away a soul."

"Who is destined to die?" asked the young man.

Rabbi Abraham looked sad; he could not bring himself to tell Jethro the full story, so he said, "That is only for the Holy Lord God to know."

Jethro raised his eyebrows, and he replied, "If that is the Divine Decree of the Lord, then we must submit to it willingly. There is a time for each of us, amen."

The Rabbi looked at young Jethro, he stroked his beard, and then he said, "Listen, young man, I will give you some advice: be certain to follow it. At your betrothal ceremony, when the time comes for the blessing and when the people are seated around the table, then sit down with them too. But do not eat or drink. Just watch quietly.

"Soon an old man will come with an uncovered head and with disheveled hair. His clothes will be torn. He will walk with a cane. As soon as you see him enter the room, get up from the table. Go and welcome him. Invite him to sit at the head of the table, among the distinguished guests. And if he refuses, then sit next to him wherever he sits and make him feel comfortable and important. I advise you, Jethro – be sure to follow these instructions."

Jethro listened carefully and he promised to follow the advice of the Rabbi. Jethro looked at the Rabbi, and the Rabbi looked at Jethro. Neither man said anything more. Then Jethro went on his way.

Jethro ben Mordecai continued his rounds, inviting various people to his wedding as if nothing unusual were about to happen. Later, he returned home and he said, "Well, Father, I have finished; I personally invited all the guests to my wedding."

The father felt sad, and the son felt sad, but neither mentioned Dumah to each other or to anyone else. Then Mordecai made all the other preparations for the wedding. Both father and son tried to ignore the impending visit of Dumah, the Angel of Death.

Eventually, the wedding day arrived. The bridegroom got dressed and left his house – and he was not supposed to return until the ceremony was over. People arrived at the Jewish city hall for the formal betrothal ceremony, the blessing to precede the actual wedding itself. The guests sat around a large table; they talked, waiting to eat and to drink. The bridegroom sat with them, and he looked very sad. "Who of these friends and relatives is doomed to die?" he wondered. People noticed that Jethro was upset, but no one knew why.

After they had been sitting for a while, a man in patched clothes came into the room. The stranger was bareheaded. He shuffled and he supported himself with a crabstick cane; he coughed quietly. But have no doubts, Rabbi – actually, it was Dumah, the Angel of Death: Dumah had come to Cologne disguised as a poor old man, just as Rabbi Achselrad had foretold.

Jethro looked up and saw the stranger. The old man had thin white hair. He had shaky hands. He squinted and he stooped. Then Jethro saw his eyes – the deep black eyes that could peer into the depths of a man's soul, staring for ever and a day – and Jethro knew that Dumah, the black Angel of Death, had entered the room. Jethro stood. He went up to the old man. The young man took the black angel by the hand, and he said, "Come with me, sir. Sit at the head of the table."

The old man refused. So the bridegroom took the shabby old man by the hand and placed him by his own side at the table. Mordecai ben Simon had been watching. He, too, knew that Death had entered the Jewish city hall, but bravely he stood and said the betrothal benediction:

Blessed be You, O Lord our God, King of the World, Who has sanctified us by Your commandments and Who has commanded us concerning the forbidden relations and Who has allowed unto us the wedded couple, through the marriage canopy and the wedding sanctification. Praised be You, O Lord our God, Who sanctifies Israel through the wedding canopy and the wedding sanctification, amen.

All the assembled people repeated "amen." Then Jethro brought a variety of good foods to the beggar; however, the old man refused to eat, and Jethro also did not eat. The other guests sitting at the table were surprised at the honor that the bridegroom paid to this unknown old man. At the same time, Jethro found himself shivering, and he could scarcely speak clearly.

Finally, the old man said to Jethro, "My son, I am going to ask you a question: If you are building a house and if you need straw to mix with the clay, where would you get the straw?"

The young man was surprised at this strange question, but he answered, "I would go to a farmer, probably some man with a large storage shed, and I would buy the straw from him."

The old man nodded, and then he said, "Now, imagine that after you have used the straw, the farmer comes and asks to have his straw back. What would you do?"

Jethro raised his eyebrows. He replied, "Well, the straw is already used, so I would pay him for the straw. Or I suppose that I could give him some other straw instead."

The old man continued: "Ah, but suppose that the farmer insisted on having his own straw returned. Suppose that he refused to accept any replacement – then what would you do?"

The young man answered, "The only honorable thing to do would be to break up the clay bricks, to take out the straw, and to give it back to him."

The old man nodded sadly, and he said, "The fearsome Lord God, blessed be He, is the Master of the barn. The straw is the soul of man. And I, young Jethro, am Dumah, the Angel of Death. Now the Lord is asking for the straw that He gave you. I am afraid that He refuses to accept any other straw. I am sorry, young man – I am here to take away your soul."

Everyone had been listening quietly to this strange dialogue.

When the guests heard the final declaration, they were stunned into absolute silence. Men turned pale. Women gasped. Jethro ben Mordecai ha-Levi was tremendously frightened. He could scarcely believe that it was him of all people whom Dumah wanted to carry off. After a few minutes of silence, Jethro said in a hoarse voice to the black angel, "If it is the will of the Almighty Lord God that I should die, then do me one last kindness, holy angel. Allow me first some time to see my father and my mother and my bride. I must bid them all farewell."

Dumah was silent. Jethro continued in a whisper: "Then, O Dumah . . . I shall die quietly."

Dumah, the Angel of Death, looked at Jethro for many minutes, and then he said in his dry and ancient voice, "Very well, Jethro – you have been so kind and so attentive to me, a beggar and a stranger, that now I will let you go and do as you have requested." And Dumah, the Angel of Death, disappeared.

Jethro went to his father and mother. To each parent, Jethro gently said that he was about to die. Jethro said his good-byes, and there was much weeping and crying and hugging and clinging. And Mordecai, the father, closed his eyes and began to pray intently.

Next, Jethro went to his bride to say good-bye. The young woman stared at Jethro in disbelief. "I cannot accept this," she said. "You are a good person, Jethro. This cannot be the will of the almighty and compassionate Lord God. There must be some terrible mistake. Listen to me, Jethro – it was Rabbi Abraham who first advised you. Let us go to see him again."

So the two young people hurried to the synagogue. They stepped in the front door, they went through the anteroom, and they walked into the main prayer hall, which was filled with wooden benches. Jethro and his bride passed the twelve stained glass windows with their colored lions and snakes, they looked up at the Holy Ark made of stone, and they walked to the door of the back study room. There, the Rabbi was bent over a book, and seven old scholars of Cologne were seated on the worn benches, talking quietly among themselves.

The bride spoke first. "Rabbis," she said, "we need your advice desperately! My poor husband-to-be, Jethro ben Mordecai ha-Levi, is to die today, before we even wed." And she began to cry and cry and cry.

White-haired Baruch ben Jacob looked at the young couple, and he asked, "Who is it that wants to take your life?"

"It is no ordinary person," said Jethro sadly.

A younger scholar, Elisah ben Samuel, stroked his beard, and he said, "Obviously it is Dumah, the Angel of Death."

Joshua ben Eliezer frowned, and he said, "This is the holy house of the good Lord God (blessed be He). Wait here, and you will be safe."

But Lewe ben Anselm said, "No place is safe from Dumah."

And Menahem ben Joel said, "Then you had best begin reading the Torah, Jethro. A man cannot die while he is studying."

However, Moyses ben Nathan said, "This sounds like a trick, Reb Menahem. You cannot fool the all-knowing Lord or any of His messengers."

Old Shimshon ha-Zaken shook his head. He coughed, and he asked, "What shall we do, Rabbi?"

Rabbi Abraham was listening with a creased brow. After a minute, he said, "We must quickly marry the couple."

Fortunately, neither the bride nor the groom had eaten that day, so the wedding ceremony could take place immediately. The groom was escorted into the prayer hall by five of the scholars, who carried candles. Rabbi Abraham took his place in his ceremonial robes before the Holy stone Ark. The two young people came and stood before him. Elisah ben Samuel and Joshua ben Eliezer held an extra prayer shawl as a wedding canopy over the couple.

Then Rabbi Abraham performed a speedy wedding ceremony. After the initial benedictions, a dash of ashes was dabbed on the groom's forehead. His *tallis katan* was gently draped over the head of the bride. The wedding prayers were recited. No glass dish was available to be broken, so the Rabbi ruled that a clay plate could be substituted; a plate was found, and it was stepped on and broken by the groom. Some wine was poured onto the floor and some salt was sprinkled over the couple. Finally, the bride marched three times around her new mate.

At last, the Rabbi recited the "to a newly-married couple" verse from the Book of Genesis:

> May God rain gentle dew –
> Showers from the West –
> Then may He give to you
> The richest fall harvest

> Under His warm sunshine,
> With corn, oats, and barley
> And honey and mellow wine
> All in luscious plenty.

Just as the Rabbi finished these words, thunderclouds began to gather outside the old wooden building. A wind came up, and Dumah, the Angel of Death, entered the synagogue. Darkness flowed from the main prayer hall. It spilled over into the anteroom in the front and into the small study room in the back, and it rolled like a vast tidal wave throughout the yeshiva. The Rabbi stood quietly. The scholars sat unmoving. The newly married couple froze in fear.

There stood Dumah, the Angel of Death, in all his fearsome nakedness, covered from head to foot with unwinking eyes. He held a drawn and bloody sword, and his breathing was like the sound of dry leaves, rustling and rustling in the blank autumn wind. And, in the most ancient and dusty voice, he repeated the holy words of the psalmist:

> As children are by their father known
> Likewise God understands His fold –
> The good Lord knows our inmost bones
> For He formed us from the dust of old.

> God made man like the wildflowers,
> We blossom in a springtime roar
> But after windy autumn showers
> The fields have no flowers anymore.

The Angel of Death stood motionless and said, "I am here for you, Jethro, son of Mordecai ha-Levi."

Rabbi Abraham said, "Are you the spirit who wants to take the soul of this bridegroom?"

And Dumah answered, "Yes."

The Rabbi stood, and although he felt weak and small, he said, "Then I ask you, O Dumah, please go back to the merciful Lord God (blessed be He) and say to Him: 'Is it not written in the Holy Law (in the Book of Deuteronomy) that a man who marries shall be free for a whole year to rejoice with the wife that he has taken?' "

Dumah frowned, and he said, "Rabbi Abraham, you are bending the meaning of that verse. You will recall that the specific context is conscription":

> When a man is newly married, he shall not be liable for military service or for any other public duty. He shall remain at home, exempt from service for one year, and he shall enjoy the wife that he has taken.

And the Rabbi said, "Ah, fearsome Dumah – is it not true that death is the ultimate conscription? So, will the good Lord God, blessed be He, violate His own law?"

Dumah, the Angel of Death, listened silently. Then he looked at Jethro. Dumah remembered the kindness and the respect that the young man had shown at the wedding ceremony. He remembered Jethro's sad resignation to the Decree of Death. And Dumah, the Angel of Death, felt pity for the couple. So Dumah waved an arm, and instantly he flew up to Heaven and he returned to the Throne of Glory where sits the omnipotent Lord God, blessed be He forever, amen.

Dumah, the Angel of Death, related the story of Jethro ben Mordecai ha-Levi to the great Lord Almighty, our Heavenly Father. Other angels joined in, and of course Jethro's father, Mordecai ben Simon ha-Levi, was also praying continuously and fervently. The good Lord God (blessed be He) listened, He nodded His radiant head, and He took pity on the boy. "We can look upon these events as a test of the young man and of his family," declared the Most Holy One, and He tore the Decree of Death into sixty times sixty pieces. Then God prolonged Jethro's life seven more years, corresponding to the seven days of the wedding festivity. And in Cologne, the thunderclouds suddenly disappeared. A fresh wind arose and it blew a sunny sky into place – and a joyous wedding reception finally took place.

Yes, Rabbi, my grandmother (may her soul rest alongside the souls of her parents) reminded me that this story is like those famous verses of Psalm 145:

Just is the Lord, God of the cherubim –
He completes the work He starts
And He is near to those who seek Him,
Who call to Him through their inmost hearts.

He grants the wishes of the pious victim
He hears their cry and protects His people,
God watches over all who love Him,
He tests them – and rewards the faithful.

The good Lord God continually tests men. He tries and He presses. He examines and He monitors. He watches and He checks. And then if there is any sign of goodness and unselfishness, if there is hope for true gentle pious behavior, if there are streaks of beauty (even if they are hidden amidst mars and stains and taints), then He delivers the faithful from their pains. The great Lord Almighty softens our griefs – hallelujah and amen. For the Lord is an ever hopeful, loving, and optimistic Father.

ood evening, Rabbi – I was just resting my eyes. Please, join me here by the stove. (I think that you will be too hot on that bench: try the one nearer to the wall.) An old man like me can doze forever by a warm stove; I suppose that is because so many of my friends have passed on to their reward in the Great Hereafter (may they all be blessed forever, amen).

What do I mean? Why, Rabbi, I miss my old friends, and now I hope to meet them while I sleep. When your body is asleep, your soul slips out from your heart. It flies about, wandering over the face of the earth, and then it reports its experiences to the sleeping mind. Did you ever dream of meeting a distant friend? Actually, it was your two souls that made contact – dreams can reduce a thousand kilometers to the breadth of one hand.

And, Rabbi, why do we dream about the dead? It is because their immortal souls still haunt the earth; therefore, they can meet our own wandering souls at night. And when you *do* come across the shade of a departed person, be certain to notice its aura. If it has a warm rosy glow, then the person was charitable during his life. Charity gives warmth to souls – and it is the same for angels. The Angels of Charity also radiate warmth and gentleness. . . . What is that, Rabbi? Well, such matters are not well known nowadays. I heard about the Angels of Charity from my grandmother many years ago, and she took as her authority the mystical Abraham Achselrad; he was a medieval rabbi who often had dealings with angels.

Angels were everywhere in medieval times, and Jews were always encountering new angels because each angel has its own unique job—each angel is responsible for a specific category of Divine orders. (But, Rabbi, do not imagine that this division of labor gives the angels any leisure time. If you think that, then I had best tell you what Eliazer ben Judah, the mystic of Worms, said: "Angels never rest. They are the messengers of God. The Almighty Lord sends them forth to do His innumerable specific biddings. This work keeps them occupied constantly at whirlwind speed: so many tasks await them that they must dash about ceaselessly in order to complete their present assignments and to fulfill the new requests.")

In those days, Jews disagreed about angelic independence. How much initiative is allowed to an angel? Rabbi Eliazer claimed, "Angels can do nothing of their own will. They act only upon the command of their Master, the good Lord God"—this was the traditional rabbinic position. On the other hand, the common folk saw angels as the agents of magic: angels could act on human requests without direct orders from the Almighty Lord God. The Kabbalists, too, believed in magic; they said that angels carry information *both* ways—that is, to and from Heaven—and many of the Kabbalistic rites were designed specifically to strengthen the communication between earth and Heaven.

Abraham Achselrad wrote in his Kabbalistic treatise, the *Keter Shem Tov*:

> Angels are everywhere. They have free access to the full and incondens-
> ably complex domain of the great Lord God (blessed be He). God
> Himself presides over everything, and the angels are His aides. Angels
> can appear to us in any guise, even as humans, as they enact God's
> orders. Angels also carry our hopes and prayers and wishes up to
> Heaven—and here on earth, they can reward righteousness, holiness,
> and charity, and they can punish sin, evil, and venality.

And this was the view of the Jews of medieval Cologne. For instance, let me tell you about a conversation among the seven old men who sat daily in the back room of the Cologne yeshiva:

One morning, white-haired Baruch ben Jacob was saying, "Angels have direct access to the secret knowledge of Heaven. In fact, it is the angels who give wisdom to our holy mystics. Angels inspire the pious and the learned, and angels give magic to the devout and the righteous."

"Amen," murmered the other men, nodding and stroking their beards.

A quiet thoughtful silence followed. After a few moments, a younger scholar, Elisah ben Samuel, said, "There certainly are a *host* of angels. I must confess, gentlemen, that I can barely remember all the angels' names that I have heard."

Joshua ben Eliezer said, "Well, Elisah, that is not surprising, for there are angels and angels and more angels. Each angel has a special function and name. Each is a deputy for the Lord. Each has been born from a Heavenly commandment – and, of course, there are endless holy commandments, my friend."

Lewe ben Anselm nodded. "Yes, gentlemen," he said, "here is the great challenge for the mystic. The pious holy man must know an incredible number of names: in a successful prayer or incantation, he must invoke just the right angel for the particular conditions and the exact requirements at hand."

Reb Lewe's neighbor, Menahem ben Joel, nodded also. "Exactly, my friends – and there is no doubt that learning all these names would be an impossible task were it not for one important fact: angels are named after their jobs. For instance, there is Shamriel, a guardian angel – his name is built on the word *shomer* or guardian. And there is Hasdiel, an angel of benevolence – his name is built on the word *hesed* or benevolence. The orderliness of these names helps the mystic remember which angel is which."

But Moyses ben Nathan said, "Well, personally, gentlemen, I think that the mystics go too far: frankly, mystics are immodest. Angels are embodiments of the Holy Wishes. Who are we mere mortals to try and categorize them? How dare we propose to understand their names? I say that we can only accept them humbly and then respect them."

"Amen," said Baruch.

Old Shimshon ha-Zaken coughed, he cleared his throat, and he said, "Now, now, my good colleagues, we must strike a balance here.

On the one hand, the great archangels are so clear and so commanding and so forceful that even we poor mortals can remember them and can begin to understand them. But it is different with most other angels. The innumerable minor angels are subtle thoughts from the mind of the Most Holy One. These must remain to us only names–albeit mystical and holy names. Yes, friends, the vast Host of angels shall forever remain a wondrous cloud of sacred wills, wishes, and wonderments from the good Lord God (blessed be He)–hallelujah and amen."

Then the many scholars nodded and murmured holy words among themselves. And, Rabbi, if you were to have looked into the back study room from the prayer hall on that fine bright summer morning, it would have seemed as if the old men of Cologne were enveloped in a wondrous cloud of sacred gentle piety–hallelujah and amen.

Undoubtedly, continued my grandmother as she told this story to me, the gentle holy cloud that pervaded the back room of Achselrad's yeshiva in medieval Cologne was due to angels, angels, and more angels. And among the countless angels that wandered the Rhinelands during the Middle Ages was Aniel. . . . Aniel? He is one of the good Lord God's many Angels of Charity. My grandmother was extremely charitable, Rabbi, and it was the angel Aniel who was responsible for her amazing health. When she was older than me she rarely felt dizzy or sick or weak and she could walk into town and back twice a day. Grandmother spent all her free time sewing: she sewed small prayer shawls–*tallis katan*–that she then gave to the poor. "Aniel has blessed me with good health–and it is all due to my charity," my grandmother would say, patting her half-completed embroideries.

As I mentioned, my grandmother learned of the powers of the Angels of Charity from tales of the old mystic Achselrad of Cologne. For example, once upon a time, in the medieval city of Cologne, there lived two poor Jewish beggars. One was named Eliakim ben Anselm ha-Kohen–he was blind. The other was named David Ephraim ben Asher–he was lame. In the Jewish community of Cologne, begging from door to door was tolerated only on Fridays. On other days, Eliakim and David Ephraim joined the needy citizens sitting in front of the synagogue. They sat along the yeshiva wall without actually begging; instead, they thought holy thoughts and hoped that passersby would take pity and would be charitable voluntarily.

Now it was the hot summer month of *Av*. For three dry sunny days few worshipers passed by. Eliakim and David Ephraim were very, very hungry. They felt tired, dusty, and desperate, and they prayed continuously to the good Lord God. Over and over, they chanted the verse from Psalm 102:

> My days are consumed like smoke
> My bones are as brittle as the dead
> My heart is like a withered oak,
> For I have neglected my daily bread.

"And where shall we find our daily bread today?" said Eliakim sadly to David. The two men shook their heads, and they continued chanting.

Now, Rabbi, if you were to have seen Eliakim or if you were to have come across David Ephraim, then you would have said, "These are good men. They are kind. When they had money, they contributed to charity. They have not forgotten their God, and they have tried to do what is right." Yes, Rabbi, Eliakim and David Ephraim were good men: it was just that the unpredictable wheel of fortune had revolved and now they had suffered repeated reversals and sad consequences. Therefore, the wondrous Lord God (blessed be He) finally took pity on Eliakim and David, and He sent a vision to Rabbi Abraham. The vision came in the form of an old pilgrim, who instructed the Rabbi to make an amulet.

Rabbi Abraham set down his pen. "An amulet, you say? I should inscribe a sacred talisman?" he asked. The pilgrim nodded. "Well, sir," said the Rabbi, "I am always happy to write a holy charm – if it will be used to fulfill the wishes of the Almighty Lord God, blessed be He."

"And so it shall," said the pilgrim. This stranger had a warm reverent glow, he was wrapped in a holy white aura, and the Rabbi had no question that his visitor was in fact a Divine messenger. In fact, the pilgrim was really the angel Aniel. "Now," said Aniel, "write a holy healing charm – and of course, write it in red ink."

"It must be in red ink?" asked the Rabbi, raising his eyebrows.

"Yes, good Rabbi. As you know, red is the color of healing."

The Rabbi looked at the meager supplies on his desk. "And where am I to get this ink?" he asked.

"Do you know the weed called *madder*?" asked the holy stranger.

"Yes," said the Rabbi.

"Go to a field and collect some roots of the *madder* plant," said Aniel. "Grind them in a little warm wine, mix in the white of an egg, and you will have a healing red ink." Rabbi Abraham Achselrad listened carefully and nodded. Then the Angel of Charity stepped from the yeshiva and he disappeared back to Heaven.

The Rabbi prepared the ink and he sat down to write a mystical charm on a piece of kosher parchment. He finished the charm by drawing a *Magen David* surrounded by seven repetitions of the Ineffable Name. Finally, the Rabbi rolled the parchment into a tight scroll, which he then tied with seven fine white threads. Again, Aniel appeared in the doorway. Abraham felt a gentle breeze and he looked up. "Rabbi," said the angel, "walk outside the synagogue. In the courtyard, you will find a good use for this amulet."

The Rabbi set down his pen. He tapped his chin, he stroked his beard, and he shrugged his shoulders. Then he stood up from his chair, and he walked out of the back room. Achselrad passed the Holy stone Ark as he walked through the main prayer hall; sunlight glowed through the twelve stained glass windows with their colored lions and snakes. The Rabbi stepped around the wooden benches, and he walked through the anteroom and out the front door of the holy house of learning – in a medieval Cologne of long, long ago.

The Rabbi walked into the courtyard, and there he came across the two poor men sitting near the yeshiva. Rabbi Abraham said to them, "Eliakim, David – again I find you sitting here. I hope passersby have given you some money. As you know, our poorbox is empty."

The Rabbi looked at the men and he looked at the parchment scroll in his hand. "Listen, gentlemen, let me try and help you in another way," he said. "Here is a healing amulet – I suspect that it is for you." Then the Rabbi handed the amulet to Eliakim, and David also put his hand on the parchment scroll. As they touched the charm, both men felt a warmth radiate through their bodies.

The Rabbi laid his hands on the heads of the two beggars. He closed his eyes, and he said:

> May the Lord bless you and watch over you
> May the Lord make His face to shine upon you

May the Lord be gracious and good to you
May the Lord look kindly on you
And may He give you peace, amen.

The two men repeated "amen."

"Now, gentlemen," said the Rabbi, "you are receiving a Divine blessing. Please be very humble. Do not forget that all good fortune is merely a loan from the holy Lord. Remember: you are only caretakers of your earthly treasures. And, my friends, always show mercy and kindness to your fellow men." The two men nodded many times. They thanked the Rabbi – they even tried to kiss his hands. Then both men returned to the hut that they shared.

Within a week, the blind Eliakim and the lame David began to heal. First, Eliakim could recognize shapes; then he saw details, and one day he could read again. Lame David hobbled about daily – soon he found that he could walk comfortably, and one day he actually ran. The two men felt young and energetic and happy. A week later, when they were walking and talking outside the old southern gate of the city, they discovered a sack of jewelry. They shook hands. They hugged each other. Then they went to the marketplace, they sold the jewels, and they divided the money equally between themselves.

With their new wealth, the two men set up businesses. Eliakim became a gardener; he worked day and night, and in a few years he owned vast fields of vegetables. David Ephraim bought oxen and sheep and goats; he too put in long hours. The men were serious workers, and in a short time both became rich.

One year passed and then two. Seven years came and seven years went, and one day the angel Aniel returned to the Rhinelands. When he came to Cologne, he thought: "Will the two beggars still remember their old poverty? Will they remember their responsibilities to the less fortunate?" Aniel took on the shape of a man with only one arm. He stopped in the synagogue, and he asked the Rabbi to accompany him on a tour of the Jewish community. After some time, they reached the house of David Ephraim ben Asher, once a lame beggar and now a wealthy trader in oxen and sheep and goats.

"Please have pity on a poor man," pleaded the angel. "Would you give me of one of your oxen, so that I can feed my wife and children?

For your kindness, God Almighty will protect you from ever becoming a cripple like myself."

Thus spoke the the angel Aniel. The Rabbi stood by, watching silently. David Ephraim shook his head and said, "I am sorry, but this is not the best time for me to give out charity. It has been a difficult year and many of my animals are sick. Moreover, I give regularly to the poorbox in the synagogue. Come back in a few weeks. I may be able to help you then."

The angel said, "I cannot wait a few weeks. Besides, compare our situations – even if it is hard for you to help me, it is even harder for me to go without your help."

But David said, "I am afraid that you will just have to accept my answer." And he turned to leave.

Aniel frowned. He looked at Rabbi Abraham, and he looked at David Ephraim ben Asher. Then the angel said, "Very well, David. However, I wish to remind you of the scriptural Proverb –"

> Never rob a defenseless man –
>   Aid him selflessly,
> And never scorn a hungry man
>   Nor plague his family.

> God is our Protector
>   He shields the humble and the weak,
> He will punish the wicked braggart
>   Then He will redeem all the meek.

David nodded, he shrugged his shoulders, and he turned away. Angrily, the holy angel Aniel left the house of David Ephraim ben Asher, and Rabbi Abraham hurried along behind him.

As they turned the corner, the angel suddenly became a blind man. He groped for a wall, and the Rabbi took his hand. "Lead me to the house of Eliakim ben Anselm ha-Kohen," said the angel. When they reached the house, Eliakim himself came to the door. "I am in desperate straits, my friend. Would you help me out?" begged the angel Aniel. "Give me some food for me and for my family. God will repay you tenfold for your charity and kindness."

Of course Eliakim remembered his own blindness. Now Eliakim had lush bountiful gardens, gardens that were warm and inviting, and you know the old Hebrew proverb: "As is the garden, so is the gardener." Therefore, the gardener Eliakim brought the beggar-angel Aniel into his house, he gave him meat and wine, and he made the angel a present of two fresh loaves of bread and also cucumbers, grain, pumpkins, and squash.

The angel looked at the Rabbi, and he smiled. Eliakim was looking at the table for a moment, and Aniel suddenly resumed his wispy spiritual shape and, light as a spring breeze, he flew off to Heaven. The Rabbi was left alone, standing next to Eliakim. Eliakim looked around. "Where did that beggar disappear to?" he asked.

"It does not matter," said old Achselrad. "It only matters that – praise the good Lord God – you have a generous heart. God will shelter you to the end of your days. Remember the scriptural Proverb –"

> He who is generous to the poor
> Lends to the Lord Himself
> And God will repay the charity-doer
> From the fullness of His shelf.

Rabbi Abraham patted Eliakim ben Anselm ha-Kohen on the shoulder, and he returned to the yeshiva.

One day passed, and then a second came and went. Soon a plague struck the animals of David Ephraim. His oxen, his sheep, and his goats fell ill and died. Then his creditors would not give him any more money – and it was not long before David became quite poor again. He even found it difficult to walk smoothly and easily, and friends thought that his old limp was returning when he walked too quickly.

Eliakim heard of this sad turn of events; therefore, he took in his lame friend. "Come, David," said Eliakim, "I would like you to live with me." David smiled, he took Eliakim's hand, and he accepted the invitation.

Eliakim ben Anselm ha-Kohen and David Ephraim ben Asher remained fast friends, and the two men lived together happily ever after. Eliakim shared his money with David, and David, although never again rich, was content. David followed Eliakim's lead and became a gardener too. Their gardens were always filled with beans, beets, and basil, and with cabbage, carrots, and corn. And both of the men gave to charity and they went to the synagogue twice a day— twice daily the two gardeners went to the Garden of the Law of the Lord. And, Rabbi, my grandmother said that soon after moving in with Eliakim, David no longer limped at all—but perhaps he was no longer in a hurry when he walked.

abbi, I am glad to see you here alone. I want to apologize for my outburst during the service this evening. It was just that Reb Anton was playing with his gold wedding ring – he was actually tossing it into the air!

What is that, Rabbi? A casual gesture? Well, it seems to me that this is a serious matter. In the olden days, in the strict and pious days of our forefathers, men considered their marriage rings to be solemn symbols; they were never toyed with. The rings were always plain solid metal with no jewels, and this symbolized the solid cohesive family bond. Such fundamental symbols are certainly not to be trifled with, Rabbi.

But besides their symbolism, rings have hidden powers too. Nowadays magic is not invoked as frequently as it once was, but in the medieval Jewish communities, rings were always inscribed with mystical symbols, such as the *Magen David*. Engraved rings were used in cures; you would encircle an abscess or a rash or a painful spot with a ring while reciting a healing incantation. Rings could also divine the future. How? Suspend a ring of pure gold over a goblet of water, and swing the ring. As it strikes the side of the cup, its different tones will reveal clues to future events.

Rings have always been serious and important, both ceremonially and magically. My grandmother treated all rings with respect and with reverence – and it was grandmother who told me the famous story of Rabbi Petahiah and the magical ring. Rabbi Petahiah – that is, Petahiah ben Jacob of Regensburg – was a traveler who toured the entire world, and he wrote about his adventures in a book called *Sivuv ha-Olam* ("Around the World"). During his travels, Petahiah also wrote letters to his friend Abraham ben Alexander, Achselrad of Cologne. One letter had to do with a gold ring and with the sudden poverty and the eventual redemption of a famous rabbi of Syria.

"My dear Rabbi Abraham – [began the letter]

"I have just met a fine young man, a Jew from Augsburg. He has agreed to carry this letter to my good friend, Rabbi Joedelyn of Augsburg, who I am certain will then arrange to transport it to you. I write to wish you and your family well, to convey my fondest greetings to all the Jews of your blessed community in Cologne, and to praise the good Lord God (blessed be He) and His Almighty Name for ever and ever, amen.

"I will not trouble you with the details of my many wagon rides and my subsequent sea voyages. Suffice it to say that they safely brought me here to the Oriental regions, regions that are so near to the great Holy Land where someday the Messiah shall return and deliver us and resurrect all souls and rebuild the Temple on Zion, amen. I write now in order to record for you some details of the lands and the peoples that I have seen in these old and foreign realms. The bright and glorious hand of God is visible everywhere, if only we look – praise the Lord Yahweh-Elohim.

"As you might imagine, my old friend, I have had many, many adventures in traveling here. I hope – if the good Lord is willing – to relate more of these events to you in person. For now, let me just say that after touring the Holy Lands of Palestine, I turned north through Syria. First, I passed through the pleasant port city of Jebeil, and most recently I have found myself in the ancient town of Tripolis.

"Tripolis is the chief town in a large coastal region of Syria known as Beirut. (I might mention that there is also a city, a port town, named Beirut.) Tripolis itself is inland on a peninsula – the town center is perhaps five kilometers from the seaport of Al-Mina. The peninsula juts out into the Mediterranean Sea, and the great sea walls, each with its own imposing tower, are visible from the town.

"Everywhere there are evidences of Phoenicia and of Rome, for this was a center of commerce in those biblical days. Tripolis itself is fortified with walls and with brick garrisons, reminders of its many sieges by the Arabs and by the Greeks. And man has not been the only ravager here: the city was totally destroyed by an earthquake five hundred years ago. When the townspeople tell about that terrible devastation, they can still point to a vast crack in the ground.

"Tripolis is thick with people – it must have at least twenty thousand residents. The main ruling family is called 'Ammar, and they are patrons of culture. The 'Ammar library has over one hundred thousand books, but unfortunately Jews are not allowed to use it. The major industries in Tripolis are sugar refining and papermaking. Fancy glassware – glass pieces cut with the figures of eagles, griffins, and lions, and glass beakers, flasks, goblets, mosque lamps, and vases, all with intricate enameled designs – is exported from here to Venice. In addition, the town has more than four thousand looms for weaving fine linen.

"As is typical for the Syrian coast, the weather is cloudless and warm in the summer, and the nights are damp but not unpleasant. The rainy season begins in the fall, in the month of *Tishri*, and it ends in the spring in *Iyar*. Being so near to the sea, Tripolis is greener than the inland regions of Syria, and there are many evergreen shrubs and date palms.

"Tripolis has long had an active Jewish community, and I easily met a number of wealthy Jews who made me feel quite welcome. To my eye, the Syrian Hebrews appear to have mixed repeatedly with the Arabian and Aramaean races: no doubt, all the Semitic tribes of the Holy Lands have intermixed over the centuries. In Tripolis, the Jews are sunny and outgoing, just like the climate. I and my new friends have passed many warm and pleasant hours in praising the glory of the good Lord God and in reviewing the local Jewish history. Among the many tales that I heard, there is one in particular that I would like to record so that you may share it too:

"Once upon a time (I was told) in the city of Tripolis, there lived a distinguished rabbi named Johel ibn Moses. Johel was wealthy and well educated. He knew the seventy languages of mankind. He prayed devoutly, and he did his best to adhere to all aspects of the holy Law. By trade, Rabbi Johel was a glass merchant. With his own money he supported a yeshiva that educated more than one hundred pupils a year. Also, he funded the local Benevolent Society, and his family served daily meals for poor and homeless Jews.

"As you know, Abraham, the world goes on and the great wheel of fortune turns–and, as the proverb goes: 'When the rope finally becomes too tight, further strain makes it snap.' One year troubles overstretched Johel ibn Moses, and suddenly his good fortune snapped and he became poor. Business turned sour in the winter. Employees defrauded him. In the spring, he was robbed. Then new taxes appeared, and glass shipments dropped precipitously. By the summer, the pious Rabbi Johel found himself absolutely penniless. He was now so poor that he could barely support his family. He could afford no money for charity. His yeshiva was forced to close. Rabbi Johel himself could not concentrate on his teaching, and he soon became of little help to his family, his followers, or his students.

"Nightly, poor Rabbi Johel tossed and turned in bed. He was constantly tired. He lost his appetite. His head ached. The Rabbi thought to himself, 'What shall I do now? Before this, I always gave money and help freely, for the good Lord's sake. I have done many good deeds for other people–at least, I have tried my very best. Now I myself am desperately poor. And I am feeling terrible; perhaps I have some fatal disease.'

"All manner of possible maladies rolled about in Johel ibn Moses' imagination. 'What shall I do?' he worried over and over again. 'Ah, well–I will accept my fate. Everything is determined by the good Lord God, blessed be He, Who does no injustice. However, I cannot help wondering what sin I have committed?'

"In the mornings, when the the day was still cool and when the sun shone brightly, the Rabbi tried to pull himself together. 'What is the good of complaining?' he thought. 'So I am poor–there are always those who are in worse situations than I am.'

"Then he would continue to talk to himself. 'Now, Johel,' he would say, 'take some action. . . .' And one day, he thought, 'Let me see–there *is* one constructive thing that I can do. I can take a pilgrimage. I can get some perspective. I can go out into the world and regain my strength and begin again. But I had best leave town quietly: it will upset the fewest people this way. Perhaps I can recover my balance and return strong and rested. I may even be able to think of a way to make some money. Then I can resume my old charitable lifestyle. Maybe I can even reopen the yeshiva. Certainly I should be able to provide a better life for my family–if only I can earn some money and stop worrying constantly.'

"Rabbi Johel called his favorite pupils together. He said to them, 'Young men, I have done my best to help you up until now. I have given you food and clothing. I have taught you the Torah and the Talmud. Now I will tell you a secret–and I hope that you will act toward me as I have acted toward you.'

"The young men were worried. First they were quiet, but then they all talked at once, saying, 'Rabbi, by all means tell us your secret.' 'Perhaps we can help.' 'Certainly, we will stand by you.' 'Rabbi, what can we do?' and 'We will be faithful to you as long as the Almighty Lord God grants us life.'

"Ah, my old friend Abraham, it always helps to hear that others love you and will help you. Johel ibn Moses had support. Was the day suddenly brighter? A surge of strength ran through his arms and legs. He had the devotion of friends–and so Rabbi Johel took heart. He sat down on a wooden prayer bench, and he said, 'Listen, my young friends, I have become poor. But why is this? Has the great wheel of fortune revolved in its inexorable way and have I just fallen underneath? Or have I sinned by mistake? I am afraid that I cannot tell. When you are in the middle of a complex situation, you lose your perspective: little things become mountains–at the same time you can miss seeing the truly big and important matters.'

"The Rabbi sighed. 'So,' he continued, 'there is no other course for me than to leave Tripolis.'

"The students began to protest. 'Just a moment, young men,' said the Rabbi. 'I have given this much thought. If I have sinned, then I must go on a pilgrimage and repent. Or, if I have just fallen on hard times, then I must regain my balance in life. In any case–I must leave. Please do not think badly of me. I have done my best for you and for the others who touch my life.'

"The pupils looked at one another. One young man said, 'Rabbi, although you are clearly suffering, you are still a comfort to us. We will miss you if you go.'

"The Rabbi smiled, and he said, 'Thank you for saying that. However, I need to get some distance from the difficulties here. My trials have become a continuous storm. My reversals and the uncertainties of my future roll around in my mind continuously. At the moment, I do not have sufficient strength to help you too.'

"The students listened and they talked among themselves. Finally one of them said, 'Rabbi, we will do whatever you want. We will share our money and our clothes with you. In fact, perhaps we can join you on your pilgrimage.'

"The Rabbi shook his head, but the boys insisted. They talked back and forth, and eventually Johel ibn Moses agreed to take five of his best pupils with him. So, one morning, Rabbi Johel said to his wife, 'My dear, I must go on a holy pilgrimage, and I do not know when I will return. If you need anything, contact my brother in Sidon or my uncle in Tyre–they can help in times of trouble.'

"Rabbi Johel's wife raised her eyebrows. She looked at her husband. 'Very well,' she sighed. 'Take care of yourself, dear, and do not be gone too long. You *do* need a vacation. Be sure to walk slowly, though: you know that your heart is weak.'

"Johel ibn Moses nodded, and he kissed his wife good-bye. Then Rabbi Johel met his five best students outside the city walls, and they began to walk north and east. And neither the students nor anyone in the Jewish community of Tripolis knew where the group was going– for the Rabbi himself could not say.

"The Rabbi left, and finally people realized that he had suffered very serious problems. The Jews of Tripolis had always assumed that Rabbi Johel was a rock, a stable boulder in their community. People were shaken to see that even the strongest hills can be decimated by the unpredictable storms of fate.

"Meanwhile, the Rabbi and his five students traveled; they roamed the Holy Lands and the surrounding countries for two long years. Their clothes became torn. Their money was quickly exhausted. And they became pious beggars, totally dependent on charity.

"The wayfarer's life was tiring, monotonous, and lonely. At first it had seemed an adventure, but eventually one of the students said to Rabbi Johel, 'When will this wandering end? We have no clothes and no money. People close their doors in our faces – they consider us to be useless vagrants.'

"And another young man asked, 'How can you regain your financial position by just rambling from town to town?'

"A third boy commented gently, 'And, Rabbi, you still seem depressed.'

"The other youths nodded. Then one said, 'We mean no disrespect, sir, but perhaps we should return to our parents. We can go back to our studies. Then we can marry and we can raise families.'

"Finally, the fifth student said, 'Yes, Rabbi, it is time for us to return to Tripolis.'

"Rabbi Johel listened quietly. Then he said, 'My boys, I have nothing but praise for your loyalty. And now you are correct – my problems are beginning to distort your young lives too. You should return home. However, let me ask you for a favor. Stay with me four days more, until after the next Sabbath. Then I will let you go, in the Name of the great Lord God (blessed be He). You see, I feel that this week God may send us something good: perhaps through the great mercy of our wonder-working Lord, through His amazing grace, we may still be able to return home together.'

"The students looked at one another, and one boy said, 'Certainly, Rabbi – we have been together so long now that we may as well remain for a few days more.' So they all continued their travels.

"Later that morning, the Rabbi and his companions came to an oasis, with a few small trees surrounding a thick tangle of underbrush. Jipijapa plants crowded together, interwoven with knotroot grasses. Windhovers, turnstones, and tanglepickers wheeled and soared in the warm breezes overhead. Johel ibn Moses had a sudden dizzy feeling: his head felt light, his stomach tightened, and his legs became weak. 'Young men,' said the Rabbi, 'I think that I need to rest a moment. Go on ahead; I will be with you soon.'

"The pupils walked ahead, talking among themselves and discussing various points of Law. Meanwhile, Rabbi Johel sat on the ground by a tree, but the dizzy feeling did not pass. Was he going to die? His heart was beating too fast. He felt very strange and very uncomfortable. He closed his eyes. Then he heard a noise, and he looked around. A small animal, a gerbil, was hopping nearby in the dried grass.

"'How curious,' thought the Rabbi, 'to see this nighttime animal in the daylight.' As the Rabbi watched, he saw an even more unusual sight. The gerbil bounced to the small marshy spring nearby. It lapped at the water, and it washed its paws. The Rabbi moved to get a better look. A branch on the ground cracked, the animal looked up suddenly and it hopped and leaped and it bounced away; and as it left, something gold and shiny fell to the ground.

"The Rabbi got up. He walked over to the place where the little animal had been. There was a gold ring on the ground. Rabbi Johel picked up the ring, and he turned it around and around in his hand. The ring was worn and scratched. Inside was etched the *Magen David* symbol, and the word 'Shaddai' was written seven times. What was this? Was it a holy omen? The Rabbi held the ring, and he felt better. He was no longer dizzy; he felt calm again. Perhaps this was the beginning of something new and good.

"Rabbi Johel put the ring on his finger. He felt stronger. He hurried to catch up with the boys, who were now far ahead. When he joined them, they were discussing the Book of Isaiah; Rabbi Johel listened for a moment and then he began to comment. Because their talk was intense, their walk seemed short, and soon they reached the next town. Now the Rabbi had an animated glow. His clothes were worn and dirty, but he had the air of a man one should respect. The Rabbi was welcomed by the small Jewish community there: in fact, he was greeted as a *hakham*, a wandering rabbinical scholar and an interpreter of the Law.

"People asked him questions, and the Rabbi answered in a deep mellow voice. Rabbi Johel spoke so forcefully and so insightfully and so eloquently that his listeners were spellbound. He recited detailed portions of the Holy Scriptures and the Talmud. He made his points with fascinating tales and even his simplest examples were drawn with vivid pictures. The local Jews vied for the Rabbi's attention. They gave him and his students food and clothes. They asked if he would stay as a permanent teacher. Then the Rabbi and his students remained in the village for another week, studying, praying, and teaching, and the people treated them like scholarly princes.

"Finally, however, it was time to go. 'Now we will return to Tripolis together,' said the Rabbi to his students. But as he was about to leave, Rabbi Johel was approached by a Gentile. 'Rabbi,' said the man, 'may I speak to you alone?'

"The two men went off, walking by themselves through the marketplace. 'Rabbi,' said the man quietly, 'I am a Jew. However, because of many family and business complications I cannot admit this openly. In fact, such a confession might cost my life and perhaps the lives of members of my family. I have heard you preach – and frankly, I am stunned by your wisdom and your holy thoughtfulness. If only I could be like you! I know that I cannot atone for all the sins of my life, but within the limits of my weak personality, I try my best.'

"The two men were silent for a while as they continued walking. After a few minutes, the man continued: 'Rabbi, I should like to give you a thousand gold coins. I know that with this money you will do good deeds. You can put the money to far better use than I can.'

"The Rabbi stopped walking, and he looked intently at the man. 'Of course, sir,' said Rabbi Johel, 'this would be a wonderfully gracious and tempting gift. Nonetheless, you must think and rethink your offer. First – can you really afford to give away this vast sum of money? Second – will it make you feel any better in the end?'

"The man began to say, 'Oh yes, I –'

"But the Rabbi interrupted him: 'Please, go home, my friend, and sleep with the idea tonight. If you still feel the same way in the bright sunlight of tomorrow morning, then I will accept. On the other hand, if in the dawn of a new day the idea appears unrealistic, then I will also understand. Remember, the holy Lord God (blessed be He) appreciates this gesture of yours in any case.'

"The Rabbi patted the man on the back, and the two men parted company. The next morning, after prayers, a boy came looking for the Rabbi. The boy gave Rabbi Johel a heavy sack. The Rabbi did not open it – he knew that it was filled with coins. This is the good Lord God's money, thought Rabbi Johel, and I am only a temporary custodian. Then Rabbi Johel told his five faithful pupils that it was now time to leave the town and return to Tripolis. The young men gathered their belongings. With the well-wishes of the townsfolk ringing in their ears, the small group of pilgrims left the town and headed home.

"Johel ibn Moses had been gone from Tripolis for two long years, and it was a warm summer afternoon, on the twenty-ninth day of the month of *Tammuz*, when he returned. Word spread quickly. People asked each other, 'Where has the Rabbi been?' and 'How does he look now that he has returned?' and 'What are his plans for the future?' In the synagogue, people who had not known Rabbi Johel stared with envy at those who had been his friends, and everyone crowded around him. The five students also talked and nodded and answered endless questions. They told their adventures in detail, and in the telling, the days of travel seemed surprisingly fine. But the Rabbi himself said little – only repeating, 'Friends, I am back, and I hope to resume my old life.'

"With five hundred of the gold coins, the Rabbi restarted his glass business. With two hundred of the gold coins, he repaired the old yeshiva, and with one hundred coins, the Rabbi revived the local Benevolent Society. Another one hundred coins began a special fund for orphans and needy children. With fifty of the gold coins, the Rabbi paid a debt that the Jewish community had owed the governor of Tripolis. And the Rabbi set aside the final fifty gold coins for a future emergency. Then the Rabbi resumed his teaching, and people said that he was more inspiring than ever before.

"These gifts built a solid foundation for the Jewish community of Tripolis and their effects can still be felt today. After he returned from his magical pilgrimage, Rabbi Johel was fond of saying, 'We each must do our best in this unpredictable world. We can do great things, if only the Lord gives us the strength.' At times like these, observant listeners noticed that the Rabbi would absently play with his scratched gold ring – gently he would rub this ring, and he would smile.

"Well, that is the whole story – and I must end my letter now. I think of you, Abraham, as you read this in your holy study in Cologne; I know that you are sitting there quietly in the bright warm magic light of our golden Lord God. Do you have a gold ring, my friend? I cannot remember at the moment, try as I might. Ah, but why do I bother to ask – of course you have a golden ring! For the beneficent Lord gives wondrous gifts to us as children and He lets us keep them into our old age. And I remember that long ago He gave us magic grasslet rings – rings that once we wove in our childhood, on mystical magical summer afternoons on the banks of the River Rhine. They were golden grasslets from golden days – and that is gold enough for me, my friend. Hallelujah and amen, good Abraham; hallelujah and a golden amen.

*"Your childhood friend,
Petahiah, the son of Jacob"*

Hello, Rabbi, I will be with you in a moment. I cannot leave until every tablecloth is folded, otherwise the day has not ended properly. . . . There, now I am finished at last and I can sit next to you by the stove.

Frankly, I am not sleepy either. Everyone says that old people are always falling asleep, but I sleep less now that I am old. It is the nature of old men to go into their last days awake and open-eyed. It gives me more time, but then I seem to muse away the hours and not much actually gets accomplished. I sit and remember and review. It is just like my grandmother, who was always reminiscing to herself. Sometimes when she talked to me it seemed as if she were just taking up in the middle of a single story that she was telling herself continuously. Perhaps, Rabbi, there *was* only one long story and I just picked up parts of it when she happened to be speaking aloud. In fact, that is exactly how she described her favorite old rabbi, Abraham ben Alexander, Achselrad of Cologne. He was a continuous story-teller. He lived to be seventy years of fine old age, and during that time he was always writing or talking or having visions – his life was one long story of gentle adventure upon adventure upon adventure.

For example, my grandmother told me that one time, in his

younger years, Abraham visited King Ferdinand II of Castile in Spain. (Although on that trip, Abraham called himself "Nathan Alexander" for some unknown reason.) Ferdinand II was King of Leon. What is that, Rabbi? I have already told you this? Did I also tell you about Gamaliel's letter to God? No, it had nothing to do with Spain—it is a story from old Cologne. You see, one night, while writing his famous *Keter Shem Tov*, Rabbi Abraham ben Alexander looked up, and in the yellow light of the candle on his desk he found Gamaliel standing sadly in the doorway.

Rabbi Abraham had been writing about angels and the wind. "Although demons are associated with storm winds," wrote Achselrad, "angels are the true powers behind the winds, especially the gentle spring breezes." Achselrad paused. He tapped his chin. His teacher, the mystic Eliazer of Worms, had said, "Angels come and go in the winds. They are made of the most tenuous substance. In fact, to men, angels appear as unsubstantial as the wind, and the holy word *ruach*—wind—is also the word for spirit." Just as old Achselrad was remembering these words, the light of his candle began to flicker. The Rabbi looked up, and there stood Gamaliel ben Simon ha-Kohen.

Gamaliel was very, very poor. His family was often hungry and they were always dressed in rags. Now it was the end of the winter, the Passover holiday was approaching, and Gamaliel found that he had barely enough food for his children. Gamaliel was weak and lame, and he could not work. The Jewish community had helped as best as they could, but it was a difficult year for everyone; all the sources of extra money were gone. Gamaliel felt desperate. Therefore, he had come to talk with the Rabbi, hoping perhaps to devise some new plan.

"My friend, how do you manage to get any money at all?" asked the Rabbi.

"It is my wife who earns us money," said Gamaliel. "My wife is wonderful, Rabbi. She is beyond all worth, like the scriptural Proverb":

> Who can appraise a capable wife?
>   Her worth is beyond all else in life—
> Like a ship that is laden with merchandise
>   She brings from afar good food and spice;
> And for the needy she opens her door:
>   A good wife is generous to all the poor.

"Recently my wife had temporary work in the *matzoh* bakery."

(As you probably know, Rabbi, *matzoh*-making employed bakery
women in Cologne for about a month at the end of the winter. After
Hannukah, the flour traders began to buy extra flour, and before *Purim*,
the owners of the *matzoh* bakeries prepared the halls where the *matzoh*
would be baked. All furniture was removed and the walls were
whitewashed. The boards on which the dough would be rolled were
brought down from the attic, and they were freshly planed; also, a
special table was fitted with a metal sheet for perforating the *matzoh*.
   The baking itself began right after *Purim*, and, once it had started,
baking continued from the early morning until ten or eleven at night.
Several times a day, the work was interrupted to reheat the ovens;
during these breaks, the workers rested and ate their meals. The work
was hard – it often lasted seventeen hours a day – but the bakeries were
always cheerful, and the women sang as they worked.
   In addition to the private bakeries, large Jewish communities,
such as the one in Cologne, had a community bakery where *matzohs*
were baked for the poor families. The community bakery was run by
volunteers from the Benevolent Society. Flour was bought with community council funds, and wood was donated for the ovens. Two
volunteers also spent the week before Passover taking a cart from
house to house, and every housewife tried to contribute at least a little
something. In this way, the poor received a bit of meat and wine and
vegetables and even some old clothes when they got their *matzohs* for
the holidays.
   In the week before Passover, all the baking was completed and all
the *matzohs* had been bought or had been given away. Housewives
looked forward to that day, for they would say, "Once the *matzoh* is in
the house, then half of Passover has already arrived.")

In any case, Rabbi, now the bakery work had ended. Moreover,
this particular year, the Jewish community of Cologne was unusually
poor. There was little *matzoh* to be distributed to the needy. No extra
meat was available and there were few spare vegetables. Gamaliel's
family had received only a small basket of *matzohs*. Gamaliel felt
entirely at a loss, and he asked himself, "Whatever shall I do?"

Gamaliel's wife tried to cheer him up. "If we have *matzoh*," she said, "then half of Passover is already in the house."

But Gamaliel asked, "And where, my dear, will the other half come from?"

No answer was forthcoming, so Gamaliel had gone to consult the Rabbi. And now Gamaliel was explaining to the Rabbi how his wife's temporary income had just barely kept the family alive. Passover was almost upon them, and Gamaliel's poverty looked especially bleak. "Rabbi," said Gamaliel, "my family and I are really suffering. You know the old talmudic proverb: 'There are three things that are hard for man to bear: heart disease, intestinal affliction, and, worst of all, an empty purse.' "

Rabbi Abraham listened sympathetically. "The poorbox in our synagogue is completely empty—this is a hard year in Cologne, my friend," said the Rabbi sadly. "I hear that it is very bad throughout all of northern Europe. Sometimes we must be patient, Reb Gamaliel. Remember the other talmudic proverb: 'Charity, fervent prayer, and repentance can modify any decrees of Providence that may have been issued against us. A devout petition can bring about Divine help.' "

"Yes, yes, Rabbi, I understand," said Gamaliel. "But I cannot provide sufficient food for the Passover holiday with prayer alone. Whatever shall I do?"

The Rabbi closed his book. He bent his head to the side, and he stroked his beard. Then he closed his eyes. Rabbi Abraham seemed to be asleep. After a few minutes, Gamaliel ben Simon said quietly, "Rabbi?"

Old Achselrad opened his eyes. "My good friend," he said quietly, "I have had a vision."

Gamaliel looked at the Rabbi uncertainly. Rabbi Abraham was an old man. There were wrinkles at the edges of his eyes. His eyebrows were grey—and now it seemed as if the Rabbi's eyes were closing again. Gamaliel ben Simon asked gently, "You have had a vision, Rabbi?"

"Yes," said the Rabbi, "and here is what I have seen: I have seen the Heavens with their fine and warming breezes. These winds are really the angels flying about and ruffling the great silver-haired mane of the Most Holy One as He sits upon His Throne of Glory, amen." Old Achselrad stroked his beard; he was smiling, and he looked far away, beyond the little back study room. "Gamaliel," he continued,

"you must write a letter. Write a letter to the Almighty Lord God,
blessed be He. Ask Him to provide for your Passover holiday."

This seemed like very strange advice, and Gamaliel said, "I should
write a letter to God? How shall I send it?"

"Just release it to the wind; the angels will take care of it from
there," said Rabbi Abraham ben Alexander, Achselrad of Cologne.

Gamaliel ben Simon ha-Kohen stood uncertainly. Was he
hearing correctly? Rabbi Abraham was a holy mystic, but sometimes
he said things that were strange even for a mystic. Gamaliel waited.
However, the Rabbi was looking down at his book; therefore, Gamaliel turned in the doorway, and he went back home. Gamaliel thought
about the Rabbi's counsel, and after a while, Gamaliel wrote a letter.
Carefully, he listed the few things that he and his family needed. He
wrote:

To my good Lord –

I write to ask humbly for a favor; I need some help. As You know, I am
not well and I cannot work. The Passover holidays are almost here, and
I would like very much for my children to remember them always as
special times. (You know how memories of the special times of childhood carry you through the hard times to come.) A little extra food,
some meat, and some vegetables would be welcome. And is there any
way to get a new shirt for my son Jacob? He shivers on cold days, and
this makes me feel sad. I thank You for the health of my family.

> Reverently,
> *Gamaliel, the son of Simon*
> *A poor Jew in the city of Cologne*

The letter was finished. Now what should he do with this
request? He felt foolish just throwing it into the air, but the Rabbi had
said to release it to the wind. So, late that night, when no one was
looking, Gamaliel climbed onto the roof of the house next door. His leg
was weak and painful, and he went very slowly. When he reached the
top, he stood on the roof and he held onto a carved gable. Gamaliel
waited and waited. One hour passed and then a second came and went.
Suddenly he felt a breeze and then a wind. Was now the time?
Gamaliel shivered. He took the parchment. He tossed it up into the air.

The wind grabbed it, and off it flew into the night. Gamaliel watched as the letter disappeared. But in his heart of hearts, Gamaliel despaired; some sages claimed that the wondrous celestial Heaven was a distance of three thousand five hundred years journey. How could this little piece of paper ever find its way to the good Lord God?

Soon, Gamaliel could no longer see the paper, and slowly he climbed down from the roof of the house. Meanwhile, the wind blew and blew. A small gale arose, and the letter of Gamaliel ben Simon flew along on the wings of the wind. It sped all night, and in the early morning hours it landed near the house of Henry, the count of the Palatinate of the Rhine region. The Palatinate counts ruled various districts along the Rhine valley, and in those years the counts lived in the castle of Juttenbuhel, near Heidelberg–and it was to Juttenbuhel that the letter of Gamaliel ben Simon ha-Kohen rushed, with the aid of the angels of the northerly winds of medieval Germany, amen.

That morning, Count Henry was out in his garden with his dogs. The letter blew in, and it fell at his feet. The count bent down. He picked up the parchment. He read the thin careful handwriting. "I wonder," he thought, "who is so desperate as to send a letter to God?"

Count Henry brought the letter in to his wife, and, over breakfast, she read it also. "Listen, husband," she said. "All of Germany honors you as its lord, and this Jew must feel the same way. Clearly, Mr. Gamaliel Simon of Cologne had in mind a god on earth–that is to say, you, his liege lord, the Palatinate count. This Jew has written to you, asking for help, and he wrote in a most reverent and respectful fashion."

The count thought a moment, and he smiled and said, "Yes, of course–this is very appropriate. I wonder what I should do?"

Then his wife said, "My dear, the request is so modest; you should fulfill it."

"You are certainly right," said Count Henry. After breakfast, the count ordered a royal cart to be filled with food and clothes, and he immediately sent it north to poor Gamaliel's house. The wagon left the castle of Juttenbuhel, and it traveled the old river road: it went north along the River Rhine, past Mannheim, Worms, Mainz, Coblenz, and Bonn, until finally it came to Cologne.

When he arrived, the wagon driver asked directions to the Jewish Quarter, and soon the fancy wagon was rolling down Judengasse

Street. People stared. Children ran behind. Eventually, the driver stopped at the house of Gamaliel ben Simon ha-Kohen. Gamaliel and his family could not believe their eyes. It was a gift from the great Count Henry?! What had this poor Jew done to receive such charity from the count? No one knew, and Gamaliel did not dare to tell them about his letter. Neighbors came and helped unload the goods. Besides meat and vegetables and extra clothes, the treasures included imported spices, newly packaged and pure for the holidays, and there were also foreign sugars from Candia and myrtle and citrons from the Mediterranean coast.

When Rabbi Abraham heard about the arrival of the wagon, he too came to Gamaliel's house. He smiled when he saw the tremendous load of goods that had arrived, and he smiled when he saw how Gamaliel was sharing it with everyone who came by. But most of all, the Rabbi smiled when he saw the round and unbelieving eyes of Gamaliel's little children. And as they stood by the wagon, which seemed to take hours and hours to unpack, the little ones' hair blew gently in the Passover wind, a gentle mystical medieval wind that rushed and whispered through the Jewish Quarter of old Cologne, once upon a time with the angels from long, long ago.

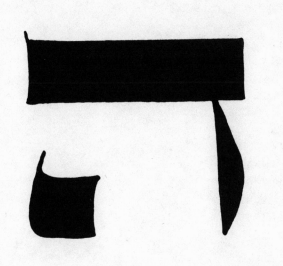

ood evening, Rabbi. Of course, please sit here by the stove: the night fire helps me to become sleepy also. You and I are not blessed like old Reb Elbaum. Once again I saw him nodding off during the last prayers this evening. He has learned to sway piously even while asleep. Sometimes he even smiles, as if in a happy dream. Reb Elbaum must have inherited some magic from the mystic Achselrad – and I suppose that tonight you and I could use a dose of Achselrad ourselves.

Rabbi Achselrad – that is, Abraham ben Alexander of Cologne – had many mystical abilities, and he was always conjuring visions in the synagogue. I doubt whether he would be tolerated nowadays, but my grandmother said that Rabbi Abraham was also a scholar; and he himself always claimed that his visions came from devout and pious study. In any case, many an astonishing event took place during his rabbinate – or so my grandmother (blessed be her memory) was told. For example, one day Rabbi Achselrad's vision from Psalm 90 saved a poor old man named Sheshet; I will tell you how it happened.

As I have said, Abraham Achselrad was a scholar. Night and day you could find him working on a set of Kabbalistic tomes of mystical knowledge; the most famous of these was the *Keter Shem Tov*. (This book was never published, and now it exists only as a secret manuscript hidden above the ancient Cologne yeshiva.) It was one afternoon while writing this very book that the Rabbi heard a noise, and he looked up. One of the Rabbi's congregants, Benjamin ben Elia, was standing fearfully in the doorway. "Please," called Benjamin, "come quickly and help rescue old Reb Sheshet. He has been charged with grave-robbing!"

And what is the background for this terrible charge? It is this:

Many, many years before, two young boys of Cologne, Sheshet ben Aleydis and Ksil ben Moshe, had been fast and inseparable friends. One day, the boys were walking down Hohestrasse Street, the main street of medieval Cologne. They were near the Waid Markt area, when three angry young Gentiles stepped up to them and said, "We do not let Jews dirty our streets around here."

One of the Gentiles had a knife. He grabbed Ksil. Ksil froze, but Sheshet pushed the ruffian away. Then, quick as a wink, Sheshet turned and he pulled Ksil along after him. The two young Jews ran, ran, ran, and safely they made their way back to the Jewish Quarter. The boys ran directly into the synagogue; then they stood panting in the anteroom and it seemed as if it were many hours before their breathing was calm and easy again.

Over the years, the boys grew apart, but Ksil never forgot that incident. Eventually, Ksil and Sheshet went their separate ways entirely, and Ksil ben Moshe became rich while Sheshet remained poor. As he aged, Ksil quietly decided to set aside one hundred gold coins for his boyhood friend, Sheshet ben Aleydis.

Years came, and years went. Seven cycles of seven years passed, and one day Ksil took ill. On his deathbed, the rich man said to his children, "I have left you much wealth, and, of course, I bequeath you all my love for ever and ever, amen. Also, my dear ones, you must do me this one last good deed. There are one hundred gold coins in the sack under my bed. Please bury this money with me."

Then Ksil sent for Sheshet. When Sheshet arrived, Ksil asked the other people to leave his room, and he said in a low voice to Sheshet, "I have always remembered how you bravely saved my life, old friend."

Sheshet was puzzled. "When was that?" he asked.

"It was when we were boys walking down Hohestrasse Street and we were attacked by the three men with a knife," said Ksil.

"Oh, yes," said Sheshet, "but it was not real bravery. I was as scared as you were."

"You are too modest, Sheshet. In any case, I have never forgotten your help. If you ever come into dire straits, if you ever have a terrible emergency, then I have set aside a large sum of money for you. To protect it, I am requesting that the money be buried with me. If you need it, take it from my grave – the Almighty Lord God (blessed be He) will forgive you, and He will even bless you, amen."

The rich man was worn out from this speech. He closed his eyes and lay back in his bed, breathing heavily. Then Ksil continued to weaken, and two days later he died. Ksil ben Moshe had been a fine and respected man; many members of the community participated in the seven days of mourning – and no one in the family washed or shaved or wore shoes, and each member of the family and all the close friends tore a rip in their clothes.

Years continued to slip by, and the wheel of fortune turned in its unpredictable revolution. Now Sheshet was an old, old man. He had always been poor, but one day Sheshet ben Aleydis found himself completely helpless. His wife fell ill. His boss closed his workshop and left Cologne. The weather turned foul for weeks, and food became very expensive. Sheshet desperately needed money. Night after night, he tossed and he turned, trying to think of ways to earn more money. Slowly, he sold all the valuables from his house. Still there was not enough money. Finally, Sheshet built up his courage. He prayed all night. He said the *Shema* three times. Then, after prayers the next day, he went to the graveyard in the early afternoon in order to claim his special emergency inheritance.

Sheshet took a small shovel, and he walked to the Cologne Jewish cemetery, the *Am Toten Juden*. Since Roman times the *Am Toten Juden* had been at the south of the city, outside the walls, outside the town limits, and some distance from the Jewish Quarter. In those days, the Jewish cemetery was a quiet place, unwatched by the Gentiles, and burial was permitted without any hindrance and without any tax.

As Sheshet approached the *Am Toten Juden*, he surveyed the area. The cemetery was on a small rise. No one was about, not even Jewish visitors. The tombstones stood smooth and silent. Sheshet walked in and he found old Ksil's grave. As quietly as possible, Sheshet ben Aleydis began to dig. However, a Gentile workman soon passed by. He noticed the Jew digging and he called the city guards, who came immediately. The officers found poor Sheshet with an open grave and with the sack of money that he had removed. Therefore, the guards dragged Sheshet to the local court.

Meanwhile, a friend of Sheshet's, Reb Benjamin ben Elia, was delivering some linens to the court building. He heard the guards discussing the case and immediately he hurried off to the synagogue. When he reached the old house of study, Benjamin stepped in the front door, he went through the anteroom, and he walked into the main prayer hall, which was filled with wooden benches. Quickly, Benjamin passed the twelve stained glass windows with their colored lions and snakes. He took no time to look up at the Holy stone Ark. He rushed through the door of the back study room. There, the Rabbi was bent over a book, and the shammas, Chayim ben Meir, was dozing on a bench along the wall.

Rabbi Abraham listened to Benjamin. Then he put on his hat and his coat. Without another word, the two men left for the ecclesiastical courthouse, and Shammas Chayim followed behind. That afternoon, the Archbishop himself was in court; this was Archbishop Adolph of Cologne, a noble and honorable prelate. Archbishop Adolph knew the Rabbi. "Rabbi," said the Archbishop sadly, "I am afraid that one of your Jews has committed grave-robbery. There is no question that he has desecrated a grave. We have accusers, witnesses, and evidence, including money recovered from the grave–unfortunately, Mr. Sheshet Aleydis must be jailed."

"I see," said Rabbi Abraham. Abraham Achselrad looked at the witnesses. He looked at the sack of money, he looked at Sheshet, and then he looked up at the Archbishop. Rabbi Abraham closed his eyes for a moment. Then he asked, "Have you a Bible here, good Archbishop?"

"Of course," replied the Archbishop, and he instructed one of the officers to pass a leather volume to Rabbi Achselrad.

"Let us read from the Book of Psalms," said the Rabbi.

"I respect your religious views, Rabbi," said Archbishop Adolph, "but is this really relevant now?"

Rabbi Abraham Achselrad was holding the Holy Scriptures.

Suddenly his eyes opened wide. Then they closed tightly. Old Achselrad became weak, he sat on a nearby chair, and he took a deep breath – then he gently set down the Bible.

"Are you all right, Rabbi?" asked the Archbishop.

"I have just had a vision," said Rabbi Abraham. "I have seen the majestic Heavens."

There was silence for a moment. "Yes, I have seen the majestic Heavens and the Holy Throne of Glory. I have seen the firmament of the good Lord God (blessed be He) – He Who sees all and Who demands justice for all, especially for His children, the Jews. In addition, I have seen that Psalm 90 is quite important," said Abraham Achselrad. "And, if you will be so good as to hand me that holy book again, then I will read a bit of that Psalm":

> In each age with Your sanctification
> We have held our souls in trust –
> Then at the end of every generation
> You turn man back to dust;
>
> You say, "Crumble and disappear
> My mortal custodian" –
> To You a thousand years
> Are but a brief timespan.
>
> Men are just passersby
> Like grass we wither and we dry
> Like eagles our brief days quickly fly,
> Our years melt like a whispered sigh.
>
> Life is seventy years of journeying –
> Perhaps eighty for the strong –
> The hurrying years are tiring
> But they fade away before long;
>
> Now give us days of gladness
> For those earlier trying years,
> Give us wealth and contentedness,
> Even beyond the grave's final tears.

The Rabbi stopped, and he bowed his head. After a moment, the Archbishop said, "Of course that is a most serious and holy sentiment, Rabbi."

"It certainly is," said the Rabbi. "Now, my good Archbishop, you are a noted cleric. What would you say that this verse means?"

"What does it mean? Why, clearly it means that all men must die but that the Lord watches over the living."

Rabbi Abraham nodded. "Yes, good sir – and I would say that it means even more than that," said the Rabbi.

"You would?" asked the Archbishop. "Then pray tell, Rabbi Achselrad: What else do you read into this Psalm?"

The Rabbi looked to Heaven. "I would say, Archbishop Adolph, that the life of a mortal is short. Nonetheless, the good Lord God (blessed be He) watches over everyone. He takes care to help the unfortunate and to repay the kindly and to reward the just and the pious and the righteous, and He even reaches beyond the grave in order to help the living," said the Rabbi.

"Exactly what are you saying, Mr. Alexander?" asked the Archbishop.

"I am saying this, Archbishop: I have had a vision. I have seen that the man, Sheshet ben Aleydis, who presently stands accused, is in fact innocent."

"How can this be?" asked Archbishop Adolph. "No one can deny that Mr. Aleydis dug up a grave and took the money that was buried inside."

"My good Archbishop," said Achselrad, "let me show you the whole story. Let me share my vision with you."

The Archbishop conferred with his councilors. After a brief argument, the Archbishop of Cologne said, "If you can prove what you say, then I will reconsider my decision."

Rabbi Abraham Achselrad sat down again, and he closed his eyes. He began to sway. He shook strangely. The members of the court raised their eyebrows, and they looked at one another. Then the pious man opened his eyes, and he took a small parchment scroll from his pocket. The Rabbi covered the top of his head with a handkerchief, and he wrote a charm with holy names on the paper. The Archbishop could see that the charm began with a quotation from the Book of Exodus: "For I am Yahweh, your Restorer – I, the Lord God, am your

Healer . . ." but Archbishop Adolph could not make out the remainder of the words.

When the Rabbi finished writing, in his neat and tiny script, he rolled the parchment into a tight scroll and tied it with a cotton thread. The Rabbi tied and untied the thread – he knotted and unknotted it seven times – then he placed the charm on a table. There was silence. A dark cloud passed over the sun, although just moments before it had been the middle of a bright afternoon.

"Now," said the Rabbi, "we must send someone to the cemetery."

The Archbishop had seen the Rabbi's mystical workings before. Archbishop Adolph was fascinated by these holy conjurings and he agreed that the Rabbi's shammas, Chayim ben Meir, would go to the cemetery in the company of one of the guards. The shammas left the courthouse. He got a bowl of oil and honey, and he set off for the cemetery. As he walked along, Chayim watched for a white stick. When he found one, he picked it up and he carried it with him.

Soon Chayim and the guard reached the *Am Toten Juden*. Chayim stood at the head of Ksil's grave. After a moment, Chayim built up his courage – he struck the tombstone with the stick, he held the glass dish filled with oil and honey, and he recited:

> I conjure you, O spirit of the grave, Nahinah, who rests upon the bones of the dead. Accept this offering from my hand, and do my bidding. Bring to Rabbi Abraham the dead man Ksil son of Moshe. Make him stand erect and speak without fear; have him tell the truth without hesitation.

Nervously the guard looked around, but nothing happened. After a few minutes, the two men returned to the center of Cologne. When Chayim ben Meir reappeared in the courtroom, he handed the white stick to the Rabbi. The air remained dark. Suddenly, Chayim pointed to a blank side wall. Was a figure materializing? A dread fear fell upon all present. Some men shut their eyes. Everyone sat as if they had been frozen in their seats. But Rabbi Abraham said, "O spirit, we, the earthly court of justice, command you to speak. Tell us the truth, O shade of the departed one: What really happened?"

The room darkened still further. A vague shape could be seen, waxing and waning and wavering on the wall. This was the spirit of the dead man, the rich man: it was the shade of Ksil ben Moshe. Everyone remained as still as stone. After a while, the spirit began to speak. "It is true, Rabbi," said a mournful voice. "Sheshet was digging up my grave, and he was taking the money that I had instructed to be buried with me."

The Archbishop frowned, and he looked down at Sheshet ben Aleydis. The spirit of Ksil seemed to sigh, and then it continued to speak: "Once, my friends, I was alive like you. I was happy and wealthy. I had a fine family; memories of my family comfort me still, and I love them dearly—blessed be the Name of the Lord.

"I hope," said the spirit, "that the good Lord will bless Sheshet, too. You see, one day long, long ago, when we were just boys, this man—Sheshet ben Aleydis, the old Jew who stands here accused— saved my life. At that time we were only children. But in many ways, we remain children all our lives, and I have never forgotten his help. Good Sheshet never even hinted at any reward. He is a fine man, amen.

"When I was about to die, I decided that in order to pass to the Great Hereafter with no debts and with no regrets, I should leave some money for my boyhood friend. Therefore, I had my family bury me with one hundred gold coins for Sheshet ben Aleydis: I thought that the money would remain absolutely safe in the grave. Then I com-manded Sheshet—in the sight of the good Lord God, blessed be He—to take the money when he was most in need. I see that the wheel of fortune has turned and my childhood friend finds himself in desperate straits. Sheshet is a proud man, and he is a good man. He has only fulfilled my last and sacred request. Please do not punish him for this."

There was silence. Then the spirit of Ksil ben Moshe disappeared, and the room brightened once again.

Everyone was stunned. The Archbishop looked intently at Sheshet, he looked at the sack of money, and he looked at the wall, which was now blank and dull. Then Archbishop Adolph nodded, and he motioned to the guards. Sheshet ben Aleydis was released from custody, and he returned to the synagogue with the Rabbi. And Sheshet was given the money from the grave.

In the main prayer hall, Rabbi Abraham patted Sheshet on the shoulder, and the Rabbi said a prayer for old Sheshet, who repeated the words himself and felt calmer. Then the two men walked back to the cemetery. Evening was coming, floating lightly down the wide dark River Rhine. The two old men–the Rabbi and Sheshet ben Aleydis–walked quietly into the *Am Toten Juden*. They stood over the grave of the rich man, Ksil ben Moshe. Together, they said the benedictions for the dead, concluding:

> Help us to to live piously. In this way, the purity and the righteousness of our lives may bring honor to the memory of the gone and darkened ones, who now dwell in peace with You–thus shall we erect for them their eternal testament, their lasting memorial among men. May the soul of our departed friend be bound up in life everlasting. Praised be You, O Lord our God, Who gives life and Who takes it away again. Amen.

Sheshet bent down and patted the dirt on the newly covered grave. Then the Rabbi sprinkled another handful of good black earth over the bones of Ksil ben Moshe, who now rested in a gentle holy peace in the Great Hereafter, happy for ever and ever more.

h, good evening again, Rabbi. Yes, I know – it is always hard to sleep on the night of the full moon. Well, put your feet up on the side bench here and I will open the stove door.

Let me push the coals back. There is nothing like that white glow; it washes away the cares of a hard day. I heard your final benediction tonight, Rabbi. Do not try and deny it – you are overworked. Oh yes, even a shammas like me can tell. I kept one eye on you when I cleaned the dishes and I saw that you were watching the door, hoping that Reb Elbaum would leave early. But then Reb Anton stayed to argue about the scriptural passage – of course you are still worn out.

What is that? A story from me? Rabbi, all I know are the old children's tales, the grandmother fables. You need something new and fresh to keep your mind keen. Otherwise you will become a dreamy old man like me, and you will find yourself constantly musing and dozing and nodding off in front of the stove.

What do you mean you are already an old man? Do you really think that sixty years is old? Why, you are still a child. When you reach eighty, *then* you will be old. You doubt that you will live to see eighty years? If so, Rabbi, then you will never grow old. . . . All right, all right—let me see about a story.

Tonight you were talking about charity. I always feel reassured when I hear your favorite scriptural Proverb, the one that you repeated to Reb Anton:

> Wealth is a light commodity
>   On Judgment Day,
> But goodness, alms, and charity
>   Shall heavily weigh.

> Generosity and virtue,
>   Kind words with each breath—
> These will protect you
> From a sad and early death.

This Proverb reminds me of my grandmother's tale of old Heinrichus from medieval Cologne. Did you ever hear her tell about Heinrichus ben Jacob ha-Levi? You never knew her? That is too bad; you missed a fine woman. Ah well . . . anyway, Rabbi, I first heard about Heinrichus from my grandmother, may her soul visit happily with her parents forever.

Once upon a time, said my grandmother to me, there lived in Cologne on the River Rhine a pious scholar named Rabbi Abraham ben Alexander, Achselrad of Cologne. In Rabbi Abraham's congregation was an old man named Heinrichus ben Jacob ha-Levi. Heinrichus was always in a hurry to be charitable—and of course there were many, many opportunities in those days. One had only to listen, for word of needy people passed continuously through the Jewish community. Ah, but the availability of extra money was a fleeting thing then as it is today, Rabbi.

Anyway, one day Heinrichus was walking home after the morning prayers. Two men were talking in the courtyard outside the synagogue. "In a nearby town," said one of them, "there is a young girl who is ready and waiting to be married, but her family cannot raise a dowry and they cannot afford any of the wedding expenses." The other man shook his head sadly.

"I should help this girl," thought Heinrichus. "What more wonderful act of charity could one do? As Psalm 106 says":

> Happy are they who live life justly,
> Who are helpful and generous again and again –
> And please, O Lord, recall my charity
> When You reward Your loving children.

And then Heinrichus nodded to himself, because he remembered that in the Talmud this particular verse is said to refer especially to one who helps children.

So Heinrichus stopped in the courtyard of the yeshiva, and he asked the two men for more information. "Well, Heinrichus," said the first man, "this girl lives in Wahn. Both of her parents are dead. Now she is staying with a large family of cousins. The father in the family is ill and he begs for money, food, and discarded household goods; the mother sells rags. At the moment, the Jewish community of Wahn is penniless. The local Benevolent Society has been disbanded, and no one can contribute enough money to make even the smallest dowry. The poor girl does not have a dress: she wears an old coat, and she cannot afford to buy any clothes. Still, she hopes against hope to marry a fine young yeshiva student named Moshe. And Moshe himself is as poor as a synagogue mouse."

It was a sad but often repeated story. Heinrichus felt a tear come to his eye. He hurried home, and he gathered all the money that he had saved. Then that very afternoon, he walked southeast to the neighboring town of Wahn. Heinrichus ben Jacob located the girl, and he gave the money to her caretaker, her uncle. The family wept. They thanked good Heinrichus; they even clung to his coat.

Heinrichus cried too. He refused to tell the family his name, and as soon as he could, he left their house and headed back to Cologne. By now it was late in the day. Heinrichus walked and he walked and he walked. On the way home, the weather began to darken. Soon, Heinrichus was stopped by a rainstorm. The rain fell in a gray curtain on all sides. However, in the lightning, Heinrichus could see that the Jewish cemetery, the *Am Toten Juden*, was not far off, on a rise to the left of the road. Tombstones stood calmly in neat and even rows–the small hill of the *Am Toten Juden* sat alone but not lonely in God's mighty storm.

As he was sitting there under a tree, lightning flashed and thunder crashed and the wind blew. Heinrichus looked down the road and he looked up the road. A curtain of rain hid the distance. Suddenly, a huge and fearsome-looking man was bending over Heinrichus. "Are you Heinrichus ben Jacob ha-Levi?" asked the stranger.

Heinrichus began to shiver. "Yes, that is me," he answered.

"Your destiny is in my hands," said the stranger. "Your end is near."

The stranger had a drawn and bloody sword. And yes, Rabbi–it was Dumah, the black Angel of Death. Heinrichus ben Jacob was old. He knew that his death was near. Heinrichus turned pale, he lifted his eyes to Heaven, and he said, "O Lord, my holy God, I know that I am old. I know that I have had a long and full life. In fact, now that I have given away all my money, I suppose that I have only hard days ahead. Nonetheless, when actually faced with my end, I would rather live."

Dumah, the Angel of Death, said, "A holy Decree of Death has been written, Heinrichus. Your time has come. But you are a good and charitable man; therefore, I will allow you to reach your house and to lie down in your own bed, if you so wish."

Heinrichus shivered and he shook, but he nodded his head, so Dumah, the Angel of Death, disappeared. The storm ended. Slowly, Heinrichus continued on his way. As he walked the dark wet streets of Cologne, he saw the alleyway leading to the old yeshiva. "I had best pray one last time," he thought. Therefore, instead of going directly home, Heinrichus went into the synagogue building, where Rabbi Abraham was studying in the back room.

Heinrichus ben Jacob stood in the doorway to the Rabbi's study room. He was wet and pale; he was weak and tired. The Rabbi gave him a warm welcome, but Heinrichus shivered and he shook, and he trembled and he coughed.

"What is the problem?" asked Rabbi Abraham.

Heinrichus sat heavily on a bench, and he told his story to the mystic Abraham Achselrad.

The Rabbi listened intently. He stroked his beard, and he closed his eyes. After a moment, he opened his eyes again and he said, "Let me see what we can do, Heinrichus. Certainly the good Lord God Almighty (blessed be He) will protect a pious charitable man against an untimely death."

"I am an old man," said Heinrichus. "Undoubtedly, my death is now appropriate."

But Rabbi Abraham said, "Good Heinrichus, you have just done a fine and noble deed. I would hope that you can still have a little time to enjoy the wonderful feelings that come from your act."

"My fate is fixed," sighed Heinrichus.

"We will see what we will see, my friend," answered the Rabbi. "Stay here a while."

Heinrichus felt worn out; he had no energy at all. He sat quietly on one of the prayer benches while the Rabbi continued his writing. After a while, it began to get darker and darker. The house of study was filled with an ancient silence. A dog whined outside somewhere far, far away, but within the building all was absolutely still. The doorway to the small back study room became blacker and blacker. Then a dark figure appeared. Again it was Dumah, the Angel of Death. Now he stood covered from head to foot with unwinking eyes, he held a drawn and bloody sword, and his breathing was like the sound of dry leaves, rustling and rustling in the cold autumn wind.

Dumah, the Angel of Death, stood darkly in the doorway. The air seemed thick and blank and empty. Was there a voice – was Dumah speaking? The Rabbi squinted. He peered into the darkness, and he thought that he heard the words of the Holy One, as repeated by the Prophet Joel, the son of Pethuel:

> Here is God's Great Day of Oblivion –
> And now comes the Judgment Requiem:
> Darkened are the moon and sun
> The stars and the planets all go dim
> God rains stormclouds down from Zion
> He thunders out of Jerusalem.

And then the Rabbi heard that once again the rainstorm had begun. Wind splattered the rain. The storm was like heavy wet curtains; it beat and beat against the outside of the yeshiva, an old wooden building near the River Rhine in the medieval Cologne of long, long ago.

And there stood the Angel of Death, and in the oldest and dustiest voice of all, he said, "Rabbi Abraham, the final hour has come for Heinrichus, the son of Jacob ha-Levi." Thus spoke Dumah, the Angel of Death, as he claimed the soul of old Heinrichus ben Jacob.

Rabbi Abraham looked at the black angel. The Rabbi felt small and old and sad. "O Dumah, esteemed angel, give this man some time longer," said the Rabbi. "Heinrichus has led a pious life. Now he has done another fine deed of charity. Let him enjoy the feelings of his kindness for a few years more."

"The Decree of Death has been signed," said Dumah, the Angel of Death. "The matter is out of my hands."

The Rabbi looked at Heinrichus, and then he began to pray:

O Mighty Lord our God, Creator of the World, blessed are You for ever and ever. Heinrichus ben Jacob sits here before You. Dear Lord, Heinrichus has always been a devout and righteous person. He has always tried his best. He has given charity and alms. And now he has given all his money to a young orphan whom he hardly knew. I recall: *Tzedakah Tatzil Mimavet*–charity is a safeguard against an untimely death. Heinrichus has been generous, merciful, kind, and charitable. Can You perhaps spare him from a sad death, at least for a short while longer?

Then the Rabbi sat silently, with his hands in his lap. Dumah stood absolutely unmoving. Nothing happened, no one stirred, and no sounds were heard.

Many minutes passed. The Rabbi had tears in his eyes. Then Heinrichus said, "Good Rabbi, let me tell you something. A wave of warm and wonderful feeling has suddenly passed over me. I do not know exactly what it is, but somehow, as I remember the faces of that family in Wahn, I feel very happy."

Heinrichus smiled, and he closed his eyes. Then swift as an eagle, Dumah reached over. He slipped the silver soul from out of the old gentleman. Dumah, the Angel of Death, pulled the light and holy soul from the white-haired head of Heinrichus ben Jacob, and they sped off to Heaven. And as the black angel passed through the nighttime celestial vault, the soul glinted and shone in the wondrous Heavenly starlight of the eternity of forever.

ood evening, Rabbi. No sleep for the weary? That is what my grandmother said, and she said it almost nightly. If you are cold then sit down here on the bench and I will stoke up the oven. This stoker? It is one of the iron shoe scrapers from the front hall—you probably do not recognize it because it is covered with soot. (Also, I bent it in order to make it fit through the oven door.) Of course there are still two scrapers in the anteroom for dirty shoes. But I myself am of the old school: I think that all pious men should remove their shoes before entering the synagogue and that they should then pray barefoot. Scholars should work barefoot too. And did you know that Nachmanides participated in his famous debate barefoot?

Exactly, Rabbi—that was the debate in medieval Barcelona in the thirteenth century. You remember: a converted Jew, Pablo Christiani, had persuaded the King of Aragon to put the question of the Messiah to a public trial. "Order Moses Nachman, our foremost Jewish scholar, to debate," demanded Christiani. "Then I will force this rabbi to admit that the Jewish book called the Talmud proves that Jesus is, in fact, the true Messiah." The King agreed, and Rabbi Moses ben Nachman—Nachmanides—was summoned to the court. In the royal hall, Rabbi Moses argued barefoot in his Sabbath robes. But although he won the debate, the Rabbi ended up exiled, and local Jews suffered reprisals, including the confiscation of their sacred books.

It all began when Pablo Christiani took on the task of converting other Jews. After his own conversion to Catholicism, Christiani had become a Dominican. The Dominicans were called the "Preaching Friars." They were trained in theological reasoning. They wandered throughout the continent, preaching and refuting the arguments of heretics, and later, because of their skills in argumentation, the Pope had them conduct the Inquisition. The two most distinguished Christian academics of the thirteenth century, Albertus Magnus and Thomas Aquinas, were Dominicans, and eventually Dominicans dominated the European universities.

What is that, Rabbi? Yes–apparently there actually was a man named "Dominic." Saint Dominic was born at the end of the twelfth century. He founded one of the two orders of wandering Christians (the Franciscans were the other)–they were somewhat like the Jewish *maggidim*. In the beginning, when Dominic first asked the Pope, Innocent the Third, to sanction this new order, the Pope hesitated. Then one night the Pope had a dream. He saw the Church of the Lateran in Rome leaning precariously–it tottered, it seemed about to collapse. The Pope was afraid, but miraculously the vast structure remained upright; the entire Church remained standing, and at the bottom stood Dominic supporting its weight with his shoulder. Needless to say, the next day, the Pope gave the Dominican movement his official blessing.

In the beginning there were only sixteen Dominicans. However, the Dominican order was highly organized, and by the first half of the thirteenth century it comprised sixty monasteries scattered over western Europe. And what was the essence of a medieval Dominican? A contemporary described them as "wandering on foot over the face of Europe, under burning suns or chilling blasts, rejecting gifts of money but receiving thankfully whatever coarse food might be set before them, enduring hunger in silent resignation, and taking no thought for the morrow. Ceaselessly, they busied themselves in snatching souls from Satan; they lifted men up from the sordid cares of daily life, they ministered to men's infirmities, and they brought to men's darkened souls a glimpse of Heavenly light."

These, then, were the Dominicans. In contrast, Rabbi Moses ben Nachman was not like this at all. He did not aspire to save souls. He did not see life as burdened by sad difficulties. Rabbi Moses was a pious gentle man, and he was an optimist. Like his predecessors, Maimonides and Abraham ben Ezra, Nachmanides was a scholar of wide learning. Like Maimonides, he was interested in medicine as well as in the Talmud, and like ben Ezra, Rabbi Moses wrote an analysis of the Torah – the "Commentary on the Pentateuch." Nachmanides also wrote two well-known homiletic books, "Epistle on Sanctity" (*Iggeret ha-Kodesh*) and "Law of Man" (*Torah ha-Adam*), discussing ritual customs.

But Nachmanides was not a dry academic scholar: he was a dreamer and a mystic. Maimonides and ben Ezra emphasized reason and intellectualizing and philosophy. On the other hand, Nachmanides liked simple pious spiritual explanations. Old Rabbi Moses ben Nachman was more interested in the religious attitude – the spiritual feelings – of the average Jew than in the depth of his thinking. . . .

What is that, Rabbi? Yes, it is true that Nachmanides was a physician and that he had studied science. And, yes, he wrote highly respected commentaries, annotations, and analyses of the Talmud. Nonetheless, Nachmanides hoped to preserve the aethereal and mystical threads that had long been woven into Jewish traditions. Unlike Maimonides, Nachmanides did not use human logic and reason as the universal test for a particular point of Judaism. Nachmanides began with the Holy Scriptures and the Talmud; then he happily built his explanations on miracles – on wonders such as the creation of the world from nothingness, the complete omniscience of the good Lord God, and the inexplicable blessings and gifts of Divine Providence.

There is no avoiding it, Rabbi, Moses ben Nachman was a mystic at heart – just as was Abraham ben Alexander, Achselrad of Cologne. The two men never met (Nachmanides was much younger), but Rabbi Moses ben Nachman did journey once to Cologne. Have you heard of that trip? No? Then let me tell you about it:

As you know, Rabbi, all manner of wanderers came through Germany each week in those olden days. Strange men appeared at all times of the day and night in the Cologne yeshiva; for, in medieval Europe, wayfarers were constantly journeying to and from the southern lands. One springtime afternoon, Rabbi Joel ben Isaac – the father of the famed legal scholar Eliezer ben Joel, and the successor to

Rabbi Abraham ben Alexander–looked up from his writing, and he saw an elderly gentleman standing in the doorway.

"Hello," said Rabbi Joel.

"My greetings to you, Rabbi," returned Moses ben Nachman. "May I come in?"

"Certainly," said Joel ben Isaac, and he cleared a place on one of the worn benches along the wall.

"I am Moses ben Nachman of Spain," said Nachmanides, and Rabbi Joel opened wide his eyes. . . .

What? Yes, yes, Rabbi, I am about to continue. I was just thinking quietly here in the glow of the stove. Now, where was I? Oh yes, Nachmanides came into the rabbi's small study room in the Cologne yeshiva, and he set his satchel on the floor. Strapped to the outside was a strange clay tablet.

Nachmanides saw Rabbi Joel looking at the old flat clay brick. Rabbi Moses smiled. "This is a handprint, good Rabbi," said the traveler. "When we were all much younger, I had an inspiration one day–and I bless the good Lord God for putting this wondrous idea into my head. My oldest boy Nahman, my dear little son, was two years old. Ah, what a fine tiny time that was."

Rabbi Moses smiled again, and he seemed to be looking somewhere far away and long ago. After a moment, he continued: "Anyway, one holy morning, we went out and bought some of the best pottery clay, and carefully we made a print of his little two-year-old hand. Then we had the clay dried and fired–and I have carried it everywhere with me since. I cannot tell you what happiness it brings to me." Nachmanides put the clay tablet in his lap, and he covered the small print with his own wrinkled hand.

Rabbi Joel was silent, but he smiled also. Nachmanides looked up at Joel ben Isaac. "Rabbi Joel," he said, "I have been looking forward to this visit to Cologne. I am happy to meet you finally–you, a man who allows demons a considerable play in this great wide rich world of ours."

Rabbi Joel raised his eyebrows. "I am happy to meet you also, Rabbi Moses. But what is this that you are saying about demons?"

"Oh, I only mean that so many of my colleagues allow no mystery into the world any longer," said Nachmanides. "They are denying a great and holy side of things: it is the incondensably complex and unknowable fabric of the universe that is often lost nowadays. I know, Rabbi Joel, that you are a student of the mystic Achselrad. Ah, the great Achselrad, who wrote about all matters hidden and magical in his many Kabbalistic books!"

Rabbi Joel nodded, although he was a bit uncertain as to how to respond. At the moment, Joel ben Isaac was more a Talmudist than a Kabbalist. Talmudists were most interested in legal – that is, halakhic – matters. The Kabbalists, in contrast, delved into the secret and mystical underpinnings of Judaism: they were immersed in the fantasies, symbols, and magics that God has let loose in the world. The good Rabbi Joel was an academic, not a mystic.

But Nachmanides was an old man, and he had his own old man's vision and his fixed old man's ideas. To Nachmanides, Cologne was synonymous with the strong mystical spirit of Achselrad. To Nachmanides, even years after the rabbinate of Abraham Achselrad, the color and the magical flavor of hidden Kabbalistic lore still permeated the back room of the yeshiva of Cologne. Rabbi Joel saw this, and he did not know what to say; so he simply sat, and he remained silent.

Nachmanides went on talking, and he seemed to be speaking to himself: "Of course, I cannot say that I am really a Kabbalist myself. No, I am a more ordinary rabbi, in spite of the claims of my colleagues. Do you know that there is actually a little verse written about me? Meshullam En-Vidas Dafiera (who is an opponent of Maimonides) set me alongside Ezra and Azriel, the mystic Kabbalists of Gerona and students of old Isaac the Blind":

> The son of Nachman knows the Lord:
> With Ezra, Azriel, and Blind Isaac,
> Nachmanides finds God's hidden word;
> Seeking the Lord with holy magic
> They are priests with secret swords –
> Mystic seers of rhetoric –
> Deciphering Torah's sacred words
> And dazzling both the dead and quick.

Then Nachmanides smiled. He looked off, far away. Was he having a mystical vision? Perhaps he was looking south, past the dark

River Rhine, to the warm Mediterranean Sea beyond. Perhaps he even saw the suntanned hills of the Holy Land, hills dotted with tiny colorful flowers, under the springtime smile of the good Lord God. Or perhaps he was just musing absently and happily. In any case, after a moment Nachmanides said, "That poem goes a bit too far. Although it is true that I believe in miracles. For example, I am convinced (in contrast to Maimonides) that angels can be seen."

Nachmanides looked at Rabbi Joel. "Have you ever seen an angel?" he asked.

Rabbi Joel hesitated. "I do not think so, Rabbi Moses," he said.

"Ah, that is understandable," said Moses ben Nachman. "They are not a common sight. Moreover, they require especially keen and pious vision."

Nachmanides became silent, and he creased his brow. Rabbi Joel waited patiently.

"It has been a long time since I saw an angel, Rabbi Joel," said Nachmanides softly. "It has been a long, long time."

Again, Moses ben Nachman was silent. The sounds of Cologne were far away – the rabbi's little back study room seemed isolated and floating by itself.

"I am leaving Europe," said Nachmanides.

"Why is that?" asked Rabbi Joel.

"It was the debate," said Nachmanides.

Rabbi Joel nodded. The great debate in Barcelona was well known throughout the Jewish communities of both northern and southern Europe. A year earlier, Nachmanides had been forced into a public presentation, a debate with a baptized Jew, Pablo Christiani, who had taken as his personal mission the conversion of all other Jews.

The debate was held in the court of James the First, the Conqueror, King of Aragon. James was a giant of a man and he was astute and patient and intelligent. During his reign, he was much occupied with the warring Moors in Murcia and with the politics of southern France. Nonetheless, he was also interested in literature, and he wrote a fine chronicle of his own life. In addition, he was a religious man, and when he fell very ill in his sixties he resigned his crown, hoping to retire to the monastery of Poblet; however, poor King James died before he could carry out his last dream.

For the debate, Nachmanides came into the royal court in Sabbath robes and barefoot, out of piety and humility. The dialogue in the Spanish court lasted three days. Each morning the Rabbi arrived calmly, and each evening he left quietly. After the first day, the Jews of Barcelona asked him to break off the debate. "Your frankness is being carried too far," they said. "In the end, the Dominicans will become uncontrollably angry, and we will all suffer."

Nachmanides nodded politely, but he returned the next morning.

On the third day, King James called Rabbi Moses aside. "Mr. Nachman," said the King, "I do not agree with you; however, I have never heard a more skillful defense of an incorrect doctrine."

The Rabbi remained silent. "Let me ask you, Mr. Nachman," said the King. "Do you consider that Jesus held sterling ideals and that he preached many holy truths?"

"Yes," said Rabbi Moses.

"Then," said the King, "why do you Jews not believe that so noble and spiritual a person as Jesus was the Messiah? You pray for the coming of the Messiah too, do you not?"

"Your Honor," said Nachmanides, "if I may be so bold, then I should like to begin my reply with a question."

"Very well."

"King James, what would you consider to be your most important occupation?" asked Nachmanides.

The King thought a moment, and then he answered, "Although I wish it were otherwise, I am occupied by the threats of the Moors. I must organize resistance and even conduct war against my enemies in order to protect my people from external forces. At the same time, I must keep watch over the local officials and the courts in order to protect the kingdom from selfish misguided internal forces."

"So I have seen, Your Honor," said Nachmanides. "And such duties fall on the shoulders of all good rulers. But here you, yourself, have given me the answer to your question–you see, good King, the coming of the Messiah is to be followed by Peace and by Justice."

The two men were silent a moment. Then Rabbi Moses ben Nachman continued: "King James, in that great era, the gift of the Messiah will be Peace–Peace forever, amen. In the days of the Messiah, finally man will be free from the trammels of war; man will be able to devote all his time and all his concentration and all his energy to the study of wisdom. Finally – praise the Lord Almighty – men will live only to study and to fulfill the good Lord God's holy Laws.

"As the psalmist has written":

> Lord, I praise You to all men
> Among the widespread nations
> I will tell Your glory again
> And sing You warm ovations.

> I will chant these glad refrains:
> "Eternal faith the Lord maintains,
> His king forever ever reigns –
> *Peace* it is that God ordains."

"Until the world is at peace, good King, we Jews cannot believe that the Messiah has finally come."

And King James was silent, for what could he say to that?

Finally, the debating and arguing and presenting ended. The Dominicans claimed that Nachmanides' fancy speeches were unconvincing and that the Rabbi would quickly leave the city in shame. However, Nachmanides remained in Barcelona for another full week. Therefore, Pablo Christiani formally charged Nachmanides with religious blasphemy; the Dominicans were angry, and at their urging, Pope Clement the Fourth wrote a severe letter to King James. In the end, Nachmanides was banished from Spain for the remainder of his life.

So, at the age of seventy, Nachmanides left his fatherland and went into permanent exile. Nachmanides followed out his claim that it is the religious duty of every Jew eventually to dwell in Judaea. However, Rabbi Moses first traveled around Europe to say good-bye to the European Jewish communities. And so it happened that he appeared in Cologne one day, and there he talked with Rabbi Joel ben Isaac. The two rabbis sat upon the worn benches in the old back room where rabbis had sat and talked and prayed since time immemorial. Rabbi Moses ben Nachman stayed in Cologne for one day and one night, and then he continued on his trip. A few months later, he landed in the ancient suntanned Holy Lands, and he settled in the walled city of St. Jean D'Acre, the chief town of Palestine.

During his three years' stay in Palestine, Nachmanides wrote many letters to his native Jewish communities in Spain. In these letters, he described the condition of the ancestral Jewish country. For instance, from Jerusalem he wrote:

Many of the sights here can only be described in sorrow. At the present time, only one Jew lives permanently in the town; he is a dyer, and he is persecuted, oppressed, and despised. Occasionally, when Jews come from the surrounding areas, they can sometimes gather a *minyan*–but that is rare. In general, the few Jews in the vicinity are a wretched folk, without a stable home, occupation, or trade; they consist of wanderers, pilgrims, and beggars. And this sorry state is in spite of the fact that the fruit of the land is still magnificent and its harvests are rich. Indeed, Palestine is a blessed country, flowing with milk and honey.

I feel for these Jewish brothers, for I too am a man who has seen affliction. I am banished from my home table. I have been removed far away from my friends and my kinsmen. At my age, the distance that separates us is too great for me ever to bridge it again. My sons and my daughters are in Spain, where lives my soul also; my heart and my soul will dwell with them in Europe forever, amen.

I tell myself that these losses are balanced by the joy of being here in the Holy Land, where I will die before the Great Day of Resurrection. Here there is the ruin of the great Temple of Solomon. Here there are the ancient stones, walked upon by the Patriarchs. Here there is the dust of our forefathers' fathers. At times, I tear my garments–and I am relieved by my tears. But here, after a storm, there are rainbows too, just as in my native Spain, amen.

Not long after this, Nachmanides passed the holy age of seventy-three; then he died and he was buried in Haifa, the Palestinian town at the foot of Mount Carmel on the south side of the Bay of Acre. Old Rabbi Moses ben Nachman left an ethical will for his eldest son Nahman. The will included a small poem:

And, my son, when prayers you start
Remove all taints, all mundane notions
All earthly feelings from your heart
Cleanse your soul of base emotions
Set your worldly self apart
Before you say your first devotions.

In this way the words you've sent
Will all be holy, good, and true,
Your prayers will all be innocent
As once more I remember you
When you stood young and reverent—
As innocent as the sky was blue.

This is what old Rabbi Moses left for his son. And what did the son, Nahman, leave for his father? The little clay handprint, of course. The clay tablet was buried with Moses ben Nachman—and gently now it rests forever in the hands of the old man, Nahman's loving father, amen.

ood evening, Rabbi. You are having difficulty sleeping again? Put your feet up on the side bench here and I will open the stove door. Let me push this coal back – there is nothing like the white glow of the oven to wash away the cares of a hard day.

I heard your final prayers tonight, and there is no use denying it, Rabbi – you are overworked. Even an old shammas like me can tell. I kept one eye on you when I was cleaning the dishes, and I saw that you were watching the door, hoping that Reb Elbaum would leave early. But then Reb Anton stayed late to argue about that passage from the Book of Isaiah:

> This is what the good Lord God (blessed be He) has said: "Maintain justice and do what is right, for My salvation is close at hand, and My truth and righteousness will soon be revealed. And most especially blessed is the man who keeps the Sabbath without desecrating it and who refrains forever from evil.

> "To him, I will give, within My temple and its walls, a memorial and a name better even than sons and daughters; I will give him an everlasting name that will not be cut off.

"To those who serve Me, who love the Name of the Lord their God, who hold fast to My covenant, and who keep the Sabbath without desecrating it, to these I say: I will bring you to My holy mountain, I will give you joy in My house of prayer, and I will shine upon you a dawning light for ever and ever."

Ah, Rabbi—you put it so well when you reminded Reb Anton that the Lord's Sabbath is the clear vision of light. And your explanation of that scriptural passage reminded me of Rabbi Jehuda ben Saul. I remember how one day old Jehuda was giving a sermon to his yeshiva students:

"My unformed young men," began the Rabbi, "open wide your eyes on the Sabbath."

Rabbi Jehuda opened wide his eyes, and he stared down at the young men seated on the worn prayer benches. "Open wide your eyes!" he repeated. "And use the Sabbath."

The Rabbi looked around the room. "You do know how to use the Sabbath—do you not?" he asked.

The boys looked puzzled, so the Rabbi continued: "Remember, my quiet students, the Sabbath is the clear vision of light. In fact, that is why the recital of the *Kiddush* in the synagogue on Friday evenings is a remedy for weak eyes."

At first, there was silence. Then a brave student, young Moshe ben Samuel, asked, "Excuse me, good Rabbi—did you say that the *Kiddush* is said in the *synagogue*?"

"I did," answered old Jehuda.

"But Rabbi," said Moshe, "I thought that the *Kiddush* is a wine blessing for the *home* on the Sabbath."

Rabbi Jehuda nodded. "That is true," he said.

Moshe looked puzzled, so the Rabbi said, "Let me ask you, young man: Can you describe the *Kiddush* ceremony to me?"

"Well, Rabbi," began Moshe, "on a Sabbath evening, everyone in the family gathers around the table for a special meal. But the Sabbath evening actually begins with the *Kiddush* before the meal."

"Very true," said the Rabbi, "and how does the *Kiddush* itself begin?"

Moshe stood up to answer. "It begins with a cup of wine," said Moshe. Rabbi Jehuda raised his eyebrows, but Moshe ben Samuel was looking at his friends and he continued: "The father holds up a cup of wine, and he says":

Blessed be You, O Lord our God, King of the world, the Creator of the fruit of the vine.

Blessed be You, O Lord our God, King of the world, Who has sanctified us by Your commandments. In love and in favor, You have given us the holy Sabbath for a heritage; it is a memorial to the work of Creation. Blessed be You, O Lord our God, Who hallows the Sabbath. Amen.

Moshe smiled and he sat down again. Rabbi Jehuda leaned on the *almemar*, the reading desk, and he stared at his charges. "Is this correct?" he asked. No one answered and there was an uncomfortable silence.

Finally, Jehuda ben Saul said, "Moshe, let me give you a hint, young man – does the *Kiddush* not begin the Sabbath celebration?"

"Yes, it does," said Moshe.

"And is the Sabbath not the memorial of the end of the Creation of the World?"

"Yes," said Moshe.

"So – what would be the most appropriate remembrance to recite in the *Kiddush*?" asked the Rabbi. He looked from student to student, but no one answered.

"Think, my boys!" said the Rabbi. "Do you not perhaps recall this passage from the Book of Genesis?"

Evening came and morning came, a sixth day.

Thus, Heaven and earth were completed, with all their mighty throng. On the sixth day, the great Lord God completed all the work that He had been doing. And on the seventh day He ceased from all His work. The Lord God blessed the seventh day and He made it holy, because on that day He ceased from all the work that He had set Himself to do.

The students nodded, and Rabbi Jehuda nodded too. "This is the beginning of the first Sabbath in Genesis. So of course it is also the appropriate beginning for *all* Sabbaths ever after," said the Rabbi.

"*First* we remember the initial Sabbath. *Then*," said the Rabbi, looking at Moshe, "then and only then, do we bless the wine. Then and only then, do we drink the wine. And afterward, of course, we all share the joy of the wine and the bread and the food of the Sabbath.

"The Sabbath has a pure white glow, my boys. And why is this? It is because after the first Sabbath, the earth and the Heavens had finally been set forth in their full brilliant pure light and radiance – and finally the great God Almighty could rest content. And now, the Sabbath remains a gift of that first full and holy light, and it is a rest for all Jews everywhere, amen."

The Rabbi looked up to Heaven, and he closed his eyes. There was silence. After a moment, Moshe ben Samuel built up his courage and he asked, "But Rabbi, what about the *Kiddush* in the *synagogue?*"

Moshe and the other boys looked up at the Rabbi, but Rabbi Jehuda had put his head on his desk and it seemed that the old man had fallen fast asleep.

Old Jehuda ben Saul had fallen asleep, Rabbi, but as he suggested, the *Kiddush* wine once *did* have a special place in the synagogue. And, of course, you remember the miracle of the *Kiddush* wine in the synagogue of medieval Cologne. You do not know about that miracle? Then let me tell you:

Traditionally, the *Kiddush* is a ceremony for the home. However, as Rabbi Jehuda reminded us, the *Kiddush* was sometimes recited in the synagogue. In the Geonic period – in the early Middle Ages – synagogues were hostels for Jewish travelers, and during the late Middle Ages, many European communities continued this tradition. Homeless strangers would eat and sleep in the synagogue building. These transients, wanderers, and pilgrims were quite poor. When staying at the synagogue, they received only the simplest of meals, and they could not recite the *Kiddush* because wine was expensive. But how could any Jew be denied the holy joys of the Sabbath? Therefore, the congregations would recite the *Kiddush* in the synagogue at the end of the Friday evening service; in this way, those who could not say a wine blessing with their Friday night meal would at least hear the prayers and they would be able to say a holy Sabbath "amen" at the conclusion.

The Sabbath wine was stored in a small cabinet beside the Holy stone Ark and the shammas was the keeper of the synagogue's special bottle of wine. In medieval Germany, in the days of Abraham ben Alexander, the mystic Achselrad of Cologne, the shammas of Cologne was a devout man named Chayim ben Meir. One night after the Sabbath evening services and after the wine bottle had been carefully replaced in its case and after everyone else had left the building, Chayim closed up the synagogue, and he went home. It had been a long tiring day. Soon Chayim was fast asleep, and late in the night he had a strange and frightening dream.

In the midst of his sleep, a bearded old man suddenly appeared to the shammas. There was a bright and blinding light. The old man was shouting, "Chayim—Chayim! Get up! Hurry back to the synagogue. The Holy Ark is in danger!"

The shammas awoke. He was shaking and worried. He sat up. He looked about him. Was there a fire? Were there robbers in the synagogue? He could not forget the dream. He was sweating and he continued to tremble. Something terrible was afoot. Chayim got out of his bed, he washed his hands, and he began walking up and down the room. He paced and he paced. Somehow, this dream was a warning.

It was the dark dead hours of the night. Chayim looked out his window at the synagogue building. Was there a dim light in the main prayer hall, or were his eyes still remembering his dream? The shammas pulled on his clothes, and he walked across the alleyway to the synagogue building. He unlocked the front door. He stepped into the anteroom. There was silence throughout the building.

As always, Chayim removed his shoes. Then he walked into the main prayer hall. The building was thick with old silence, but a dog whined outside somewhere far, far away. Chayim peered into the dark hall. No one was about. Slowly, Chayim walked through the worn wooden benches. He passed the twelve stained glass windows with their colored lions and snakes. Chayim reached the Holy stone Ark. Carefully, he opened the carved doors. There was no smoke or fire. The Holy Scrolls were standing neatly in their places, and nothing seemed amiss.

Chayim shivered again. He knew that dreams can bring secret knowledge. As the Book of Deuteronomy said:

> There are things that are hidden, and these belong to the Lord our God—but what is revealed belongs to us and to our children forever.

Chayim felt that things had been revealed, but what things were they? Chayim began to look around the Ark more closely. He opened the small cabinet where the Sabbath wine was kept. The bottle was pushed far over into a corner. Why, it was not even the usual flask of wine—a new bottle had been substituted for the old one.

Chayim ben Meir became very worried. He opened the bottle, and he tasted the wine. But this was not wine: it was blood!

At first, Chayim stood frozen. Then he looked around, and he listened. Silence still shrouded the old synagogue. Chayim took the bottle. He ran out into the courtyard. There, in a corner behind a bush, he scraped a hole in the dirt and he poured out the terrible blood. He pushed dirt over the blood, and he stamped it down with his foot. But what about the bottle itself? Chayim went to another corner of the yard. Again he dug a hole. He pushed the bottle in. The top stuck out of the ground and Chayim cracked it with a rock. Then he covered the hole and the broken glass with dirt.

The shammas felt cold and he felt weak. He began to shake, but he knew that there was more to be done. Quickly he ran back home, and he got a new bottle of wine. Then, still in his stocking feet, Chayim stepped into the synagogue and went directly to the main prayer hall. He stood in the back a moment, listening. The old building remained blanketed in silence. A shiver ran through Chayim's back. He felt as if someone must be hidden near the Ark or in the rabbi's study—but there was absolute silence throughout.

Finally, Chayim walked through the worn wooden benches. He passed the twelve stained glass windows with their colored lions and snakes, all of which were now dark and lifeless. Chayim reached the Holy stone Ark. Carefully he opened the cabinet where the Sabbath wine was kept. He set the new bottle of wine in its proper place, he closed the doors, and he stood, listening and listening. There was nothing—there were no other sounds. As quietly as he could, Chayim walked back to the anteroom, and he put on his shoes. He stepped out the front door of the yeshiva, closing it gently behind him, and gently and silently, he walked back to his own house. When he got to his bedroom, he sat on the edge of his bed, he stared at his feet, and for many minutes he did not move at all.

Finally, the trembling Chayim took off his clothes, and he lay down on the bed. How could the blood have gotten into the synagogue? Was it a demon or was it an evil person? And what troubles would tomorrow, the Sabbath day, bring? The old shammas tossed and turned in his bed, and he could not fall asleep again that night.

The morning dawned blank and gray. Chayim felt dizzy. He had not slept and he was not hungry. He mumbled his prayers, he put on his clothes, and he crossed the alleyway and opened the synagogue for the Sabbath. The morning services were uneventful, but Chayim remained ill-at-ease. Eventually, the Rabbi and the old scholars retired to the back study room. Chayim stood uncomfortably in the anteroom, unable to concentrate on his chores. The day felt tense, and Chayim was worried.

Suddenly there was a heavy knock at the front door of the yeshiva. Chayim opened the door. The Archbishop of Cologne was standing outside; beside him were three official guards and another man – a thin man with an angry look. "We have come to speak to Mr. Abraham Alexander, the Rabbi," said one of the guards. Chayim's eyes widened. He hesitated for a moment; then he invited the company in, and he led the way back to the Rabbi.

The Archbishop and his attendants stepped in the front door, they went through the anteroom, and they walked into the main prayer hall, which was filled with wooden benches. The men passed the twelve stained glass windows with their colored lions and snakes. They looked up at the Holy Ark made of stone, and they followed the shammas through the door of the back study room. There, the Rabbi was bent over a book.

Archbishop Adolph knew the Rabbi, and Rabbi Abraham knew the Archbishop. "Rabbi," said the Archbishop sadly, "I am afraid that I have come here on a very serious matter."

Archbishop Adolph hesitated a moment, and then he said, "We have been told that you are using blood instead of wine for your religious services."

Rabbi Abraham listened quietly. The Archbishop continued: "In fact, it has been suggested that it may be the blood of a child – a Christian child."

The thin angry man standing next to the guards frowned and he nodded his head several times.

The Rabbi stroked his beard. "Your Honor, this is a terrible accusation," he said.

"Yes," replied the Catholic cleric, "and that is why I cannot ignore it. I know that you are an honorable person, Mr. Alexander – but the charge is so serious that we must investigate."

"I see," said Rabbi Abraham. Abraham Achselrad looked at the Archbishop, he looked at the guards and the thin angry man, and he looked at Shammas Chayim, who was pale and shaky.

"Reb Chayim," said the Rabbi, "please get the Sabbath wine, and bring it here."

Chayim felt very weak. He could not look at the Archbishop. Instead, he kept his eyes on the floor and he turned and went into the main prayer hall. He was followed by one of the guards. Chayim went to the cabinet beside the Holy stone Ark. He took out the bottle of wine. "Is this still real wine?" he asked himself silently, and he cast a worried glance toward the Heavens. Chayim began to turn the bottle around in his hands, but the guard immediately grabbed the bottle and he marched it into the small back study room where he set it on the desk in front of the Rabbi and the Archbishop.

The Archbishop picked up the sealed bottle, and he peered at it. "This looks like wine to me," he said.

"I can assure you," said Rabbi Abraham, "that is exactly what it is."

The Archbishop turned the bottle around in his hands; meanwhile, Chayim stepped quietly into the room. After studying the wine flask, the Archbishop said, "In order to be certain, Rabbi, we must taste the wine."

Rabbi Abraham looked at the wine bottle. Then he stared intently at the shammas for a moment. Finally, the Rabbi closed his eyes. Suddenly he opened his eyes again, and he said to the Archbishop, "Your Honor, let me read you a passage from the Book of Psalms."

"I respect your religious views, Rabbi," answered Archbishop Adolph, "but is this really relevant now?"

Old Abraham Achselrad was holding a copy of the Holy Scriptures. He seemed about to stand, when suddenly his eyes opened wide and then they closed tightly. The Rabbi took a deep breath, and he leaned back in his chair. Then he gently set down the Bible.

"Are you all right, Rabbi?" asked the Archbishop.

"I have just had a vision," said Rabbi Abraham. "I have seen the Heavens at night."

There was silence for a moment. "Yes, I have seen the Heavens at night. I have seen the firmament of the good Lord God (blessed be He) – He Who sees all and Who demands justice for all, especially for His children, the Jews. In addition, I have seen that Psalm 75 is quite important," said the Rabbi. "Here is a bit of those verses":

> God offers us the Sabbath wine –
> Each man gets a keg –
> The good find mellow Sabbath wine
> But the wicked get the dregs.

"Well, of course," said the Archbishop, "that is a fine and holy sentiment."

"It certainly is," said the Rabbi. "Now, my good Archbishop, you are a noted cleric. What would you say that this verse means?"

"Clearly it means that the Lord rewards good men."

"Yes, I agree. However, I think that it means even more than that," said the Rabbi.

"You do? Then pray tell, Rabbi Abraham: What more do you read into this Psalm?" asked the Archbishop.

"I would suggest this, Your Honor: the good Lord God offers everyone – Jew and Gentile alike – the opportunity to enjoy His holy Sabbath. However, those who scorn His grace, those who live selfishly, and those who hurt others are destined to find bitterness in the end," said the Rabbi.

"Speak more directly, Rabbi. Exactly what are you saying?" asked the Archbishop.

"I am saying this, Archbishop: I have had a vision. I have seen that some ill-intentioned man has made a false, devious, and dangerous accusation about this sacred wine."

Then one of the officers laughed, and he said, "The Psalm has told you all this, old man?"

"Yes, it has," said the Rabbi. "My good Archbishop, what are you going to do? A terrible and destructive accusation has been made. Will you let it go unpunished when you know that it is false?"

"At the moment, Rabbi," said the Archbishop, "I must say that I cannot honestly deny the charge."

Rabbi Abraham Achselrad closed his eyes. He began to sway, and he shook strangely. The guardsmen raised their eyebrows and they looked at each other. Meanwhile the pious old Rabbi opened his eyes. He took a small parchment scroll from his desk. Then he covered the top of his head with a handkerchief, and he wrote a charm with holy names on the paper. When the Rabbi finished writing, in his neat and tiny script, he rolled the parchment into a tight scroll and he tied it with a cotton thread. The Rabbi tied and untied the thread–he knotted and unknotted it seven times–and then he placed the charm on the table next to the bottle of wine. There was silence throughout the synagogue.

"Taste the wine, Your Honor," said the Rabbi.

The Archbishop unsealed the bottle. He poured some of the wine into a cup. He looked at it, and he smelled it. Then he tasted it. "It is only wine," he said.

The accusing Gentile–the thin angry man–could not restrain himself. "Let me taste it, Archbishop," he said. He grabbed the cup and he took a sip. "But it was blood–I am certain!" he said, looking from the Rabbi to the Archbishop.

The Archbishop stared intently at the man. "Apparently, this man knows something that you do not know, Rabbi," said Archbishop Adolph. "Perhaps you Jews are totally innocent. Or perhaps a miracle has occurred–in which case, the Lord has taken it upon Himself to acquit you already. In any event, this man is now guilty of making an evil unholy accusation."

Quietly, Rabbi Abraham said, "I cannot argue with your conclusions, Archbishop."

The Archbishop frowned, and he motioned to the guards. The thin man was held between two officers. "Now," said the Archbishop, "what shall we do with this man?"

The Rabbi looked around him. "Often, good Archbishop, in times of difficult decisions, we scholars discuss the matter among ourselves," he said.

The Archbishop raised his eyebrows, and he sat down on a worn bench. "Very well – please proceed," he said.

The old sages sitting on the other benches looked at one another and they looked at the Rabbi. After a moment, white-haired Baruch ben Jacob said quietly, "Well, Rabbi, this is the Sabbath, and in the holy Book of Exodus, the great Lord God (blessed be He) said, 'For six days you may do your work, but on the seventh day you shall abstain from all work.' "

The Archbishop looked puzzled. Hurriedly a younger man, Elisah ben Samuel, said, "More to the point, Reb Baruch, is that in the same holy book the word of the Almighty One is: 'You shall not spread a baseless rumor.' "

"Amen, Elisah," said Joshua ben Eliezer. "And the holy words of the Almighty One continue":

> If you ill-treat the innocent, then you can be sure that I will listen and I will hear. And My anger will be roused and I will kill you with the sword, and your wives will become widows and your children will become fatherless.

The sages nodded and stroked their beards, and they murmured among themselves. Lewe ben Anselm was sitting next to Reb Joshua, and after a time he said, "However, my friends, justice always must be tempered. In that same chapter, the word of the Lord is that a judge must balance the penalty against the crime":

> Wherever hurt is done, you shall give life for life, eye for eye, tooth for tooth, hand for hand, foot for foot, burn for burn, bruise for bruise, and wound for wound.

Again, the many scholars nodded and murmured among themselves. A few of them stroked their beards and tapped their chins. The Archbishop waited politely. There was silence, and then Menahem ben Joel said cautiously, "Perhaps I would remind us of the scriptural Proverb":

> The Lord curses mightily
> The evil man's kin,
> But God blesses the whole family
> Of the righteous and the genuine.

With this, Moyses ben Nathan felt brave, so he added, "Exactly, good Menahem. And then there is also the scriptural Proverb":

> God hates the prayer
>   Of the wicked person,
> But He loves forever
>   The good-hearted man.

Finally, the men looked at old Shimshon ha-Zaken. Reb Shimshon was tugging at his beard. He coughed; then he said, "Gentlemen, I would contribute this: The same chapter in the Book of Exodus – the section already invoked so eloquently by my scholarly colleagues – contains the following injunction by the great and omnipotent Lord our God":

> You must avoid all lies. You must not cause the death of the innocent and the guiltless. For I, the Lord your God, will never acquit the guilty.

"Amen," said Baruch.

The old men became silent, and the Archbishop looked at Rabbi Abraham. Abraham ben Alexander, Achselrad of Cologne, was also quiet for a moment. Then he said, "All that you say, my good colleagues, is quite true. It is true and right and holy. On the other hand, let me remind you of something else. In the Book of Exodus, the word of the Almighty One is this":

> When you come upon your enemy's ox straying, you shall take the animal back to him. When you see someone in trouble, although he may hate you, you must give him a hand, however unwilling you may be to help. And you shall not oppress the alien, for you know how it feels to be an alien – you, too, were aliens yourselves in Egypt.

The Archbishop looked at Rabbi Abraham. Now the Rabbi was silent. Archbishop Adolph stood, and he said, "Good Rabbi, thank you for your counsel."

Then the Archbishop motioned to the guards, and with the thin angry man between them, the official group left. They walked from the back room. They passed the Holy stone Ark; beside the Ark, the door to the small wine cabinet was still open. The men made their way through the many wooden benches in the main prayer hall. A glowing Sabbath light filtered in through the twelve stained glass windows with their colored lions and snakes. Then the men went through the anteroom and out the front door of the old Cologne yeshiva. The Archbishop and his three officers and the thin angry man left the synagogue, and they walked into the warm sunlight. It was the late afternoon of a fine Sabbath day—yes, Rabbi, it was a fine Sabbath afternoon in medieval Cologne, once upon a time, long, long ago.

hat is that, Rabbi? I was just resting my eyes. Please feel free to join me here by the stove. (I think you will be too warm on that bench: try the one nearer to the wall.) An old man like me can doze forever by a warm stove; I suppose that is because I no longer fear demons.

Why, Rabbi – certainly you know that your guard is let down when you sleep. Your soul leaves your body when you dream; therefore, you are particularly susceptible to demonic attack during the night. As my grandmother would say: "When the tenant leaves town, then there is no one to look after the house." That is why the fear of demons keeps you awake, especially when you are young. But now that I am old and evil spirits are just hollow winds to me, I am sleepy all the time.

Of course, youth always looks to the holy bright dawn for protection. The new day is *ki tov*: it is so good that no demons dare to show their evil faces in the bright morning smile of the good Lord God (blessed be He). Exactly, Rabbi – we learn that the dawn is *ki tov* from the most holy words in the Bible:

In the beginning of Creation, when God made Heaven and earth, the earth was without form and it was void; darkness covered the face of the abyss, and a mighty wind swept over the surface of the waters.

And God said: "Let there be light"–and there was light. And the Lord saw that the light was *ki tov*, it was good, and He separated the light from the darkness. He called the light "day," and He called the darkness "night." So evening came and morning came, the first day.

Yes, the dawning day is called *ki tov* because it is good and bright and holy and light–and it is a friend to the Jews. I have heard it said that Ki Tov lives in the synagogue, with a *tallis* and with *tefilla*. And why is that? It is because one must first say his morning prayers with prayer shawl and *tefilla* in order to greet the new day properly. The *ki tov* dawn is strong and it is safe. My grandmother said that a man should always enter and leave under the sign *ki tov*. She meant that a traveler should plan always to reach some resting place, such as a friend's house or a synagogue or an inn, while it is still daylight–while it is still *ki tov*. Likewise, never leave for a trip after dark. . . .

What? No, no–do not get up on my account, Rabbi: I was just resting my eyes a moment. I was resting and musing. . . . Well, to tell you the truth, Rabbi, I was thinking about the bright *ki tov* dawn and about a story that my grandmother told me:

Once upon a time, said my grandmother to me, in the congregation of Rabbi Abraham ben Alexander, Achselrad of Cologne, there was a devout man named Meyer ben Asher ha-Kohen. Meyer had some business in the town of Julich. Do you know Julich, Rabbi? It is an old town on the River Roer, about forty kilometers west of Cologne. Meyer went to the morning prayers in the Cologne yeshiva. Then he returned home, he organized his last-minute business matters, he packed his satchel, he kissed his wife good-bye, and he gave her some instructions; finally, he left on his trip in the early afternoon.

At that time in the countryside between Cologne and Julich, there was an innkeeper who was really a demon (may the good Lord God always protect us from them, amen). This innkeeper had a large old house on the main road beside the River Erft. When people passed by the inn, they were often too late to reach other lodgings; therefore, they would stop and spend the night at this evil old house.

And what was so evil about this house? I will tell you. When a traveler had settled in, the demon-innkeeper would ask him: "And where might you be going, my friend?" And the demon would also ask: "And what road do you plan to take?"

The traveler would say to the demon: "Oh, I am going this way." Or he would answer: "Oh, I am going that way." Then the innkeeper would always say: "Well, fancy that! It just so happens that I am going the same way myself."

Then, at about midnight, the demon-innkeeper would wake up the traveler, and he would say: "Get up, my friend. It is almost dawn, and we need an early start."

The traveler would get up, and he would go with the innkeeper. The unsuspecting person would feel safe; he would be happy to have a companion with him as they passed through the uninhabited countryside. But when they came out of the old inn and into the darkness of the night, the traveler would often comment: "My goodness, it is much earlier than I thought."

"Never fear," the demon-innkeeper would say. "We shall get to our destination that much quicker." However, as soon as they had entered an especially dark area, with wild forest like walls on either side of the road, then the demon would kill the traveler and he would steal all the man's possessions.

At the time of this story, it was the autumn month of *Elul*, and because Meyer ben Asher ha-Kohen did not leave for Julich until the early afternoon, it began to get dark when he was only about halfway there. Meyer could not reach the next town by daylight. Therefore, he decided to spend the night in the demon's inn, on the edge of the River Erft to the west of the small town of Horrem.

Meyer arrived in the evening. Three stars were already visible in the darkening sky. Meyer entered the inn. He sat down at one of the large oak tables. As Meyer was eating dinner, the demon-innkeeper came up to him.

"Hello, friend," said the demon. "Where are you headed tonight?"

"I am going no farther tonight," replied Meyer. "However, tomorrow morning. I intend to continue on to Julich."

"Julich? Well, well – what a fine coincidence. I happen to be going there myself tomorrow; we can travel together."

And Meyer said, "Good, I shall be very glad to have company."

After dinner, Meyer ben Asher went up to his room. He locked the door, and he went to sleep. When it was midnight, the demon-innkeeper came along. He knocked on Meyer's door. "Get up, my good sir, it is almost morning. We should be getting an early start if we are to make any progress today."

Meyer rubbed his eyes. He yawned. Then he answered, "Thank you for thinking of me, but I am still waiting for a companion. I have promised to go with him, and he has not yet arrived."

"What? You did not tell me that you were traveling with another," said the demon.

"Yes, yes – just be patient, sir. Undoubtedly my friend will be here in a short while," said Meyer ben Asher from under the covers and behind his locked door. The demon made a grumbling noise. Meyer shivered slightly, and he recited a traveler's prayer from the Book of Exodus:

> With love and care and Grace
> You guided Israel –
> You saved that ancient race,
> Leading them safe and well
> To the gentle resting place
> Where You ever dwell.

Then Meyer went back to sleep.

An hour passed, and the demon-innkeeper came and woke Meyer again. "My friend," he said, "it is getting later and later. We must set off. It is time to dress and to eat so that we can leave for Julich."

Meyer opened his eyes. It was still pitch black, and he said, "I am not ready to go yet. I have taken a solemn oath to wait for my friend, and he has still not arrived." The demon-innkeeper made a low rumbling sound. Again, Meyer nervously recited the prayer from the Book of Exodus:

> With love and care and Grace
> You guided Israel –

You saved that ancient race,
Leading them safe and well
To the gentle resting place
Where You ever dwell.

And again Meyer went back to sleep.

Another hour came and another hour went. The demon-innkeeper returned and he knocked at Meyer's door. "It is getting late. I have been waiting patiently, but this is the last time that I can call you. This is a dangerous part of the world. Do you not want some experienced companionship? It is time to get up. Get dressed, my friend, and come down and eat. We must get an early start on our trip if we are to arrive in Julich at a decent hour." So called out the demon through the locked door.

Meyer ben Asher ha-Kohen opened his eyes. He saw that it was still quite dark and he said from under the covers, "Once again, I thank you for your concern. Unfortunately, my companion seems still not to have arrived. I am afraid that I must wait longer."

The demon growled. Meyer shivered and quietly recited the traveler's protection prayer:

With love and care and Grace
You guided Israel –
You saved that ancient race,
Leading them safe and well
To the gentle resting place
Where You ever dwell.

The demon-innkeeper gritted his teeth. He clenched his fists. He coughed and he hissed. "What is the name of this friend of yours?" he asked.

"His name is Ki Tov," said Meyer.

"Ki Tov? What kind of a name is that?" asked the demon. "I have never heard it before."

"It is a Hebrew name. It is a very old name – and it is a very good name," replied Meyer ben Asher.

"Oh?" responded the demon. "And where does this Ki Tov live?"

"He lives in the synagogue, in my home town of Cologne."

"He lives in the synagogue? He must be a religious man. Is he a rabbi?" asked the demon.

"No," said Meyer ben Asher.

"Well, when did Ki Tov leave Cologne?"

"He left last night," said Meyer.

"Then he should be arriving soon," said the demon-innkeeper.

Meyer saw the first lightening of the dawn sky, and he smiled and said, "Yes—so he should."

Then Meyer got out of his bed, and he put on his *tefilla*. He put on his hand *tefilla*—winding the black leather strap seven times around his arm below the elbow—and he recited thanks to "He Who has commanded us to lay *tefillin*." Next, Meyer put on his head *tefilla*; the special knot sat behind his head and the black leather straps hung down his neck. Meyer recited: "Thanks be to He Who has commanded us about the duty of *tefillin*." Finally, Meyer wrapped the strap of the hand *tefilla* around his hand and fingers, reciting from Hosea:

> I pledge my troth a thousand-fold
> To be a righteous truthful ward.
> I speak in modesty. This is told
> Full humbly and with God's accord:
> I betroth myself, to have and hold—
> And then will I truly know the Lord.

"What is going on in there?" growled the demon.

"I am saying my prayers," said Meyer.

"Well, hurry up," said the demon-innkeeper. "It is almost dawn."

Meyer ben Asher said the morning benedictions, beginning: "Blessed are You, O Lord our God, King of the world, Who has formed the dawning light," and ending: "Blessed are You, O Lord our God, King of the world, Maker of the great and luminous lights of the Heavens." The sky was now pink. Meyer smiled. He opened the window in his room, and he called out, "Ki Tov?" Then a small light, bright, and holy voice answered, "I am here." And Meyer ben Asher ha-Kohen unlocked the door and he strode past the demon and he left the inn. Meyer marched out and left behind him all the demons of the night—and safely and happily, he walked to the town of Julich.

abbi, I am glad to see you here alone. I want to apologize for my outburst during the service this evening. Reb Anton had said that he always slept poorly on Thursday nights and that this must be due to demons. Demons indeed! Everyone knows that Thursday nights, especially during the fourth hour after sunset, are very, very holy. Thursday is a fine day – it is a special day and it is a holy day. My grandmother told me that it is the day most associated with love. What did she mean? Undoubtedly she was referring to a Thursday egg. (The Thursday egg? You take the egg laid by a black hen on a Thursday – the day during Creation when the good Lord God first made birds – and you feed it to someone. Then that person will immediately fall in love with you.) And of course Thursday is the day when widows are allowed to marry.

But speaking of widows reminds me that Thursday weddings need not always bring happiness – perhaps Reb Anton was thinking of this too. . . . What is that, Rabbi? Well, I was remembering the story that Rabbi Petahiah reported about a widow who married on a Thursday, in Egypt of long ago.

Exactly, Rabbi – that was Petahiah ben Jacob, the brother of Rabbi Isaac ben Jacob ha-Lavan (Isaac "the Wise") of Prague. Petahiah toured the entire world at the end of the twelfth century, in the days of Achselrad and well before Asher ben Yehiel was the Chief Rabbi of Cologne. When Rabbi Asher was the leading scholar in Cologne, he spent most of his time writing and reading; he was always studying the Torah and the Talmud in the little back room of the yeshiva. This room was where the Cologne rabbis had passed endless hours working and thinking and arguing with themselves. Above the back study room was a loft for storage. One day (I think that it was a Thursday), when he was rooting around among the manuscripts in the loft, Rabbi Asher found a letter from Rabbi ·Petahiah of Regensburg to Rabbi Abraham ben Alexander, Achselrad of Cologne.

"My dear Rabbi Abraham – [began the letter]

"I have just met a fine young man, a Jew from Salzburg. He has agreed to carry this letter to my good friend Rabbi Yitzchak, who I am certain will then arrange to transport it to you. I write to wish you and your family well, to convey my fondest greetings to all the Jews of your blessed community in Cologne, and to praise the good Lord God (blessed be He) and His Almighty Name for ever and ever, amen.

"I will not trouble you with the details of my many wagon rides and my subsequent sea voyages. Suffice it to say that they brought me here safely to the Oriental regions, regions that are so near to the great Holy Land where someday the Messiah shall return and deliver us and resurrect all souls and rebuild the Temple on Zion, amen. I write now to record for you some details of the lands and peoples that I have seen in these old and foreign realms. The bright and glorious hand of the Lord is visible everywhere, if only we look – praise the Lord Yahweh-Elohim.

"Yes, my old friend, I have had many, many adventures in traveling here. I hope – with the good Lord willing – to relate more of these events to you in person. For now, let me just say that after touring the Holy Lands of Palestine, I turned west and I ventured into Egypt. In essence, Egypt is the Nile and the desert, and if it were not for the River Nile then there would be nothing here to differentiate this particular country from all other parts of the vast dry Sahara. Egypt is warm and rainless and there is a north wind almost all year long, but the River Nile splits the Egyptian desert and overflows its banks each year, depositing rich wet life-giving mud.

"All the chief towns of Egypt are in the narrow valley of the Nile. Most recently, I have been in the city of Cairo. As you may know, this city was invulnerable to the crusading princes, and now Saladin (the ruler of the area) has made Cairo his stronghold. Cairo sits on the eastern side of the great River Nile, stretching north from an old Roman fortress that is known locally as 'Babylon.' Saladin is constructing a new citadel on the edge of the Mokattam hills, and standing on the ramparts of this modern fortress, you have a view of incomparable beauty. Below lies the city, with its walls and towers and gardens and squares; there are palaces and mosques with carved domes. The whole scene is filled with milling people. From here, you can see the port and the gardens and the palaces and the broad River Nile, studded with islands. Then, on the northern horizon, there are the great stone pyramids. And if you look east? All that you see are barren cliffs, backed by an endless waste of sand.

"Cairo is divided into many quarters, and each district has its own walls and its own gates; there is a Mohammedan district, a Christian district, and a Jewish district. The town is filled with diverse races, with distinctive faces, and with all manner of skin colors. People flow everywhere through the narrow streets. Buildings jut out above your head, so that the houses nearly meet. Fountains are everywhere, and they can be two stories tall, with rooms on the second floor for rest and study. The poorer houses are dirty and broken, but the wealthy houses are elaborate. The rich have shaded windows and projecting cornices and graceful woodwork and ornamented stained glass. You walk into these fairyland houses by a winding passage that leads through decorated doorways and into a court. In the center there is an oasis with palm trees shading a fountain or a pool. And all the rooms are paved with marble and hung with lanterns.

"Great cities are great trading centers. In Cairo, the many, many shops are small and open to the street. Each trade has its shops clustered together. Merchants sit in front of their stores. Musical street-cries ring out, as vendors of fruit, sherbet, and water call for your attention. I am told that there is a high death rate here, Abraham, and I can believe this because the city is crowded and many areas are quite dirty. Nonetheless, the remarkable variety of goods distracts you from the dirt that fills every corner—there are cotton, gum, hides, indigo, ivory, ostrich feathers, shawls, sheep, sugar, and woolens of all imaginable kinds.

"Of course, I have spent most of my time visiting the old settlements here in the Jewish Quarter. You may not know that Rabbi Moses ben Maimon has recently come to Cairo, after living for a time in Jerusalem (where he had fled from Morocco)–his family was already living in old Cairo (in Fostat) before he came. Rabbi Moses is not as well known here as I would have expected from his European reputation. He and his brother David live together quietly, carrying on the jewelry trade. David is younger than Moses, and he takes the more active role, traveling on business as far as India. In contrast, Moses stays at home, studies, and also works as a physician. Unfortunately, I have not had the opportunity to meet with him yet because he has been away from Cairo during the last few weeks.

"In general, things have gone well here for Egyptian Jews in the past few years. The Fatimite Caliph died and was replaced by the great Saladin, a gracious leader who is sympathetic to the Jews. The chief Jewish congregation in Egypt is in Cairo; it has two thousand Jewish families and it includes many men of great wealth. Jews here are optimistic. Families laugh. Children run about and pop up in every corner, and there is a warm happy feeling throughout.

"I have been made quite welcome here and have lived for more than a week with a fine Jewish family. Just yesterday afternoon we sat idly on their shaded porch in the heat of the day. We were lazy and quiet. We chatted about this and that–talking of every imaginable and silly thing. We talked of knotroot grass and demons' eyes and cabbages and kings. We rambled on and on dreamily, and after a while one of the old men asked whether I had heard of the cow and the golden footprints. I said that I had not, so he proceeded to tell me a strange tale; here is what he said:

"Once upon a time, in an outlying region just south of Cairo, a young Jewish girl lived happily with her father and mother. The father was handsome and strong, and a nearby widow fell in love with him. The widow could not get the man out of her mind. She watched him from a distance. Day and night she thought of him. Then she had an idea, and she befriended the little girl.

"The girl was just a small child, and soon the neighboring widow became almost like a second mother. One day, the widow said, 'We will play a trick on your mother. Do you know her big clothes chest?

Good! Well, when you find that it is open, crawl behind it. You can hide and then call out to your mother. Pretend that you are caught inside. When your mother looks in to find you, just push the lid down.' The widow smiled and patted the child. The little girl nodded seriously, and she went home. She found that the chest's heavy lid was already open, so she hid behind the chest. After a moment, she called out. Her mother came and looked into the chest. The girl pushed down the lid, it fell on her mother's neck, and the poor woman died instantly.

"In Egypt, Jewish funerals include a number of local customs. While the neighborhood women washed and shrouded the corpse, they chanted and wept. The body was laid out on the floor overnight. The following morning, there was a procession to the cemetery: first came the poorest members of the community, next came the husband and his friends, then came the children, and finally there was the coffin accompanied by the women. After the burial, the funeral party returned and everyone washed his hands and entered the house. Inside, all the furniture in the sitting room was turned upside down. Then, of course, there were seven long days of mourning. And as for the little girl? Well, Abraham, I am told that she would not speak for weeks afterward.

"Eventually, though, daily life resumed, and one day the father became betrothed to the neighboring widow. As in Europe, the favorite wedding day for Jews in Egypt is Friday. However, the bride was a widow, so the marriage took place on a Thursday. The couple fasted that morning, and then they went to the synagogue. After the ceremony, the little girl walked in front of the newly married couple and she tossed barley and nuts in their path. Slowly, the wedding procession reached home. Beggars stood at the door and bowed as the groom gave them each a gold coin. The groom bowed in return, and he turned and stepped over a small lamb that had been placed on the threshold. Then all the procession went in, and the wedding feast began.

"One week passed and then two. Seven weeks came and seven weeks went, and after seven cycles of seven weeks, the man and his new wife had another daughter. Meanwhile, however, the scriptural Proverb proved all too true":

Charm is illusion,
   Beauty is just a ghost—
It is the God-fearing woman
   Who should be honored most.

"The new wife's apparent good nature was only skin deep. Instead of being well treated by her stepmother, the older daughter was continually criticized and was given endless chores and was forced to be alone all the time.

"Now, this family was a farm family. Alongside their house were rows of irrigated gardens of cotton and barley. In addition, the family had a few chickens, some black sheep, and one cow. The cow was small and short-horned, and it must have been a wedding present from God, for it had wandered onto their farm shortly after the man had remarried. The young girl immediately made friends with the cow, stroking its nose and scratching its ears. The girl talked to the cow endlessly, and sometimes she thought that the cow actually answered. Was she imagining this? I cannot believe that the cow talked, good Abraham, but my story-telling friend was quite certain himself. In any case, the cow was the one bright and happy spot in the girl's bleak little life.

"After a time, the father grew fond of the cow, and he also spent time talking to it. 'What is going on here?' wondered the stepmother. 'This cow has become an evil distraction in our household routine.' Therefore, she told one of the servants to have the cow slaughtered for its meat. 'The old cow is not giving much milk,' said the stepmother. 'And we need the meat.'

"Ah, my good Abraham, it is as the psalmist sang in Psalm 49":

A man soon bequeaths his house
And riches to his son—
Yes, men are like the cows:
Their lives are quickly done.

"So, I am afraid, *this* cow's earthly life was quickly done too, amen. When the servant brought the meat back from the *shochet*, the

girl was assigned to wash the meat in the River Nile nearby. Sadly she
dragged the heavy basket to the edge of the river, and she put some of
the meat into the stream. Suddenly, the strong current carried the meat
off and the girl ran after it along the river bank.

"The girl followed along the rushing river. She could see the
meat, but she could not quite catch up to it. The girl ran along the river
bank, past date palms and wild vines and thick thorn bushes. In the
water, the meat slid by the reeds and the rushes and the water lilies.
Eventually, the meat flowed into a deep pool filled with a swirl of
wings, with ducks, herons, spoonbills, and storks fluttering about and
diving and splashing in the water; then the meat sank and was lost
forever.

"At the edge of this pool was a mud hut, and sitting on the front
porch was an old woman – an old clay-colored woman who could have
been a mud statue. The girl saw the woman, and she was frightened.
But the old woman said, 'My little daughter, I know that you have lost
your meat. But do not be sad – I have a gift for you.'

"The girl looked up at the old woman curiously. There was
something comforting and almost familiar about her. The woman
continued: 'Listen, little girl, go back home. Do not be afraid. As you
walk, you will leave golden footprints behind. You can pick them up,
and you can give them to your father. Then he will become rich.' The
girl did not know what to say and she remained quite still. 'Go along
with you now,' said the old woman, waving the girl away.

"The child began to walk home. As she stepped along, she left
golden prints in the mud. She looked back wonderingly, and every
once in a while she picked up a footprint and put it in her apron.

"When the girl returned home, she showed the gold to her father.
He could not believe his eyes. He hugged his daughter. He jumped up
and did a joyous Sabbath dance. The stepmother smiled, but she was
very jealous and angry, and later she made the little girl recount the
entire incident in detail.

"The next morning, the stepmother picked up her own infant
daughter, and she walked along the river bank toward the pool and the
mud hut. When the woman and her daughter arrived, the sky was dark
and the pool was surrounded by falcons, hawks, ospreys, and vultures.
Again, the old mud-colored woman was sitting in front of her hut. 'Old
woman,' called the stepmother, 'you gave my other daughter – my

stepdaughter – golden footsteps. To be fair, you should also give golden footprints to my real daughter.'

"The old woman stared at the stepmother and her daughter, but she said nothing. 'Perhaps this is just a statue,' thought the stepmother. She moved closer to the mud-colored woman. When she was standing right next to the old woman, the stepmother said loudly, 'I said – you should treat both girls equally. Please give the golden blessing to my real daughter too!'

"The old woman stared, unmoving. The stepmother became very angry. Holding her infant daughter in one arm, she struck the old woman with her free hand. The old woman was like mud. The stepmother's hand stuck fast. 'Let me go!' cried the stepmother. But the old mud-colored woman fell from her chair and she rolled down the path and the stepmother was dragged along. The tangle of people rolled and slid down to the river, and the old woman and the young woman and the infant daughter fell into the pool of water; then they were swept along in the strong currents of the River Nile, and they were never seen again.

"Well, that is the entire tale – and yes, it *is* a strange story, but I report it to you just as I heard it myself yesterday afternoon. Now I must end my letter. My dear Abraham, think of me as you read this in your holy study in Cologne, far from the golden sun of Egypt. Think of me, and remember that even when adversity strikes, the good Lord God watches over His children. The blessed Lord gives us wondrous gifts. He loves us as children in the golden beginnings of our lives, and He redeems us again as children in the golden ends of our old age. And in the glorious days of our Resurrection, the world will be adazzle with His radiance, and He will lead us all with golden footprints to that warm and Holy Land again. Hallelujah and amen, good Abraham – yes, I wish you a most golden hallelujah and amen.

"Your childhood friend,
Petahiah, the son of Jacob"

ello, Rabbi, I will be with you in a moment – I cannot leave until every tablecloth is folded, otherwise the day has not ended properly. . . . There, now I am finished at last and I can sit next to you by the stove.

No, I am not sleepy either, but there will be plenty of time to sleep in the grave, in the shadow of a tall gray Jewish tombstone. Did you know that, in medieval Germany, Christian tombstones cast no shadows? *Flat* gravestones were the rule for Christian graves – erect tombstones were the mark of Jewish graves: it was the Jews who brought to Europe the Oriental practice of placing headstones upright.

In those days – the Middle Ages – Jewish gravemarkers could be of almost any shape and size: some were more than half a meter thick and two meters high. The tombstones were never gaudy; nonetheless, medieval Jewish gravestones often had small emblems and symbols. There were dragons, bears, and lions. Also, there were stars (both pentagrams – the "Wizard's Foot" – and hexagrams – the *Magen David* or "Solomon's Seal"). Other mystical tombstone symbols included:

Kohanim had two open hands on their tombstones in order to symbolize the priestly benediction. The tombstones of the Levites had the symbol of a water jug. The tombstone of Rabbi Abraham ben Alexander, the mystic Achselrad of Cologne, had the carving of a bloody sword. Why was that? Well, I am not certain, Rabbi, but perhaps it is related to a story that my grandmother told me:

Once upon a time, said my grandmother to me, there lived in medieval Cologne a very pious man named Symon ben Aleydis ha-Kohen. In his old age of seventy years, Symon finally took sick. Symon had no family whatsoever; so when Rabbi Abraham heard about Symon's illness one afternoon, he shook his head sadly. "We must be certain," he said, "that Reb Symon is not left alone."

Many of the community scholars volunteered to maintain a vigil at the bedside. As the men stood watch, they read mystical prayers. Frequently they repeated the prayer *Ana Be-Khoah*, which says:

Lord, we beseech You to release Your captive nation by the mighty strength of Your right hand. Accept the joyful shout of Your people. Lift us and purify us, O revered God. O Mighty One, guard us as the apple of Your eye—guard those who meditate upon Your steadiness and Your unity and Your constant love. Bless them, purify them, have mercy on them, and bestow forever Your righteousness upon them. O powerful and holy Being, in Your abounding goodness, lead Your congregation. You Who are the only and exalted God, turn again to Your people, who humbly acknowledge Your holiness. Accept our prayer and listen to our cries, You Who know all secrets.

Candles were lit beside Symon's bed to drive away the demons. A loaf of bread was laid at his right side to help straighten his limbs. And now his bed itself was only a sheet and a board: feathers or straw will prolong the final moment before death. Rabbi Abraham forbade any loud noise nearby, because it frightened the soul and prevented it from leaving the body when the decreed time finally arrived. All was done to ensure that death would be as smooth and quiet and gentle as a light afternoon rain. As the old hymn said:

And then, fair friend, death with no fears
Awaits for you like rainy mist —
Quiet, gentle, soft like tears
Drifting in now to assist
When you are tired with seventy years.

Eventually, late one afternoon, Dumah, the Angel of Death, appeared in Symon's bedroom. Dumah was covered from head to foot with unwinking eyes. He had a drawn and bloody sword and at its tip was a drop of poison. Symon ben Aleydis saw the black angel, and he shook and he shivered. Dumah was a fearsome sight, and in his surprise, Symon opened his mouth. Immediately, the messenger of death thrust forward his sword and dropped the poison into the old man's mouth. Then Dumah washed his sword in a dish of water that he found at the bedside. Next, Dumah reached out with a long cold hand. Fast as the swiftest eagle, the Angel of Death slipped Symon's soul from his white-haired head and then Dumah and the soul flew off to Heaven, with the soul glinting and gleaming in the celestial starlight of an eternal forever.

In this way, old Reb Symon died before the three evening stars arrived. The women came from the Burial Society, and they washed the body in salt and water. Symon's body was dressed in a clean Sabbath robe. He was placed on a plain board, his eyes were closed, and spices were sprinkled throughout his robes. Then Symon's favorite prayer shawl was laid over his shoulders and a candle was set at his head. The Rabbi came, and he marched seven times around the body — and each time, he recited the funeral quotation from the 32nd chapter of the Book of Jeremiah:

O great and mighty God Divine
Whose Name the world extolls,
Your secrets are a Grand Design
And wondrous are Your hidden goals.

You watch all men, assess their needs
And justly You reward each one
According to his acts and deeds
And as his lifetime works were done.

The next day, old Symon was buried under the shadow of a simple erect gray tombstone. He was laid to his final rest in the *Am Toten Juden*, just outside the southern gates of medieval Cologne.

When he returned to the synagogue after the funeral, Rabbi Abraham felt worn and weary. "Every day is not a happy day," thought old Achselrad. Then he sighed, and he forced himself to write. Rabbi Abraham Achselrad worked late into the night on his mystical tome of Kabbalistic knowledge, the *Keter Shem Tov*, and eventually, in the deep dark hours of the night, he fell asleep. Yes, Rabbi Abraham fell asleep in the little back study room, and he dreamt that he himself was at the point of death and that Dumah, the Angel of Death, appeared at the head of his bed.

In his dream, Rabbi Abraham heard a noise. He opened his eyes and he saw Dumah, the Angel of Death. The black angel stood covered from head to foot with unwinking eyes. He held a drawn and bloody sword, and his breathing was like the sound of dry leaves, rustling and rustling in the blank autumn wind. The Angel of Death bent over the Rabbi, slowly and silently and smoothly and darkly. Was he speaking? The Rabbi thought that he heard the holy words of the Book of Job:

Hearing this, poor Job stood up, and he tore his cloak; then he shaved his head and fell prostrate on the ground, saying:

Naked was I when I came from the womb
And naked I shall reach my Reward.
The Lord gives life and He sends to the tomb –
Blessed is the Name of the Lord.

Dumah, the Angel of Death, bent over the Rabbi, and in the oldest and dustiest voice of all he said, "Your time has come, Abraham, the son of Alexander."

The Rabbi began to shiver and to shake. He could not speak for many minutes. The black angel remained close and unmoving. Finally, Rabbi Abraham said in a hoarse voice, "I am afraid, O Dumah."

"All men must meet their end," said Dumah, the Angel of Death. "You have been a pious and charitable man, and a place in Heaven awaits you."

The Rabbi blinked his eyes, and he said, "Good angel, could you show me first my place in Paradise? If I saw, for just a moment, my small space in the Great Hereafter, then I think that I would feel calmer. That would make it easier for me to depart gently and smoothly from this life on earth."

"Very well," replied Dumah. "Come with me; I will show you."

Then, in the dream, the Angel of Death, touched old Achselrad's hand, and the two beings swiftly sped off to the farthest celestial regions, slipping through the glorious nighttime skies above.

They went through the clouds and past the stars, and the Rabbi peeked and poked and he looked and leaped on his journey, while the black angel glided along, swift and silent and steady. It seemed to take hours and hours, and Rabbi Abraham began to glance nervously at the drawn sword of his companion. The sword looked sharp and cold and cruel and it dripped blood as they sped through the air.

Finally, the Rabbi built up his courage. He looked at the black angel, and he said quietly, "O great Dumah –"

The Angel of Death did not reply. After a moment, Rabbi Abraham said again, "O great Dumah – if I can be so bold as to interrupt your thoughts, I must say that your sword puts a great and terrifying fear deep into my heart."

"And well it might," responded Dumah, the Angel of Death. "It is the sword of death."

The Rabbi was silent, and then he said hesitantly, "Perhaps, O Dumah, you might let me hold your sword. I am shaking with fright, and I would like to feel assured that you will not use the sword until we return to Cologne."

"Humans cannot be trusted with this sword, Rabbi," said Dumah, the black Angel of Death. And the angel looked away, far into the nighttime sky.

The two beings – the old Rabbi and the black Angel of Death – sped like the night wind through the celestial skies, beyond the far ends of the earth. As they passed the edge of the world, the Rabbi looked out and down into the deepest blue, with night-silver clouds floating below as far as the eye could see. Then the Rabbi looked up, and he saw that all was a golden gray. And when he looked straight out there was no horizon at all, and the stars and the moon and the planets rolled along in the Heavenly blue far beyond to black.

And now rushing like the night wind toward the blue-black
Heavens which rolled away before him, the Rabbi passed shooting
stars and bits of planets, all carried on the endless astral tides. And what
was that shimmering in the distance? Could it be the long silver robes
of the cosmic Lord God Himself? The dark blue did not end. The far-off
spaces were deep and vast. And the Rabbi was small and trembling and
afraid. "I understand what you are saying, O great angel," said Rabbi
Abraham in a shaky voice that seemed to disappear into the celestial
night.

Again, Dumah looked ahead, and he did not reply. The Rabbi
continued: "Dumah, I understand what you are saying. Nonetheless, I
cannot control my feelings. I am an old man. I am a small mortal, and
I am afraid when I see the sword, sharp and shining and bloody in your
hand – may the merciful Lord God convert all evil hearts to good,
amen."

The Angel of Death knew Rabbi Abraham to be a righteous and
a holy man. Dumah looked for a moment at the old Rabbi, and Dumah
felt pity for him. So the black angel reached over to the Rabbi, and he
gave him the sword of death. Abraham Achselrad held the sword in
both hands, and he found the weapon to be as cold as ice and to be very,
very heavy indeed.

It seemed hours longer, but finally they arrived at Paradise.
Dumah, the Angel of Death, stopped on a cloud outside the gates to the
Great Hereafter. With a long and cold and steady hand, the black angel
pointed, and he showed Rabbi Abraham the place reserved for him.
There, beyond the Golden Gates and amidst the scores of happy
curly-haired bearded rabbis, was a fine empty seat with blue satin
cushions and with golden bowls of food and goblets of wine at its side.
Wondrous music filled the air, and angels were singing Psalm 100:

> All people on the earth shall dance
> And sing to God with a cheerful voice;
> Acclaim Him with full reverence,
> Come before Him and in song rejoice.
>
> The Lord, our Father, will provide;
> He created man from primal dust,
> We are His flock, He is our guide –
> He clothes and feeds and shelters us.

Enter His Gates with joy today
Rest along His river banks;
Sing, laud, and bless His name and ways –
To Him, we owe eternal thanks.

All creatures here and Hosts above
Praise God from Whom all blessings flow,
Forever lasts the Lord's warm love
That radiates down from long ago.

Suddenly the Rabbi felt joyous and light, and he could not resist the pull of the wondrous life of Eternity. Rabbi Abraham jumped from the cloud and he sprang forward and tried to leap through the great Golden Gates of Paradise. The Angel of Death seized hold of the Rabbi by his robe in order to pull him back. Rabbi Abraham had the shining sword of Dumah, the cold sword of death. The Rabbi reached back. With a swing of the sword, he cut his robe and freed himself from the black angel. Then he began to run and run, running toward the final Paradise of Eternity.

"Stop!" called Dumah, the black Angel of Death, and the huge Golden Gates of Paradise slowly and inexorably swung closed.

The massive Golden Gates swung closed before the Rabbi could get into Heaven – and Rabbi Abraham stood outside looking in. The Rabbi looked in at the Gan Eden, which measures eight hundred thousand years wide. He looked at the five glorious chambers inside: One chamber was cedar with a ceiling of crystal, one was cedar with a ceiling of silver, one was silver and gold with a ceiling of pearl, one was olivewood with a ceiling of rubies, and one was made of emeralds with a ceiling of rosewood. He saw these five glorious chambers, and he saw the many holy rabbis and he saw the empty place reserved for him. And Achselrad was both happy and sad, and he felt light and overwhelmed and calm and nervous all at once.

"Return the sword!" called Dumah, the black Angel of Death. But Rabbi Abraham was still looking into the Great Hereafter; he stood at the Golden Gates, mesmerized and speechless. "Abraham, son of Alexander," continued Dumah, "you have been overwhelmed by the holy spirit of Heaven. However – you must go back to Cologne with me. You must die in the proper fashion. At the moment you are not dead at all, and you cannot enter Heaven."

Rabbi Abraham was weak and almost dazed from the powerful spirtuality of the glorious Great Hereafter. He felt confused. He was afraid that he would not really be allowed into Heaven. So the Rabbi stood unmoving, and he refused to give up the sword.

By now the angels had gathered on the other side of the Gates of Heaven. They watched Dumah and they jostled each other. They talked and they wondered. If the good Rabbi retained the sword of death, not only would he be unable to enter the Great Hereafter—*no* human would ever be able to enter Paradise. Would death be abolished from the world? Would men continue to live on earth forever?

The noise of the angels increased. Dumah began to call in deep bell-like tones over and over again, and slowly he stepped toward the Rabbi. Rabbi Abraham felt cold and he began to tremble and to shiver. And then, suddenly, there was silence.

Suddenly there was silence, and the celestial nighttime skies became black. The Lord God Almighty had stepped from his great Throne of Glory, and He strode across the Heavens, radiant and omnipotent, and no one dared to look up. The magnificent Lord God, the most Holy One Himself, walked from His Throne. Thunder rolled from His shoulders. Lightning flashed from His eyebrows. And then all was silent.

The fearsome Lord God, the Most Mighty of the Holies, reached down His powerful right hand. He knocked the sword of death from the hands of the Rabbi. The Almighty One had raised His arms and He had waved His hands, and the bloody sword of death had flown from the Rabbi's hands. It dropped through a cloud. It glinted in the newly lit starlight of the celestial nighttime skies. The sword plummeted: it dropped to earth and it stuck like a silver tombstone in the center of the *Am Toten Juden*, the Jewish cemetery of Cologne—yes, Rabbi, it stuck like a tall fearsome cold tombstone casting a sharp black shadow beyond the outer walls of old medieval Cologne. Swift as an eagle, Dumah, the Angel of Death, flew down too, and he stood beside his sword. And the great and awesome voice of the eternal Lord God roared from Heaven, *"Man must continue to die!"* And then, the Rabbi awoke.

ood evening, Rabbi. Of course—please feel free to sit here by the stove: the night fire helps me to become sleepy also. You and I are not blessed like old Reb Elbaum. Once again, I saw him nodding off during the last prayers this evening. He has learned to sway piously even while asleep: he must have acquired some magic from the mystic Achselrad. I suppose that you and I could also use a dose of Achselrad tonight. My grandmother said that he could put men into a sleep trance by waving a gold coin before their eyes.

Rabbi Abraham Achselrad was always conjuring visions in the synagogue. Often, he saw two men when others saw only one, and one night he claimed to have seen the Golem of Worms walking down Judengasse Street in Cologne. With all his phantasms, I doubt whether old Achselrad would be tolerated nowadays—but my grandmother said that Rabbi Abraham was also a scholar, and he himself claimed that his visions came from devout and pious study.

This same Abraham Achselrad was a writer too. He authored many Kabbalistic tomes of mystical knowledge, including the *Keter Shem Tov*; unfortunately this work was never published—now it exists only as a secret manuscript hidden in the old Cologne yeshiva. Rabbi Abraham had learned much strange and occult lore from his old

268

master, Rabbi Eliazer. What is that? Eliazer? Why, yes, Rabbi, I will gladly tell you the history of Eliazer ben Judah, the mystic of Worms:

Once upon a time, in medieval Germany of the twelfth century, there lived a pious scholar named Judah. Judah was the Chief Rabbi of Worms. One year, on the first night of Passover, Judah's wife gave birth to a son, a little wrinkled red potato of a boy who cried strongly when he was hungry and who waved his fists and smiled when he was fed. In those days, the Jews were suffering many persecutions. Rabbi Judah shared the hope of others that the good Lord God soon would hold out His mighty right arm and shelter the Jews. Some men wondered whether this Divine Providence might work through one of the German Jews. Judah looked at his little baby. Would this vigorous new son one day help to protect his people? Judah prayed and prayed, and in his heart he felt that he should name the newborn boy "Eliazer," which means "God has helped."

Judah's son grew up strong in body and strong in mind. He became a great scholar, and he was well versed in the Holy Law. In addition, Eliazer quickly mastered many foreign languages. As a young man he traveled throughout Europe. Eliazer disappeared from record for two full years, and during this time he learned the mystical knowledge of the Kabbalists. After his travels, he settled in Frankenthal. When the old rabbi of Frankenthal retired, Eliazer ben Judah was asked to head the local yeshiva. A few years later, Eliazer's father died, and Eliazer left Frankenthal to become the Chief Rabbi of the Jewish community in Worms.

In those days, terrible forces were loose in the Rhineland countryside. Demons whispered that Jews used the blood of Christian children during the Passover ceremonies. Public denials from Jews and Gentiles alike were of no use. The evil spirits merely laughed and hissed and coughed, and then they whispered the monstrous accusation anew. Rabbi Eliazer prayed and prayed, for it seemed that only the Almighty Lord God Himself had the strength and the wide-ranging power to silence these malign whispering winds.

The demons of the German countryside were not content with rumor: they also stirred up attacks. Eliazer ben Judah took over the rabbinate of Worms not long after the Jewish community had been ransacked by a mob of crusaders. The angry force had come to Worms from Speyer. The local cleric of Worms – the Bishop Allebrandus – sheltered as many Jews as he could, but in outlying areas other Jews were killed, their houses were destroyed, and their goods were stolen. Then on a Sunday, the 23rd day of the month of *Iyar*, the Worms synagogue and the Holy Scrolls were burned.

The angry crowds remained in Worms for seven long days. They laid siege to the Bishop's estate. Bishop Allebrandus could not protect the Jews forever. "You must convert to Christianity," he said to them. "This is your only chance to escape a certain death."

The Jews requested time to consider; then many of them killed themselves. At this, the enraged mob stormed the Bishop's residence and murdered most of the remaining Jews. Eventually the mob of crusaders left town, and almost eight hundred Jews were finally buried by the survivors. The black memory of those days had darkened the Jewish community of Worms for years. It was no wonder that almost a decade later, Rabbi Eliazer ben Judah spent much of his time worrying and praying, almost in a state of mourning.

In the world beyond the little Jewish community of Worms, power struggles continued between the local bishops, the wealthy citizens, and the German kings. Finally, King Henry the Fifth acquired Worms, in the treaty of Wurzburg. King Henry built a castle in Worms, and he granted the citizens formal independence from Church domination. This worried Rabbi Eliazer, for it was well known that the King did not like the Jews. Rabbi Eliazer frequently shook his head, and he said to his pupils, "I fear King Henry. He is like Goliath, the contemptuous Philistine giant. To balance this malevolence, we must find some countervailing hero, someone with the strong spirit of brave King David."

Eliazer ben Judah prayed and prayed for help from a heroic figure. One night in the cold month of *Shevat*, Rabbi Eliazer fell asleep in the small back study room of the old yeshiva of Worms. The Rabbi fell asleep, and he dreamt a strange and wondrous vision. In his dream, Aniel, an angel of the Lord, appeared barefoot, in white robes, and amidst a gentle spring breeze, and he said:

Ato Bra Golem Devuk Hakhomer V'tigzar Zedam Chevel Torfe
Yisroel.

"Rabbi Eliazer – in order to defeat the tormentors of the Jews, you must fashion a Golem out of clay. Make an animated human image of new clay; in this way, you can protect Israel from its enemies."

The Rabbi awoke. He looked about him. The dream was still fresh and clear in his mind. The words rang in his ears. So, Rabbi Eliazer ben Judah wrote out the Hebrew command of the holy angel Aniel – and he found that the message formed a *minyan*, ten holy words beginning with the first ten letters of the alphabet.

The Rabbi stared at the words. He stared until the letters seemed to fade away. Then he took out the most ancient and mystical Kabbalistic book, the *Sefer Yetzirah* – the "Book of Creation" – and he began to read. Eliazer ben Judah read chapter after chapter. And it was late in the night when Rabbi Eliazer ben Judah discovered the secret. Suddenly he opened wide his eyes: he realized how to rearrange the ten mystical words in the command of the holy angel Aniel into *zirufim* or formulas that would allow him to make a living being from inanimate clay. Rabbi Eliazer had learned how to create a Golem.

The Rabbi could not sleep. He viewed and reviewed his *zirufim*. He did not dare to leave the exact words written on a paper: they were too dangerous and too powerful for anyone else to see. Therefore, he burned the paper in the stove – and the flames turned a bright and holy blue. Then the Rabbi sat at his desk. He sat unmoving until dawn, and no one knows what it is that he thought. I can only say, Rabbi, that had you seen him, you would have thought that he had grown much older and more worn during the night.

The next morning, Rabbi Eliazer sent for two associates: his son-in-law, Isaac ben Shimshon ha-Kohen, and a special pupil, Jakob ben Chayim Sasson ha-Levi. "My friends," he began, "I need your assistance." The Rabbi told them that the Jews' troubles had become so serious that they now needed special Divine aid. The Rabbi lowered his voice. "I have had a holy vision," he said. "I have been instructed to make a Golem, a clay man who can be our protector."

The two men, Isaac and Jakob, did not know what to say. They looked at each other and then they looked at the Rabbi. Rabbi Eliazer continued: "To do this secret and holy deed, we must work together. We must mix the four elements: *Aysch* (Fire), *Mayim* (Water), *Ruach* (Wind), and *Aphar* (Earth). Each man can contribute the spiritual force for only one element. Isaac, you must represent Fire. Jakob, you will represent Water. I shall represent Wind, and the good Earth will give us Clay. Together, and with the power of the holy *zirufim* taught to me by the angel Aniel, we shall create a Golem."

Isaac looked at Jakob, and Jakob looked at Isaac. After a moment, Isaac said, "Good Rabbi, do we dare to do this thing? It is true that you are a holy man, but the creation of life is something beyond the province of man."

The Rabbi nodded. "*True* creation is beyond us," said Eliazer ben Judah. "But in the end we will not have a real man, Isaac—we will have a Golem. We will have a clay-colored creature with the shape of a man but without a complete human spirit."

Jakob ben Chayim Sasson shifted his weight on the worn bench, and he tapped his foot nervously. "Rabbi," said Jakob, "the thought of this makes my stomach feel tight, and it makes my head ache. Are you certain that we are about to do the right thing?"

And Rabbi Eliazer answered, "I can only say, my friend, that it is a commandment from the Lord. In matters of creation, we dare not question the will of the good Lord God (blessed be He). Remember the old story from the Talmud:

"When the Almighty Lord God first planned to create man, He began by making a company of ministering angels. The golden glimmering Hosts leaped and jostled one another and laughed with the gentle ringing voices of the Heavens. They flew about, swooping and soaring and gliding among the celestial clouds—clouds that stretched on and on beyond the ends of the world and into the deepest blue nighttime skies beyond. The angels soared where the iridescent skirts of the majestic Lord God flowed like shimmering curtains, amidst the stars and the planets and the astral tides, for ever and ever and ever.

"The Lord sat on His Great Throne of Glory, watching these wondrous and perfect creatures. Then He turned to them, and He said, 'I intend to make another creature, which I will name "man." I will make him in My image. You shall be responsible as My messengers and caretakers for this creature.'

"The angels talked among themselves, and they asked the Lord, 'O Sovereign of the World, what is it that man will do? What will be his great deeds?'

"Then the Lord replied, 'He has no specific tasks. He must only behave justly and rightly, and he must respect My Laws.'

"And the angels said, 'This is all? Great King, You can do anything by Yourself. Why bother to create man? Will this creature have some new, special, and wondrous powers?'

" 'No,' said the great Lord Almighty, 'man will be a complex, impure, and rather weak creature.'

"The angels lifted their eyebrows–all the holy Host looked puzzled. 'Man will be ordinary? In fact, he will be impure? Then why should You make this creature *man*? Already, we can see that there will be troubles. Clearly there will be taints and turmoils and misdeeds and misfortunes if You put this imperfect being into Your incondensably complex world. Why should we waste our time ministering to him?'

"The fearsome Lord God frowned, but some of the angels continued: 'Do not take offense, O Most Holy Master–but this course of action looks like wasted effort on Your part. This plan of creation is not pure and holy; it seems doomed to cause problems and complications and grief forever.'

"The Lord creased His holy brow. He said, 'Creation of the simple, the pure, and the untainted is a waste of My effort. But this creation of man is special. We cannot predict its future–that makes it the most special creation of all.' And the Almighty Lord God stretched out His little finger and scattered the angels aside, and He reached down into the dust of the earth–the warm dust of the original Holy Lands amidst the suntanned golden hills–and He shaped the shape of a man, and then He breathed into him the warm spirit of life. And God created man.

"Yes, in the beginning, the Lord created man in His own complex and unfathomable image, amen."

Jakob listened quietly. "And what does this tale teach us, Rabbi?" he asked after a moment.

"It teaches us that we cannot understand, and therefore that we cannot question, the good Lord God on matters of creation," answered the Rabbi.

"Very well, Rabbi," said Jakob. And then he asked, "So, what must we do first?"

Rabbi Eliazer leaned back in his chair, and he tapped his fingers on his desk. "First, we must become clean, pure, and holy," said the Rabbi. "For one week we must be penitent, we must pray constantly, and we must eat only bread and drink only water."

Therefore, the three men prayed and they fasted. Then one week later, on the second day of the cold month of *Adar*, the three men went to the ritual bathhouse after the evening prayers. In a small side room, they removed their prayer shawls and their clothes. They set the shawls and the clothes on a green stone shelf cut into the wall, and they wrapped themselves in clean white sheets. Then they entered the main bath room, where the ceiling was supported by seven stone pillars. Eliazer ben Judah, Isaac ben Shimshon ha-Kohen, and Jakob ben Chayim Sasson ha-Levi stepped down the stone steps into the spring-water bath. In accord with the old tradition, they immersed themselves completely in the water seven times. Meanwhile, Rabbi Eliazer said, "Thus is it written in the Holy Scriptures":

> So he went down and he dipped himself into the River Jordan seven times, as the man of God had told him. And his flesh was thereby restored as a little child's, and he was clean once again.

"Amen," said the Rabbi, and the other men said "Amen." Then they returned to the synagogue.

The men sat silently in the back study room; they sat barefoot on the floor and they chanted the midnight liturgy. It was now six hours after sunset. Rabbi Eliazer slowly and sadly recited the *Haztot*, the midnight Lamentation for Jerusalem. And eventually it was the fourth hour after midnight on that second day of *Adar* in medieval Worms of long, long ago.

Now the men arose, and without a word, they walked to the outskirts of the city of Worms, to the banks of the River Rhine. There they found a loam pit, and in the black mud they located a pocket of pure gray clay. The men dug by torchlight. Soon, they had formed the figure of a large person from gray Rhine clay. There before them, inert and blank, lay the image of a man two and a half meters long. It was the beginning of a Golem – and it lay on the river bank, with its blank eyes turned toward the nighttime Heavens above.

The men stood around the figure. It was empty and lifeless; it was a blank soft statue of a man. The Rabbi looked up to the nighttime Heavens. There were faint twinkles in the sky. Were the silver souls of the newly departed glinting in the celestial starlight, somewhere far, far overhead? Rabbi Eliazer stared into the sky. Then he sighed, and he bent down. Neatly and carefully, he inscribed the word *emet*–truth–in the soft clay of the forehead of the future Golem of Worms.

The three men stood at the feet of the Golem-to-be. They stared at the word *emet*. The clay body lay empty and unmoving. The Rabbi looked up to Heaven, and he began to chant: he recited the mystical incantation that comprises the alphabets of the two hundred and twenty-one numinous Gates of Knowledge, and he recited this chant over every single part of the clay figure.

"Now, Isaac," said the Rabbi softly, "you must walk seven times around the clay body from right to left." And as Isaac passed the Rabbi, the old man whispered quiet *zirufim*. The inert body became red like fire–it gleamed like a coal in the black, black night of medieval Worms.

"Now, Jakob," said the Rabbi, "you must walk seven times around the clay body from left to right." And as Jakob passed the Rabbi, the old man whispered quiet *zirufim*. The men poured water from the river on the Golem. It sprouted hair on its head. Nails appeared on its fingers and its toes. After a moment, the inert body again became as gray as the clay in the banks of the River Rhine.

Then Rabbi Eliazer ben Judah himself walked seven times around the clay body, whispering quiet *zirufim*. The Rabbi took a tiny tablet from his pocket. On the tablet was written the *Shem* –the Ineffable Name of God–in seven mystical forms. Gently, the Rabbi put the tablet into the clay man's mouth. The Rabbi bowed to the east and to the west. He bowed to the south and to the north. And then, facing Jerusalem, the three men recited together the verse from the Book of Genesis:

> Then the Lord God formed a man from the dust of the ground, and He breathed into his nostrils the holy breath of life. Thus, the man became a living creature.

A wind arose. It blew the men's hair and their clothes and their arms. The men closed their eyes. The wind passed and the men looked down, and there before them, they saw that the clay figure had come alive. The Golem had opened his gray eyes, and now he was alive.

The two younger men, Isaac and Jakob, looked at the Golem and they looked at the Rabbi. But Rabbi Eliazer ben Judah kept his eyes on the clay man. "Stand," said the Rabbi. "Stand, and defend the Jews."

And slowly, the Golem stood.

The Golem stood, and the Rabbi said, "We have fashioned you from clay to help protect the Jews. I shall call you Joseph, after Joseph Sheda, a spirit who helps rabbis. 'Joseph' means 'the Lord increases,' and through you the Lord will increase the strength of the Jews." Silently, the Golem nodded his massive clay-colored head.

The Golem stood and he stared at the three men, but he said not a word. (The Golem did not speak because he could not speak – the mystical *zirufim* did not convey the power of speech – and this was one sign that the Golem was not fully human.) Then the men dressed the clay creature in the clothes of a shammas, and to all outward appearances, the Golem became a large clay-colored lumbering man.

And at daybreak, on the morning of the second day of the cold month of *Adar*, the four figures went home. Yes, four individuals walked home through the gray streets of medieval Worms – four walked, Rabbi, where once there had been only three.

h, good evening again, Rabbi. Yes, I know – it is always hard to sleep on the night of a bright half moon. Put your feet up on the side bench here and I will open the stove door. Let me push this coal back. There is nothing like the glow of the oven; it washes away the cares of a hard day.

I heard your final benediction tonight, Rabbi. Do not deny it – you are overworked. Oh yes, even a shammas like me can tell. I kept one eye on you as I cleaned the dishes and I saw that you were watching the door, hoping that Reb Elbaum would leave early. But then Reb Anton stayed late in order to wrestle with the scriptural passage from the last pages of the Book of Genesis:

> When their father was dead, Joseph's brothers approached Joseph and they said: "In his last words to us before he died, your father gave us this message for you: 'Joseph, my dear son, I ask you to forgive your brothers' crime and wickedness – although I know that they did you harm.' So now, Joseph, forgive us, we beg you. For we, too, are servants of your father's merciful God."

> When they said this to him, Joseph wept. And like the ever merciful Holy One (blessed be He forever), Joseph forgave his brothers, for they had cared for their father Jacob in his old age.

The warring emotions of forgiveness form a complex tangle; after trying to unravel them for Reb Anton, of course you are still worn out. . . . What is that? A story from me? Rabbi, all I know are the old-fashioned children's tales, the grandmother fables. You need something new and fresh to keep your mind keen. Otherwise you will become a dreamy old man like me, and you will find yourself constantly musing and dozing and nodding off in front of the stove.

What do you mean you are already an old man? Do you really think that sixty years is old? You are still a child. When you reach eighty, *then* you will be old. You doubt that you will live to see eighty years? If so, Rabbi, then you will never grow old. . . . All right, all right, I know no special stories but listening to you and Reb Anton put me in mind of Isaac the crude *shochet*, whom the Lord forgave. It was my grandmother who told me about Isaac, and now I will tell you:

Once upon a time, said my grandmother to me, in the days when Abraham ben Alexander was the Chief Rabbi there lived within the family of the Jewish community of Cologne a pious man, named Meshulam ben Jesse ha-Levi. Meshulam was righteous, honest, and upright. One of his special virtues was his attendance at funerals. As you know, Rabbi, the Jewish cemetery of Cologne, the *Am Toten Juden*, was located outside the old southern gate of the city, far from the houses—in order to fulfill the old custom of burying the dead in a garden that was at least fifty paces from the nearest home. Meshulam's house was on the street leading from the synagogue to the cemetery, and all funeral processions passed by his door.

Whenever someone in the town had died and was being carried to his grave, Meshulam ben Jesse ha-Levi stopped whatever he was doing and he joined the funeral procession. Meshulam had been a yeshiva student when Yehudi ben Solomon was the Chief Rabbi of Cologne. Rabbi Yehudi had told his pupils: "Young men, recall the words of the Holy Scriptures":

> The good Lord God is testing you to discover whether you love the Lord your God with all your heart and with all your soul and with all your might. So remember: you must follow the ways of the Lord.

Rabbi Yehudi looked down sternly at his charges. "And, my boys, how does this teach us about funerals?" he asked.

The boys looked at the floor, and there was silence. So the Rabbi said, "I will *tell* you how this teaches us about funerals: just as the good Lord God Himself attended to the burial of His dead (such as His fine servant Moses), so must all men follow the ways of the Lord and attend humbly to the burial of their own dead, amen."

Meshulam never forgot this lesson. Therefore, Meshulam always followed the ways of the Lord: specifically, he always followed the funeral processions as they passed by his front door. Meshulam went to every single burial. In fact, it was Meshulam who always recited Psalm 91 seven times on the way to the cemetery and then again seven times as the body was lowered into the grave. Meshulam would begin:

> You who enjoy God's protectiveness
> Resting in His Heavenly shade
> Admit that the Lord is your fortress
> Your refuge and your barricade.
>
> The Holy One will soon subdue
> The fiercest gales that rainstorms bring
> For He is ever guarding you
> Within the shelter of His mighty wing.

And he would end:

> "When he calls to Me I will answer
> I will help him in his strife
> Then I will bring him lasting honor
> And will give to him long life.
>
> "So a good and humble person—
> He who trusts and follows Me—
> Will enjoy My full salvation
> Through a glorious Eternity."

Meshulam was a good man and a humble man: he trusted and believed in the Almighty Lord God, and he knew that he would enjoy the fullness of God's salvation, to the end of his long and joyful days.

Meshulam was getting old now. His legs became weaker and weaker; finally, they often refused to carry his body. Eventually, he could not walk up stairs or down stairs, and it took two canes and many, many minutes for him to travel the shortest distance. Then suddenly Meshulam's walking deteriorated even further: now Meshulam could barely walk at all.

Meanwhile, there came a mild and gentle Sabbath on which a well-respected colleague died. The next morning, when the funeral procession was forming in the synagogue, Meshulam found himself unable to stand. Tears came to his eyes, and Meshulam ben Jesse prayed to the good Lord God:

> Lord of the Universe, You have restored sight to the blind and You have made lame men walk again. Now my limbs are weak. Please listen to my prayer. I send my plea high up to Your Golden Throne of Glory from my lowly bed of sorrow and suffering. Give me strength enough to rise and to accompany to his grave every honorable, pious, and upright man who dies in this town—blessed be You, amen.

Then Meshulam bowed his head and he repeated the verses from Psalm 31:

> You ignore the idol worshiper.
> And You redeemed me, great God of virtue,
> I am grateful, and now I'm holier—
> I put my fullest trust in You.

> I will rejoice, I will be glad:
> With mercy and with kindness
> You saw the afflictions that I had
> And You helped, in my distress.

> Now my life is worn with sorrows,
> It is filled with daily groans;
> I stumble under a load of woes
> And disease is in my very bones.

Upon Your humble follower
Send Your radiance from above;
Be my critical examiner –
But then shine down Your warmest golden love.

Ah, Rabbi, we can take heart; for the good Lord God (blessed be He) hears all the prayers of the righteous. Therefore, the Most Holy One tilted His radiant head and He listened with His wondrous ears. Meshulam's prayers were a tiny noise from a far-off town on the River Rhine, but the Almighty One heard them clearly. Therefore, the Lord sent down his messenger Hasdiel, an angel of benevolence. Hasdiel sped through the Heavens down to the Rhinelands, down to medieval Cologne, and he appeared to Meshulam as a holy man dressed in pure white Sabbath robes. Hasdiel said gently, "Good Meshulam, your prayers have been heard. Your request has been granted." Then Hasdiel disappeared.

And so it came to pass that whenever a truly honorable, pious, and upright man died, and whenever the funeral procession was passing the house of old Meshulam ben Jesse, Meshulam miraculously regained his strength. Once again, old Meshulam followed the funerals, reciting Psalm 91 and praying fervently for the soul of the newly departed.

This went on for many, many months. Soon it was the summer, the month of *Av*, and Alexis ben Moshe, a well-known member of the Cologne Jewish community, died unexpectedly. Alexis had always been thought to be upright and God-fearing. He gave much charity unasked. He prayed regularly in the synagogue. He spoke kindly to everyone. After he died, the whole community was sad. When the funeral procession of Alexis ben Moshe passed Meshulam's house, the old man tried to stand. But what was this? His legs would not hold him. He collapsed on the floor. Meshulam tried again, but it was of no use. His legs remained weak, and the funeral procession proceeded to the *Am Toten Juden* without Meshulam ben Jesse.

As the funeral passed Meshulam's house, people turned to look at Meshulam's old wooden door. It remained closed. This was very strange. The pious men in the procession opened wide their eyes and they raised their eyebrows, but they continued on. The other people in the community were puzzled too when they heard of this – and of course Meshulam himself could make no sense of it at all. Could it be that Meshulam had finally gotten too old and too weak to help with the funerals? Perhaps he had already fulfilled his holy mission here on earth and now it was time for him simply to rest. "Well," thought Meshulam sadly, "if this is the will of the Omnipotent One, then so be it—praise the will of the Lord."

The next week, another Cologne Jew died. This was Isaac ben Reuben—"Rude Isaac," as he was nicknamed. Isaac was a *shochet*. He was not very smart, he was quarrelsome, and he had done many rough and questionable things in his lifetime: Isaac was not really a bad man, but he was not someone you would want as a companion. As the funeral procession of Isaac ben Reuben was passing Meshulam's house, the old man tried to stand. Why, he stood with no difficulty! He held onto a chair in case he should fall. But, no—he was quite steady. In fact, Meshulam found that he could run out the door. So, Meshulam joined the procession. Then he recited the funeral Psalm seven times on the way to the *Am Toten Juden* and seven times as the body was being lowered into the grave. Meshulam walked home by himself. When he reached his bed, his legs began to feel tired again, and after a few minutes his full weakness returned.

This strange turn of events surprised Meshulam, and it surprised the Jews of Cologne. "If Meshulam could still miraculously accompany funerals, then perhaps Alexis had not been such an upright man. And perhaps Isaac had not been such a bad man," thought the people.

The men of Cologne talked and talked about this upside-down possibility. Finally, the sages in the congregation decided to investigate. White-haired Baruch ben Jacob said, "Gentlemen, we have talked this matter back and forth and up and down. We need more information."

"I agree, Baruch," said old Shimshon ha-Zaken, "for I believe in the scriptural Proverb—"

> The Almighty turns His radiant head,
>   Standing aloof from the wicked crowd;
> But the good Lord listens closely instead
>   To the prayers of the righteously endowed.

"In other words, are we witnessing here the fact that the true characters of these two men, Alexis and Isaac, were in fact the opposite of what we had thought?"

The old scholars muttered and murmured among themselves and there was much stroking of beards. After the full seven days of mourning, Baruch ben Jacob and Shimshon ha-Zaken went to visit the widow of Isaac the *shochet*. "Tell us, good woman," began Baruch, "what kind of man was Isaac?"

"Well, gentlemen," she answered, "Isaac was not always pleasant. He yelled too much. He did not have good things to say about others. We were never rich, but even then I think that he could have contributed more to charity. He did not go to the synagogue every day. In many ways, he was difficult to live with."

Baruch and Shimshon nodded: this description matched what they remembered about Rude Isaac. But the wife was continuing: "On the other hand, Isaac surprised me recently. You see, Isaac's father, Reuben ben Avram, was more than ninety years old when he came to live with us, a few years ago. Do you remember old Reuben? He died during Passover last year."

Again, Baruch and Shimshon nodded. "Reuben was very old. Isaac used to dress the old man and to feed him; he took gentle care of his father. In the end, Reuben died happily."

Baruch and Shimshon looked at one another. Then they thanked the widow, and they bid her good-bye.

The two old scholars walked down Judengasse Street. "I think that the story is becoming clearer," said Baruch. "Shall we visit the widow of Alexis?"

"Yes, I think that we should," said Shimshon.

Baruch ben Jacob and Shimshon ha-Zaken found the widow of Alexis ben Moshe still red-eyed and sad. "Tell us, good woman," began Baruch. "What kind of man was your husband?"

The wife sat down on a chair, and she put her hands in her lap. "Oh, gentlemen, Alexis was the best of husbands," she said, and she began to cry and cry. After a moment she stopped, and she wiped her eyes. "Excuse me, sirs—whenever I think of him, I miss him so much."

The widow took a deep breath. "Let me see. During all our married life, Alexis never spoke a harsh word to me. He was always kind to the children and to our friends and even to strangers. He recited his prayers three times each day. In fact, he was so pious that he would arise at midnight and go into his private study and pray for at least an hour."

Baruch and Shimshon both raised their eyebrows, and they looked at each other. "What is in this private study?" asked old Shimshon.

"Why, I do not know exactly," she answered. "Alexis kept the door locked, and I was never in the room."

Then white-haired Baruch said, "Perhaps you would be so good as to let us take a look inside."

"I do not see how that could upset Alexis now," she answered sadly. Then she went to her bedroom. From her husband's drawer she removed a heavy key, and she gave it to the two old sages of Cologne.

The men asked the wife to wait in the bedroom. They went into the hallway, they located the door to the study, and they opened it with the key. Inside, they found a small Christian shrine, with a cross and a crucifix and a statue of the Mother Mary. In addition, there were keys, a sword, and an icon of a fish – all the symbols of Saint Peter, the saint of fishermen and the prince of the Christian Apostles.

Baruch and Shimshon did not touch a thing in the room. Carefully, they locked the door. When they returned to the bedroom, the wife asked, "And what was in the study?"

Baruch looked at Shimshon, and Shimshon looked at Baruch. "It was nothing of any interest to a fine Jewish woman such as yourself," answered old Shimshon. "Let us leave it as a private memorial to your husband."

"Very well," said the widow, and she sighed and tears came to her eyes.

Then Baruch said, "We should give this key to the Rabbi to keep, good woman."

"Do you really think that is the best thing?" she asked.

"Most definitely," answered Baruch.

So the two old sages left the woman, and they took the key back to the Rabbi. When they returned to the synagogue, they found Rabbi Abraham ben Alexander reading in the back room. He looked up, he sat back in his chair, and he listened quietly to the story. Then the Rabbi closed his eyes. The two sages looked at one another. Eventually, they set the key on the Rabbi's desk. Then white-haired Baruch ben Jacob and old Shimshon ha-Zaken both shook their heads, and they left.

For many minutes, the Rabbi sat silently in his chair. Finally he opened his eyes, he picked up the key, and he walked from the old building. Rabbi Abraham walked down Judengasse Street. He passed the house of Meshulam ben Jesse, and he went through the town and out the southern gate to the *Am Toten Juden*. Old Achselrad walked to the grave of Alexis ben Moshe, and he pushed the key into the damp earth at the foot of the grave. Then the Rabbi turned, and without looking back, he walked home into the Jewish Quarter. Rabbi Abraham Achselrad walked back along the route of the funeral processions and he returned to his small Jewish family in the medieval city of Cologne.

ood evening, Rabbi. No sleep for the weary? That is
what my grandmother said, and she said it almost nightly. If you are
cold then sit down here on the bench and I will stoke up the oven. This
stoker? It is one of the iron shoe scrapers from the front hall – you
probably do not recognize it because it is covered with soot. Of course
there are still two scrapers in the anteroom for dirty shoes. But I myself
am of the old school: I think that all pious men should pray barefoot
and that holy men should always write barefoot. I have even been told
that some *hazans* will only sing barefoot; apparently, this began in
Europe with Rabbi Mordecai ben Hillel.

Exactly, Rabbi – I am speaking of the same medieval German
rabbi who wrote the famous two volumes of *Responsa* and who also
wrote the great Halakhic legal work now known as the "Mordecai."
Sadly, this wonderful rabbi, Mordecai ben Hillel, and his wife and five
children were killed by an anti-Semitic mob in Nuremberg during the
very last years of the thirteenth century.

But let me return to happier things. You may not know this,
Rabbi, but Mordecai was not only a scholar, he was a *hazan* too. In
those days music was not commonly a part of the synagogue ritual in
northern Europe. Music still had a secular feel; in fact, Rabbi Morde-

cai's music—like all the music of Europe—was strongly influenced by
the songs of the wandering minstrels. In medieval France, Germany,
and Italy, troubadours traveled from court to court carrying the
southern French poetry and customs. The troubadours and the jon-
gleurs came north from the Mediterranean regions. They sang about
the gay and polished society of the feudal princes; they brought with
them those beautiful songs that were the glory of the Provençal tongue.
Of course, there were no Jewish troubadour songs—although some of
the musicians were Jewish. Nonetheless, Jews saw and heard and felt
this special lyrical music. The songs were sweet and touching, and to
the Jews of Germany the songs were a window into a dream world, a
fantasy world, a world that seemed like magic.

At that time, all manner of wanderers filtered through the Jewish
communities of Rhineland Germany. These travelers came wide-eyed
and worn and filled with wondrous tales and with reports of ever new
potential Messiahs. Occasionally, the pilgrims were singers: sometimes they were transients from minstrel troops, and sometimes they
were itinerant *hazans*. Strangers were always appearing in the old
Cologne yeshiva, and one mild autumn afternoon, in the month of
Tishri, Rabbi Hayyim was working in the small back study room when
he heard a beautiful new voice singing in the main prayer hall.

As you know, Rabbi, Hayyim ben Yehiel was the Chief Rabbi of
Cologne at the end of the thirteenth century. (Hayyim was three rabbis
after the mystic Abraham Achselrad.) Now it was a gentle *Tishri*
afternoon, and Rabbi Hayyim suddenly had a mystical feeling. He
lifted his head. He looked to the door, and he heard a wonderful chant:
Mordecai ben Hillel had wandered into the synagogue, and he was
singing a holy psalm of prayer.

Hayyim ben Yehiel lifted his head in the back study room in the
old Cologne yeshiva. He raised his eyebrows. He opened wide his eyes.
He listened to the fine singing that floated back from the main prayer
hall. Hayyim listened for many minutes. Then he stood and he walked
to the doorway. Sitting on a wooden bench before the Holy stone Ark,
in the golden light of the afternoon sun filtering through the twelve
stained glass windows with their colored lions and snakes, was a man
in a dark coat. The man had his eyes closed, and he was singing a
wondrous hymn. Rabbi Hayyim waited. The singer stopped, and he
opened his eyes. "Hello, Rabbi," said the stranger, smiling at Hayyim.

"Hello," said Rabbi Hayyim. "Welcome to our synagogue."

"Thank you," said the man.

"Would you like to join me in the study room? I can offer you some bread and some wine."

"That is very kind of you, Rabbi," said the stranger. "Let me introduce myself. I am Mordecai ben Hillel from Nuremberg. I am on my way north to a meeting in Dusseldorf. Perhaps you have heard about it. Rabbi Simcha of Dusseldorf has asked a number of us to attend a conference; we hope to rework the Halakhic code for dealing with erroneous decisions of a *Bet Din*."

"Ah, Rabbi Mordecai," said Rabbi Hayyim, "it is a great honor to have you visit us here."

Warmly, the two men shook hands, and they went into the back study room. Rabbi Hayyim gave Mordecai the seat of honor behind the rabbi's desk. The two rabbis talked for many hours. When evening came, Rabbi Mordecai led the prayers. Afterward, Rabbi Mordecai and Rabbi Hayyim talked late into the cool night.

Although the men began by discussing Halakhah, Mordecai's talk turned to singing as the hour grew late and as the night deepened. "I grew up as one of eight children," he was saying. "We lived in a small house outside of Nuremburg. It was a farmhouse with a thatched roof and dirt floors."

Rabbi Hayyim leaned back on the bench and nodded.

"My mother always kept her linens white and clean and spotless, and throughout the house there was the smell of warm freshly baked bread," continued Mordecai. "What fine memories it brings back." He smiled, and he took a deep gentle breath.

The two men were quiet, each remembering his own warm freshly baked childhood days.

After a time, Mordecai ben Hillel said, "My father and my mother were both weavers. They worked at home, and in the evenings the whole family sang together while my parents made cloth. Singing was their life and their redemption. Of course, we sang only at night: we lived in the business district of a small Gentile community, and during the days our neighbors did not tolerate Jewish singing. But in the evenings, when the next-door shops were closed and when the Gentiles had retreated to their homes, we sang. There were even competitions among local Jewish singing groups."

"There were competitions?" asked Rabbi Hayyim.

"Yes – we called these 'song nights,' " said Mordecai. "Another Jewish family, or sometimes two or three, would come over. We would serve honey cakes, and we would take turns singing."

Mordecai was silent for a moment. "You know, Rabbi Hayyim," he said, "now that I think of it, there were probably only a handful of 'song nights.' But they were such wonderful happy times that now I seem to remember them with a crystal clarity, as if they happened every night."

Again there was silence.

Mordecai sighed. "Then I grew up," he said, "and I went to the yeshivas in Nuremberg and in Wurzburg. I did fairly well, and I was rewarded with a rabbinate. Now I have a wife and five children. I suppose that I should have been completely happy. Certainly, I was blessed by the good Lord God, amen."

"Amen," responded Hayyim.

"I should have been happy," continued Mordecai, "but something was missing. It was something spiritual, but at the time I did not recognize exactly what it was. Then, one day I began singing a hymn in my congregation. I do not think that I had sung in public since I was a child."

Mordecai's voice became a bit quieter, and he said, "And then the clouds parted and the day dawned. It was as the great poet, Jehuda ha-Levi, wrote":

> We will live together in peace again –
>   once more the nation Israel
> Under God's golden sunshine mane
>   which sweeps dark clouds beyond the hill.

"Yes, suddenly a wondrous feeling swept over me; I think that many of the congregants felt it too."

(What is that, Rabbi? Well, as I mentioned, in those medieval days, true singing was not yet heard in most European synagogues. The northern congregations were conservative: they maintained the old Oriental ways. The men chanted in the simplest Jewish plainsong. They used the ancient musical formulas from the early days of the

Holy Lands – these were chants that could be learned easily and that could be sung by almost anyone.

But in the days of Rabbi Mordecai, the adventurous congregations were beginning to employ a *hazan*, a singer who had a special proficiency in music. As *hazans* proliferated, unique European Jewish melodies were developed. The *hazans* traveled, and the new Jewish songs passed from town to town. Well-known *hazans* even attracted crowds; their beautiful songs moved the congregations to tears. And soon, true music – full, complex, and emotional music – seeped into the life of the Jewish communities throughout Europe. Nuremberg had been a conservative congregation, but through Rabbi Mordecai, music suddenly filled the souls of the Nuremberg Jews.)

"Then, Rabbi Hayyim," Mordecai ben Hillel was saying, "once I had begun singing, I could not stop. We extended the service hours. A new spirituality enwrapped our little community. The holy music was like preaching. When you preach, you speak of the wonders of the Lord,and the listeners find love and comfort and happiness. In the same way, songs also talk of love and comfort and happiness. They speak of forgiveness and of joy – and they seem to speak directly to the soul, more directly than any plain words. With beautiful song, all is right with the world, amen."

Rabbi Mordecai smiled; then he continued, "My mind raced on and on when we sang. What new melodies could I find? I listened to the wandering troubadours. Yes, I must confess that I stood for hours before the minstrels at the Fair each fall.

"Then," said Mordecai, "one night I had a dream. Ah, Rabbi, I had a Great Dream, a wondrous God-given dream. You know the kind. It is a dream filled with mystical emotions. It is a dream where your soul floats free through the celestial skies and it sees and tastes the Paradise of the Great Hereafter. I am certain that you know what I mean."

And Rabbi Hayyim nodded, for he knew what Mordecai meant.

"I dreamt," said Mordecai, "a dream of a new kind of harmony; it was a harmony of music chanted to the deep prayers and the mystical psalms and the hidden holy verses. In the dream I was inside a synagogue, a huge bright synagogue. And, wonder of wonders, the little Jewish children floated back and forth to the ceiling, which was like a sunny morning sky. Everyone – babies and parents and grand-parents alike – was barefoot. All around us was the most gentle ancient melody and a glorious rich harmony and there were innumerable voices singing and singing and singing.

"But, good Rabbi, the words were not real words – no, they were 'song words' and hums and holy low chants. This glorious music of Paradise seemed to float on for hours and hours, and at the same time it seemed to be contained in the wink of an eye. And then at the end of the dream, I heard a deep mellow voice intone from the Book of Exodus":

> I will sing to the Lord Almighty
> Who has risen in wondrous triumph,
> Our voices blend in joyful harmony
> For He shall reign for ever and ever.

Mordecai closed his eyes, and he was silent. After a few minutes, Rabbi Hayyim said gently, "And then what happened, Rabbi?"

Mordecai smiled. "And then, good Rabbi, I awoke," he said.

Rabbi Mordecai nodded. "Then, I awoke," he said. "And imme-diately I began to try to recapture the music of this dream. I hummed and I chanted to myself, but this did not work: I could recreate some of the music, but the holy reverent sound was missing.

"Then it came to me. The sound, the sacred wondrous sound of my dream, was from a chorus and not from one man. The next day I hurried through the morning prayers. I was very excited, and I think that this made my congregants a bit unsettled. After the service, a group of men and boys stayed as usual to chant with me. I sat them down. I tried to tell them about my dream. At first, the singers did not understand at all what I was after. I was discouraged. I sang to them as best I could, but no one individual voice could capture the rich thick sound that I had heard.

"One day passed, and then the second came and went. And, as Genesis says: 'Evening came and morning came, a third day.' And it was on the fourth day after my holy dream that we had a blessed experience. It was at night. Only a few men were left in the prayer hall. As usual, they were chanting and I was singing a harmony along with

them. Soon, we fell to repeating an old mystical phrase that I had heard
from a wandering Kabbalist:

Anaktam Pastam Paspasim Dionsim

"We were tired. I began to tap out the rhythm with my foot.
After our pious prayers we were all barefoot and the other men began
gently to tap their bare feet also. A strange rhythm came forth. A low
holy tune happened. Where did this old harmony come from? No one
could say. Suddenly, a harmony, a chant, a sacred sound was hum-
ming through us. We were afraid to stop. For a moment I heard again
the sound of my dream. It was our ancients, our forefathers, who were
guiding us."

Rabbi Mordecai seemed to be listening to a sound from far away
and from long ago. "How can I describe that music to you?" he asked.
He paused a moment; then he said, "There is a deep gentle hum. It fills
the air. Then there are many voices blending in a quiet low harmony,
and in the background is the feeling—only the feeling, mind you, not
the sound—of a celestial tapping of hollow logs."

He was quiet; then he smiled. "I have not heard the dream music,
with its ancient celestial sound, since that glorious night," said Mordecai ben Hillel. "But I know, good Hayyim, that someday I shall hear
it again."

ood evening, Rabbi. You are having difficulty sleeping again? Well, just put your feet up on the side bench here, and I will open the stove door. Let me push this coal back; the white glow of those coals will wash away the cares of a hard day.

I heard your final prayers tonight and there is no use denying it, Rabbi–you are overworked. Even an old shammas like me can tell. I kept one eye on you when I was cleaning the dishes; I saw that you were watching the door, hoping that Reb Elbaum would leave early. But then Reb Anton stayed late to discuss the morning Sabbath Psalm, Psalm 136, which ends:

> God gives food to all His creatures,
>   And His love endures forever;
> God gives shelter to His children,
>   And His love endures forever;
> So give thanks to the God of Heaven –
>   For His love endures forever.

I had to smile when I listened to that Psalm; it is a happy and hopeful verse. The good Lord God *does* protect His children, especially

on the Sabbath, even under the most trying of circumstances. I remember a Sabbath protection story that my grandmother told me – it
was the tale of a difficult Sabbath long ago, when with the help of old
Rabbi Abraham Achselrad, the good Lord once again saved His children. This took place in the town of Ohligs, which is a half day's walk
north of Cologne. Have you heard of the dream of the evil tax-collector
of Ohligs? No? Then let me tell you what my grandmother told to me:

As you know, during the last half of the twelfth century
Abraham ben Alexander was the Chief Rabbi of Cologne. In those
days, the rabbinate of Cologne was the spiritual head of all the small
Jewish congregations nearby – that is, Deutz, Kalk, and Mulheim.
Rabbi Abraham was also responsible for the outlying communities of
Bensberg, Berg, Gladbach, and Immekeppel to the east, for Bruhl,
Rondorf, Sechtem, Sieburg, and Wahn to the south, for Bedburg,
Bergheim, Horren, Kerpen, and Kastor to the west, and for Hitdorf,
Neukirchen, Opladen, Stommeln, and Ohligs to the north. This last
town – the city of Ohligs – is a small flour-milling, brewing, and brick-
making community on the River Rhine, and while Abraham Ach-
selrad was the Chief Rabbi in Cologne, a greedy man named Henry
von Merscheid was appointed as head tax-collector of Ohligs.

In medieval Europe, merchants were taxed regularly, and local
tax-collectors were free to set their own rules. Traveling traders faced
the payment of endless tolls, duties, and tariffs as their goods passed
through town after town and fiefdom after fiefdom. Duties were
exacted on the highways, on the bridges, and at the fords. In addition,
landowners who had estates on a river blocked the stream and then
demanded payments to let merchant vessels through. Usually, these
various passage fees were small, but there was no standard, and greedy
tax-collectors could become quite wealthy.

Henry von Merscheid was a greedy man. Von Merscheid saw
the Jews as a special source of income, and, unfortunately, in Ohligs
there were no sympathetic officials to overrule Henry's capricious
decrees. One Sabbath morning in the hot month of *Elul*, the Jews of
Ohligs had just recited Psalm 136 – now they were concluding the
Nishmat prayer:

And the great God Almighty slumbers not at all: He does not sleep. In
fact, He wakes the sleeping man and He rouses those who have sunk

into a stupor. He causes the dumb to speak. He loosens the captive and the bound man. He supports the falling. He raises those who are bowed down. To Him alone do we give our heartfelt thanks, amen.

At that moment, during the morning hours of that holy Sabbath service in *Elul*, Henry and his men entered the synagogue. With no warning, von Merscheid arrested fifteen of the most influential Jews of Ohligs, including the wealthy Saul ben Isaac and also Natronai ben Solomon, the son of Rabbi Solomon Amora. Henry von Merscheid charged these Jews with failing to pay a special tax on Jewish merchants, a tax that he had just instituted; then he set their release at one hundred gold coins each. The Jews had no choice. The money was raised, and the hostages were released.

This new tax was ad hoc – von Merscheid levied it whenever he decided that the specific economic or political conditions required extra money. A few months later, Henry von Merscheid decreed that the special tax was again needed. Again, he raised the money by arresting the same fifteen Jewish merchants on another Sabbath morning during the service.

The local rabbi protested, but von Merscheid said, "You know quite well that you Jews are misers. On your own, you barely contribute to the general community of Ohligs. We have a great many expenses, and you live off the hard work of decent Christian citizens. You keep all of your charity for yourselves. Moreover, it is not me who made up the expression: 'To get a Jew to pay, you must squeeze his pockets.' You Jews have forced us to use these extreme methods of taxation."

Not long afterward, Henry set in motion a third round of taxation by ransom. Now the leaders of the Jewish community of Ohligs felt desperate. Therefore, they sent Saul ben Isaac down the River Rhine to Cologne in order to consult with Rabbi Abraham. Early one Friday morning, Saul packed a satchel, he kissed his wife good-bye, and he traveled south to Cologne. It was late in the afternoon when he reached the old synagogue behind Judengasse Street. There, Saul found the Rabbi reading a book in the small back study room, and a number of scholars were seated on benches along the wall, talking quietly among themselves.

The Cologne sages greeted the merchant from Ohligs. They listened to his sad tale. Then they offered their counsel.

First, white-bearded Baruch ben Jacob shook his head and he said, "There is no excuse—clearly, this is outright greed and thievery."

All the men nodded solemnly. Then a younger scholar, Elisah ben Samuel, said, "Perhaps the Book of Proverbs will guide us here, good friends. For instance—"

> A selfish, greedy man
>   Brings trouble to his kin,
> But the modest citizen
>   Prospers through thick and thin.

Elisah's neighbor, Joshua ben Eliezer, said, "Amen. And, gentlemen, let us not forget the other scriptural Proverb":

> Greed is like bad health;
>   It is better to be content—
> Although you have no wealth—
>   Than to be unhappy and affluent.

"How true, good Joshua," continued Lewe ben Anselm. "The Book of Proverbs also tells us":

> Most dishonest money
>   Quickly slips away
> But money that's earned honestly
>   Remains for many a day.

Saul looked around the room. The sages were nodding seriously and they muttered and stroked their beards. Rabbi Abraham sat quietly, with his eyes closed. After a moment, Menahem ben Joel said, "Of course, there is also the scriptural Proverb":

> Wealth is a light commodity
>   On Judgment Day,
> But goodness, alms, and charity
>   Shall heavily weigh.

Generosity and virtue,
    Kind words with each breath –
These will protect you
From a sad and early death."

And Moyses ben Nathan offered: "Then, too, there is the apt Proverb":

Through justice that is tolerant
    A king steadies his entire realm,
But a greedy, selfish tyrant
Destroys his kingdom from the helm.

The sages nodded and nodded and said many "amens," and finally old Shimshon ha-Zaken coughed, and in a hoarse voice he said, "Yes – the Proverbs say much that is useful here, my friends. I would also remind you":

Do not worship wealth and ease;
    Be sensible and give up greed.
Before you turn, up comes a breeze –
    Gold disappears, wealth will recede,
Money grows swift wings and flees
Like an eagle, a fleet bird of speed.

Saul raised his eyebrows and listened uncertainly. No one said anything further. The old men all seemed to be waiting for a word from Rabbi Achselrad. So after a moment, Saul said, "And what do *you* think, Rabbi?"

Abraham Achselrad opened his eyes, and he looked at Saul. "Reb Saul," said the Rabbi, "I have no doubt that a demon has been at work in Ohligs. Yes, it is a wicked demon, or perhaps it is even Samael himself. However, we can take comfort from the scriptural Proverb":

Do not exploit the poor
    Just because they're weak –
Do not crush a helpless creature
    In your powerful beak;

For the Mighty Lord of Heaven
Will champion their cause
And will ruin those evil men
Who disregard His Laws."

"Amen," said Baruch.

"Yes–amen," repeated Saul. He hesitated a moment, and then he said, "Thank you, Rabbi. I do take comfort from these holy Proverbs."

Rabbi Abraham smiled and nodded and he stroked his beard. Saul looked at the many sages sitting on the worn benches, and he looked at his hands. Then he said, "It sounds like the good Lord God will ensure that justice triumphs in the end. . . . But perhaps, Rabbi, there is something that I can do to help God speed matters up in this situation."

The scholars were very quiet. The Rabbi stared at Saul. He wrinkled his forehead, and he tapped a finger on his desk. Then he slowly closed his eyes–in fact, Rabbi Abraham put his head down on his desk, and his breathing became even and heavy. Saul looked around the room. The seven sages of Cologne were watching the Rabbi intently. Saul looked again at the Rabbi. After a few minutes, he said gently, "Rabbi?"

There was no answer, so Saul said a little louder, "Excuse me, Rabbi."

Suddenly Rabbi Abraham opened his eyes. He sat up. "Saul," he said, "you *do* need special help–in fact, you need Divine help."

The Rabbi frowned, and he looked among the pile of papers on his desk. Then he reached into a drawer and he pulled out a clean piece of white parchment made from the skin of a kosher calf. On one side, he wrote the *Shema* followed by seven mystical words. On the other side he wrote:

Mighty is Yahweh-Elohim, Who communicates with Israel through dreams. May the blessed Lord save Saul, the son of Isaac, and his pious colleagues from all manner of evil overlords. As it is written in the holy Book of Genesis: "And the Lord was with Joseph and kept faith with him; thus, Joseph won the favor of the governor."

May the great Lord God bless Saul and the Jews of Ohligs–in the names of the angels Aniel, Gabriel, Hasdiel, Kabshiel, Metatron, Michael, Rahab, Raphael, Ridyah, Sandalfon, Shamriel, and Uriel– Yah, Yah,

Yah, Yah, Yah, Yah, Yah, Yah, Eheyh, Ahah, Ahah, Ahah, Ahah, Yehu, Yehu, Yehu, Yehu, Yehu, Yehu, Yehu, Yehu, Yehu. Amen, eternally hallelujah – thus shall be Your will, *selah* and amen.

The Rabbi wrote this in Hebrew in his small neat script. Then he rolled the parchment into a tight scroll; he tied the scroll with seven white threads, and in each thread he put seven neat knots. The Rabbi tapped the amulet on his desk. Then he handed the scroll to Saul.

"Reb Saul," instructed the Rabbi, "you must slip this into the house of the tax-collector. Then, my good friend, trust in the Almighty Lord God, for His love endures forever."

"Amen," said Baruch ben Jacob.

"Amen," repeated Saul. He took the scroll. He thanked the Rabbi, and he thanked the other scholars of Cologne. And then Saul ben Isaac returned to Ohligs.

Saul returned to Ohligs, and it was night when he arrived in the old brickmaking town. Saul went directly to the house of Henry von Merscheid. He was shaking when he got there.

Von Merscheid lived in a large stone house surrounded by a wall. It was late at night, and no one was about. The shadows seemed to hide demons and dybbuks. Saul waited by the back gate for many minutes. Finally, he built up his courage. Slowly he pushed the gate; it creaked, but it opened. Saul stepped into the yard. He walked gently toward the back door. When he got to the house itself he bent down, and with a trembling hand, he slipped the tiny scroll under the door. Then as quietly as he could, Saul backed away, and without closing the gate he ran, ran, ran back to the Jewish Quarter of Ohligs and into his own warm home, and he bolted the door behind him.

This was the Sabbath eve, the night when each Jewish home becomes holy and is infused with the Divine presence. South of Ohligs in Cologne tiny bright stars were brushed like fine sugar in the sky. Rabbi Abraham had long finished saying:

For You, O Lord, have chosen us and have hallowed us above all nations. And You have given us, in love and in favor, Your holy Sabbath for a heritage. Blessed be You, O Lord our God, Who hallows the wondrous Sabbath.

The Rabbi had drunk from the wine cup, he had washed his hands, and he had said the prayer over the bread, cutting one loaf, taking a piece for himself, and distributing the rest for the others at his table. Then Rabbi Abraham ben Alexander, Achselrad of Cologne, had closed his eyes, and he had said a silent prayer for the Jews of Ohligs.

And late that night, in Ohligs to the north, Henry von Merscheid was sleeping fitfully in his bed. He dreamt that an aged white-haired man, dressed in a bright white robe, appeared in his bedroom. The old man reached down. Slowly and inexorably, he began to strangle Henry. "Stop, stop!" begged the choking tax-collector, but the old man continued to tighten his grip. Henry von Merscheid felt his life slipping from him. He was choking, and he heard the old man intoning the words of the Almighty Lord God from the Book of Leviticus:

> You shall not steal, and you shall not bribe or cheat or deceive a fellow countryman. You shall not mistreat your neighbor or rob him. When an alien settles with you in your land, you shall not tyrannize or oppress him. He shall be treated as a native born among you. You shall fear your God—for I am the Lord.

> If, in spite of all this, you do not listen to Me and you still defy Me, then I will strike you in anger. I Myself will punish you seven times over for your sins.

Henry thrashed about in his bed. He coughed and he choked; but he remained asleep, and he remained alive.

The next morning, Henry von Merscheid awoke worn and sore. He was hoarse. He could barely speak. His wife asked why there were red handprints on his neck. Henry was scared and shaky. He could not eat his breakfast. He paced and paced. He had a headache, and he felt miserable all day. And that night, the same dream was repeated. Then, after a third terrible night, Henry arose early, he walked into the town, he went to the official courthouse, and he resigned his post as tax-collector. The next week, Henry moved his family back to his original home town of Dusseldorf, hoping that the evil dreams would remain far behind him. . . .

What is that, Rabbi? Yes, amen—dreams *are* holy messages. They are holy, and they are spiritual. Old Abraham Achselrad had a great reverence for dreams, and he often cited the passage from Deuteronomy about dreams:

> There are things that are hidden, and these belong to the Lord our God—but what is revealed belongs to us and to our children forever.

Have you ever dreamt of old departed friends? Ah, I have too—and this reminds me of another dream, one that slipped later into the life of Saul ben Isaac. Well, actually, it was the dream of Saul's child, a little girl named Hannah.

As you know, Rabbi, most European Jews did not have pets in the Middle Ages—although in the surrounding Gentile communities pets were often used for hunting and other rough sports. Perhaps the rarity of Jewish pets stemmed from strong Jewish feelings against cruelty toward animals. Or perhaps it was simply that the Talmud declares:

> A person is not permitted to acquire for himself a domestic animal or a wild beast or a bird unless he has arranged for it to be housed and fed properly.

And, of course, in those days most Jews were quite poor.

However, Saul ben Isaac was wealthy, and his little four-year-old daughter Hannah had a dog. It was a fine old dog, and it was named Greta. Greta became sick, and one day she died while Hannah was out playing. Saul's wife had a neighbor remove the body immediately, while the little girl was not at home. The neighbor took the dead animal and threw it in a trash heap.

When Hannah came home, her mother told her that the dog had died and had been taken away by the neighbor. The little girl cried and cried. Her mother held her in her arms and she recited a bit of Psalm 136:

> God gives food to all His creatures,
>   And His love endures forever;
> God gives shelter to His children,
>   And His love endures forever;
> So give thanks to the God of Heaven—
>   For His love endures forever.

Hannah could not be comforted. All afternoon she sat with tears in her eyes. She did not eat any dinner. Then, late that night, Hannah had a happy dream—she dreamt that Greta was still at home, warm and furry and wagging her tail. But when she awoke, Hannah discovered that it had been only a dream.

"Tell me about the hole," she asked her mother that morning.

"The hole?" asked the mother.

"Yes—people are buried in a hole in the ground. Tell me about the hole where Greta is buried," said Hannah.

The mother looked sadly at her daughter, and then she said, "Well, my little girl, the hole is in the woods, where Greta liked to play."

"I hope that it is a pretty place," said Hannah.

"I am sure that it is," said her mother.

hat is that, Rabbi? No, I was just resting my eyes—
please feel free to join me here by the stove. (I think you will be too
warm on that bench: try the one nearer to the wall.) An old man like
me can doze forever by a warm stove. I suppose it is because we old
men have worn our *tefillin* so long that by now they are almost a part of
us.

What does this have to do with sleep? Why, Rabbi, certainly you
know that *tefillin* drive off the demons that keep us awake at night. In
the Middle Ages, *tefillin* were placed on babies who had been frightened
out of their sleep by demons—and, of course, good sleep is necessary for
good health. My grandmother told me that living in a very pious
household surrounded by many holy *tefillin* accounted for her amazing
health in her old age. When she was older than me, she could still walk
for a full hour and then argue for another hour with the shopkeepers in
the marketplace. And why was this? My grandmother always said, "I
have been blessed by the holy emanations of the *tefillin*."

I know that this sounds like mysticism—but it is *sacred* mysticism.
Rabbi, you yourself have often told us that there are many sacred
things that we can never hope to understand in this world: it is a
mystical magical world and it has been woven with a thick tangle of

incondensable complexity by the good Lord God (blessed be He). Of course, that was also the view of the mystic Achselrad, Rabbi Abraham ben Alexander of medieval Cologne. How could he think otherwise, when daily he and his congregants were forced to wrestle with demons, dybbuks, devils, and all manner of ill-intentioned spirits. For example, I remember one story that my grandmother told me about Natronai Hayyim and the old woman-demon. Have you ever heard it? No? Then let me tell you:

Once upon a time, in the days of the mystic Achselrad of medieval Cologne, there lived a pious but poor man named Natronai Hayyim ben Aaron ha-Kohen. Natronai's faith was as strong as a rock. This was a great irritant to the many demons living nearby in the shadows, the wells, the cellars, and the dark corners of Cologne. One demon in particular shivered and shook uncontrollably every time she saw Natronai – and because she lived in a cave near Natronai's house, she saw him every day.

As you know, Rabbi, demons can change their shapes. One day, this demon appeared in the shape of a weak old woman, shaking and shivering on Natronai's doorstep. "Reb Natronai, my good fellow," she said, "I need some help and some protection. I must go out to the forest tomorrow in order to get wood. Would you come out and cut the wood for me?"

Natronai had never seen this woman before, and he was very suspicious. Could this be a demon in disguise? Natronai knew that certain spirits – called *ruhin* – are completely disembodied and formless. On the other hand, among the various kinds of demons (the *mazzikin*), the *shedim* can take on human forms and they eat and drink like people. The *lilin*, too, can have human forms, but they have wings. In all cases, however, female demons have no hair on their heads. (This is why, in the Holy Scriptures, Boaz placed his hand on Ruth's head when he awoke and found her at his feet. When he discovered that she had hair, he knew that this was no demon, he relaxed, and he asked: "What person are you?")

Anyway, Rabbi, poor Natronai stared at the old woman. He saw that she was wearing a cap. "Oh no! This woman has no hair: she is a demon! May the good Lord God protect me," thought Natronai. "I had best be very, very careful."

Natronai cleared his throat, and he rubbed his hands together. "Why are you hesitating, my good man?" asked the old woman. "I am weak and shaky. Certainly you must be aware that the Lord does not look favorably on someone who refuses to help the poor and the old and the helpless."

Now Natronai became more worried. Perhaps this truly was a needy weak old woman. Perhaps she did have some wispy white hair beneath her cap. It was his sacred and holy responsibility to be charitable to the needy and to donate his time to the elderly. On the other hand, what if this old woman really were a demon? In this case, if he refused to help then she might turn him into a cabbage or a cricket.

Natronai was stuck – demon or not, this old woman must be helped. Therefore, he said, "Very well, madam. However, do not take the trouble to come here for me. I will meet you in the usual woodcutting clearing in the forest tomorrow morning. If I arrive before you, then I will begin to cut wood and to put it in a sack. And if I should finish and if you should by some chance miss me, then feel free to take the sack of wood home yourself."

"Thank you very much," said the old woman and she left Natronai's house.

The next morning, Natronai Hayyim arose very early. He said the *Shema* as soon as he had washed and dressed. He put his arm *tefilla* in one pocket and a special parchment scroll in another pocket. He took his axe, a small sharp knife, and a large heavy sack, and he hurried off to the forest. Natronai arrived long before the old woman, and he cut down a great deal of wood. Then he filled the sack with the wood. Natronai thought to himself, "There! I have fulfilled my obligation to the old woman, be she demon or human; now I can hurry home safely."

However, just then he heard the old woman coming toward him through the woods. Natronai looked around. There was no place to hide, so he hollowed out a space in the center of the sack of wood. Then he climbed into the empty space, and he tied up the sack around himself. Now Natronai felt safe because he knew that demons have no power over things that are tied securely. (How did he manage to tie up the sack from the inside? Frankly, Rabbi, I do not know and my grandmother did not tell me.)

The old woman shuffled along in the forest. When she arrived at the woodcutting clearing, she smelled Natronai, but she could not see him. She waited and waited, but Natronai Hayyim did not appear. She looked at the sack of wood sitting on the ground. "This must be the wood that Natronai cut for me," she said aloud. "I had hoped to eat that irritatingly pious Jew. However, if I cannot have a good lunch, then at least I might as well get some wood from this ill-fated venture."

The demon put the sack upon her back, and she began to walk off. "What is this?!" thought Natronai. "Not only is this a demon – she is a *hungry* demon too! And to think that I was almost her midday meal." For a moment, Natronai Hayyim felt very angry. As soon as the demon had gone a few steps, Natronai gave her a stab with his knife through the sack.

The demon jumped. Then she coughed and she hissed and she spat. "Hmm," thought the demon, "that foul Natronai must have cut some sort of thorn tree." She shifted the sack on her back and she continued walking. Again Natronai gave her a stab with the knife, and again the demon shifted the sack. This went on all the way back to the demon's cave.

When finally she reached the cave, the demon was quite sore, and she was very, very angry. She coughed and she hissed and she spat and she cursed. She threw down the sack, and she went to find some ointment – and as the wood in the sack tumbled on top of him, Natronai bit his tongue so as not to make a noise. The demon rooted around in her cupboards. She looked on all her shelves. She searched under her bed. There was no ointment anywhere. Where *was* her ointment? She coughed and she hissed and she spat and she cursed, but since she was a demon, she decided that she would make a healing egg in order to soothe her painful back.

What, Rabbi? Well just be patient, and I will explain how the demon made a healing egg. First, she took a needle and she pricked a hole in each side of a fresh egg. Gently she blew out the white, and gently she blew a bit of saffron into one end of the egg. She sealed the egg with bits of wax. Then she shook the egg. Unfortunately for this malign demon, the saffron was old and bad; it was light yellow with black tinges – there was hardly any of the bright orange saffron that makes saffron cakes so sweet. Therefore, the egg broke, the power seeped away, and the spell did not work. The demon coughed and she hissed and she spat and she cursed, and she felt even more sore and more achy and more angry than she had before.

Then, Rabbi, the old woman-demon lost her composure and she made her final mistake. She said, "Ever since I brought home this load of wood, I have had problems. I wonder what is in that accursed sack."

What is that, Rabbi? Why, certainly you know what it means for a demon to utter the word "sack"! You recall that after the primordial Great Flood, the men of the world journeyed in the East. They came to a plain in the land of Shinar and they decided to build a tower. The tower was called the "gate of the gods": it was called "Babel." (Just a moment, Rabbi – I will get back to the demon in a minute.)

As I was saying: the tower was called "Babel," and it was designed to reach to the top of Heaven. As the building progressed, the good Lord God looked down, and He thought to Himself, "What is this? Here they are, one people with one single language. Now they have started to make this single towering monolithic architecture. They are trying to reach Heaven itself. What monumental thing will they do next? With a concerted effort, nothing that they have a mind to do will be beyond their reach."

The Almighty One called together His Host of angels, and He said, "You had best go down to the men below, My holy Host. We will scatter them. We will garble their speech. We will confuse their communications and divide them into a multitude of idiosyncratic diversity."

The angels were a bit surprised at this command, but they descended from Heaven, and they dispersed the men from the land of Shinar and scattered them all over the face of the earth. Then the good Lord God waved His mighty arms, and He made a babble of the languages of the world.

Forever after, the speech of men was a diverse tangle of colorful individual idiosyncratic words. This was a great wonder and mystery to rabbis in succeeding generations. What was the original unifying powerful language? Sages worked late into the night, attempting to unpuzzle the primal universal speech. The original language still remains a mystery. However, my grandmother told me that the mystic rabbis of medieval times succeeded in discovering one fact:

the last common word, the last word uttered by any of the original men before the human tongues were confounded at Babel, was "sack."

Therefore, when the demon uttered "sack," Natronai knew that at last he was safe: "sack" would be last word that this demon ever uttered too. Natronai Hayyim ben Aaron took heart and he became brave. He removed the *tefilla* from his pocket. He wrapped it in his parchment charm – a paper on which was inscribed the anti-demonic incantation:

> Deny a witch or a sorceress life;
> Life to a witch must be denied;
> Deny the life of a sorceress;
> A witch is to be denied her life;
> Life is denied to a sorceress.

> I charge you, Mchashpiel, Ktasiel, and Sandriel, in the name of what I am and what I shall be, in the names of the angels Aniel, Gabriel, Hasdiel, Kabshiel, Metatron, Michael, Rahab, Raphael, Ridyah, Sandal-fon, Shamriel, and Uriel, and in the Name of the good Lord God Jehovah – in the Name of the Lord of Hosts, Who presides over the angels – that all these names shall nullify any sorcery committed against Natronai Hayyim, the son of Aaron ha-Kohen, from now until eternity. Thus shall be Your will – amen and *selah*.

Natronai held this makeshift amulet tightly in his left hand. His hands were damp. He shivered slightly. In his pocket, Natronai also had some fine white salt wrapped in a cloth. Carefully, he took out the salt. With his right hand, he slowly reached out of the top of the sack in which he was hiding. Natronai reached out, and he tossed a pinch of finely ground salt toward the demon.

The salt flew up into the air, and then in slow motion like gentle snow, the salt fell down onto the shoulders of the demon. As the first grains floated lightly onto the demon, she looked up in horror. She yelled and she cursed and she coughed and she hissed. And in a puff of smoke, the evil spirit dissolved into a pile of old gray dust – dust that was mixed with a few holy white grains of fine, fine salt.

Natronai peeked from the sack. He saw the smoke drifting up to the ceiling. He saw the pile of dust on the floor. Natronai jumped from the sack and he leaped out the door and he ran and ran and ran. On the way, a wind arose; a huge tree limb fell down and it just missed hitting Natronai. "Bless the good Lord God, amen," said Natronai Hayyim ben Aaron ha-Kohen—and then he continued running until he reached his home, whole and safe and sound.

What, Rabbi? Yes, that is the whole story; there is no more.

abbi, I am glad to see you here alone. I want to apologize for my outburst during the service this evening. You see, I heard Reb Anton say that old Reb Gershom had been stingy. Exactly, Rabbi, that is the Gershom who died last spring. Imagine, speaking ill of the dead like that – and in the synagogue no less! Why, in the olden days, in the strict and pious days of our fathers, Reb Anton would have been ordered to leave and never to return. As you well know, the dead are quite aware of everything that is said here on earth. If you say something good about the spirits, then you will be rewarded – but if you speak unkindly, then you will certainly be punished.

The spirits of the dead are watching us: they see all our earthly actions, especially those things that we do in their memory. Of course memorial deeds – pious acts such as prayer, charity, and lighting candles – are humbling, and so they make *us* better people. But, in addition, these acts brighten the souls in the Great Hereafter. In fact, all our kind, thoughtful, and pious actions make the spirits of the dead proud and happy. For instance, when a son studies the Torah, when he gives charity, and when he does what is right and good at all times, then his dead father smiles and is content in the Land of Eternity, amen.

Yes, the good deeds of the living are appreciated by the dead. And good will goes the other way also: the spirits of the departed pray for the health and happiness of the living. (Even empty remnants of the departed have special powers that can help the living. I have been told [although, of course, I have no direct personal knowledge of this, praise the Lord] that dice made out of the bones of a corpse will win a man as much wealth as he wishes.)

In any case, the dead are like the living. They want a gentle and happy existence. And they want all their friends and relatives—both living and dead—to be at peace. For this reason, the spirits of the dead float through the cemeteries, filling them with a holy peaceful calm. Jewish cemeteries are restful gardens. They have names like "The House of Life" and "The Holy Garden" and "The Field of Life." This is because, even for the living, the cemetery is the last refuge from the many trials and the inevitable day-to-day storms in any Jewish community.

All Jewish cemeteries are Gardens of Life. I remember how my grandmother used to sit happily by her mother's grave in one of these Gardens, embroidering for hours and hours in the good weather. Calm warm breezes of the departed spirits gently caress the living in these parks. The light winds blow into the park from the cities— they come down the alleyways and into the old quiet cemeteries, which are usually at the end of a back street in the ghetto. Jewish Gardens of Life are far from the houses in order to fulfill the ancient custom of burying the dead at least fifty paces from the nearest home. That is why my grandmother would say to me, "Walk fifty steps, my golden young man, and you will always find a quiet lasting happiness, amen."

Jewish cemeteries are peaceful places—and they were very important to my grandmother. Through cemeteries, we maintain the deepest contact that we ever need: we touch our loves, long gone though they may seem. And that was what had happened to sad Rebeka. Which Rebeka? Well, Rabbi, I am speaking of Rebeka of medieval Cologne, the wife of Jokshan ben Lavan and the daughter of Benjamin ben Jesse. It was my grandmother who told me the famous ballad of Rebeka. My grandmother recited it to me, once upon a time, and now I will tell it to you:

A nighttime spirit came windblown
To poor Rebeka's door,
It sighed and gave a grievous groan
Then it sighed a few times more;

It rapped three knocks quite light
Like a tiny, tiny stone
In the dark dead hours of night
And Rebeka answered faint and lone:

"Is that my father from Heaven's land?
Or is it my departed Isaac?
Or could it be my long-gone husband
From far shores now come back?"

"It is not your father Benjamin,
It is not your brother Isaac,
Yes – it is your husband Jokshan
From far shores I have come back.

"Rebeka my darling wife –
Tell me, I pray you, dear:
Do you still love me in your life
As I love you from my bier?"

"My dearest you have my full love,
I will be yours for all my days,
Come join me in the rooms above;
We will stay together always."

"No, I cannot enter where you lead –
I cannot heed your call,
My cold dead bones have long been buried
Beyond Cologne's southern wall."

Rebeka opened wide the door
And reached out for the shade:
"Here is my hand, take it once more,
Hold me now before you fade."

She stood there as a child lingers
Hoping he would gently hold her,
Three times she reached her trembling fingers
Out toward his misty shoulder.

But as she grasped, he drifted slow
Sifting through her hands,
Impalpable as the shadows go
Like a mist in the evening lowlands.

This brought the sadness and the fright
Of lonely hours without moonlight
And Rebeka cried into the night:
"O Jokshan stay here within my sight.

"Would your lap provide me rest
Here outside death's darkest place?
Can you hold me to your breast
So that I may weep in your embrace?"

The soul just wavered in the wind
Pointing south with his misty hand,
Again Rebeka called to him
But he floated silent across the land.

Rebeka stepped onto the path
Gathering her long dark dress,
She sadly walked behind the wraith,
Following into the blackness;

They walked the nighttime darkling sea
Past sleeping shuttered enclaves,
Down empty streets and silently
South to the Jewish graves.

"Is there room atop your winding-sheet?"
Asked Rebeka, teary-eyed.
"Is there space beyond your cold, cold feet
Or else along your right-hand side?"

"There is no room beside my head,
No space along my right
Nor at the foot of my death bed –
The coffin is too tight."

Then suddenly came the lightening dawn,
The sky was pale and gray.
"Rebeka, I fear you must be gone,
Now you must go away."

Thus ended Rebeka's ghostly tryst,
For with a grievous groan
Jokshan vanished in a nighttime mist
And he left her all alone.

"O stay my only love!" she sighed:
The worn Rebeka sat and cried,
Her cheeks grew pale by the cold graveside,
She lay her down – and there she died.

Hello, Rabbi, I will be with you in a moment – I cannot leave until every tablecloth is folded, otherwise the day has not ended properly. . . . There, now I am finished at last, and I can sit next to you by the stove.

Although it is late, I am not sleepy either, Rabbi: I am old and awake and happy. Something keeps me up at night; I think that I have been hearing some Heavenly nighttime noises – some music, some celestial sounds crafted afar in the great Paradise of Eternity. They remind me of the old craftsman's hymn:

> Hearing Your amazing Grace
> (How sweet the celestial sound)
> And feeling now Your warm embrace,
> I am surely Heaven-bound.

> And when a rainbow is my door
> And when Your morning light
> Wakes me for a thousand years or more,
> Each day will still dawn bright –

And through those glorious centuries
I will be an artisan
Crafting artworks at my ease,
As Your humble journeyman.

I wonder if these graceful Heavenly sounds also kept old Abraham Achselrad awake, when he worked all night? Achselrad was like that hymnist: he and the other rabbis of the Middle Ages were handicrafters, artisans, and artificers. As the Talmud says: "Handicraft and manual labor are great things, for they reward their practitioners with artifacts of honest beauty." Rabbis were spiritual laborers. They used the Torah as a spade and they dug into the spiritual life of the heart and the soul just as gardeners dig into the natural life of the fields and the gardens.

In his own way, each medieval rabbi aspired to be a master handicraftsman. Rabbi Abraham was a craftsman of writing, and he happily worked and reworked his compositions. At any hour of the night or day, his congregants could find him crafting and polishing his tome of mystical Kabbalistic knowledge, the *Keter Shem Tov*. The *Keter Shem Tov* is a vast and wondrous treatise, but it has never been published; I am told that even today it remains hidden in the loft above the old Cologne yeshiva. Most of the time, Rabbi Abraham labored late into the night – but the good Lord God (blessed be He) works in strange ways. As my grandmother used to say, "The magnificent Lord whirls and twirls our little earth in His holy palm." And one day the Almighty One whirled and twirled the earth and Rabbi Abraham was surprised to find himself suddenly walking out the front door of the synagogue when it was still early in the evening.

It was early evening in the autumn. Yes, it was autumn, and the sky was blue and warm and near, and the clouds were gray and cool and far. And where was he off to, that old mystical Rabbi? He himself did not know.

Rabbi Abraham ben Alexander felt holy, and he felt happy – and be began to walk. First, he walked down Judengasse Street. Then, he turned down Engegasse Street. And as he was walking down Engegasse Street, in medieval Cologne on an early autumn evening, the mystical Rabbi Achselrad met Shelomi ben Isaac ha-Kohen going home.

And who was Shelomi ben Isaac? Well, I will tell you:

Once upon a time there lived in medieval Cologne a very pious man named Shelomi ben Isaac ha-Kohen. Shelomi had been a salesman for much of his life, and he specialized in small wooden utensils. Shelomi sold wooden beaters and dippers and forks and ladles, mixers, scrapers, and spoons; he also sold candleholders, combs, cutting boards, dishes, plates, racks, saucers, and trays. Of all the myriad and sundry woodcrafts, Shelomi liked the wooden combs best: combs made him the happiest. To Shelomi, there was something about a fine wooden comb that seemed holy.

Shelomi liked the combs, but he also liked all the other wooden utensils. "I love the smell of carved wood," he once said to Rabbi Abraham. "On the other hand, I do not like to sell things – although I must admit that I am a good salesman."

Selling utensils may have been uninteresting to Shelomi; nonetheless, he did it well. It seemed to be a gift of the good Lord God. Shelomi did not push his wares on people, but somehow they always bought his wooden items. Shelomi would sigh and shrug his shoulders and repeat the business passage from the Book of Genesis:

> If the good Lord, the God of my father, the God of Abraham, and the Fear of Isaac, had not been with me, then you would have sent me away empty-handed and with no success. But the Lord saw my labor and my hardships; thus, He has sustained me and He shall make me prosper in my work.

Yes, Shelomi successfully sold utensils. He sold them so well that after a while he had some extra money. And what did he do with this extra bit of cash? Half of the money he gave to charity, and half he used to buy a few combs for himself – and he chose only the finest combs with engraving along the edges. His wife said to him, "Shelomi, my dear, whatever are we going to do with ten more combs?" Shelomi ben Isaac ha-Kohen looked at the combs, but he had no answer.

In those days, Rabbi, Jewish communities were held at a distance from the surrounding Gentiles. Still, ours is a world of vapors and emanations; therefore, German culture seeped into the Jewish Quarter of Cologne. These hints of Christian life seemed otherworldly and magic. And to Shelomi, the magic of the Gentile world shone most brilliantly in its prayer books: he could not tear his eyes away from the beautiful illuminations.

In medieval Europe, book illustrations – illuminations – were the most accessible paintings. Medieval books were handwritten and each illumination was painted in each book directly on the parchment page. The artists used tiny brushes and brilliant colors with a generous portion of gold. Monks were the chief scribes, and monks became the chief illuminators, decorating the breviary, the Psalter, and the Book of Hours with pictures of the lives of the saints and the events of biblical history. Shelomi saw these books on his travels, and he was stunned by their artistry.

And where exactly did Shelomi travel? Why, Rabbi, he roamed the whole of western Europe. Medieval Jewish merchants like Shelomi were the heart of international commerce. They knew the local needs of each region. They had access to Jewish money-lending. They were mail carriers for an informal international postal service. Shelomi himself regularly made the rounds of the Great Fairs in Frankfort-on-Main, Frankfort-on-Oder, Leipzig, Lyons, Troyes, and, of course, Cologne. He had a gentle manner and a warm smile. He was well liked, and he was entertained by wealthy Gentiles as well as by Jews. Thus, Shelomi had many opportunities to pore over illuminated books and other intricate handcrafted objects. Soon, Shelomi began to dream of being an artisan himself.

Shelomi's life went on this way for many years. Eventually, a wealthy Gentile took over the wholesale business that Shelomi represented. The Gentile had little interest in the utensil trade, so Shelomi took more and more responsibility. He traveled farther. He went to more fairs. It was not long before he became the chief bargaining representative for the utensil business of Cologne. Shelomi expanded their trade into imported wooden spice boxes and ornamental jewelry cases and glassware from the Mediterranean regions. Frequently, he traveled as far east as Lemberg and Lublin and as far south as Granada. At the same time, Shelomi's unease with his life increased. He felt tense and tired continuously. His neck frequently ached. His stomach was often knotted.

One day, Shelomi was driving his wagon back to Cologne. He had spent the previous night in Bonn, on his return trip from Coblenz,

Mainz, and Frankfort-on-Main. "The sky is blue," thought Shelomi. "The air is bright and cool – I should be happy." But he was not. He mused and he dreamed and his mind drifted, and he did not notice a small fox that was sitting on the edge of the highway. As the wagon approached, the fox darted out. Shelomi swerved to avoid hitting the animal, but the wagon skidded and skittered and it fell over the edge of the road and overturned in a ditch.

Shelomi crawled from his seat. He had strained his back, and he had banged and scraped his leg. He felt stunned. He sat still for a moment. Then he stood, and he limped back to the wagon. With a large stick as a lever, he managed to right the wagon. He gathered his fallen belongings, he re-tied the horse's harness, and he slowly climbed back into his seat; then he returned to Cologne. When he reported to his boss late that afternoon, the man said, "Well, I hope that you will be able to continue tomorrow. As you know, we have an important account in Bremen."

Shelomi ben Isaac ha-Kohen went back to his house. He was tired and sore and discouraged. He looked at his supply of utensils. He looked at the combs again and again. Shelomi shook his head. He talked to himself. He paced the room, and then he returned to his boss. "I am afraid that I must quit," said Shelomi.

"What?!" said the man. "Whatever for?"

Shelomi felt a great tiredness. He was quiet for a moment; then he said, "I am going to make combs."

"You are a salesman, Mr. Isaac," said the Gentile. "You are on the way to becoming a wealthy man. You would be foolish to give up a regular income."

"Perhaps," said Shelomi.

The man looked at Shelomi and frowned: "You know that Jews cannot join any of the craft Guilds."

"I know," said Shelomi. The Gentile shook his head, but he said nothing more. Shelomi left the room, and he went home and told his wife about his decision.

Shelomi's wife patted him on his shoulder. "The good Lord knows best," she said.

Shelomi sat in his kitchen, and he looked at some of his combs. Most of them needed more waxing and polishing. One comb had a deep gouge. Another was badly warped. Many combs had uneven teeth, and none of the engravings was done with care. "I will do better," he thought, and he smiled.

The next day, Shelomi told two people that he was going to make combs. Each of these people told two others, and within a month, Shelomi had orders for more combs than he could make. Now Shelomi ben Isaac ha-Kohen had become a comb-maker.

Yes, Rabbi, Shelomi was a comb-maker, and he did this for many years. And early one evening in autumn, when the skies were the gentle brown-gray of the falling leaves, Rabbi Abraham met Shelomi just as the comb-maker was returning to his home.

"Hello, Rabbi," said Shelomi. "Will you come in?"

"Well, just for a moment," said Rabbi Achselrad.

The two men went through the kitchen and into the back room where Shelomi worked.

"What do you make your combs of?" asked the Rabbi.

"I use oak," said Shelomi. "Oak is long-lasting and tough, but it is not too hard for woodcarving."

The woodworker took down an oak rectangle. "First," he said, "I cut flat pieces about the size of a man's hand. I smooth them to look like this, then I bury them for a few months."

The Rabbi raised his eyebrows. "You bury the wood? Why is that?" he asked.

Shelomi sat down, and he smiled at his guest. "That is an interesting question, Rabbi. Frankly, I do not know exactly how this works. An old workman, whom I met once in Duren, told me that the deep earth sweetens the wood, through the mysteries of the good Lord God. Burial seems to make the wood stronger and more bendable: it makes my combs special and long-lived."

Although it was the evening, Shelomi began to work as the two men continued talking. "People speak highly of your craftsmanship," said the Rabbi. "They call you an artist."

Shelomi looked at his wood. Then he said, "I have traveled quite a bit, Rabbi."

Shelomi ben Isaac wiped his hands on his old coat, and he straightened up in his seat. "I would say, Rabbi – well, actually I would *hope* – that comb-making *is* an art, somewhere between sculpture and painting.

"You see, Rabbi," continued Shelomi, "as I traveled from town to town, I met wonderful artists of all varieties. The sculptors are dusty men; their faces are coated with marble powder. In fact, a sculptor looks like a baker. He is covered with white; he is dusted with little chips of marble. He looks as if he had come in from a snowstorm. And, then, his house! It is in complete disarray. Why, his house is not only full of stone splinters and dust and grit, it is also noisy.

"At the other end of the spectrum, there is the painter of canvases or the illuminator of manuscripts. This artist sits in a clean room. He is comfortable, easy, and quiet. He can wear whatever clothes he likes. He works with light brushes, dipping them in wondrous colors. And his house is neat and clean and peaceful."

Shelomi stopped talking as he tightened a piece of wood in a vise. Then he continued: "The comb-maker works more quietly than the sculptor, and he works more noisily than the painter. We wood-workers can have a neater workroom than the sculptor–but our homes are never as clean as the painters' homes. Nonetheless, I would like to think that we all are brother artists."

Shelomi worked while he talked to the Rabbi. He wore an old brown cloak coated with dust and wax. The wood in his vise had come from his stockroom–and the wood in the stockroom came from the yard, where underground alone it lay, warm at night and cool by day.

Here in the workroom, filing was the first step in shaping a comb. But before he took each piece into the workroom to file, Shelomi heated it ever so gently in a coal fire; this gave the oak a warm dappled graceful burnish. And now a piece of this very oak wood, gently burnished, was tightened in Shelomi's vise. Evenly, patiently, and methodically, Shelomi filed the general shape of a comb, using a rough file. As he filed, Shelomi interrupted his talk to recite the craftsman's verse from the Book of Exodus:

> Then came the craftsmen who
> Made the holy Tent
> Of ten sheets magnificent
> Delicate and finely woven
> Of violet, scarlet, and blue
> With threads of argentine;
> And cherubs were weavers too–
> Humans and angels blending in
> Smoothly, as if God simply drew
> One complex Heavenly artisan.

The rough filing went on and on. And what would come next? It was more filing. Tomorrow, Shelomi would begin the fine filing: he would carefully file the comb's teeth with a very small file. After all the filing was completed, Shelomi engraved a design. Then he polished the comb. For polishing, Shelomi used a special smooth stone and he also rubbed the comb with a harsh cloth. Finally, he shined the wood with animal wax, using a smooth leather cloth.

Usually, the rough filing took one afternoon and the fine filing took two days. Shelomi spent the next morning engraving a tiny latticework design along one edge – and the last rubbing, polishing, and shining needed one hour, or sometimes two or three. All in all, it took half a week to make each comb.

That evening, Shelomi ben Isaac was just beginning the three days that it took to make one of his fine wooden combs. As he worked, he said to the Rabbi, "I do not make much money, Rabbi. Nonetheless, I carve fine oaken combs. I make them as best I can. At night, before I fall asleep, I think about these combs out there in the city of Cologne and beyond. They are almost like my children."

Shelomi continued to file the wood. He was quiet for a few minutes. The night was deepening, and finally, Rabbi Abraham Achselrad said, "I must be going, Shelomi."

"Goodbye, Rabbi," said the comb-maker. Shelomi smiled and nodded his head to Rabbi Abraham; but he did not wave – instead he maintained the smooth even rhythm of his filing. As the Rabbi left, he walked down the street, slowly and peacefully and quietly, and he heard Shelomi ben Isaac ha-Kohen singing an old song – as he made his way down Engegasse Street, Rabbi Abraham heard the comb-maker singing:

> Hearing Your amazing Grace
> (How sweet the celestial sound)
> And feeling now Your warm embrace,
> I am surely Heaven-bound.
>
> And when a rainbow is my door
> And when Your morning light
> Wakes me for a thousand years or more,
> Each day will still dawn bright –

And through those glorious centuries
I will be an artisan
Crafting artworks at my ease,
As Your humble journeyman.

ood evening, Rabbi. Of course, please sit here by the
stove: the night fire helps me to become sleepy also. You and I are not
blessed like old Reb Elbaum. Once again, I saw him nodding off during
the last prayers this evening. He has learned to sway piously even
while asleep; he must have inherited some magic from the mystic
Achselrad. I think that you and I could use a dose of Achselrad
ourselves tonight. My grandmother said that he could put men into a
sleep trance just by waving a gold coin before their eyes. . . . Exactly,
Rabbi, that is the same German mystic whom I have told you about
before—Rabbi Abraham ben Alexander, also called Achselrad of Cologne; he was the most famous pupil of Eliazer, the mystic of Worms.

Old Abraham Achselrad was always having visions. I doubt
whether he would be tolerated nowadays, but Rabbi Abraham was
also a scholar—and he claimed that his visions came from devout and
pious study. Night and day, old Rabbi Abraham could be found writing
and reading in the little back study room of the yeshiva. He worked
continuously on a set of Kabbalistic tomes of mystical knowledge; the
most famous of these was the *Keter Shem Tov.* My grandmother said
that it was one afternoon while writing this very book that Rabbi

Abraham looked up and, in the waning light of that cool autumn day, he saw a crowd of his congregants; they stood fearfully in the doorway. "Please, Rabbi," called one of them, the respected Levi ben Alexis ha-Kohen, "can you come to the Archbishop's Court? I am about to be charged with delinquency on a huge tax bill. I simply cannot pay, and now my businesses will be completely ruined and the Archbishop will put me in prison."

And, Rabbi, this is what had happened:

In medieval Germany, King Henry the Lion, Duke of Saxony, appointed his son – who was also named Henry – to be the count of the Palatinate of the Rhineland. All rulers needed wealth. Otherwise, how could they pay their servants, their ministers, and their troops? And how else could they maintain their castles and their luxurious lifestyles? Count Henry looked at his treasury and he frowned. "I need a new set of taxes," he thought.

The count decreed triple taxes on the Jews, he instituted an extra church tithe to be paid twice yearly by all non-Christians, and he set a new duty on imports by non-Christian merchants. Moreover, young Henry had an efficient plan: the Church, said Henry, will collect these moneys. One quarter of the funds would go to the local parish, one quarter would go to the regional bishop, and the remainder would be sent to the count. Then, Henry sat back and waited for his money.

In Cologne, Archbishop Adolph set Henry's plan in motion. Soon it was clear that the new taxes would bankrupt Jewish businesses. Levi ben Alexis was an aggressive Jewish banker. Recently he had loaned out much money, he had signed a variety of contracts with long-term agreements, he was speculating in seasonal goods, and he had even mortgaged his properties, living with short-term financial pressures for the long-term reward. But suddenly Levi found himself in serious trouble. All his available cash together with all the money that he could raise by selling his house would not cover the new taxes that he owed. Count Henry pressured the local church districts for regular payments, and the local church districts demanded the full taxes from the Jews. Levi ben Alexis had already postponed payment for two weeks. He was due in court for a final accounting today. What could he do? In desperation, Levi and his friends hurried to the synagogue.

There they found Rabbi Abraham Achselrad writing in the back room. It was a cool afternoon in the autumn month of *Heshvan*, and the daylight was already fading.

Rabbi Abraham knew of the new taxes, and he listened to Levi's brief and discouraging story. Carefully, the Rabbi set aside his papers. He put on his hat and his coat. He left the small back study room of the yeshiva and he walked through the main prayer hall, which was filled with wooden benches. Rabbi Abraham passed the twelve stained glass windows with their colored lions and snakes, he went by the Holy Ark made of stone, he stepped out of the front door, and he strode off to the courthouse.

Levi ben Alexis followed the Rabbi. Before entering the court building, Levi quietly said the protective verse from the Book of Exodus:

> Terror and dread fell upon them
> Through the great might of Your arm—
> Stone-still they stood by helpless
> While Your people passed safe from harm.

Archbishop Adolph himself was there in court. "Ah, Rabbi," said the Archbishop, sadly shaking his head, "I am afraid that I have no choice. Count Henry has ordered me to sign this bill of special taxation. I must not be influenced by sentiment. Unfortunately, it applies especially to your wealthy Jews, such as Mr. Levi Alexis. Today, Mr. Alexis owes us nine hundred gold coins. We have already given him an extension on his payment. I hope that he has brought the money—otherwise, he must be imprisoned and his assets will be confiscated."

"Archbishop Adolph, these taxes are crushing our Jewish businesses," said Rabbi Abraham.

"I am sorry for that," said the Archbishop. "However, we all live within the larger German community. We—both Christians and Jews alike—are dependent on the protection of the great German rulers, and we must submit to those community obligations that are designed for the common good."

"I see," said the Rabbi. Abraham Achselrad looked around the courtroom. He looked at Levi ben Alexis ha-Kohen, and he looked at the Archbishop. Rabbi Abraham closed his eyes for a moment; then he asked, "Have you a Bible here, Archbishop?"

"Of course," replied the Archbishop, and he instructed one of the officers to pass a leather volume to Rabbi Achselrad.

"Now – let us read from the Psalms," said the Rabbi.

"I respect your religious views, Rabbi," said Archbishop Adolph, "but it is quite late in the day, and I wonder whether this is really relevant now."

Rabbi Abraham Achselrad was holding the Holy Scriptures. Suddenly his eyes opened wide; then they closed tightly. The Rabbi became weak, he took a deep breath, and he sat on a nearby chair. Then, gently he set down the Bible.

"Are you all right, Rabbi?" asked the Archbishop.

"I have just had a vision," said Rabbi Abraham. "I have seen the Heavens and the Holy Throne of Glory on God's great mountaintop."

There was silence for a moment. "Yes, I have seen the Heavens. I have seen the firmament of the Omnipotent Lord God – He Who sees all and Who demands justice for all, especially for His children, the Jews. In addition, I have seen that Psalm 3 is quite important," said Abraham Achselrad. "And, if you will permit me a moment, then I will read a bit of those verses." The Rabbi stood and he read aloud:

> In difficulty, when contrite
> I call to God of the Israelite
> In His glorious Heaven bright
> In His celestial mountain height;
> And then He sends me brave sunlight
> And also strength and keen insight.

> Therefore I can lie down then
> Sleeping without dread or fright
> And I will awake tomorrow again
> Calm and warm and sound and tight –
> For the good Lord holds me safely when
> I brave the terrors of the darkling night.

The Archbishop was a bit puzzled. When Rabbi Abraham did not seem to have anything further to say, the Archbishop ventured, "Of course that is a most serious and holy sentiment."

"It certainly is," said the Rabbi. "Now, my good Archbishop, you are a noted cleric. What would you say that this verse means?"

"Clearly it means that the Lord watches over and guides the faithful."

"Yes," said the Rabbi, "and I would say that it means even more than that."

"You would?" asked the Archbishop. "Then pray tell, Rabbi Achselrad: What more do you read into this Psalm?"

"First I would say, Archbishop Adolph, that the good Lord God (blessed be He)–He Who is the Guardian of all Israel–watches over and guides the faithful. Now and in the past and in the future, the Lord will not desert His people Israel. When there is misery, then help is at hand," said the Rabbi. "Moreover, Psalm 3 reminds us that the great Lord God can help us through sleep, through special dreams: sometimes, the miraculous Lord works His protective ways through a sacred sleep."

"Exactly what are you saying, Mr. Alexander?" asked the Archbishop.

"I am saying this, Archbishop: I have had a vision that can help the financially oppressed Jewish businessmen. Let me share this vision with you."

One of the officers laughed, and he said, "You have had a vision? You are just repeating a Psalm, old man."

The Rabbi turned to Archbishop Adolph: "My good Archbishop, let me continue."

"All right," said the Archbishop, "I will give you a few minutes more, Rabbi."

Rabbi Abraham nodded and he said, "Thank you, Your Honor."

Abraham Achselrad remained seated and he closed his eyes. He began to sway; he shook strangely. The members of the court raised their eyebrows, and they looked at one another. Then the pious man opened his eyes. He took a small clean piece of kosher calf parchment from his pocket. The Rabbi covered the top of his head with a handkerchief, and he wrote a charm with holy names on the paper. The Archbishop could see that the charm began with a quotation from Exodus: "For I am Yahweh, your Restorer–I, the Lord your God, am your Healer"–but Archbishop Adolph could not make out the remainder of the words.

When the Rabbi finished writing, in his neat and tiny script, he rolled the parchment into a tight scroll and tied it with a cotton thread. The Rabbi tied and untied the thread – he knotted and unknotted it seven times. Next, he strung the small packet on a thin white string, stood up and gently placed the parchment necklace around the Archbishop's shoulders. Finally, old Achselrad pronounced seven mystical Names of the Lord God Almighty and also the one mystical name of the Angel of Dreams. There was silence. A dark cloud passed over the sun.

The Archbishop yawned, and he said, "I am feeling quite weary. Perhaps it is the cool autumn season – or maybe it is just the late hour of the day. In any case, I know that this is unusual, but I think that I will take a short nap, Rabbi. If you will sit down a moment, good sir, then I will just close my eyes."

The Rabbi sat, and he said, "Archbishop, recall the passage in Deuteronomy about dream divination":

> There are things that are hidden, and these belong to the Lord our God – but what is revealed belongs to us and to our children forever.

Then Archbishop Adolph nodded, and he yawned again and he put his head down on his desk and he fell asleep. And as he slept, he dreamt a dream, a strange and mystical dream":

The Archbishop dreamt that he was in his court receiving a messenger. One of the nearby princes, Bernhard the Count of Munster, who ruled much of the Westphalian countryside, had sent a letter to the Archbishop:

> *"To his honor, Adolph, the Archbishop of Cologne –*

"It is appropriate, sir, that you take responsibility for the spiritual guidance of the communities near Cologne. Clearly, however, regions farther afield must care for themselves. Thus, we are forced to depend upon our own sovereignty. Of course, this means that we must set our own rules and must be responsible for our own finances. Consequently, we are dissolving our past temporary obligations to Cologne.

> "Respectfully,
> *Bernhard, the Count of Munster"*

Specifically, Count Bernhard refused to pay his yearly taxes. Bernhard represented a number of other princes of Westphalia, and Archbishop Adolph worried that the revolt would spread to closer regions of the Rhinelands. Therefore, the Archbishop called a local council meeting where it was decided to declare war without delay against the rebellious group.

And the dream continued. Quickly, an army was collected, and the Archbishop himself led the troops. The plan was to capture the Cathedral of Munster and to dethrone Count Bernhard. The Archbishop's army traveled up the River Rhine to Dusseldorf; there they turned northeast and inland. Eventually, the army reached the old walled town of Munster. But Count Bernhard had been forewarned: he was fully prepared, and in the very first battle he defeated the Archbishop's troops. Many of the Cologne soldiers were killed, and the few remaining men from the Rhine valley were captured and were imprisoned.

Archbishop Adolph was also taken captive. He was locked within the fortified walls of the city of Munster, in the main dungeon under the town hall, the *Rathaus*, which is just south of the marketplace and southeast of the large Cathedral Square. The Archbishop was put in this small dark basement prison, and during the day he would stand at the tiny window in his cell and look out on the cold distant world beyond. The Archbishop stared out blankly at the city of Munster, and his mind was numb.

Now, Rabbi, you know the old Hebrew proverb:

> Many are the friends before
>   The golden palace gate,
> But at the prison door
>   Few visitors stand and wait.

So, in the dream, twelve long years went by, and the Archbishop had no friendly visitors at all.

One day, the Archbishop was looking out his little cell window. Through the bars he saw Levi ben Alexis, the Jewish banker from Cologne, who had come to Munster on business.

"Mr. Alexis!" called the Archbishop. "Mr. Alexis! I need your help!"

Levi ben Alexis ha-Kohen looked around. He saw the Archbishop shouting from the small dungeon window. Levi was afraid. He stared at the Catholic cleric, but he did not dare to come close to the prison. He was a Jew—would he be arrested also? Reb Levi glanced nervously about, and soon he hurried off. The next day, when he returned to Cologne, he reported his experience to Rabbi Abraham. The Rabbi closed his eyes and he opened his eyes, and he nodded his head and stroked his beard. Then he said, "I see that I must accompany you on your next trip west." A week later, Levi returned to Munster, and the Rabbi went with him.

The two Jews passed the prison. Levi stayed far away, but Rabbi Abraham walked over to the small window. As usual, the Archbishop was watching the distant world outside his cell. When he saw the Rabbi, he shouted, "Rabbi! Good Rabbi Abraham—please, rescue me!"

The Rabbi approached the little window, and he extended his hand to the prisoner. "Be calm, Archbishop, the Lord will provide help," said the Rabbi.

"Ah, Rabbi, I have tried to be patient, but I have waited for almost twelve long years," said the Archbishop sadly.

The Rabbi looked up at the sky, and he looked down at the earth. Then he said, "I have an idea. However, if I should free you from this situation, then I would like your help in return. Will you agree not to sign Count Henry's orders, the orders condemning Jews to unreasonable taxes and to overbearing financial strictures in Cologne?"

The Archbishop shook his head and he said, "I have been here in prison for more than a decade. Is there anything left for me to do in Cologne after all these long years?"

The Rabbi smiled. "The good Lord God condenses all time into the wink of an eye," he said.

"Very well," said the Archbishop, "I will try to protect the Jews."

"Thank you, Archbishop. Now, sir, be patient a little longer, and I will do my best to help you," said the Rabbi. Then he left. He went to the small yeshiva in Munster, and he prayed quietly all afternoon. When night came, the Rabbi walked through the city and out the western gates. There, under the high and holy open sky, Rabbi

Abraham ben Alexander, the mystic Achselrad of Cologne, recited the
end of Psalm 30:

> Terror comes from nighttime sorcery
> But joy returns with each new dawn;
> One morning I woke happy and carefree –
> The evil night-fears had withdrawn.
>
> But, Lord, it was Your grand design
> To shatter then my light dawn dream,
> You hid Your radiant face Divine
> And woes rained in a dreary stream;
>
> Then I cried – but now I dance
> For You removed my mourning coat
> And clothed me with Your radiance;
> I sing Your praise with every note –
>
> I chant Your glorious Name abroad,
> O wondrous Lord my holy God.

Then the Rabbi returned to the center of town.

Rabbi Abraham stood in front of the prison building. It was the
black hours of the night. He raised his arms and waved a small metal
amulet. Could it have been a *mezuzah*? My grandmother told me this
story, but she herself was not certain. In any case, Abraham Achselrad
waved the amulet, he said seven mystical words, and with a whisk of
his old rabbinical hand he pulled the Archbishop out through the small
window – and then the Archbishop suddenly awoke in the courtroom
in Cologne.

The Catholic cleric shook his head and he rubbed his eyes. He
looked about him uncertainly. "What is going on here?" he asked.

The courtiers hesitated. Finally, one of Adolph's councilors said,
"Your Holiness, you dozed off for a moment."

"How long was I asleep?"

"It was only a moment, Your Honor."

The Archbishop looked intently at Rabbi Abraham. Then the
Archbishop said to the Rabbi, "Before I fell asleep, you reminded me of

a passage from the Book of Deuteronomy. I know that particular section quite well: it is from Chapter 29. In the next section, God says":

> If you and your sons take My commandments to heart, and if you help your fellow countrymen, then I, the Lord your God, will show you compassion and I will restore your fortunes.

Rabbi Abraham nodded, and he stroked his beard.

"And earlier," continued the Archbishop, "in Chapter 19, it is written":

> You shall not pervert the course of justice. Justice – and justice alone – you shall pursue, in order that you may live honestly and so occupy the holy blessed land that the Lord your God is giving to you.

Again, the Rabbi nodded. After a moment of silence, the Archbishop continued: "I think, Rabbi, that I shall not sign these financial papers. Mr. Levi Alexis and the other Jewish businessmen are now free to go."

"Thank you, Archbishop," said the Rabbi. And the delegation of Jews returned to the warm synagogue for the evening prayers, on that cold *Heshvan* evening once upon a time, long, long ago.

What happened to the charm? Well, Rabbi, my grandmother said that when the Archbishop awoke and shook his head and rubbed his eyes, the necklace fell to the floor. Later, one of the councilors looked under the Archbishop's desk, but the small parchment scroll was nowhere to be found.

ood evening again, Rabbi. Yes, I know: it is always hard to sleep on the night of the new moon. Put your feet up on the side bench here and I will open the stove door. Let me push the coals back; the white glow will wash away all the cares from your hard day.

I heard your final benediction tonight, Rabbi. There is no use denying it—you are overworked. Oh yes, even a shammas like me can tell. I kept one eye on you when I cleaned the dishes, and I saw that you were watching the door, hoping that Reb Elbaum would leave early. But then Reb Anton stayed to argue about the scriptural passage from Ecclesiastes.

Ah, Ecclesiastes, what a difficult book. How can anyone feel comfortable when reading such verse as:

Again I looked, and I saw all the oppression that was taking place under the sun. I saw the tears of the oppressed—and now they have no protectors. Unfortunately, all the power is on the side of the oppressors, and the trammeled and the downtrodden have no comforters.

A man may have a hundred children, and he may live many, many years. Yet no matter how long he lives, if he cannot enjoy his prosperity

334

and if he does not receive a proper burial, then a stillborn child is better off than he. And so I declare: "The dead – those who already have died – are happier than the living, who are still alive. Moreover, better than both are the unborn. For the unborn have not yet seen the evil that is done under the sun."

With such gloomy thoughts still reverberating in your mind, of course you are worn out. . . . What is that? A story from me? Rabbi, all I know are the children's tales, the grandmother fables. You need something new and fresh to keep your mind keen. Otherwise you will become a dreamy old man like me, and you will find yourself constantly musing and dozing and nodding off in front of the stove.

What do you mean you are already an old man, Rabbi? Do you really think that sixty years is old? Why, you are still a child. When you reach eighty, *then* you will be old. You doubt that you will live to see eighty years? If so, Rabbi, then you will never grow old. . . . All right, all right, I know no special stories but listening to you and Reb Anton put me in mind of old Sasson ben Johel, who was a friend of Rabbi Achselrad. Sasson was a good and holy man, and it was for him that Dumah, the Angel of Death, also recited a verse from the Book of Ecclesiastes. But, Rabbi, this was a more hopeful verse; it was:

I have seen the burden that God has laid on men – however, He has made everything beautiful in its time. He has also set Eternity into the hearts of men. Nonetheless, men cannot hope to fathom all the incondensably complex things that God has done from the beginning to the end. . . .

What? Of course there is more, Rabbi: I only closed my eyes for a moment – can an old man not take a little rest? Now you have interrupted my thoughts. Let me see, where was I? Yes, yes – as my grandmother (may her soul visit happily with her parents forever) told me:

Once upon a time, in medieval Cologne on the wide River Rhine, there lived a pious scholar named Sasson ben Johel ha-Levi. Sasson was a friend of Rabbi Abraham ben Alexander, the mystic Achselrad of Cologne. Sasson ben Johel was getting very old, and he was becoming very weak. His skin turned yellow, his belly got large, and he could not eat: it seemed that soon he was to die.

One day, in the cool autumn month of *Heshvan*, Sasson took to his bed and could not get up, and Rabbi Abraham came to visit. The Rabbi was a holy mystic man. He saw quite clearly that Dumah, the Angel of Death, stood at the head of Sasson's bed. The black angel stood with a drawn and bloody sword and he was covered from head to foot with unwinking eyes. Yes, Dumah, the Angel of Death, stood there unmoving, and his breathing was like the sound of dry leaves that rustled and rustled in the blank autumn wind. When Achselrad entered the room, he looked at Dumah for many minutes, and Dumah stared back at the Rabbi. Finally, Dumah said, "Rabbi, the time has come for Sasson the son of Johel ha-Levi to die."

A tear came to Rabbi Abraham's eye. Abraham looked down at the old man lying in the bed. To the Rabbi, Sasson looked like a pale weak child. Could it be that the Almighty Lord was now to take away this little child, his old friend, the good and pious Sasson ben Johel? Perhaps this was just a passing illness. Perhaps a guardian angel would intervene. Was a holy angel passing by the window right now? If so, then certainly it would open wide its bright angelic eyes, it would listen well with its softest and tiniest ears, and then it would fly up directly to Heaven and petition the great and merciful Lord God Almighty to tear up His hasty Decree of Death.

Abraham ben Alexander thought that he heard a flutter of angel's wings outside the window – but no, it was only the sound of Dumah breathing like the rustling of the dry blank autumn leaves. Dumah, the Angel of Death, made an ancient dusty rustling noise, and then he began to intone these words from the Book of Jeremiah:

> Sovereign Lord God, You have made the Heavens and the earth by Your great power and with Your outstretched arm. You show love to thousands. But also You bring punishment to the children for their fathers' unatoned sins. O great and powerful God, Whose Name is the Lord Almighty, great are Your purposes and mighty are Your deeds. Your eyes are open, ever watching the ways of men: You reward everyone according to his conduct and as his deeds deserve – and Your ways are holy, amen.

Sasson seemed to weaken more and more, and he did not move at all. Rabbi Abraham knew that if Dumah remained at the head of the bed, then soon Sasson's breathing would cease altogether. At that point, quick as the swiftest eagle, Dumah would slip Sasson ben Johel's soul out from his head and carry it off through the celestial nighttime skies.

What could the Rabbi do? Clustered in the doorway of the sickroom was a group of quiet scholars who had followed Rabbi Abraham from the synagogue: there were the white-haired Baruch ben Jacob, the younger Elisah ben Samuel, Joshua ben Eliezer, Lewe ben Anselm, Menahem ben Joel, Moyses ben Nathan, and old Shimshon ha-Zaken. The Rabbi looked at these men, and he said, "Help me lift and turn the bed, gentlemen."

The old sages raised their eyebrows, and they looked at the Rabbi. The Rabbi was a strange man, and sometimes he made strange requests. The scholars looked at one another. Then they shrugged their shoulders, and they followed the holy man's orders. The eight men took hold of the bed. They lifted it from the floor, and they began to turn it. They turned it slowly, and they turned it quickly; they turned it to the right, and they turned it to the left. But no matter how they moved, the Rabbi found that Dumah flew ahead of them – the black angel remained always by the head of the poor sick man, Sasson ben Johel ha-Levi.

Rabbi Abraham stood looking intently. Then he said, "Dumah, shall we have a death here soon?"

Dumah, the Angel of Death, said, "I do not pass my time lightly at the head of a bed. As you well know, Rabbi Abraham, a Decree of Death has been signed by the Most Holy One."

Now the Rabbi was very, very worried. "Gentlemen," he said to the scholars, "please say the *Shema* for Reb Sasson – and repeat it three times, very slowly." The old sages began to chant, and the Rabbi hurried home. In his pantry, Rabbi Abraham picked up a large harvest melon, he hid it under his coat, and he returned to Sasson's house. The men were just finishing their benedictions. Dumah, the black Angel of Death, stood grimly at the head of the bed. The Rabbi set a lit candle, a cup of water, and a small dish of salt on the small table next to the head of the old man, Sasson ben Johel ha-Levi. Dumah, the Angel of Death, stood unmoving – simply watching.

Next, the Rabbi sat down at a table in the sickroom. He wrote the *Shema* followed by seven mystical words on a small piece of white parchment. He rolled the parchment into a tight scroll. He tied the paper with seven white threads, and in each thread he put seven neat knots. Then he said to Dumah, "O great angel, will you take this, my entreaty, to the Almighty Lord God (blessed be He)? Will you then request that the Decree of Death be postponed?"

Dumah said, "This is a waste of time. However, you are a holy and pious man; therefore, I will do as you ask."

Dumah, the black Angel of Death, took the parchment scroll. He flew up to the Great Throne of Glory, where sits the Amighty One. The awesome Lord God raised His massive white eyebrows. Silently, He read the parchment, but He said nothing and He turned away. Then Dumah, the Angel of Death, flew back to earth, and he returned to the sickroom of Sasson ben Johel ha-Levi.

As soon as Dumah had left, the Rabbi turned the sick man around in his bed. Sasson's feet were at the top of the bed. His head was under the covers at the foot of the bed. Then the Rabbi took the woven skullcap of his old friend Sasson, he put the cap on the melon, and he put the melon at the sick man's feet. Rabbi Achselrad covered the melon with the blanket, as if it were the head of Sasson ben Johel lying properly and only covered by his blankets. Now the melon with Sasson's skullcap lay at the head of the bed next to the lit candle, the cup of water, and the dish of salt.

Then the room darkened, and Dumah returned. A drawn and bloody sword was in his hand and he was covered from head to foot in unwinking eyes. "Well," asked the Rabbi, "what has the good Lord God decided?"

Dumah stared at the Rabbi for many, many minutes. Dumah, the Angel of Death, had black eyes that seemed as deep and as empty as those of a skull. Rabbi Abraham felt small and afraid. "Who are you to question the Almighty Lord God?" asked Dumah in the oldest of voices, rustling like the wind on a cold blank autumn night.

And now Dumah was standing at the foot of the bed, beside the covered head of old Sasson–and the Rabbi despaired. Dumah, the black angel of the Lord God Almighty, looked down at the dying man, and he looked at the sad Rabbi. Dumah stood, he stared, and he said, "Do not feel so badly, my good Rabbi. Recall the verse from Ecclesiastes":

I have seen the burden that God has laid on men–however, He has made everything beautiful in its time. He has also set Eternity into the hearts of men. Nonetheless, men cannot hope to fathom all the incondensably complex things that God has done from the beginning to the end.

The Rabbi looked up at Dumah. Slowly, old Achselrad uncovered the blankets at the foot of the bed, and gently he kissed the cheek of his old friend, Sasson ben Johel ha-Levi. The room was dark, but it was not lonely. The oak table at the side of the bed had a warm worn sheen – it was burnished as brown as the suntanned hills of the Holy Land. The candlelight in the room felt gentle and holy. And Dumah stood beside the Rabbi.

"Abraham," said the dark figure of death, "remember the hopeful words of the Book of Deuteronomy":

I will proclaim the Name of the Lord. Praise the greatness of our God. He is the Rock, His works are perfect, and all His ways are just. A faithful God is He – is He Who does no wrong – although His ways are often beyond the comprehension of man. Upright and just is He, is He, is He.

And the Rabbi only nodded. By then Sasson had stopped breathing, and with the swiftest of movements Dumah, the Angel of Death, reached down and pulled the soul of the old man, Sasson ben Johel, from out of his white-haired head. Quick as the speediest bird of prey, Dumah, the Angel of Death, flew off to the great celestial Heavens above, carrying the old man's soul, and the silver soul gleamed and glinted in the starlight as it passed by the white moon of the holy nighttime sky, amen.

Thus, Sasson ben Johel ha-Levi died a quiet gentle death. Later, the empty body of the pious old man was washed and it was dressed in his full clean holy *tallis*. Old Sasson ben Johel ha-Levi was curled into the position of an unborn child, so that someday, on that great day of resurrection, he might roll smoothly into the Holy Land beyond the grave. Rabbi Abraham ben Alexander conducted the burial service, the *Tzidduk ha-Din*. And Sasson was buried in a peaceful spot in the *Am Toten Juden*, the Jewish cemetery outside the southern town walls of old medieval Cologne.

After the ceremony and before they left the cemetery, Rabbi Abraham tossed a tuft of grass onto the grave, and he said some quiet words. Was he speaking to himself? My grandmother was not certain, but she thought that the Rabbi had said:

> May the great Name of the Almighty Lord God Yahweh-Elohim be magnified and be sanctified in this world. And someday, may this world be created anew. May the Almighty Lord God quicken the dead, and may He raise them to life eternal. Until that wondrous day, may Sasson be reunited with his parents and his friends in the Great Hereafter—hallelujah, O Lord, and amen.

And many years later, Rabbi Abraham himself was buried in the Cologne *Am Toten Juden*, on the right-hand side of Sasson ben Johel ha-Levi. And, Rabbi, I like to think that Abraham Achselrad once again found his old friend Sasson in the Great Hereafter and that now the two men walk and talk together, somewhere beyond the edge of the dark wide River Rhine, the old medieval River Rhine.

ood evening, Rabbi. I see there is no sleep for the
weary. That is what my grandmother said, and she said it almost
nightly. If you are cold, then sit here on the bench; I will stoke up the
oven. This stoker? It is one of the iron shoe scrapers from the front hall.
Of course, there are still two scrapers in the anteroom for dirty shoes.
But I myself am of the old school: I think that all pious men should
pray barefoot. And scholars and scribes and even popular writers do
their best work barefoot too. As my grandmother said, "To write
barefoot has always been most holy." Undoubtedly, my grandmother
was thinking of the poet Judah ben Solomon al-Harizi, who composed
the *Tahkemoni*, the famous set of adventure stories—al-Harizi always
wrote barefoot. Did you know that he once came to Cologne? No?
Well then, let me tell you about his visit:

Once upon a time, on a fall day in medieval Cologne, a thin
traveler wandered into the back room of the yeshiva, where Rabbi Joel
ben Isaac was working. In those days, all manner of pious pilgrims
came through Germany each week from the Holy Land, and wanderers appeared at all times of the day and night in the old synagogue in
Cologne. These strangers walked in, weary and wide-eyed, brimming

with wonder tales from distant lands and from far-off shores. In just this way, on one fall day, a traveler arrived in the synagogue and respectfully removed his shoes in the anteroom; then he padded barefoot into the back of the old wood building, where he found Rabbi Joel. As you know, Joel ben Isaac was the successor to the mystic Rabbi Abraham Achselrad and he was the father of the great legal scholar (and chess player) Rabbi Eliezer ben Joel.

Rabbi Joel looked up. The stranger smiled. "Hello, Rabbi," said the young and dusty man. "May I come in?"

"Certainly," said the Rabbi.

"My name is Judah ben Solomon al-Harizi," said the stranger.

Rabbi Joel nodded, and he stroked his beard; he had heard of young Judah. Judah al-Harizi was a Hebrew poet from Spain. Even as a young man, Judah wrote and lectured and traveled and he had been to lands as far away as Palestine and Armenia. Al-Harizi was quick and energetic and proficient in languages. He translated many works from Hebrew into Arabic and from Arabic into Hebrew, and today he is well known for his translation of Maimonides' *Guide of the Perplexed*.

As a poet, Judah al-Harizi introduced into Hebrew a form of verse devised by the Arabic writer Hariri of Basra. What is that, Rabbi? You have never heard of Hariri? Hariri was Abu Mahommed ul-Aasim ibn 'Ali ibn Mahommed al-Hariri. He had lived a century earlier, near Basra (a city south of Baghdad). Hariri was a country gentleman, with an estate of eighteen thousand date palms in the village of Mashan; in addition, he held a minor government position. However, his true love was the study of the Arabic language, and early in his life he wrote a long intricate linguistic poem entitled "Grammatical Recreations." Hariri also composed fifty rhymed essays on Arabic grammar and rhetoric, all thickly interwoven with details of Arabian history, litera-ture, and traditions. Hariri wrote in light unmetrical rhymes – that is, in rhymed prose. His poetry was fresh and new. It captivated young people, and it was this innovative style that al-Harizi adopted for his own Hebrew verse.

Now the Hebrew poet, young Judah ben Solomon al-Harizi, had appeared tired and barefoot at the door of the back room of the old yeshiva in Cologne. Rabbi Joel looked up. He set down his pen. "Please come in, Judah. Sit down and rest," said the Rabbi.

"Thank you very much," said al-Harizi. He stepped lightly into the room, he moved a pile of prayer books, and he sat on the floor, leaning against one of the worn benches. Rabbi Joel smiled at Judah, and Judah smiled back.

"Are you just passing through Cologne?" asked the Rabbi. "Or do you plan to stay for a while?"

"Well, Rabbi, I am going to visit a distant cousin in Dusseldorf," said Judah. "May I spend the night here on my way north?"

"Certainly," said Rabbi Joel.

Al-Harizi continued to smile. After a moment, the Rabbi said, "Tell me a little about yourself, young man."

The Rabbi sat back. Judah ben Solomon stretched his bare feet out in front of him. "I am a Jew from Spain, Rabbi. I am a writer."

Rabbi Joel nodded. Al-Harizi smiled again; then he too nodded. "Yes, Rabbi, I am a writer," said the young man. "Actually, I am a story-teller. Originally I worked only on translations, but when I was in the Holy Lands I discovered the most fascinating set of poems. They were in Arabic by the famous Hariri of Basra.

"These poems are not limited to simple repetitive chants: they do not have a plain monotonous meter. Instead, they are much freer— wonderfully free. In fact, I would call them rhymed prose. It was really a revelation to see this kind of verse, and it was just what I needed for my *Tahkemoni*," said Judah ben Solomon al-Harizi, and he leaned back happily.

Rabbi Joel looked at the poet. Should he know the *Tahkemoni*?

"Oh, I know, Rabbi," said Judah, nodding his head, "you are wondering: What is this *Tahkemoni*?"

Rabbi Joel began to say something, but al-Harizi was continuing: "Clearly you cannot know about the *Tahkemoni* yet—it is still unpublished. But I will tell you the basic plots. You see, this is a collection of stories. The *Tahkemoni*—'He Who Makes Wise'—is a cycle of stories and poems and fables, and they are all rather loosely tied together as a mythical journey through a forest. I have been working on this book for three years. As I wrote, the *Tahkemoni* developed into a sequence of life episodes, the adventures in the life of one Asher ben Jehuda. Do you know any Asher ben Jehudas?"

"Well, I—"

"Yes, yes, of course you do, Rabbi," said al-Harizi. "We all know an Asher ben Jehuda. In this case, he is my narrator. I like him, and his intentions are good but he is always having difficulties. If he meets a fine young woman, then she does not like him. Or if she likes him, then her father does not like him. Or if she and her father both like Asher, then her brothers or her mother do not like him. Sometimes Asher mistakenly trusts thieves. Sometimes his friends betray him. And everything that I tell, every single event and adventure, is rhymed, of course." Abruptly, al-Harizi stopped talking, and he looked intently at the Rabbi.

Rabbi Joel raised his eyebrows. "Of course," said the Rabbi, "but—"

"Yes, yes," said al-Harizi, "I know that you are surprised that I can write sixty adventures in verse. It has been difficult, but I have kept at the project patiently. And, of course, you know what language this is all written in."

"Well, I suppose—"

"Yes, Rabbi, *exactly*—it is written in Hebrew," said Judah, nodding again and stroking his curly black beard. "Now, I must admit that I did borrow a bit from the Holy Scriptures. I also interwove old Oriental stories that I heard in the Holy Lands. But it is natural that these events should appear: history repeats itself, and these particular adventures seem to have re-emerged in the course of Asher's strange life.

"As I said, the *Tahkemoni* is basically an unfulfilled romance: poor Asher tries his best, but he seems to fail most of the time. You see, Asher is usually wandering about in the forest, looking for his true love—that is, he is looking for one of a continuous stream of true loves. Then, at other times, he is following his companions (when they are not following him). You know how these adventures go—do you not, Rabbi?"

"Well, I am not certain. The first—"

"Exactly, Rabbi—even the first adventure leads to trouble. That is absolutely required in stories of this type," said Judah. "After losing most of their money, Asher and his friends wander through the countryside. There, they meet a variety of beautiful women, they fall in and out of love, and they are accosted by all manner of thieves and robbers. Also, the young men have a number of wild feasts. Eventually, they become bored. They become bored—but what is this? Suddenly, Asher finds a mysterious letter from a woman who has fallen in love with him. (In the *Takhemoni*, letters turn up in the oddest of places; in this case, the letter has blown into the forest from a nearby city.)

"Asher is fascinated by the poetry of the unknown woman who has written to him, so he sets out to find her. Soon, he discovers a harem. The harem master is a grim man with a bad temper and with thick arms; of course, the man is really Asher's lady-love in disguise. (I know, Rabbi, that this is a rather expected plot, but I did not want to write anything too unusual.) In the end, Asher discovers that everything, all the griefs and the troubles and the coincidences and the misadventures, were merely an elaborate joke of one of his friends — and then, naturally, everybody ends up living happily ever after."

Judah nodded to himself. He tapped his chin, and he patted his leg absent-mindedly. "Yes, Rabbi, I cannot say that it is great art. But it is light and enjoyable and good-natured. And it is the common stories, such as these, that we all remember. Why, the *Tahkemoni* is much like the collected Persian tales that are so popular. You know the ones — they are sometimes called *A Thousand and One Nights*."

Al-Harizi was silent for a few moments. His forehead creased, and he seemed to be listening to something far away. Finally, he yawned and he said, "Ah, Rabbi, when I think of it, *all* the *Tahkemoni* stories are rather obvious and simple." He paused, and then he added, "And now that I think of it, I suppose that my introduction to the stories was the obvious choice too. It is that famous passage from the introduction to the Book of Proverbs":

> These are tales that lead
> To shrewd and keen judgment —
> These words can be a creed
> For every manner of men —
>
> Here are rules, vintage
> Advice both just and wise,
> Basic principles, sage
> Truths in pocket size.
>
> The simple will see wisdom
> The wise will review the truths
> The young will hear old maxims
> The old will remember their youths;

Always some insightful stroke
Shines through these words which have survived
Through generations of common folk
Leading full and complex lives.

Judah stopped reciting. He yawned and he rested his head on the bench behind him. "Excuse me, Rabbi," he said in a fading voice, "I seem to be quite tired."

Judah moved his shoulders a little. He settled back into the corner by the bench, and he said, "Rabbi, do you mind if I just rest here for a moment?" And before Rabbi Joel could answer, al-Harizi closed his eyes. The Rabbi sat quietly for a few minutes. Then he walked softly over to Judah, and he covered the sleeping poet with a blanket, which he tucked carefully around the young man's bare feet.

As you know, Rabbi, it was this very book, the *Tahkemoni*, that brought Judah his lasting fame. The *Tahkemoni* is pure entertainment; it is light and fun and filled with a happy Judaic spirit. And even when working on these simple adventureful fables, the bright-hearted al-Harizi always wrote barefoot, with the complete innocent humility of a pious spirit. Judah ben Solomon al-Harizi died in the year 1230 – and do you know what the epitaph on his grave is? My grandmother told it to me; it is:

> *Judah al-Harizi wrote stories and poetry*
> *And good Judah wrote barefoot, humbly*
> *For the greater glory of the Lord Almighty.*

ood evening, Rabbi. You are having difficulty sleeping again? Just put your feet up on the side bench here and I will open the stove door. Let me push the coals back; the white glow will wash away all the cares of your hard day.

I heard your final prayers tonight, and there is no use denying it, Rabbi – you are overworked. Oh yes, even an old shammas like me can tell. I kept one eye on you when I was cleaning the dishes, and I saw that you were watching the door, hoping that Reb Elbaum would leave early. But then Reb Anton stayed late to argue about the scriptural passage from the Book of Judges:

> Then the Philistines bound Samson with two ropes, and they brought him up from the cave in the Rock. Samson came to Lehi, and when the masses met him, the Philistines shouted in triumph. However, the spirit of the Almighty Lord God suddenly seized Samson, and the ropes on his arms became as weak as burnt hemp and his bonds melted away. Samson looked down. He found the raw jawbone of an ass; then he picked it up, and he slew a thousand men.

Samson and the other eleven Judges were heroes for the Jews. They were men sent by the great God Yahweh to rescue the faithful, in the days when the Israelites were settling the land of Canaan. And when I think of heroes and Judges, I am always reminded of the teacher of Rabbi Abraham ben Alexander of Cologne. Yes, Rabbi, I am referring to Achselrad's mentor, Eliazer of Worms. I have told you about this old German rabbi before. Eliazer was a mystic, and he had taken part in a very strange and very mystical creation; it was the creation of a medieval Judge of sorts.

As you know, the mystic Eliazer ben Judah was the Chief Rabbi of Worms. To protect his people in those grim and difficult days, he had used holy occult powers to create a huge dumb creature from clay. Eliazer had made a Golem, but the true nature of this medieval Judge was kept a secret. Initially, Rabbi Eliazer announced to his household: "On the way to the ritual bath, I met a stranger, a beggar. The poor man is honest but simple-minded, and he is completely speechless. Apparently he is homeless, so I brought him back to the yeshiva to live and to work as a shammas." Rabbi Eliazer named this lumbering giant "Joseph Golem." (The Rabbi had called the man of clay "Joseph" after Joseph Sheda, who is mentioned in the Talmud; this Joseph was half human and half spirit, and he had helped many rabbis, frequently saving them from great trouble.)

For many of those dark years, the Golem haunted medieval Worms, and he guarded the Jews. Have you ever been to Worms, Rabbi? No? Worms is an ancient city in the Wonnegau plain along the River Rhine. The old town was an irregular patchwork, with buildings scattered here and there. Near the center, the large Cathedral of the Saints Peter and Paul stands silently, with four round towers and with two domes and a choir at each end. Worms has always been a trading town, manufacturing cloth and leather products. Goods move easily year-round through its harbor, and it exports chicory, slates, and wool – also, the famous Liebfraumilch wines come from Worms.

The Jewish synagogue in Worms is one of the oldest in all of Germany. Joseph Golem was assigned to be a shammas and to work as the custodian for the synagogue and its accompanying school. When he was not working, the Golem sat motionless on a bench in the corner of the yeshiva, with his head resting on his two hands. He stared at the floor; he seemed almost senseless. The Golem did not initiate any activity. He paid no attention to the others around him. Rabbi Eliazer told his confidants that this passiveness came from a lack of fear: neither fire nor sword nor water could harm the Golem.

The Golem appeared to be a dull, strong, and obedient man, and usually he just sat silently in the house of study. Rabbi Eliazer said that the Golem was not to be a personal servant. He warned his family not to ask Joseph Golem to do any housework. But the Rabbi's wife saw the Golem just sitting, sitting, sitting, day after day. "Joseph Golem is a shammas, a servant of the religious community," thought the woman. "Certainly he can help out with some of the ritual chores."

Now, as you know, Rabbi, one of the strict biblical admonitions deals with the removal of *hametz* or leaven from the house before Passover: nothing made with yeast or other fermenting substances can remain. As the Book of Exodus declares:

> For seven days, no leaven may be found in your houses. And anyone who eats anything fermented shall be outlawed from the community of Israel, be he foreigner or native. You must eat nothing fermented— wherever you live, you must eat your cakes unleavened.

In other words, even the minutest crumb, the most infinitesimal bit of *hametz*, must be removed. This requires a thorough and meticulous house-cleaning—and the *hametz*-cleaning soon became a general spring-cleaning.

In medieval Worms, the Passover house-cleaning began long before the actual holiday. Soon after *Purim*, almost a month before Passover, houses were cleaned and washed. The furniture was taken out-of-doors. All clothing was hung out in the sun and the breeze. In addition, when the weather was pleasant, the books were put on boards outside and they were opened to be aired in the wind. Next, the floors were scraped and swept. Most houses had wooden walls and ceilings, and these were freshly whitewashed with lime. (For a touch of color, some people added a little blue paint to the lime.) Then all the furniture was washed and wiped before being taken back into the house. Finally, the women decorated the houses with early spring flowers and with ornaments cut from colored cloth.

That year, just before Passover, Rabbi Eliazer's wife found herself behind schedule. Her sister was sick, and the Rabbi's wife visited her daily in order to help out. Rabbi Eliazer's wife had to divide her time between her sister and her own house-cleaning chores. The Rabbi's wife felt overwhelmed; she was short of help, she was tired, and she was harried—therefore, she decided to ask the Golem to help.

The Rabbi's wife stepped into the synagogue. "Joseph Golem," she said, "I need some water in order to prepare for the holiday of Passover. Please fill the water buckets and pour them into the two large kegs in the Rabbi's kitchen. This is an important ritual task; as the Rabbi's wife, I must be certain to have the household absolutely clean and orderly for the holidays." The Golem stood, and he nodded silently.

Slowly and steadily, the Golem took the three water pails from the kitchen. Then he walked to a nearby brook. Rabbi Eliazer's wife could not believe how deliberately and unhurriedly the huge man moved. Just watching him made her feel itchy—she wanted to push him along, to whisk him on his way with a broom. The Rabbi's wife had to turn away and not look at the Golem. However, she soon became occupied with other chores and she forgot all about the slow water-carrying Golem.

The Rabbi's wife finished scraping and cleaning the front steps. The Golem had not returned from his first trip to the stream. The woman looked toward the stream, she shrugged her shoulders, and she went off to her sister's house to prepare a meal for her nieces and nephews. Soon, other relatives appeared, and the women talked and argued and gossiped. Several hours passed. After a time, passersby began to call out: "There is a flood in the Rabbi's house—a river is running out of the kitchen!" Eventually, the Rabbi's wife heard the report. Fearing the worst, she ran home. There she found the Golem continuing to obey his orders: he was still pouring water into the kitchen kegs, which had been filled to overflowing long, long before. Now the courtyard was flooded with water.

"Stop!" yelled the wife. The Golem put down his pail. The Rabbi, too, had heard the uproar, and he had arrived home at the same time. He looked at the emotionless Golem, he looked at the water running like the River Rhine through the house, and he looked at his appalled wife. "Well," he said, "I see that you have found a tireless water-carrier."

The wife did not know whether to be angry or to be embarrassed. "This man has no common sense," she replied.

"Joseph Golem obeys orders literally," said the Rabbi. Then he said to the Golem, "Follow me." And slowly and silently, the lumbering giant followed Rabbi Eliazer ben Judah back to the yeshiva. . . .

What is that? Of course there is more, Rabbi: I only closed my eyes for a moment. Can an old man not take a little rest? Now you have interrupted my thoughts. Let me see, where was I? Yes – Rabbi Eliazer used the special strength and the invulnerability of the Golem to defend his people against outside threats. The worst of these were the blood-accusations, from which the Jews of Worms suffered greatly in those days. My grandmother reported that whenever the mystic Rabbi sent the Golem on such missions, an amulet written on kosher parchment was hung like a necklace around the clay creature's neck. Supposedly, this talisman made the Golem invisible. Frankly, Rabbi, I find this difficult to believe – but my grandmother told me that many unbelievable wonders occurred in those medieval days and that I should not question the possible deeds that can be accomplished in the Name of the Great Lord God Almighty (blessed be He).

Each year, said my grandmother, Rabbi Eliazer put this necklace on the Golem in the evenings during the week before Passover. Then the Golem was told to patrol the streets of the Jewish district; he was to watch especially for Gentiles carrying suspicious-looking sacks. On one occasion, such a bundle contained the bloody heart of a pig. The pig heart was supposed to look like the heart of a child – it was wrapped in a Jewish prayer shawl, and an evil man tried to put it in the house of a prominent Jew. Fortunately, however, the Golem prevented the terrible consequences of this act, and here is how it happened:

In those long-ago days, there lived in Worms a Jewish philanthropist and wealthy community leader named Mordecai Meisel ben Simon. Reb Mordecai was a moneylender by trade. (In the Middle Ages, the Church felt that it was wicked to lend money for interest because this took advantage of the misfortunes of others. Priests refused to give a religious burial to moneylenders, and they declared the wills of such businessmen to be invalid. Thus, money-brokering, a critical realm of the economy, was left entirely to the Jews.)

Actually, Mordecai Meisel was more than a moneylender; he was also a private banker, advising, investing, and crediting for various

businesses. One of Reb Mordecai's clients was a Mr. Havlicek, who
was a local Gentile butcher and an officer of the Butcher's Guild.
Havlicek owed Mordecai five hundred gold coins, but he refused to
repay his loan. Repeatedly, Mordecai asked for the money. One week
went by, and then two passed. Seven weeks came and seven weeks
went, and after seven cycles of seven weeks, Mordecai ben Simon filed
a formal charge, and Havlicek was ordered to report to the court.
Havlicek had long before used all of his available funds – there would be
no way for him to repay the loan or to pay any fines. He did not want
to go to prison; therefore, he devised a plan to trap Mordecai before the
court session took place.

Passover was coming, and this was a season when it was easy to
stir up bad feelings against the Jews. One night, Havlicek went into the
public slaughterhouse – the *Kuttelhofe* – which stood on the edge of a
stream leading into the River Rhine. That night, Havlicek was the
only person in the slaughterhouse. He took the heart from a newly
killed pig, and he wrapped it in a Jewish *tallis katan*, a prayer shawl that
he had stolen.

It was a dreadfully dark night, as if the Almighty Lord God had
poured blackness over everything in the world. At about midnight,
Havlicek placed the pig heart, wrapped in the prayer shawl, into a
wagon, and he drove through the Jewish Quarter. Havlicek reached
Reb Mordecai's house. The house was built of gray stone. It was large,
and it was surrounded by courtyards with vegetable gardens. Havlicek
looked nervously around, but he saw no one. He stepped into a side
courtyard. Most of the windows were barred, but two cellar windows
could be pushed open. As quietly as possible, Havlicek opened one of
the cellar windows.

Yes, the night was black – but, Rabbi, we Jews must always take
heart. As it says in Psalm 121:

> The Guard of Israel never sleeps
> The Lord defends your soul –
> No foes will strike from the nighttime deeps
> No evil will crawl from the midnight hole.
>
> God guards against all evil things
> He protects against ill winds and blight
> He shelters you with mighty wings
> Throughout the blackest night.

In those distant days, in the Jewish district of old Worms, it was the Golem who was the Lord's nighttime guard of Israel: the Golem was the medieval Judge. That night, the Golem was standing nearby, but he was invisible to most men. He stood by Mordecai's house, and he caught sight of the wagon. He watched the wagon stop in front of the house. He saw Havlicek get down quietly and take a sack from the wagon, and he watched Havlicek open the cellar window. Usually the Golem was a slow plodding clumsy creature. But the good Lord God (blessed be He) works wonders. Thus, quick as a wink, the Golem reached over and he caught up Havlicek in his huge cold clayey hands.

Havlicek was a butcher and a man of thick arms and strong shoulders. He felt the heavy hands grab him. Was it someone hidden in the dark shadows? Havlicek tried to lash out, but he could barely move. He had no chance against the huge invisible clay man: the Golem was a medieval Samson. With what seemed like no effort at all, the Golem lifted Havlicek, he tied him up tightly, and then he drove the butcher and his wagon and his bloody package toward the office of the city magistrate.

Wildly, the wagon flew through the dark streets. There was a large cold moon in the sky. The great Cathedral of the Saints Peter and Paul, with its basilica of four round towers and two large domes, cast a bleak shadow, through which the invisible Golem drove and drove and drove with his bound charge.

When they reached the magistrate's building, the Golem needed to get the attention of the officials. He was invisible, and he could make no sound with his voice. Therefore, the strange clay man raised his great fist and he smashed it down. He smashed his mighty right arm onto the boards of the wagon. The seat broke in two. Then the Golem ran off into the night and he returned to the old synagogue in Worms, where once again he sat quietly on a worn wooden bench along the wall, with his head resting in his hands.

The noise of the boards cracking brought the guards rushing out of the building. Havlicek lay in the wagon, shaking and dazed and bound. The city officials stared at the broken wagon. They looked at the tied man. The guards untied the butcher, and they found the bloody prayer shawl lying at his feet. Feebly, Havlicek said that some Jews had beaten and tied him. He said that inside the prayer shawl was the heart of a child that was destined for the Jewish Passover ritual.

The officials looked carefully at the heart; they found that a pig's foot was also wrapped in the prayer shawl. And where had this come from? Havlicek began to tremble. He was known to be a butcher and an officer of the Butcher's Guild, and although he denied any wrong-doing, the officials remained suspicious of his story. Of course, Havlicek was too frightened to try his evil deed again. Thus, once more and with the help of the Golem, the ever-watchful Lord God – the Guardian of the Jews both in the Holy Lands and abroad – had protected His children in the nighttime deeps, amen.

      Yes, it is true, Rabbi – Germany is far from the Holy Lands: it is far in space and it is far in time. And even in those old medieval years, it was far distant from the times and the places of the biblical Judges. Nonetheless, the good Lord Yahweh watched over Jews everywhere, as He continues to watch over them today. As my grandmother (may her memory ever be blessed) would recite from the Book of Leviticus:

      Then the Mighty Lord God said to Moses: "Always, I will remember My covenant with Jacob and My covenant with Isaac and with Abraham. Even in the lands of the enemies of Israel – even in distant lands and in far-off times, in day and in night – I shall neither reject nor spurn the faithful. I will judge mankind, and I will never break My covenant with them – because I am the Lord, their eternal God."

hat is that, Rabbi? No, I was just resting my eyes—please feel free to join me here by the stove. (I think you will be too warm on that bench. Try the one nearer to the wall.) With a warm stove, an old man like me can doze on and on and on. I suppose that is because my nights seem to flow on and on and on.

What do I mean? Actually, Rabbi, I am not certain. I only know that my grandmother told me that *she* was sleepy because her nights seemed to flow on and on without end when she got old. And she told me that the Talmud says:

> Night was created for endless sleep. In contrast, sleeping at dawn is like a rough edge on iron: morning sleep is jarring, and it puts a man into a coarse world. Thus, a man is forbidden to sleep during the daytime any more than can a horse (which is only sixty breaths of sleep).

I remember my grandmother telling me this when she was shaking out her apron one morning after a long night's sleep. I never knew why she always had crumbs in her apron in the mornings. Whatever the reason, she would shake them out vigorously and recite a number of prayers. To my grandmother, every day was just like the first day of *Rosh Hashanah*, when people go to a river or stream or lake in order to perform the Tashlik ceremony.

No, Rabbi, I do *not* think that Tashlik is superstitious. I go through the Tashlik ritual every year – and I know many other people who do it too. At the end of the Book of Micah, it is written:

> Once more You smile on me
> With affection tenderly
> And You wash me clean and guilt-free
> Casting my sins and my misdeeds
> Down to the depths of the sea.

So, in the fall, we go to some nearby water and shake the dirt and lint and crumbs out of our clothes: we cast our sins into the depths of the seas. My grandmother told me that by keeping her apron neat and clean, without a speck or a spot or a spiven of dirt, without the least hidden crumb, she was able to live happily into a ripe old age; it was because of regular Tashlik that she could walk for an hour without resting, even when she was older than me – and I am eighty, you know.

Why, Rabbi, how can you doubt such a holy ceremony? Remember the other sacred verse that is part of the Tashlik prayers:

> Jehovah, your Lord, is a God compassionate and gracious, long-suffering and true. He is ever constant to thousands of His children. He forgives iniquity, rebellion, and sin. He does not casually sweep away the guilty. However, He does hold the sons and the grandsons responsible for the unexpiated misdeeds of their fathers, for the sins that have not been properly cast off.

With such holy prayers in hand, the pious Jew walks to the nearest big river, such as the River Rhine in Cologne, and he lets the rushing waters carry off all the evil and the bad luck that may have accumulated during the past year. The mystic Kabbalist Achselrad of Cologne said that after reciting the Tashlik prayers you must also shake your clothes very vigorously. In this way, you remove any clinging demons. . . . No, Rabbi, this does not sound like a pagan custom to me – it sounds very prudent. Demons, dybbuks, and devils crowd about us constantly, and with their thick and hairy claws, they cling even to the most pious of men.

I wonder whether it was somehow in connection with Tashlik that poor Etan ben Anselm ha-Kohen was beset by a river-demon. What do you think? You do not know the story of Reb Etan of Cologne? Then let me tell it to you:

Once upon a time, said my grandmother to me, in the congregation of Rabbi Abraham ben Alexander, the mystic Achselrad of Cologne, there was a devout man named Etan ben Anselm ha-Kohen. Etan was a gardener and he grew cabbage, cucumbers, lettuce, melons, and onions.

Now, one day in the autumn of his life, Anselm ben Mannus, Etan's father, felt that his death was fast approaching. Therefore, he said to his son, "Etan, my first love, I am almost in the hands of the good Lord God (blessed be He). My time has come to die."

"This is not true, Father," said Etan. "You are just feeling weak today. I am certain that you still have many fine years left."

"No, young man," answered Anselm. "When a Decree of Death has been signed, then a man knows. But I have lived a good life, and I am content. Still, son, I must ask you a favor."

"Ask anything," said Etan.

Anselm was out of breath, and he rested for a moment. Then he said, "Etan, I would like you to continue a small tradition of mine."

"What is that?" asked the son.

"It is simply this: I have been in the habit of going down to the river every day and throwing bread crumbs to the fish," said the father. "As you know, I walk through the marketplaces and down to the old Roman bridge; then I stand on a rock, a gray-green rock, over the River Rhine."

Anselm closed his eyes and was silent again. Etan waited patiently. After a few minutes, Anselm said, "Do you think that you can continue this, son? You are aware of what I have been doing—are you not?"

"Yes, of course I know what you do," said Etan. "But let me ask you, Father: Why do you do it?"

"Actually, I am following the custom of my mother (may she rest forever in the bosom of the holy Lord God, blessed be He, amen)."

"Amen," said Etan.

"Yes–amen," repeated the father. "This is a very religious custom. You see, son, in the Bible, Moses told the wandering Israelites that–"

"Your feeding the fish has something to do with Moses in the desert?" asked Etan.

"Let me finish, son. As I was saying–Moses told the wandering Israelites that there would be no Manna available from the Heavens on the seventh day, on the Sabbath. Therefore, Moses advised the Israelites to collect twice as much food on Friday. Specifically, Moses said":

> The Lord has given you the holy restful Sabbath; therefore, He also gives you two days' food every sixth day. On the Sabbath, let each man stay where he is–no one may stir from his home on the seventh day, the day of rest.

Anselm coughed, and he too rested. Etan remained quiet. After a few minutes, his father continued:

"Ah, my good son, even we Jews are a mixed lot. I am sorry to say that there were some angry and sinful men in the camps of the Israelites: there were some opponents of Moses. These men wanted to prove that the old Patriarch and Law-giver had in fact been wrong. Therefore, on the Sabbath morning, these wicked men arose very early, before the dawn. Quietly, they went out into the surrounding countryside, and they scattered some of the Manna that they had gathered on the previous day.

"Had this 'new' Sabbath Manna been discovered, then Moses would have been embarrassed. But the good Lord God is ever watchful. He sent down birds and animals and even fish (in the streams); the creatures came, and they ate all the scattered food before the Israelites awoke and discovered it.

"Now, was that not a fine thing for them to do? The descendants of these creatures surround us, even here in the Rhinelands. And it was in gratitude to these wild animals that my mother scattered bread crumbs each morning, along the edges and into the depths of the wide and dark River Rhine."

Etan raised his eyebrows. "Well, I never would have imagined this," he said. "It seems like a daily Tashlik. But of course I will follow your wishes, Father."

Anselm smiled. "That would make me very, very happy," he said. "You see, son, by now the fish of the River Rhine have come to depend on me."

And Etan nodded his head.

Anselm had more to say. "I hesitate to ask this, my son, but this small matter is so important to me that I wonder if you would be willing to take a solemn oath to do this deed."

"Of course, Father," said Etan, "I solemnly promise." Then Etan took hold of the fringes of his father's *tallis katan*, his prayer shawl, and Etan repeated, "I solemnly promise – in the sight of the good Lord God (blessed be He)."

Happily, Anselm ben Mannus closed his eyes and he breathed gently and easily. Etan had tears in his eyes. He said that he hoped that the Lord would spare his father's life. However, the old man died soon after, on a Sabbath in the early autumn month of *Tishri*, and he was mourned deeply for seven long and sad days. On the eighth day, the son remembered his solemn oath. Early in the morning, Etan took some bread crumbs, and he went down to the River Rhine and he fed the fish.

Although the weather turned cool, Etan ben Anselm ha-Kohen continued to take bread crumbs to the river each morning. He developed a simple routine. At dawn, he would work in his garden. After a few hours, he ate his breakfast, he collected the leftover crumbs, and he went down to the wide dark River Rhine. Etan stood on a gray-green rock. He threw the crumbs into the water. Windhovers and turnstones soared far overhead. Shore birds with long legs pecked at the bits of bread near the bank, and ducks snapped the crumbs in midstream. Fish swarmed and they swirled – they flashed to the surface to grab the floating crumbs, they swished through the water to snatch the bits of food that lazily drifted down to the black and murky depths, and they churned up the cold River Rhine from side to side and from end to end.

Now, it is an unfortunate fact, but a demon lived under a rock at just that point in the river. (May the good Lord God protect us from all such evil spirits forever, amen.) The demon did not like to have Etan bothering him. This malign spirit stayed awake all night and he slept all day, and he wished to sleep calm and undisturbed. When Etan arrived each morning, the fish flipped the demon hither and thither with their strong fishy tails—each day, the grumpy demon was awakened and he was battered and bruised. Therefore, late one night, the demon angrily dug a large pit in front of the gray-green rock at the edge of the medieval River Rhine.

The next morning, Etan came to feed the fish. Absently, he walked where he always walked. Without thinking or looking, he stepped where he always stepped, and suddenly he fell into the hole, he hit his head, and he became unconscious. Etan ben Anselm ha-Kohen lay unconscious in a ditch beside the broken jipijapa plants and the trampled knotroot grasses, and the demon laughed and it hummed and it hissed and it coughed.

Just at that moment an angel of the Lord was passing by. This angel was Nahaliel, the angel of streams, rivers, and lakes, and he saw Etan fall and hit his head and he heard the demon laugh and hiss and cough. The good angel Nahaliel opened wide his bright, bright eyes. He listened well with his softest and tiniest ears. Then he flew up directly to Heaven. "O Lord my God," said the angel, "a young man has fallen prey to a demon." And then Nahaliel told the story to the good Lord God.

The Most Holy One nodded His radiant head. "Go and find Rabbi Abraham ben Alexander of Cologne," said the Lord. "He will know what to do."

So the angel Nahaliel flew back down to Cologne. Nahaliel took the shape of a winged human, and he stepped in the front door of the synagogue. The holy angel was barefoot. Lightly he went through the anteroom, and he flew into the main prayer hall, which was filled with wooden benches. He floated past the twelve stained glass windows with their colored lions and snakes, he looked up at the Holy Ark made of stone, and he glided to the door of the back study room. There, the Rabbi was bent over a book—well, actually, Rabbi, old Abraham Achselrad was asleep, having worked all night on his mystical tome of Kabbalistic knowledge, the *Keter Shem Tov*.

A gentle wind rustled through the yeshiva building. Nahaliel the angel bent down and he whispered in the Rabbi's ear. "Rabbi Abraham," he said, in an airy holy voice, "go down to the river and rescue poor Etan ben Anselm ha-Kohen."

The Rabbi awoke with a start. He looked around. No one was

there. Rabbi Abraham raised his eyebrows. He sat quietly a moment, and then he put on his hat and his coat, and he went down to the banks of the cold dark River Rhine. Abraham Achselrad walked through the marketplaces and over to the old Roman bridge. There, at the edge of the river by the gray-green rock, the Rabbi found poor Etan lying unconscious in a deep pit. A foul demon sat laughing at the edge of the pit.

"What is the meaning of this?" asked the Rabbi.

"What is the meaning?" hissed the demon. "Why, the meaning is quite clear, old man."

"It may be clear to you," said the Rabbi, "but you live in mud and darkness. Perhaps you will just explain this sad situation to me."

"Certainly, Rabbi," said the demon, and it hissed and it spat and it laughed a cruel laugh. "This discourteous man has been bothering my sleep. Do you think that a spirit can stay awake all day as well as all night? Well, if you think this, then you are sadly mistaken. Moreover, every day he throws garbage into the River Rhine – right here by my underwater rock! This Jew messes up the quiet water, and he attracts all manner of noisy boisterous fish. Therefore, I have decided to put an end to his rude behavior."

"Oh, you have, have you?" said the Rabbi. "This man is a member of my congregation. He is a humble gardener, you foul demon; he means you no harm."

"Well, there is an old proverb: 'As is the garden, so is the gardener.' And I think that this gardener has an annoying garden," answered the demon, who hissed and spat and laughed and snapped his pointy demonic fingers seven times.

"Enough discourtesy is enough, evil one," said the Rabbi angrily. Rabbi Abraham reached into his pocket, and he tossed a handful of salt into the river; for it is written in the Second Book of Kings:

> The people of the city Jericho said to the prophet Elisha: "You can see that our city is located in a fine and pleasant area. However, the water is polluted, and now the country is troubled with evil spirits and with miscarriages and other diseases."
>
> Elisha responded: "Fetch me a new bowl, and put some salt in it." When the citizens had gotten the bowl and the salt, Elisha went out to the

spring of water. He threw a handful of salt into it, and he said: "This is the word of the Lord: 'I now purify this water. It shall cause no more death, disease, miscarriage, or other evil.'"

And in fulfillment of Elisha's holy words, the water in that area has remained pure until this very day.

So, in this tradition, Rabbi Abraham threw a handful of salt into the River Rhine, saying: "I now purify this water. It shall cause no more death, disease, miscarriage, or other evil." Next, the Rabbi pronounced seven mystical Names of the Lord God Almighty.

The demon began to tremble. He tried to fly away, but he found that he was rooted to the spot where he sat. Rabbi Abraham's voice became louder and louder: "In the Book of Leviticus the Almighty Lord spoke to Moses, saying":

Do not resort to ghosts, spirits, or demons. Do not make yourselves unclean by seeking them out or by associating with them in any way: they are not among My sphere of holy children—and I am the Lord.

Just at that moment Etan ben Anselm awoke. He felt strange and ill-at-ease, as if he had just been jarred awake into the coarse world from a morning's sleep. Suddenly Etan saw the demon, and the gardener shrank back in fear. Now, however, the Rabbi was again invoking the seven mystical Names of the Lord. The Rabbi waved an amulet. The sky darkened and the Rabbi chanted:

> Now I exorcise you far beyond
>   The cottages of the dead,
> Fly back across the bleak cold pond,
>   Fall down the caves of dread.
> Never will you see a child
>   Wide-eyed, laughing in the sun,
> Never will a newborn smile
>   And hold his fist around your thumb;
> God will smite you blind—reviled
>   Forever you'll be blank and dumb:
> The fierce Lord sends you far from here,
>   He only holds the gentle near.

Clouds covered the sun. There was a clap of thunder. Etan winked and he blinked. Then the demon shriveled with a hiss and a shriek, and all that was left was a wet pile of blank gray mud.

Wearily, the Rabbi put his hands at his side. "Hallelujah, and amen forever," said the old mystic softly. Etan raised his eyebrows and he looked at the Rabbi – but the Rabbi was already walking quietly and slowly back to the synagogue. After a few minutes, Etan too turned from the river, and slowly he walked home to his garden. Etan walked back home, as the clouds began to float away far and high and as the sun shone brightly over medieval Cologne, once again and forever.

ell, Rabbi, I am glad to see you here alone. I want to
apologize for my outburst during the service this evening. It was just
that Reb Anton said that his bones ached; he said that in his old age
they were failing him and that they were not worth a fig. Imagine
speaking ill of one's bones! Why in the olden days, in the strict and
pious days of our fathers, Reb Anton would have been ordered to leave
and never to return.

What? How can you not remember the many sacred words
about bones, Rabbi? The famous section in Psalm 35 says:

> Now I shall rejoice in the Lord
> And delight in His love and mercy.
> My very bones shout to the Adored:
> "O Lord, who is like unto Thee?"

And bones are also holy records. The Kabbalah tells us that your
sins are written on your bones, and after your death, those bones that
have sins inscribed on them are transformed into demons. Bones also
have much medicinal value, although I was never privy to the details of
exactly how they should be used.

Bones are very holy, Rabbi. My grandmother told me that bones were a part of the most holy of holy artifacts: the original sacred Ark of the Covenant. The great Ark of the Covenant was a chest of acacia wood, overlaid with gold; it was carved with sacred symbols and words, and it had four gold rings as handles. The wandering Israelites took it with them on their travels to Palestine. At first, said my grandmother, the sacred Ark contained the bones of the Patriarch Joseph – later, of course, it contained the Holy Scriptures.

For all these reasons, bones were most important to my grandmother, and it was she who told me the famous story of the bones of Johel Shimshon. No, Rabbi, he was not Johel *ben* Shimshon – he was just plain Johel Shimshon. . . . Well, if you will just be patient a moment, then I will tell you why he was not Johel the son of Shimshon, but only Johel Shimshon. Now, I first heard about Johel Shimshon from my grandmother (blessed be her memory), and she had learned this strange tale from a letter of Rabbi Petahiah.

Exactly, Rabbi – that was Petahiah ben Jacob (the brother of Rabbi Isaac "the Wise" of Prague). Rabbi Petahiah undertook a tour of the entire world, and eventually he wrote about his adventures in a book he called *Sivuv ha-Olam* ("Around the World"). His travels took place in the days of old Achselrad, well before Asher ben Yehiel was the Chief Rabbi of Cologne. Why do I mention Rabbi Asher? When he was the leading scholar in Cologne, Asher spent all his free time writing and reading. Rabbi Asher continuously studied the Torah and the Talmud in the little back room of the yeshiva where for centuries the Cologne rabbis had worked and thought and argued with themselves. Above the back study room was a loft for storage. One day, late in the cold autumn month of *Heshvan*, when he was rooting around among the manuscripts in the loft, Asher found a letter from Rabbi Petahiah of Regensburg to Rabbi Abraham ben Alexander, Achselrad of Cologne.

"My dear Rabbi Abraham – [began the letter]

"I have just met a fine young man, a Jew from Nuremburg. He has agreed to carry this letter to my good friend, Rabbi David of Nuremberg, who I am certain will then arrange to transport it to you. I write to wish you and your family well, to convey my fondest greetings to all the Jews of your blessed community in Cologne, and to praise the good Lord God (blessed be He) and His Almighty Name for ever and ever, amen.

"I will not trouble you with the details of my many wagon rides and my subsequent sea voyages. Suffice it to say that they safely brought me here to the Oriental regions, regions that are so near to the great Holy Land where someday the Messiah shall return and deliver us and resurrect all souls and rebuild the Temple on Zion, amen. I write now in order to record for you some details of the lands and the peoples that I have seen in these old and foreign realms. The bright and glorious hand of God is visible everywhere, if only we look – praise the Lord Yahweh-Elohim.

"Yes, my old friend, I have had many, many adventures in arriving here. I hope – with the good Lord willing – to relate more of these events to you in person. Recently, I have been touring the Holy Lands of Palestine. Now I find myself in Gaza. (This city is also called 'Azzah and Ghuzzeh.) Gaza is the most southerly of the five ancient and princely Philistine cities; it lies near the sea, at the meeting point of the old trade routes to Syria from Egypt, Arabia, and Petra.

"There are almost five kilometers between Gaza and the sea, and the intervening land is principally sand dunes. Gaza has no natural harbor; instead, the Gazans use a small port area called the Mineh. To the east of Gaza are the remains of a Greek racecourse, with corners marked by granite shafts. To the south is a remarkable hill, quite isolated and bare, with a small mosque and a graveyard. This southern rise is called el Muntar ('The Watch Tower'). Do you recall this place from the Holy Scriptures? Samson carried the gates of Gaza to el Muntar – you remember that section in the Book of Judges":

Samson went to Gaza. There he met a beautiful woman, and he spent the night with her. When the people of Gaza heard that Samson had come, they planned to capture him at dawn and then to kill him; therefore, the Gazans surrounded the woman's house, and they waited for him all that night, near the city gate. However, at midnight Samson arose, and he slipped out of the house. When he came to the city gates, he seized hold of the great doors and he uprooted the two huge posts. Samson pulled them out with their heavy wood and iron bars, he hoisted them onto his shoulders, and he carried them to the top of the hill called 'el Muntar,' east of Hebron.

"Even in those biblical days, Gaza was a strongly walled, thickly gated fortress town, and it was a place of commercial importance. Today, Gaza is divided into four quarters, one of which is built on a low hill. To the north, a magnificent grove of olive trees forms an avenue six kilometers long. There are lofty minarets in various parts of the town, and there is a lovely mosque built of ancient materials. Since the Crusade, there is also a new Catholic church toward the south side of the hill. And on the east is the tomb of Samson.

"As usual, I politely questioned everyone I met, and I quickly discovered a fine friendly man, a Jew named Kalonymus ibn Johel ben Shimson. Reb Kalonymus welcomed me into his home, and then he and I spent many days wandering the Gazan markets. Kalonymus is a potter, and pottery is everywhere in Gaza – the local earthenware is black, and it overflows the marketplaces in piles and piles.

"One day, after walking through the crowds and talking about the clay works, Kalonymus took me down an alley, past an open park, and then beyond the park into an old cemetery. The climate of Gaza is dry and healthy, but now in the summer it is very hot, and the two of us were quite warm. The land around the cemetery was partly dried cornland and partly waste, and we sat and rested, appreciating the calm cool garden of the dead, amidst the dry heat of the desert.

"The cemetery had a clump of small trees – white mulberries – and Kalonymus and I sat on a bench between the trees and the graves. With the afternoon warmth flowing over me in waves, I was daydreaming and I was not listening carefully. After a while, I realized that Kalonymus was saying: '. . . on a farm not far from here. He was a Jew, living in a small hut next to his field, which he leased from a shrewd and rather greedy Mohammedan landowner. At the same time, this Jew tried to get into the linen exporting business. Unfortunately, he was not a very good businessman, and he lost all of his investment. The poor man had borrowed money from neighbors, from acquaintances, and from the landlord; suddenly his crops also failed, his one worker quit, and soon he found himself absolutely penniless and in great debt to his landlord.

" 'And what did the landlord do? First, he had the Jew arrested. That gave the landlord no reward, so he took the Jew back into his custody and made him a virtual slave. The Jew was not especially able-bodied, and he was depressed and weak: in fact, he was completely worthless as a workman. The landlord became angry, and he locked the Jew in a storeroom. Was it a mistake, was it neglect, or was it cruelty? I suppose that we will never know. In any case, the Jew died soon thereafter, with his huge debts still unpaid.'

"A warm wind blew the sun's heat over our arms and our hands. Kalonymus ibn Johel took a drink of water from the skin bag at his side.

" 'So, this poor Jew died,' said my companion. 'He had no money, no friends, and no relatives. The Mohammedan landlord thought, "Perhaps this wretched creature will have some use in death, if not in life." Therefore, he buried the Jew in the mud by a river bank. After a year, only the bones were left. The landlord dug up the bones. He put them in a wooden box; then he took them to the market, and he offered to sell them.

" 'Of course, human bones can be used in many magic rituals and it would be easy to sell a box of bones – especially a box of Jewish bones. The landlord took the bones into the marketplace, and he sat on the porch of a pottery shop, talking idly with the owner. It was a steamy morning, and I was walking by the open shop. As I passed, the shopkeeper called out, "Bones for sale! Buy the magical bones of a Jew!"

" 'I stopped. The men did not recognize that I too was a Jew. I asked how it was that they had happened to have this box of Jewish bones. The Mohammedan landlord was an easy talker. He told me the whole story. "Now," he said, "I need to recoup my losses. In essence, I am holding these bones for ransom."

" 'The shop owner laughed, and the two men returned to talking among themselves. I stood there for a moment, looking at the box. It was rough cedar wood. The edges did not meet evenly, and there was no top. I tried to picture what the Jew had looked like. Was he tall? Did he have dark black eyes? At one time those bones were inside a little child. Had he run through these very streets? Had he splattered mud on his tunic in the rainy season? Had he leaped and jimped and jumped on sunny evenings in the spring? I stood, and I stared. Then I remembered the passage from the Book of Deuteronomy in the Holy Scriptures'":

> When a man is found to have kidnapped an Israelite and to have treated him harshly and to have sold him, then he shall be punished and die – and you shall do all you can to right the crime and to rid yourselves of this wickedness.

" 'I thought of these holy words,' said Kalonymus. 'Then I turned and hurried home, and I collected all the money that I could. Next, I returned to the bazaar. "Let me buy those bones," I said. The shop-keeper shrugged his shoulders, and we traded the bones for a large sum of cash.

" 'I took the box of bones home. I washed them. Then carefully, I wrapped them in my *tallis katan*, and I covered them with spices. I took apart the box, and I glued it neatly together again (in order that no sharp nails snag the soul of the poor dead Jew). Then I brought the bones and the box here to the cemetery.'

"Kalonymus stood, and I followed him to a child-size grave, with a flat gray headstone that had a *Magen David* scratched neatly on both sides.

" 'I buried the bones as best I could, reciting the prayers that I remembered. I also set a small clay jar of water in the grave,' said Kalonymus.

"Although I was silent, Abraham, I must have raised my eye-brows, because Kalonymus looked at me and said, 'Why did I do this? A jar of water is a holy memorial; in Psalm 56 it says'":

> Record now my laments, O Lord, I ask –
> Store every salty tear of dew
> In Your golden mourning flask –
> Then my enemy will bow his head
> When I finally call to You
> With no tears from my calm deathbed.

"And Kalonymus continued: 'The famous bar Kappara – Rabbi Eleazar ben Eleazar ha-Kappar, who had his school at Caesarea not far from here – said: "'Water symbolizes tears, and tears shed for good and righteous men are counted by the Lord and are placed in His treasury. In fact, gentle rain is also like tears. Thus, may rain soak the graves of all the righteous dead. May the departed ones forever taste soft rains upon their sleeping faces, and may light storms gently wet their holy bones, amen."'

"Kalonymus ibn Johel bowed his head for a moment. 'I carried out the funeral rites myself,' he said. 'I hope that this was not too presumptuous. After the last prayer, I tore up some grass and earth, and I tossed it behind my back. Is this ritual somehow about Resurrection? I do not know, but I have seen the rabbis do it, so I did it too.

"'The next day I found a flat gray stone, and I set it up here as a headstone. You can see that I carved a Star of David on both sides. Then I needed to inscribe the name. But who was this Jew? I did not know. I was afraid to return to the landlord and ask – perhaps he would do me some harm when he discovered that I too was a Jew; certainly he would try and extort further payment of the debt from me. So I thought to myself, "In the Great Hereafter this poor dead man knows his own name. And obviously the Almighty Lord God knows the man's true name. For this one last time here on earth, let me just lend him a good name." So I called him Johel Shimshon, after my own father,' said Kalonymus.

"I looked carefully at the headstone, and I could see, written in small neat script":

Here lies a pious Jew

He can be called Johel Shimshon

"I looked at Kalonymus ibn Johel. He was smiling. He patted and neatened some of the dried dirt at the edge of the grave. We stood together for a moment, quietly. Then we walked back into the warm city of Gaza, at the edge of the eternal Holy Lands.

"That is the whole story, Abraham, and I must end my letter now – but, dear friend, think of me as you read this letter in your holy study in Cologne. You are called Abraham, and I am called Petahiah. These names are fine loans to us on this good and dusty earth. But are these the names by which the wondrous Lord God knows us in His pure and glorious Heaven? Someday we shall find out. Someday we will be redeemed in the true names of our childhood—although it will be in the light of our old age. Then the springtime showers will soak our graves again; yes, soft rains we will forever taste upon our sleeping faces and light storms will gently wet our holy bones for all eternity. So, hallelujah and amen, my good young Abraham, hallelujah and a fond amen.

"Your childhood friend,
Petahiah, the son of Jacob"

Hello, Rabbi, I will be with you in a moment – I cannot leave until every tablecloth is folded, otherwise the day has not ended properly. . . . There, now I am finished at last and I can sit next to you by the stove.

I am not sleepy either. Sometimes staring at the stove helps: everything fades into a bright white sleepy fog. After taking my eyes from the glow of the firelight, details of my world seem to melt away – I certainly cannot read the writing inscribed on the wall over there. It is as if the writing has disappeared. Yes, it is *disappeared writing,* and perhaps this is the way that all the stories about disappeared writing began. You do not know those tales, Rabbi? Then let me tell you one of them. I will tell you a story that my grandmother told about the disappeared writing on an amulet made by old Abraham Achselrad:

Once upon a time, said my grandmother to me, there was a very pious man named Natronai ha-Kohen. Natronai was a baker who lived in medieval Cologne. Natronai's wife Ruth was a good and loving mother, but her newborn baby boy had sudden and repeated attacks of crying. The baby was called Samuel, and he was their only child.

Little Samuel's fits got worse and worse. Soon he would cry for hours on end and nothing whatsoever could calm him down.

Samuel was only two months old. He did not seem to be sick. For a time, he would be normal and happy, especially in the mornings. But in the afternoon or the evening, he would begin to cry loudly and continuously. His face became red. His stomach grew fat and round, his feet became cold, and he clenched his hands into fists. He would cry and cry and cry and it seemed that he stopped only when he was completely exhausted.

The poor mother tried all manner of remedies. She held the child upright and she held him upside down. She patted him on the back. She rocked him, and she pulled his left ear when he sneezed. She put red ribbons on his crib. She walked in a circle around his bed seven times. She put a knife under his mattress, she put salt under his pillow, and she put silver coins under his blankets. She washed his face with his own urine. She pierced a clove of garlic with holes and then put the cloves on a necklace around the child. (And, of course, she *never* put Samuel's clothes on him inside out.) When he cried, she would snap the fingers of her left hand seven times. Nothing worked. After weeks and weeks, the woman was at a loss, and finally she went to consult with Rabbi Abraham ben Alexander.

It was a weekday evening. The Rabbi was working in the back room of the old Cologne yeshiva, concentrating on a particularly difficult chapter in the *Keter Shem Tov*, his mystical treatise of Kabbalistic lore. The Rabbi heard a noise. He looked up. Ruth was standing in the doorway. The Rabbi nodded, and he invited the young woman to sit on one of the wooden benches. Ruth wasted no time – quickly she explained her problem to the old man, and she waved her hands and shook her head as she spoke. Rabbi Abraham closed his eyes and he stroked his beard, and after a few minutes he said, "I had best see the child myself."

So Rabbi Achselrad went with the woman to her home, and for many minutes he looked intently at the infant. The child was sleeping. The Rabbi inspected the room very carefully. Then the pious old man said, "First, we must remove the *mezuzah* from the doorpost."

"You must take off the *mezuzah*?" asked Ruth.

"Yes," said Rabbi Abraham, "but only temporarily."

This they did, and gently they set the *mezuzah* in a linen cloth on the doorstep. Rabbi Abraham sat at the kitchen table. He took a clean piece of kosher calf parchment from his pocket, and he wrote a secret and mystical incantation on one side; on the other side he drew a *Magen David* inscribed with the Ineffable Name of the Great Lord God. The Rabbi rolled the parchment into a tight scroll. He tied the scroll with seven white threads, and in each thread he put seven neat knots. Ruth watched silently as the scroll was put in a little silver box and as the box was strung on a heavy red thread. Finally, Rabbi Abraham closed his eyes and he pronounced seven mystical Names of the Almighty Holy One.

The Rabbi opened his eyes. He laid his old hands on the holy necklace. Rabbi Abraham was silent a moment. He nodded his head, he took the silver box in his right hand, and he put it up to his ear. Old Achselrad set the amulet against his ear – and he smiled. Then he said, "My good woman, hang this around your son's neck whenever he cries. It will calm him down immediately."

Ruth took the little silver box with its parchment scroll, and she looked at it carefully.

"I must caution you," said the Rabbi, "it is best not to open the amulet." Ruth shrugged her shoulders and she said, "Very well, Rabbi."

Then the Rabbi replaced the *mezuzah* on the doorpost, and he returned to the yeshiva.

Ruth set the amulet on a shelf in the child's room. The first time that the baby cried uncontrollably, Ruth put the charm around the child's neck. Within an hour the infant calmed down, and he soon fell asleep. The second time that he cried, the charm worked in five minutes. By the third time, the child calmed down immediately and he fell asleep quite happily. Thereafter, whenever the baby cried, his mother would put the amulet around his neck; Samuel would instantly become calm and contented, and he would fall into a warm and happy sleep.

Young Samuel grew up. In a few months, the amulet was no longer needed. Ruth put it on a shelf in the kitchen and she forgot about it. One day, two or three years later, Ruth was cooking. She reached back on a cupboard shelf, and her hand touched the amulet. She took it down. There was no one else in the house, and she could not restrain her curiosity. With a knife, she pried open the little silver box. She unrolled the amulet, but she found only a blank piece of paper –

nothing was written on it. Had the holy letters flown away? Were they written in invisible ink? How had the incantations disappeared?

Ruth was a bold and curious woman. Therefore, the next morning she went to Rabbi Abraham. He was sitting in the little back study room, staring absently at his desk.

"Rabbi," said Ruth, "do you remember the amulet that you gave me? My son Samuel no longer needs this holy necklace, and I must confess that I have opened it up. I found that there is nothing written on the parchment."

The Rabbi tapped his fingers on the table, but he did not answer. After a few minutes Ruth said, "Rabbi?"

"Oh, excuse me, my good woman," said the Rabbi. "What were you saying?"

"I was saying that a few years ago you gave me an amulet in order to stop my little son from crying. The charm worked. It was wonderful. My Samuel is cured, and I no longer use the holy necklace. Now, Rabbi, I have taken the liberty of looking inside it," said Ruth. "However, the parchment is blank."

The Rabbi nodded, he stroked his beard, and then he said, "Are the details of that old incantation really important? What *is* important is that, through the amazing grace of the good Lord God, the charm has worked, amen."

Ruth looked at the Rabbi. "Amen," she said. She was silent a moment. The Rabbi was rubbing his finger along the edge of his chair. Ruth did not get up to leave; instead, she said, "Tell me, Rabbi – was there ever anything written on the parchment? Or," and here she lowered her voice, "is this a case of *disappeared writing*?"

" 'Disappeared writing'?" mused the Rabbi. The Rabbi stroked his beard, and he smiled at Ruth. "My good woman, before you arrived I was just reading Psalm 3," he said. "Let me recite a bit of those verses for you":

> Therefore I can lie down then
> Sleeping without dread or fright
> And I will awake tomorrow again
> Calm and warm and sound and tight –
> For the good Lord holds me safely when
> I brave the terrors of the darkling night.

"May the Almighty Lord God (blessed be He) convert all evil hearts to good, amen," said the Rabbi.

"Amen," said Ruth somewhat uncertainly. Old Abraham Achselrad looked down at his desk. Then he said, "Let me make a suggestion, Ruth. Give the charm to your son. He can keep it as a sacred memento."

Ruth raised her eyebrows. She felt a bit puzzled, but for some unexplainable reason she also felt better. So Ruth went home, and that evening she gave the small silver box on a red string to her son Samuel. Samuel's eyes brightened, and he ran off to his room.

Years passed. Seven years came and seven years went, and the child grew up and became a pupil in Rabbi Abraham's yeshiva. Eventually, he went on to become a well-known rabbi of Cologne, the Rabbi Samuel ben Natronai. In those later years, Rabbi Samuel was a judicial colleague of Rabbi Eliezer ben Shimson and Rabbi Ephraim ben Jacob, who together made up the famed and far-reaching rabbinate of the Rhinelands. Rabbi Samuel was warm, good-hearted, energetic, and insightful, and his father-in-law, Rabbi Eliezer ben Nathan, often referred to him as "a mighty spiritual jouster."

But before those elder days, and while he was still young, Samuel had studied with Rabbi Abraham. One day, after a Talmud session, young Samuel waited until the other boys had left, and he went to see the Rabbi. This was when the little boy had become a young man and when Abraham ben Alexander was quite old.

For a moment, Samuel stood by the worn wooden benches in the main prayer hall. He looked up at the twelve stained glass windows with their colored lions and snakes. He stared at the Holy Ark made of stone. Then he walked to the door of the back study room, where old Rabbi Abraham was bent over a book.

Samuel peered into the open doorway. "Excuse me, Rabbi," he said.

Rabbi Abraham ben Alexander looked up. "Yes?" said the Rabbi.

"You may not know me," said the young man. "I am the boy who had crying fits when I was a baby and for whom you made up a magical amulet. You gave this to my mother, and she says that it worked, by the blessings of the good Lord God, amen."

The Rabbi squinted and he winked and he blinked, looking

intently at the young man. "Yes, yes–I remember, Samuel," said Rabbi Achselrad.

"Here is the amulet," said Samuel. "But it has changed."

Rabbi Abraham set down his book, and he raised his eyebrows. "It has changed?" he asked.

"Yes–you see, I remember that old charm quite fondly," said the young man, "but it was different. Once, it was so red as to almost glow, and the silver had a magical glint, even in the dark. I remember that this little box was warm in the winter and that it was cool in the summer."

Young Samuel was quiet for a moment. "Rabbi, you may not believe me," he said, "but I think that it actually hummed me to sleep at night when I was little."

The Rabbi said nothing. "Now look at it," said Samuel. "This necklace is dull red, and the box is old and gray and scratched and cold."

Samuel turned the amulet over in his hand. "It has become tarnished and unmagical with time," said Samuel ben Natronai. "Moreover, Rabbi, my mother claimed that at one time there had been some writing inside of it. But now the parchment is blank."

The Rabbi took the charm, and he examined it carefully. He took it up in his old worn hands. He peered at it. He squinted and he rubbed it, and he studied it for many, many minutes. "My boy," said the Rabbi, "this is exactly the way that it always was. This is the identical charm, down to the last detail, that I once gave to your mother, years and years ago."

Rabbi Abraham held the silver box in his right hand, and he put it up to his ear. He set the amulet against his ear–and he smiled. Then he gave it back to Samuel. "It is exactly the same," said the Rabbi. "And if you sit very quietly, and if you listen to it gently with your littlest and newest ears, then you can hear that it still hums with a fine and holy magic. Samuel, it hums now in the same way that it always did– and in the same way that it always will." Gently, the Rabbi handed the amulet to Samuel; then the old man turned back to his books, and he went on reading.

ood evening, Rabbi. Of course, please sit here by the stove; the late night fire helps me to become sleepy also. You and I are not blessed like old Reb Elbaum. Once again I saw him nod off during the last prayers this evening. He has learned to sway piously even while asleep: he must have inherited some magic from the mystic Achselrad.

I suppose that you and I could also use a dose of Achselrad tonight. My grandmother said that old Achselrad could put men into a sleep trance by waving a gold coin before their eyes. Yes, not only the hidden saints but the holy rabbis too had these magical powers – and they also had the power to make one feel young enough to dance a happy Sabbath dance. What is that, Rabbi? You do not know about the hidden saints? I first learned about them from my grandmother. She once told me a tale about these secret pious men; it was the story of a saint who lived hidden in medieval Germany at the time of Rabbi Abraham ben Alexander, the mystic Achselrad of Cologne:

Was it in the early spring, or was it in the late winter? At the moment I forget – but in any case, I do know that old Rabbi Abraham was dozing in the back room of the Cologne yeshiva. He had stayed awake all night writing in his mystical tome of Kabbalistic lore. Before he fell asleep, Rabbi Abraham had been muttering to himself, *"Lamed Vav Tzaddikim,"* and this set the other men in the room to talking—quietly the many scholars sitting on the wooden benches along the wall were discussing the hidden saints.

White-haired Baruch ben Jacob said as if lecturing, "The Jewish saints are called the *Lamed Vav Tzaddikim*. And Rabbi Abaye has said in the Talmud: 'In every generation, there live in the world not less than thirty-six *Lamed Vav Tzaddikim*—thirty-six righteous persons upon whom rests the *Shekhinah*, the holy radiance of the good Lord God (blessed be He).' "

"Amen," said Moyses ben Nathan. The other men nodded. A younger scholar, Elisah ben Samuel, added, "Yes, good Baruch—but these *Lamed Vav Tzaddikim* are so modest that they conceal their virtue. They hide. They are humble and quiet. Sometimes, they even seem dull and clumsy. And they are always poor."

Joshua ben Eliezer looked around at his colleagues. "I hear," he said, "that these hidden saints live among us as manual laborers: they could be blacksmiths, farmers, millers, shoemakers, tailors, or wood-workers."

"Exactly," said Lewe ben Anselm, "they are never rabbis or scholars. So the Jews around them never suspect their true identity."

Menahem ben Joel nodded. He sighed and stroked his beard, and he said, "True—and I hope that there is a hidden saint or two living near here. I would feel safer. When danger threatens the Jews, then the *Lamed Vav Tzaddikim* finally emerge. They have much Kabbalistic power, you know. They can counteract evil and they can rescue helpless people."

"Amen," said old Baruch.

"Amen," repeated Moyses ben Nathan. "Of course, after helping us out, the saint is unmasked. He has revealed his true nature—he is no longer hidden in his own community. Now he must move and go off somewhere where he is still unknown; he must hide in some other Jewish community."

"These sound like itinerant holy spirits, like traveling angels," said Reb Menahem.

Old Shimshon ha-Zaken coughed, and he cleared his throat. "No, no, Menahem," he said, "the thirty-six hidden saints are humans and mortals. They fall prey to disease, illness, maltreatment, and poverty just like anyone else."

"Ah, praise the Lord," sighed Menahem ben Joel.

"Amen," said the scholars.

A light breeze seemed to whisk through the back room, and suddenly Rabbi Abraham awoke with a start. The Rabbi was puzzled. He looked about him as if he did not recognize the other scholars. Old Achselrad had just had a vision. As you know, Rabbi, Abraham Achselrad had been a pupil of Eliazer, the mystic of Worms, and the aging Achselrad was somewhat of a mystic himself. And now Rabbi Abraham had had a mystical dream. He had dreamt of Passover, and he had dreamt of a poor congregant of his, named Samuel. And here was the cause of Achselrad's visionary dream:

Just outside the city of Cologne there actually lived one of the thirty-six hidden saints. This was in medieval times, and it was so long ago that now I can safely tell you his name: it was Samuel ben Aleydis ha-Kohen. Reb Samuel was a junk hauler. He was one of the thirty-six saints, but he hid his powers. Samuel ben Aleydis was poor and humble and good and righteous – and he was happy, because he believed in the scriptural Proverb:

> The sweet fruits of righteousness
> Fill the Tree of the Lord –
> And he who serves with humility
> Will harvest a rich reward.

The story that I am telling you, Rabbi, happened during a difficult year. A cruel winter passed. As the Passover holiday came near, this meek saint, good Samuel ben Aleydis, fell gravely ill. No longer was he able to earn even his few crusts of bread. His family relied on stews made from vegetable scraps and bones, and on most days they were hungry. There seemed no chance at all that they would have sufficient money to buy *matzohs* and wine for the holidays. And, of course, there were few friends to help, because (as the old proverb reminds us) when poverty slips in through the door then friendship escapes through the window.

Yes, Rabbi, the family was extremely poor, but Samuel would

not allow anyone to know how poor they actually were. And also, Rabbi, although Samuel ben Aleydis himself was quite ill, he would not tell anyone how ill he actually was. Samuel consoled his family in a weak voice: "I am just feeling a bit tired, and we are just suffering a few temporary business reversals. Have faith in God – He raises the fallen, amen."

"Amen," said his wife. She looked at her pale husband, she hesitated a moment, and then she said, "Samuel, my dear, we must be practical. We have an old and valuable copy of the Holy Scriptures. Let us sell this book; then we can celebrate the holiday properly."

But Samuel ben Aleydis said, "What good is the holiday without the Holy Scriptures? In fact, what is the purpose of living at all if we do not have God's holy words? No, we cannot sell this book."

Samuel and his family went to bed hungry in the evenings. But no one in Cologne knew this man's full sufferings – rather, no *human* knew the sufferings. However, Shamriel, an angel of the Lord, was passing by and he heard the conversation between Samuel and his wife. The angel Shamriel opened wide his bright blue eyes, he listened well with his softest and tiniest ears, and then he flew up to Heaven. "O Lord my God," said the angel, not able to look directly at the blinding radiance of the great Lord God Almighty, "one of your *Lamed Vav Tzaddikim*, a man named Samuel ben Aleydis ha-Kohen of Cologne, is suffering greatly at the moment."

The most holy Omnipotent One said, "Then return to earth, My angel. Give a holy dream to Rabbi Abraham of Cologne – he will know what to do."

Therefore, Shamriel, a guardian angel of righteous men, flew down to Cologne just as the sages were talking in the yeshiva. Shamriel swept into the synagogue, flying over the wooden prayer benches, under the twelve stained glass windows with their colored lions and snakes, and past the Holy stone Ark. The angel slipped into the back room where the scholars were talking and where the Rabbi was sleeping, and like a gentle Passover wind he whispered a holy word into the Rabbi's ear. And then old Abraham Achselrad had a fine and mystical dream.

Shamriel whispered a holy word, and the Rabbi had a mystical dream. Old Achselrad dreamt that he heard a gentle voice reciting from Psalm 149:

Praise the glorious Lord:

Sing to the Lord a fine new song
Cry His praise to the faithful crowd,
Let all rejoice in their Creator strong
Sending hosannas to the highest cloud.

The needy laugh with joy aloud
The poor can praise His Name in dance
The weak will sing Him psalms of joy now,
For our God bestows luxuriance.

In his dream, mists cleared, the Rabbi looked up, and he saw a man who looked familiar. Could it be Samuel ben Aleydis ha-Kohen, a quiet, poor, and humble member of his congregation? The man was hiding behind the door of a small hut. The hut was tiny, but it glowed with a shining white and radiant light. The bright white light woke Rabbi Abraham, right in the middle of his dream.

Rabbi Abraham awoke. He looked around, but he did not seem to see the many scholars on the benches. Instead, he again saw the bright white and radiant light. As if still in his dream, Rabbi Abraham ben Alexander, Achselrad of Cologne, took off his clean prayer robes, and he put on an old coat and a hat, which he pulled down low over his forehead. He rubbed some dirt on his face. He put a knapsack over his shoulder. The old sages stared at the Rabbi, but they said not a word. Then the Rabbi took all the money from the poorbox, and he set out for the house of Samuel ben Aleydis ha-Kohen.

Rabbi Abraham walked down Judengasse Street and out of the city. . . . What is that, Rabbi? No, I cannot tell you exactly where Rabbi Abraham went; my grandmother said that she could not reveal where the hidden saint lived. However, old Abraham Achselrad knew, and after a time he reached the house of the hidden saint. Rabbi Abraham stood looking at the wooden house, which was so tiny as to be almost a hut. All was quiet. The Rabbi sat down on the small front porch and he waited.

Rabbi Abraham waited one hour and then two. It was cool outside. The tangleberry bushes had not yet put out their tiny green shoots; the knotroot grasses by the edge of the road were still brown.

The Rabbi looked up at the turnstones and windhovers that soared high and far among the clouds. Rabbi Abraham waited patiently. After a while Samuel's son Jacob came out on an errand. He saw the Rabbi sitting on the front steps; strangers were uncommon there and the boy went quickly back inside the house.

"Father," said Jacob, "a stranger has come to our door."

But Samuel ben Aleydis was just finishing a recitation of the *Shema*:

If you pay heed to the commandments that He has given you this day – if you love the Lord your God, and if you serve Him with all your heart and soul – then He will send rain for your land in season, both autumn and spring showers. And you will gather plentiful corn and new wine and oil, and He will provide pasture in the fields for your cattle: then you shall eat your fill.

Remember to take these words of His to heart and to keep them in mind. In fact, bind them as a sign on your hand and wear them as a phylactery on your forehead. Teach them to your children, and speak of them indoors and out-of-doors, when you lie down and when you rise up. Write them on the doorposts of your houses and on your gates. Then you will live long and happily, you and your children and your children's children, in the land that the Lord swore to your forefathers to give them, for as long as the Heavens are above the earth.

Then Samuel completed his prayer, and his son said, "*Barukh Hu U Barukh Shemo*, blessed be He and blessed be His Name."

"Amen," said the father.

"Amen," said the son, and then he repeated, "Father, a stranger has come to our door."

"All right, Jacob – I will go and see what he wants," said Samuel. The sick man and his wife walked slowly to the door, with the good woman supporting her husband.

"*Sholom aleichem*," said Rabbi Abraham.

"*Aleichem sholom*," returned the couple. "Are you looking for someone?"

"No, but I am in trouble," sighed the Rabbi. "Here I am, a stranger in town, and I have no place to spend the holy Passover."

The husband and the wife looked at each other. "Well, we have very little to offer," said Samuel ben Aleydis ha-Kohen. "Nonetheless, you are welcome to come in and to spend the holiday with us: even the poorest Jew must have a chair in which to relax on Passover."

"Thank you, I think that I shall accept," said the Rabbi.

Abraham Achselrad smiled at Samuel and his wife, and he said, "I know that your house must have been searched for *hametz* – for the least crumb of leaven – last night." Therefore, before he stepped in the door, he turned his pockets inside out and he brushed off his clothes thoroughly. Then the Rabbi walked in, saying, "Of course, I will need some food and wine if I am to last until the seder meal."

The couple looked sadly toward their empty kitchen. But before they could say anything, the Rabbi turned to Jacob, the son, and he said, "Young man, you can help out. Here is some money. Go to the marketplace and buy us some food." The Rabbi gave the boy all of the charity money that he had brought. "Be sure to buy vegetables and *matzoh* – and get some wine too," the Rabbi reminded him. The boy's eyes opened wide, and he ran off to buy food for the family. Samuel looked at his wife, and the wife looked back at her husband.

Rabbi Abraham was continuing to talk: "You know, good friends, I have just remembered a very important errand that I must attend to. Now, it is possible that I may not be able to return before the holiday meal begins. If so, start the seder without me. And be sure to have a most sweet and joyous Passover."

And before the couple could say a word, the Rabbi jumped up and he ran out the door. Rabbi Abraham felt light and strong. He could not help running. And on the way back into Cologne, old Rabbi Abraham Achselrad jumped and he leaped and he did a Sabbath dance; for Samuel ben Aleydis ha-Kohen, the hidden saint, had suddenly made the Rabbi feel young once again.

Then Rabbi Abraham ben Alexander, Achselrad of Cologne, returned to the synagogue. The scholars raised their eyebrows when they saw him come back. Old Rabbi Abraham took off his hat and his coat. He wiped his face clean, he yawned a large and holy yawn, and he put his head back down on his desk. The Rabbi immediately fell asleep, and again he dreamt his holy dream with its white bright and radiant light, and the many sages saw him sigh and smile. And then a gentle wind passed through the old back study room on the late afternoon of a Passover eve, whispering of saints and angels, once upon a time in the medieval Cologne of long, long ago.

h, good evening again, Rabbi. I know that it is always hard to sleep on the night of a bright half moon. Just put your feet up on the side bench here and I will open the stove door. Let me push the coals back. There is nothing like that white glow: it washes away all the cares of a hard day.

I heard your final benediction tonight, Rabbi; clearly you are overworked. Oh yes, even a shammas like me can tell. I kept one eye on you when I was cleaning the dishes, and I saw that you were watching the door, hoping that Reb Elbaum would leave early. But then Reb Anton stayed to discuss the scriptural passage from the Book of Judges:

> Then Samson called on the good Lord God, saying: "Remember me, O Lord my God. Remember me: give me strength only this once. Let me, at one stroke, be avenged on the Philistines for my two eyes, which they have so cruelly put out."

> Samson put his arms around the two central pillars, which supported the temple. He put his right arm around one pillar, and he put his left arm around the other pillar. Then he braced himself and he turned his

head Heavenward, and he said quietly: "And let me die with the Philistines."

The mighty Samson leaned forward with all his strength, and the temple fell on the Philistine lords and on all the people who were in the building. And the dead, whom Samson killed at his own death, were more than those he had killed in his entire life. Then his brothers and all his father's family came down, they carried him up to the grave of his father Manoah, between Zorah and Eshtaol, and they buried him there. And at that time, Samson had been Judge over Israel for twenty long years.

I listened carefully as you reread and discussed this passage with Reb Anton. Such thoughtful scriptural analysis always takes energy: of course you are still worn out. . . . What is that? A story from me? Rabbi, all I know are the children's tales, the grandmother fables. You need something new and fresh to keep your mind keen. Otherwise you will become a dreamy old man like me, and you will find yourself constantly musing and dozing and nodding off in front of the stove.

What do you mean you are already an old man, Rabbi? Do you really think that sixty years is old? Why, you are still a child. When you reach eighty, *then* you will be old. You doubt that you will live to see eighty years? If so, Rabbi, then you will never grow old. . . . All right, all right, I know no special stories but listening to you and Reb Anton put me in mind of another Judge, a medieval Judge. Of course I am speaking of the Golem of Worms. And the story that comes to mind involves *Lag B'Omer*. My grandmother loved *Lag B'Omer*, and each year she would look forward to the time when the holiday of *Shavuot* arrived. When I was young, my grandmother always had a story or two to tell about the *Shavuot* season—and some of them were very strange tales indeed. In particular, I remember one about the end of the Golem:

Once upon a time, said my grandmother to me, in medieval Germany, there lived a pious and mystical scholar named Rabbi Eliazer ben Judah of Worms. Rabbi Eliazer was a Kabbalist: some even said that he was a sorcerer. Now, Rabbi, the most awesome feat for any mystic is *creation*. In the Middle Ages even the most accomplished magicians could create only crude and massive objects, such as rocks and logs and piles of mud–common magic did not work for fine and delicate things. Actually, the medieval magician owed his creative powers to demons, and it is well known that demons cannot create anything smaller than a barleycorn and that they cannot create anything that is complex, like camels, camellias, or camomile.

Anyway, this was for profane earthly magic. On the other hand, old Rabbi Eliazer was a holy man, and the Talmud recognizes a second method, a more holy method, of creation. Sacred creation avoids demons and other spirits. Instead, holy magic uses the "Laws of Creation." By means of these Laws, one might create an entire world, inhabited by men and other living creatures. I have heard, Rabbi, that certain old sages and holy rabbis used to sit every Friday studying the "Laws of Creation." Eventually, these sages created a three-year-old calf, which they then ritually slaughtered and ate. And exactly how did this creation work? No one knows for certain, but Rashi has suggested that these rabbis discovered how to combine the letters of the Ineffable Holy Name. (In fact, this was also the way in which the world itself was first created.)

Later, after the Dark Ages had begun to fade, Rabbi Eliazer ben Judah learned the holy rules of creation too. Where did Rabbi Eliazer learn these mysteries? Well, the ten basic words were told to him in a dream by the angel Aniel. But the Rabbi himself spent many hours studying these words and reflecting on the most difficult passages in the original Kabbalist book, the *Sefer Yetzirah*. The *Sefer Yetzirah*–the "Book of Creation"–is quite ancient: it originated with the patriarch Abraham, and it was put into its final form by the great Rabbi Akiva. With the help of this book, Rabbi Eliazer ben Judah eventually discovered how to rearrange the ten mystical words in the command of the holy angel Aniel into *zirufim* or formulas. And thus, Rabbi Eliazer learned how to make a living being from inanimate clay.

So it came to pass that, in the medieval days in the Rhineland of Germany, an animated figure–a huge lumbering lout of a man–was created by *zirufim* from the clay of the River Rhine. It was built from new clay, clay that no man had touched before, and it was given the spirit of life by the holy mystic, Rabbi Eliazer ben Judah of Worms. On its forehead was incised the single word *emet*–truth.

Eliazer named the creature Joseph Golem. Many years later, one of Rabbi Eliazer's confidential assistants, his son-in-law Isaac ben Shimshon ha-Kohen, asked the Rabbi, "Why did you choose the name Joseph?"

Rabbi Eliazer stroked his beard. He looked down at his hands, and he said, "Actually, I did not decide until the final moments of his creation, Isaac. Suddenly, as the clay figure began to stir, two mystical spirits appeared to me: one was named Joseph, and the other was named Jonathan. I chose the name of the spirit Joseph because he had already helped many of the sages of the talmudic days."

Rabbi Eliazer paused. Again he stroked his beard a moment. Then he continued: "I gave him a full name, but as you have seen, the Golem himself never possessed a full spirit; for example, he did not have the power of speech. Instead, the force animating the Golem was a sort of animal vitality – it had a limited intelligence and only rudimentary common sense and wisdom."

Isaac ben Shimshon nodded, remembering many times when the Golem had been clumsy or crude or thoughtless. The Golem had no innate drive either for good or for evil – he only followed orders. But Joseph Golem was strong and powerful, and even when something was ten meters above the ground or ten meters under it, he could reach it easily. And then, once he had begun, nothing would stop him from completing a task.

"And yet," said Eliazer, "although the Golem did not have a human soul, I noticed something strange: on the Sabbath his face became friendlier. I must confess that this worried me."

Isaac listened quietly. The Rabbi looked off somewhere far away. Was he picturing that clay-colored face with the one holy word *emet* incised on its forehead? There were many minutes of silence. A wind blew outside and it shivered the walls. "I was worried," repeated Rabbi Eliazer. "Would the holy Sabbath somehow infuse this half-human creature with a stronger soul? Would the Golem of Worms become immortal? Would our hybrid creation perhaps even be worshiped as an idol?

"I could not take this chance. I knew that someday the Golem would have to be destroyed. But until then, I took out the small tablet from his mouth on the eve of each Sabbath. You remember that tablet, Isaac: written on it were the Ineffable Holy Name and certain mystical *zirufim.* These words were necessary to keep the Golem animate. Therefore on each Friday evening just before sunset, the Golem lay down and he slept the sleep of the dead until I replaced the tablet after the holy Sabbath had passed safely."

Isaac sat silently. He listened to the Rabbi–but Isaac too had a faraway look in his eyes. Isaac was remembering the night of *Lag B'Omer* many years before, when he had helped in the final destruction of the Golem. You see, Rabbi, Eliazer ben Judah had created the Golem originally as a protection against the continuous violence that Jewish communities suffered throughout northern Europe. When King Henry the Fifth acquired Worms, in the treaty of Wurzburg, things turned from bad to intolerable. Henry was power-hungry. He was selfish and treacherous; at one point, he actually sent his army against the citizens of Worms, and the Jews suffered heavily in the street battles.

However, a year after these cruelties, King Henry died in Utrecht and he was buried at Spires. Henry had no children. His nephew, Frederick the Second of Hohenstaufen, the Duke of Swabia, took over many of King Henry's rights and responsibilities. At this point, things improved for the Jews. The evil feelings incited during the Crusade had eased, the countryside demons were occupied with other matters, and, at least temporarily, the Jews were being left alone. Therefore, one night the angel Aniel again appeared to Rabbi Eliazer in a dream. "The time has come," the angel said, "to pass on to other things. The Golem has fulfilled his mission. Now his life must end."

Rabbi Eliazer awoke in the dead of the night. He remembered the dream, and there was little doubt in his mind as to how to proceed. Once a year there was a sacred night of destruction: it was on the night of *Lag B'Omer*, the night before *Shavuot*, the Feast of Weeks. Thus, one full season after Passover, after forty-nine days had been counted, after seven cycles of seven days, the Golem came to an end one dark night in Worms.

"Do not spend the night in the prayer hall," said the Rabbi to the Golem. "Instead, lie down in the bed in the small loft over the back study room." As he was told, the Golem retired to the attic of the yeshiva of Worms at midnight, six hours after the beginning of a medieval *Lag B'Omer*, once upon a time, long, long ago.

The Golem lay as always, quiet and passive, with his eyes staring toward the Heavens. When two o'clock in the morning came—at the eighth hour after sunset—Rabbi Eliazer entered the attic with his son-in-law, Isaac ben Shimshon ha-Kohen, and with his faithful pupil, the scholar Jakob ben Chayim Sasson ha-Levi. Each man carried one white candle. They stood at the head of the bed. Rabbi Eliazer said, "My good and faithful Golem, you have defended the Jews. We thank you. Now your job is at an end. Close your eyes." And the clay-colored man closed his eyes.

The Rabbi removed the clothes of the Golem. Then old Eliazer ben Judah walked once around the blank clay figure. He removed the small tablet from its mouth; in its place he put a parchment scroll inscribed with the *Shem* (the holy Name of the Almighty Lord God) in seven mystical forms—but here the inscription was written backwards. The Rabbi bowed to the north and to the south and to the west and to the east. Then he stood with his back to Jerusalem, and he recited from the Book of Genesis: "And then he died."

Now Jakob ben Chayim Sasson ha-Levi walked seven times around the clay body from right to left. As Jakob passed the Rabbi, the old man whispered quiet *zirufim*. Soon the Golem's body began to glow red. The Rabbi sprinkled the body with water; the hair disappeared from its head and the nails faded from its fingers and toes. Next, Isaac ben Shimshon ha-Kohen walked seven times around the clay body from left to right. As Isaac passed the Rabbi, the old man whispered quiet *zirufim*, and the clay body became cold and gray once more.

The Rabbi looked down at the large clay lump. It was an empty silent statue in the shape of a man. Eliazer ben Judah removed the parchment from inside the clay mouth. Gently, Eliazer took his finger and he erased the "e" from the clay forehead: now the word truth— *emet*—was changed into the word death—*met*. The medieval Judge was rendered River Rhine clay again. The Golem was no more.

The three men stood for a moment, each remembering when the Golem had roamed the town. Then they covered the lifeless hulk with prayer robes and with old Hebrew books from corners of the loft. And there it lay, in the attic of the old yeshiva of Worms.

By now the candles had burned down to small flat stumps, and the men blew them out. Then one by one, the three men walked silently down the ladder. At daybreak, three men walked down from the loft above the back room of the yeshiva in medieval Worms – three walked where once there had been four. That was on a *Lag B'Omer* of long, long ago, but is it possible that the Golem is still there? And if so, will he ever again be revived? Ah, I wonder, good Rabbi – yes, often I wonder.

ood evening, Rabbi. No sleep for the weary? That is what my grandmother said, and she said it almost nightly. If you are cold then sit down here on the bench and I will stoke up the oven. This stoker? It is one of the iron shoe scrapers from the front hall. You probably do not recognize it because it is covered with soot. Of course, there are still two scrapers in the anteroom for dirty shoes. But I myself am of the old school: I think that all pious men should remove their shoes when they enter the synagogue and that they should then pray barefoot. Did you know that Rabbi Amram of medieval Cologne prophesied that the Messiah will appear barefoot? Well, we can always hope.

As my grandmother said to me, "We must always hope, my little one. Is it a delusion to hope in these difficult times? It does not matter, for hope is happiness." She said this often, and of course how could you question a great saying like that? Sometimes she would even tell stories about hope. In particular, I remember my grandmother's tale about the hopes of Hayyim ben Meyer, the shammas of the little congregation of Bensberg. That was in those old and mystical days when Rabbi Abraham ben Alexander, Achselrad of Cologne, was the spiritual head of all the surrounding Jewish communities, including Bensberg (which, as you know, is only about a three-hour walk east of Cologne):

Once upon a time, said my grandmother to me, in the small town of Bensberg, there lived a pious man named Hayyim ben Meyer. Bensberg had a tiny Jewish community, and Hayyim was the shammas. The community was so small that there were only two officials in the synagogue (beside the rabbi): there was the parnas, a wealthy man named Simcha ben Eli, and there was the shammas, Hayyim ben Meyer, who was also the gabbai, the treasurer.

Hayyim was the record-keeper for the congregation. He was the custodian and the overseer of the synagogue. He was the executor of the sentences of the local religious court, the *Bet Din*. Then, too, Hayyim was the town crier. On Friday afternoons he went around to the workshops and he knocked three times to remind all Jews that work was soon to cease. (On the Friday afternoons before the major Festivals, Hayyim followed the old Palestinian custom: instead of knocking on doors, he stood on the low rooftop of the yeshiva and he blew three blasts on a *shofar*.) The Jewish community of Bensberg was so small that all the men were needed for funerals. When someone died, Shammas Hayyim went around from door to door collecting men. Again, Hayyim knocked on doors–but instead of three knocks, he gave only two–and at the sound of two knocks, each man's heart sank a bit and his stomach became tight.

Shammas Hayyim was responsible for making announcements in the synagogue. He was the local mailman: he carried messages, invitations, and summonses. In addition, he did his best to ensure that there was a *minyan*–ten adult men–at all major prayer sessions, especially on the New Year and on the Day of Atonement. You may know, Rabbi, that in the Middle Ages, Jewish communities often appointed certain men to form a permanent *minyan* for all services; these men, the *batlanim*, were scholars, and sometimes they even received a salary for this service. However, small communities (such as Bensberg) did not have sufficient men or money for the luxury of a regular core of *batlanim*.

In Bensberg, ten worshipers could not always be collected for a formal service. Shammas Hayyim would go around frantically searching out Jewish men, but he could not always find them. As a last resort, Hayyim would stand hopefully at the edge of the city. Every so often, strangers happened through. Would a wandering Jew appear? Hayyim could always hope. When a newcomer did appear, it became a communal occasion. The townsfolk competed for the honor of offering him hospitality, and every word the wayfarer spoke was listened to intently and his stories were reviewed for weeks afterward.

One year, on the eve of the Day of Atonement, the community was short one worshiper for the evening service. A death in Cologne had called away two of the stalwarts of the congregation, another man was in Regensburg on business, and one of the old congregants was very ill and could not move from his bed. Where would they find another man to pray? In order to be hallowed by the Divine presence, in order to deserve the official designation of *kehillah kedoshah*—a holy congregation—the service needed to have at least ten adult worshipers. The shammas was beside himself. What would happen on this *Yom Kippur*? How could the service proceed? But unfortunately there was nothing more that Hayyim could do. He stood sadly at the edge of the city, and he looked down the empty road.

Evening was coming. The sun was already low and soon it would set. The first star could be seen in the eastern sky. No travelers were in sight on the cooling evening road. Suddenly, Hayyim thought that he saw a movement far, far down the road. Was it possible? Yes— an old man with a long white beard was walking toward Bensberg from the direction of Cologne. His clothes were dusty, and he seemed to be barefoot. Hayyim rubbed his eyes and he squinted. Then he ran toward the old man.

"Peace to you, my friend!" called out Hayyim.

The old man smiled, and he said, "Greetings, sir."

"I almost dare not ask, but are you a Jew?" asked Hayyim.

"Yes, I am," answered the stranger.

Hayyim looked up at the Heavens. Then he led the man straight to the synagogue. The two men walked in the front door. Hayyim removed his shoes; the stranger was already barefoot, even on that cool autumn evening. "Well," said Hayyim, "you have come just in time for the Atonement service."

"Yes," said the stranger, "I have."

The second and the third stars were shining in the darkening sky.

Eight other men had gathered in the main prayer hall. It was still before nightfall, and a religious court of expiation, a *Bet Din*, was convened with the ten Jewish men. Two Torah scrolls were taken from the Holy stone Ark and they were held by two of the men. The stranger was invited to be the reader. He stood between the men holding the scrolls. Then he chanted the *Kol Nidre* in an ancient and solemn melody:

All vows and prohibitions, all bans and devotions for sacrifice, all swearings and avowals and other oaths that we have taken or those things that we have forbidden to ourselves from this Day of Atonement to the next Day of Atonement – may they all come in peace, amen. We have repented of all of them. Let all of them be dissolved, abandoned, put to rest, voided, and annulled; let them be invalid and unenforced. Our vows are no vows, our prohibitions are no prohibitions, and our oaths are no oaths, amen.

The stranger chanted the *Kol Nidre* three times. The other nine men stood barefoot and silent around him. Then the full set of ten men repeated three times the verse from the Book of Numbers:

They made penitential offerings to the good Lord God for their inadvertent sins. Then the whole community of Israelites and the aliens residing among them and the strangers passing through were all forgiven.

And so the Day of Atonement was properly begun.

That night and the next day there were prayers and scriptural lessons and, of course, fasting. During the services, the worshipers recited the seven penitential Psalms, taking turns reading from the Holy Scriptures. When it was the stranger's turn, he closed his eyes and he recited Psalm 130:

In the depths I sigh –
Consider my humble plea
O Lord hear my cry
And look down compassionately.

If all our sins were shown
Then who would dare to speak aloud?
But You forgive us if we've grown
And You let us stand unbowed.

My soul waits to embrace
The most radiant Holy One,
I search for His good Grace
As flowers watch for the sun.

O Israel revere the Lord;
Now let us celebrate
For God forgives his ward,
His redeeming power is great—

The great Lord will not bother
With every tiny sin,
God is our loving father
And we are His young children.

The stranger had an old and mellow voice, and a shiver of holiness swept through the others as they listened to his chants.

Late on the afternoon of the Day of Atonement, the *Neilah* prayers were recited to close finally the gates of prayer. The sun was setting, the shadows were lengthening, and all the worshiping men strained: the prayerful men shivered and they shook. They made their supreme effort to reach the Divine Throne of Glory and to move the merciful One (blessed be He) to grant atonement to His penitential children. Finally, the stranger shouted out, "The Lord is God, the Lord is God!"—and then the evening of the day after the Day of Atonement was upon them, hallelujah and amen.

The sun had set—the solemn service was over. The men stood around in the prayer hall. They chatted quietly and happily, planning for the night meal that would end their fast. As they stood around, the men of Bensberg cast lots to decide who should have the honor of entertaining the stranger in his own home. The lot fell to the shammas; Hayyim ben Meyer could not believe his good fortune.

Hayyim and the stranger began to walk back to Hayyim's home. They reached the door, and Hayyim turned to let the stranger precede him into the house. But where was the old man? Suddenly, the stranger was gone.

Hayyim looked up the street and he looked down the street. No one was in sight. What had happened? Was it a holy event, or was it profane? Tears came to Hayyim's eyes. He went back to the syna-gogue. Some of the men were still standing in the main prayer hall talking–they listened to the shammas, and they could not believe Hayyim's story. Had the shammas actually lost the holy stranger? No one had seen the old man: he seemed to have disappeared completely from Bensberg.

Rabbi, you remember the quotation in Deuteronomy about dream divination:

> There are things that are hidden, and these belong to the Lord our God – but what is revealed belongs to us and to our children forever.

Well, so it was for the good shammas of Bensberg. Later that night, the shammas finally fell asleep–but when he had lain down, he was so upset that he forgot to remove his shoes. Shammas Hayyim fell asleep with his shoes on, and soon he dreamt a dream in which things were revealed that belonged to Hayyim ben Meyer and to his children forever.

In Hayyim's dream, an old wise man appeared. This sage looked like the stranger of Bensberg, but now he was clothed in magnificent robes and his face shone with a white, bright, and radiant light. The stranger was white- robed and he was radiant and he was barefoot. He stood a moment, and he smiled down at the sleeping shammas, Hayyim ben Meyer of Bensberg. The sage smiled, and gently he whispered into Hayyim's ear. What did he say? I do not know. But it was only one or two words, for in a wink the stranger disappeared and Shammas Hayyim fell into a calm and dreamless sleep.

When Hayyim awoke in the morning, he found that his shoes were neatly laid out at the side of his bed; therefore, Hayyim said his morning prayers barefoot. Hayyim ben Meyer remembered his dream and he smiled, and the sun shone brightly in his window on a glorious golden fall day–yes, Rabbi, it was a bright new barefoot dawn on the day after the Day of Atonement.

ood evening, Rabbi. You are having difficulty sleeping again? Put your feet up on the side bench and I will open the stove door. Let me push these coals back. The white glow will wash away all the cares of your hard day.

I heard your final prayers tonight, and there is no use denying it — you are overworked. Even an old shammas like me can tell. I kept one eye on you when I was cleaning the dishes; I saw that you were watching the door, hoping that Reb Elbaum would leave early. But then Reb Anton stayed late to discuss the scriptural passage from the Book of Numbers:

> So Moses gave no wagons or any of the common goods to the Kohathites, because they were required to carry the most sacred of things. The Kohathites were responsible for the holy articles, and these they must carry on their own shoulders.

You know, Rabbi, I remember old Jehuda ben Saul discussing that exact passage in a lecture to his yeshiva students one day:

> " 'These they must carry on their own shoulders'!" recited Rabbi Jehuda, and sternly he looked at the young men on the benches. The

Rabbi stared at the boys, the boys looked at the floor, and there was silence – so the Rabbi said, "All holy men are like Samsons."

The Rabbi beat his hand on his reading desk, the synagogue's *almemar*. "Yes, boys, holy men must be very strong men," the Rabbi said strongly.

"They carry us weak sinners on the shoulders of their devout prayers," continued the Rabbi.

"Now, young men," said the Rabbi more quietly, "tell me: Which are the most powerful prayers?"

The students looked down. A thick silence blanketed the room. Eventually, a brave young man named Moshe ben Samuel said, "The *Shema* is a powerful prayer."

Rabbi Jehuda nodded: "Yes, Moshe – the *Shema* is quite strong. Can you name any other mighty prayers?"

No one volunteered an answer. Rabbi Jehuda stared down at the boys. Dust seemed to accumulate in the corners of the room. After many, many minutes, the Rabbi said, "Do you not know the *Minhah*? The *Minhah* is a powerful winged prayer." Then the Rabbi pounded the *almemar* desk at which he stood. "The *Minhah* is forceful – it is stout, it is like a giant!"

Again, the Rabbi looked at his charges. "You can tell me, of course," he said, "what the *Minhah* prayer is – can you not?"

Moshe nodded and he answered, "Well, Rabbi, there are three daily prayers. The morning and the evening prayers follow the *Shema*. The afternoon prayer session is the *Minhah*."

"Correct, Moshe," said the Rabbi. "And why is it called *Minhah*?"

There was silence, so the Rabbi said, "Perhaps, my untutored young scholars, you need a hint. *Minhah* means 'gift' – it means 'offering.'"

The Rabbi looked down expectantly at the students. The students looked at Moshe, but Moshe said nothing. Finally, Rabbi Jehuda ben Saul sighed. "Ah, well," said the Rabbi, "I will tell you. The *Minhah* began as the afternoon service – which was originally an afternoon offering of food and thanksgiving to the Lord – at the Great Temple in Jerusalem."

Rabbi Jehuda sighed again, and he repeated quietly, "The Great Temple in Jerusalem." Then with a faraway look he said very, very softly, "The Great Temple. . . ." And he closed his eyes, and his voice faded away. After a moment, some of the students began to stand in order to leave.

Suddenly the Rabbi opened wide his eyes. He stared out beyond his students. Loudly he said, "Happy are they who!"

The boys looked at one another, and they sat down again.

"*Ashre!*" said Rabbi Jehuda. "Happy are they who!"

"Now, why do I proclaim *Ashre?*" asked the Rabbi. He drummed his fingers, he tapped his foot, and he stared at the students – but no one had anything to say.

"Come now, boys," said Rabbi Jehuda. "The *Ashre* is the joyous introduction to the *Minhah* prayer – is it not?"

"Yes, it is," said Moshe ben Samuel. "The prayer says":

> Happy are the people in Your temple
> Continually they sing praise to You,
> Happy are they who follow Your Law,
> Whose hearts revere Your ways of Truth.

> Happy are they who are our people
> Happy are they who are the faithful
> Happy are they who trust in You, Lord
> Happy are they whose God is All.

The Rabbi nodded. "Very, very good, Moshe," he said. "Now, why is it that we begin the *Minhah* with this joyous Psalm?"

No one answered. "Well, Moshe, what do you think?" asked Rabbi Jehuda.

"To be honest, Rabbi, I do not know," said Moshe ben Samuel.

"Think, young man!" said the Rabbi. "Is it not true that before starting any serious prayer, it is necessary to get into the right frame of mind? One cannot enter the synagogue and immediately start to worship – can one?"

Several students shook their heads.

Rabbi Jehuda shook his head also. "Certainly not," he continued. "Now, my boys, chanting a Psalm puts you in a prayerful mood. Also, certain Psalms have mystical properties. And that is definitely the case for the next Psalm – the one that follows the 'Happy are they who' prayer – namely, Psalm 145, which begins":

I ring out Your amazing grace
I announce Your complete perfection
I proclaim Your eternal kindness
I praise Your words and every action.

"This is how Psalm 145 begins – and, my young charges, you do remember how it ends, do you not?"

No one answered, so Rabbi Jehuda said, "Well, I will remind you: it ends":

He answers the prayers of all His children
He hears them from His holy room;
Yes, God protects the righteous men –
But sends the wicked to their doom.

I will sing, my tongue shall shout
The praises of the loving Lord;
All men shall bless without a doubt
His wondrous Name for ever more.

The Rabbi smiled and he nodded, and he looked up toward the Heavens. "The Sages of the Talmud have said: 'Whoever recites Psalm 145 three times daily is sure to inherit the great and glorious world to come.' And what pious Jew does not aspire to immortality? Therefore, boys, never forget to chant Psalm 145 three times with your prayers, every single day of your lives – may they be long and happy lives, amen."

Again, Rabbi Jehuda smiled, and he closed his eyes. The yeshiva students hesitated. After a moment, young Moshe ben Samuel said, "But, Rabbi, do prayers really have such magical powers?"

Moshe looked up at the Rabbi, but old Rabbi Jehuda had put his head down on his reading desk and he seemed to have fallen asleep.

Ah, the great Jehuda ben Saul is a reminder to us all, Rabbi: prayers are powerful things. For instance, I remember that my grandmother once told me a story about the mystical power of the *Minhah* prayer:

Once upon a time, began my grandmother, in medieval Cologne there lived a young man named Jedaya ben Moshe ha-Levi. Jedaya was a rationalist. He was a follower of the Spanish philosopher Abraham ben Ezra, and he could not believe in the supernatural. Most especially, Jedaya doubted the mystical powers of the Kabbalists, those magical holy men like old Achselrad of Cologne. One Friday, Jedaya had been arguing with his friends about the limits of magic and of occult knowledge. Another young man said, "Not all people have these powers. But, Jedaya, certain holy men do know sacred and magical incantations."

Jedaya shook his head. "I cannot accept hearsay," he declared. "I must see this in action myself." Therefore, he stood up, and he went off to speak directly to Rabbi Abraham ben Alexander, the famed mystic Achselrad of Cologne.

Jedaya walked down Judengasse Street. People were milling about. There were horses and wagons; there was noise and dust. As he walked by a storefront, the warm smell of sourbread filled the air. "This is the real world," thought Jedaya as he strode along. "Our world is quite fine – but it is not magical."

Jedaya stepped in the front door of the yeshiva. He went through the anteroom, and he walked into the main prayer hall, which was filled with wooden benches. Jedaya passed the twelve stained glass windows with their colored lions and snakes, he looked up at the Holy Ark made of stone, and he walked to the door of the back study room. Seven old sages of Cologne were sitting on the benches, and the Rabbi was bent over a book.

Jedaya surveyed the men, and he said straightaway, "Good Rabbis, often I hear that our benedictions are more than holy."

The old men raised their eyebrows, and they stroked their beards. Jedaya continued: "Miracles and enchantments have been attributed to the sacred words. Gentlemen, I find this to be stretching matters a bit. However, I have an open mind. I know that it sounds presumptuous, but if it were possible, then I would like to see a little of these wonder-working magical prayers in action."

There was silence. So Jedaya said, "My friends, I would like to know: Are Jewish prayers occult and wondrous? Are they cryptic and transcendental and mystical? If so, then I certainly ought to be able to see these magical effects here, in this famous old synagogue. And that is why I have come today – if it would not be too much trouble, perhaps we could ask the Rabbi to work a small miracle for me." And Jedaya sat down on a bench, he folded his arms, and he looked at the Rabbi.

The old sages were very quiet. They raised their eyebrows. They stroked their beards. They looked at one another. After many minutes, white-bearded Baruch ben Jacob said, "Jedaya, it is not the Rabbi who works wonders – it is the good Lord God, blessed be He. As Psalm 5 says":

> Lord, heed my quiet words
> And consider my humble plea:
> Provide my basic needs –
> You are my Sustaining Tree.
>
> At dawn when I float my prayers
> Into Your holy boughs
> Then please grant my few requests
> And hear my solemn vows.

"Amen," murmured the other scholars. Then a younger sage, Elisah ben Samuel, nodded and he said, "Prayer is not magic, and it is not wonder-working. Prayer is a holy obligation. And certainly prayer is not only for rabbis: it is for you yourself, Reb Jedaya. You can pray anywhere – here in the synagogue or in your workroom or in the field."

"Exactly, good Elisah," said Joshua ben Eliezer. "And, Jedaya, I remind you that if you are unable to pray in your workroom or in your field, then pray in your home or even when you are out walking. Humble prayer should always be in your heart."

And Lewe ben Anselm said, "Amen, Reb Joshua. The Talmud reminds us that this is the meaning of the verse in Psalm 4":

> God hears whenever you speak;
> Thus this is what I advise:
> Though your heart may be angry or weak
> Keep holiness before your eyes.

Although you feel hurt and sore
Do not speak hateful and grim,
Instead pray quietly to the Lord –
Be humble and trust in Him.

"Amen," said Baruch.

"Yes, yes," said Jedaya, "I understand all this, gentlemen. And believe me, good scholars, I find that prayers are a great spiritual comfort."

Menahem ben Joel raised his eyebrows. "They are a spiritual comfort, Jedaya?"

The scholars fiercely stroked their beards. "Did you say that they are merely a *comfort*?" repeated Menahem. "No, young man, you are missing the point. Your prayers should not be merely a comfortable routine: they must be a plea before God for mercy and grace and truth."

"Hallelujah!" said Moyses ben Nathan. "Prayers raise us from gloom and from idleness. They transport us into the wondrous joys of religious fervor!"

And old Shimshon ha-Zaken coughed and he added, "What is the true, innermost service of the heart? What is the hidden, mystical exercise of the soul? Simply, it is devout and regular prayer."

The other scholars nodded. Jedaya nodded too, but he said, "I have no doubt that prayer is fine and holy and necessary. But is it truly *magical*? Is it mystical? Certainly we Jews can pray without being sorcerers."

Sorcerers?! How could a pious Jew say that in the synagogue? The old scholars looked at one another and only shook their heads.

Meanwhile, Rabbi Abraham had been very quiet. Was he sleeping? Often he worked late at night on his Kabbalistic treatise, the *Keter Shem Tov*, and by the afternoon of the next day, the Rabbi's thoughts seemed adrift in deep and holy matters. Now the Sabbath was approaching. The Rabbi opened his eyes. He took a deep breath. He stretched, and he rubbed his arms. Rabbi Abraham stood, and he bent and touched his toes. Then old Abraham Achselrad slowly turned his waist from side to side. Jedaya looked at the holy old man, puzzled. "What is the Rabbi doing?" he asked.

White-haired Baruch said, "Rabbi Abraham is preparing for the *Minhah* prayers."

"But it is still early," said Jedaya.

"Wait and watch," said old Shimshon ha-Zaken.

After a few minutes more, Rabbi Abraham closed his eyes and he began to pray. (Of course, Rabbi, you know that even in medieval times, the *Minhah* service was essentially a set of Psalms followed by the *Tefillah* prayer ritual. In those days, the congregants at the service recited their prayers silently; the main reciter–in this case, Rabbi Abraham–also prayed silently, although he often finished by repeating the appropriate *Kedushah* benedictions aloud.)

Now, when the mystic Rabbi Achselrad said the benediction, he remained standing motionless on his feet for an entire hour. His forehead became damp with perspiration. His muscles were tense. Sometimes he trembled and he even shook. Finally, he took a deep breath, and he ended his silent prayer. "Amen," said the Rabbi aloud.

"Amen," said the scholars.

Jedaya stayed and watched the entire service. Later he asked Rabbi Abraham, "Why did it take you so long to say the benedictions? And why were you so weak afterward?"

The Rabbi was sitting tiredly on one of the worn benches. "Come back on the afternoon before the next Sabbath, young man," said Rabbi Abraham. "Then I shall teach you how to say the benedictions as I say them–and you will see matters for yourself."

On the next Friday, Jedaya ben Moshe ha-Levi returned to the house of study. He stepped in the front door. He went through the anteroom, and he walked into the main prayer hall, which was filled with wooden benches. Jedaya passed the twelve stained glass windows with their colored lions and snakes, he looked up at the Holy stone Ark, and he walked to the door of the back study room. Again the scholars were talking quietly among themselves, and again the Rabbi was bent over a book.

"Excuse me, good Rabbi–I have come to learn how you pray," said Jedaya.

The Rabbi looked up from his reading. He raised his eyebrows and he looked at the scholars, but he himself said nothing. White-haired Baruch ben Jacob looked at the Rabbi; then Baruch said, "My respected colleagues, perhaps we should say a few words about prayer."

The other sages nodded and stroked their beards and murmured among themselves. "Now," said Reb Baruch, "I always like to begin with the Holy Scriptures. One of my favorite stories is that of Jonah in the whale–I remember how Jonah prayed to God, in his dark wet whaley cave":

Then the Almighty Lord arranged that a great fish should swallow Jonah, and Jonah was inside the fish for three days and three nights. From inside the fish, Jonah prayed to the good Lord, his eternal God.

And Jonah said, "In my distress, I call to You, my Lord. The engulfing waters threaten me, the blue deep surrounds me, and seaweed is wrapped around my head. My life is ebbing away, but I remember You, O Lord, and my prayers rise to Your holy temple. With a song of thanksgiving, I will sacrifice to You forever. What I have vowed, I will make good–for true salvation comes only from the Lord."

Then the fearsome Lord God spoke to the fish, and it spewed Jonah out safely onto the dry land.

The other scholars nodded and they smiled and stroked their beards. And a younger man, Elisah ben Samuel, said, "As you turn to the Holy Scriptures, Reb Baruch, so I turn to the Talmud. In relation to prayer, the *Sanhedrin* chapter of the Talmud reminds us: 'The merciful One desires the prayers of our heart, and He listens to them intently.' "

"Ah, yes," said Joshua ben Eliezer, "we can always bask in the fine and thoughtful Talmud, amen."

"Amen," repeated Baruch.

Then Reb Joshua continued: "The Sages of the Talmud also say (in the *Berakhot* section): 'Invariably, God's presence can be found in the midst of a congregation that is devoutly praying.' "

Jedaya listened patiently. The scholars nodded and muttered, and after a moment, Lewe ben Anselm said, "Friends, the Talmud is all well and good, but I would return to the most sacred of sacred words, the Holy Scriptures themselves. In the First Book of Chronicles, King David reminds us all, as he speaks of prayer to his son Solomon":

And you, Solomon my son, be certain to acknowledge your father's God. Serve Him with a whole heart and with a willing mind; for the great Lord God (blessed be He) searches all hearts and He discerns every whim and invention of men's thoughts. If you look deeply for Him and for His ways and His wishes, then He will let you find Him.

"Ah, gentlemen," said Menahem ben Joel, "the most sacred of sacred words are certainly beautiful and inspiring; in relation to prayer, I myself always remember Psalm 116":

> I love the Lord.

> I am blessed: the good Lord hears
> My voice, my hopes, my prayers;
> The Lord is righteous, He reveres
> Even one who errs.
> With His kind compassionate gaze
> God uplifts the fallen man –
> Once I fell to evil ways
> Yet God has saved my soul again.

> In my heart I held to Him
> (Even when I said in spite:
> "Men despise the cherubim.")
> Now I greet the Lord, contrite
> In His House where truth is read
> In His Courts I bow my head
> With others whom He's shepherded –
> I will praise the Lord till my deathbed.

> O praise the Lord.

"Amen," said another scholar, Moyses ben Nathan. "We could go on and on like this forever, Jedaya. Prayer is the essence of communicating with God. As Psalm 96 tells us":

To the holy Lord bow down
In the splendor of His glory
And dance for His renown
All you creatures transitory.

Declare to every nation:
"God is our great Illuminator.
Pray to Him, our Foundation,
The eternal world's Prime Creator."

Then old Shimshon ha-Zaken coughed; he seemed to be having a bit of trouble with his throat. The other scholars waited respectfully. Finally, Shimshon said hoarsely, "The holy Book of Jeremiah says":

If you invoke Me and pray to Me, then I will listen to you. When you seek Me, you shall find Me. Remember: if you search with all your heart, then I will let you find Me–thus says the Lord.

The old men nodded and they stroked their beards and they said many "amens."

Meanwhile, the Rabbi had set aside his book and he had been listening quietly. As the men talked, the afternoon wore on. Finally, the Rabbi turned to Jedaya ben Moshe ha-Levi. "You have asked to see for yourself the power of prayer, and now I will show it to you."

The old scholars sat silent on the benches. "Now," continued the Rabbi, "you can recite today's *Minhah*. You must recite it silently. It is one of the most powerful of all prayers, and it becomes mystical when one word is substituted: this word is the secret Word of the Will. Before you begin the prayers, you must say this word, and you must substitute it in all the appropriate places. Then, young man, you will understand why it is that I spend more than an hour laboring over this sacred benediction on the afternoon before each Sabbath eve."

The Rabbi looked very serious. Jedaya felt strangely weak. He looked around at the many scholars sitting immobile on the worn benches. The scholars stared back at him. Jedaya looked at his feet. Finally, Jedaya said, "Very well, Rabbi, I am ready." So the Rabbi leaned over, and he whispered the secret Word of the Will to young Jedaya ben Moshe ha-Levi. Jedaya closed his eyes. He repeated the Word, and he began to say *Minhah*.

Now, as you know, Rabbi, there are certain spiritual moments of communication – certain special windows of prayer – that occur during ritual ceremonies. (For example, on *Rosh Hashanah* it is possible to ask for wealth, wisdom, and a male child when the *Kedushah* prayer is recited, just before the third benediction.) By using the secret Word of the Will, mystic holy men had access to one of these spiritual windows of request each Sabbath.

Normally, as the Sabbath was being welcomed, Rabbi Abraham would utter the secret Word of the Will. For a short time, this broke the bonds of all dead souls. Suddenly, thousands of these freed souls flew about. They would rush like the wild winds from the nothingness of their eternal wanderings. They would swarm and flow around the holy man, begging him to put them into his prayers, in order that at last on the strong wings of the prayers of a pious holy man, the souls could be carried up to Heaven and could reside in the glories of the Great Hereafter forever, under the golden smile of the Most Holy of Holies, blessed be He, hallelujah and amen.

Old Abraham Achselrad would be enveloped, entangled, en-wrapped, and enmeshed by the pleas and the entreaties of the innumerable souls flying at him from all directions like the winds of the wildest storm. The lost souls begged him to speed them aloft with his most holy of prayers, and Rabbi Abraham always did his best.

You see, Rabbi, during *Minhah*, Achselrad recited the mighty second benediction – the *Gevrot* (the "Powers") – which begins:

You are mighty forever, O Lord. You revive the dead. . . .

and which ends:

Who is like You, Master of mighty deeds? Who compares with You, O King Who kills and Who brings to life again and Who causes salvation to grow and to flourish – You and You alone are entrusted to revive the dead. Blessed be You, O Lord our God, Who revives and Who quickens the dead.

And it was then – at the moment when the Rabbi uttered the words "quickens the dead" – that suddenly he would be overwhelmed by the innumerable exiled souls. One by one, the good Rabbi sent them to Heaven. But even a strong and holy man like Abraham ben

Alexander was only human. After one hour or two, he would tire. Soon, he would find that he could carry fewer and fewer souls. And then finally, he would hear a *Bat Kol*, the solemn and sacred Daughter of the Voice. The *Bat Kol* would call out: "Holy! Holy! Holy!" At this point, the Rabbi knew that no more souls could be admitted into Heaven on that particular day, and so, wearily, Rabbi Abraham would take a deep breath, and he would end his prayer.

Yes, this is what happened each time that Rabbi Abraham went through the *Minhah* service on the afternoon before the Sabbath eve. However, today the Rabbi waited, and he did not begin to pray. Instead, he stood quietly and he watched, absently fiddling with the fringes of his prayer shawl. Rabbi Abraham Achselrad waited and waited, until at last Jedaya came to the words: "quickens the dead."

At that instant, there came a terrible rush of souls. Thousands upon thousands of dead souls came flying at young Jedaya. A great crowd, weeping and shrieking and begging, pressed down around the praying man. The souls flew like the great winds of a hurricane. They came like the inexorable breath of the fiercest of storms. They swarmed and they cried and they pleaded, in an overwhelming torrential wave of the dead. And Jedaya ben Moshe ha-Levi opened his eyes wide, and then he fainted with fright.

The old scholars lifted poor Jedaya onto a bench, and after a moment he weakly opened his eyes again. But for many minutes afterward, he could say no words. Meanwhile, Rabbi Abraham closed his eyes and he stroked his beard. Then the Rabbi opened his eyes. He took a deep breath. He stretched, and he rubbed his arms. Rabbi Abraham stood, and he bent and he touched his toes. Then old Abraham Achselrad slowly turned his waist from side to side. Again, the Rabbi closed his eyes – but this time he began to pray.

The Rabbi of Cologne began to say the afternoon *Minhah* prayer. When the mystic Rabbi came to the *Gebrot* benediction, he remained standing motionless on his feet for an entire hour. His forehead became damp with perspiration. His muscles were tense. Sometimes he trembled and shook. Old Abraham Achselrad helped many thousands of souls into Heaven that day. Finally, he took a deep breath, and he ended his prayer. "Amen," said the Rabbi aloud.

"Amen," said the scholars.

"Amen," whispered Jedaya ben Moshe ha-Levi.

That was in medieval Cologne, a great many years ago. But my grandmother reminded me that even today, and in the most trying of times, there always are strong holy men. There always have been, and there always will be, holy men with strong shoulders and with powerful prayers and with a mighty piety, on whose swift and sacred benedictions we can rest easily as we are carried up to the good Lord God's glorious celestial city of Heaven in the sky.

W hat is that, Rabbi? No, I was just resting my eyes—
please feel free to join me here by the stove. (I think that you will be too warm on that bench: try the one nearer to the wall.) An old man like me can doze forever by a warm stove. I suppose that is because I am not hungry. As you know, the Talmud says that food induces sleep—although my grandmother preferred the insect-bone.

What is the insect-bone? Well, to cure insomnia my grandmother would push a small insect into a hollow bone. She would seal the bone, and then she would hang it as a necklace around the sleepless person's shoulders. Now, insect-bones are all well and good for sleeplessness, but *food*, Rabbi, is better than charms or even medicines for disease. My grandmother told me that there are illnesses completely insensitive to charms and incantations—illnesses impervious to the greatest potions and medicines—but good foods and careful eating will cure these diseases completely.

So, Rabbi, food is a great cure. And certainly food is a necessity. But when it comes to healing, then there is a greater power even than food—it is *sunshine*. The warm smile of the good Lord God heals the body and rejuvenates the soul, as it radiates to us from afar, from somewhere over the cloudless suntanned hills of the Holy Land. My grandmother made it a point to sit in the sun every day that it shone. Some sunny mornings, she would knit at the edge of her mother's grave. At other times, she would just sit on the bench in our yard by the garden. Grandmother said that sunshine accounted for her amazingly good health when she was older than me (and now I am eighty, you know). Yes, sunshine kept my grandmother healthy, just as it cured Mannus ben Aleydis. You do not know about Mannus? Then let me tell you:

Once upon a time, said my grandmother to me, in the congregation of Rabbi Abraham ben Alexander, Achselrad of Cologne, there was a devout young man named Mannus ben Aleydis ha-Kohen. One day this pious Jew fell ill with a long list of strange and diverse problems and complaints.

Like every large Jewish community, the Cologne Juden Viertels had a hospital – a sort of medical hostelry – but the medieval Jew's first choice was to remain at home when he was sick. (Of course Jews believe that it is a sacred obligation to attend the sick; therefore, whether the patient was at home or in the hospital, he was well looked after.) At first, Mannus ben Aleydis ha-Kohen was treated at home. However, after many weeks, poor Mannus continued to be ill. He had problems breathing. He had pains in his chest and in his stomach. He sweated in the cool weather. He felt faint, and he trembled. His heart raced for no apparent reason. He felt too weak to walk any distance. Sometimes things around him seemed distant and unreal. Frequently he was very dizzy. Always, he was sad and tired.

Finally, the local Jewish doctors advised Mannus to move to the hospital. There, the doctors listed his complaints, and they treated the problems one by one. In the Middle Ages, physicians used all manner of charms and potions – and this was the special regimen that the doctors of Cologne instituted for poor sick Mannus ben Aleydis:

They began with two general remedies. A round stone that looked like a crystal and that had been found in the stomach of a chicken was wrapped in a clean linen cloth; this was put under Mannus's pillow. A poultice was made of pepper, mustard, and salt, all ground together with a little wine and wrapped in a white cloth; this was put around Mannus's chest each morning.

For Mannus's lungs, he was fed a mixture of bay leaves and wine, spread on fresh bread. For Mannus's stomach, he was given an apple that had been baked in a thin coating of wax. For Mannus's heart, he ate ground walnuts and white flour boiled in fat. For Mannus's sweats, he drank vinegar and garlic.

On some days, Mannus felt better and the world seemed brighter. But on other days the symptoms returned. The nurses were discouraged; they shook their heads. After another two weeks, the doctors consulted among themselves and they decided to add a pennyroyal cure.

(Pennyroyal is a wonderful herb, Rabbi. It helps every possible ailment, and my grandmother used it all the time. Pennyroyals are mints – the crushed leaves smell like spearmint – and they grow around here in damp gravelly places, especially near pools. In case you ever have need of pennyroyals, you can recognize them by their square stems and their thick clusters of small red-purple flowers.)

Each morning, Mannus drank ground pennyroyal in wine and he ate ground pennyroyal in porridge. Each evening, he ate pennyroyal baked in bread. On the first day, Mannus felt wonderful. But on each succeeding day, Mannus felt worse and worse, until finally he thought that he was even more ill than when he began the treatment.

Jewish doctors visited their patients after the synagogue service on Sabbath mornings. One Sabbath, the two chief doctors for the Cologne Jewish community met in the hospital. They examined Mannus and they shook their heads. One of the doctors said, "Clearly, a very bad demon is at work here." And the other doctor said, "We have done our best. Now there is no alternative: Mannus must consult with Rabbi Achselrad."

Therefore, Mannus ben Aleydis ha-Kohen returned to live at home, and on one cold evening on the last day of the month of *Kislev* Rabbi Abraham came to consult. The Rabbi listened to Mannus's story and nodded. "What do you think, Rabbi?" asked Mannus weakly.

The Rabbi stroked his beard. "Yes, Mannus," said old Abraham Achselrad, "clearly a very bad demon is at work here."

Rabbi Abraham thought quietly for a few minutes. "Just a moment," he said. The Rabbi walked out the front door. Carefully, he removed the *mezuzah* from the doorpost, and gently he laid the *mezuzah* on a clean linen cloth. The Rabbi returned to the sickroom. He lit a single white candle, and by the candlelight he wrote seven mystical words on a clean parchment from a kosher calf. The Rabbi rolled this parchment into a tight scroll. "Here, Mannus," said Rabbi Abraham, "hold this in your right hand." And the Rabbi went out and he replaced the *mezuzah* on the doorpost.

Next, Mannus and the Rabbi bundled themselves warmly, and they walked out of the house together. A chill wind blew. Mannus walked slowly and the Rabbi held his arm. The two men made their way toward the synagogue. They turned into the alleyway leading to the house of study. It was late and cold and dark, and Mannus ben Aleydis ha-Kohen was frightened. The men stopped. The Rabbi set his hands on Mannus's head and he recited from the Book of Numbers:

> May the Lord bless you and watch over you
> May the Lord make His face to shine upon you
> May the Lord be gracious and good to you
> May the Lord look kindly on you
> And may He give you peace, amen.

Mannus felt a little better, and the two men proceeded toward the old wooden building.

It was the dark dead hours of the night. Normally, when the shammas (or any other authorized person) entered the synagogue door at an unusual hour, he would knock three times. This was to warn the spirit worshipers. (You do not know about spirit worshipers, Rabbi? These are the wandering souls of Jews, and they gather—clothed in strange prayer shawls or even in shrouds—in empty synagogues for their own midnight services. At the sound of a knock, the spirits fly out through the cracks in the doors and the walls, and they vanish into the deep dark night.) This time, however, Mannus and the Rabbi did not knock. Instead, they opened the door very, very quietly. They removed their shoes; silently, they walked into the main prayer hall. Mannus was weak and dizzy, and he was trembling uncontrollably.

The building was thick with old silence, but a dog whined outside somewhere far away. Mannus peered into the dark hall. There, past the worn wooden benches, beyond the twelve stained glass windows with their colored lions and snakes, stood a faint luminous figure at the Holy stone Ark. The figure turned–it turned, and Mannus saw that the specter looked exactly like him. Was this Mannus's own spirit? Or was it a double from the spirit world?

Mannus stood frozen. He could not move. He and the Rabbi remained absolutely silent and unmoving. After many minutes, Mannus thought that he heard some words. Were they spoken aloud? Perhaps they were only words that he remembered in his mind. In any case, Mannus thought that he heard a verse from the Book of Ecclesiastes:

> Consider God's handiwork. Who can straighten what He has made crooked? When things go well, when times are good, then be glad. But when things go ill, remember this: God has set the one alongside the other; He has mixed the good with the bad. Therefore, a man can never be certain what is to happen next.

In a whisper, the Rabbi said to Mannus, "Mannus, at this point I must not move. You, on the other hand, must walk to this spirit, and you must give him that holy amulet from your right hand."

Mannus looked at the Rabbi. His throat was dry. His arms and his legs would not move. "Mannus," said the Rabbi quietly, "give the parchment scroll to the spirit."

How did Mannus manage to walk? I do not know, Rabbi–but somehow he did. Slowly, shakily, and weakly, Mannus stepped toward the Holy stone Ark. The walk seemed to take hours. The spirit radiated waves of fear that pushed against Mannus. Mannus stopped. Softly, the Rabbi said, "Go on, Mannus. You must continue walking." Mannus took one step. Then he took two. After seven cycles of seven steps, Mannus was within reach of the spirit. Waves of black fear pushed Mannus backwards, and he felt that he would fall over. "Reach out, Mannus," said the Rabbi. Mannus could not make his hand move. The spirit extended its right hand. Mannus could see through the arm as if it were a cloud or a fog. The spirit hand was coming closer to the right hand of Mannus. The spirit hand would have touched the right hand of Mannus, could a spirit hand touch a human hand. The misty hand reached the parchment scroll, and slowly Mannus opened his clenched fist. Then the scroll passed into the hand of the spirit.

It seemed that the blackness deepened. A low rushing rumbling sound began. The spirit grew larger and larger. It filled the prayer hall. It filled the synagogue. Did it reach out beyond Cologne, swallowing trees and fields and mountains and oceans? Mannus trembled; he shook and shook. A blackness covered all, and the abyss of the endless night enveloped the little wooden synagogue of Cologne.

Then suddenly there was nothing. The building was empty and dull and blank. And Mannus, too, was completely empty. He sat upon a prayer bench. Rabbi Abraham took a deep breath, and he walked slowly into the back study room. Mannus stayed on the prayer bench. He sat blank and numb and dulled and empty. When the shammas came in to open the building the next morning, he was astonished to find Mannus sitting there already. Mannus was pale, he sat looking down at his knees, and Shammas Chayim knew to ask no questions.

Mannus sat through the morning service. He said nothing, and it seemed that he heard nothing. Later, a friend walked him home. Mannus went immediately to bed, and he slept the dreamless sleep of the dead until the next morning. During the next day, Mannus felt a bit stronger. He ate some stew, and he walked out into his yard. One week came and one week went, and then the next week passed and then two more. Each week, Mannus felt a little stronger, and the days seemed a little brighter. After five weeks, after six weeks, after seven cycles of seven days, Mannus ben Aleydis ha-Kohen was regularly attending the synagogue, and he was even working two days a week.

One day, Mannus came to the synagogue and he walked into the back study room. Rabbi Abraham was reading a book.

"Rabbi—" said Mannus.

"Yes?"

"Rabbi, I think that I am healing," said Mannus.

"I am glad to hear that," said Rabbi Abraham, holding open his book with one hand.

"It is slow progress," said Mannus.

"I understand," said the Rabbi, "but that is to be expected."

Mannus ben Aleydis looked down at his feet. He rubbed his hands on the sides of his pants. Then he looked up at the old Rabbi. "I am in a hurry to be completely well again, Rabbi. Is there anything else that I might do?" asked Mannus.

Rabbi Achselrad closed his eyes a moment. There was a long

silence. "Well, Mannus, there *is* something," said the Rabbi finally. "Sit out in the sun. Sit in the springtime sun, every single day."

"I should sit in the sun?"

"Yes," said the Rabbi, "in the sunshine the disease will finally begin to abate completely."

The Rabbi looked at the wall, as if he could see the sunshine beyond. "You see, my friend," said old Achselrad, "the sunshine is the warm smile of the good Lord God (blessed be He). It heals the body and it rejuvenates the soul, as it radiates to us from far off, over the cloudless suntanned hills of the Holy Land."

Rabbi Abraham smiled his own sunshine smile. "Once upon a time, Mannus," continued the Rabbi, "there was a golden radiant precious stone that hung around the neck of the patriarch Abraham. When a sick man looked at it, then he was healed – he was healed warmly, radiantly, and completely. And what happened to this golden stone? When Abraham died, then the good Lord God placed the stone in the sun. Now it shines down upon us from the radiant springtime sun."

The Rabbi smiled, and Mannus ben Aleydis smiled – and then Mannus ben Aleydis ha-Kohen left the old yeshiva. Mannus went home. Each day he sat in the warm sunshine of the Lord's holy smile. Mannus sat in the sun, and he ate healthful foods. And there came a day when suddenly he knew that he was healed. Was it that the air was warm and fresh again? Was it that the day was bright and young? Was it that a wind of gentle embracing contentment had slipped up to Cologne, between the cool European breezes, from the far-off shores of the Holy Lands? Mannus felt that it was all of these things, and Mannus knew that at last he was completely and happily cured forever.

abbi, I am glad to see you here alone. I want to apologize for my outburst during the service this evening. You see, I heard Reb Anton say: "I swear that the writing in these prayer books is getting smaller each day." Imagine, uttering an oath in the synagogue! You should never swear to anything casually, and you should *never* swear in the synagogue. "Let no oath rise to your lips," said the Sages. "Stay far from frivolous vows, light-minded oaths, and hasty solemn promises. In other words, swear not at all, amen."

My grandmother always reminded me that a false oath, even if made with honorable intent, is a great sin, and it will be punished with the full wrath of the omnipotent Lord God (blessed be He). Now *you*, Rabbi – you are much too easy on your congregation. I have heard you releasing men from all manner of hastily made vows. However, in the olden days, in the strict and pious days of our fathers, rabbis would not forgive a solemn vow: the strict rabbis did not absolve men from thoughtless oaths.

I remember that my grandmother would say:

> If you solemnly swear only to what is true
> Then the good Lord God will give healthy children to you.

Ah, but false oaths are a different matter: the great Lord God Almighty punishes wrong vows with a vengeance. Therefore, the stern German rabbis did not allow sacred oaths to be sworn in the synagogue or in the *Bet Din*. Of course I suppose that was the German style. German Jews were more extreme than the Jews of any other country; for instance, the German Jews fasted for two consecutive days at *Yom Kippur* instead of fasting for one day. My grandmother often used Rabbi Meir of Rothenburg as an example of this strictness. At the time of Rabbi Meir, French rabbis allowed the yeshiva to be warmed on winter Sabbaths by Gentile custodians. But as for Rabbi Meir—he insisted that no fires could be lit by anyone on the Sabbath, not by Gentiles and certainly not by Jews. Instead, Rabbi Meir ordered that in the cold weather the doors and windows of the houses and the synagogue be tightly fastened in order to save the heat before the Sabbath began.

You knew this already? Did you also know that one time Rabbi Meir found that a Gentile servant had made a fire in the yeshiva stove on the Sabbath? Therefore, the Rabbi bolted shut the oven doors every Friday afternoon. Oh, you knew this too? Then undoubtedly you must know of Rabbi Petahiah and the Kuweti Jew who never took an oath. No? It is a curious tale. . . .

Exactly, Rabbi—I am speaking of Petahiah ben Jacob, the brother of Rabbi Isaac ben Jacob ha-Lavan (Isaac "the Wise") of Prague. Petahiah undertook a tour of the entire world. He traveled through Poland, Russia, the land of the Khazars, Armenia, Media, Persia, Babylonia, and Palestine; then he wrote about his adventures in a book called *Sivuv ha-Olam* ("Around the World").

Rabbi Petahiah's travels were at the end of the twelfth century, in the days of Abraham Achselrad and well before Asher ben Yehiel was the Chief Rabbi of Cologne. Why do I mention Rabbi Asher? It is simply this—when he was the leading scholar in Cologne, Asher spent most of his time writing and reading. Rabbi Asher continuously studied the Torah and the Talmud in the little back room of the yeshiva. This room was where for centuries the Cologne rabbis had passed hours on end, working and thinking and arguing with themselves. Above the back study room was a loft for storage. One evening, when he was rooting around among the manuscripts in the loft, Rabbi

Asher found a letter from Rabbi Petahiah of Regensburg to Rabbi Abraham ben Alexander, the mystic Achselrad of Cologne.

"*My dear Rabbi Abraham* – [began the letter]

"I have just met a fine young man, a Jew from Mainz. He has agreed to carry this letter to my good friend Rabbi Nahman of Mainz, who I am certain will then arrange to transport it to you. I write to wish you and your family well, to convey my fondest greetings to all the Jews of your blessed community in Cologne, and to praise the good Lord God (blessed be He) and His Almighty Name for ever and ever, amen.

"I will not trouble you with the details of my many wagon rides and my subsequent sea voyages. Suffice it to say that they safely brought me here to the Oriental regions, regions that are so near to the great Holy Land where someday the Messiah shall return and deliver us and resurrect all souls and rebuild the Temple on Zion, amen. I write now in order to record for you some details of the lands and the peoples that I have seen in these old and foreign realms. The bright and glorious hand of God is visible everywhere, if only we look – praise the Lord Yahweh-Elohim.

"I have had endless adventures while traveling here. I hope – with the good Lord willing – to relate many of these events to you in person. For now, let me just say that after touring the Holy Lands of Palestine, I turned south and west, and I ventured across the Arabian desert. Most recently, I have been in the port city of Kuwet, on the northwestern angle of the Persian Gulf south of Basra.

"Kuwet (also known as al-Kuwait) is a walled town, and it has a wonderful natural harbor with a good anchorage of almost ten fathoms of water. The town is bright and clean and low-built, and it is filled with industrious people. The surrounding country is entirely desert, and the Kuwetis depend upon the sea and sea-trade for their livelihoods. Kuweti sailors are the most skillful and trustworthy on the Persian Gulf, and for all the surrounding regions, Kuwet is the main port of entry for rice and grain and it is the main port of exit for goats and mules and sheep.

"I have located a few Jews living here and working as middlemen in the shipping trades. One of them took me into his house; it was not long before we became fast friends. One evening, we began to talk of the dangers of vows and oaths and promises. As in Europe, solemn oaths are held to be serious and complex matters throughout the Orient too. Of course, the Holy Scriptures clearly warn *all* peoples against taking vows lightly. As you know, when Moses reports God's universal Laws in the Book of Deuteronomy, he says":

> And when you make a vow to the Lord, do not put off its fulfillment. For the Almighty One will require its honest completion, and any procrastination will be a sin.

"All the great rabbis have considered vows to be extremely serious. They discouraged sacred oaths, and they helped their congregants to annul misspoken vows. Undoubtedly in Cologne you follow the rule that on the first day of the New Year men should declare, 'All the vows that I make this year are to be void.' My host here in Kuwet had never heard of this practice. When I told him that we do this in Regensburg, he was led to tell me a story, the tale of a local Jew who was so humble and righteous that he never took an oath. I must confess that the story seemed vaguely familiar. Do you recognize it? Here is what I heard:

"Once upon a time, not far from here along the coast, there lived a rich Jew named Kaleb ibn Benjamin. Kaleb had never sworn a holy oath in all his life. When he was about to die, Kaleb made an ethical will that ordered his children never to take a holy oath for any reason. In his will, Kaleb wrote:

" 'My dear children, all my wealth and happiness came to me because throughout my life I never took a sacred oath. Of this I am firmly convinced. I never swore a holy vow; therefore, I have always had a clear conscience and the benevolent Lord God has let me prosper, amen.

" 'My good and obedient children, especially beware of holy oaths. For example, do not make a promise when holding onto the fringes and the tassels of a prayer shawl. And how do I know that this is a sacred oath? I learned it from the famous oath in the Book of

Genesis. At one point, Tamar asks her father-in-law for a holy oath that he would truly keep his promise'":

The man asked: What pledge shall I give to you?

And Tamar replied: Swear by your seal and your cords and by the staff that you hold in your hand.

" 'In other words, my children, the father-in-law was required to forge his promise with his signet ring, his fringes and tassels, and his walking stick. Such solemn and serious pledges are the oldest and most sacred rituals for an oath: one must avoid them at all costs – although, I am sad to say, I have seen these holy oaths taken quite casually nowadays.

" 'I have said that my reverence for oaths has brought me prosperity – and that is what I believe. But the deepest joy and benefit of this principle is that I have lived a fully truthful life, humble and free of the immodesty of excess holy oaths, and that forever, since you were very little, I could enjoy your happy laughter honestly, in the warm clean open sunshine of the good Lord God's Heavenly smile, amen.'

"Of course, Kaleb's final testament went into a great many other matters too. Before he died, he read the ethical will aloud to his children one afternoon, and they agreed to abide by all his wishes and to try to profit from the experience that he had written down carefully and had recorded for them in detail.

"Not long afterward, Kaleb ibn Benjamin died. After seven bleak and tearful days of mourning, the children reread the will together. Sadly they repeated all the injunctions, and sadly they divided the estate evenly and fairly among themselves. And each of them agreed most solemnly never to take a sacred oath in any form. Then each child went his own way except for one son, Judah, who remained in his father's house on the outskirts of Kuwet and resumed the duties of his father's businesses, in accord with his father's last wishes.

"Ah, good Abraham, not all the world is populated by righteous people. Evil men are found everywhere. But then who are we to question the ways of the awesome most Holy of Holies (blessed be He)? As it is said in the Book of Proverbs":

> There is a special end
> For everything God made –
> He even made the wicked friend
> So that other men could say:
> "These evil men are destined
> For the final Destruction Day."

"In any case, the town of Kuwet contained a number of wicked men. People talked about the unusual will of Kaleb ibn Benjamin, and it was common knowledge that Kaleb had instructed his children never to take a holy oath. 'This is a most delicious situation,' laughed one local Jew (of whom, I must say, Abraham, we could not in any way be proud). This unscrupulous character went to Judah ibn Kaleb and asked him to return the five hundred gold coins that, said the wicked man, the father, Kaleb, had owed him. The son denied the claim. Therefore, the greedy man had Judah summoned before the local *Bet Din*, the religious court of the Jewish community of Kuwet.

"In the court, Judah was ordered to take a sacred oath – to swear on the fringes of his *tallis katan* – that he knew nothing of the claim. But Judah thought to himself, 'In the Midrash *Tanchuma*, the Talmud reminds us never to declare a sacred oath for nonreligious matters, even to assert a truth. Moreover, if I take the required holy oath, then I shall be breaking my father's will. It is better for me to pay this money than to disregard my father's last wishes.' So Judah ibn Kaleb paid the rogue.

"When the word was spread that Judah absolutely refused to take any holy oaths, other evil men rubbed their hands together. Again and again, people invented charges and demanded large sums of money. Soon, Judah ibn Kaleb found himself penniless, without possessions, and owing money to all manner of unsavory characters in Kuwet. Matters continued to degenerate, and, eventually, Judah was put in prison.

"Judah was now more than sad and more than depressed, he was almost incapacitated. He could not sleep. He could not get up in the mornings to exercise – he simply lay in bed. He had no appetite for his food. He was always dazed. Then, while Judah was in prison, his wife died, and out of pity for his children, Judah was released. You would think, my old friend Abraham, that Judah would now be unable to function at all. But this was not the case. Judah had two little children, and for their sakes he continued on.

"Judah had nothing in Kuwet, so he hoped to start anew somewhere else. Poor Judah ibn Kaleb took his little children by the hand, and he went away with them. Where were they going? Judah did not know. But movement was life, and as long as they traveled at least they were alive.

"After a day, Judah and his children came to a river, but there was no ferryman to take them across. Judah took off his heavy coat. He made it into a sling, and he carried his two young children through the rushing water. By the mercy of the great Lord God (blessed be He), the small family reached the other shore safely. But where were they now? Judah had walked on blindly, and he had crossed the river blindly. Now he was lost and alone. Judah was wet and cold, and he had the charge of two little children.

"The night was coming. Judah looked up the river, and he looked down the river. Far down the river bank, he saw a man. Judah walked in that direction, carrying his children. The man was standing by a flock of sheep.

" 'Hello,' said the man.

" 'Hello,' said Judah.

" 'Where are you going?'

" 'Nowhere,' answered Judah.

"The man looked at Judah, and he looked at the two little children, quiet in Judah's arms. Judah was wet and tired. 'Perhaps,' said the stranger, 'you need a place to spend the evening.'

" 'Yes, I certainly do,' said Judah.

" 'Then come with me,' said the man. He led Judah and the children to his house, a brick and mud building not far away. The man's wife fed them dinner, and she helped to put the children to bed. The man watched Judah carefully, but he asked no questions. After a while, the man said, 'Sir, I could use a shepherd. Do you need a job?'

" 'Yes,' said Judah.

" 'Then I will try you out,' said the man.

"The man could not afford to pay Judah; however, he allowed Judah and his children to live in a small hut on his land. Judah did not talk much, but he took good care of the flocks. The children were happy with the landlord's wife, and she was happy to mother them.

"One afternoon, Judah was sitting on a rock. He stared at the sheep. He stared at the sky. It was a fine day, but Judah felt that a curtain hung over the world. Once he had been rich. Once he had had a fine wife. Once he had lived in a large and busy city. Judah ibn Kaleb had studied in a yeshiva when he was young. He had thought that he would be a scholar and that he would age among the thoughtful rabbis and that he would contribute to the community charities and that he would see his children marry and that he would be the grandfather of many, many fine scholars. Now he sat on a rock. He had no money and he had no future. He remembered the verses in the Book of Lamentations":

> Look down, Lord. Be merciful
> For I am ignored and despised
> And I am clearly pitiful
> To the men who pass me by.
>
> I stare around in disbelief—
> Is such suffering man's true lot?
> God has brought me extra grief
> In His anger fierce and hot.
>
> From on high He sent down searing heat
> Seeping it deep into my bones,
> He roughened the path beneath my feet,
> Setting obstacles and sharp stones.
>
> He made me weak and broken
> And desolate all day long;
> My sins, they bind me like a yoke
> And my youthful strength is gone.

" 'Perhaps,' thought Judah wearily, 'it would be better for me to die rather than to live.'

"Judah did not cry, and he did not move. He just sat on the rock. He sat and he looked out blankly on the world. Then, in the distance, he heard a noise. It was a noise that he had heard every day; it was the happy shout of one of his children, playing in the fields on that warm afternoon. What was that verse from the Book of Proverbs?"

Start a boy on a road that's true
And even late in his old age
He won't stray far from that avenue
He will grow to be a happy sage,
And you will die happy too.

"Judah listened to the far-off child – and the sky seemed blue and the clouds were white and the dirt was warm. Then Judah got up from his rock, and he walked back toward his hut. And I think that he even smiled.

"Well, that is the whole story, Abraham, my childhood friend. I must end my letter now – but, Abraham, think of me as you read this in your holy study in Cologne, for I think of you. I think of the springtimes when we were small yeshiva students; those were spring-times when we played in the fields outside the city walls and when we lay on the dusty banks of the wide River Rhine in warm weathers with rain falling gently all around. Was it really like that long ago, one afternoon in the gentle rain? Could it have been as fine and good and warm as I remember? We were so poor, in tattered clothes and always shoeless. We were so young and penniless. Did we actually have such rich grand full years together? Well, that is what I now remember. And how can it possibly have been otherwise, dear Abraham – I see it so clearly now, and I know that it is the truth.

"Your childhood friend,
Petahiah, the son of Jacob"

ello, Rabbi, I will be with you in a moment. I cannot leave until every tablecloth is folded, otherwise the day has not ended properly. . . . There, now I am finished at last and I can sit next to you by the stove.

If I stare at the hot coals, I sometimes think that I can already see the Holy Land into which – the good Lord willing – I will roll someday smoothly like a round, round bottle beyond the grave. The stove door is the mouth of a cave and I am looking through it and into the bright warm sunshine of that great golden land with its ancient suntanned hills. Do you know the story of the cave to the Holy Land, Rabbi? No? My grandmother told it to me when I was just a boy – it begins with a dairyman in old Cologne.

In the medieval days of the mystic Rabbi Abraham Achselrad, Cologne was a major trading center in the German Empire. Cologne was known for its goldwork and its armor. Cologne had exquisite woven cloths, and it exported herring and wines. Many Cologne Jews were wine manufacturers and wine dealers, because Jews preferred wine prepared by members of their own religion. (At the same time, Jews often supplied the wine used in church ceremonies, just as they sometimes made the vestments of the Catholic bishops. Oh yes,

Rabbi–it is true: I am not inventing this.) Besides wines, the Rhineland Jews traded in all manner of other farm produce, including corn, geese, horses, poultry, and cattle. But although manual labor was respected (many rabbis were artisans and workers themselves), the Jews of medieval Europe considered dairymen to be lower-class workers. And this is a tale of one dreamy European dairy-farmer, a man who was hardly noticed by his neighbors.

One day, Rabbi Abraham was studying in the small back room of the Cologne yeshiva. Papers were piled in disarray on his desk. It was the morning. Suddenly, a fresh breeze, a light morning wind, arose; it blew open his copy of the Holy Scriptures to the Book of Psalms. The Rabbi raised his eyebrows. Then he looked down at his desk, and he read these verses from Psalm 104:

> From His cloud-filled blue domain
> He waters the suntanned hills
> And His gentle springtime rain
> Brings golden daffodils.

> God makes grass grow for the cows,
> Green grasses show their leafy charms
> Under man's rough iron ploughs
> In rich brown fertile farms;

> And from the earth, grain He imparts
> For bread to build our bones
> And then gives wine to warm our hearts–
> Even quietly when we are alone.

Somehow, in these sacred verses, the word "cows" seemed to glow in the morning light. "Cows?" thought Rabbi Abraham. "This is curious. What holy mysticism is afoot this morning?" Then the Rabbi looked up, and there he saw a woman standing in the doorway. The woman was Hannah, the wife of Dan ben Moshe. Why had she come to the Rabbi that morning, and why had she come alone–and what had this to do with cows? Well, Rabbi, I will tell you exactly what my grandmother told to me:

Once upon a time, in the countryside just outside of Cologne, there lived a poor daydreaming dairyman named Dan ben Moshe; Dan lived quietly with his wife Hannah. Every Sabbath, Dan went to the synagogue in Cologne, in order to pray and to study. And what did he do the rest of the week? No one knows. Only this is known: Dan ben Moshe had two cows and they gave very little milk. In the morning, Dan's wife would let the cows loose in the fields behind their home. In the evening, she would tie them up again in the fenced yard. Dan and his wife sold butter, cheese, and milk, but they earned very little money and they themselves depended on the food from these animals and from their garden in order to stay alive.

One evening, Hannah went to milk the cows. The animals were not in their usual meadow. Hannah called for her husband. The man and his wife searched for the cows in the woods beyond the fields, but the animals were not there either. Then the wife remembered that she had forgotten to tether the cows together in the morning. (Normally, she tied them together by a long rope to restrict their wanderings.) Hannah began to cry and to berate herself and even to shout.

Dan patted her on the shoulder. "Calm down, my dear," he said, and he smiled. "Listen, my good wife, everything is ultimately a gift from Heaven. This too may prove to be a gift."

"But Dan—these are our cows! They are our entire livelihood," she said. Again she began to cry and cry.

Dan ben Moshe sat down next to his wife. He put his arm around her shoulder. "I am not upset, and I am not worried. All will work out, Hannah," he said.

Hannah looked into her husband's eyes. How could he still be smiling? Something mysterious was afoot. Hannah hoped that this mysterious something was holy and that all *would* truly work out well in the end.

Dan simply patted her hand. Then he said, "Let us have a little food. This will take our minds from our problems." So Hannah took a deep breath. Then she stood, and she began to warm the cold lentils from the night before. As she worked, Hannah remembered back many years. Ever since they had been married, her husband had hoped to buy some cows, even when the couple had owned only a small plot of land and when they had made all their meager living from their vegetable garden. After buying the animals, Dan had discovered that they gave very little milk, but he had insisted on keeping them anyway. "It is the will of Heaven," Dan ben Moshe had said at the time.

After their dinner, the couple went outside again. There, quietly nibbling at the grass and the weeds, were the two cows. Hannah ran up to them, she patted them on their sides, and she led them back to the cowshed. Hannah milked them immediately, and the cows each gave more milk than usual. Although she was no longer young, Hannah practically skipped into the house.

The next morning, Hannah let the cows out. Carefully, she tethered them together. Then she stopped; for she had just had a strange feeling. A shiver went down her back. She untied the rope between the two animals. Then she let them loose. Later, when she went to check on them, the animals had disappeared. "Was I a fool to be so daring and hopeful and careless?" she wondered. In the early evening, the cows were still gone. Hannah was worried. She could hardly bring herself to speak to her husband at dinner, but Dan ben Moshe was daydreaming and he did not seem to notice. After dinner, Hannah hurried outside. Again the cows had come home by themselves, and again they gave much more milk than usual.

So, Hannah stopped tethering the cows together each morning and she stopped looking for them in the early evenings. The cows returned home later and later. Each day their milk was richer and richer, and the cream and the cheese had a special otherworldly flavor and a warm golden color. Hannah was very, very happy. And Dan smiled his usual absent-minded smile.

Soon the couple began to have more dairy products to sell in Cologne, and they got a reputation for very fine milk and cheese indeed. The townsfolk said that the milk from these cows was not just healthful, it was actually healing. People claimed that the sick were restored to health when they drank the milk from Dan's cows, and Hannah wondered whether this was in fact true.

Six days passed and then there were seven. Six weeks came and six weeks went, and then seven more days went by. Soon, seven cycles of seven weeks passed, and Dan and his wife lived more and more comfortably. They began to buy extra things for the house. They bought a new kitchen table. Hannah bought some boots for the winter. Dan finally bought a wool coat. The couple felt content and happier than they had ever been before.

Dan continued in his quiet life of study and prayer. Then one morning, as he was leaving for the long walk into Cologne, he looked at the road and he looked at the fields to his right. "I wonder," he thought. "Where do the cows graze each day?" Instead of walking off to Cologne, Dan decided to follow his cows when they disappeared into the woods that morning.

Dan stepped from the road. He walked through a small clump of oak trees until he reached the open field. The cows were slowly walking in single file, up beyond a ridge. Dan hurried after them. Soon the cows walked past the meadows and into the woods, and Dan followed. The cows ambled on and on, deeper into the woods. The trees were tall and the forest was dark and thick. Then up ahead, Dan saw a large pile of rocks. No–it was more than just a collection of boulders: it was the rocky opening to a cave. The mouth of the cave was only the width of one cow, and the two animals entered, one behind the other. No wonder that they needed to be untethered–they would never have fit through the opening if they were roped together. The cows disappeared into the cave, and Dan went in after them.

Dan ben Moshe followed the cows. He went in, and never once did he consider how in the world he might get out again. The tunnel went straight on for some way. Then it dipped suddenly down, so suddenly that Dan had not a moment to think. He stumbled, but the ground was soft: Dan seemed to have fallen onto a heap of sticks and dry leaves and he was not hurt at all.

Dan ben Moshe stood up, and he found himself inside a winding tunnel. Dan looked toward the ceiling, but all was dark overhead. Before him was another long passage, and far, far ahead, he thought that he saw the cows walking slowly away from him. The ceiling was dark; nonetheless, the cave had a gentle glow. Dan walked after the cows. As he went along, stones fell from the walls and there seemed to be water dripping along his right. And were there demons in the shadows? Reremice and blanktees fluttered along the dark damp ceiling. The many recesses were gloomy places, but somehow Dan was not afraid. He walked on and on. His faith in Heaven kept him calm—although, in truth, he did not have the courage to look too closely into the many small side tunnels that he passed.

After a while, the gentle glow became brighter and brighter, and Dan ben Moshe ha-Kohen found himself walking out through another opening in the cave. There before him were dry suntanned hills, and Dan seemed to be standing in the Holy Lands, with their warm sands and with the good Lord's sunshine smile overhead. All around him the ancient dusty hills of our forefathers stood warm and thoughtful. And grazing contentedly in front of him were the two cows. Dan took off his shoes and he walked barefoot for a while. Dan was in no hurry and there was no one else around. Dan walked and walked, and then he stopped. He was happy. He was not thirsty, he was not hungry, and he was not tired. He felt the slow easy pace of the holy old countryside.

Then Dan saw a weathered wooden building. Perhaps it was a yeshiva—to be honest, Rabbi, I do not know. Dan stepped in the open door. Inside, it was empty of people, but there was a small cedar desk. On the desk were pens and sheets of parchment. Dan raised his eyebrows, he looked around, and then he sat down and he wrote a letter to his wife:

"My dear wife Hannah,

"I am here in the Holy Land. Somehow I know that this is the great country to which we shall all roll someday, as smoothly as a round bottle, when the good Lord digs a tunnel from our graves and whisks us gently from the cold Rhinelands to the warm dry home of our forefathers, amen. And how did I come here? It was the cows—they found a cave that leads directly to this fine holy blessed place. Enjoy their milk, dear Hannah. I love you, and I hope to see you soon.

"With great and joyous love,
Your husband Dan, the son of Moshe"

Dan took the parchment note and he rolled it tightly into a scroll. Then he tied the scroll to the rope trailing behind one of the cows. The cows paid no attention: they continued chewing on the grasses and the stackburs and the field cedar. The day wore on. Dan lay on his back and he was warmed by the radiant smile of the good Lord's glowing sun. As evening approached, the cows wandered slowly and easily back toward the cave. They ambled into the opening. Soon, they had disappeared through the tunnel and were on their way back to the Rhinelands of medieval Cologne.

Dan did not come home for dinner that night, and Hannah was worried. She ate a little food, but she jumped up from the table at the least sound. Eventually the cows returned at nightfall, heavy with rich and holy milk. But where was her husband? Hannah was so worried that she did not notice the letter tied behind one of the cows. Hannah walked around and around through the rooms of the house, and she did not sleep at all that night.

Poor Hannah waited one day and then two. She could not eat, she could not sleep. Each morning she let out the cows. Each evening she watched for Dan, and each night the cows returned home alone. Six long days passed, and then there were seven – and on the seventh day, Hannah finally noticed the letter. It was muddy from being dragged through the dirt, but it was still legible. She read it once and she read it twice, but what did it mean? Was her husband dead, or was he alive? Was he really in the Holy Lands? Would he ever return?

The next morning, Hannah walked into Cologne, and she took the letter to Rabbi Abraham. She stepped in the front door of the synagogue. She was weak, and she was worn. Her face sagged. Her arms were heavy. She walked slowly, passing blindly through the anteroom and the main prayer hall. She did not notice the twelve stained glass windows with their colored lions and snakes. She did not look up at the Holy stone Ark. Hannah walked directly to the door of the back study room, and there the Rabbi was bent over a book.

"Rabbi," began the woman, "I need your counsel."

Her voice was quiet. She did not sit down. She told the whole story to the Rabbi, and he listened without saying a word.

The Rabbi stroked his beard, and he closed his eyes for many minutes. Hannah waited, very still. After some time, the Rabbi opened his eyes: "Hannah, my good woman, the Talmud tells us that if a husband wants to go to the Holy Lands, then the community should encourage his wife to follow."

Hannah looked at the Rabbi. She looked down at her feet. Then she handed the parchment letter to old Abraham Achselrad.

"Please keep this letter for me," said the woman. There was silence. Then she said, "Rabbi –"

Rabbi Abraham raised his eyebrows, but he said nothing. After a moment Hannah said very quietly, "Rabbi, I am so lonesome that I could cry." Then Hannah turned, and she left.

Yes, Hannah left the old Cologne yeshiva, and slowly she walked home. The Rabbi never saw her again. Did she ever find the cave? And what became of the letter? My grandmother said that the muddy parchment message was still to be found in the loft above the old yeshiva in Cologne – but I myself do not know if it is still there or if it is not.

ood evening, Rabbi. Of course—please sit here by the stove: the night fire helps me to become sleepy also. I see that you and I are not blessed like old Reb Elbaum. Once again, he nodded off during the last prayers this evening. He has learned to sway piously even while asleep; undoubtedly he acquired some magic from the mystic Achselrad. Yes, Rabbi, we too could use a dose of Achselrad tonight: my grandmother said that he could put men into a sleep trance by waving a gold coin before their eyes.

Ah, old Abraham Achselrad—he was always conjuring visions in the synagogue. I doubt whether he would be tolerated nowadays, but my grandmother said that Rabbi Abraham was also a scholar and he himself claimed that his visions came from devout and pious study. Many an astonishing event took place during his rabbinate—or so grandmother (blessed be her memory) was told. For instance, one dark and cold day he saved poor Gumpertus ben Avigdor with a holy conjured vision in the Archbishop's Court.

This was in the winter, in medieval Cologne. As you know, Abraham Achselrad worked night and day on a set of Kabbalistic tomes of mystical knowledge. The most famous of these was the *Keter Shem Tov*. (This was never published, and now it exists only as a secret manuscript hidden in the loft of the ancient Cologne yeshiva.) My grandmother said that one cold afternoon in the winter month of *Shevat*, while he was writing this very book, Rabbi Abraham looked up, and in the waning light of the day he saw a crowd of his congregants huddled fearfully in the doorway. "Please," called one of them, "come quickly and help rescue Gumpertus ben Avigdor. He has been charged with murder!"

Now, Rabbi, this is what had actually happened:

As you know, Cologne was a major trading center in the Middle Ages. (It is for this reason that many Jews settled there.) The city had been destroyed during the Norman invasion at the end of the ninth century, but it soon rebounded. Its yearly fair became famous throughout the continent. Commerce dominated Cologne. By the middle of the tenth century, the most powerful secular organization was the Merchant's Guild of St. Martin, which was centered in the district lying between the River Rhine and the Roman Wall.

In large medieval German towns, merchants and craftsmen all belonged to Guilds. The Guilds were political as well as commercial. (In fact, the official town charters were written contracts between the local lord and the Guilds; these charters were both birth certificate and constitution for the town: they set the city limits, they defined the taxes, they outlined the laws, and they described the chain of legal authority.) Jews could not formally be members of the Guilds. Nonetheless, Jews became intertwined with Guild operations at all levels, from the workmen to the top officers. And this was the case for Gumpertus ben Avigdor ha-Kohen, who became the main advisor to the warden, the head of the Merchant's Guild.

Gumpertus was an astute Jewish businessman. He was quite wealthy. He lent money to various independent merchants of the city, and he advised many of the Gentile burghers. After a time, Gumpertus became the main councilor to the Guilds, instructing them on investments and on legal matters; frequently, he gave confidential advice to Karl von Hohenheim, the warden of the powerful Merchant's Guild of Cologne.

Karl von Hohenheim had grown up as a poor man. Now he was rich and influential. Along the way, he had always hoarded money and power. In order to reach the top of the Merchant's Guild, he was constantly making deals and agreements and balancing precarious plans and projects. One day, von Hohenheim heard that the local count was being threatened and that his tenant farmers were being harrassed by a rival from Westphalia. The count was in desperate need of money to pay for extra troops. Von Hohenheim suspected that he could use funds from the Merchant's Guild treasury to put the count in his debt.

"I will lend the count money from the Guild treasury," thought von Hohenheim. "Then I will collect the interest myself." As part of the payback agreement, the warden would also reduce the regular yearly taxes that the Guild owed to the count; then von Hohenheim would pocket that difference too. The plan seemed sound–but what were the precise details of the count's finances? Were any other organizations offering him money? To negotiate most strongly, von Hohenheim needed to know exactly how much leverage he had; therefore, he sent for Gumpertus ben Avigdor.

It was in the cold winter. The two men stood together in front of a blazing fireplace. The warden gave Gumpertus a goblet of wine and then he said, "Mr. Avigdor, you know the government finances; you are discreet and trustworthy, and we have had many satisfactory dealings together, my friend."

Gumpertus nodded, but he said nothing. "What is coming next?" he wondered. Karl von Hohenheim rubbed his hands together in front of the fire. He looked at Gumpertus. "I know that you have the interests of us honest merchants at heart. At the moment, we have the opportunity to strengthen our position a bit in relation to the count."

The warden looked intently at the Jew. "Apparently the count is in some financial difficulty. Of course the problems of the count are ultimately the problems of the entire community. I would like to help him out, but I need to know exactly how bad are his problems. Also it would be best for us to keep this quiet, so as not to panic anyone else– I assume that the other Guilds are not privy to this information?"

Gumpertus looked down at his wine cup. "I have heard some rumors," he said slowly.

Gumpertus said nothing more. Karl von Hohenheim frowned; then he continued talking. "Now, now, my good man," he said, "you know more than rumors. You lend money to the count. You see him frequently to advise him. You know the details of the situation, Mr. Avigdor–if you will just set out the basic information then we can analyze this matter together. I assure you that anything you tell me will go no farther than this room."

Gumpertus said, "My good friend, I can tell you nothing. I cannot break the confidence that the count has in me. I am entrusted to be discreet."

"Listen," said von Hohenheim, pacing before the fire, "I will tell you a secret. The Guild of the Rich—the aristocratic *Richerzeche*—is trying to monopolize the support of the count. But if I can lend the count the appropriate funds then he will owe us a large favor. Frankly, the Merchant's Guild needs this help, Gumpertus, because (as you well know) the *Richerzeche* has old family wealth and all manner of other influences. The *Richerzeche* is powerful and it is selfish, and we are always second to them in the count's mind. Certainly you can understand that it is for the good of the common citizens that I ask for your help."

Gumpertus was very uncomfortable. He said, "Sir, believe me, I appreciate your problem. However, my silence is often worth more than my advice, and my clients must trust my word. You have to understand that honor and honesty are critical assets in my business— I simply cannot share any confidential information with you."

The warden could hold back no longer. "This is a serious matter, Mr. Avigdor: think it over when you are alone. I expect you to come back tomorrow. And if you do not tell me what I want to know then I am afraid that things will go very badly for you—yes, they will go very, very badly indeed."

Worriedly, Gumpertus ben Avigdor returned home. The next day he went back to the warden. "Perhaps," said Gumpertus, "there are others who can give you the information that you need, Mr. von Hohenheim."

"No," replied the warden, "only *you* know the true financial situations of all the parties involved. This information is crucial if I am to plan correctly. To make the right moves, I must know all the details."

Gumpertus looked at his feet. "I am afraid that I cannot tell you anything," said the Jew quietly.

"You dare to refuse?" cried Karl von Hohenheim. He stood up. He walked about the room, pacing back and forth. He threw a book at the wall. At that moment, a pageboy opened the door, mistakenly bumping the warden. Von Hohenheim was a huge man. He struck the young boy on the back of the neck – the boy fell to the floor, he hit his head, and he died.

Gumpertus stood frozen. Von Hohenheim opened wide his eyes. Suddenly Karl von Hohenheim called in the guards, and he accused the Jew of murder. Gumpertus was dragged to the local ecclesiastical court; as he was being pulled into the court building, poor Gumpertus remembered to recite the protective verse from the Book of Exodus:

> Terror and dread fell upon them
> Through the great might of Your arm –
> Stone-still they stood by helpless,
> While Your people passed safe from harm.

Word passed through the surrounding parishes; rumor of the death spread quickly. Gentiles came from the St. Laurence parish and also from the St. Albans parish. Angry people collected at the court building, and they demanded an equal punishment. "This Jew has killed one of our boys," someone shouted. "He himself must be put to death!" Was a riot in the making? Terrified Jews rushed into the synagogue, where Rabbi Abraham Achselrad was writing in the back room.

Rabbi Abraham listened to the confused and fearful reports. He stroked his beard. His forehead creased. Then he stood, and he put on his hat and his coat. The Rabbi left the small back study room of the yeshiva. He walked through the main prayer hall with its many wooden benches. He passed the twelve stained glass windows with their colored lions and snakes. He went by the Holy Ark made of stone, he stepped out of the front door, and he strode off to the courthouse.

The Archbishop himself was there in court; this was Archbishop Adolph of Cologne, a noble and honorable prelate. Archbishop Adolph knew the Rabbi. "Rabbi," said the Archbishop sadly, "I am afraid that one of your Jews has committed murder. We have accusers, and we have the body. I have no choice, Rabbi – Mr. Gumpertus Avigdor must be hanged."

"I see," said Rabbi Abraham. Old Abraham Achselrad looked at the accusers. He looked at poor Gumpertus and again at the accusers –

the chief of whom was Karl von Hohenheim. Rabbi Abraham said to von Hohenheim, "Sir, have you nothing else to contribute to these proceedings? Did you have no role at all?"

Karl von Hohenheim frowned and said, "Archbishop, you know that a Jew will beat you up and then shout 'Help!' "

"Cruel remarks do not help, sir," said the Rabbi.

But the warden set his mouth tightly and he answered in a firm voice, "I am a respected member of the community. My conscience is clear. The Jew is guilty."

Rabbi Abraham closed his eyes for a moment; then he asked, "Have you a Bible here, good Archbishop?"

"Of course," replied the Archbishop, and he instructed one of the officers to pass a leather volume to Rabbi Achselrad.

"Let us read from the Book of Psalms," said the Rabbi.

"I respect your religious views, Rabbi," said Archbishop Adolph, "but is this really relevant now?"

Rabbi Abraham Achselrad was holding the Holy Scriptures. Suddenly his eyes opened wide and then they closed tightly. He became weak, he sat on a nearby chair, and he took a deep breath. Then the Rabbi gently set down the Bible.

"Are you all right, Rabbi?" asked the Archbishop.

"I have just had a vision," said Rabbi Abraham. "I have seen the Heavens and the Great Throne of Glory."

There was silence for a moment. "Yes, I have seen the Heavens. I have seen the firmament of the good Lord God (blessed be He)–He Who sees all and Who demands justice for all, especially for His children, the Jews. In addition, I have seen that Psalm 88 is quite important," said old Achselrad. "And if you will be so good as to hand me the Holy Book again then I will read a bit of those verses":

> I am in prison
> An innocent victim;
> My sight is failing
> It is growing dim
> With fear of death
> From Dumah's sword,
> Daily I pray
> For help O Lord.

Why work wonders
For dead men only?
Can departed spirits
Sustain You alone?
Only live men can
Your memories save –
Our children preserve You
Out beyond the grave.

The Rabbi bowed his head and he closed his eyes, so the Archbishop said, "Of course, Rabbi, that is a most serious and holy sentiment."

"It certainly is," said the Rabbi. "Now, my good Archbishop, you are a noted cleric. What would you say that this verse means?"

"Clearly it means that the Lord helps and is sustained by the living."

"Yes, Archbishop – and I would say that it means even more than that," said the Rabbi.

"You would?" asked the Catholic cleric. "Then pray tell, Rabbi Achselrad: What more do you read into this Psalm?"

"First, I would say, Archbishop Adolph, that the good Lord God (blessed be He) helps the living and He is sustained by the living. In addition, God is the Guardian of all Israel. He has seen who has caused this murder; He will avenge it and He will protect His people against false accusations. The Almighty Lord God will even reach beyond the grave, where a child will save the innocent – amen," said the Rabbi.

The Archbishop looked at his councilors, he looked at the Rabbi, and he pursed his lips. "Can you be a little more specific?" asked the Archbishop. "Exactly what are you saying, Mr. Alexander?"

"I am saying this, Archbishop: I have had a vision. I have seen that a man who presently stands unaccused is in fact the murderer in this very case."

Then one of the officers laughed, and he said, "The Psalm has told you all this, old man?"

"Yes, it has," said the Rabbi. "My good Archbishop, what are you going to do? An angry mob has collected. Will you allow innocent people to be hurt or to be killed, when you know well enough that none of us Jews is guilty?"

"At the moment, Rabbi," said the Archbishop, "I must say that I know no such thing; in fact, I have been told exactly the opposite."

"Slander is a powerful weapon, Archbishop," said Rabbi Abraham. "As the scriptural Proverb says":

> The wicked witness, who with a false word
>   Denounces an innocent man,
> Strikes like the club or like the sword
>   Of a cruel barbarian.

The Rabbi nodded to himself. "Now, in this case, another man, a Christian, has committed slander – in fact, he is the guilty party," said Rabbi Abraham. "And I can prove this to you."

Karl von Hohenheim began to look pale, and his throat became dry. However, the Archbishop was not watching the warden; instead, he tilted his head a bit and he looked intently at old Achselrad. Then Archbishop Adolph conferred with his councilors. After a brief argument, the Catholic cleric said to the Rabbi, "If you can prove what you say, then no harm will befall any of you Jews." And he gave orders that the people in the court and the people in the street should all remain quiet.

Rabbi Abraham nodded again, and he said, "Thank you, good Archbishop. First, let me ask that you lock the court, so that the murderer will not be able to escape."

Karl von Hohenheim looked around him. He felt very weak. The Archbishop instructed his officers to stand by the doors.

Rabbi Abraham Achselrad sat down again. He closed his eyes. He began to sway. He shook strangely. The members of the court raised their eyebrows, and they looked at one another. Then the pious man opened his eyes, and he took a small piece of white kosher parchment from his pocket. The Rabbi covered the top of his head with a handkerchief, and he wrote a charm with holy names on the paper. The Archbishop could see that the charm began with a quotation from the Book of Exodus: "For I am Yahweh, your Restorer – I, the Lord God, am your Healer. . . ." But Archbishop Adolph could not make out the remainder of the words.

When the Rabbi finished writing, in his neat and tiny script, he rolled the parchment into a tight scroll and he tied it with a cotton thread. The Rabbi tied and untied the thread—he knotted and un-knotted it seven times—and then he placed the charm on a table next to a large gray blank wall. There was silence, and a dark cloud passed over the sun.

For a moment, nothing happened. Then, suddenly, it seemed as if a small hazy shape was wavering along the wall. The shape expanded. It became a dark aura. It rose up, and it appeared to be the dead page-boy, larger than life and sad and young and grim. Silently, the shape raised a wavering arm, and the arm pointed directly at the warden, Karl von Hohenheim. Von Hohenheim shouted, "No, no—stop! It was not me: it was the Jew!" But the image of the dead child pointed and it pointed, and it seemed to grow larger and to fill the room, in the silence of a dark and cold winter's day. There was a pressure in the air. It was irresistible. It inflated the wavering spirit, which grew larger and which pointed and pointed and pointed. The warden jumped up. "Stop!" he yelled. "Please stop! O Lord, have pity on me. All right, I admit it! I struck him, but it was a mistake!"

The wavering arm continued to point. The outstretched hand seemed to reach for the warden. Karl von Hohenheim fell back in his seat, and he looked away and he shook and he wept.

Then suddenly the shape was gone. The wall was blank, the room was empty, and every single person was weary and worn: everyone felt stunned and broken and silent.

No one moved. Karl von Hohenheim wept silently. Eventually, the Archbishop frowned, and he motioned to the guards. They stood beside the warden. "Well," said the Archbishop, as he turned to the Rabbi, "what do you suggest here, Mr. Alexander?"

Rabbi Abraham shook his head sadly and said, "I believe Mr. von Hohenheim. And if the death was unintentional, then the court should have mercy. This is a religious court, good Archbishop, and in the Book of Deuteronomy, it says":

This is the rule concerning a man who kills another and then flees in order to save his own life: he may be allowed to live if he has killed unintentionally, without malice aforethought. For instance, a man may go into the forest with his neighbor, in order to cut wood, and as he swings his axe to fell a tree, the axehead may fly off and hit his neighbor and kill him. The killer may then flee to another city in order save his life. The culprit, even if negligent, may flee without reprisal from the grief-stricken community.

Rabbi Abraham concluded: "Mr. von Hohenheim claims that the death was accidental. Therefore, I suggest that you send him away from Cologne, forever."

The Archbishop nodded, agreeing with the Rabbi. An official decree was issued: the warden, Karl von Hohenheim, was banished from the city. Gumpertus ben Avigdor was released immediately, and he returned home safely. And once again the ever-watchful Lord God Almighty had saved the Jews in that medieval city along the wide and dark River Rhine—yes, God again protected the Jews, on one cold winter day in old medieval Cologne.

h, good evening again, Rabbi. I know that it is always hard to sleep on the night of the full moon. Put your feet on the side bench here, and I will open the stove door. Let me push the coals back. There is nothing like the white glow of the stove; it washes away the cares of a hard day.

I heard your final benediction tonight, Rabbi—clearly you are overworked. Oh yes, even a shammas like me can tell. I kept one eye on you as I cleaned the dishes, and I saw that you were watching the door, hoping that Reb Elbaum would leave early. But then Reb Anton stayed to discuss the scriptural passage from the Book of Ecclesiastes:

Remember your blessed Creator in the days of your youth, before the days of trouble come. Remember Him before the elder years approach, when you will say: "I can find no pleasure any longer." Remember Him before the sun and the light and the moon and the stars grow dark and before the clouds return after the rain—at that time, the keepers of the houses will tremble, the strong men will stoop, the millers and grinders will cease because they are few and old, and the vision of those looking through the windows will grow dim. At that time, the doors to the street will close, and the sound of milling and grinding will fade; then men will awake at the sound of birds, but all their songs will grow faint; then men will be afraid of heights and of dangers in the streets; and then the almond tree will blossom but the grasshopper will drag himself along, and desire will no longer be stirred. And man will go to his eternal home, and mourners will wander about the streets but no bells will ring—and there will be a sad and respectful silence all around.

That is certainly anguished verse, Rabbi: of course it would wear you out.

What is that? A story from me? Rabbi, all I know are the children's tales, the grandmother fables. You need something new and fresh to keep your mind keen. Otherwise you will become a dreamy old man like me, and you will find yourself constantly musing and dozing and nodding off in front of the stove.

What do you mean you are already an old man, Rabbi? Do you really think that sixty years is old? You are still a child. When you reach eighty, *then* you will be old. You doubt that you will live to see eighty years? If so, Rabbi, then you will never grow old. . . . All right, all right, I know no special stories but listening to you and Reb Anton reminded me of bells and of mourners, it reminded me of the streets of Cologne and the evil gatekeeper. . . . Now, let me see, where shall I begin? I guess that I had best start with the tale just as my grandmother told it to me:

Once upon a time, said my grandmother to me, in the medieval Cologne of old Rabbi Abraham ben Alexander, there lived a city gatekeeper who was a very wicked man. What exactly was a city gatekeeper? Well, first let me remind you, Rabbi, that in those days the Juden Viertels, the Jewish Quarter of Cologne, was located in the eastern corner—the sunrise corner—of the old town. It was close to the ancient Roman wall, where the main street led to the River Rhine through the gate called the "Porta Principalis Dextra," which was later known as the Market Gate.

At that time, there were four major city gates and each of these gates was manned day and night by a gatekeeper. At each gate, there was a bell called the "Thor Glocke," which was used to signal the opening or the shutting of the city gates. In Cologne, as elsewhere, the Jewish cemetery (the *Am Toten Juden*) was located outside the town limits, beyond the walls; to get to the cemetery, a funeral procession had to pass through the southern gate, which was formally in the parish of St. Severin. In the days of Rabbi Abraham ben Alexander, the gatekeeper for the southern gate was a shriveled little man whose unfriendly smile made your stomach tighten. He had no family and no friends. He lived in the gate tower. All day long, he sat in the tower and he reminded himself about the many bad things that others had done to him. Usually, he blamed the Jews, and whenever a Jew died and when the body was being carried through the southern gate, the gatekeeper tolled the bell loudly, over and over and over, and he laughed. . . .

What? Of course there is more, Rabbi: I only closed my eyes for a moment—can an old man not take a little rest? Now you have interrupted my thoughts. Let me see, where was I? Ah, yes—as my grandmother said, "The three gates to Heaven have no bells—no one tolls your entry into the Great Hereafter." Did you ever hear her say that, Rabbi? You never knew her? That is too bad; you missed a fine woman. Anyway, Rabbi, I first heard about Makir and the gatekeeper from my grandmother, may her soul visit happily with the souls of her parents forever. What is that? Who was Makir? Just be patient, Rabbi:

Once upon a time, said my grandmother to me, in the early days of the Jewish communities in Germany—at the time of Rabbi Abraham ben Alexander—there lived in Cologne, on the River Rhine, a pious scholar named Makir ben Jesse ha-Levi. As Makir got older, his eyes became weaker, his sense of smell diminished, and his sense of taste became dulled. But Makir seemed to hear better and better. Well, Rabbi, perhaps it was not that Makir's sense of hearing became more acute—perhaps he had become more sensitive to sounds. And the one thing that bothered him particularly was the tolling of the bell at the southern gate. Whenever the evil gatekeeper rang the bell, Makir would shiver, and it would take many minutes for him to feel calm again.

Old Makir ben Jesse could barely leave his house, so his friend, the shammas Chayim ben Meir, would try to visit every day. One day, Makir said, "Chayim, the Thor Glocke scares me. I wish that it would never ring."

Chayim shook his head sadly. "My friend, you are hoping for a different world. The gatekeeper is an ill-tempered old coot. He rings the bell simply to annoy people – especially, to annoy us Jews. He tolls the Thor Glocke just as each Jewish funeral passes through his gate, and then he laughs."

"I do not think that I would like him to ring the bell at my funeral," said Makir.

"Ah, Makir," sighed Chayim, "if wishes had weight, then we Jews would be heavy people indeed." And Makir sighed too.

Old Makir had lived a long and contented life, and one day in his gentle old age, he became ill and he knew that soon he would die. And how did he know this? Ah, Rabbi, how does anyone know – Makir ben Jesse ha-Levi looked up one night, and there standing at the head of his bed was Dumah, the Angel of Death. Dumah stood at the head of the bed. He stood covered from head to foot with his unwinking eyes. He stood with a drawn and bloody sword – and in the oldest and dustiest voice of all, he said, "As the Almighty Lord God said to Moses, before appointing Joshua son of Nun as his successor: 'Moses, my child, the time of your death is drawing near.' "

Makir had been ill for some time. His head ached. He was feverish, and frequently he was dizzy. His heart pounded. His nose was sore and stuffy. He coughed a rattling cough continually, and his chest hurt when he breathed. Seeing the black angel Dumah, Makir opened wide his eyes, and then he sneezed. But there was no one nearby to say: "God bless you" – there was no one around who could say: *Hayim tovim*, "For a good life." Unfortunately, Rabbi, no one was there to give old Makir the little extra lifetime allowed to an ill man who sneezes. Dumah himself remained silent. Therefore, when Makir ben Jesse ha-Levi sneezed, he closed his eyes, and he died. Then Dumah swiftly drew old Makir's soul from out of the top of his wispy-haired head, and the angel and the soul flew up to Heaven with the fine old soul glinting and gleaming as it passed through the starlight of the blessed celestial regions, far, far away.

Old Makir ben Jesse died contentedly, and he was reunited with his parents in the Great Hereafter. Then old Makir was young again, and he heard the beautiful voice of his father Jesse, who was a *hazan*, singing him soft songs at night. And father and son were at peace together forever – and the mother, too, amen.

On the following day, when the shammas, Chayim ben Meir, came to check on Makir after the morning services, he found that the sick old man had died during the night. Chayim bowed his head, and he said a small prayer. Then he returned to the synagogue and he arranged for the Burial Society to prepare for the funeral.

The body of old Makir ben Jesse ha-Levi was washed, and he was dressed in his fine Sabbath robes. He was laid out overnight on a plain clean board. Spices were sprinkled on his clothes, underneath his prayer shawl. The next morning, the body was put into a plain wooden box, which had been glued together. (No nails were used so that Makir's spirit would not be snagged as it traveled back and forth between this world and the next.) Then the funeral procession assembled, well bundled, for it was a cold, cold morning in medieval Cologne.

It was in the month of *Tevet*. The shammas and the other men carried the coffin, and slowly they walked toward the *Am Toten Juden*. As they marched to the southern gate of the city, they passed down the street of Meshulam ben Jesse. Whenever someone in the town had died and was being carried to his grave, this pious man always left whatever he was doing, and he joined in the procession. It was Meshulam who chanted the funeral Psalm (Psalm 91) seven times, beginning:

> You who enjoy God's protectiveness
> Resting in His Heavenly shade
> Admit that the Lord is your fortress
> Your refuge and your barricade.
>
> The Holy One will soon subdue
> The fiercest gales that rainstorms bring
> For He is ever guarding you
> Within the shelter of His mighty wing. . . .

and ending:

> "When he calls to Me I will answer
> I will help him in his strife

Then I will bring him lasting honor
And will give to him long life.

"So a good and humble person –
He who trusts and follows Me –
Will enjoy My full salvation
Through a glorious Eternity."

Meshulam had a fine and mellow voice, and he chanted the Psalm in beautiful singsong tones.

As the funeral approached the southern gate, the gatekeeper heard Meshulam chanting. The evil gatekeeper smiled. He reached up, he pulled the heavy hemp rope, and he began to toll the Thor Glocke bell over and over and over. Then he began to laugh.

The southern gate was a sign of the strength of the city. The belltower was high: it was a watchtower, and it was visible from afar. The bell rang, the gatekeeper laughed – and a wind began to blow. The wind came from out beyond the city. It came from deep in the north. It flowed over the roofs of Cologne, and it rushed toward the tall southern gate. The belfry rang out. The wind blew in. And, suddenly, the gatekeeper sneezed.

The gatekeeper sneezed and immediately he fell over dead, and the bell ceased its tolling and the belfry crumbled and it collapsed in the snow. The Jews felt the wind pass over their heads. They shivered and pulled their coats about them. When the bell fell silent, the whole land fell silent, but the funeral procession continued on. The solemn marchers reached the gate. They walked unimpeded through the rubble and out beyond the city limits. Then they reached the *Am Toten Juden,* and Makir was given a quiet burial on that cold, cold medieval *Tevet* day.

And that is the story, exactly as my grandmother told it to me. If you do not believe this tale, Rabbi, then go to Cologne, and you will see for yourself that a belfry has never been rebuilt on the old southern gate. In fact, even today this is a place where the sun and the light and the moon and the stars seem to grow dark; it is a place where the clouds return after the rain and near which the homeowners sometimes tremble; it is a place where men are afraid of heights and of dangers in the streets and where no bells ring anymore and where always there is a sad and respectful silence. And why is this? Ah, Rabbi, that is one of the many mysteries that shall remain a secret forever in the town of Cologne on the edge of the dark wide River Rhine, the ancient River Rhine.

ood evening, Rabbi. No sleep for the weary? That is what my grandmother said, and she said it almost nightly. If you are cold then sit down here on the bench and I will stoke up the oven. This stoker? It is one of the iron shoe scrapers from the front hall. Of course, there are still two scrapers in the anteroom for dirty shoes – but I myself am of the old school: I think that all pious men should take off their shoes, enter the synagogue humbly, and pray barefoot. Did you know that Abba Mari not only prayed barefoot, he also wrote barefoot? Well, that is what I have heard.

Bare feet are quite holy: they symbolize humility. They also signify the most serious of intents. In the Book of Ruth, it is written:

> In those olden days, when property was redeemed or exchanged, it was the custom for a man to pull off his sandal and to give it to the other party; this was the form of solemn avowal in Israel.

Oh, I know that some rabbis are critical of exposed feet, but they are referring to unlaced shoes or to those showy shoes with no tops. Barefoot is humble, and I am certain that barefoot is holy. Remember – Abba Mari himself always worked barefoot. Of course this barefoot piety was just one example of Abba Mari's strong reaction against the secularism and the rationalism that was sweeping Europe in those days. . . . Exactly, Rabbi–that was at the end of the thirteenth century; Abba Mari ben Moses ben Joseph grew up in the late Middle Ages in Lunel, near Montpellier, France.

As a young man, Abba Mari was brilliant. Soon he became a rabbi and he devoted himself to the defense of orthodox religion. In those days, parallel rationalist movements were ongoing in both the Christian and the Jewish communities. In the late Middle Ages, the Christian universities had immortalized Aristotle; they called him *"The Philosopher."* Full courses were devoted to each of his major treatises– the *Physics*, the *Metaphysics*, and the *Ethics*. Even devout Christian theologians (such as Albertus Magnus of Cologne and his student Thomas Aquinas of Paris) were fascinated by Aristotle's organized reasoning, and Christian doctrine was organized and explained in the style of Aristotle's philosophy.

And what of the Jews? Well, as I am talking about Abba Mari, let me begin in Montpellier, in the south of France. Montpellier was the clearinghouse for trade between northern Europe, Italy, and the countries of the eastern Mediterranean. Montpellier was a Jewish commercial center and it had a famous medieval rabbinical college. Abba Mari was one of the intellectual leaders in Montpellier–and in Montpellier, Abba Mari continually worried over the Aristotelian rationalism that had seeped into the strong tried-and-true spiritual traditions of Judaic philosophy.

"It was Maimonides," thought Abba Mari, "who let the pagan and unspiritual philosophy of Aristotle into Jewish culture. Now the extremists who follow Maimonides are threatening the authority of the Torah. They deny miracles. They deny revelations. They exclude the unknowable and the suprahuman. They are losing the Divine spirituality of religion."

Abba Mari could not sit quietly and watch the destruction of all that he considered truly wondrous–truly holy–in Judaism. He lectured, and he argued. Then he wrote a set of letters to Jewish leaders throughout Europe. Strengthen the traditional teachings! he wrote. The letters that Abba Mari ben Moses sent to Rabbi Solomon ben Abraham ben Adret of Barcelona have been collected and published as *Minhat Kenaot*, the "Jealousy Offering." Among the other famous rabbis who received a letter from Abba Mari was Asher ben Yehiel, while he was still in Cologne. This letter arrived in Cologne with a traveling merchant Jew from southern France. The letter came one cold winter afternoon in the month of *Tevet*—it arrived on one afternoon when the tiny white sun had a keen bite to it.

"My dear friend and holy colleague,
Asher, the son of Yehiel—[wrote Abba Mari]

"I have heard of the thoughtful scholarship that flourishes under your direction in the Jewish communities of the rich Rhine valley. I know that the good Lord God (blessed be He) has shined down His warm smile and His loving kindness on you and all your colleagues and on the many eager young children in your yeshivas, amen.

"I write because, frankly, I am afraid. My dear colleague, I feel that some unspiritual temptations have crept into the old and holy Judaic traditions. These are subtle demons, and they entice the young in ways that will work against us all in the long term. Specifically, I am speaking of the trend to try and explain everything in simple and rational terms. There is an arrogance overtaking the philosophical side of our theology. We Jews have many clever and even brilliant young men, and their quickness often makes them arrogant. However, as you and I both know, a great religion is not about brilliant arrogance. Arrogance is selfishness, and the great gift of the Almighty Lord is just the opposite: it is selflessness—it is humility.

"Selflessness appears in many forms. At base, however, selflessness is the true understanding that there is more in the world than just us. There are things beyond our grasps, both physical and mental. For example, there are miracles. Unfortunately, modern rationalism denies miracles. In the choice between Moses and Aristotle or between the authorities of the Talmud and the upholders of *logical philosophy*, give me Moses and the Talmud. I sometimes wonder that it is even necessary for me to say such things aloud—and, Rabbi Asher, I despair. Nowadays book after book seems smoothly to justify a simple and completely comprehensible universe, but this position threatens the dissolution of all Judaism.

"My good friend, what can we do? I have had much correspondence with the well-known Rabbi Solomon ben Adret of Barcelona.

He, too, is worried. As he says: 'Strangers have forced their way through the gates of Zion.' Ben Adret even encouraged me to organize a conservative union; he would have it oppose the extreme scientific teachings of glib rationalists. However, I think that a formal conservative organization would be too divisive. Instead, I am writing to our many colleagues in order to present my views.

"I hesitate to push forcefully any dictums. Nonetheless, I would encourage one specific measure: perhaps we should restrict the literature that is available to malleable young minds. Some of the rationalist writings are simply too seductive. They must be presented in a balanced context; otherwise, they can overwhelm the quieter and humbler traditions. These traditions, of course, are the modest and mature understandings upon which our long-lasting Judaism has been built.

"Now, Rabbi, should secular literature be prohibited from Jewish youths until their thirtieth year? By age thirty, men are mature. They have already filled their minds with the Holy Scriptures and with the Talmud. Only then should Jews be allowed to warm themselves by the strange fires of *logical philosophy* and *natural science*.

"Well, my friend, that is the essence of my suggestion – I leave it to you to judge its merit. Let me now turn to a political matter. You may have heard of a dispute between myself and another Montpellier scholar, Jacob ben Machir Tibbon. The truth of the matter has been distorted, and now it threatens to obscure the more important problem – an issue on which both Reb Jacob and I agree. Both of us are quite worried about the blind acceptance of scientific, overly logical explanations of our God-given World.

"But, Rabbi Asher, there I go dragging out my old hobby-horse again. I had best tell the story from its proper beginnings. As I was saying: here in Montpellier lives an esteemed scholar named Jacob ben Machir Tibbon. I have known this man for many years. He was schooled both in Judaism and in the secular sciences – in fact, he practices medicine quite successfully. (I am told that his mathematics is also highly respected by astronomers and that he has said some profound and accurate things about the tilt of the world as it rolls though God's great celestial skies – hallelujah and amen.)

"Moreover, Reb Jacob knows Arabic, and he has translated many secular books into Hebrew. Jacob Tibbon hopes to show the Gentile world that we Jews can hold our own in this new age, with its rationalistic explanations of all phenomena. 'In happier times,' Jacob Tibbon has said, 'Jews were immersed in all the aspects of culture. I would like to demonstrate that nowadays we continue to participate in the advance of knowledge on all fronts.' Nonetheless, Reb Jacob has told me that he, too, does not want the true, holy, and mystical underpinnings of Judaism to be lost in the process.

"Therefore, I approached Jacob Tibbon with my idea – namely, restricting the access of secular literature for our impressionable youth. Unfortunately, Tibbon would not listen. On this subject, he has a blind spot: he has invested so much of his time and energy in making the profane literature available in Hebrew that he could not admit the necessity for my proposal. Even the strong endorsement of the Barcelona rabbinate could not overcome Jacob Tibbon's attachments to the flawed secular literature.

"In fact, it was over a thoughtful communication from Rabbi Solomon ben Adret that things degenerated. As you have probably heard, Rabbi Solomon of Barcelona sent me a closely reasoned and supportive letter. It was essential that we air these views here in the college in Montpellier. Thus, my colleagues and I convened a special meeting of the local scholars in the synagogue, on a Sabbath during last *Elul*.

"Before the meeting, Reb Jacob asked me not to present formally the letter from Barcelona. Clearly this plea was based on a purely emotional response. How could it be otherwise? Is Jacob ben Machir Tibbon not a proponent of completely free speech? Why, he has even taken the position that one must listen politely to the antireligious rhetoric of the secular rationalists!

"Excuse me for that tirade, Rabbi Asher. You can see that I feel quite strongly about these problems. As I was saying: we convened a special meeting one Sabbath. I remember it well – it was a hot and sticky day in the month of *Elul*. We read Rabbi Solomon's letter, and there was much lively discussion. A number of supporters of Reb Jacob gave impassioned speeches. They claimed that we were 'enslaving the intellect.' Certainly we all realized that we were being forced to suggest drastic measures. The restriction of literature is a painful step. Some thoughtful men refused even to participate in our group decision. In the end, we could not come to an agreement, and the meeting dissolved with much bad feeling. However, since then, twenty-five esteemed members of our congregation have signed a petition in favor of our position, and I have sent this document to Rabbi Solomon.

"The followers of Jacob Tibbon were angry. They suggested that I had some personal animosity against the good Reb Jacob. Such slandering does not help. I am truly sad that we were forced to suggest extreme measures. At the same time, I cannot accept the arguments put forth by the secularists. They have made such statements as: 'If a man is not familiar with science before his thirtieth year, then he will be permanently incapable of studying it.' Now I ask you, good colleague, do you believe this? As our age advances, do we become incapable of reasoning, of understanding, of insight, or of further learning? Why, that goes against all that we hold dear! Jews revere wisdom, and wisdom comes with age. A child is born with a clean gray slate in his mind, and over the years we continue to write on that slate. And, my friend, the writing never ends. That is why we have the obligation to study until the very day that we die, amen.

"In any case, I think that finally reason has prevailed. Both Rabbi Solomon and I have sent copies of our resolutions throughout Spain, France, and Germany. Of course, every Jewish congregation is independent—resolutions of one community have no official standing in any other. Nonetheless, many Jewish communities have endorsed our position. Specifically, I might mention the formal statements from the leaders of Aix, Argentiere, Avignon, Beaucaire, and Lunel, besides, of course, the active support of the respected scholars of Barcelona.

"And so, my holy colleague, I write to keep you fully informed and to enlist your support also; we would appreciate the encouragement of the thoughtful and spiritually devout communities of the Rhinelands. I know that you are committed personally to these same goals. I know that you, too, hope to hold at bay the glib and facile rhetoric of those who would speak solely with their minds and not with their hearts. A Jew must be modest and humble—he must listen intently to his God-given soul.

"The great Lord God made man different from the animals. And exactly how are we unique? Do we differ from animals in our tools, in our constructive use of materials? No, my friend, for birds build nests using straw and sticks and mud. Do we differ from animals in our ability to communicate? No—birds sing to each other, and in fact all baby animals 'talk' to their mothers. Then do we, perhaps, differ from animals in our clothes? No again, for it is exactly the opposite: many animals are clothed in feathers and fur, while holy men work, study, and pray barefoot.

"Of course, Rabbi Asher, there are our wonderful creative minds: our agile minds distinguish us somewhat from other creatures. However, even more fundamentally, there are our souls. Our souls are deep and compassionate. These souls set us apart from all other creatures. The human soul is an inscrutable gift of the Lord. It is a gift of selfless mystery. And *this* is the humility that I spoke of before: it is the honest humility of the unfathomable human soul.

"The soul is the witness of our humble role. The good Lord God and His world are greater than any mortal man – this we learn clearly and humbly by looking deep within our unknowable soul. There is simply no honest place for arrogance. In the end, we must openly admit that our God and our world are not fully knowable. We are not complete masters of our wondrous and incondensably complex world – our soul is simply too deep. The unfathomable mystery of the world is the unfathomable ineffable mystery that is forever captive within our God-given human soul.

> *"Your humble friend and colleague,*
> *Abba Mari, the son of Moses"*

ood evening, Rabbi. You are having difficulty sleeping again? Put your feet up on that side bench and I will open the stove door. Let me push the coals back. There is nothing like the white glow of the night oven to wash away the cares of a hard day.

I heard your final prayers tonight. You are overworked, Rabbi— even an old shammas like me can tell. I kept one eye on you when I was cleaning the dishes, and I saw that you were watching the door, hoping that Reb Elbaum would leave early. But then Reb Anton stayed late to discuss one of your favorite passages from the Book of Deuteronomy:

> If a man is poor, then do not sleep in the cloak that he has pledged to you, even if he now owes it to you. Instead, give it back to him at sunset as charity so that he may sleep in it. Return his cloak and give him a blanket besides, and he will bless you. Then such good deeds will be counted to your credit in the sight of the Almighty Lord God ever after.

Listening to Reb Anton and Reb Lavan discuss this passage, I could almost hear *you* reminding us of the importance of charity.

But when I closed my eyes, it was no longer you, but rather it seemed to be my grandmother telling one of her many, many stories. She was relating an incident from the study hall of Achselrad of Cologne; Achselrad was her favorite rabbi, an old mystical scholar from those dim medieval days in Germany, along the wide dark River Rhine.

Once upon a time, said my grandmother to me, in the congregation headed by Abraham ben Alexander, Achselrad of Cologne, there was a pious man named Nahum ben Isaac ha-Levi. Nahum recited his prayers three times a day; then in gentle succession, these holy devotions ascended to Heaven like the daily sacrifices formerly offered on the altar. Good Nahum was a happy man who kept strictly to the rules. He was righteous and proud, and he had made a vow never to accept a gift from anyone. At the moment, Nahum was quite poor, and every day he went to search in the dust bins, in the garbage piles, and in the local waste dumps, trying to find some useful discard.

Surprisingly, modest Nahum had an ostentation: there was one special bit of finery that he treasured. It was a vest. As poor as he was, Nahum wore a beautiful vest every day. This was a vest that his father, Isaac, had received as a gift from a wealthy man, years and years ago. Originally, the vest came from Venice. It was made of closely woven cloth, a mixture of silk and wool. It was stitched with geometric designs, and at the edges it was interlaced with a pure gold thread. When Nahum wore this vest, he felt very good indeed.

At the same time, Nahum was at peace with himself deep inside his soul. Therefore, one day, one cold wintry day, when Nahum's child became quite ill and food was in short supply, Nahum sold his vest with no second thoughts. Nahum ben Isaac pawned his vest with a clothes broker for three gold coins.

Other than the vest, Nahum had no fine clothes and he had no other special pleasures in life. Now, Rabbi, the good Lord God Himself is often occupied with deep and serious matters at the far corners of His thick and tangled world. However, just as the world is awash with thousands of demons, dybbuks, and devils, so it is also filled to overflowing with a myriad of wandering angels. When Nahum pawned his vest, Hasdiel, a holy angel of the Lord, was passing by.

Hasdiel opened wide his bright eyes, he listened well with his softestand tiniest ears, and then he flew up directly to Heaven. "O Lord my God," said the angel, "You know poor Nahum ben Isaac ha-Levi (as You know all Your creatures, both man and beast)."

"Ah, yes," replied the Omnipotent One, "Nahum is a fine and righteous Jew in Cologne."

Hasdiel nodded, but he could not look directly upon the brilliant radiance of his Master, so he looked at the Lord's feet. "My good Lord," said Hasdiel, "Nahum is humble. He has had a life of misery. Now he has been forced to pawn his one pleasure in life, the vest that his father gave to him."

"Well," said the glorious Lord God, "by all means go back to earth and help him out, Hasdiel. Begin by giving him eight gold coins."

So Hasdiel, the archangel of benevolence, slipped from the Holy Court of the Lord, and he returned to Cologne. There the angel found poor Nahum walking home from his daily search for useful discards in the trash heaps. Hasdiel floated down to the ground, and he appeared to Nahum in the form of a human.

"My good sir," said Hasdiel, "I have been assigned to give you eight gold coins."

Nahum raised his eyebrows. "Eight gold coins," he repeated. "That is too kind of you. However, I have vowed never to accept a present." Then Nahum quickly turned away and he began walking off in the other direction.

"Just a moment," said Hasdiel. Nahum stopped.

And Hasdiel continued: "This is no gift."

Nahum turned back toward the angel. "This is no gift," repeated Hasdiel. "Actually, it is a loan. I have been instructed by a Benefactor (Whom I am not at liberty to name) to give you a loan of eight gold coins, without interest."

"It is a loan?" asked Nahum.

"Yes," said Hasdiel.

"For how long?"

"It is a loan for one year," replied Hasdiel, holding out the money.

Nahum's eyes opened wide. Hesitantly, he took the coins. "How will I find you to pay you back?" he asked.

"Do not worry," said the angel. "*I* will find *you*."

Nahum looked down at the coins in his hand, and when he looked up again, the angel had disappeared.

As he walked home in wonderment, Nahum passed the shop of the clothing pawnbroker. Nahum stopped. He walked in the door, and he saw that his vest had not yet been sold.

"I would like to buy back my vest," said Nahum.

"Very well," said the pawnbroker, "that will be four gold coins."

"But you only paid me three coins for it, just a few days ago," said Nahum.

"True, but I have expenses," said the man. "Furthermore, just this morning, a gentleman came in and said that he would probably return to buy the vest for five gold coins. Out of sentiment, though, I will let you have it for four – if you have the money right now."

Nahum hesitated, but then he took out four of his new gold coins, and he traded them for the vest.

Nahum felt happy. He had his vest again, and he had four gold coins in his pocket. Therefore, he walked directly to the synagogue. Nahum stepped into the anteroom, where he removed his shoes, which were old, dirty, and tattered. He walked into the main prayer hall. He sat down and he looked up at the Holy stone Ark – and although it was a cold day outside, he felt warmed by the sun passing through the twelve stained glass windows with their colored lions and snakes.

"My son is getting better. We have some food in the house. And I have my father's fine vest again," thought Nahum. Therefore he stood and he put three of his remaining gold coins into the poorbox. Now he felt very good indeed, and he put on his shoes and he began to walk home.

Nahum decided to walk through the marketplace, in the hope of finding some discarded item that he might sell or at least bring home. As he passed by the clothing shops, a stranger walked up to him.

"Just a moment," said the man. "Where did you get that vest?"

Nahum stopped. "Well, sir, it was handed down to me from my father."

"Would you consider selling it?" asked the stranger.

Nahum looked down at his vest. "I think not," he said.

"Listen, my friend – sell me that vest. I will pay you twenty-four gold coins."

Nahum was amazed. He raised his eyebrows, and he opened wide his eyes. Again he looked down at his vest. He hesitated, and then he said, "That is very tempting—but I think that I must say no."

This made the other man all the more interested. "No? Not even for twenty-four gold coins?" asked the man. He stood silently a moment and tapped his chin. "My friend, that is a beautiful vest. Twenty-four gold coins is all that I have with me at the moment. How much money would you need in order to sell it to me?"

Nahum looked down at his vest again. Gently he rubbed his fingers on a smooth spot that he liked especially. "Thank you, sir," said Nahum, "but I would rather not sell my vest. It came from my father."

"Hmm, it is a patrimony," said the man, stroking his chin. "Well, then why not turn it into a patrimony for your children?"

"What do you mean?" asked Nahum.

"I will be honest with you," said the stranger. "I deal in fine linens, as well as many other goods. The vest you have is a rare and wonderful work. I immediately recognized it as a treasure from Italy, probably from Venice, and I would love to own it. I will buy it from you for one hundred gold coins."

Nahum could not believe his ears, and he took a step backward. The man thought that Nahum might leave. "Just a moment, my friend—not only will I give you one hundred gold coins for that vest," said the man, "I will also give you a stock of wine, so that you may begin in the wine wholesale business. Soon you, too, will be wealthy. In this way, your vest will remain a patrimony: it will have turned into a financial inheritance that you can pass on to your children."

Nahum was stunned. Finally he nodded his head. "Good, good," said the linen merchant happily. "You come to my shop on Hohestrasse Street tomorrow morning. Bring the vest, and we will make all the arrangements. And please take good care of that invaluable vest!"

Nahum turned around and he walked home in a daze. He told his wife that a miracle had occurred. She patted him on the shoulder and then she dished out a plate of stewed cabbage.

The next morning, after his prayers, Nahum ben Isaac ha-Levi found the linen dealer's shop in the market area of Hohestrasse Street. Exactly as he had been promised, Nahum traded his vest for one hundred gold coins and arrangements were made to set him up in the business of wholesaling wine.

Nahum worked hard. Soon he became rich. He bought houses and shops and land. He had warehouses, and he even owned trading ships and barges for moving his goods up and down the River Rhine between Bonn, Cologne, and Duisburg, and between Dusseldorf, Karlsruhe, Mainz, Mannheim, and Rotterdam. But as business improved, Nahum had to deal with all manner of difficulties. Middlemen complained about shipping schedules. One of his workers stole an entire load of engraved swords. Bonn levied a special shipping tax on Jews. A Cologne merchant accused Nahum of not paying a debt. Then one of Nahum's sons began doing very poorly in the yeshiva, and the boy was asked to find another school at which to study.

Nahum worried constantly. He did not sleep well. Frequently he could not get to the synagogue to pray, even once a day. Although he seemed prosperous, much of Nahum's financial dealings involved risk and credit, and he always worried about money. One day a poor man came to Nahum's main office and asked for some money; Nahum sent him to see a clerk, who gave the beggar nothing. Later that week, the gabbai from the Cologne congregation called on Nahum for an extra contribution, but Nahum said that things were going very poorly at the moment and that he could not afford any extra charity.

Of course, these acts did not escape the far-seeing and ever-watchful Lord God Almighty. Therefore, the angel Hasdiel was again sent to the Rhinelands to visit Nahum ben Isaac. Hasdiel came one evening, in the form of a human. He came to the house of Nahum, he knocked on the door, and when Nahum's son answered, Hasdiel said, "Is your father at home?" The boy did not invite the stranger in. After a moment, Nahum appeared. "Yes?" he asked.

"Do you remember me," asked Hasdiel.

It was dark. Nahum frowned for a moment. Then he said, "Oh yes, you were the kind man who lent me eight gold coins some time ago."

"I have come to reclaim my loan," said the angel Hasdiel.

"Very well," said Nahum. He turned and he went into the kitchen; then he took eight gold coins from a moneybox and he brought them back to the front door. "Here," said Nahum, handing the money to the angel. "Thank you very much for the loan."

Hasdiel carefully studied the coins. As Nahum turned to go back inside, the angel said, "Just a moment, sir."

"Yes?"

"These are not the coins that I gave to you," said Hasdiel.

Nahum raised his eyebrows again. "What do you mean?"

"I mean simply this: you have given me eight gold coins. However, I want the *same* eight gold coins that I gave you one year ago."

"That is silly," said Nahum.

"Give me your cashbox," said the angel.

Nahum frowned. He looked at the angel. The angel looked like an ordinary man, but somehow the world seemed to darken and Nahum felt afraid. Nahum went back into his kitchen. He returned with a locked wooden box. He unlocked the box and held it open in front of Hasdiel, the Lord's angel of benevolence.

Hasdiel looked into Nahum's eyes and not at the box. The angel reached into the cashbox. Swiftly he pulled out eight gold coins. "Are those the original coins?" asked Nahum.

Hasdiel said nothing but continued staring into Nahum's eyes. Nahum looked away. When he looked back, the angel had disappeared.

Nahum's stomach tightened. He went back into the house, but he slept poorly that night. Nahum felt uncomfortable throughout the next day. Restlessly, he walked about the kitchen; then he paced the yard. In the afternoon, the weather turned cold. Nahum was too upset to pray at all that day.

On the following day, Nahum went to work. Things seemed quiet, and Nahum felt that everything was normal again. Over the next few weeks, however, business began to deteriorate. A building that he owned along the edge of the River Rhine caught fire. One of his wine suppliers died and many scheduled deliveries had to be canceled. Two of Nahum's barges were found to be so rotted that they had to be abandoned at the docks in the city of Kehl. A cold and wet week caused Nahum's stocks of corn to turn moldy. Creditors took legal action, and he was forced to sell much of his remaining merchandise and buildings. And by the middle of the bitter winter, Nahum was once again poor. Nahum had nothing to pawn, and, of course, he no longer had his vest. Now Nahum was destitute, unhappy, and ashamed.

It was the cold, cold winter, the month of *Kislev*. Nahum was depressed. The other merchants and businessmen avoided him. At best, Nahum's neighbors considered him unlucky. Some said that he had bad judgment. Others speculated that he might actually be dishonest. Now no one would hire Nahum and he could not earn any money. Therefore, Nahum again took to looking for saleable discards in dirty corners and in trash heaps: every day he went to search in the dust bins, in the garbage piles, and in the local waste dumps, trying to find something useful to salvage.

One afternoon, Nahum was so cold that he went into the synagogue in order to get warm. Nahum ben Isaac stepped in the front door. He removed his tattered snowy shoes. He went through the anteroom, and he walked into the main prayer hall, which was filled with wooden benches. He passed the twelve stained glass windows with their colored lions and snakes, he looked up at the Holy Ark made of stone, and he walked to the door of the back study room. A number of the community scholars were sitting, warming themselves on the benches by the stove, and the Rabbi was bent over a book.

The sages nodded to Nahum, who returned their greeting. Nahum walked over to the stove. He rubbed his cold hands. "How are you today?" asked the white-haired Baruch ben Jacob.

"Not too well, Reb Baruch," said Nahum ben Isaac.

"We do not see you here often," said a younger man, Elisah ben Samuel.

"I have had many difficulties in my life," said Nahum. "Recently, I cannot seem to get enough money to support my family."

"None of us is rich," said Joshua ben Eliezer.

Nahum nodded silently.

Another sage, Lewe ben Anselm, said, "Not long ago, Nahum, you had much money, but in the Book of Proverbs it is written":

> Do not worship wealth and ease,
> Be sensible and give up greed;
> Before you turn, up comes a breeze –
> Gold disappears, wealth will recede,
> Money grows swift wings and flees
> Like an eagle, a fleet bird of speed.

The other scholars stroked their beards, and they murmured "amen."

"Ah, my good colleague Lewe, that is an apt quote," said Menahem ben Joel. "And it reminds me of another useful statement from the Book of Proverbs":

> Wealth is a light commodity
>   On Judgment Day,
> But goodness, alms, and charity
>   Shall heavily weigh.

> Generosity and virtue,
>   Kind words with each breath–
> These will protect you
>   From a sad and early death.

Again, the other scholars nodded and they murmured "amen."

Moyses ben Nathan had been standing near the stove. His coat was getting hot so he went over to a bench and sat down again. Then he said, "We can never have enough of the Book of Proverbs, Nahum; for instance, in those holy chapters it is also written":

> The sweet fruits of righteousness
>   Fill the Tree of the Lord–
> And those who serve with humility
>   Will harvest a rich reward.

Finally, old Shimshon ha-Zaken coughed, and he said in a hoarse voice, "How true, gentlemen–how true. And then do not forget the scriptural Proverb":

> He who is generous to the poor
>   Lends to the Lord Himself,
> And God will repay the charity-doer
>   From the fullness of His shelf.

Nahum was sitting sadly on one of the benches. "Good scholars," he said, "that counsel is for some other man. I am a poor beggar. I *do* remember a man named Nahum ben Isaac ha-Levi. He was a man with my name and with my face. But this man was wealthy, and I am poor."

Nahum shook his head. "What went wrong?" he asked, staring at his feet.

The scholars looked at one another. After a minute, white-bearded Baruch ben Jacob said again, "We have not seen you here recently, good Nahum."

"Yes—as I said, I have been beset by problems," said Nahum.

The younger scholar, Elisah ben Samuel, said, "We all have problems, my friend."

Nahum nodded, but he said, "My daily life requires all my energy, Elisah."

Joshua ben Eliezer said, "You do not seem happy, Nahum."

Nahum was silent, so Lewe ben Anselm said, "Nahum, something is missing. You have forgotten something."

And Menahem ben Joel added quietly, "Yes, Nahum—you have forgotten to pray."

The other men nodded, and Moyses ben Nathan said, "In the Book of Proverbs, it is said":

> The Almighty turns His radiant head,
>   Standing aloof from the wicked crowd;
> But the good Lord listens closely instead
>   To the prayers of the righteously endowed.

And old Shimshon ha-Zaken coughed, and he said in a hoarse voice, "How true, gentlemen—and then do not forget the other scriptural Proverb":

> If you ignore the Law
>   Then even fervent prayer
> Invokes the Lord God's wrath,
>   And by leading the unaware
> Along an evil path
>   Then in your own cruel snare
> You will be caught at last—
>   But you will get a Heavenly chair
> By holding to God steadfast.

The scholars nodded and they shifted on the benches and they murmured among themselves. Nahum ben Isaac ha-Levi sat silently, staring down at his hands. Old Rabbi Abraham had listened quietly during these interchanges. Finally he said, "Nahum, may I put in a word here?"

"Certainly, Rabbi," said Nahum slowly.

Rabbi Abraham closed his book. "I would follow my colleagues, Reb Nahum, by reminding you of another passage from the Holy Scriptures – this is the last verse in the Book of Ecclesiastes":

> Now all has been heard. Here, then, is the conclusion of the matter: revere God and keep His commandments, for this is the whole duty of man. In the end, the great Lord God (blessed be He) will bring every deed into judgment, including every hidden thing, whether it be good or evil.

The scholars all nodded, and some of them said "amen."

Rabbi Abraham was silent. He looked at the ceiling. After a moment, Nahum asked, "Exactly what are you saying, Rabbi?"

"Reb Nahum," said Rabbi Abraham ben Alexander, Achselrad of Cologne, "simply go home and be good – and be sure to be charitable to the best of your means."

Nahum was about to speak, but the scholars had again begun to talk among themselves and the Rabbi had turned back to his writing. After a moment, Nahum quietly left the back room of the old yeshiva behind Judengasse Street.

It was a cold, cold afternoon in the month of *Kislev*. Nahum stuffed his hands into his pockets. He walked slowly, looking at his feet. Nahum walked slowly, and he thought, "I was poor before – but at least I was happy."

And, Rabbi, I remember that at this point in the story, my grandmother stopped and she looked up at me. She looked up from her embroidery – the handwork with which she busied her old fingers each day when she sat at the edge of her mother's grave – she looked up, she smiled, and then she said, "My little one, you are young and you look forward, but I am old and I look backward. And with my backward-looking eyes, I see that of all the many things that I have done, the best has been helping others – you and the rest of my family, and even strangers. Charity means making other people a little happier. In the end, you will look backward also. And you too will rest content if, because of your charity, you can remember the happy faces of others."

And what happened to Nahum? Instead of going home and instead of continuing to search for old discards, he turned around. Nahum ben Isaac ha-Levi went back to the yeshiva. He stood a moment in the anteroom. Again he removed his tattered snowy shoes, and he walked into the main prayer hall, which was filled with wooden benches. Nahum sat on one of the benches. He looked up at the Holy Ark made of stone. The twelve stained glass windows with their colored lions and snakes let in the late winter light. Nahum sat for many minutes. He remembered his vest – but he was no longer sad. Nahum remembered his vest, and he smiled. Then he stood, and he put on his shoes and he walked out into the snowy streets. As he stepped along, he gently patted the shoulder of a young man that he passed. For even if he had no money, he could at least give someone a friendly touch.

ood evening, Rabbi. I was just resting my eyes – please, join me here by the stove. (I think you will be too warm on that bench: try the one nearer to the wall.) An old man like me can doze forever by a warm stove; I suppose that is because I try not to sin.

How does sleepiness relate to sins? Well, Rabbi, my grandmother used to tell me that a sinful man cannot sleep at night – or perhaps it was that not sleeping at night is a sin. Let me see if I can remember exactly what she said. . . . I think that she would begin with a quote from the Talmud, where it says:

> It is impossible for a human being to live without sleep for three consecutive days. This is implied in the law: "If a man says that he will not sleep for three days, then he is to be criticized or even punished. And he must sleep forthwith, because he has sinned: he has made a vain oath that is impossible to fulfill except with fatal consequences."

Attempting to stay up for three or more days is a sin. Of course, it is a very strange sin, and if one acquired it, then one might not easily get rid of it. What is that, Rabbi? Onion juice? Rabbi – wherever did you hear that? Onion juice is a cure for baldness, not for sins. No, in order to rid yourself of sins – sins such as sitting for an hour without thinking of the good Lord God (blessed be He) and sins such as forcing yourself to go without sleep for three or more days – you must put some bread crumbs in your pocket and go to a river. Yes, yes, Rabbi – I am speaking of Tashlik: Tashlik can expiate *any* sin.

You do not believe in Tashlik? Now listen to me, Rabbi: Does not *Rosh Hashanah* begin the Ten Days of Penitence, ending with the holy Day of Atonement? Well, as the first act of penitence, you must cast off last year's sins – that is, you must perform Tashlik. My grandmother told me that the Tashlik rituals originated in the Rhinelands, at the time of the mystic Abraham Achselrad. In those days all pious Jews took a pilgrimage to the River Rhine on the afternoon of the first day of *Rosh Hashanah*; there, they recited the verse from the Book of Micah:

> Once more You smile on me
> With affection tenderly
> And You wash me clean and guilt-free
> Casting my sins and my misdeeds
> Down to the depths of the sea.

The penitents would toss bits of crumbs and lint and fluff from their pockets into the waters, to symbolize the casting off of their sins. Fish swarmed around and ate the bits of food that rained down on them. (My grandmother said that demons, dybbuks, and devils also hid in her pockets and that she had to shake them out vigorously along with the sins when she reached the river. . . .)

What? No, no – do not get up on my account, Rabbi: I was just resting my eyes a moment. I was resting and musing. . . . Well, to tell you the truth, Rabbi, I was remembering the Tashlik of medieval Germany – I was thinking of a Tashlik story that my grandmother told me, from the days when old Abraham Achselrad was the Chief Rabbi of Cologne:

Once upon a time, said my grandmother to me, in the town of Gladbach east of Cologne, lived a vain self-centered young man named Nathan ben Aaron. Nathan was losing his hair, and every morning he rubbed his head with onion juice. Nathan was also a sinner; he was a very great sinner. In fact, he committed one sin after another. "What does it matter if I sin twice or if I sin sixty times?" he asked. "At the end of the year, I simply take all my sins, I drag them down to the edge of the water, I throw them into the lake, and that is the end of them. Then for the New Year I am a clean man again."

Yes, Rabbi, I am afraid that Nathan ben Aaron was an unrepentant sinner. (But may God not punish me for these words—because as the Book of Ecclesiastes says: "The world contains no man so righteous that he can do right always and never do wrong: there is not a man who never sins." So I suppose that we must let the great and final Arbiter, the good Lord God, blessed be He, judge Nathan in the end, amen.) However, I think that most people would agree that Nathan lived in sin from year to year. Each year on the first afternoon of *Rosh Hashanah*, he performed the Tashlik ceremony. Each year, the bundle of sins that he brought down to the edge of the water was greater than that of the year before. And each year, the lake by his home became a little blacker because of the terrible sins that he threw into it.

Now, Rabbi, many countries have special sin-eating demons in their deep and cold lakes, lakes that are actually bottomless and that extend down to the depths of the earth, to the very edge of the abyss of Sheol. I have heard that Scotland has such a demon; it is shaped like a huge serpent and it rolls and swims endlessly in one of the black crystalline fathomless Scottish lakes. Sweden, too, has a famous water-demon. My grandmother told me that it is a worm-like monster ten meters long and that its large neck waves back and forth like a horse's mane. These demon sea-serpents are imprisoned in the lakes for eternity; they feed on the sins that men cast into the waters, and they get longer and fatter from the Tashlik each year.

Nathan ben Aaron lived beside a deep dark lake, east of Cologne. In this lake lived an ancient Tashlik demon. "Fortunately, the lake is close to my house!" laughed Nathan. "I have not far to carry my sins; I might as well add a few more to the bundle." And the young and wild Nathan ben Aaron sinned all the more.

But his wife said, "Nathan, I wish you would stop your evil ways. We are all suffering—I and our relatives and our neighbors. And then, do not forget that we are extremely poor: because of your constant sinning, God keeps money from coming our way."

"Do you really think so?"

"Yes I do," said his wife.

"Well, perhaps you are right," said Nathan ben Aaron, and he thought no more about it. Instead, Nathan rubbed some onion juice in the thinning hair on his head.

I am afraid that there is no avoiding it, Rabbi—Nathan was simply a terrible sinner, and that year Nathan committed a sin that was even uglier than all his previous sins. This sin was huge and shapeless. It was like a great gruesome sponge, oozing and dripping with mud. It was moist and sticky and foul; to tell you the truth, Rabbi, it was quite dreadful.

Nathan ben Aaron could hardly find a place to store and to hide this nasty sin until the end of the year, when he could finally throw it into the lake. Eventually he put it in the cellar of his house. But there, the sin seemed to grow larger. Was the sin actually expanding? Yes, it must have been growing, because soon the cellar was not high enough to hold it. The smell and the mud of the sin began to squeeze through all the cracks. The sin began to ooze into the other rooms; it filled every corner of the house with its damp crawly odor. Finally, Nathan and his wife were forced to move into a small hut, where they had once kept goats.

At last, however, the New Year's Day came. Nathan took hold of the sin with both his arms. He pulled with all his might, and he managed to squeeze the foul thing out through the cellar door. Nathan tugged and he sweated. He got the sin out of the house. Then he pushed and pushed and he rolled it down to the lake.

Nathan ben Aaron rested. He took a deep breath. "There!" he said, as the sin sank into the water. "I am rid of that!" And he laughed and rubbed some onion juice on his head.

The lake was unsettled and upset. How could there be a sin so large and so ugly and so distasteful? The sin-eating Tashlik demon could barely force itself to look at Nathan's sin. The serpentine demon hissed and it shook itself. The poor water-demon heaved upward. It rolled from side to side. It thrashed about. But the sin could not be removed from the lake—it could not be hurled back into the air. In the primeval days of Creation, the Almighty Lord God had ordained that Tashlik demons must devour all the sins of man on the first day of each

New Year. Therefore, the poor frustrated sin-eating demon slowly began to gnaw at the sin, and after many, many days, the black waters became calmer again.

One week passed and then came two, and finally, after seven cycles of seven days, the lake became quiet – but the water was dark and black, and it had an unhealthy smell.

At this point in her story, my grandmother reminded me that the Book of Proverbs says:

> Do not thoughtlessly begin:
>   "My conscience is a clean board –
> I am purged from all my sin
>   And my innocence is restored."
> For a denial that is not genuine
> Is unacceptable to the Lord.

But Nathan must have forgotten this verse, for he went on sinning. Each year, the lake became blacker and more murky. At the same time, Nathan's few remaining hairs became grayer and thinner, and each morning he frowned and he rubbed more onion juice on his balding head. One day, his wife passed away, but Nathan could not bring himself to sit quietly for the full seven days of mourning.

And now Nathan lived totally alone. Did he continue to sin? Frankly, Rabbi, I do not know, and my grandmother did not tell me. In any case, Nathan and his wife had never had any children and Nathan got older and older all by himself, in his little dank house at the edge of a deep black murky medieval lake.

Eventually, Nathan died too. The women of the Burial Society prepared his body, and there was a short funeral that no one but the required scholars of the yeshiva attended. Into Nathan's casket one of the women of the Burial Society put two dried onions, at the side of the body. Later – just before the next New Year, said my grandmother – a wild onion plant grew over the grave of Nathan ben Aaron. But that was only the first year: nothing at all grew there forever after.

abbi, I am glad to see you here alone. I want to apologize for my outburst during the service this evening. Reb Anton was whispering about fruit–I distinctly heard him say "Apples."

I know that you are thinking: "What is the problem with fruit?" And I must admit that fruit is fine in its proper place. But where is its proper place? It is in the kitchen–fruit belongs in the kitchen, not in the prayer hall. (And then I suppose that fruit also belongs in dreams; for the Talmud tells us that dreams of fruit foretell prosperity.)

What is that? Well, all right, Rabbi, I admit that fruit can also have a religious place. Now that I think of it, I remember how my grandmother sometimes recited Psalm 17 in relation to apples:

> Bend down Your ear to me,
> Please listen to my petitioning
> And attend to my humble plea.

> Show me warmth and kindness,
> Give me Your love unfailing
> And grant me happiness.

Am I the apple of Your eye?
Then shelter me with Your mighty wing—
And shatter evil with Your war cry.

Likewise, in the Book of Deuteronomy it is said:

In the desert God cared for Israel,
In a waste both barren and dry;
He protected Jacob and He trained him well—
Israel is the apple of His eye.

Yes, exactly, Rabbi—the "apple of your eye" is the mysterious pupil. It is a special portal that is round like an apple and that is a window into the soul—so of course the "apple of your eye" is something near and dear and close to the soul. If we are the apples of the good Lord's eye, then undoubtedly apples are special to the Lord. Certainly apples have guarded many a Jew. What do I mean? Well I was thinking of Berachiah ben Jesse ha-Levi and the healing apples. You do not know about Berachiah? It is a curious tale. My grandmother told the story to me, and I gladly will tell it to you:

Berachiah ben Jesse ha-Levi was born long, long ago, in the little town of Strassebersbach, just north of Marburg. A Jew must be trained to the best of his ability, so the parents of young Berachiah scrimped and saved and they sent their son to study in Marburg, where a famous scholar, Rabbi David Tov, was the head of the yeshiva. Berachiah ben Jesse worked diligently for many years; he was an outstanding pupil and he learned much Torah and Talmud.

Rabbi David Tov had a beautiful and intelligent daughter named Leah. Leah was the Rabbi's only child, and one day she would inherit the family financial responsibilities. The Rabbi was in a hurry for her to marry so that she would not have to become a businesswoman and so that she would have a fine large family, and in this way she would speed the day of the arrival of the Messiah, amen.

Rabbi David talked with his wife, who said, "It is simple, David—look among your students for a good husband." The next day when the Rabbi went to his yeshiva, he looked thoughtfully at the young men while he lectured. When the Rabbi finished his talk, the boys began to leave the study hall. Rabbi David stroked his beard as he watched them go.

The Rabbi said to himself, "Old man, have you a student who is an outstanding scholar? Is there someone you would be happy to have as a son-in-law?" He thought about the various boys. Then he answered, "Yes, two young men are especially good students. One is Johanan, and the other is Berachiah. And I think that I prefer Berachiah." Rabbi David Tov returned home. He told his wife that there were two fine marriageable young men in his yeshiva. Both were good scholars. One was called Johanan and the other was called Berachiah, and Berachiah was a very special young man—when Berachiah talked, you might raise your eyebrows, but he always said something interesting. Rabbi David's wife nodded in approval.

However, interesting speech was not everything. David Tov still had to face a decision. Although Berachiah was brilliant, he was also very poor. Johanan, on the other hand, was rich and handsome as well as being a good student. The Rabbi said to himself, "I am old, and I have only one daughter. Today or tomorrow, I shall die—certainly, someday soon my end will come. Then there will be no one left to protect Leah. I had best decide soon. But who shall it be? One boy is rich and handsome, and one boy is especially well educated but poor." Rabbi David thought of these alternatives, and he worried all night long.

The next day, the Rabbi talked with his advisory scholars in the yeshiva. "Friends," he said, "I am old and I would like to see my daughter married. My two choices for a son-in-law are Johanan ben Israel and Berachiah ben Jesse. But I cannot decide which young man is best."

The men talked among themselves. Finally one of the old scholars said, "Both of the young men are worthy sons-in-law—they are good students, although one is rich and one is poor. Why not test their practical business sense? I suggest that each of these boys be given fifty gold coins and sent off to buy merchandise. Whoever brings home the best goods shall marry your daughter."

The Rabbi nodded—he thought that this was a fine idea. The next day he went to the yeshiva, he waited until the pupils were leaving, and then he asked both Johanan and Berachiah to remain for a moment. The Rabbi said, "Young men, you have learned much here under my guidance. I am proud of you both. I would like one of you to become my son-in-law."

The two boys looked at each other in amazement. Rabbi David continued: "I do not know how to choose between you. Therefore, I am giving each of you fifty gold coins. Now go off, young men, and buy things; buy any manner of goods. Whichever of you returns with the best values shall marry my daughter. You each have ten full months. Ten months from today, we shall have a wedding – this is my decree."

The boys opened wide their eyes, and they looked at one another. Hesitantly, they took the money from the Rabbi. Then they went to their homes. The boys packed their knapsacks, and they returned to the yeshiva. From there, they set out on their journey, with the Rabbi's blessings sounding gently in their ears. The two young men went away together – it was the cold winter month of *Kislev*, but the boys were full of warm joy in their hearts. They were good friends, and they were happy. They knew that the son-in-law of a rabbi often succeeded his father-in-law in the yeshiva. Each young man had golden visions, and it felt as if a delicious fried pigeon had flown, fully cooked, into their mouths.

After a time, the boys came to Mannheim, a beautiful town built around the castle of Eicholzheim. In the town itself, there was much fine merchandise for sale. Johanan bought precious stones with his money: he bought agates and amethysts, emeralds and onyx, and rubies and sapphires. Berachiah went to the other side of the marketplace, and he bought fine linens – exquisite pieces of baldachin, damask, samite, sarcenet, sendal, silk, and velvet, each with an intricate woven design.

Both young men were proud of their purchases. Together they started back for Marburg. When they were halfway home, they spent the night in an inn, outside the town of Darmstadt. Johanan's gems fit in a small sack, which he kept under his pillow. Berachiah's linens took up two large packs, which he set by the door. In the middle of the night, a thief silently entered the room and stole Berachiah's expensive linens. In the morning, the young men awoke to find that everything Berachiah had purchased was gone without a trace.

The boys were stunned. Finally, Johanan said, "My good friend, let me lend you some of my gems; then we can both return home early. Somehow the Rabbi will decide who should marry his daughter."

But Berachiah could not do this. He said, "That is a wonderful offer, Johanan. However, I cannot accept. Instead, you go back to Marburg alone. I still have many months, perhaps the good Lord God will yet bless me with something valuable to bring home."

Sadly, the two young men parted. When Johanan ben Israel came home with his goods, the townspeople asked him about Berachiah. Johanan replied, "I do not know where he is. We were forced to part company, and Berachiah decided to take the long road home."

The Rabbi saw the fine precious stones that Johanan had brought back with him to Marburg. "Well, I guess that Leah will end up marrying Johanan," thought Rabbi David. He shook his head, and he sighed. "I still think," he said to himself, "that Berachiah would have made a very good son-in-law."

Aloud, the Rabbi said, "Johanan, you have done well. We will wait and see what comes of Berachiah's adventure." And the Rabbi and Johanan and the other members of the Jewish community of Marburg settled back into their daily routines.

Meanwhile, Berachiah sat at a worn wooden table in the inn. "Now what shall I do?" he wondered. After a while, he thought sadly, "I must admit that I have failed: I have nothing valuable to bring back to Marburg, and I have spent all my money." He sat with his head in his hands. "Well, if I cannot fulfill my practical mission," he thought, "then at least I can make some good use of my remaining time. Here I am, out and about, away from home. What better can I do than to learn a bit more of the holy law and lore?"

Therefore, Berachiah ben Jesse ha-Levi traveled southeast from Darmstadt, in the opposite direction from Marburg, and eventually he reached Regensburg on the River Danube. In Regensburg lived Rabbi Juddah he-Hasid (the son of Samuel he-Hasid of Speyer). Rabbi Juddah was, of course, the famed mystical scholar who knew the whole Torah by heart and who knew many other strange and wondrous things besides. In Regensburg, Berachiah was more than one hundred and fifty kilometers away from Marburg, so Rabbi David Tov and his daughter Leah and Johanan ben Israel and all the other members of the Marburg Jewish community heard nothing directly from Berachiah ben Jesse ha-Levi for many long months.

Berachiah studied hard with his mystical teacher Juddah he-Hasid, and the young man became well versed in holy lore and in arcane knowledge. Berachiah learned the three great healing charms from Psalm 118. He learned the seven mystical signs and the seven holy Names. He learned the nine Divine symbols. In addition, Berachiah learned the two hundred and twenty-one sacred descriptions of the two hundred and twenty-one numinous Gates of Knowledge.

At the same time, Berachiah also learned archery. (Did you know that Rabbi Juddah was an accomplished archer? I am not inventing this, Rabbi: my grandmother, blessed be her memory, swore that it was true.) One day, Rabbi Juddah was instructing young Berachiah in the advanced mental art of archery. "Hold the bow taut," said the Rabbi. "Close your eyes and concentrate on that most holy set of letters *gimel* and *dalet*." Berachiah stretched the bow. He stood firm and he stood calm, and he thought of *gimel* and then of *dalet*. Suddenly the letter *dalet* reminded him of the name "David," and "David" brought to mind his old teacher, Rabbi David Tov.

"Oh my goodness," thought Berachiah, "if I am not in Marburg in a week with a treasure of valuables, then Leah will marry Johanan."

Berachiah ben Jesse set down his bow. Rabbi Juddah raised his eyebrows, and he looked at his pupil. "Rabbi," began Berachiah, "here is my problem. . . ." And Berachiah told the entire story to his teacher.

"Ah, Rabbi Juddah," concluded Berachiah, "what can I do? Even if I travel back to Marburg, I have no gifts. I have collected no valuable merchandise."

Berachiah sat sadly. He shook his head. "I may as well stay here. There is no hope of my marrying Rabbi David's daughter."

Old Rabbi Juddah looked intently at Berachiah. Something sparkled in the corner of the Rabbi's eye. Was it the morning sun glinting off the edge of an eyelash? Was it the hint of the moon to come? Rabbi Juddah smiled, and he said quietly to young Berachiah: "Remember—the truly devout, the truly learned, the truly humble and holy man need have no fear."

"Yes, yes, I know that, my good teacher. But how will this help me return to Marburg, strong and pious and successful?"

"Well, Berachiah, we must always begin by trusting in the good Lord God (blessed be He)," said Rabbi Juddah.

Berachiah nodded dejectedly.

"Now," continued the Rabbi, "you must begin your return journey immediately."

"But, Rabbi, how can I return? What will I bring back with me?"

"You bring *yourself*, Berachiah," said the Rabbi.

"Of course," said the young man.

"And," said the Rabbi, "let me put a holy thought into your mind."

Juddah he-Hasid closed his eyes, he laid his hands on Berachiah's head, and he said, "Apples."

Berachiah looked up at the old man. "Apples?" he asked.

"Yes," said Rabbi Juddah, "apples—and then, of course, you must trust in the Lord."

Berachiah was unsure what the holy man meant, but Rabbi Juddah was a strange and mystical man whose sayings often took time to become clear. Therefore, Berachiah shrugged his shoulders, and he took heart. Then he packed his few belongings, and he left Regensburg with the blessings of Rabbi Juddah sounding softly in his ears.

The young man followed the River Altmuhl, which runs between the Danube and the Rhine, winding interminably among weird and romantic gorges. After a while, the day began to darken. Soon Berachiah found himself outside a strange woods, somewhere just north of the town of Ansbach. Berachiah hesitated. Then he began to walk along the edge of the forest.

Berachiah walked and walked, and he became very, very hungry. He was starving. He was famished—in fact, he felt that he might die of hunger. Suddenly he came upon a beautiful apple tree. "Ah, thank the good Lord Almighty," said Berachiah. He shook some of the apples down, and he ate them. But soon he developed a terrible rash. His skin had blotches and red patches. He felt weak and dizzy. His stomach ached, and he itched all over. Yet strangely, Berachiah felt as hungry as ever.

Berachiah was quite frightened. He looked into the tree. There he saw a little beast, a creature that some demon had made in the shape of a lizard. And the animal radiated coldness: it was so cold that fire could not burn it. I know that you have heard of this small animal, Rabbi. This is the creature called "salamander," and it often climbs into apple trees, where its touch poisons the apples. (Also, when it falls into a well, the water becomes evil and causes death or disease.)

Berachiah recognized the creature, and he was certain that he would soon die. The young man was weak and itchy and dizzy, but he started to walk. "Perhaps I can find a comfortable place to lie down for my final rest," he thought miserably.

Soon Berachiah saw another apple tree. Carefully, he studied the branches. He saw no sign of salamanders. There were not many apples, but each one looked red and delicious, and now he was even more hungry than before. "Ah, well," thought poor Berachiah, "I may as well eat some of this fruit. If it is healthy, then I will feel better; if it is poisonous, then at least I will be put out of my misery."

Berachiah shook down some of the apples. He picked one up, and he looked at it. It seemed to be a normal apple. Tentatively, he tasted it. "Well," he thought, "there is no problem yet." So he shrugged his shoulders and he finished off the apple. Berachiah sat down on the ground. He waited. Nothing happened. He felt no worse and he felt no better. Therefore, Berachiah picked up another apple–and in a few minutes, Berachiah had eaten seven juicy red apples.

Apparently the good Lord God was watching out for young Berachiah, the apple of His eye. After a few minutes, the boy became sleepy and he slept the sleep of the just, the righteous, the innocent, and the holy, and when he awoke he was cured. (And, my grandmother said, Berachiah was more handsome and even more learned than before–however, I suspect that it was only that he *felt* more handsome and more learned than before.) In any case, Berachiah awoke the next morning feeling as fine and as fit and as strong as an apple tree.

Berachiah was lying under the apple tree. "Undoubtedly," he thought, "this is what the old prophet, Rabbi Juddah, meant when he said to me, 'Apples.' " Therefore, Berachiah gathered the few remaining apples that he found, he stuffed them into his sack, and he continued on his journey.

Berachiah wandered on and on. Late that day he arrived in a small town. "Hello," he said to the first person that he met. "What is the name of this place?"

The man said, "This is Atzvut"–and then he sighed.

Berachiah opened wide his eyes. "Atzvut?" he asked. "You call this place 'Sadness'?"

The man nodded. "Yes, my friend–you see, our old Rabbi has become gravely ill. And although he does not seem on the verge of death, he is moaning constantly. He is unhappy, and we are unhappy."

"What do your physicians say?" asked Berachiah.

"We have only one doctor here, and he has given up all hope."

"Perhaps I can be of some assistance," said Berachiah.

The man shook his head. "It is kind of you to offer. And certainly the wonders of the good Lord God are great. However, we have tried everything possible – and unfortunately nothing works."

Then the man walked away. Berachiah wandered about and soon he located the little wooden yeshiva building. Inside, the Rabbi was lying on a cot, groaning. He was attended by three old men, who were saying prayers. Clearly, the poor Rabbi was suffering terribly, and the other men had tears in their eyes.

Berachiah ben Jesse walked into the room. The men stopped praying, and they looked at him. "I should like to try and help the Rabbi," said the young man.

One of the old scholars said, "Ah, my good sir, so would we all."

"Listen, gentlemen," said Berachiah, "I would like to use a healing incantation that I learned in Regensburg. However, in order to begin, I must remove the *mezuzah* from the front door."

"Never!" said one of the scholars immediately, and the other men frowned. In the background, the poor old Rabbi moaned and he groaned.

Berachiah said, "My good sirs, for any magic to work, we must remove the *mezuzah* from the doorpost of the yeshiva for a moment."

The three old men emphatically shook their heads "no." But what was this? It seemed as if the Rabbi was trying to speak. The Rabbi made a strange sound. Berachiah bent his head toward the old Rabbi, and then he said, "I think that he said 'yes.' "

The other men looked at each other doubtfully. Had the poor sick old Rabbi said something? And if he had, was it "yes" or was it "no"?

Well, Rabbi, I am afraid that we shall never be certain, because Berachiah took the sound to be a "yes," and before the three old scholars could stop him, Berachiah removed the *mezuzah* from the doorpost, and gently he laid it on a clean linen cloth on the front step. Then he took out one of the healing apples from his knapsack.

The old scholars stood watching uncertainly while Berachiah set to his work. From the mystic Juddah he-Hasid, Berachiah had learned the three scriptural healing verses. Berachiah took an apple and he cut it into three equal pieces. Then he sat on a prayer bench, and with the fine point of his knife he inscribed the following section of Psalm 118 on one of the pieces of the apple:

> I will not die – I shall live free
> To praise God with every breath.

Berachiah reread the inscription to himself, and he took the apple to the Rabbi. The old men watched silently. Berachiah tried to get the Rabbi to eat the fruit, but the poor old man did not open his eyes. Finally, Berachiah put the slice of apple into the Rabbi's mouth, and after a few minutes it disappeared down the Rabbi's throat.

The Rabbi continued to moan and to groan. The old men looked puzzled. One of them was about to speak, but Berachiah held up his hand for silence. Again Berachiah sat on a prayer bench, and with the fine point of his knife, he inscribed the following section of Psalm 118 on the second piece of the apple:

> In the past the good Lord punished me
> But He saved me from cruel Death.

Then Berachiah took the apple to the Rabbi. The old men watched intently. Although Berachiah tried to get the Rabbi to eat the fruit, the poor old man would not open his eyes. Finally Berachiah put the slice of apple into the holy man's mouth, and after a few minutes it disappeared down the Rabbi's throat.

Still the Rabbi continued to moan and to groan. The old men looked sad and worried. One of them was about to speak, but Berachiah held up his hand for silence. Berachiah sat on the prayer bench, and with the fine point of his knife he inscribed the following section of Psalm 118 on the last piece of the apple:

> God is a refuge eternally
> Better than all the earthly kings,
> Though evil is surrounding me
> I am safe under His mighty wings.

Berachiah looked down at the piece of apple in his hand. "Amen," he whispered. Then he took the apple to the Rabbi. The three old men watched in silence. Berachiah tried to get the Rabbi to eat the fruit. The poor old man moaned and he groaned, and he would not open his eyes. Finally Berachiah put the slice of apple in the old man's mouth. After a few minutes it disappeared down the Rabbi's throat.

Nothing seemed to change. The old men waited expectantly. Eventually one of them said, "Well? What do we do now?"

Berachiah tapped his chin, and he said, "We must wait through the night."

Berachiah carefully replaced the *mezuzah* on the front doorpost of the yeshiva. The old men continued their prayers, and Berachiah lay down in a corner and he fell asleep.

In the morning, the Rabbi was no longer groaning. He was very weak, but his eyes were open. Berachiah mashed one of his remaining apples in cream and he fed it to the Rabbi with a spoon. Later that day, the Rabbi said a few words. After two more days, the Rabbi could sit up in bed – clearly, he was improving daily.

One morning, the Rabbi said, "My good friend, I do not even know your name."

"I am Berachiah, the son of Jesse the Levite."

"How did you learn the healing arts?" asked the Rabbi.

"Well, sir," said Berachiah, "I spent many months with a pious old mystic in Regensburg. However, this was the only healing charm that I learned."

"Well it certainly was the *right* healing charm. The omnipotent Lord God has watched over me, and he has sent me a wondrous gift in you and your one healing charm, my friend," said the Rabbi. "Whatever can I do to repay you?"

"I am not certain, Rabbi," said Berachiah. "I must be on my way back to Marburg. I think that I should leave today, or tomorrow at the latest. It is a long journey, and I hope to arrive with some miraculous gift from the good Lord God (blessed be He)."

Then Berachiah looked a bit sad. "I suppose that it is too much to hope for miracles, however," he sighed.

The Rabbi looked at Berachiah strangely. "Young man, I think that a miracle has occurred here."

"Perhaps it has," said Berachiah. He paused a moment, and then he added: "But it was a miracle for *you*, good Rabbi – not for me."

"Listen, young man," said the Rabbi. "I do not have much experience with miracles. But let me give you a present. In our congregation, we have a sacred and holy amulet. Many years ago, it was given to me by the pious Samuel he-Hasid of Speyer. I am a *Kohen* (as are most of the Jews in this town), and I cannot use it. Old Rabbi

Samuel said that someday this should be given to a Levite. You are a Levite, and I am convinced that it must be for you. So, Berachiah, now I will give the amulet to you."

Berachiah said nothing, but he knew that the good Lord God was at work, for Samuel he-Hasid of Speyer was the father of Rabbi Juddah he-Hasid, the mystic scholar of Regensburg.

The Rabbi stood. He was still weak; he steadied himself with his hand on a chair. Slowly he walked to his desk, and he took a small square amulet from a drawer. It was a silver box containing a parchment. On the front of the box were nine magical numbers:

$$2 \quad 7 \quad 6$$
$$9 \quad 5 \quad 1$$
$$4 \quad 3 \quad 8$$

These numbers added to fifteen in any row or column or even diagonally. On the back of the box were inscribed two lines from the Holy Scriptures:

For I am *Yahweh*, your Healer

and

I am that is Who I am

Inside the box was a parchment, on which was written:

By the power of all the holy names and seals in this charm, I command all impure and malignant powers, all evil spirits, and all the plagues that molest human beings to remain afar and to fear the Levite who bears this amulet.

Demons, dybbuks, and devils must not annoy him, either by day or by night, when the bearer is awake or when he is asleep. May he also obtain a perfect cure from all diseases which are in the world and from a beclouded mind, convulsions, epilepsy, fright, headaches, oppression, palpitations of the heart, paralysis, trembling, and worms. May the bearer be guarded from bondage, disease, cruel visions, witchcraft, and other evil powers.

By the names of the angels Aniel, Gabriel, Hasdiel, Kabshiel, Metatron, Michael, Rahab, Raphael, Ridyah, Sandalfon, Shamriel, and Uriel, may all good things fall upon the Levite who owns this charm. May the bearer of this amulet be shielded henceforth and for ever after by the power of Yahweh-Elohim. May this blessing be established and confirmed by all that is holy—*selah* and amen.

It was a beautiful and holy gift. Berachiah smiled and thanked the Rabbi. Then Berachiah packed his few belongings, and with the blessings of the Rabbi sounding gently in his ears, Berachiah left Atzvut and again he set off for Marburg. Berachiah walked all night and all the next day.

It was now the day on which Rabbi David Tov had decreed that his daughter Leah must be married. Early that morning, the Rabbi awoke suddenly. He looked around. Had someone called out his name? He searched his house, but his family was still asleep and no one else was there. The sky was gray. Something very strange was in the air. The Rabbi washed and dressed, and he said his morning prayers. Then he went to the synagogue and he sat, just watching the Holy Ark.

As you know, Rabbi, Marburg is a beautiful town on the banks of the River Lahn. That morning the river seemed ill-at-ease. A wind arose, and it blew and it whistled. The wind shivered the branches in the trees, and it swept leaves and grasses through the streets. People bent down as they walked; they shielded their eyes from the flying dust. And then, walking into town in that strange autumn wind, came young Berachiah ben Jesse.

At first, no one in the town saw the young man. And Berachiah himself hardly saw the townsfolk: he was tired, and he seemed dazed by the wind. In fact, Berachiah was unsure as to where he was. Then he recognized the yeshiva building, and in he went. He removed his shoes in the anteroom. He walked into the main prayer hall, which was filled with wooden benches, and he sat down beside Rabbi David Tov, who could only open his mouth in silent surprise.

Then the Rabbi hugged Berachiah and he patted him on the back. "You have returned just in time for the wedding day," said the Rabbi. "What valuables have you brought home with you?"

Berachiah looked down at his feet. "I am afraid, my good Rabbi, that I have brought nothing with me but this pack." Berachiah was sad, and Rabbi David, too, seemed sad. Then Berachiah remembered the beautiful amulet. "Just a moment, Rabbi," said the young man hurriedly. He tore open his pack and he emptied all the belongings onto the yeshiva floor. The amulet was not there. Berachiah pushed aside his few bits of clothing, his holy books, a clean linen handkerchief, and one old apple. There was nothing else. The amulet was gone.

The Rabbi looked at Berachiah, and Berachiah looked at the Rabbi.

The two men said nothing for many minutes.

"I guess that Johanan will marry your daughter," said Berachiah softly.

"I guess that he will," said the Rabbi.

That afternoon, Leah was married to Johanan. The groom was escorted by five young men carrying candles, and the candles were thrown into the air as the procession reached the courtyard of the synagogue. Rabbi David Tov accompanied the party to the synagogue, where he himself performed the marriage ceremony. After the first prayers, a dash of ashes was dabbed on the groom's forehead. Then the groom's *tallis* was gently draped over the head of the bride. The Rabbi pronounced the blessings, the groom stepped on a glass dish, some wine was poured on the ground, and a pinch of salt was sprinkled over the couple. Finally, the bride marched three times around her new mate, and all the assembled company clapped and cheered and hugged each other.

Berachiah ben Jesse stood quietly through the ceremony. Afterward, the wedding feast was held in the synagogue too. Most people reported that Berachiah remained standing alone, there in the back of the synagogue, and that he said nothing and he ate nothing. However, my grandmother said that while young Berachiah ben Jesse stood quietly in the background, he ate the one old apple from his pack—yes, Berachiah ate the shriveled apple, and a tear was in his eye.

ello, Rabbi, I will be with you in a moment. I cannot leave until every tablecloth is folded, otherwise the day has not ended properly. . . . There, now I am finished at last and I can sit next to you by the stove. I see that your head is nodding–a demon must have sneaked up on you. Perhaps you remember that this is exactly what happened to the mystic Rabbi Achselrad of Cologne. No? Well, I will tell you about it–it is a story that I heard from my grandmother, a tale from long, long ago in the dim medieval ages of Germany

This was when Cologne was already a major trading center in the German empire. In those days, when you heard "Cologne" you thought of wine and herring, and you thought of woven cloths, goldwork, and armor. Cologne was a bustling city. Its marketplaces grew rapidly, and the annual Cologne Fair became one of the major European trade expositions. Merchants moved into Cologne from the countryside, emigrating from Bonn, Duren, Dusseldorf, Eschweiler, Remscheid, and Siegburg.

Soon, the central city of Cologne spilled into its surroundings, and the once independent towns of Niederich, Oversburg, and St. Aposteln became suburbs. The rush of people, with their goods and carts and wagons, was overwhelming, and this frantic everyday commerce crowded the myriad shadowy spirits from their usual haunts. Demons, dybbuks, and devils slipped off to try and sleep in the few out-of-the-way corners and crevices that still were available to them; evil spirits flitted here and there, trying to find a quiet resting place. On occasion, some malign spirit would even sneak into the old synagogue building in the Jewish Quarter at the end of the alleyway off Judengasse Street – and this is exactly what happened one night, during the tenure of the old mystic Achselrad.

As usual, Rabbi Abraham Achselrad was studying in the small back room in the yeshiva. He had worked late after the evening prayers. Papers were piled in disarray on his desk. Unbeknownst to the Rabbi, on that very night a wicked spirit was rolling and flowing through the streets of Cologne. The spirit was grim and angry. It whipped like a chill wind up one street and down the next. Eventually, it whirled and whisked through a crack under the front door of the yeshiva building. The demon slipped under the door. It rushed along the corners of the main prayer hall, and it flowed into the little back study room when the Rabbi was not looking.

The evil spirit was like a wind. It blew open the Rabbi's copy of the Holy Scriptures to the Book of Psalms. The candlelight flickered. Rabbi Abraham looked up, with his eyebrows raised. The Holy Scriptures were open in front of him, and silently the Rabbi read the first verses of Psalm 132:

> O Lord, remember good king David
> And the hardships he endured,
> Recall the vows he solemnly said
> When to the Lord he gave his word.

> He said: "I will not take my bread
> I will not sit and eat
> Nor will I climb into my bed
> Nor will I rest my feet –

> "I will not dare to fall asleep
> Nor shut my eyes before
> I find our God's most holy keep,
> A secure temple for the Lord."

The Rabbi read this verse, and he creased his brow. "Something strange is afoot," he thought.

Then the Rabbi yawned. He rubbed his eyes. His lids felt heavy, and his head nodded.

Yes, a wicked demon had sneaked into the holy synagogue of Cologne. Quietly, it hummed and it hissed and it spat and it laughed, and it made the Rabbi very, very sleepy. The Rabbi was so exhausted that he could not concentrate. Perhaps a walk would clear his mind. But could he even manage to stand and to pull himself together?

With a tremendous effort of will, the Rabbi stood. He put on his coat. His arms felt weak. His legs were shaky. His head was warm. Nonetheless, the Rabbi stood and he dressed, and slowly, he walked – Rabbi Abraham Achselrad walked from the small back room and into the main prayer hall, with its many worn wooden benches. Then he passed through the anteroom, and he stepped out the front door of the old yeshiva building. Rabbi Abraham stood in the courtyard, and he yawned.

It was nighttime. The sky was dark; the moon had not yet risen, although the stars were out. The Rabbi was exhausted. He walked up the alleyway that led from the synagogue building out to Judengasse Street. The Rabbi turned left. Blindly, he walked up Judengasse Street toward Engegasse Street.

The Juden Viertels, the Jewish Quarter in Cologne, was located in the eastern corner – in the sunrise corner – of the old city, close to the ancient Roman wall. This was where the main street led to the River Rhine through the principal gate on the right (the "Porta Principalis Dextra") – in later days, this came to be known as the Market Gate. The Jewish Quarter itself was bounded by Budengasse Street (Klein Budengasse) on the north, Obenmarspforten Street on the south, the Alter Markt area on the east, and Unter Goldschmied Street on the west. Judengasse Street ran from north to south through the center of the district.

The Rabbi continued walking north on Judengasse Street. He crossed Budengasse Street, and he walked on unsteadily. Judengasse Street changed its name to Unter Taschenmacher Street in the Christian areas, and now the Rabbi was walking on Unter Taschenmacher. Rabbi Abraham ben Alexander, Achselrad of Cologne, felt dizzy. He needed to sit or, better yet, to lie down. Was there any place to rest?

The Rabbi saw a wagon at the side of the road. The open back was filled with cloaks and empty wine barrels. Wearily, the Rabbi climbed in and he lay down. It was cold. He pulled a few cloaks over himself, far up over his head. Soon, he was fast asleep.

The night wore on, the inns closed, and eventually the owners of the wagon returned. They did not notice the Rabbi, and they set about on their way, collecting empty wine barrels on a regular, winding route. They rolled down the narrow dark streets and lanes. They passed through market after market, the Domhof, the Waid Markt, the Alter Markt, and the Heu Markt. They rumbled down Hohestrasse Street. They passed the great Catholic cathedral–the Dom–in which the three kings of Cologne are buried. (Those kings–Kaspar, Melchior, and Balthazar–were the three wise men who came from the East to see the infant Jesus.)

The night was dark, the two men were tired, and as they pushed empty wine barrels onto the back of the wagon, they did not notice the sleeping Rabbi. The wagon wove in and out of the city streets. Now they made one final stop to collect a load of discarded cloaks. The two wagonmen worked in silence. Then the wagon rumbled on. Soon, on the left was the Ravenstone, the bleak black stone gibbet, little used but always a heavy-lidded grim warning. Then, tiredly, the men turned south.

Bonn was south–and it was toward Bonn that they rolled, following the course of the wide dark River Rhine. They had passed out of Cologne through the south Severn Gate. Vaguely, the Rabbi heard the gatekeeper ringing and ringing the Thor Glocke bell, but the tolling seemed to echo a long way off and a long time ago. The wagon rumbled on, past the old Jewish cemetery, the *Am Toten Juden*, where the gravestones shone like white fingers sticking up from many giant Jewish hands that reached and pointed toward the nighttime Heavens. And then, had Rabbi Abraham been awake and had he looked back, he would have seen that the city of Cologne was a fortress on the Rhine; yes, Cologne was a vast semicircle on the broad and dark River Rhine, the wide medieval River Rhine.

The wagon rolled on and on, along the southerly Rhine road. Cologne disappeared. The travelers passed the outer neighborhoods of Rondorf, Kierberg, Bruhl, and Sechtem, continuing southward–south to the medieval city of Bonn.

It was hours later when the Rabbi awoke. One of the men in the front of the wagon was singing an old hymn:

> Swift as the fleeting deer
> Time flows on out of sight
> With endless streaming years
> In its windswept flight.
>
> Each dawn dissolves like ocean spray
> Splashed up into the morning's light;
> Short-lived is each passing day –
> Soon there comes the endless night.
>
> Yesterdays are fleet fugitives
> Returning nevermore,
> Taken from today's brief lives
> And left on distant shores.
>
> But no day dissolves to nothing,
> For inscribed in Time's Book of Yore
> It becomes a permanent marking
> On Eternity's pebbled shore.
>
> Parting from our aging parents
> We leave our childhood door –
> And soon *our* children's sustenance
> We then provide to them no more.
>
> The worldly bonds are finally torn
> And we disappear heartsore
> From the family in which we're born,
> To lands beyond the distant shore.

The Rabbi awoke; he turned and he stretched, and he knocked over an empty barrel. The two wagon drivers jumped. Was there some evil spirit in the wagon? Were they being robbed? Quickly they pulled the wagon to a stop. Their hearts were pounding. One of the men leaped off the cart.

The Rabbi sat up. He looked around, and he saw the wide-eyed drivers. "My friends," he said, "please excuse me for frightening you. I have just fallen asleep here."

The two drivers said nothing. The Rabbi was old and bearded; he seemed harmless. One of the men asked, "What were you doing back there?"

Rabbi Abraham said, "I am really quite sorry, gentlemen – I had just fallen asleep."

"Well," said the other man, "you had better get out of this wagon."

The Rabbi slowly got down from the back of the wagon. He shook out his coat, and he patted down his pants. "Where are we?" he asked.

"We are almost in Bonn."

"Are you by any chance going back to Cologne now?" asked the Rabbi.

"No."

"Ah, well," said the Rabbi, and he seemed bewildered as he looked around.

One of the men was beginning to feel a bit badly. "I am sorry, sir," he said to Rabbi Abraham. "We are hauling wine barrels. After Bonn, we go to Coblenz – that is where all the Rhine wine is traded."

"I see," said the Rabbi. The second man climbed back onto the wagon. The two wagonmen looked down at the Rabbi, but he was looking south at Bonn. The men shrugged their shoulders, and slowly they continued on their way.

The Rabbi looked south at Bonn. He was at the edge of the city, a beautiful old town filled with narrow streets and fine buildings. Rabbi Abraham looked up. Across the city walls, he saw the magnificent towering Munster Cathedral, with its five spires of smooth gray stone; the gray church had a cold grandeur in the starlight of those medieval Rhineland nights.

The Rabbi looked up at the towering stone church, and he looked down at the rough dirt road. Then he began to walk north, back toward Cologne, back along the Rhine River road. Rabbi Abraham walked north, through the neighborhoods of Sechtem, Bruhl, Kierberg, and Rondorf. The sky was gray. Then it was a pale light blue. Over the trees hung an orange moon. Had he ever before seen the moon so large? Why, it was as big as a tree! The Rabbi stood for a moment, looking at the moon. He felt rested, and he began to walk again. Now he could make out the details of the small stones in the road. The Rabbi felt like walking forever – and that is just what he did. The Rabbi walked and he walked and he walked: quietly and peacefully, Abraham Achselrad walked forever home to Cologne, to his old yeshiva in the Jewish Quarter of far-off medieval Cologne.

ood evening, Rabbi. Of course—please sit here by the stove: the night fire helps me to become sleepy also. You and I are not blessed like old Reb Elbaum. Once again, I saw him nodding off during the last prayers this evening. He has learned to sway piously even while asleep—Reb Elbaum must have acquired some magic from the mystic Achselrad. I suppose that you and I could use a dose of Achselrad ourselves tonight. My grandmother said that he could put men into a sleep trance by waving a gold coin before their eyes.

As you know, Rabbi Abraham ben Alexander, also called Achselrad of Cologne, was a pupil of Eliazer the mystic of Worms. Old Abraham Achselrad was always conjuring visions in the synagogue. I doubt whether he would be tolerated nowadays, but Rabbi Abraham claimed that his visions came from devout and pious study. In any case, many an astonishing event took place when he was the Chief Rabbi of Cologne—or so my grandmother (blessed be her memory) was told. For example, one day his vision from Psalm 140 saved poor Lemhule ben Anselm ha-Kohen. . . . Yes, Rabbi, I will gladly tell you about Lemhule—although he had nothing to do with Spain.

Did you not ask about Spain? Then I suppose that I was drifting off—for a moment I was thinking of the time when Rabbi Abraham visited the Spanish King Ferdinand II in his court in Leon and made a young pageboy disappear during dinner. Oh? You knew this already? Then perhaps you have heard about Achselrad's vision from Psalm 140. You have not heard about this vision? Ah, then I will tell you exactly what I learned from my grandmother:

As you know, Rabbi Achselrad is the author of the mystical treatise the *Keter Shem Tov*; unfortunately, this book was never published—now it exists only as a secret manuscript hidden in the loft of the old Cologne yeshiva. Grandmother said that it was one cold winter night while writing this very book that Rabbi Abraham looked up, and in the light of the candle he saw Lemhule ben Anselm ha-Kohen standing in the doorway, pale and shaken. "Rabbi," said Lemhule, "I need your help. I am about to be arrested for theft."

This, in fact, is what actually had happened:

The medieval Jewish Quarter of Cologne was just north of the Christian parish called St. Laurence, and beyond St. Laurence was St. Albans parish; St. Albans was named after the beheaded Christian martyr of England. Lemhule was the son of a struggling businessman named Anselm ben Moses. When he was young, Lemhule had lived as a carefree boy in St. Albans parish—that is, he had lived as carefree as a poor young Jew could in those days.

Lemhule lived the good life—a life of eating and drinking and gambling. His father did not make much money, but Lemhule showed no concern; he even stole food money from his mother. When he was a child in the yeshiva, Lemhule would throw pieces of dirt and bits of dust at his classmates. He would make faces. Often he skipped the lessons and followed the older boys into the back alleys. When he grew older, he slept late and he never attended the synagogue. He rarely talked with his parents, and he obeyed none of their rules. During the afternoons, Lemhule sat in one of the inns that allowed Jews. In the evenings, he would plan small thefts with a group of other boys, most of whom were Gentiles, and sometimes they would steal for an older man, who mysteriously received orders from someone in France.

One day, one of the boys, a Gentile named Henry, came in excitedly. He had heard that a shipment of valuable gems, including many emeralds, had been stored in an old warehouse on the Rhine River side of the Alter Markt. The young men had never stolen anything so expensive. They were nervous – they planned quietly and they joked loudly.

That night, long after dark, Lemhule, Henry, and two other youths slipped down the narrow street leading to the warehouse. Henry and the two other boys broke the lock and went inside; Lemhule stayed outside to watch for trouble. Suddenly there was a shout. The two boys came running out. Lemhule ran after them. They ran and ran until they reached a dark courtyard many streets away. "Henry was killed by a guard," said one of the boys in tears. Crumpled in a shadow-enshrouded corner, the three young men sat stunned and motionless until the morning.

As the dawn dragged a gray light through the city, each of the boys slunk home. Lemhule walked into his room. He lay in his bed. "What will become of me now?" he thought. "I, too, can be killed at any time."

Lemhule lay in bed all morning. He did not answer his mother when she called to him. He was not hungry. "What can I do with my life?" he wondered.

Lemhule stayed in his bed all afternoon and all evening. His father looked in at him and only shook his head. "What happens now?" thought Lemhule blankly.

The night came, and it lay heavily on Lemhule. Lemhule stared at the ceiling. "What does everything mean?" he said.

Then he thought, "In the end, undoubtedly I shall lose my life. I hardly know my parents, and it appears that I will have no children. Why will I have bothered with all this living?"

Lemhule was staring at a far corner of his room. Was there a spider in the darkness there, or was it merely the edge of a shadow? Lemhule could not bring himself to get up and to look more closely: he was too dulled to move. "There may be a spider in that corner," thought Lemhule. "Who is to say that there is no spider there?" Lemhule looked at the shadow-spider. Was it sitting in a web? Was it happy? Was Lemhule better off than the spider? Lemhule and the shadow-spider were the only two living things in his room. It seemed that perhaps Lemhule and the spider were the only two living things in the world. And now, Lemhule felt like he was just a shadow also.

"Nothing makes any sense. I cannot figure this out alone," thought poor Lemhule. Minutes passed in dull silence. Eventually, Lemhule said to himself, "I had best go and talk with someone. . . . Perhaps I should see Rabbi Abraham." Lemhule had lived in Cologne all his life, but he could not remember ever having spoken to the famous old Rabbi. Nonetheless, this seemed like the only thing to do.

Lemhule did not fall asleep. After an eternity, the day dawned with a bland gray sky. Lemhule washed and he dressed. He thought of trying to say a prayer, but he felt that perhaps he was too wicked for prayers. He shook his head sadly. Then Lemhule ben Anselm ha-Kohen walked out of his house, and with his shoulders drooping, he went up Unter Goldschmied Street, across Engegassse Street, and down Judengasse Street to the synagogue building in order to find Rabbi Abraham ben Alexander, the mystic Achselrad of Cologne.

As usual, Rabbi Abraham was reading in the back room of the yeshiva. The Rabbi was alone. Lemhule walked slowly through the main prayer hall. He stood in the doorway of the rabbi's study room. After a moment, the Rabbi looked up. "Yes, young man?" he said.

Lemhule looked at his shoes. "Rabbi," he began, "my name is Lemhule. My father's name is Anselm ha-Kohen. I have wasted my life – I need your help."

The Rabbi stared at young Lemhule. "I think that you had better sit down, Lemhule. Now, tell me what this is all about."

Lemhule sat on a bench, far from the Rabbi. He began to talk slowly, but soon he spoke more quickly, and after an hour he had said all that there was to say.

The Rabbi sat unmoving. Now there was only silence. The Rabbi closed his eyes. After many minutes, young Lemhule said, "Rabbi? Excuse me, Rabbi – are you awake?"

Rabbi Abraham opened his eyes. He spoke in a firm voice. "Now listen to me carefully, Lemhule. There is only one thing that you must do –"

"What?! There is only one thing? How can this be?"

"Lemhule," said the Rabbi sternly, "do not interrupt. As I was saying, there is only one thing that you must do to cure all of your problems."

"Yes, Rabbi?" asked the boy.

"Just trust in the Lord and never lie."

Lemhule raised his eyebrows. "That is all?" he asked. "Just trust in the Lord and never lie?"

"Exactly," said the Rabbi.

Lemhule took a deep breath. "This is an easy task," he said. "I thought that you were going to send me away from Cologne or that I would have to do some incredible penance." Lemhule stood up. "I can do this with no trouble, Rabbi," he said. "You will see."

But Rabbi Abraham held up his hand. "Just a moment, young man," he said. "If you intend to keep your promise, then you must swear to me a solemn oath that you will never tell a lie."

"Of course, Rabbi—you have offered me a very simple cure. I agree. And I so swear before God, amen," said young Lemhule, and he went away happily.

Lemhule felt much better. He returned home, he ate his breakfast, and he spoke politely to his parents. He avoided his friends. He began to think of what he might do in order to earn a living.

Lemhule's parents were amazed. Still, they remained unsure, and for a time they did not dare to talk with Lemhule about anything serious. Instead, they talked of meals and shopping and relatives. Lemhule chatted with them happily about any subject. At the same time, Lemhule's former companions wondered why he never appeared any more in the alleyways or the inns or in the shadowy back rooms of stores.

Not far from Lemhule's home in the St. Albans parish was the house of a widow named Rachel. Rachel took care of other people's children, and if the parents went on an overnight trip, Rachel also guarded some of their valuables. One evening, about a week after his visit to the Rabbi, young Lemhule was passing by the widow's house. The kitchen window was lit brightly and Lemhule looked inside. By the candlelight, Lemhule saw that a number of valuables were piled on the table—there were candlesticks, books, a purse filled with money, and some fine linens.

Somehow Lemhule could not take his eyes from all these fine things. After the widow had put the children to bed and after she had straightened up the house and after she herself had locked the doors and had retired to her room, Lemhule found himself still standing at the window. "It would be so easy," he thought, "to open the window quietly and take those things." Lemhule stood there, staring and staring. Then Lemhule pushed the window. It was loose. It slid backward. Lemhule climbed inside. His heart was beating very fast. His hands were damp. Now that he was inside the house, he was worried and weak. He took the things from the table, and he began to climb out the window.

Lemhule began to climb out the window – and then he heard a voice. For a moment, he felt that his heart had stopped beating. It was the voice of Rabbi Abraham! Then Lemhule realized that the sound was in his mind: Lemhule was hearing again something that the Rabbi had said to him the other day. It was: "Remember, Lemhule, the Talmud tells us that lying is the equivalent of theft. Specifically, the Sages say: 'There are seven classes of thieves, and first among them all is he who steals the mind of his fellows through dishonest lying words.' "

Lemhule stood stock-still. "I am stealing," he said to himself. "And therefore, I am lying." Lenhule still felt weak, but he began to put the items back; quickly he set the candlesticks, the books, the purse, and the fine linens on the kitchen table. Unfortunately, just at that moment a group of Gentile boys, who knew Lemhule, walked by on the street. They saw the open window. They stopped at the house, and they looked in.

"Ah, what have we here?" said one of them. "Our old friend Lemhule – who has made himself so scarce recently – is back to his usual tricks. And he has not been sharing with us."

Lemhule's heart began to pound even faster. He looked at the window, and he looked behind him at the closed cellar door. But his legs were too weak, and he could not move.

Another one of the boys said, "That is not very friendly, Lemhule."

The boys nodded to each other. Two of the youths jumped in through the window. One of them grabbed Lemhule. The other took the purse and threw it out the window to his companion, and this third boy immediately ran away. Then the remaining boys began to call out loudly. Soon, two guards arrived. "We have caught this Jew robbing a poor old widow," said one of the boys. The boy let go his grasp on Lemhule, who, with all his remaining strength, jumped out the window and ran, ran, ran up Unter Goldschmied Street, across Engegassse Street, and down Judengasse Street to the synagogue building.

Ah, but the Gentile boys knew Lemhule's name and they knew where
he lived, so they accompanied the guards to the Court – and there they
formally swore a charge of theft against Lemhule ben Anselm ha-
Kohen.

Meanwhile, breathless and pale, Lemhule arrived at the door of
the back study room in the yeshiva. Rabbi Abraham looked up, and he
listened to the story that was told by young Lemhule. Then the
mystical old man closed his eyes. After a moment, Achselrad opened
his eyes, he stared at the ceiling, and he recited from the Book of
Proverbs in the Holy Scriptures:

> Gentle blessings enwreathe the head
>   Of the honest, pious citizen,
> While cruel and evil thoughts unsaid
>   Enchain the hearts of wicked men.

The Rabbi took a deep breath. He stood, and he put on his hat and
his coat. Without glancing backward, he left the small study room of
the yeshiva. Rabbi Abraham walked through the main prayer hall,
which was filled with wooden benches. He passed the twelve stained
glass windows with their colored lions and snakes, he went by the
Holy Ark made of stone, he stepped out of the main door, and he strode
off to the courthouse, with Lemhule hurrying behind.

By now it was well after dawn, and the Archbishop himself was
in the courtroom; this was Archbishop Adolph of Cologne, a noble and
honorable prelate. Archbishop Adolph knew Rabbi Abraham. "Rabbi," said the Archbishop, "one of your Jews has robbed a poor widow
named Rachel. We have witnesses who have sworn that young Mr.
Anselm took the valuables. I see that you have brought the accused,
and I appreciate this – I am afraid, Rabbi, that Lemhule Anselm must be
imprisoned."

"I see," said Rabbi Abraham, stroking his beard. Abraham Achselrad looked at the witnesses, he looked at Lemhule, and he looked at
the Archbishop. The Rabbi closed his eyes for a moment. Then he
asked, "Have you a Bible here, good Archbishop?"

"Of course," replied the Archbishop, and he instructed one of the
court officers to pass a leather volume to Rabbi Achselrad.

"Now let us read from the Book of Psalms," said the Rabbi.

"I respect your religious views, Rabbi," said Archbishop Adolph, "but is this really relevant now?"

Rabbi Abraham Achselrad was holding the Bible. Suddenly his eyes opened wide and then they closed tightly; he became weak and he sat on a nearby chair. Then the Rabbi gently set down the Bible.

"Are you all right, Rabbi?" asked the Archbishop.

"I have just had a vision, Your Honor: I have seen the Heavens at night. I have seen the Omnipotent Lord God (blessed be He) Who never sleeps—and now I have seen also that Psalm 140 is quite important," said Abraham Achselrad. "If you will be so good as to hand me the Holy Book again, then I will read a bit of those verses":

> Rescue me, Lord, from villain's dreams,
> Keep me safe from violent men
> Who daily execute wicked schemes
> Inciting hate toward me again.
>
> Their tongues are sharp as a keen-edged knife
> Their lips have scorpion's venom
> Their seductive words can end your life
> Their lies are like opium.
>
> Guard me, Lord, from injury
> Keep me safe from the evil tide—
> For murderous men plot to behead me
> And then to thrust my poor body aside.

"Yes—that is serious verse," said the Archbishop. And when Rabbi Abraham remained silent, the Archbishop added, "It is certainly a noble and holy sentiment, Rabbi."

The Rabbi nodded. "Now, you are a noted cleric, Archbishop Adolph. What would you that say this verse means?" asked the Rabbi.

"Clearly it means that God helps to protect us against slander," said the Archbishop.

"I agree—and I would say that it also means more," said the Rabbi.

"You would?" asked the Archbishop. "Then pray tell, Rabbi Abraham: What else do you read into this Psalm?"

"First, I would say, Archbishop, that the good Lord God (blessed be He) protects us against slander. I would also add, sir, that the Almighty and Omnipotent One protects us against those who would behead us," said the Rabbi.

The Archbishop raised his eyebrows. "'Behead us,' Rabbi? Exactly what are you saying, Mr. Alexander?"

"I am saying this, Archbishop: I have had a vision—I have seen a headless man, and he shall save the Jews."

Archbishop Adolph looked at his councilors and he looked at the Rabbi. "Rabbi," said Archbishop Adolph, "I have often gone along with your mysticism. But I must confess that I am confused here. Exactly what are you proposing?"

"I have had a vision, Your Honor—let me share it with the Court," said Rabbi Abraham.

"Very well," said the Archbishop.

The Rabbi sat at a nearby table, and he wrote seven mystical names on a small piece of white parchment. He tied the paper with seven white threads, and in each thread he put seven neat knots. Then the Rabbi strung the small packet on a slender white rope.

"Archbishop," said the Rabbi, "I should like your permission to put this around the neck of one of the boys who made the accusation."

Archbishop Adolph nodded. Rabbi Abraham walked over to the two youths who had brought the charges. They shrank away, but a guard held them by the shoulders. Then Rabbi Abraham gently placed the parchment necklace around the shoulders of one of the boys.

The boy began to shake. Suddenly he called out, "Oh my God! Who is that man there? He looks like a spirit. He is dressed in white. . . . Look! he is carrying his head in his hands. And—he is pointing at me! Now he is walking toward me. Save me, please!"

The boy pushed himself backward as if to escape from some demon that no one else could see. The courtroom was silent and heavy and dark. The boy was still shaking as Rabbi Abraham removed the amulet. Now Archbishop Adolph was silent too. He stared intently at the boy, who was pale and who trembled uncontrollably. Finally, the Archbishop said, "A white-robed man carrying his head—it must be Saint Alban. Yes, it is Saint Alban, who was beheaded and who died a martyr." Archbishop Adolph nodded to himself: "This must symbolize the St. Albans parish, where you boys live and where the crime was committed."

The Archbishop tapped his finger on his desk. "Saint Alban was pointing at you, young men," said the cleric. "Apparently, you boys are guilty too."

The boys were shocked and stunned, and one of them said, "Yes, yes – it is true, we were trying to take the valuables also, and we put all the blame on Lemhule. In fact, our friend William has still got the purse of money."

The Archbishop frowned at the boys. He looked at Lemhule, he looked at Rabbi Abraham, and then he looked back at the two Gentile youths. "Do you not know that in the Bible it says":

You shall not steal. You shall not cheat or deceive a fellow countryman. You shall not oppress your neighbor, nor shall you rob him.

The boys looked away from the Archbishop. But the clergyman continued angrily: "And in the Bible it also says":

You shall not wrong an alien nor be hard on him. You shall not spread a baseless rumor. You shall not join with a wicked man by giving malicious evidence.

"Moreover," said the Archbishop, "in the Bible, God decrees":

When a malicious witness comes forward in order to give false evidence against another, then you shall treat him as he intended to treat his fellowman.

The Archbishop turned to the other officials of the court. "These young men have stolen, and they have deceived; they have oppressed and robbed and spread baseless rumors maliciously," he said.

"Specifically, these young men robbed a widow, and they attempted to put the full blame on another. Therefore, we find these two men, and their friend William, guilty of theft, along with Mr. Lemhule Anselm," declared the Catholic cleric.

There was a moment of silence. Then the Archbishop turned

back to Rabbi Abraham. "Now, my good sir," said the Archbishop, "you have helped to solve a crime. What do you suggest as a punishment?"

"Your Honor," said Achselrad, "as this is a religious court, I suggest that we follow the dictates of the Holy Scriptures. As you know, in the Book of Exodus it says that a thief must restore two-fold the goods that he has stolen. Therefore, I suggest that William return the money that was actually stolen. Then I would propose that all four young men or their families must pay the widow an additional equivalent amount of money as punishment for the theft and as compensation for the poor woman's troubles."

"That," agreed the Archbishop, "is a fine solution, Rabbi."

Thus, Lemhule ben Anselm ha-Kohen and the three Gentile youths were each required to pay a restitution. Lemhule's family was very poor, so Lemhule borrowed the money from Avigdor ben Jacob ha-Kohen, a wealthy member of the Jewish community.

To repay Reb Avigdor, Lemhule began to work for him as a deliveryman and a warehouse porter. Lemhule worked hard. Avigdor soon discovered that the young man was agile with accounting and figures; so after a time, Lemhule became Avigdor's bookkeeper.

Lemhule ben Anselm grew up quickly, and as a man, he was scrupulously honest. ("An almost unique trait," said Avigdor frequently.) Soon Lemhule was advising Reb Avigdor on sales, on investments, and on purchases. Avigdor began to rely more and more on Lemhule's counsel, and together the two men expanded the business, with new connections into Dusseldorf, Bonn, and Coblenz. One day, Lemhule married Avigdor's second daughter. Then, eventually, with the blessings of the good Lord God, Avigdor ben Jacob retired, and Lemhule ben Anselm ha-Kohen took over his father-in-law's business – and Lemhule had a fine family and he became as prosperous and as happy as he had ever hoped to be.

h, good evening again, Rabbi. Yes, I know—it is always hard to sleep on the night of a bright half moon. Put your feet up on the side bench here and I will open the stove door. Let me push the coals back; that fine white glow washes away all the cares of a hard day.

I heard your final benediction tonight, Rabbi. There is no use denying it: you are overworked. Oh yes, even a shammas like me can tell. I kept one eye on you when I cleaned the dishes, and I saw that you were watching the door, hoping that Reb Elbaum would leave early. But then Reb Anton stayed to argue about the scriptural passage from the Book of Genesis:

> After Isaac had finished blessing his son Jacob, who was disguised as Esau, and soon after Jacob had left his father's presence, his brother Esau came in from hunting. He, too, prepared some tasty food and brought it to his father. Then Esau said to Isaac: "My father, sit up and eat some of my game, so that you may give me your blessing."
>
> But his father Isaac asked him: "Who are you?"
>
> "Who am I? Why, I am your son," he answered. "I am your firstborn, Esau."

Isaac trembled violently and he said: "Then who was it who already hunted game and brought it to me? I ate it just before you came, and I blessed him – therefore, he will indeed be blessed!"

When Esau heard his father's words, he burst out with a loud and bitter cry, and he said to his father Isaac: "Do you have only one blessing, my father? Please bless me too, my father, my only father!" But sadly Isaac bowed his head, and then Esau wept aloud.

That was a sad and difficult fate for Esau – I see, Rabbi, that you are still worn out from facing the old tale. . . . What is that? A story from me? All I know are the children's tales, the grandmother fables. You need something new and fresh to keep your mind keen. Otherwise you will become a dreamy old man like me, and you will find yourself constantly musing and dozing and nodding off in front of the stove.

What do you mean that you are already an old man, Rabbi? Do you really think that sixty years is old? You are still a child: Adam lived for nine hundred and thirty years, you know. Perhaps you will feel old when you reach eighty or ninety. You doubt that you will live to see eighty years? If so, Rabbi, then you will never grow old. . . . All right, all right, I know no special stories but listening to you and Reb Anton put me in mind of Shelah, who was a midwife and who was the widow of Salemannus ben Johel ha- Levi. . . .

What? Of course there is more, Rabbi: I only closed my eyes for a moment – can an old man not take a little rest? Now you have interrupted my thoughts. Let me see, where was I? Oh, yes – as my grandmother (may her soul visit happily with her parents forever) said:

Once upon a time, there lived along the wide and dark River Rhine a pious scholar named Rabbi Abraham ben Alexander, Achselrad of Cologne. (Now do not interrupt, Rabbi.) As I was saying, Rabbi Achselrad was the spiritual leader of all the Jewish communities in the Rhinelands near Cologne. In those distant medieval days, there lived in Cologne two wealthy friends, Jesse ben Yehutiel and Hananiah ben Solomon. Jesse and Hananiah were partners in business, and they were very successful.

Both men were married. Together they bought a huge stone house on Budengasse Street; Jesse and his family lived in the upstairs section, and Hananiah and his family lived downstairs. The families shared their belongings, and they helped each other out. Yes, Rabbi, the two families lived closely and they were similar in many ways – but there was one striking difference. Jesse's children were healthy and strong and apple-cheeked. In contrast, Hananiah's children were sickly and weak and pale.

This took its toll. Jesse's wife was carefree and confident, but Hananiah's wife was always trembling: she worried constantly that her children would fall ill and die suddenly. Like their husbands, the two women were good friends, and Hananiah's wife tried to hide her fears and her feelings but at times they showed through. Hananiah's wife was always afraid – and one person who saw this fear most clearly was Shelah. Shelah was the widow of a poor man named Salemannus ben Johel ha-Levi. For many years, Shelah had worked as a maid and a midwife for the two families in the large house on Budengasse Street, and she had become a confidante of both wives.

It happened, one year, that both wives were pregnant and that they went into labor on exactly the same night. In fact, they both gave birth to a child within an hour of each other, and both babies were boys. In each case, Shelah, the midwife, had said the appropriate biblical incantation from the Book of Exodus:

> Then all your courtiers and servants will come to me. They will prostrate themselves and bow down and cry: "Get yourselves out – go away, you and all the people who follow at your heels." And after that, I will get out and go away.

Then, of course, both births were smooth and easy. The babies were washed, and they were wrapped tightly in bandage-like cloth (in order to prevent them from becoming cripples). The midwife handed each child to its mother and wished the mother *mazel tov*. And on the first night, the newborn children and their mothers were protected from demons, devils, and dybbuks by tying a red ribbon to their beds and by placing a knife underneath the mother's pillow.

As Shelah washed each newly born, red wrinkly little baby, she thought, "Just this once, it would be so nice if Hananiah had a strong child." Shelah looked at both boys. Jesse's son seemed much stronger and healthier. It cried more loudly, and it kicked more vigorously. Then Shelah did a startling thing. Quickly she substituted one boy for the other. Shelah passed Jesse's son to Hananiah's wife and said, "*Mazel tov.*" Next, Shelah gave Hananiah's son to Jesse's wife and said, "*Mazel tov.*" And once she had done this amazing deed there was no turning back. The two boys were forever switched, and Shelah tried never to think of this frightening act again.

Of course, it was only Shelah who felt any awe or terror or fear. Each of the mothers was quite happy, nursing the child that she imagined to be her very own son. In fact, a calm and joyous night passed – and then there were many happy days and weeks and years. And over the years, the two boys grew up together, but they never knew that each was really the neighbor's child. And did Jesse's true son grow stronger and more healthy and more apple-cheeked than Hananiah's true son? To be honest, Rabbi, I do not know, and my grandmother never told me. In any case, both boys grew innocently side by side, and Shelah carried her secret knowledge to the grave.

The two neighboring boys grew up and became young men, and soon it was time for them to marry. Hananiah ben Solomon called his neighbor Jesse ben Yehutiel down to his kitchen one evening. "My good friend," said Hananiah, "I propose that my youngest son marry your daughter."

Jesse smiled. "I hope that you have some wine ready, Hananiah," he said. The two men hugged, and they drank a cup of wine together. It was not long before the young man and the young woman were taken to the synagogue, and a deed of betrothal – the *ketubah* – was written:

> Blessed be You, O Lord our God, King of the World, Who has sanctified us by Your commandments and Who has commanded us concerning the forbidden relations and Who has allowed unto us the wedded couple, through the marriage canopy and the wedding sanctification. Praised be You, O Lord our God, Who sanctifies Israel through the wedding canopy and the wedding sanctification, amen.

The boy and the girl each sipped from a cup of wine. The bridegroom took the bride's hand, and he said, "Behold, you are now consecrated unto me by the law of Moses and of Israel." In those days, the bride's father gave an engagement ring to the groom; therefore, Jesse ben Yehutiel gave a beautiful gold band to the young man as a sign of the marriage agreement. Then Hananiah ben Solomon gave a finely bound prayer book to the bride, as her betrothal present.

Seven days later it was the day of the wedding ceremony. Rabbi Abraham ben Alexander was presiding. The Rabbi began to recite the first benediction over a cup of wine. Suddenly the cup broke in his hand and it fell to the ground and red wine spilled on the floor and ran into the cracks in the old wooden boards.

All the guests were very silent. Had the Rabbi squeezed the cup too hard? Had he absently let it slip from his fingers? Or was something more ominous happening?

The Rabbi raised his eyebrows. He looked at the broken cup on the floor. Hurriedly, Chayim ben Meir, the shammas, brought a second cup of wine. He handed it to the Rabbi. Again, Rabbi Abraham was preparing to say the benediction, when the wine cup literally exploded into many pieces. Dark red wine ran upon the floor and it flowed into the cracks in the old wooden boards.

The guests were frozen. The Rabbi stood grim and silent. He closed his eyes and he trembled. He swayed back and forth. No one spoke, and no one moved.

After many minutes, Rabbi Abraham opened his eyes and he looked intently first at the bridegroom and then at the bride. They looked amazingly similar to each other. Rabbi Abraham creased his forehead and he stared. Then he said, "My friends, a strange and difficult matter is transpiring here." The Rabbi stroked his beard. Then he continued: "We have been drawn into a very complex web of events. I must ask you all to be seated, until we find a holy resolve to these tangled circumstances."

People shifted their weight from foot to foot. Hananiah's wife felt hot and weak, and she sat down heavily on a prayer bench. The many guests were not sure what to expect. Was the wedding still to take place, or had it been canceled? What complex web was the Rabbi thinking of? People found places to sit on the worn benches. There was weak talk. The bride began to cry. But the Rabbi took no notice. Rabbi Abraham was holding a copy of the Holy Scriptures. Suddenly his eyes opened wide and then they closed tightly. He sat on a nearby bench. Then he took a deep breath, and he gently set down his book. Rabbi Abraham gestured to the shammas, who came over to him, and the two men talked seriously and quietly for many minutes.

Rabbi Abraham stood, he went into his back room, and he returned with an oak walking stick. He whispered a set of instructions to Shammas Chayim. Chayim opened wide his eyes. He took a step backward. The Rabbi said aloud, "It is necessary, my good shammas." So Chayim took the oak staff and he got a glass bowl with oil and honey from the yeshiva's small back room. Then Chayim ben Meir walked through the main prayer hall and he went out the front door of the old synagogue building behind Judengasse Street.

Chayim walked as fast as he could through the gray streets of medieval Cologne. A dog barked, somewhere far away. The day was cool. Chayim looked up and he saw turnstones and windhovers soaring high in the sky. Shammas Chayim continued walking south until he reached the *Am Toten Juden* cemetery beyond the old stone city walls. There, he went straight to the grave of Shelah, the midwife.

Chayim was trembling. He stood at the head of the grave. He struck the grave three times with the oak walking stick. He held out the glass bowl with the oil and the honey, and then he said:

> I conjure you, O spirit of the grave, Nahinah, the angel who rests upon the bones of the dead. Accept the offering from my hand and do my bidding. Bring me Shelah (the wife of Salemannus ben Johel ha- Levi), a woman who is now dead. Make her stand erect and speak aloud. Have her tell the truth without fear – and we, in turn, shall not be afraid of her.

Then without looking back, Chayim ben Meir walked quickly to the Juden Viertels and into the old synagogue building. Chayim felt a chill breeze at his heels, and his knees were weak. As he entered the old wooden building, a cloud covered the sun. The many wedding guests suddenly felt a heavy fear. They saw the shammas, and behind him, they saw a darkness – a vague shape – and everyone was very, very still indeed.

Rabbi Abraham was standing by the Holy stone Ark. He rested one hand on the reading desk, and he said, "Now, O shade of the departed–it is time for the truth." And a silence, the silence of the eternal abyss, blanketed the room.

The thick silence of the eternal abyss lay heavily upon the room, and from somewhere far away, a muffled voice was heard. Did it come from the dark spirit hovering in the doorway? The voice said, "Rabbi Abraham–Rabbi Abraham, I am Shelah. I was the wife of Salemannus ben Johel ha-Levi. This now is the truth of what happened many, many years ago–I so swear by the Almighty Lord God–" and Shelah related the entire story from its very beginning to its very end.

All the guests heard every word. No one spoke. It seemed, in fact, that no one breathed. Then Shelah said, "Such is the truth, amen. And now, good Rabbi, let me rest."

The Rabbi took the oak staff from the hands of Shammas Chayim, and he slowly beat upon the reading desk three times. Then Rabbi Abraham ben Alexander said:

> Now I send you quietly
>   To that place whence you came
> To rest forever gently
>   In the warmth of His Name.

The soul of Shelah flowed out of the room like a cool thin wind, and the room brightened and the people began to breathe more easily again. But still no one spoke. All eyes were fixed on the Rabbi.

Rabbi Abraham looked around at the many people sitting before him. "We have come for a wedding," said the Rabbi. "What shall we do now?"

There was silence. The Rabbi smiled. "We should have a wedding," he said quietly.

Rabbi Abraham walked over to the bridal party. He took the brother of the bride by the hand and he said, "You know, my boy, this is not really your sister. Your father is actually Reb Hananiah. How would you like to marry this fine young woman?"

Shyly, the boy looked down at his feet.

Rabbi Abraham said to the bride, "Well, what do you think, young woman?" And the girl smiled at her newly discovered groom.

The various guests began to whisper among themselves. Rabbi Abraham stepped back. Quietly, he called the shammas aside, and he had Chayim heat a brick in the synagogue stove. (As you know, Rabbi, this ensured that the new couple would fall deeply in love.) However, it turned out that there was no need for such measures: it was immediately apparent that the couple would marry happily. The true brother and sister embraced, and they agreed to renounce their inappropriate vows. A new decree of betrothal was written, right then and there, and a glorious wedding followed.

A happy wedding can overcome the most sad and shocking of events – and so it was for the two families. A joyous ceremony ensued. This was the last unmarried child in Hananiah ben Solomon's family; therefore, after the wedding, Hananiah and his wife stood in the center of a circle of dancing wedding guests, and everyone clapped and cheered and laughed and was happy. Finally, the Rabbi gathered the couple together again, and he recited the "to a newly married couple" verse from the Book of Numbers:

> How finely your tents have stood,
> Wondrous homes at gentle ease,
> Like rows of shady palm tree hoods
> Like rich and fragrant river trees
> Like God's tall gracious eaglewoods
> Like cedars in the evening breeze;
> And now your smooth cool waterjars
> Shall always overflow,
> And you will have children like the stars –
> Bright, numerous, and aglow.

And at the wedding feast, in contrast to the patriarch Isaac of biblical times, the two fathers in medieval Cologne gave their full blessings to each and every child – for during those many years since the days of Isaac, Jacob, and Esau, the Jews had stored up sufficient blessings for all the children of even the largest of families. Then the guests sang and sang, and they danced around the parents and they placed garlands of flowers on the parents' heads. And everyone was very, very happy ever after, amen.

ood evening, Rabbi. No sleep for the weary? That is
what my grandmother said, and she said it almost nightly. If you are
cold, then sit down here on the bench and I will stoke up the oven. This
stoker? It is one of the iron shoe scrapers from the front hall–you
probably do not recognize it because it is covered with soot. Yes, there
are still two scrapers in the anteroom for dirty shoes. But I myself am
of the old school: I think that all pious men should pray barefoot. Did
you know that, when he arrives, the Messiah will walk barefoot into
the city of Jerusalem? It will be through the third gate to Heaven, for
the Talmud tells us that there are three entrances to the *Gan Eden*: the
first is in the wilderness, a second is in the sea, and the third is in
Jerusalem, amen.

Ah, but now Jerusalem is quite far from us–and it has always
been far from Lunel too. Lunel? Why, certainly you know the little
city of Lunel. Lunel is a vineyard town that is famous for its white
wines; it is just west of Montpellier, in the south of France. At one
time, in the Middle Ages, Lunel was an important city. In those days,
the Jewish college of Lunel–with a congregation of more than three
hundred regular members–rivaled the talmudical school of Norbonne

for scholarship, and it was attended by students from all over Europe and even from distant lands.

The chief rabbi of Lunel was Meshullam ben Jacob. Meshullam was a wealthy scholar. He was known for his strong, clear, and constructive decisions. Moreover, he always put learning above other considerations, and he encouraged his local scholars to study a wide range of subjects. Rabbi Meshullam commissioned the translation of many Arabic works into Hebrew, and in Lunel grew up a famous family of translators, the Tibbon family, descended from Judah ibn Tibbon.

Judah ben Saul ibn Tibbon was born in Spain, in Granada. Later, he emigrated to southern France in order to escape the persecution of the Jews by the Almohades who came in from North Africa. These were the same problems that drove Maimonides from Cordova – and, like Maimonides, Judah also practiced medicine. Judah's first love, however, was books.

Judah ibn Tibbon was a fanatic reader, writer, and book collector. Judah was a perfectionist, and he irritated people around him with his insistence that all details should be just so. His books needed to be in exact order on the shelves. His papers were in careful geometric piles. His handwriting was precise and neat. And as to his clothes? They had to be spotless, with no loose threads anywhere. Likewise, Judah's translations were absolutely faithful: he spent hours finding the exact parallel for every word and phrase. Unfortunately, his literal translations were stiff and clumsy, and often the new renditions lost the easy idiomatic flow of their original language.

In those days, most important Jewish works had been written in Arabic, the language of the Spanish Jews. Judah knew Arabic thoroughly. In Lunel and with Rabbi Meshullam's encouragement, Judah ibn Tibbon translated from Arabic into Hebrew: Bahya ben Joseph ibn Pakuda's "Duties of the Heart," Solomon ibn Gabirol's "Ethics" and his "Necklace of Pearls," Jehuda ben Samuel ha-Levi's philosophical works, Joseph Marinus ibn Janach's important grammatical and lexicographical treatise called the "Critique," and Rabbi Saadia ben Joseph Gaon's "Book of Beliefs and Convictions."

With Judah as a model, his son Samuel and his grandson Moses both became fine translators too. Each of the Tibbons made original contributions to philosophy and even to science, but it was through their translations that they had the deepest impact: these three men – over the unbroken cord of three generations – rendered into Hebrew all the chief Jewish writings of the Middle Ages. . . .

What is that? I was just resting my eyes, Rabbi. Let me see, now where was I? Oh yes, once upon a time in the town of Cologne on the wide River Rhine, there lived a fine old rabbi named Abraham ben Alexander. (Yes, yes, Rabbi, I will get to the Tibbon family in a moment – just be patient.) In those medieval times, Cologne had strange dark nights, and it was on one of those mysterious nights that a thin traveler arrived in the back room of the yeshiva, where Rabbi Abraham was hard at work.

It was a strange night, a dark night, a mild night. It was nearing the springtime, and a hint of the wonderful mysteries of new spring- times came to Cologne with this thin traveler. Old Abraham Achselrad could feel the spring slipping into the synagogue that night, and he looked up.

The stranger smiled. "Hello, Rabbi," he said, in a mild springtime voice.

"Hello to you," said Rabbi Abraham. "It is rather late to be out and about."

"Yes, it is, good Rabbi," said the man, "and I am tired. May I spend the night here?"

"Certainly," said the Rabbi, and he cleared a place among the benches. Rabbi Abraham got out two blankets that he kept folded behind his desk. Then he and the stranger arranged a makeshift bed in a corner on the floor.

"This is very kind of you, Rabbi," said the young man.

The Rabbi stood looking. Finally he asked, "And who are you, my good man?"

"My name, Rabbi, is Samuel ibn Tibbon," said the traveler. "I come from the town of Lunel, in southern France. By profession, I am a scribe."

"Ibn Tibbon?" said the Rabbi. "Are you related to the famous Judah ben Saul?"

"Yes – I am his son," said Samuel.

The Rabbi nodded. "Do you translate literature also?" he asked.

"Well, Rabbi, I do my best," said Samuel. "At the moment, I am working on translating Rabbi Moses ben Maimon's *Moreh Nebhukhim* – the 'Guide of the Perplexed' – from Arabic into Hebrew."

"I see," said the Rabbi thoughtfully. "That is quite a task you have taken on yourself."

"True," said Samuel, "but it is a wonderful book, and the European Jews deserve to have direct access to it."

The Rabbi nodded. The two men sat quietly for a while. Then Rabbi Abraham asked, "What brings you to Cologne, Samuel?"

Samuel ibn Tibbon was quiet for a minute. He studied his hands; then he said, "To be honest, Rabbi, I needed a vacation from my father."

Samuel was leaning against the wall, with the blankets around his legs. He pushed his knapsack back under a prayer bench. "You see, Rabbi, my father is a strong-willed man. He believes that there is only one correct way to do things. I know that he loves me, but he pushes and pushes, trying to drive my life in his own chosen direction. He had me study Arabic and medicine – just as he had done. And he chose a wife for me, when I was a boy.

"Yes, we have had many difficult times, my father and I. One day, I tried to go into business with a friend. We had some complications: a rather shady wholesaler promised us a large shipment of spices but he never delivered it (after we had already paid him an initial fee). In the end, I needed a loan from my father, and although he gave it to me as a present, he has never let me forget my debt."

Again, Samuel was quiet for a moment. "In any case, now I am spending all my time translating. But I have to do it on my own, away from the smothering influence of old Judah ben Saul."

The two men stopped to listen to a creaking sound that came from somewhere outside the old yeshiva building.

"You say that you are working on the philosophical tracts of Rabbi Moses ben Maimon?" asked Abraham Achselrad.

"Yes, I am," said Samuel. "In addition, I have just finished translating a wonderful manuscript by the famous talmudist, Rabbi Nissim of Kairouan (in North Africa). The book is called the *Sefer ha-Ma'asiot* – the 'Book of Gestes and Exempla.' Have you ever heard of it?"

"No," said Rabbi Abraham. "I have not heard of the book or of its author."

"Oh?" said Samuel. "I am surprised. Rabbi Nissim ben Jacob ibn Shahin lived about two centuries ago. I was told that he was very poor when he was a child; however, he eventually became the head of a famous school of talmudic study in Kairouan, a link between the old schools in the Holy Lands and the newer schools in Spain. Among his other achievements, Rabbi Nissim compiled and wove together a collection of popular stories – fables really. The tales came from all manner of traditions, Jewish, Christian, and Mohammedan; most of them ended with a moral saying. Originally, Rabbi Nissim wrote this book for his father-in-law, who had been desolated by the loss of his only son."

Samuel ibn Tibbon looked serious, and then suddenly he smiled. "I love these tales. They emphasize something essential that differs between my father and me. My father is primarily a man of words – frankly, he is rather cold and technical. I am more a man of deeds and of things that cannot always be put into words."

Samuel went on: "Old Rabbi Nissim, too, was fond of fables that pointed out how the Lord requires the heart and not the words. For example, here is one of his stories":

"It was the afternoon of the eve of the Day of Atonement. A Jewish villager, a farmer named Eben who had no schooling, got into his wagon and set out for the city in order to go to the synagogue. Unfortunately, along the way he hit a rock and a wheel broke. Eben got down from the wagon. He looked at the splintered wheel. Poor Eben had no tools with him, and he sat down sadly on an old log.

" 'I cannot believe that this is happening,' he thought. For a few minutes, Eben just sat there. Then he realized that the day was moving on, even if he – Eben – was not. Should he try and walk to the synagogue? That would take at least four hours. Or should he turn back and walk home? That would take two hours. Perhaps he should improvise some sort of wheel. But Eben was certain that a crude patchwork would not hold up either for a journey to the city or a journey back home.

"Eben just sat and sat. Slowly, the surrounding forest began to cool and to turn gray. The holiday was fast approaching. 'Now,' thought Eben, 'I will have to spend the Day of Atonement here, at the edge of the woods, with no one else around.' Eben's legs felt heavy. His mind was not working quickly. 'I have no prayer book,' he said. 'But of course I cannot read one anyway.'

"The sun began to set, and the first three stars shone in the darkening sky. Eben shook his arms and he rubbed his legs. 'Let me see,' he said to himself. 'Now, this is no way to act. I had best say some prayers. . . . But how do they begin?' Eben could not remember. He wrinkled his forehead. 'Undoubtedly I am safe with the *Shema*.' So he recited, 'Hear, O Israel, the Lord is our God; He is our one Lord, and you must love the Lord your God with all your heart and soul and strength.'

"Eben stopped: this was all that he could recall. He repeated the lines two more times. 'Is this sufficient for the Day of Atonement?' he worried. He knew that many, many benedictions were missing. 'What can I do?' he thought sadly. Then he remembered a scriptural Proverb:

> The Almighty turns His radiant head,
>   Standing aloof from the wicked crowd;
> But the good Lord listens closely instead
>   To the prayers of the righteously endowed.

" 'Very well,' he thought, 'I have done my best to be a righteous man. Therefore, I hope now, O Lord of all the world, that You will be so good as to listen closely to my prayers. In fact, perhaps You will help me out a bit here. I will do my part–' and then slowly and carefully, Eben recited the entire *alef-bet*. Finally, Eben said, 'This, O blessed Lord God, is the raw material. Would You just arrange those letters in the proper order for the Day of Atonement prayers? Thank you very much, and amen.' "

Samuel paused, and he smiled to himself. "Or, Rabbi," he continued, "there is the tale of a young boy who leaped over a ditch every daybreak. And why did the little boy do this? It was in honor of his departed father:

"Once upon a time, there was a little boy whose father had died suddenly during the winter before. The child could not understand what had happened. Where had his father gone? Why had the Almighty One done this? Was his father really gone forever? Would he not walk back home again one day–happy and strong and warm, just as the child remembered? The boy knew that his father would come back. And he could hardly wait. Therefore, when the sun first came up and when it was only the tops of the trees that were orange and gold and when the bottoms of the trees were still brown and black, then the boy jumped once and he jumped twice, over a ditch by his home.

"And why did he do this? The boy did not know how to pray; he could not say the *Kaddish* prayer. Instead, he jumped over the ditch for his father. The little boy remembered how his father had once patted him on the back for being so brave as to leap and hop and skip over that same ditch. Somehow, the boy knew that his father would come home and would say, 'My golden little man, I am proud of you for leaping and hopping and skipping each morning.' And the father would pick up his boy in his arms and he would carry him home, and then they would all live happily together for ever and ever and ever, amen."

Old Abraham Achselrad stroked his beard. Samuel sat quietly. After a while, the young man yawned and he said, "I am rather tired, good Rabbi. Do you mind if I lie down and go to sleep?" And Samuel smiled, he put his head back, and he relaxed and closed his eyes – and soon he was fast asleep. . . .

What is that, Rabbi? Yes, that is the whole story; there is no more.

ood evening, Rabbi. You are having difficulty sleeping again? Put your feet up on the side bench here and I will open the stove door. Let me tap the coals a bit; that white glow will wash away all the worries of a hard day.

I heard your final prayers tonight, and there is no use denying it – you are overworked. Even an old shammas like me can tell. I kept one eye on you when I was cleaning the dishes; I saw that you were watching the door, hoping that Reb Elbaum would leave early. But then Reb Anton stayed late to argue about the passage in Psalm 60 where it says:

> The Lord has proclaimed His stratagem,
> He has spoken from on high in Heaven:
> "I will go out and partition Shechem,
> The valley of Succoth shall have this plan:
>
> "First, to the North, Gilead and
> Manasseh shall be My coffer,
> Ephraim is My golden headband
> And Judah My royal scepter.

528

"South, Moab is My watering spa;
My shoes I fling at old, dry Edom.
And as to cruel Philistia?
I beat it like a broken drum."

That passage reminded me of ruby necklaces. Yes, yes–I said "ruby necklaces." You see,, Rabbi, my grandmother once told me a story of shoes and a ruby necklace and the barefoot smile in old Cologne. . . . You have never heard of a barefoot smile? Well, actually, Rabbi, I myself do not know exactly what it is, but here is what my grandmother told me:

Once upon a time, said my grandmother, in the city of Cologne there lived a man named Martel ben Simon ha-Levi. Martel was a jewelry salesman. He was a kind-hearted and honest man, and his customers all had complete confidence in him. In those days, Jews were the leading traders in jewelry and gems. Medieval Europeans were especially interested in agates, amethysts, and beryls, and in emeralds, jaspers, onyx, rubies, and topazes, and each of these stones was known for its own special magical property. Somehow, Rabbi, it seems that these magics have begun to drain out of the world nowadays. In olden times, amethyst protected against evil spirits, emerald brought financial success, jasper restrained the blood, onyx attracted the admiration of important people, ruby prevented miscarriages, and topaz cooled the body. Have people only forgotten these powers today? Or is it as my grandmother said: the magics have become weaker and weaker as the long centuries pass.

In any case, it was one dark night in those far-off magical times. A long complicated business deal had just been concluded. Five men had been meeting; one of the wealthiest men took Martel aside and showed him a necklace, and he said quietly, "Listen, Martel, finances are very tight for me at the moment: frankly, I need five hundred gold coins. I want you to sell this necklace for me. But be sure to accept no less than five hundred pieces of gold." Martel ben Simon looked at the beautiful item of jewelry, and he agreed to act as a middleman.

The necklace was breathtaking. It was made of finely hammered metal and it had a lovely ruby in the center. Martel carried the necklace everywhere, cautiously searching for a buyer. One day, Martel was

meeting with a Jew who was affiliated with the local Merchant's
Guild. Formally, Jews were not allowed to be members of any of the
Guilds. However, a selfish Jew named Anschel ben Berachiah had
become an unofficial assistant to the warden of the powerful Cologne
Merchant's Guild. Anschel lived a very secular life: he was rich, and he
and his wife lived in the style of the local Gentiles. Anschel, the Guild
assistant, met Martel to arrange for some special financing for the
Guild warden. After a while, Martel showed Anschel the necklace, and
Anschel's eyes lit up.

"Sir," said Martel, "this necklace has been entrusted to me for
sale. I must ask five hundred gold coins for it."

"Five hundred gold coins?! That is outrageous," said Anschel.
"However, it certainly is a nice necklace. Now, my good friend, this
looks like a ruby in the center."

"Yes, it is," said Martel. "It is a beautiful perfect ruby."

"Ah, rubies prevent miscarriages. My wife would like this necklace. I suppose that I would be willing to help you sell it–perhaps I
could offer you as much as two hundred gold coins."

"No," said Martel ben Simon, "I am afraid that I cannot take a
penny less than five hundred coins."

Anschel tried all manner of arguments, but Martel held firm.
Anschel continued to turn the shining neckband in his hands. Finally,
Anschel seemed worn down. "All right, Martel," said Anschel. "Let
me take the necklace to my wife–if she really likes it, then we will pay
you the full price."

Martel trusted his customers and they trusted him. Therefore,
Martel said, "Fine, Anschel." And he gave the necklace to the Guild
assistant.

Yes, Rabbi, Martel gave the metal and ruby necklace to Anschel,
and he waited patiently for one day and then for two. Soon, seven days
came and seven days went. Martel had difficulty sleeping. He became
more and more worried. Finally he went to the house of the Guild
assistant.

Martel knocked on the door. Anschel came out. He looked at
Martel and he raised his eyebrows, but he said nothing. Martel was
very uncomfortable. "Ah, good sir," said Martel ben Simon, "have you
had enough time to decide about the necklace? Would you like it, or
should I sell it to someone else?"

The Guild assistant frowned. "I do not know what necklace you are talking about," he said.

"What necklace?!" asked Martel in disbelief. "Why, I mean the metal and ruby necklace. It is the one that you took from me last week in order to show it to your wife."

"You are mad," said Anschel. "You are fortunate that I have a sense of honor and dignity. Otherwise, I would have you arrested for making slanderous accusations." Then Anschel went back inside, and he slammed the door behind him.

Martel became frightened. He stood there for a moment. Then he went straight to the synagogue. He stepped in the front door, he went through the anteroom, and he walked into the main prayer hall, which was filled with wooden benches. Martel passed the twelve stained glass windows with their colored lions and snakes, he looked up at the Holy Ark made of stone, and he walked to the door of the back study room. There, Rabbi Abraham was bent over a book.

Martel ben Simon was pale. The Rabbi looked up, and he saw that something serious was afoot.

"What has happened?" asked the Rabbi.

"Rabbi," said Martel, "I am in great trouble. I am almost afraid to tell you what has happened. I was entrusted with something valuable, something very expensive. Foolishly, I let it out of my hands, and now I have lost it."

"Tell me everything," said Abraham Achselrad.

"But will you believe me?"

"In the end, it is the Almighty Lord God (blessed be He) Who will judge," said the Rabbi, leaning back in his chair.

"Very well," said Martel, and he told his story.

Rabbi Abraham sat silently. Then he said, "Martel, let me think and pray." Rabbi Abraham ben Alexander closed his eyes. His breathing became slow and regular. Seven minutes came, and seven minutes went. Then more time passed. After an hour, Martel left quietly.

On the following day, the Rabbi sent an invitation to the Guild assistant to come to the synagogue. Anschel ben Berachiah felt that he was an important member of the community; when the messenger arrived, Anschel raised his eyebrows and he nodded his head. Then Anschel finished his business and he went to the old yeshiva building.

Anschel walked through the courtyard, he stepped in the front door, and he went into the anteroom. There, the shammas was waiting. "Ah, good Reb Anschel, the Rabbi would like your advice," said the shammas, Chayim ben Meir. "I remind you, of course, to remove your shoes."

"Oh, certainly," said Anschel, and he took off his shoes.

Now, Rabbi, Anschel was what one might call a casual Jew—certainly he was no scholar. Anschel could not tell you the reason why bare feet were symbols of respect, but Anschel and his wife and all the other Jews of Cologne had grown up knowing that bare feet were most definitely pious. Anschel could not tell you exactly why, but I will:

Bare feet had two meanings. On the one hand, all pious men prayed barefoot, and devout men removed their shoes whenever entering the holy synagogue. On the other hand, removing one's shoes was also a ritual in Jewish business transactions: you could seal an agreement by handing over your shoes. Of course, Rabbi, you know that this action was derived from a verse in the Book of Ruth which says:

> In those olden days, when property was redeemed or exchanged, it was the custom for a man to pull off his sandal and to give it to the other party; this was the form of solemn avowal in old Israel.

Jews brought this custom to Europe. In the Middle Ages, shoes were the first items left by the buyer inside a new house, and shoes were placed on the center of a newly purchased piece of land. Shoes became a standard token of business transactions: they could be substituted for the object purchased, if it was not yet available, and this was a commonly understood practice.

However, it was for the first reason—that is, out of respectful piety—that Anschel walked barefoot into the main prayer hall, which was filled with wooden benches. Barefoot, he passed the twelve stained glass windows with their colored lions and snakes. Barefoot, he looked up at the Holy Ark made of stone. And barefoot, he walked to the door of the back study room, where the Rabbi was bent over a book.

Anschel cleared his throat. The Rabbi looked up. "Thank you for coming, Anschel," said the Rabbi. He set his book aside, he put his fingers together, and he tapped his chin through his beard. "Reb Anschel," said Abraham ben Alexander thoughtfully, "in my capacity as a judge in the *Bet Din,* I often need a bit of advice."

Anschel nodded and he smiled. "I am happy to be of help to the Chief Rabbi of Cologne," he said, and he sat on one of the worn benches along the wall.

"Now, Reb Anschel," began the Rabbi, "as you know, the sale of complex objects, things like houses and ships, often entails unforeseen complications."

Anschel was not certain what the Rabbi meant, but he nodded his head again. The Rabbi was continuing: "In one section of the Talmud, a sage suggests that if one sells a house, then he has not necessarily sold all the annexes and the adjoining structures, unless they have been expressly included in the bill of sale—of course you know all this."

Anschel nodded slightly.

"But," said Rabbi Abraham, "there are many variant opinions, for example. . . ." And the Rabbi began to list case upon case upon case.

The Rabbi detailed many examples. Anschel listened and nodded. Meanwhile, the shammas put on his black coat and a tall hat, he wrapped a scarf around his chin to disguise his face, and he hurried off with the Guild official's shoes—just as the Rabbi had instructed him earlier.

Shammas Chayim went to the house of Anschel the Guild assistant. He knocked on the door, and Anschel's wife answered.

"Good woman," said Chayim, "your husband Anschel has asked me to bring him the fine necklace that he gave you the other day. He wants to show it to his friends."

The wife looked at Chayim. She frowned. "I have never seen you before. How do I know that you are telling me the truth? My husband said nothing to me of this."

"Ah, your husband warned us that you are a careful woman," said the shammas.

The wife nodded. "I certainly am," she said.

"Therefore," said Chayim, "he sent his shoes. As you know, shoes can be left as a token in trade for valuables. You do know this, do you not?"

Again, Anschel's wife frowned. Chayim continued quickly:

"Have you not heard how shoes can be stand-ins, substitutes for things that are purchased? Your husband told us that you have a good business sense–apparently, he relies on your opinion frequently."

"He does?" asked the wife.

"Oh yes," said the shammas, "at least, that is what he tells us."

"Well–I do speak my mind," said the woman, nodding. "And now that you mention it, I do recall that shoes are used in business transactions."

"Of course they are," said Chayim. He reached under his coat, and he pulled out Anschel ben Berachiah's shoes. "Therefore, respected wife, here are your husband's shoes."

Carefully, Anschel's wife studied the shoes. She turned the shoes around in her hands. She looked at the shammas; then she looked at the shoes again. Finally she said, "Yes–these are definitely Anschel's shoes. They are the ones that he was wearing this morning."

The woman looked at the shammas. "Well, I suppose that I can make this trade," she said. Again, Anschel's wife hesitated, but then she shrugged her shoulders and she went back into the house. A few minutes later she came out, and she handed the necklace to the shammas. Chayim left the shoes with the woman, and he hurried back to the synagogue. Quietly the shammas appeared in the doorway of the little back room, and silently he signaled to the Rabbi.

Anschel was saying, "Of course, Rabbi, we in the Merchant's Guild often see the sale of large lots of wine, and if any of the wine has turned to vinegar, then there are always complaints. But what can the poor wholesaler do? I would say–"

"Well, Reb Anschel, I appreciate your coming today. I thank you for your advice," said the Rabbi.

Anschel raised his eyebrows. "I only want to he helpful, Rabbi, and there is much more that I could say."

"And I would be happy to hear your ideas–if it were not for a very important appointment that I have now," said the Rabbi, standing and gently ushering the Guild assistant out of the back room.

Anschel shrugged his shoulders. Barefoot, he walked past the twelve stained glass windows with their colored lions and snakes. And barefoot, he skirted the wooden benches that filled the main prayer hall. Anschel reached the anteroom. He looked around for his shoes.

"Where are my shoes?" he asked.

Chayim looked at the Guild assistant in amazement. "Your shoes?" he asked. "I thought that you came barefoot to the holy house of study out of piety."

Then Shammas Chayim hurried out of the anteroom, through the main prayer hall, and into the rabbi's back study room. Meanwhile, Anschel looked in all the corners of the anteroom. Then he looked through the main prayer hall. He even looked outside the front door of the synagogue. All the while Anschel became angrier and angrier. "How dare someone steal the shoes of an important man!" he muttered. Eventually, however, he stepped out the front door, and barefoot, he stomped home.

Anschel went into his house. He was muttering to himself, and his feet hurt. Anschel's wife said, "Well, dear, did your friends appreciate your necklace?"

"Whatever are you talking about?" asked Anschel ben Berachiah.

"I mean that beautiful necklace with the red ruby," said the wife.

"I know which *necklace* you are talking about. I mean what is this about my friends?" asked Anschel.

Anschel's wife became worried. She did not know what to say next.

"Wife," said the Guild assistant, "listen to me: What did you do with our necklace?"

The woman hesitated. "I gave it to that servant who came this morning. You know who I mean – I could not see his face completely, but he had a black coat and a tall hat. He traded your shoes for the necklace."

"My shoes?!" said the man, and then Anschel suddenly realized what had happened. He sat down heavily on a chair. Clearly, he could not reclaim the necklace – and now there was nothing for him to do.

That afternoon, Rabbi Abraham returned the necklace to Martel ben Simon. Martel had tears in his eyes when he took it, and he held it fondly in his hands. Two days later, Martel sold the jewelry for six hundred gold coins, and so he made a profit of one hundred pieces of gold. Martel was overjoyed. He returned to the old yeshiva building. "Whatever can I do to repay you, Rabbi?" he asked.

As usual, old Rabbi Achselrad was working on his vast mystical treatise, the *Keter Shem Tov*. He looked up from the page on which he was writing. The Rabbi looked up at Martel, and then he looked down at Martel's shoes. Rabbi Abraham ben Alexander smiled. "Martel," he said, "my good, humble, and pious Martel, I think that it would be nice if you would remember to take off your shoes when you come here to pray. Leave them in the anteroom when you enter – and bring in only your pious barefoot smile."

"Oh, certainly, Rabbi," said Martel. He hurried back to the anteroom, and he took off his shoes. And ever after, Martel ben Simon ha-Levi was careful to pray barefoot, humbly and piously. Yes, Rabbi, from that day forward, Martel always prayed with a very happy and very holy and – as my grandmother told me – a very barefoot smile.

ood evening, Rabbi – I was just resting my eyes. Please
feel free to join me here by the stove. (I think you will be too warm on
that bench: try the one nearer to the wall.) I can doze forever by a warm
stove; I suppose that is because I am an attendant. What do I mean?
Well, Rabbi, after all these years of sitting in the study rooms during
lessons, I have learned a bit of Talmud and I remember that the Talmud
says: "Originally, ten measures of sleep descended into the world.
Slaves, servants, and attendants took nine of them, and the rest of
mankind took one."

I guess that we attendants and caretakers are basically lazy. As the
scriptural Proverb warns: "Laziness brings on deep sleep" – and then
my grandmother told me that too much sleep saps your strength. She
took this warning from the story of Samson: as Samson slept, Delilah
had his head shaved, and Samson's wondrous strength was drained
away.

Ah, has there ever been such a strong hero for the Jews as the
Judge Samson? Do you know that Samson uprooted trees with his
bare hands? You had never heard this? Of course you know the old
Haggadah legend telling how Samson tore out two *mountains* and
rubbed them against each other. But I am speaking of trees. . . . Yes, I

know that this is never mentioned in the Holy Scriptures; nonetheless, it is a fact. Many churches in the Rhine region – churches in Limburg, Alspach, and Remagen – show Samson, with his long hair and ancient short tunic, uprooting trees.

What is that, Rabbi? Oh my grandmother heard about the uprooted trees in *Jewish* stories too. For instance, her favorite rabbi, the mystic Achselrad, wrote about Samson and his tree adventures in the Kabbalistic treatise the *Keter Shem Tov*. Old Achselrad inferred that Samson had been ridding the world of tree-demons. Tree-demons are not common nowadays. But in the olden times, in the medieval days when Abraham ben Alexander was the Chief Rabbi of Cologne, tree-demons populated the countrysides.

For example, once upon a time, just outside the medieval city of Bonn, there lived a wealthy Jew named Eli ben Asher ha-Kohen. One night, Eli had a very troubling dream. Eli dreamt that he saw the biblical Judge Samson pull up a walnut tree. Then Samson began to walk slowly toward Eli, as if the old Judge were planning to strike Eli with the thick trunk. Eli shrank back. Samson came closer and closer – then Eli woke up sweating.

The next day, Eli could not forget his vivid nightmare. One day passed and then two. Seven days came and seven days went, but every single morning, the dream preyed and preyed and preyed on his mind. Eli also had other problems in his life, and now he became very worried. So finally he traveled north, up the River Rhine from Bonn to Cologne – the dream had been so strange and so compelling and it had left him so uneasy that Eli felt he must consult the famed Kabbalist, Rabbi Abraham ben Alexander, Achselrad of Cologne.

Eli ben Asher came north alone. He arrived in Cologne at night, and he was directed to the Jewish Quarter. Rabbi Abraham was studying in the back room of the old yeshiva. Eli walked quickly through the main prayer hall, which was filled with wooden benches. He passed the twelve stained glass windows with their colored lions and snakes, he looked up at the Holy stone Ark, and he walked to the door of the back study room. It was late at night, and the Rabbi was bent over a book.

"Rabbi Abraham?" asked Eli.

The Rabbi looked up in the candlelight. "Yes?"

"Rabbi, my name is Eli ben Asher. I live in Bonn. I have had a very disturbing dream. It seems to have some sacred but foreboding meaning. If I told it to you, would you try and help me to make sense of it?"

Rabbi Abraham closed his book. "I will do my best," said the Rabbi. "Tell me about your dream, Reb Eli."

Eli ben Asher ha-Kohen sat on an empty worn bench along the wall. He looked down at his hands. "Rabbi," began Eli, "let me begin by telling you some background about my life. Recently, I have become rather wealthy, and I fear that this is related to my dream. You see, it is like this:

"I have always been a gardener at heart. It is a profession that I feel happy about. I suppose this warm feeling toward the land and growing things stems from that great scriptural passage – you know the one. It is where Moses says, in his farewell speech to the people of Israel":

For the Lord your God is bringing you to a rich land, to a land of streams, of springs, and of underground waters gushing out in hill and in valley. It will be a land of wheat and barley, of vines, fig trees, and pomegranates, a land of olives, cream, and honey. It will be a land where you will never live in poverty nor will you want for anything. It will be a land whose common stones are iron ore and gold and from whose hills you will dig copper. You will have plenty to eat, and then you will bless the Lord your God for the rich warm land that He has given you.

The Rabbi smiled, and he nodded. "In any event, Rabbi," continued Eli, "This is what has now taken place. . . ."

As he had said, Eli ben Asher was a gardener, a vegetable gardener. At the edge of his main vegetable field stood a magnificent walnut tree. One day, a tree-demon set up housekeeping in a small dark hole in the tree. The evil miasma from the demon was like a blight. The tree began to lose its leaves and it produced very few walnuts. After a time, the vegetables growing nearby became sickly too.

To Eli, it appeared that the tree had become diseased and that its sickness or the many wilted fallen leaves and stunted broken branches were now ruining Eli's garden. Therefore, Eli ben Asher said to his wife, "I think that finally I will cut down that old tree at the edge of the garden."

Eli went out to the tree. There were drops on the bark that looked like candle drippings. "Very strange," thought Eli. Then Eli looked high up in the branches. Was there a bird hanging from its beak, far up among the highest leaves? "Curiouser and curiouser," thought Eli. Eli squinted his eyes, but he could not tell if it was a bird or if it was just a bird-shaped leaf. Eli shrugged his shoulders. He lifted his axe to begin to chop. However, as Eli began to swing the axe, the resident tree-demon suddenly appeared. The demon said sharply, "Just a moment, you heartless oaf! I live here. This is my house!"

Eli jumped back. Then he said, "I am sorry."

The demon frowned and it hissed. After a moment, Eli recovered his courage: "As I said, I am sorry. However, this tree is ruining my garden. The garden is my total livelihood, and I have no choice: I must cut down the tree."

The demon hissed and it coughed and it said, "This tree is your livelihood? Well, this tree is my home! If you need money, then I will pay you rent. I will give you three gold coins every day if you will spare this tree."

Eli was a pious man, but three gold coins each day was a princely sum. So Eli said that he would think about the offer, and he took his axe and he went back into the house.

"What is going on?" asked the wife.

"Some spirit, apparently a demon, has taken up residence in our walnut tree," said Eli.

The wife thought a moment, and she said, "Husband, this is a serious situation. If you are not careful, you may bring on your own death. I have heard that you must not even shake a demon's tree, for if you anger the demon, then he will certainly harm you. And who knows what strange spell this evil spirit may weave?"

"I think that you are too timid," said Eli. "We will go along with the plan offered by the spirit—he wants to rent our tree, and this will be a fine source of income."

Demons have ways of knowing what is out and about in the world. The evil spirit knew immediately what Eli had decided; therefore, the next morning Eli found three gold coins in a neat stack under the walnut tree. In fact, Eli found three gold coins under the walnut tree the following day and for every day thereafter, and soon he became quite wealthy. Eli bought houses and he bought a vineyard. He bought jewelry and new clothes. And never once did he question the demon as to where the money came from.

Many months passed. One day, the barn behind Eli ben Asher's house caught fire. Then a wagon broke. The next week, his son became very ill. Suddenly his two warehouses were repossessed by creditors and his vineyard had to be sold in order to raise cash. Soon, with all his financial setbacks, the three daily gold coins were insufficient, and Eli became poor again. Moreover, he had headaches and stomach troubles. Eli became weak and dizzy, and he had chest pains. Then, Eli ben Asher had his fateful dream – and finally he decided that it was time to consult with Rabbi Abraham.

And now it was late at night. Eli sat in the back room of the old yeshiva in Cologne. He related the entire story to Rabbi Abraham. Eli looked down at his shoes as he talked, and the Rabbi said not a word.

Eli paused a moment. He looked up at Rabbi Abraham. "Is this too strange, Rabbi?" he asked.

"It is strange," said Abraham ben Alexander quietly. "But who is to say what is *too* strange? Only the good Lord God (blessed be He) is the true Arbiter of strangeness."

Eli looked to Rabbi Abraham. The Rabbi had closed his eyes. His chin had sunk to his chest and his breathing was heavy and slow. Reb Eli was not certain what to do. Finally he said, "Rabbi?"

Old Achselrad opened his eyes. He stared at the ceiling. He said something very quietly. Eli bent toward the Rabbi. "What did you say, Rabbi?"

The Rabbi looked at Eli. Rabbi Abraham stared at Eli as if he were trying to see inside of the man, and then the Rabbi said, "Eli, my good friend – Proverbs!"

"Proverbs, Rabbi?"

"Amen and hallelujah, Eli – the Book of Proverbs. And let me quote a certain Proverb for you":

> He who lovingly tends a fig tree
>   Will eat ripe fruit in the fall –
> And if he attends to the Lord Almighty
>   Then an early death He will forestall.

Then the Rabbi closed his eyes again. Eli was puzzled. "Yes? What does this mean, Rabbi," asked Eli.

"Listen, my friend," said Abraham ben Alexander, squinting at the man from Bonn. "There is an important old Hebrew proverb: 'As is the garden, so is the gardener.' "

"I see," said Eli uncertainly. Eli blinked; then he said, "Can you perhaps be a bit more specific, Rabbi."

"Cut down the tree," said the Rabbi.

"But, Rabbi," said Eli, "in the first place, I have come to depend on the regular income. In the second place, I fear for my life. As my wife said, if I anger the demon, he may turn me into a raisin or a spider."

Eli waited for more advice, but old Achselrad had closed his eyes; he seemed to have fallen into a deep sleep. So eventually Eli ben Asher stood up, and he slipped quietly out of the Cologne yeshiva.

Eli ben Asher ha-Kohen returned to Bonn. The next day, he took his axe and he went out to the blighted walnut tree. Hardly had he raised the axe, when the demon appeared again.

"Do not touch this tree, Eli," warned the evil spirit.

Eli put down his axe. He looked at the demon. The demon stared at Eli. It coughed and it hissed and it spat. Eli felt frightened, but he lifted the axe again.

"Stop!" shouted the demon. "I am prepared to offer you nine gold coins each day. Think of it, Eli – nine gold coins! Soon this will make you as rich as a king!"

Eli closed his eyes. He repeated the *Shema,* and then he began to chop the tree. There was a blinding flash of light and a clap of thunder. Eli began to tremble, but he kept chopping. A wind arose. Eli could hardly move his arms against the gale. Rain fell. Lightning flashed. But Eli continued to chop. The tree swayed, and Eli chopped. His arms ached, and he felt like crying. Suddenly, with a tremendous crack and a crash, the tree fell over. There was a shriek. Eli dropped the axe and held his ears and closed his eyes. When he opened his eyes, the demon was gone and the tree lay quiet and long and sad at the edge of the field. Eli, too, felt sad. He put his axe on his shoulder, and, very tiredly, he walked back to his house.

Eli ben Asher ha-Kohen had cut down his walnut tree, and he went into his house. He sat down on a chair in the kitchen. His wife sat silently across from him. After a few minutes, he said, "You know, my wife, I feel like the psalmist."

"You feel like the psalmist?" she asked.

"Yes, I am thinking of Psalm 137, the one that we say for grace before meals":

> By the rivers of Babylon
> We wept upon our knees
> When we remembered holy Zion
> There beside the willow trees.

Not long afterward, Eli's son recovered from his illness. Together, Eli and his son planted the spring vegetables – the kale, the collards, and the kohlrabi. They planted onions, peas, and melons. They planted leeks, lettuce, and parsnips. Eli ben Asher was never wealthy again, but his garden grew bright and lush and green, and each spring he would look forward to the fall – and each fall, he would look forward to the spring.

h, Rabbi, I am glad to see you here alone. I want to apologize for my outburst during the service this evening. It was just that Reb Anton was complaining again. He said his children sometimes gave him so much grief that now he wished for his earlier carefree and childless years. . . . What is that, Rabbi? A casual comment? No, this is a serious matter. In the olden days, in the strict and pious days of our forefathers, childlessness was no jesting subject. As the Talmud says: "A childless person is accounted as dead." This is because one of our principal duties is to have children; we must preserve our good name and our fine faith and our strong heritage. Children are the promise of a never-ending future. That is why children and grandchildren were so important to my grandmother – in fact, it was my grandmother who told me the famous story of Rabbi Petahiah and the unfulfilled promise of a set of magnificent twin boys.

Exactly, Rabbi, that was Petahiah ben Jacob (the brother of Rabbi Isaac "the Wise" of Prague). Petahiah was the medieval European rabbi who undertook a tour of the entire world. Eventually, he wrote about his adventures in a book that he called *Sivuv ha-Olam* ("Around the World"). Rabbi Petahiah's travels took place in the days of Achselrad, well before Asher ben Yehiel was the Chief Rabbi of Cologne. Why do

I mention Rabbi Asher? When he was the leading scholar in Cologne, Asher spent most of his time writing and reading. He was always studying the Torah and the Talmud in the little back room of the old wooden yeshiva; this room was where for centuries the Cologne rabbis had passed endless hours working and thinking and arguing with themselves. Above the back study room was a loft for storage. One night, when he was rooting around among the manuscripts in the loft, Asher found a letter from Rabbi Petahiah of Regensburg to Rabbi Abraham ben Alexander, the mystic Achselrad of Cologne.

"*My dear Rabbi Abraham* – [began the letter]

"I have just met a fine young man, a Jew from Mainz. He has agreed to carry this letter to my good friend Rabbi Dan Kemuel ha-Kohen of Mainz who I am certain will then arrange to transport it to you. I write to wish you and your family well, to convey my fondest greetings to all the Jews of your blessed community in Cologne, and to praise the good Lord God (blessed be He) and His Almighty Name for ever and ever, amen.

"I will not trouble you with the details of my wagon rides and my subsequent sea voyages. Suffice it to say that safely they brought me here to the Oriental regions, regions that are so near to the great Holy Land where someday the Messiah shall return and deliver us and resurrect all pious souls and rebuild the Temple on Zion, amen. I write now in order to record for you some details of the lands and the peoples that I have seen in these old and foreign realms. The bright and glorious hand of the good Lord God (blessed be He) is visible everywhere, if only we look – praise the Lord Yahweh-Elohim.

"At present, I am in the city of Jebeil. As you might imagine, my old friend, I have had many, many adventures in traveling here. After touring the Holy Lands of Palestine, I turned north. I passed through the seaport of Tyre, a most beautiful city. It is guarded from the sea by two towers. At the base of these towers, innumerable fine vessels ride at anchor. At night, the customs officers draw a thick iron chain from tower to tower in order to prevent smugglers, thieves, and robbers from entering or leaving the harbor under the cover of darkness. Most wealthy Jews of Tyre are either ship-owners or manufacturers of the far-renowned Tyrian glass. In addition, it is the Jews who produce the famous brilliant purple cloth of Tyre–and I am told that there are two hundred Jewish dyers living in the Jewish Quarter of this warm and happy city.

"After Tyre, I found myself in the city of Jebeil, in Syria. (This is the Phoenician city that you would know as Gebal or as Byblos in the Holy Scriptures.) Jebeil sits on a small hill near the sea, about seven kilometers north of the city of Beirut. The entire town of Jebeil is surrounded by a wall, with square towers at all the angles. There is an elegant castle in the southeast corner, and everywhere within the town itself there are granite columns and gardens. The surrounding country-side has vineyards and farms. Ah, good Abraham, the city is light and elegant throughout: it feels like a peaceful suntanned old gentleman.

"In the past, most people of Jebeil have been Mohammedans. Recently the town was taken over by the crusaders–now there is even a local bishop. The bishop is a mild-mannered man, and he is surprisingly undogmatic in his views. In fact, when he heard that I had arrived, he invited me to visit him one afternoon–I think that he misses Europeans. The bishop is quite a talker, and I hardly said a word. Instead, all manner of stories and gossip and anecdotes rolled forth in an endless stream from this voluble Catholic cleric as I enjoyed my cool drink on a hot afternoon.

"I must confess that I was daydreaming, when the bishop began to talk of meeting a Christian missionary, a priest from the far eastern Orient, somewhere beyond Persia and Armenia. This priest called himself 'Presbyter John.' He was a warrior and he said that he had led great armies against the brother kings of the Persians and the Medes. He claimed to be descended from the ancient race of the Magi. He said that he was, in fact, the rightful heir to the kingdoms of the three Indies, including Farther India, where lies the body of Saint Thomas. Moreover, he described how his wild Oriental lands harbor strange beasts and monstrous creatures, such as giant ants that dig gold and iridescent fish that when dried turn to a brilliant purple powder.

"Well, good Abraham, with the heat of the day and the gentle tones of the bishop, my head began to nod. But the bishop did not seem to notice. He talked on and on. After a while, I realized that he was reciting a poem or a ballad. It was a tale of a Syrian Jew named Aleydis and his wife Leah and their two remarkable sons. Had they lived in Jebeil? I do not recall how we got onto the subject. In any case, the bishop was quite pleased with his memory for the old poem, and he was flattered that I asked him to recite it again so that I might write it down. I am not certain where the poem originated: however, I repeat it here in order to record it for you":

> Aleydis' wife was Leah
> She bore twins of short-lived fame
> Wild thunderers for a day
> Joel and Jahath were their names.
>
> More magnificent than grown men
> They were the tallest in those lands
> The strongest ever bred till then
> Along the ancient Syrian sands;
>
> At nine years old they towered
> Almost four cubits tall,
> Agile with great power
> Manly and proportional.
>
> They had no fear – they threatened
> Furor on hills and coasts
> They shook their fists at Heaven
> And at the celestial Hosts;
>
> Neighbors began to understand
> That these two young Jewish warriors
> Would someday rule the Syrian land
> With mighty arms and iron swords
>
> And as fierce giants grown
> They might one day have reigned
> But for black Dumah alone –
> God's messenger, the ruffian's bane. ;
>
> The boys were hunting deer
> When Dumah appeared with sword
> And a silence thick with fear
> Cloaked the black herald of the Lord –

Yes, under the graying skies
Stood the darkling Angel of Death
Covered with unwinking eyes
And hissing a dry ancient breath –

The sound of his ancient breathing
Was like the torrential rush
Of dry leaves blown in the seething
Fall winds, through the underbrush.

Now Joel and Jahath each had a bow
So between them Dumah sent a deer
And suddenly each boy's powerful arrow
Sped through the animal clean and clear;

Then each swift arrow struck a brother
And still unbearded these children fell,
They were shot dead by one another
In the thick silence of a black woodland dell.

They had not even got curly beards then –
Clustered from temple to chin –
And now their hair would not whiten,
Nor would ever there be two small children

To see these magnificent boys as grown men.

"Well, Abraham, that is the poem told to me by the bishop. Now it is late, the candle is burning low, and I must end my letter. I think of you, my old friend, as I write these last words. Once we too were children together – two boys playing at hunting. And now – well, now we are old men and fathers, separated by vast seas and by long years. Yet, Abraham, I feel that we are together still. Undoubtedly, my friend, that is because we are children still. It is not just that the good Lord God has blessed us with the memories of childhood, and it is not just that He has given us children and grandchildren to remind us of how it once felt to be young and free and magnificently strong in a magical world. It is also that we always remain children, just under the thin wrinkly skin of our old age. So farewell, my good and ever-youthful Abraham – farewell and amen.

"Your childhood friend,
Petahiah, the son of Jacob"

hat is that, Rabbi? No, no – you did not wake me. I was just resting here happily by the stove; I was thinking of old Abraham Achselrad. I must confess that he is probably my favorite of all the medieval rabbis that my grandmother would talk about. You know that he was a pupil of Eliazer ben Judah, the mystic of Worms, and Achselrad himself was forever having mystical visions. I guess that is why I am so fond of him: now, in my old age, I seem always to be having visions also – at least, I see things in the glow of the stove at night.

Now? Well, Rabbi, I see a sunny morning in those white coals. Yes, it reminds me of a sunny morning, when no one is about, but when the clouds are high and white and when the sun is far and bright and when the sky is blue and light. It is just like that sunny morning when Abraham ben Alexander, Achselrad of Cologne, suddenly realized that he had been writing all night in his mystical tome the *Keter Shem Tov*.

Yes, my grandmother said that it was one bright and sunny morning while writing this very book that Rabbi Abraham looked up, and in the gentle light filtering in from the main prayer hall – a prayer hall filled with wooden benches – in the light that had passed through the twelve stained glass windows with their colored lions and snakes, in the light that was made holy as it rolled around the stone Ark and that then streamed into the door of the back study room, it was in this very *ki tov* light of the good and radiant Lord God Almighty (blessed be He) that Rabbi Abraham looked up, and he saw no one there. Yes, the Rabbi looked up, and there was no one standing in his doorway, amen.

It was very early in the morning, one day long, long ago. The sun was out, and no one was about at the old yeshiva. Rabbi Abraham stood up. He walked through the main prayer hall, and he looked out the front door. Where were all the people? The Rabbi stood still for a moment. Then he stepped out into the courtyard. Was the world empty of all mankind? How could this be? It felt so bright and so warm.

Perhaps the Rabbi was remembering Moshe ben Daniel and his wife Naomi and their four children, Saul, David, Daniel, and Deborah. When they had said the traditional prayer during their last seder meal – "This year we celebrate here, but next year we shall be in the Holy Land; this year we celebrate as slaves, but next year shall we be free?" – after breaking the middle *matzoh* and hiding the *afikoman* piece, even then the family knew what the answer would be. They had said the prayer with special fervor; and late last month, the couple and their four children had left Cologne for the Holy Land. By wagon they had gone to Frankfort and then to Venice; then by boat they had gone to Jaffa, at the edge of the holy Promised Land. Moshe and Naomi and Saul, David, Daniel, and Deborah had joined the hundreds of other German Jews who had returned to their spiritual homeland.

Moshe was a carpenter and a craftsman of wood. When they had lived in Germany, he had worked for Gentiles outside the Jewish Quarter, and he was ill-treated and unhappy. He and Naomi decided on an *aliyah*: they dedicated themselves to going up to the Holy Land, to the Land of the Hebrew Prophets, the land of their forefathers and of their forefathers' fathers. Neither Moshe nor Naomi had ever been to Palestine. They knew no one who had emigrated. Nonetheless, at night they felt the pull of the old Hebrew patriarchs. At night, Moshe and Naomi talked and talked about what the fields and trees and sands would actually look like. Ah, to garden in that most ancient and holy of soils, along the suntanned hills! Europe was a cold dark land with vast forests and with grim fairy tales, but Palestine was the sunny land of a gently smiling Lord Who reaches out with the warm embrace of the oldest and happiest childhood of all. Moshe and Naomi had read accounts of Palestine—but what would that old dry holy land feel like to their very own hands and to their very own bare feet? At these times, as they talked and wondered, Moshe and Naomi became happy. And soon, it was their days that felt like sad dreams, and it was their nighttimes that felt full real.

"We are proud of our Cologne congregation," said Moshe ben Daniel to Rabbi Achselrad one day. "However, we are going to Palestine. As Jews, it is where we feel that we belong. Everyone needs to rest in the warm embrace of a family, and Naomi and I are certain that the hills of the Holy Land are our true family."

And Naomi said, "Rabbi, we will help to rebuild the old land; we will work hard to recreate the old cities. Of course, we can take very little with us. I am afraid that we can pack only a few pots and pans and clothes, and somehow I must find room for one of my grandmother's embroideries. And the books, Rabbi—we will certainly take our holy books. But that is all that we can manage."

Then, for a while, they were a whirlwind of activity. They sold things, and they packed things. Would two shirts do instead of three? How can you live without a salt shaker? Must Uncle Samuel's carved walking stick come to Palestine? And how about the handprints? Many years ago, the children had made handprints in clay—could they take the four old dried clay bricks? Although it seemed that they packed and planned for weeks, suddenly one day Moshe ben Daniel and his wife Naomi and their four children—Saul, David, Daniel, and Deborah—were gone. And their house was silent and the cellar door was forever shut. The yard was blank and the garden was only dried sticks and leaves, and the street was empty. And it was not long after this that Rabbi Achselrad found himself looking out the front door of the synagogue, one quiet empty sunny morning. It was very early; the sun was out, and no one was about at the old yeshiva. Rabbi Abraham stood in the doorway. Where, he thought, were all the people? He stood still for a moment. Then he stepped out into the courtyard. Was the world suddenly empty of mankind? How could that be? It felt so bright and so warm.

Rabbi Abraham Achselrad stepped into the courtyard, and he walked down the alleyway leading from the synagogue out to Ju-

dengasse Street. He walked down the street. There he saw two little
Jewish boys playing. One boy was about seven years old, and the other
boy was three. And the Rabbi heard the littler boy say, "You know
what I like best in the whole world?"

"What?" said the older boy, not looking up.

"I like my little cart and having it run around and you being the
driver of it."

"Oh."

"And you know what else I like?" asked the younger boy.

"What?"

"I like when you push me on the swing. . . . And you know what
else I like?"

"What?"

"Lots of things."

"Oh," said the older boy.

"What do you like?"

"Me?" asked the older boy. "Well, I like doing grown-up things.
I like fixing things in the house with Father–I am allowed to use the
tools, you know."

"Oh–me too," said the younger boy.

"I like important things. And now I will be going to school in the
yeshiva, and I'm going to study with the famous rabbis."

"Can I come too?"

"No, you're too young."

"Then, will we play afterward?"

"Probably not–I'll be too busy."

"You will?" asked the younger boy.

"Yes, of course," said the older boy.

"But afterward, after you are busy, then can we play?"

"Oh, probably not–I will be grown up then."

"I think that I will wait for you anyway," said the littlest one.

The End.

Now grow stronger all my children
Let us all grow wise and happy:

May no harm or hurt befall
The scribe and his gentle family all,
Shield them, Lord, from all bad wills—
Demons, dybbuks, and other ills—
Until a donkey scrambles up
To the angels' wispy ladder top
Which Jacob the Patriarch of old
Dreamt at Beth-El long ago.

Amen.

ACKNOWLEDGMENTS

The present volume is a companion to:

Katz, M. J. (1988). *Night Tales of the Shammas.* Northvale, NJ: Jason Aronson.

Katz, M. J. (1991). *Night Tales from Long Ago..* Northvale, NJ: Jason Aronson.

Brief versions of some of these tales can be found in:

Abrahams, I. (1896). *Jewish Life in the Middle Ages.* New York: Macmillan.

_____ (1911). Bahya, Ibn Paquda. In: *The Encyclopaedia Britannica,* 11th ed., vol. 3, pp. 213–214.

_____ (1911). Harizi, Judah ben Solomon. In: *The Encyclopaedia Britannica,* 11th ed., vol. 12, p. 953.

_____ (1911). Ibn Tibbon. In: *The Encyclopaedia Britannica,* 11th ed., vol. 14, p. 223.

_____ (1911). Nachmanides. In: *The Encyclopaedia Britannica,* 11th ed., vol. 19, pp. 147–148.

_____ (1911). Rashbam. In: *The Encyclopaedia Britannica,* 11th ed., vol. 22, p. 911.

_____ (1911). Tam, Jacob ben Meir. In: *The Encyclopaedia Britannica,* 11th ed., vol. 26, p. 386.

_____ (1926). *Hebrew Ethical Wills*, Parts One and Two. Philadelphia: The Jewish Publication Society of America.

Ausubel, N., ed. (1948). *A Treasury of Jewish Folklore*. New York: Crown Publishers.

Bernstein, M. (1960). Two Remedy Books in Yiddish from 1474 and 1508. In: *Studies in Biblical and Jewish Folklore*, ed. R. Patai, F. L. Utley, and D. Noy, pp. 287–305. Bloomington, IN: Indiana University Press.

Bloch, C. (1925). *The Golem. Legends of the Ghetto of Prague*. Vienna: John N. Vernay.

Brewer, E. C. (1949). *Brewer's Dictionary of Phrase & Fable*. Revised & enlarged. New York: Harper & Brothers.

Cohen, A. (1949). *Everyman's Talmud*. New York: E.P. Dutton & Co.

Dembitz, L. N. (1898). *Jewish Services in Synagogue and Home*. Philadelphia: The Jewish Publication Society of America.

Gaster, M. (1934). *Ma'aseh Book. Book of Jewish Tales and Legends Translated from the Judeo-German*. Philadelphia: The Jewish Publication Society of America.

Graetz, H. (1894). *History of the Jews*. Vols. 3 & 4. Philadelphia: The Jewish Publication Society of America.

Hanauer, J. E. (1935) *Folk-lore of the Holy Land. Moslem, Christian and Jewish*. London: Sheldon Press.

Handford, S. A., trans. (1954). *Fables of Aesop*. Harmondsworth, Middlesex, England: Penguin Books.

Kober, A. (1940). *Cologne*. In: *The Jewish Communities Series*, trans. S. Grayzel. Philadelphia: The Jewish Publication Society of America.

Leach, M., ed. (1955). Sweet William's Ghost. In: *The Ballad Book*, pp. 257–258. New York: A.S. Barnes & Company.

Millgram, A. E. (1971). *Jewish Worship*. Philadelphia: The Jewish Publication Society of America.

Noy, D. (1963). *Folktales of Israel*, trans. G. Baharav. Chicago: The University of Chicago Press.

Rappoport, A. S. (1937). *The Folklore of the Jews*. London: Soncino Press. (Reprinted by Singing Tree Press, Detroit, 1972.)

Roberts, W. E. (1960). A Spaniolic–Jewish Version of "Frau Holle." In: *Studies in Biblical and Jewish Folklore*, ed. R. Patai, F. L. Utley, and D. Noy, pp. 175–182. Bloomington, IN: Indiana University Press.

Robinson, J. H. (1903). *An Introduction to the History of Western Europe.* Boston: Ginn & Co.

Rose, H. J. (1959). *A Handbook of Greek Mythology.* New York: E.P. Dutton & Co.

Sabar, Y. (1982). *The Folk Literature of the Kurdistani Jews: An Anthology.* New Haven: Yale University Press.

Scheiber, A. (1985). *Essays on Jewish Folklore and Comparative Literature.* Budapest: Akademiai Kiado.

Schwarzbaum, H. (1960). Jewish and Moslem Sources of a Falasha Creation Myth. In: *Studies in Biblical and Jewish Folklore,* ed. R. Patai, F. L. Utley, and D. Noy, pp. 39–56. Bloomington, IN: Indiana University Press.

Spoer, A.M. (1930). Notes on some Hebrew amulets. In: *Papers and Transactions. Jubilee Congress of The Folk-Lore Society, Sept. 19–Sept. 25, 1928,* pp. 293–313. London: William Glaisher.

Trachtenberg, J. (1939). *Jewish Magic and Superstition.* New York: Behrman's Jewish Book House.

Yule, H. (1911). Prester John. In: *The Encyclopaedia Britannica,* 11th ed., vol. 22, pp. 304–307.